# Application of AI in the Teaching and Learning of English as a Foreign Language (EFL)

Youssef Baba Khouya
*University of Hassan I, Morocco*

Abderrahmane Ismaili Alaoui
*Hassan II University, Morocco*

IGI Global Scientific Publishing
Publishing Tomorrow's Research Today

Vice President of Editorial Melissa Wagner
Director of Acquisitions Mikaela Felty
Director of Book Development Jocelynn Hessler
Production Manager Mike Brehm
Cover Design Jose Rosado

Published in the United States of America by
IGI Global Scientific Publishing
701 East Chocolate Avenue
Hershey, PA, 17033, USA
Tel: 717-533-8845
Fax: 717-533-7115
Website: https://www.igi-global.com E-mail: cust@igi-global.com



Library of Congress Cataloging-in-Publication Data

Names: Baba Khouya, Youssef, 1983- editor. | Ismaili-Alaoui, Abderrahmane, editor.
Title: Application of AI in the teaching and learning of English as a foreign language (EFL) / edited by: Youssef Baba Khouya and Abderrahmane Ismaili Alaoui.
Description: Hershey PA : IGI Global Scientific Publishing, [2025] | Includes bibliographical references. | Summary: "The primary objective of this book is to explore, analyze, and document the transformative role of Artificial Intelligence (AI) in the teaching and learning of English as a Foreign Language (EFL)"-- Provided by publisher.
Identifiers: LCCN 2025007852 (print) | LCCN 2025007853 (ebook) | ISBN 9798337309699 (hardcover) | ISBN 9798337309705 (paperback) | ISBN 9798337309712 (ebook)
Subjects: LCSH: English language--Computer-assisted instruction for foreign speakers. | Artificial intelligence--Educational applications.
Classification: LCC PE1128.3 .A655 2025 (print) | LCC PE1128.3 (ebook) | DDC 428.0078/563--dc23/eng/20250519
LC record available at https://lccn.loc.gov/2025007852
LC ebook record available at https://lccn.loc.gov/2025007853

British Cataloguing in Publication Data
A Cataloguing in Publication record for this book is available from the British Library.

# Table of Contents

# Detailed Table of Contents



This paper outlines two sets of information regarding the use of artificial intelligence (AI) resources in teaching and acquiring English as a foreign language (EFL). The first set presents a scientific perspective on the appropriateness of using ChatGPT, Diffit, Wordwall, and Twee in EFL instruction, with examples of practical applications provided. The second set highlights the capabilities of AI tools that support learners in the process of EFL acquisition. Tools such as ChatGPT with voice integration, Mizou, GetPronounce, Quizlet, and Duolingo function as effective AI-powered facilitators for language comprehension. The findings affirm and support the potential of AI in enhancing foreign language teaching and learning.



The combination of Artificial Intelligence (AI) and gamification in English as a Foreign Language (EFL) training has transformed how learners interact with language acquisition. This chapter addresses the unique convergence of AI and gamified learning, concentrating on the use of interactive language games to boost student motivation, engagement, and competency. The talk begins with a review of theoretical underpinnings, stressing how gamification elements such as incentives, challenges, and feedback connect with language learning goals. It then investigates how AI-powered technologies customize the learning experience by adjusting information to specific learner requirements, enabling a more engaging and successful environment. AI-driven gamification promotes real-time language practice, adaptive feedback, and contextual learning, making it a dynamic alternative to standard teaching approaches. This chapter includes practical ideas and techniques for educators and researchers hoping to harness these emerging technologies for better language learning experiences.

Artificial Intelligence (AI) which is transforming English as a Foreign Language (EFL) education, introducing innovative solutions that make learning more effective, engaging, and adaptable. These advancements have unlocked unprecedented opportunities for both students and teachers. However, these innovations come with significant challenges such as bias in language models, inadequate contextual understanding, and data privacy concerns. Ethical considerations also loom large. The evolving role of teachers raises questions about the balance between human expertise and machine efficiency. Moreover, the security of learner data must be prioritized to avoid breaches that could compromise trust and safety. Addressing these challenges requires a thoughtful, collaborative approach to ensure the responsible and equitable adoption of AI in EFL education.



This study investigates the role of AI-powered chatbots in enhancing conversational English skills among learners. As digital tools become increasingly integrated into education, chatbots offer interactive, real-time language practice that traditional methods often lack. By providing personalized feedback, error correction, and continuous conversational exposure, chatbots create an engaging learning environment that fosters fluency, accuracy, and confidence. This research aims to assess the effectiveness of chatbot-assisted learning by examining its impact on learners' fluency, motivation, and retention of conversational skills. Through a mixed-method approach involving pre- and post-tests, surveys, and qualitative interviews, this study will provide insights into the potential of AI chatbots as a transformative tool for English language education. The findings are expected to guide educators in incorporating AI technologies to enhance learner outcomes and promote autonomous language learning.

The study aimed to explore the effectiveness of employing AI Praat acoustic analysis to investigate the challenges Omani EFL college students face in producing English prosodic features, particularly sentence intonation and lexical stress. The test was developed and applied to thirty students from foundation programs at a university level. Students' audio-recordings were analyzed using Praat acoustic analysis. Findings indicated that Praat acoustic analysis are very effective as it provided precise and objective methods for examining prosodic features of sentence intonation and lexical stress. The detailed acoustic data generated by Praat helped in diagnosing phonetic acoustic issues and enabled the comparison of learners' speech with native speakers' norms, fostering a deeper understanding of the challenges faced by Omani EFL learners in mastering English prosody. The results revealed significant differences between the students' intonation patterns and lexical stress placement compared to native English speakers, likely influenced by mother tongue.



Finding effective ways to incorporate Artificial Intelligence (AI) in Teaching English as a Foreign Language (TEFL) is becoming a major concern as AI literacy is in different stages of development worldwide. In Greece, the growing number of seminars on the use of AI has encouraged teaching professionals to consider possible venues for using AI-based tools in their lesson planning. This study takes the aid of Magic School AI tools to develop a film-based project on Disney animated movies for the EFL classroom. The study's main objectives are to explore ways of interacting with a reading text (i.e., the movie script), to examine opportunities for the development of intercultural communicative competence (ICC) skills through chatbot interaction with the movie characters and to facilitate the design of EFL lesson plans based on film projects. The results indicate that Magic School AI tools can respond effectively without compromising the students' creativity.

# Preface

## INTRODUCTION

The rapid advancement of Artificial Intelligence (AI) technologies has ushered in a new era of educational possibilities, transforming how we teach and learn languages across the globe. As English continues to solidify its position as the world's lingua franca, educators, learners, and institutions are seeking innovative, scalable, and effective tools to facilitate English as a Foreign Language (EFL) education. This reference book responds to this timely need by presenting an in-depth exploration of how AI can be strategically applied to EFL contexts, offering both theoretical perspectives and practical insights.

This volume brings together scholars, educators, and researchers from diverse regions and disciplines, providing a multifaceted view of AI's role in enhancing EFL instruction. Topics range from AI-powered personalization, gamification, chatbot-based learning, to ethical considerations and pragmatic competence development. Each chapter draws from empirical research or grounded theoretical frameworks to examine how AI tools are reshaping language pedagogy, learner experiences, and teacher development. Collectively, these contributions highlight AI's potential to personalize learning, streamline instruction, and address both the cognitive and affective dimensions of language acquisition.

Importantly, this book does not approach AI uncritically. While showcasing AI's benefits in augmenting EFL practices, it also addresses pressing challenges, including ethical dilemmas, bias in algorithms, and the implications for classroom dynamics. By balancing optimism with critique, this collection serves as both a guide and a reflective companion for educators, policymakers, and technologists navigating the evolving intersection of AI and EFL education.

# CHAPTER OVERVIEW

## Chapter 1: Acquisition of English as a Foreign Language and Resources for Teaching in a Time of Generative Artificial Intelligence (AI)

Building upon the discussion in Chapter 1, this chapter presents a focused look at AI applications for EFL classrooms. Emphasis is placed on the effectiveness of tools in practical classroom settings and their capacity to support learner autonomy and comprehension, reinforcing AI's value in education.

## Chapter 2: AI and Gamification: Engaging EFL Learners with Language Games

This chapter investigates the synergy between gamification and AI in EFL education. It discusses how AI can adapt language games to individual learning needs, boost engagement through real-time feedback, and create a more immersive and personalized language learning environment.

## Chapter 3: AI-Driven Personalization in English as a Foreign Language (EFL)

Focusing on speech synthesis and adaptive learning, this chapter examines how AI personalizes the EFL learning experience, enhances learner autonomy, and redefines pedagogical approaches. It explores both the pedagogical implications and ethical considerations of personalized learning.

## Chapter 4: Artificial Intelligence–Assisted Error Analysis: Developing Pragmatic Competence in EFL Learners

This chapter addresses how AI tools can diagnose and correct pragmatic language errors. By analyzing speech acts, politeness strategies, and cultural appropriateness, AI helps learners develop nuanced communicative competence necessary for cross-cultural language use.

## Chapter 5: Challenges and Ethical Considerations of AI in English as a Foreign Language

Here, the focus is on the ethical and technical challenges of AI integration in EFL. The chapter critically assesses bias, privacy concerns, and the evolving role of teachers in AI-mediated environments, calling for responsible and equitable implementation strategies.

## Chapter 6: Chatbots for Conversation: AI's Role in Transforming English Learning

This chapter delves into the role of AI chatbots in improving conversational fluency. It highlights the benefits of interactive dialogue, personalized feedback, and learner motivation, and presents empirical findings from studies evaluating chatbot effectiveness.

## Chapter 7: Employing Praat AI to Analyze the Production of Sentence Intonation and Lexical Stress Placement Produced by Omani Learners of English

This empirical study investigates how Praat AI can be used to assess phonetic and prosodic features of speech among EFL learners. Findings demonstrate its effectiveness in diagnosing learner challenges and providing precise acoustic feedback to improve pronunciation.

## Chapter 8: Experiencing Film Literacy through Magic School AI

By integrating AI tools with film-based instruction, this chapter explores how AI can foster creativity, intercultural competence, and learner engagement. It presents a case study using Disney films and Magic School AI to design interactive, media-rich lesson plans.

## Chapter 9: Roles of AI in Supporting Ongoing EFL/ESL Teacher Development

Focusing on professional development, this chapter explores how AI can provide customized training, reflective teaching support, and on-demand resources for EFL/ESL instructors. The discussion blends practical strategies with broader implications for teacher education.

## Chapter 10: The Relationship Between AI Tools Usage, Information Retrieval and Research Output Among Moroccan Novice Researchers

This quantitative study investigates how AI tools influence research productivity. It identifies information retrieval as a critical mediating factor, providing insights into how EFL researchers can leverage AI to enhance scholarly work and academic output.

## Chapter 11: University Students' Sense of Belonging in AI-Mediated EFL Classrooms: Classroom Rapport and Management

This chapter explores the emotional and relational aspects of AI in EFL settings. It highlights how AI can affect students' sense of belonging and classroom interaction, influencing teacher approaches to management and rapport-building in AI-integrated environments.

# CONCLUSION

The collective insights presented across the chapters illustrate the vast and varied potential of AI in transforming EFL education. From empowering learners through personalized and gamified content to supporting teachers in professional growth and classroom management, AI's integration into language education is both dynamic and multifaceted. However, the rapid adoption of AI also prompts a reevaluation of long-standing pedagogical traditions, classroom roles, and the essence of human interaction in education.

AI is not a panacea, and its deployment in EFL contexts must be approached with caution, critical reflection, and ethical awareness. This volume surfaces key concerns such as bias in algorithms, data privacy, and the loss of cultural nuances in automated instruction. It urges educators and stakeholders to adopt AI tools thoughtfully—balancing efficiency with empathy, personalization with inclusivity, and innovation with accountability.

Ultimately, this reference book invites continued dialogue and exploration at the intersection of AI and language education. It serves as a resource for educators, researchers, and policymakers seeking to navigate the complexities and opportunities that AI brings to EFL teaching and learning. By embracing this technological shift with informed intentionality, the field can move toward more inclusive, effective, and learner-centered language education.

# Chapter 1
# Acquisition of English as a Foreign Language and Resources for Teaching in a Time of Generative Artificial Intelligence (AI)

**Natalia Shumeiko**
https://orcid.org/0000-0002-7859-7519
*Department of English Language, Bratislava University of Economics and Business, Slovakia*

**Mária Spišiaková**
*Department of Romance and Slavic Languages, Bratislava University of Economics and Business, Slovakia*

## ABSTRACT

*This paper outlines two sets of information regarding the use of artificial intelligence (AI) resources in teaching and acquiring English as a foreign language (EFL). The first set presents a scientific perspective on the appropriateness of using ChatGPT, Diffit, Wordwall, and Twee in EFL instruction, with examples of practical applications provided. The second set highlights the capabilities of AI tools that support learners in the process of EFL acquisition. Tools such as ChatGPT with voice integration, Mizou, GetPronounce, Quizlet, and Duolingo function as effective AI-powered facilitators for language comprehension. The findings affirm and support the potential of AI in enhancing foreign language teaching and learning.*

DOI: 10.4018/979-8-3373-0969-9.ch001

## INTRODUCTION

Language education is an area within the educational landscape where artificial intelligence (AI) can assist by supporting pedagogues' work, automating routine tasks, and helping learners acquire English as a foreign language (EFL). AI can facilitate language acquisition in various ways. AI-powered resources have the potential to make language learning and teaching easier. AI-powered technology expands today's possibilities, offering numerous opportunities for both pedagogues and learners. The use of AI-powered resources in the teaching process, when specific settings are configured automatically or by the teacher, enables knowledge assessment, grading, and feedback provision. In turn, AI-powered language learning platforms can enhance language acquisition. Recent research (Boeru, 2024; Fu et al., 2023; Kim, 2022; Kushmar et al., 2022; Mohamed, 2024; Shumeiko, 2024) on AI in language teaching supports this perspective. Scholars have also examined the options provided by ChatGPT (Khiem et al., 2023; Lee et al., 2024; Mohamed, 2024; Tsai et al., 2024). A recent study investigating academic paper writing emphasized its significance in educating medical students for whom English is not the first language, aiming to assess the effectiveness of employing large language models, particularly ChatGPT, to improve their English academic writing skills (Li et al., 2024). The use of AI in foreign language teaching and learning remains a central research focus (Çakmak, 2022; Chen et al., 2022; Zeng & Fisher, 2024). Recent studies have also explored AI applications in higher education (Crompton & Burke, 2023). Shumeiko and Osadcha (2024) offered perspectives on applying AI in higher education to develop learners' soft skills. Regarding AI in education, it is important to note that "the rapid expansion of learning analytics and AI in education offers new scalable, data-intensive systems but raises concerns about data privacy and agency" (Alfredo et al., 2024, p. 1). From historical and social viewpoints, AI has also captured scholarly attention (Williamson, 2024), with the author highlighting the ethical and legal issues related to AI integration in education. Holmes and Tuomi (2022) examined AI systems in education, distinguishing between knowledge-based AI (symbolic AI), hybrid AI, and data-driven AI (machine learning).

In today's fast-moving world, new opportunities are emerging daily, drawing the attention of researchers. Figure 1 shows the number of publications related to AI categorized by field of study. The data indicate that the volume of publications on linguistics remains relatively limited. Therefore, this monograph chapter contributes to advancing research in linguistics alongside the educational sphere.

*Figure 1. The number of publications related to AI by the field of study from 2010 to 2022*

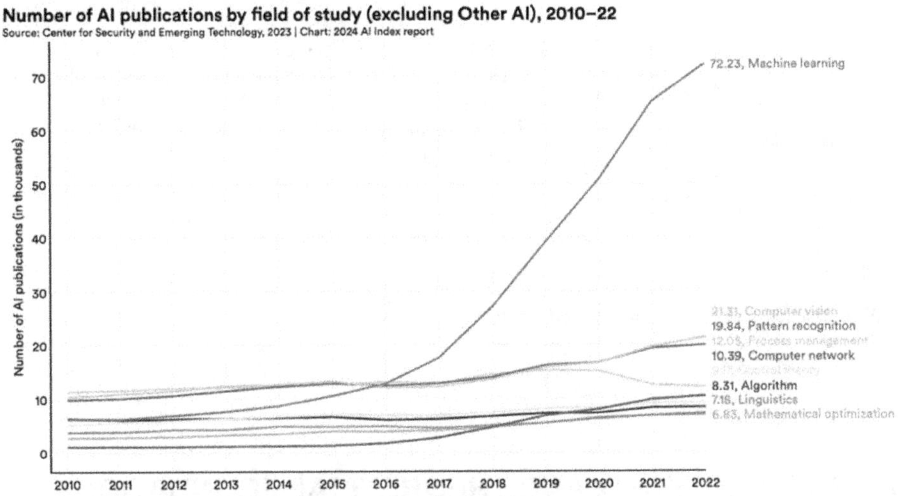


*Note. AI = artificial intelligence. Adapted from AI Index (2024).*

This paper aims to delineate selected AI resources, such as Diffit, Wordwall, and Mizou, for teachers and learners of EFL. To accomplish this aim, the study was guided by the following research questions (RQs):

RQ1: What AI resources are helpful for pedagogues in teaching EFL?
RQ2: What AI resources can potentially support learners' language acquisition?

## METHODOLOGY

This paper's methodology is defined as a theoretical exploration of selected AI resources (Twee, Diffit, Wordwall, Mizou) that enhance the learning and teaching of EFL. The graphical method was employed to visualize AI publications by research field from 2010 to 2022 and to display learners' preferences for AI-powered language learning applications. SmartArt figures were used to create visually compelling diagrams of the research structure (Figure 2) and to illustrate the core functions of AI resources for teachers and learners.

*Figure 2. Diagram of the research structure on exploiting AI for language acquisition*

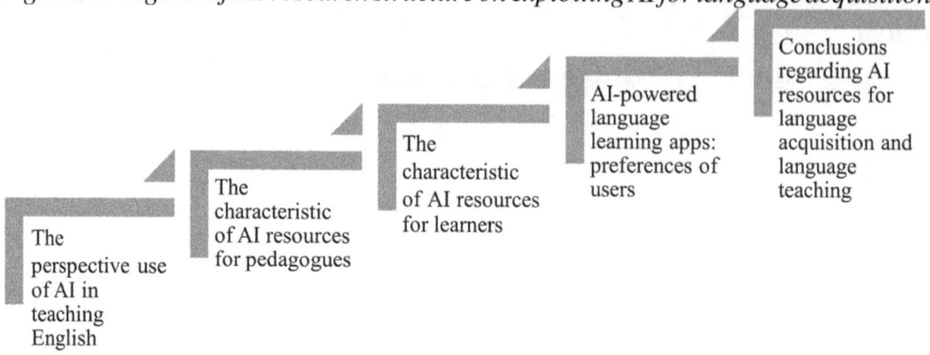


*Note. Source: Own work. AI = artificial intelligence.*

## LITERATURE REVIEW AND THEORETICAL FOUNDATIONS

### Publications Review (2024–2025): The Major Topics

Table 1 depicts the major topics addressed in recent scientific articles published in 2024–2025, which comprehensively explore the implementation of AI in learning EFL. These studies focus on learners' and teachers' perspectives on using AI in second language acquisition and examine the potential of AI-powered technologies. The present study addresses the practical application of AI-based resources, including ChatGPT, Diffit, Wordwall, Twee, Mizou, GetPronounce, Quizlet, and Duolingo, in EFL learning and teaching, contributing to the scientific novelty of this research.

*Table 1. Research-Related Publications (2024–2025)*

| Source | Explored topics |
|---|---|
| Zhang et al. (2025) | Examined the dynamics of AI literacy on EFL learners' willingness to communicate, focusing on Chinese non-English major university students. Used structural equation modeling to analyze the interplay between AI literacy, AI learning self-efficacy, and foreign language classroom anxiety in AI-enhanced environments. |
| Yang (2025) | Systematic review (2015–2023) highlighting the rapid growth of AI-supported L2 vocabulary acquisition research, emphasizing technologies like augmented reality and virtual reality for vocabulary learning. |
| Zhu and Wang (2025) | Overviewed AI technologies in language education, including automated writing evaluation and machine translation. Reviewed empirical studies (2013–2023; Scopus, Web of Science, Education Resources Information Center, ProQuest) and discussed practical implications, calling for research on diversity, equity, and inclusion. |
| Liu and Fan (2025) | Explored AI-mediated communication in EFL classrooms, focusing on technical and pedagogical stimuli. |
| Liu and Xiao (2025) | Examined Chinese university teachers' engagement with GenAI across different stages of foreign language teaching. |
| Xu and Wang (2024) | Conducted a meta-analysis and found that "AI had a higher effect size … on English language learning achievements" (Xu & Wang, 2024, p. 1) |
| Wu et al. (2024) | Investigated Chinese students' positive attitudes toward AI-assisted L2 learning. |
| Chen et al. (2024) | Modeled the roles of self-efficacy, anxiety, and attitude in L2 learning using an extended technology acceptance model. |
| Chen (2024) | Focused on AI chatbot interaction for semantic learning. |
| Fathi et al. (2024) | Explored improving EFL learners' speaking skills through AI-based technologies. |
| Huang et al. (2024) | Examined teachers' perspectives on the relevance of using AI in EFL acquisition? |
| Huang and Zou (2024) | Addressed methods for improving English speaking skills using AI-powered resources. |
| Han (2024) | Analyzed the application of AI-powered tools in second language learning. |
| AlAqlobi et al. (2024) | Explored the potential and challenges of using AI in language acquisition, providing a literature overview. |
| Persulessy et al. (2024) | Analyzed engineering students' perceptions of AI in language learning; ELSA received positive feedback for vocabulary acquisition and pronunciation improvement. |
| Schütze (2024) | Highlighted how virtual reality and AI technologies enhance connectivity between cognitive functions and language faculties. |
| Fatima (2024) | Analyzed AI's role in improving pronunciation in second language acquisition, finding that accurate models enhance pronunciation accuracy. |

continued on following page

*Table 1. Continued*

| Source | Explored topics |
|---|---|
| Zhang and Huang (2024) | Examined the impact of chatbots on second language vocabulary acquisition, showing that AI chatbots based on LLMs significantly enhance receptive and productive vocabulary. |
| Wu (2024) | Presented a meta-analysis on AI effectiveness in language learning, identifying key moderators (educational level, environment, interactivity, feedback, intervention duration) and emphasizing adaptive, personalized AI tools. |

*Note*. AI = artificial intelligence; EFL = English as a foreign language; LLMs = language learning models; GenAI = generative artificial intelligence; L2 = second language.

## AI and Its Components: An Overview

According to U.S. Department of Education, Office of Educational Technology (2023), AI can be described as:

> *Automation based on associations. When computers automate reasoning based on associations in data (or associations deduced from expert knowledge), two shifts fundamental to AI occur and shift computing beyond conventional edtech: (1) from capturing data to detecting patterns in data and (2) from providing access to instructional resources to automating decisions about instruction and other educational processes. (p. 1)*

AI is an umbrella term encompassing (a) machine learning (i.e., deep learning, supervised learning), (b) knowledge-based systems (i.e., intelligent agents, expert systems), (c) computer vision (i.e., image restoration, motion analysis), (d) robotics (i.e., actuation, sensing), (e) natural language processing (text, speech), (f) automated planning and scheduling, (g) optimization (i.e., evolutionary algorithms, genetic algorithms), (h) components of AI (i.e., learning, planning, communication, action), and (i) types of AI (Bhardwaj & Kumar, 2021; Greco et al., 2021; Regona et al., 2022; U.S. Department of Education, Office of Educational Technology, 2023). Components, types, and subfields of AI are visualized in Figure 3.

*Figure 3. Components of Artificial Intelligence (AI) Along With Types and Subfields*

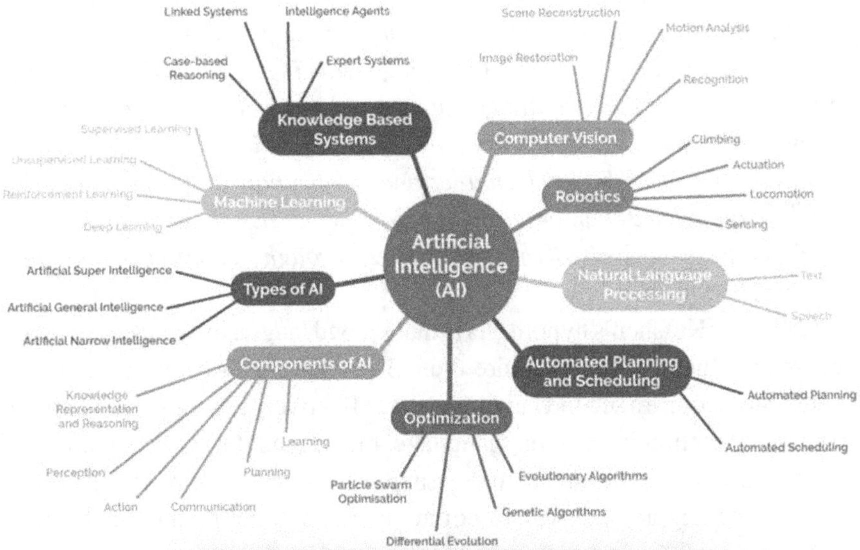


*Note. AI = artificial intelligence. Source: Adapted from U.S. Department of Education, Office of Educational Technology (2023); based on Regona et al. (2022); derived from Bhardwaj and Kumar (2021) and Greco et al. (2021).*

## AI Applications for Language Learning and Teaching: An Overview

Common trends in the use of AI technologies for second language learning direct students and teachers to several key resources: computer-assisted language learning, data-driven learning, intelligent tutoring systems, automatic speech recognition, chatbots, automated writing evaluation, natural language processing, and computerized dynamic assessment. Natural language processing enables machines to understand human language and serves as a critical tool for language learning. Data-driven learning is supported through the use of corpora (Pérez-Paredes, 2022), while automated writing evaluation provides learners with feedback on written work (Son et al., 2023).

## The Essence of Krashen's Theory For AI-Supported Learning of EFL

A theoretical analysis—the foundation of this study—was conducted to explore the relationship between AI tools and second language acquisition (SLA). This analysis addresses whether AI can enhance EFL acquisition and whether language teachers should integrate AI-based technologies into instruction. The discussion begins with Stephen Krashen's theoretical contributions. Tricomi (1986) noted that:

> *Central to Krashen's theory of second-language acquisition is his distinction between language acquisition and language learning... According to Krashen, learned competence and acquired competence develop in very different ways. In his view, language learning occurs through the formal study of rules, patterns, and conventions, a study which enables one to talk about and consciously apply the knowledge gained. Language acquisition, however, occurs quite differently, for it develops exclusively. Krashen believes, through "comprehensible input" (Tricomi, 1986, p. 60).*

The essence of Krashen's hypothesis is that second language acquisition parallels the process by which children acquire their first language. According to Krashen (1982), learners acquire a second language more effectively through natural communication and interaction in the target language, rather than through error correction or explicit instruction in grammar rules. Language is best acquired when learners focus on the meaning and purpose of communication rather than on its form. Notably, "foreigner talk"—interactions between native and non-native speakers—is considered essential for EFL acquisition. This type of communication provides simplified speech models through shorter, less complex sentences, thereby supporting learning. Similarly, "motherese"—a repetitive, exaggerated intonation style used by adults when speaking to children—has also been identified as a facilitative tool in language acquisition. Krashen's "comprehensible input" hypothesis proposes that learners acquire a second language by understanding input that is slightly above their current proficiency level, defined as "i+1," where "i" represents the learner's current level and "+1" indicates input just beyond that level. Krashen also emphasizes the role of public practice in language learning (Krashen, 1982). In light of Krashen's theory, AI can be seen as a valuable tool for simulating "foreigner talk," thereby supporting the acquisition of EFL through comprehensible and interactive input

## RESULTS AND DISCUSSION

### The Prospective use of AI in Teaching English: Theoretical Knowledge and Scientific Insights

The prospective use of AI in teaching EFL is shaped in part by its demonstrated benefits. First, AI supports the development of speaking skills. Second, it is effective in improving writing skills. Third, it enhances reading skills. Fourth, it offers pedagogical benefits by introducing new opportunities to strengthen and expand English language knowledge. Lastly, AI promotes self-regulation (Edmett et al.,

2023). A visual representation of these benefits and challenges in English acquisition is depicted in Figures 4 and 5.

*Figure 4. Benefits of Artificial Intelligence (AI)-Powered Resources in Teaching English*

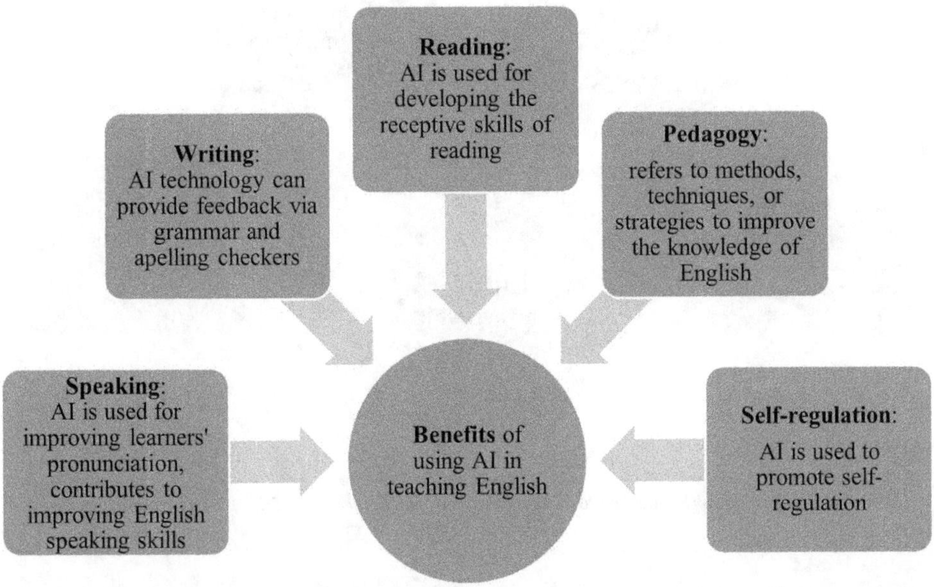


*Note. AI = artificial intelligence. Image adapted from Shumeiko (2024) and compiled from Edmett et al. (2023).*

*Figure 5. Challenges of Artificial Intelligence (AI)-Powered Resources in Teaching English*

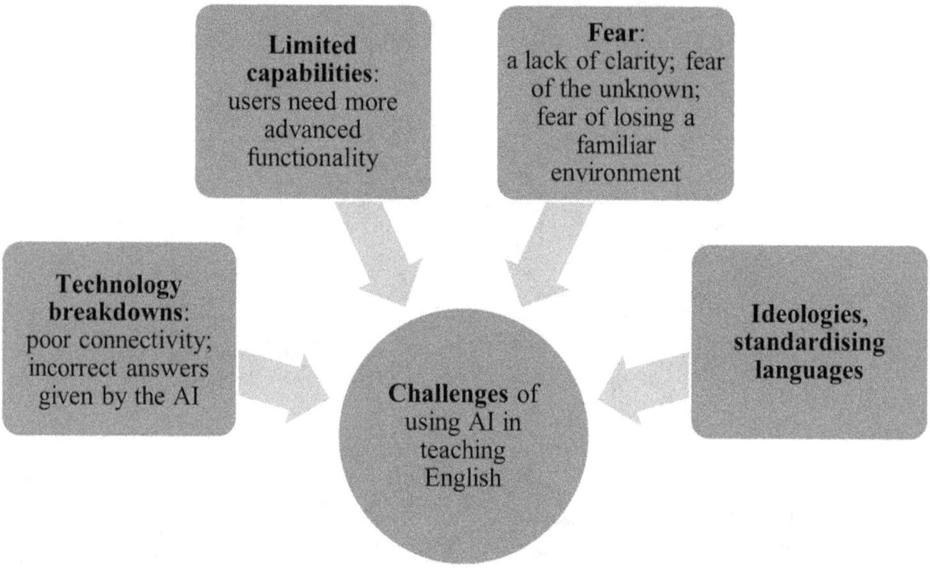


*Note. Image adapted from Shumeiko (2024) and compiled from Edmett et al. (2023). AI = artificial intelligence.*

When addressing the challenges of implementing AI-powered resources in teaching English, it is essential to recognize that teaching writing and reading in classrooms where AI use is expanding presents particular difficulties. With appropriate prompting, AI can generate impressive written content and offers considerable time-saving potential. However, despite these advantages, traditional classroom approaches should remain central, particularly in teaching reading and writing. Students should first read and analyze a text for its content, following the text as a vehicle for information approach, which focuses on understanding the main idea, identifying key points, and analyzing details. Subsequently, learners can examine the linguistic features of the text using the text as a linguistic object approach (John & Davies, 1983).

Typical text as a linguistic object activity include: (a) finding examples of specific verb forms in the text, (b) identifying lexical sets (topically linked words), and (c) analyzing the use of participle clauses. Text as a vehicle for information activities include: (a) predicting the content, (b) discussing questions related to the text, (c) marking unfamiliar information, (d) answering comprehension questions, (e) summarizing main points, and (f) sequencing events. This dual approach to reading instruction enhances students' awareness of linguistic features and strengthens their comprehension. Teachers can further support learners by guiding them in highlighting grammatical structures and analyzing sentence connections. Ultimately, the goal is to help students understand the content of what they read, fostering both language and cognitive development.

Moreover, pedagogues should encourage students to read for pleasure, which can be fostered during English classes, in reading circles, or as part of school activities. The process involves selecting a book, reading it, and then discussing it as a group. Teachers can lead class discussions on the text and enhance engagement by prompting students to change the story's ending, add or remove a character, or complete other creative tasks that stimulate student imagination. Writing, in turn, benefits from being done by hand. Writing with a pen on paper has been shown to improve memory retention and cognitive processing (Lambert, 2024). Language teachers can encourage students to write vocabulary lists, draft essays, and compose answers to discussion questions by hand before speaking. It is important to emphasize that AI is a valuable resource in today's classrooms. AI significantly reduces teacher preparation time, assists with repetitive and routine tasks, and helps generate ideas. However, limited use of AI in language learning can be most beneficial, particularly for tasks such as proofreading or helping students individually generate ideas.

## AI Resources for Pedagogues: A Scientific Vision and Examples of Practical Application

Online opportunities for language education are increasingly diverse, and AI technologies further expand these possibilities. Teachers invest considerable effort in preparing for classes, including lesson planning and material selection. ChatGPT, for example, can generate lesson plans, student assignments, discussion questions, vocabulary tasks, and questionnaires. Woodrum (2024) examined ChatGPT's use in translation, comparing its performance with Google Translate and professional translators. Tsai et al. (2024) also investigated the feasibility of using ChatGPT in education, focusing on potential challenges. Their study reported that "ChatGPT is effective in providing timely feedback to EFL English majors in an affordable manner, but it also highlights the potential for unfairness in writing evaluation" (Tsai et al., 2024, p. 22427). Many scholars recognize the value of AI-powered tools for teaching pronunciation and speaking (Al-Shallakh & Ahmad, 2024; Boeru, 2024; Liu & Hung, 2016).

It is important to note that detailed prompts, such as a single question, a series of questions, or a set of instructions, are essential for obtaining practical support from ChatGPT. For example, a teacher might provide the prompt: "Clarify the distinction between a 'linear' economy and a 'circular' economy with at least one example sentence for each term. The explanation should be suitable for advanced ESL students." ChatGPT responds: "In a linear economy, resources are extracted, used to make products, and then discarded as waste after use. It follows a 'take-make-dispose' model. Example sentence: 'In a linear economy, electronics are often thrown away when they break, contributing to large amounts of e-waste.' In contrast, a circular economy focuses on minimizing waste by reusing, repairing, recycling, and repurposing resources, creating a closed-loop system. Example sentence: "A circular economy encourages companies to design products that can be easily repaired or recycled, reducing the need for new materials and decreasing environmental impact." This example illustrates how precise prompts help maximize the educational value of AI tools in language instruction.

Another AI tool available online is Twee (twee.com), which is currently designed specifically for English language teachers. Teachers can customize requests by specifying the subject of the text—for example, "product life cycles"—along with the target vocabulary (modular, upgrade, salvage, commodity, from the outset, waste stream), learner level (advanced), genre (text), and desired length (100–250 words). In response to this input, Twee generated the following text:

*Understanding product life cycles is crucial in today's rapidly changing market. Companies design products to fulfill specific purposes and meet consumer demands. This initial phase affects the entire trajectory of the product's life. A modular approach allows for easier upgrades over time, extending its usefulness. As products mature, strategies shift from growth to maintenance. Once products decline, businesses must salvage value by treating them as reusable components or commodities. Considering the environmental impact is important. Planning for the end of a product's life reduces contributions to the waste stream. Sustainable practices help fulfill ethical responsibilities and cut disposal costs. Addressing product life cycles with foresight and innovation is essential for modern companies seeking longevity and relevance.*

To diversify student-centered teaching activities, teachers can use an AI-powered platform such as Diffit (app.diffit.me) to generate complete lesson materials. As an online tool, Diffit assists educators in creating classroom resources. Notably, "Diffit offers a variety of question formats and allows for scaffolding by providing adapted reading passages that build on students' background knowledge. Word banks can be included to enhance lexical retention" (Boeru, 2024). The teacher inputs the topic—for example, "Innovation: from idea to reality"—along with the learner level (e.g., Grade 8) and reading type (informational text). Diffit then generates a reading text or paragraph with key vocabulary and accompanying questions. Below is the text generated by Diffit on the topic "Innovation: from idea to reality:"

*Innovation is a powerful force that drives progress and helps us find better ways to do things. It's not just about having a great idea, but also about turning that idea into something real. This process is called the innovation process, and it involves several steps. The first step is to come up with ideas. This can be done through brainstorming, mind mapping, or simply observing how people use things. It's important to get ideas from different people and backgrounds to get a wide range of perspectives. Once you have a bunch of ideas, you need to figure out which ones are the best. This involves looking at things like how much it would cost to make the idea happen, if there's a market for it, and if it fits with the goals of the company or organization. The next step is to make a prototype, which is like a test version of your idea. This helps you see if your idea actually works and if there are any problems that need to be fixed. After testing the prototype, you need to make changes and improvements based on what you learned. This is an ongoing process, and you might need to make several changes before you're happy with the final product. Finally, you need to launch your new product or service. This involves getting everything ready, like making sure you have enough of the product, marketing it to people, and training people on how to use it.*

Diffit can also generate a summary, a list of vocabulary with definitions, and example sentences related to the selected topic; in this case, the topic is "Innovation: from idea to reality." In addition, the platform provides teaching guidelines to support lesson delivery (Figure 6).

*Figure 6. Teaching Guidelines for the Lesson on "Innovation: From Idea to Reality" Generated by Diffit*

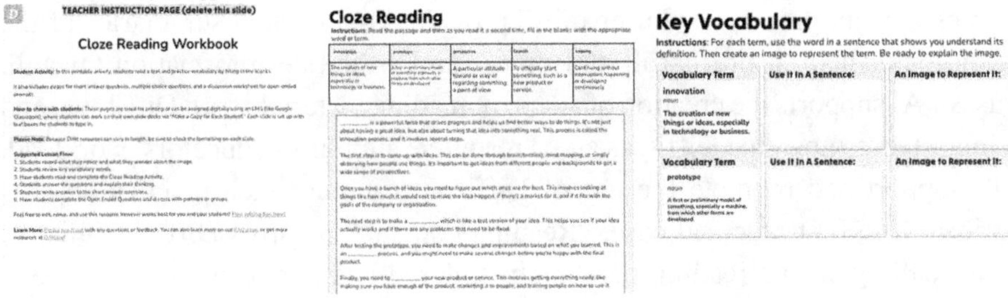


The practical application of Diffit in the educational process helps teachers optimize the potential of this AI resource and use it effectively in the classroom. Diffit offers several practical use cases, which are summarized in Table 2.

*Table 2. Practical Cases From Diffit*

| Practical case | Characteristic |
|---|---|
| Reading content | Automatically generates reading materials, including paragraphs, texts, and stories, across different proficiency levels (A1 to C2, CEFR framework). |
| Open-ended prompts | Develops open-ended questions to promote critical thinking and discussion. |
| Vocabulary and questions | Provides vocabulary lists tailored to text difficulty levels and creates comprehension questions to support understanding. |
| Google classroom | Offers an option to export tasks generated by Diffit directly into Google Classroom. |
| Summaries | Generates concise summaries of reading materials. |

*Note.* CEFR = Common European Framework of Reference for Languages; A1–C2 = proficiency levels within the CEFR scale, ranging from beginner (A1) to proficient (C2).

"Reading content" is a practical case that automatically generates reading paragraphs, allowing the teacher to select an appropriate reading level (e.g., 2nd Grade–8th Grade). "Open-ended prompts" enable the creation of open-ended questions, such as: The author mentions that accents can change over time. Think about the way you speak and how it might be different from your parents or grandparents. How do you think accents will change in the future? "Vocabulary and questions" generate tailored vocabulary lists and comprehension questions. "Google Classroom" integrates tasks directly into Google Classroom, enabling teachers to assign differentiated activities and track student progress. "Summaries" provide AI-generated summaries of the reading texts to help ensure that all students can understand key information. Overall, the use of AI supports the creation of adaptive reading materials with Diffit.me, and it is important to note that Diffit, as an AI resource, simplifies educators' workload.

To support and promote the use of Diffit in teaching, each practical case is described. The first practical case, "Reading content," involves Diffit's ability to automatically generate reading paragraphs tailored and personalized to learners' proficiency levels. Teachers can adapt any article to match students' reading abilities, offering simplified versions of thought-provoking content or providing more challenging texts for advanced learners. An example is presented in Figure 7.

*Figure 7. Example of Diffit-Generated Reading Content Adapted to Learners' Proficiency Levels. Source Text:*

**It's not what you say, it's ...**

I remember as a child desperately wanting to have an accent. My parents had moved several times when I was young, and I ended up with no significant accent at all. For a while it made me feel different, almost bereft. In my mind an accent was a sign of belonging – to a place, a community. My parents were unperturbed. At that time having a regional accent made getting some jobs more difficult, and they saw it as a benefit. Fortunately, times have changed, and accents are welcomed with open arms, employers eagerly bending over backwards to show how well they are accommodating the need for diversity.

It is curious, though, how bereft I still feel at times. My cousins live in Essex, and all speak strong Estuary English. When I visit, I know they consider me 'posh' because I speak in a different way, but that's what accents do, isn't it? They tell you all sorts of things about the speaker and can **have a bearing on** future relationships and an influence over how that person is perceived, be it rightly or wrongly. At first meetings when we are **sizing up** the other person, the unfavourable impression created by an accent that we are suspicious of can **have a lasting effect**. And by 'suspicious of' I'm referring to the fact that in addition to showing where people are from, some accents carry a form of social value, which can **lead to problematic preconceptions**. Is a person with an accent from a public school privileged and pompous? Does this accent command instant respect or irritate us? On most occasions we need to be aware of prejudice and look beyond an accent. The way a person speaks should not **taint our impression of them**.

It's perhaps this concern about my lack of obvious accent that has led to my fascination with accents. What I find quite remarkable is the range of accents existing in some shape or form in the UK – upwards of forty, would you believe – with some accents changing within a few hundred metres of each other. One reason for this is the influence of successive invading peoples, another is the isolation of communities, which allowed accents to develop in different areas. Today, with people relocating and travelling much more widely than before, many accents are blurring.

However, the accent someone uses still tells us a lot about that person. And sometimes what it tells us is about how far people consciously, or subconsciously, want to relate to those they are speaking to, **establishing an immediate rapport**. Or not. Have you ever noticed how children's accents can change depending on who they are interacting with? An associate of mine told me about her horror when her very young daughter appeared to be mocking a shopkeeper once when buying sweets. The child took the bag, opened her mouth and out came a perfect imitation of the shopkeeper's accent. But this was not done on purpose. Apparently, this is common, as all we want to do as children is to adapt and 'fit in' with a group. So important is this need to conform that children will even subconsciously **adopt** speech **mannerisms** of those around them. And contrarily, we can emphasise our own accents when we wish to establish a difference between ourselves and the other speaker, for whatever reason. Even more interesting, in my mind, is the fact that some people consciously change accents to **project a certain image**. I remember a schoolmate who was from London, who used to put on an American accent, presumably because he wanted to sound 'cool'. He didn't.

Whatever the reason for the way we accent our speech, the fact remains that it is a powerful indicator of who we are and subconsciously is often thought to be an indicator of personality, too. Currently, companies are cashing in on the influence that certain UK accents can have on listeners (particularly on the phone or in advertisements). According to a recent YouGov poll, it's the Scottish accent that is top of the list (after the Queen's English) when it comes to being perceived as trustworthy and reassuring. Manchester accents are considered creative and industrious, and a Yorkshire one wise and honest. I suppose I have finally come to terms with my lack of clear accent, but I have to admit that I still experience a little tug of envy when I meet someone whose voice immediately takes me to a particular part of the UK.

*Note. Source: Text adapted from "It's not what you say, it's ..." in Edwards et al. (2023, p. 56-57).*

*Diffit-Generated Reading Content* (for 8th-grade learners):

*As a kid, I really wanted to have an accent. My parents moved around a lot when I was young, so I ended up without a strong accent. For a while, it made me feel different, like I was missing something. In my mind, an accent was a way to belong – to a place, to a group of people. My parents didn't seem to care. Back then, having a regional accent could make it harder to get certain jobs, and they saw that as a good thing. Luckily, things have changed, and now people are happy to hear different accents. Companies are even trying to use the power of accents to make their products seem more trustworthy.*

*It's interesting, though, that I still feel a little lost sometimes. My cousins live in Essex, and they all have strong accents. When I visit, I know they think I'm "posh" because I talk differently. But that's what accents do, right? They tell you a lot about a person and can even influence how you feel about them.*

*Kids are really good at picking up accents. They'll even copy the way people talk without realizing they're doing it. This shows how important it is for us to fit in with the people around us. On the other hand, sometimes we want to emphasize our own accents to show that we're different from someone else. We might do this if we want to make a statement or if we don't trust the other person.*

*It's even more interesting that some people change their accents on purpose to create a certain image. I remember a classmate from London who used to put on an American accent, probably because he thought it sounded cool. It didn't really work.*

*No matter why we talk the way we do, accents are powerful. They tell us where people are from and can even make us think certain things about them. For example, some people might think someone with a public-school accent is privileged and stuck-up. Or they might think a certain accent sounds trustworthy or annoying. We need to be careful not to judge people based on their accents. The way someone speaks shouldn't change how we feel about them.*

*Maybe it's because I don't have a strong accent that I'm so fascinated by them. It's amazing how many different accents there are in the [United Kingdom] – over forty, can you believe it? Some accents even change within a few hundred yards of each other! This is partly because different groups of people have moved to the [United Kingdom] over time, and partly because communities have been isolated from each other. Now, with people moving around more, many accents are starting to blend together.*

*I guess I've finally accepted that I don't have a clear accent, but I still get a little jealous when I meet someone whose voice instantly tells me where they're from.*

The summary (Diffit-Generated Summary) highlights several key points. The author grew up moving frequently and, as a result, did not develop a strong accent, which made them feel as though they did not belong. Accents, as the author observes, can be powerful markers of identity, revealing a person's background and influencing how others perceive them. The author remains fascinated by the variety of accents in the United Kingdom and how they reflect the country's history and changing demographics.

Key vocabulary words drawn from the text help support language development. The term fascinated (adjective) refers to being extremely interested in something; for example, "She was fascinated by the ancient ruins." The word privileged (adjective) describes having special rights or advantages most people do not have; for instance, "He comes from a privileged family and has never had to worry about money." The verb emphasize means to give special importance to something, as in "The teacher emphasized the importance of studying for the test." The verb influence refers to having an effect on something or someone; for example, "The weather can influence our mood." Finally, isolated (adjective) means being separated from other people or places, as illustrated by the sentence, "The small village was isolated from the rest of the world."

Multiple-choice questions further support comprehension of the text. For example, why did the author feel different as a child because of their lack of a strong accent? The correct answer is that the author felt like they did not belong to a place or group of people. Another question asks why the author's parents did not mind the absence of a strong accent; the answer is that they believed it would help the author get a job. A final question addresses why the author remains fascinated by accents, with the correct response being that they are fascinated by the history of accents, how they change over time, and how they influence opinions—all of the above.

Short-answer questions encourage reflection and recall. One question asks how companies use accents to make their products appear more trustworthy, with the answer being that companies hire people with various accents to advertise their products. Another question explores how people may intentionally change their accents, such as when someone adopts an American accent because they think it sounds cool. A further question asks why so many different accents exist in the United Kingdom, with the answer pointing to historical migration patterns and the isolation of communities.

Open-ended prompts promote critical thinking and personal connection to the text. For example, students are invited to reflect on whether they have ever felt different because of something about themselves or their way of speaking and how they managed those feelings. Another prompt encourages discussion on whether students have ever judged someone based on their accent and how to avoid making such assumptions. A final prompt asks students to consider how accents may change in the future, particularly in relation to the ways they and their families speak.

Diffit generates teaching materials for the lesson on "First Impressions" (based on the text "It's not what you say, it's …" from Edwards et al., 2023), including printable activities such as fill-in-the-blank exercises and comprehension questions (Figure 8).

*Figure 8. Printable Activities Generated by Diffit for the Lesson on "First Impressions."*

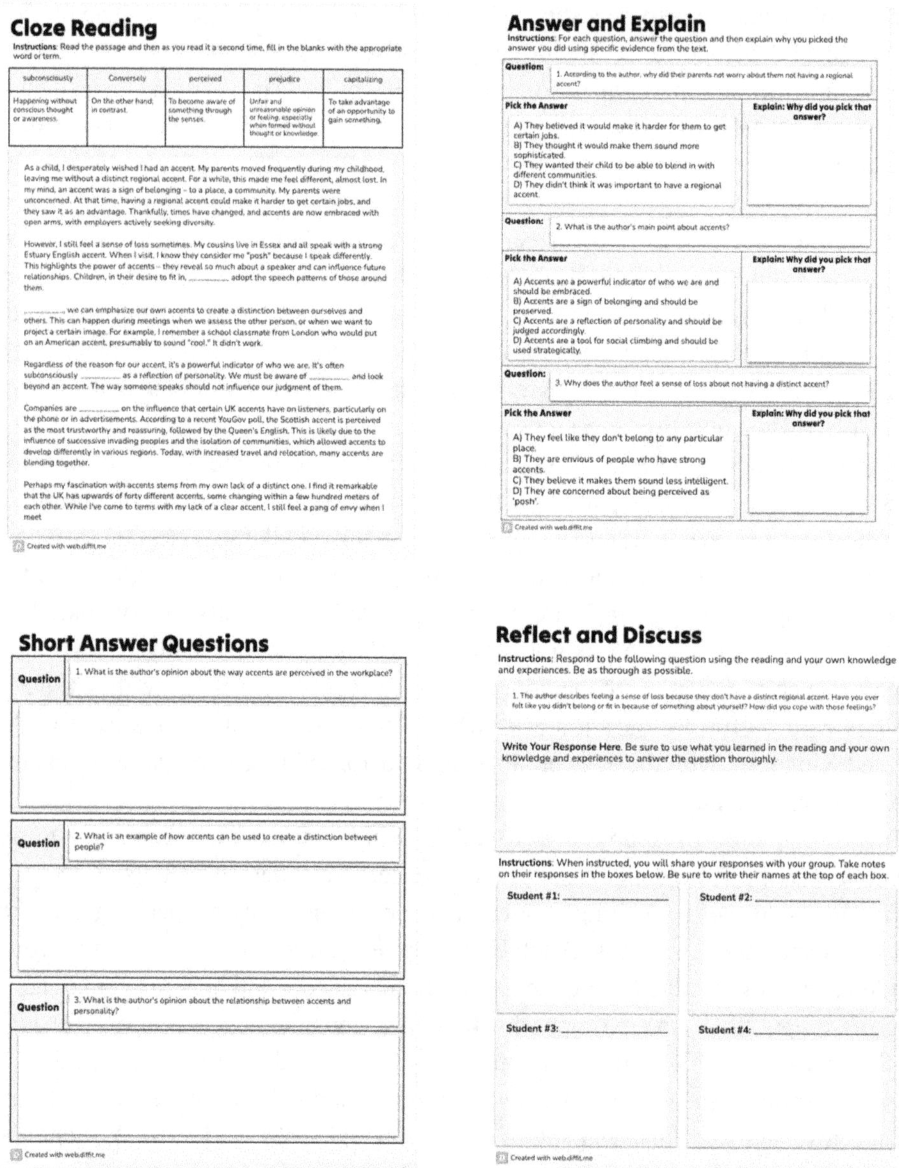


Diffit automatically generates assignments for YouTube videos that align with the lesson plan. For example, an English lesson on "Persuasion" for advanced learners can be supplemented with the YouTube video Robert Cialdini – Science of Persuasion (https://www.youtube.com/watch?v=kv0sOX6Alrk&t=4s). The assignments generated by Diffit help make the lesson more informal and engaging (Figure 9).

*Figure 9. Assignments Generated by Diffit for the YouTube Video Science of Persuasion*

The following adapted passage presents the key principles from Robert Cialdini's Science of Persuasion in simplified language for 8th-grade learners:

## The Science of Persuasion: 6 Powerful Techniques

*For over 60 years, researchers have been studying how people get convinced to say "yes" to requests. It turns out there's a real science to persuasion, and some of it might surprise you.*
*When making decisions, we like to think we carefully weigh all the information. But in our busy lives, we often use shortcuts or "rules of thumb" to make decisions faster. My research has identified six universal shortcuts that guide human behavior:*
***1. Reciprocity:** This means people feel obligated to return favors. If someone does something nice for you, you feel compelled to do something nice back. Think about it: if a friend invites you to a party, you feel like you should invite them to one of yours.*
*A great example is how restaurants use this principle. Have you ever noticed that waiters often give you a small gift, like a mint, when they bring the bill? This little gift can actually increase your tip! Studies show that giving a single mint can boost tips by 3%. Giving two mints? Tips increase by 14%! But the most surprising thing is that if the waiter gives you one mint, then walks away, but turns back and says, "Here's an extra mint for you nice people," tips jump to 23%! It's not just what you give, but how you give it.*
***The key to using reciprocity is to be the first to give something, and make it personal and unexpected.***

**2. Scarcity:** People want things more when they're hard to get. Remember when British Airways announced they were stopping their London-New York Concorde flights? The next day, everyone wanted to fly on the Concorde! Why? Because it was becoming scarce. Even though the plane didn't fly any faster or offer better service, people suddenly wanted it more.

**To use scarcity effectively, don't just tell people about the benefits of your product or service. Highlight what makes it unique and what they stand to lose if they don't choose you.**

**3. Authority:** People trust experts. Think about it: Would you be more likely to follow a physiotherapist's exercise plan if they had their medical diplomas on the wall? Probably! We tend to believe people who seem knowledgeable and credible.

**To use authority, signal your expertise to others before you try to persuade them. You can do this by having someone else introduce you as an expert, even if they might benefit from the introduction.**

**4. Consistency:** People like to be consistent with their past actions and statements. This means that if you can get someone to make a small commitment, they're more likely to make a bigger commitment later.

**For example, one study found that people were more likely to put up a big, ugly sign in their yard supporting a "Drive Safely" campaign if they had previously agreed to put a small postcard in their window supporting the same cause.**

**To use consistency, look for ways to get people to make small, voluntary commitments, preferably in writing.**

**5. Liking:** We're more likely to say "yes" to people we like. What makes us like someone? There are three key factors:

* **Similarity:** We like people who are similar to us.
* **Compliments:** We like people who give us compliments.
* **Cooperation:** We like people who work with us towards a common goal.

**To use liking, find common ground with the person you're trying to persuade and give them genuine compliments before you get down to business.**

**6. Consensus:** When people are unsure, they look to others to see what they should do. Think about hotel signs that encourage guests to reuse towels. These signs often mention the environmental benefits of reusing towels. But studies show that a sign that simply says "75% of guests reuse their towels" is even more effective! Why? Because it shows that other people are doing it, so it must be the right thing to do.

***To use consensus, show people that others, especially similar others, are doing what you want them to do.***

*These six principles of persuasion are scientifically proven and can be used to make small, practical changes that lead to big results. They can help you influence and persuade others in an ethical way. So, use them wisely!*

The extract of the adapted passage on The Science of Persuasion highlights several key points. People are more likely to say yes to a request when they feel obligated to return a favor, such as when they receive a small gift. They are also more likely to want something if it is scarce or difficult to obtain. Additionally, people tend to trust and agree with individuals who are experts or appear knowledgeable.

The key vocabulary words drawn from the passage further support language development. Reciprocity refers to the practice of exchanging things for mutual benefit, as in "The two countries signed a treaty of reciprocity, allowing their citizens to travel freely between the two nations." Scarcity means the state of being in short supply, exemplified by "The scarcity of water in the desert made survival difficult for the travelers." Authority is the power or right to give orders, make decisions, and enforce obedience, as seen in "The police officer had the authority to arrest the suspect." Consistency refers to always behaving or performing in a similar way, such as "Her consistency in her training helped her win the championship." Finally, consensus means general agreement, as in "The committee reached a consensus on the new budget."

The multiple-choice questions assess comprehension of the passage. For example, students are asked which of the following is not a key factor that makes us like someone, with the correct answer being "physical appearance." Another question asks how to most effectively apply scarcity, with the best answer being to emphasize a product's unique qualities and what people stand to lose if they do not choose it. A final question addresses the main idea of the text, with the correct response being that there are six scientifically proven principles of persuasion.

Short-answer questions encourage deeper reflection. For instance, students are asked how reciprocity works in the restaurant industry, with the answer being that small gifts like mints increase the tips customers leave. Another question asks for an example of consistency, where a small commitment, such as placing a postcard in a window, leads to a larger commitment, such as putting up a yard sign. A further question addresses consensus in hotel towel reuse campaigns, where showing that many other guests are already reusing towels increases compliance.

Open-ended prompts promote critical thinking and personal connection to the material. Students are invited to reflect on a time they were persuaded to do something and identify which of the six principles was used. They are also asked to consider ways to make themselves more likable to others, providing specific examples. Finally, students reflect on the role of experts in their lives, how they recognize expertise, and whether they consistently follow expert advice.

Diffit generated teaching materials for the lesson on "Persuasion" (YouTube video: Robert Cialdini – Science of Persuasion), including printable activities (Figure 10).

*Figure 10. Teaching Materials on "Persuasion" Generated by Diffit*

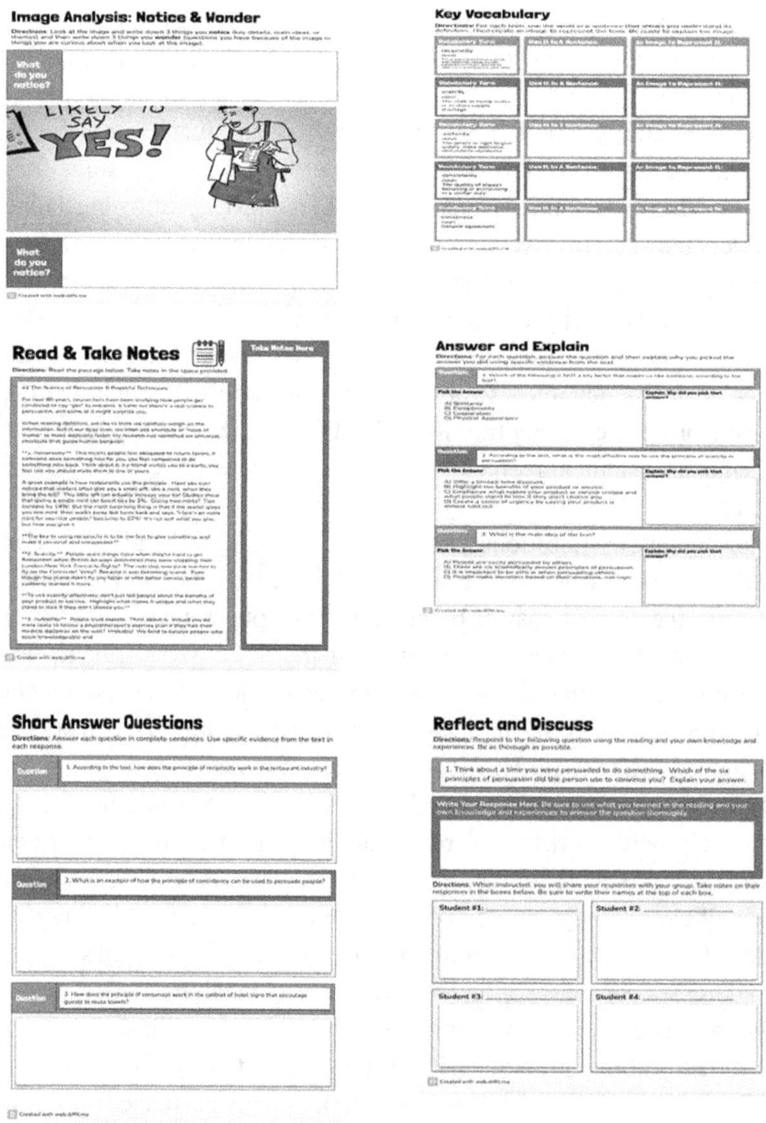

Wordwall (wordwall.net) is a valuable tool for pedagogues that enables the creation of interactive activities for foreign language learners. It allows teachers to design quizzes, word searches, and other printable or digital activities that can be used in class or completed at home. Wordwall transforms vocabulary lists into interactive games, enhancing student engagement. With this AI tool, teachers can incorporate tasks such as "Match Up," "Find the Match" (drag and drop each keyword next to its definition), "Matching Pairs" (flip pairs of tiles to check for matches), and "Group Sort." Additionally, Wordwall generates quizzes with multiple-choice questions and word games such as "Complete the Sentence" (a cloze activity where students drag and drop words into blanks). Randomizers such as speaking cards, flashcards, and "Spin the Wheel" can also be created to add variety and engagement. Examples of these applications are depicted in Figures 11 and 12.

*Figure 11. Grammar Task: Complete the Sentences, Generated by Wordwall Part 1*

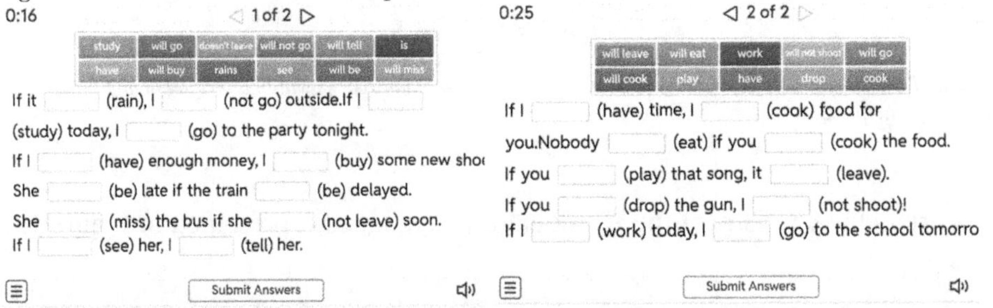


*Note. Task description: Learners drag and drop words into blank spaces within a text to complete sentences in the First Conditional.*

*Figure 12. Grammar Task: Complete the Sentences, Generated by Wordwall Part 2*

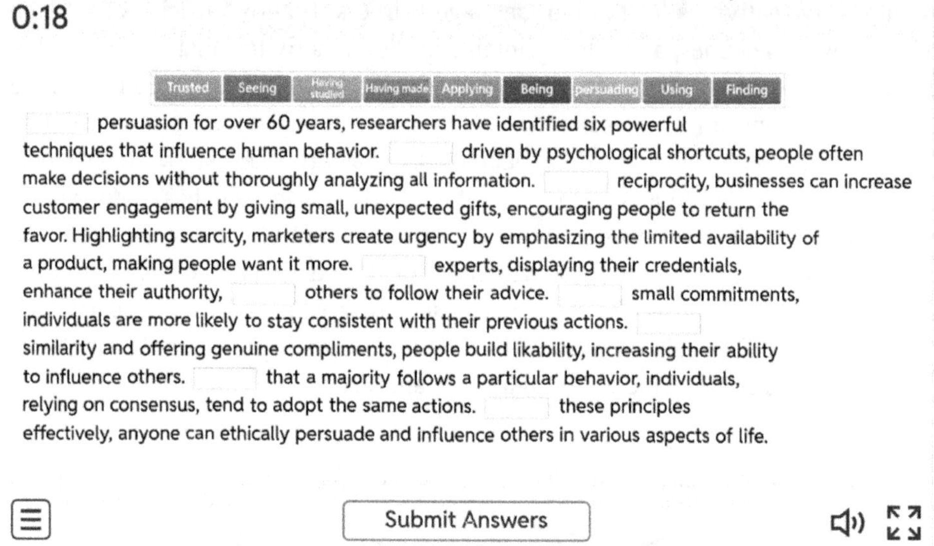


*Note. Task description: Learners drag and drop words into blank spaces within a text to complete sentences using the Participle Clause.*

A brief characteristic of the AI tools for pedagogues is presented in Figure 13.

*Figure 13. Artificial Intelligence (AI) Resources for Teachers: Core Functions*

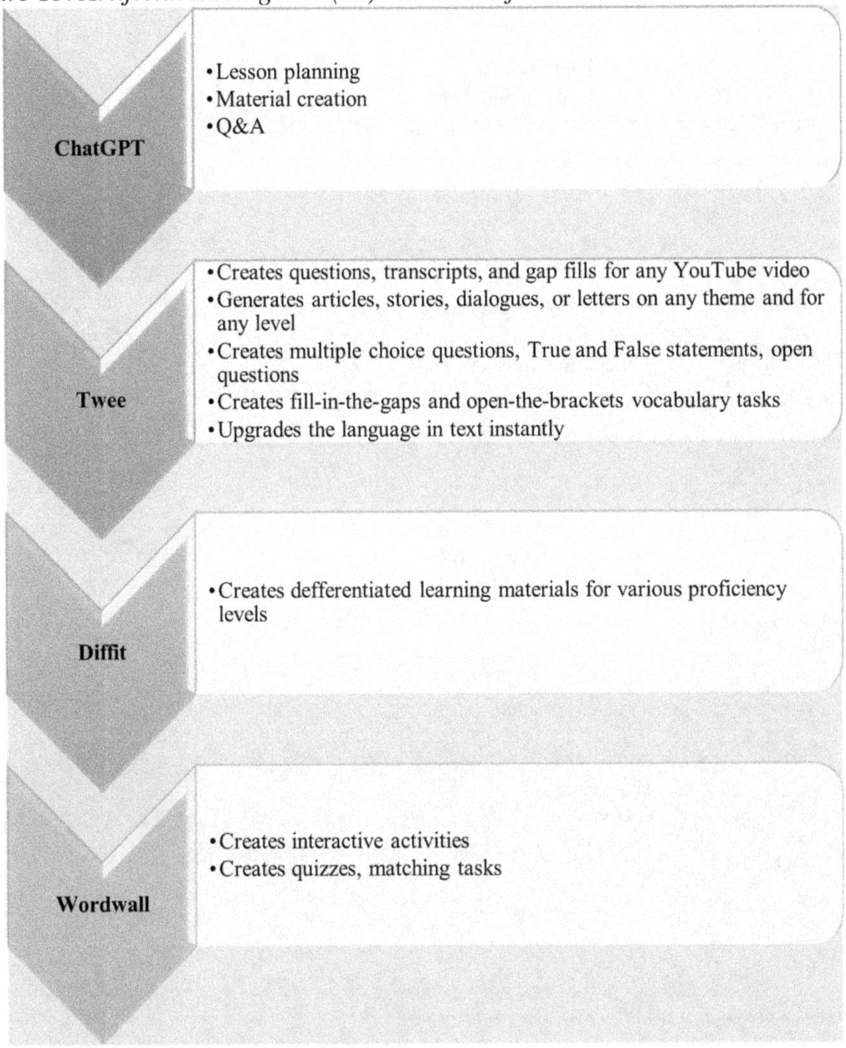


*Note. Image compiled based on Corrigan (2024).*

## AI-Powered Resources for Learners: Insights

Online opportunities for language education are increasingly diverse, and a brief overview of AI tools for learners is presented in Figure 14.

*Figure 14. Artificial Intelligence (AI) Resources for Learners: Core Functions*

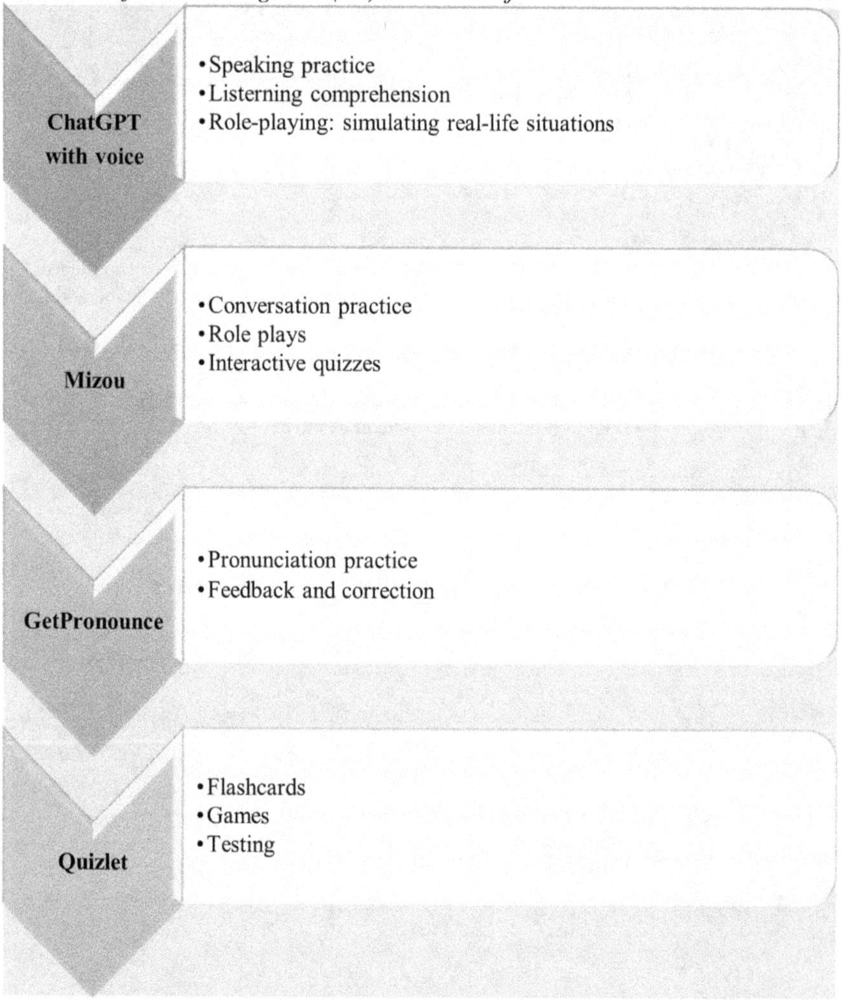


*Note. Image compiled based on Corrigan (2024).*

ChatGPT with voice integration offers an interactive way to practice speaking skills by engaging learners in spoken conversations with an AI, simulating real-life dialogue situations. While using it for speaking practice, learners receive immediate feedback on grammar and pronunciation errors. This type of language practice supports various situations and role-playing activities, such as asking for directions (for beginners) or pitching a business idea to a team (for advanced learners). Additionally, ChatGPT with voice integration enhances listening comprehension by exposing learners to natural language use.

Mizou (mizou.com) allows teachers and learners to create chatbots with specific learning objectives, enabling learners to practice speaking skills through personalized interactions. Mizou's intelligent AI algorithms tailor chatbot conversations to each learner's interests and needs, adapting in real time to learner responses. This promotes active learning, as Mizou's chatbots are both engaging and effective. Notably, teachers can either create their own chatbots for lessons or select from Mizou's online library (Nogues, 2024).

Characterizing Mizou, it is important to note that:

*Mizou offers the division in university, high, middle, and elementary schools. The software is similar to the social media platforms, which 'followers' and 'following' options available, creates a community for administrators and educators. The obvious benefit of the AI-powered learning tool is security, which is granted due to access to the task via a generated secure link without the need to log in and with the only requirement to fill in the student's name to launch the task... The unique feature is the ability of students to leave feedback for the teacher and to self-access (Rudnik, 2024, p. 18).*

GetPronounce (getpronounce.com) supports learners in improving pronunciation by recording their speech and comparing it with native speaker models. Quizlet (quizlet.com) helps students memorize vocabulary, including words and idioms, through interactive flashcards. Özdemir and Seçkin (2024) noted that:

*Quizlet, with its interactive and engaging features, emerges as a valuable tool that facilitates the learning process and is effective and helpful in the learning processes of language educators and learners. It is thought that it may be important to integrate mobile-assisted language learning resources such as Quizlet into educational practices and curricula as auxiliary tools to support foreign language learners' performance in vocabulary acquisition and to improve their attitudes positively (Özdemir & Seçkin, 2024, p. 15-16).*

Recent research also highlights that Quizlet enhances vocabulary learning and makes the study process more enjoyable and engaging, which in turn improves learners' motivation (Mykytka, 2023).

## AI-Powered Language Learning Apps: Studying Preferences of Learners

According to the statistics presented in Figure 15, Duolingo is the most popular language-learning app among AI-powered language-learning apps downloaded monthly worldwide. While other apps rank far below Duolingo, they continue to attract significant learner interest. These apps include Lingutown, HelloTalk, ELSA Speak, and Memrise.

*Figure 15. Leading Artificial Intelligence (AI)-Powered Language Learning Apps Worldwide in July 2024 by Downloads*

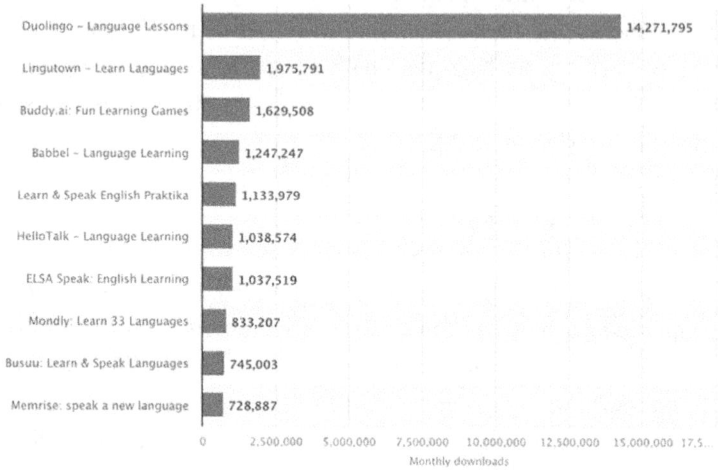


*Note. Adapted from Statista (2024).*

Within this study, Duolingo (www.duolingo.com), an AI-powered language learning app, is characterized as a widely recommended tool for foreign language learning. Recent research highlights that scholars have noted and endorsed the application of Duolingo to support language acquisition (Jiang et al., 2024; Permatasari & Aryani, 2023). This popular game-based app is an effective resource for improving language skills and offers various task types. These include translation exercises, matching tasks (such as matching pictures with words), and pairing exercises, where learners match an equal number of words from two languages. Additionally, Duolingo provides listening practice, where learners hear a short phrase and type the correct word, and speaking practice, in which learners listen to a phrase and then pronounce it (Nushi & Eqbali, 2017; Permatasari & Aryani, 2023).

## CONCLUSION

In summary, AI-powered resources have become valuable tools in language teaching. This study's characterization of Diffit, Twee, ChatGPT, and Wordwall has enabled the formulation and visual presentation of their key features. Learners, in turn, now benefit from a wide range of AI-driven platforms. Tools such as ChatGPT with voice integration, Mizou, GetPronounce, and Quizlet serve as effective facilitators in foreign language learning, alongside the globally recognized app Duolingo. Studying EFL remains a complex yet rewarding and essential endeavor. In today's digital era, AI technologies provide learners with enhanced opportunities to practice speaking skills through role-playing simulations of everyday scenarios, supported by ChatGPT with voice. GetPronounce supports pronunciation development, while Quizlet reinforces vocabulary acquisition. The teacher's role remains central in organizing and guiding the learning process. With AI tools such as ChatGPT, Twee, Diffit, and Wordwall, preparing lesson materials has become more efficient and dynamic. As interest in language learning continues to grow globally, Duolingo stands out as one of the most in-demand AI-powered apps supporting this educational journey.

## ACKNOWLEDGMENTS

This paper is a part of a research project of the Ministry of Education, Research, Development and Youth of the Slovak Republic KEGA/ePortfolio as Pedagogy Facilitating Integrative Learning 012EU-4/2023. The research was funded by the EU NextGenerationEU through the Recovery and Resilience Plan for Slovakia [grant number 09I03-03-V01-00045].

Correspondence concerning this monograph's chapter should be addressed to Natalia Shumeiko, Department of English Language, Bratislava University of Economics and Business, Slovakia. Email: natalia1shumeiko@gmail.com, natalia.shumeiko@euba.sk

## REFERENCES

Al-Shallakh, I., & Ahmad, M. (2024). Embedding Artificial Intelligent Applications in Higher Educational Institutions to Improve Students' Pronunciation Performance. [TPLS]. *Theory and Practice in Language Studies*, *14*(6).

AlAqlobi, O., Alduais, A., Alasmari, M., & Qasem, F. (2024). Artificial intelligence in language acquisition: A balancing act of potential and challenges. *Forum for Linguistic Studies*, *6*(6), 1103–1122. DOI: 10.30564/fls.v6i6.7524

Alfredo, R., Echeverria, V., Jin, Y., Yan, L., Swiecki, Z., Gašević, D., & Martinez-Maldonado, R. (2024). Human-centred learning analytics and AI in education: A systematic literature review. Computers and Education: Artificial Intelligence, 100215.

AI Index. (2024). Artificial Intelligence Index Steering Committee . https:// aiindex .stanford.edu/wp-content/uploads/2024/04/HAI_2024_AI-Index-Report.pdf

Bhardwaj, M., & Kumar, S. (2021). Scope of computer integrated manufacturing (CIM) in future technology as artificial intelligence. *Journal of Advanced Research in Electronics Engineering and Technology*, *7*, 16–20. https://thejournalshouse.com/index.php/electronics-engg-technology-adr/article/view/150

Boeru, M. (2024). Exploring the use of AI Tools in Teaching English for Specific Purposes (ESP). Scientific Bulletin'Mircea cel Batran'Naval Academy, 27(1).

Çakmak, F. (2022). Chatbot-human interaction and its effects on EFL students' L2 speaking performance and anxiety.

Chen, C.-H., Koong, C.-S., & Liao, C. (2022). Influences of integrating dynamic assessment into a speech recognition learning design to support pupils' English speaking skills, learning anxiety and cognitive load. *Journal of Educational Technology & Society*, *25*(1), 1–14. https://eric.ed.gov/?id=EJ1335942

Chen, D., Liu, W., & Liu, X. (2024). What drives college students to use AI for L2 learning? Modeling the roles of self-efficacy, anxiety, and attitude based on an extended technology acceptance model. *Acta Psychologica*, *249*, 104442. DOI: 10.1016/j.actpsy.2024.104442 PMID: 39111241

Chen, M.-R. A. (2024). The AI chatbot interaction for semantic learning: A collaborative note-taking approach with EFL students. *Language Learning & Technology*, *28*(1), 1–25. https://hdl.handle.net/10125/73586

Corrigan, S. (2024). Top 7 AI tools for language teachers and language learners. URL: https://epale.ec.europa.eu/en/blog/top-7-ai-tools-language-teachers-and-language-learners

Crompton, H., & Burke, D. (2023). Artificial intelligence in higher education: The state of the field. *International Journal of Educational Technology in Higher Education*, *20*(1), 22.

Edmett, A., Ichaporia, N., Crompton, H., Crichton, R. (2023). Artificial intelligence and English language teaching: Preparing for the future. British Council. URL: DOI: 10.57884/78EA-3C69

Edwards, L., Eales, F., & Oakes, S. (2023). Speak out 3rd Edition, Student's book and eBook with online practice, Pearson Education Limited, 176 p.

Fathi, J., Rahimi, M., & Derakhshan, A. (2024). Improving EFL learners' speaking skills and willingness to communicate via artificial intelligence-mediated interactions. *System*, *121*, 103254. DOI: 10.1016/j.system.2024.103254

Fatima, S. N. (2024). Artificial intelligence for pronunciation improvement in second language acquisition. *Journal for Research Scholars and Professionals of English Language Teaching*, *8*(41), 2–22. DOI: 10.54850/jrspelt.8.41.001

Fu, Y., Zhang, Z., & Yang, H. (2023). Design of Oral English Teaching Assistant System based on deep belief networks. *Soft Computing*, *27*(22), 17403–17418.

Greco, M., Grimaldi, M., Locatelli, G., & Serafini, M. (2021). How does open innovation enhance productivity? An exploration in the construction ecosystem. *Technological Forecasting and Social Change*, *168*, 120740. DOI: 10.1016/j.techfore.2021.120740

Han, Z. (2024). Chatgpt in and for second language acquisition: A call for systematic research. *Studies in Second Language Acquisition*, *46*(2), 301–306. DOI: 10.1017/S0272263124000111

Holmes, W., & Tuomi, I. (2022). State of the Art and Practice in AI in Education. *European Journal of Education*, 57(4), 542–570. DOI: 10.1111/ejed.12533

Huang, F., Wang, Y., & Zhang, H. (2024). Modelling generative ai acceptance, perceived teachers' enthusiasm and self-efficacy to English as a foreign language learners' well-being in the digital era. *European Journal of Education*, *59*(4), e12770. DOI: 10.1111/ejed.12770

Huang, F., & Zou, B. (2024). English speaking with artificial intelligence (AI): The roles of enjoyment, willingness to communicate with AI, and innovativeness. *Computers in Human Behavior*, *159*, 108355. DOI: 10.1016/j.chb.2024.108355

Jiang, X., Peters, R., Plonsky, L., & Pajak, B. (2024). *The Effectiveness of Duolingo English Courses in Developing Reading and Listening Proficiency. CALICO, 2024*. URL., DOI: 10.1558/cj.26704

John, T., & Davies, F. (1983). Text as a vehicle for information: The classroom use of written texts in teaching reading in a foreign language. *Reading in a Foreign Language*, *1*(1), 1–19.

Khiem, H. G., Huong, H. L., Triet, M. N., Khanh, H. V., Phuc, N. T., Khoa, T. D., Hien, N. Q., Tung, L. K., Nam, T. B., Vinh, N. T., Kha, N. H., Thuan, Q. T., Bang, L. K., Minh, N. V., Ngan, N. T. K., & Quy, T. L. (2023, November). Generative AI in English education: Harnessing ChatGPT for digital learning. In International Symposium on Emerging Technologies for Education (pp. 147-157). Singapore: Springer Nature Singapore.

Kim, N. Y. (2022). AI-Integrated Mobile-Assisted Language Learning: Is It an Effective Way of Preparing for the TOEIC Test in Classroom Environments? *English Teaching*, *77*(3), 79–102.

Krashen, S. (1982). *Principles and practice in second language acquisition*. Pergamon Press.

Kushmar, L. V., Vornachev, A. O., Korobova, I. O., & Kaida, N. O. (2022). Artificial Intelligence in Language Learning: What are we afraid of. *Arab World English Journal*, *8*, 262–273.

Lambert, J. (2024). Why writing by hand beats typing for thinking and learning. URL: npr.org

Lee, U., Jung, H., Jeon, Y., Sohn, Y., Hwang, W., Moon, J., & Kim, H. (2024). Few-shot is enough: exploring ChatGPT prompt engineering method for automatic question generation in English education. In Education and Information Technologies (Vol. 29, pp. 11483–11515). URL., DOI: 10.1007/s10639-023-12249-8

Li, , JZong, , HWu, , EWu, , RPeng, , ZZhao, , JShen, , B. (2024). Exploring the potential of artificial intelligence to enhance the writing of english academic papers by non-native english-speaking medical students-the educational application of ChatGPT. *BMC Medical Education, 24*(1), 736.

Liu, S. C., & Hung, P. Y. (2016). Teaching pronunciation with computer assisted pronunciation instruction in a technological university. *Universal Journal of Educational Research, 4*(9), 1939–1943.

Liu, X., & Xiao, Y. (2025). Chinese university teachers' engagement with generative AI in different stages of foreign language teaching: A qualitative enquiry through the prism of ADDIE. *Education and Information Technologies, 30*(1), 485–508. DOI: 10.1007/s10639-024-13117-9

Mohamed, A. M. (2024). Exploring the potential of an AI-based Chatbot (ChatGPT) in enhancing English as a Foreign Language (EFL) teaching: Perceptions of EFL Faculty Members. *Education and Information Technologies, 29*(3), 3195–3217.

Mykytka, I. (2023). The use of Quizlet to enhance L2 vocabulary acquisition. *Encuentro Journal, 31*, 56–69.

Nogues, J. (2024). Unlocking potential: harnessing AI for language teaching and learning. URL: https://www.fraubastowmfl.co.uk/post/unlocking-potential-harnessing-ai-for-language-teaching-and-learning

Nushi, M., & Eqbali, M. H. (2017). Duolingo: A mobile application to assist second language learning. *Teaching English with Technology, 17*(1), 89–98.

Özdemir, O., & Seçkin, H. (2024). Quantifying cognitive and affective impacts of Quizlet on learning outcomes: A systematic review and comprehensive meta-analysis. *Frontiers in Psychology, 15*, 1349835.

Pérez-Paredes, P. (2022). A systematic review of the uses and spread of corpora and data-driven learning in CALL research during 2011–2015. *Computer Assisted Language Learning, 35*(1–2), 36–61. DOI: 10.1080/09588221.2019.1667832

Permatasari, D., & Aryani, F. (2023). Duolingo: An enchanting application to learn English for college students. *ELTR Journal, 7*(2), 101–109.

Persulessy, S. I., Nikijuluw, R. P. V., & Jakob, J. C. (2024). Utilizing Artificial Intelligence in Language Learning: What About Engineering Students' Perception? *Journal of English Education Program*, *5*(1), 3–11. DOI: 10.26418/jeep.v5i1.71159

Regona, M., Yigitcanlar, T., Xia, B., & Li, R. Y. M. (2022). Opportunities and adoption challenges of AI in the construction industry: A PRISMA review. *Journal of Open Innovation*, *8*(1), 45–60. DOI: 10.3390/joitmc8010045

Rudnik, Y. (2024). The Use of Artificial Intelligence Chatbots in Teaching Foreign Languages as an Innovative Interactive Technology. Educological discourse, 45(2).

Schütze, U. (2024). *Virtual reality, artificial intelligence, and language learning*. John Benjamins Publishing Company., DOI: 10.1075/bpa.19

Shumeiko, N. (2024). Exploiting the potential of Artificial Intelligence in teaching English: some scientific aspects. ZBORNÍK konferencie XXXVII DidMatTech 2024. Proceedings of XXXVII DidMatTech 2024 Conference "New Methods and Technologies in Education, Research and Practice," J. Selye University - Komárno, Trnava University in Trnava, p.46-57. Article. ISBN 978-80-568-0698-2. http://didmattech.ujs.sk/proceeding/

Shumeiko, N. V., & Osadcha, K. P. (2024, October). Application of artificial intelligence in higher education institutions for developing soft skills of future specialists in the sphere of information technology. *Journal of Physics: Conference Series*, *2871*(1), 012027.

Son, J., Ružić, N., & Philpott, A. (2023). Artificial intelligence technologies and applications for language learning and teaching. *Journal of China Computer-Assisted Language Learning*. Advance online publication.

Statista. (2024). Leading language learning apps worldwide in July 2024, by downloads. https://www.statista.com/statistics/1239522/top-language-learning-apps-downloads/

Tricomi, E. T. (1986). Krashen's second-language acquisition theory and the teaching of edited American English. *Journal of Basic Writing*, *5*(2), 59–69. DOI: 10.37514/JBW-J.1986.5.2.07

Tsai, C. Y., Lin, Y. T., & Brown, I. K. (2024). Impacts of ChatGPT-assisted writing for EFL English majors: Feasibility and challenges. In *Education and Information Technologies*. URL., DOI: 10.1007/s10639-024-12722-y

U.S. Department of Education, Office of Educational Technology. (2023). *Artificial intelligence and the future of teaching and learning: Insights and recommendations*. U.S. Department of Education. https://www.ed.gov/sites/ed/files/documents/ai-report/ai-report.pdf

Williamson, B. (2024). The social life of AI in education. *International Journal of Artificial Intelligence in Education, 34*(1), 97–104.

Woodrum, C. (2024, May). ChatGPT and Language Translation: A Small Case Study Evaluating English–Mandarin Translation. In International Conference on Human-Computer Interaction (pp. 147-157). Cham: Springer Nature Switzerland.

Wu, H., Liu, W., & Zeng, Y. (2024). Validating the AI-assisted second language (L2) learning attitude scale for Chinese college students and its correlation with L2 proficiency. *Acta Psychologica, 248*, 104376. DOI: 10.1016/j.actpsy.2024.104376 PMID: 38955032

Xu, T., & Wang, H. (2024). The effectiveness of artificial intelligence on English language learning achievement. *System, 125*, 103428. DOI: 10.1016/j.system.2024.103428

Yang, Y. (2025). AI-supported L2 vocabulary acquisition–a systematic review from 2015 to 2023. *Education and Information Technologies*, 1–35. DOI: 10.1007/s10639-025-13417-8

Zeng, C., & Fisher, L. (2024). Opening the "black box": How out-of-class use of Duolingo impacts Chinese junior high school students' intrinsic motivation for English. *ECNU Review of Education*, *7*(2), 283–307.

Zhang, Q., Nie, H., Fan, J., & Liu, H. (2025). Exploring the dynamics of artificial intelligence literacy on English as a foreign language learners' willingness to communicate: The critical mediating roles of artificial intelligence learning self-efficacy and classroom anxiety. *Behavioral Sciences (Basel, Switzerland), 15*(4), 523–540. DOI: 10.3390/bs15040523 PMID: 40282144

Zhang, Z., & Huang, X. (2024). The impact of chatbots based on large language models on second language vocabulary acquisition. *Heliyon, 10*(3), e25370. DOI: 10.1016/j.heliyon.2024.e25370 PMID: 38333802

Zhu, M., & Wang, C. (2025). A systematic review of artificial intelligence in language education: Current status and future implications. *Language Learning & Technology*, *29*(1), 1–29. https://hdl.handle.net/10125/73606

## ADDITIONAL READING


Crawford, J., & Krashen, S. (2007). *English Language Learners in American Classrooms: 101 Questions, 101 Answers*. Scholastic.

DeKeyser, R. M. (2012). Interactions between individual differences, treatments, and structures in SLA. *Language Learning*, *62*(Suppl. 2), 189–200. https://doi.org/10.1111/j.1467-9922.2012.00712.x

Dörnyei, Z. (1994). Motivation and motivating in the foreign language classroom. *Modern Language Journal*, *78*(3), 273–284.

Dörnyei, Z. (2001). *Motivational Strategies in the Language Classroom*. Cambridge University Press.

Dörnyei, Z. (2003). *Questionnaires in Second Language Research: Construction, Administration, and Processing*. Routledge.

Dörnyei, Z. (2005). *The Psychology of the Language Learner: Individual Differences in Second Language Acquisition*. Lawrence Erlbaum Associates.

Dörnyei, Z. (2007). *Research Methods in Applied Linguistics: Quantitative, Qualitative, and Mixed Methodologies*. Oxford University Press.

Dörnyei, Z. (2009). The L2 Motivational Self System. In Dörnyei, Z., & Ushioda, E. (Eds.), *Motivation, Language Identity and the L2 Self* (pp. 9–42). Multilingual Matters.

Dörnyei, Z., & Csizér, K. (2002). Some dynamics of language attitudes and motivation: Results of a longitudinal nationwide survey. *Applied Linguistics*, *23*(4), 421–462.

Dörnyei, Z., & Ottó, I. (1998). Motivation in action: A process model of L2 motivation. Working Papers in Applied Linguistics, vol 4. https://nottingham-repository.worktribe.com/output/1024190

Dörnyei, Z., & Ryan, S. (2015). *The Psychology of the Language Learner Revisited*. Routledge.

Dörnyei, Z., & Ushioda, E. (2011). *Teaching and Researching Motivation* (2nd ed.). Longman.

Elahi Shirvan, M., Saeedy Robat, E., Alamer, A., Lou, N. M., & Barabadi, E. (2024). A multilevel meta-analysis of language mindsets and language learning outcomes in second language acquisition research. *Educational Psychology Review*, *36*(15). https://link.springer.com/article/10.1007/s10648-024-09849-2

Jeon, E.-Y., & Day, R. R. (2016). The effectiveness of ER on reading proficiency: A meta-analysis. *Reading in a Foreign Language, 28*(2), 246–265. https://files.eric.ed.gov/fulltext/EJ1117026.pdf

Krashen, S. (1982). *Child-Adult Differences in Second Language Acquisition*. Newbury House.

Krashen, S. (1985). *The Input Hypothesis: Issues and Implications*. Longman.

Krashen, S. (1985). *Inquiries & Insights: Second Language Teaching Immersion & Bilingual Education, Literacy*. Alemany Press.

Krashen, S. (1989). *Language Acquisition and Language Education: Extensions and Applications*. Prentice Hall International.

Krashen, S. (1991). *Fundamentals of Language Education*. Laredo Publishing.

Krashen, S. (1991). *Bilingual Education: A Focus on Current Research*. National Clearinghouse for Bilingual Education.

Krashen, S. (1992). *Free Voluntary Reading*. Libraries Unlimited.

Krashen, S. (1993). *The Power of Reading: Insights from the Research*. Libraries Unlimited.

Krashen, S. (1996). *Under Attack: The Case Against Bilingual Education*. Language Education Associates.

Krashen, S. (1998). *Foreign Language Education the Easy Way*. Language Education Associates.

Krashen, S., & Biber, D. (1988). *On Course: Bilingual Education's Success in California*. California Assn.

Krashen, S., & Tracy, D. Terrell (1983). The Natural Approach (Language Acquisition in the Classroom). Alemany Press.

Krashen, S. D. (1999). *Condemned Without a Trial: Bogus Arguments Against Bilingual Education*. Heinemann.

Krashen, S. D. (2003). *Explorations in Language Acquisition and Use*. Heinemann.

Lennon, P. (2020). *The Foundations of Teaching English as a Foreign Language* (1st ed.). Routledge., DOI: 10.4324/9780429285998

Mihaljevic Djigunovic, J., & Medved Krajnovic, M. (2025). Language Teaching Methodology and Second Language Acquisition. Encyclopedia of Life Support Systems (EOLSS). https://www.eolss.net/Sample-Chapters/C04/E6-91-13-01.pdf

Muthyala, U., & Chada, R. R. (Eds.). (2024). *Vocabulary, corpus and language teaching: A machine-generated literature overview.* Springer., https://doi.org/10.1007/978-3-031-45986-3

Myles, F. (2010). The development of theories of second language acquisition. *Language Teaching*, *43*(3), 320–332. DOI: 10.1017/S0261444810000078

Peña-Acuña, B., & Corga Fernandes Durão, R. (2024). Learning English as a second language with artificial intelligence for prospective teachers: A systematic review. *Frontiers in Education.* Advance online publication. DOI: 10.3389/feduc.2024.1490067

Shumeiko, N., & Krajčovičova, N. (2023). Testing vocabulary and grammar: Online techniques. Proceedings of V Annual Conference on Current Foreign Languages Teaching Issues in Higher Education. Retrieved from https://kamts2.kpi.ua/en/conferences-2/

Shumeiko, N., & Nypadymka, A. (2021). ICT-Supported Students' Independent Work in the ESP Cpontext: The New Reality in Tertiary Education. *Advanced Education*, *8*(18), 79–91. https://doi.org/10.20535/2410-8286.223286

Spišiaková, M., & Shumeiko, N. (2024). E-learning Resources Implementation in Teaching Business English and Testing English Speaking Skills at the University Level. Folia linguistica et litteraria. *Journal of Language and Literary Studies*, *48*. Advance online publication. DOI: 10.31902/fll.48.2024.14

Spišiaková, M., & Shumeiko, N. (2025). Using YouTube in Language Education in Non-linguistic Universities: Bridging the Theory and Practice. In Reis, J. L., Peter, M. K., Reis, L. P., & Bogdanovic, Z. (Eds.), *Marketing and Smart Technologies. ICMarkTech 2023. Smart Innovation, Systems and Technologies* (Vol. 393). Springer., https://doi.org/10.1007/978-981-97-3698-0_46

## KEY TERMS AND DEFINITIONS

**AI-Mediated Communication:** (in an EFL conversation lesson) using AI-powered chatbots, translation apps, or AI voice assistants in the teacher-student communication during an EFL (EFL = English as a Foreign Language) conversation lesson.

**AI-Supported L2 Vocabulary Acquisition:** The process of learning new words in a second language (L2 = a second language) with the help of AI (AI = artificial intelligence) tools.

**Artificial intelligence (AI):** A technology that enables virtual machines or computer systems to perform tasks that previously seemed to be manageable only by human intelligence. It comes to fulfilling such tasks (in the context of language learning), but not limited to: speech recognition, and the collection of information on a certain topic (however, this information should be checked).

**EFL Classroom:** This is a learning environment (offline, online, blended) where students learn English as a Foreign Language (EFL). Actually, it is about learning EFL in a country where English is not a state language. In such a classroom English is typically not used outside a school in everyday communication. English is learned during pedagogically structured lessons that are focused on improving students' writing, speaking, reading, and listening skills.

**Foreigner Talk:** A simplified language style for achieving effective communication. This style is used by native speakers when communicating with non-native speakers. In the process of such communication native speakers use basic vocabulary, simplify grammar, and pronounce the words clearly, and slowly.

**L2 Learning:** The process of learning the second language (L2 = a second language), after acquiring the first (L1 = a native language) language.

**Motherese:** A way of speaking (usually when adults are talking to babies) that implies clear pronunciation, the repetition of words or sentences slowly.

**Second Language Acquisition (SLA):** The process of learning a language other than the learner's native one (L1 = a native language). The method of the SLA involves the acquisition of vocabulary and grammar, and the achievement of strong communicative competence.

# Chapter 2
# AI and Gamification: Engaging EFL Learners With Language Games

**Mustafa Kayyali**
https://orcid.org/0000-0003-3300-262X
*Maaref University of Applied Sciences, Syria*

## ABSTRACT

*The combination of Artificial Intelligence (AI) and gamification in English as a Foreign Language (EFL) training has transformed how learners interact with language acquisition. This chapter addresses the unique convergence of AI and gamified learning, concentrating on the use of interactive language games to boost student motivation, engagement, and competency. The talk begins with a review of theoretical underpinnings, stressing how gamification elements such as incentives, challenges, and feedback connect with language learning goals. It then investigates how AI-powered technologies customize the learning experience by adjusting information to specific learner requirements, enabling a more engaging and successful environment. AI-driven gamification promotes real-time language practice, adaptive feedback, and contextual learning, making it a dynamic alternative to standard teaching approaches. This chapter includes practical ideas and techniques for educators and researchers hoping to harness these emerging technologies for better language learning experiences.*

## INTRODUCTION

The teaching of English as a Foreign Language (EFL) has experienced substantial development during the past several decades. From conventional classroom settings where instruction was largely professor-centered to the creative, technology-driven

DOI: 10.4018/979-8-3373-0969-9.ch002

techniques of today, the path of EFL teaching has been nothing short of spectacular. This development reflects not just improvements in instructional practices but also the ever-changing demands of a globalized society where English serves as a shared language franca. As we go deeper into the 21st century, EFL education is at the crossroads of creativity and necessity, spurred by technology breakthroughs, increasing learner expectations, and the linked character of modern society (Al Khatri, 2019). The value of English as a crucial instrument for worldwide communication, trade, and diplomacy cannot be emphasized. In practically every part of the world, English is no longer considered solely as an academic topic; it has become a gateway to chances in education, work, and cultural interaction. This fact has placed great pressure on educators to guarantee that EFL education fulfills the diverse and changing requirements of learners. The problem rests not only in providing students with language skills but also in promoting cultural competence, critical thinking, and the capacity to adapt to varied circumstances where English is used. As a result, the scope of EFL education has increased dramatically, incorporating far more than grammatical rules, vocabulary lists, and pronunciation drills.

At the heart of this revolution is the rising incorporation of technology into language training (Ally & Wark, 2020). Technological developments have opened up a world of possibilities for both instructors and students, offering pathways for individualized learning, quick feedback, and immersive experiences. Language learning applications, virtual classrooms, artificial intelligence technologies, and gamified platforms have transformed the landscape of EFL education, making it more accessible, interesting, and personalized to individual requirements. These improvements have allowed instructors to go beyond one-size-fits-all approaches, adopting ways that acknowledge the particular strengths, limitations, and learning styles of each student. Yet, the inclusion of technology is not without its obstacles. Questions of accessibility, digital literacy, and the balance between human engagement and machine-driven learning remain essential considerations (Bengsch, 2024). While technology plays a vital role in current EFL training, it is not the main engine of change. Societal transformations, particularly in the aftermath of globalization, have also changed how English is taught and learned. The old idea of English as a foreign language is giving way to a more subtle understanding of its position as a global language. Learners nowadays are not only adopting English to connect with native speakers; they are utilizing it to communicate with people from varied languages and cultural backgrounds. This transition has important consequences for EFL instruction, necessitating a concentration on multicultural communication skills, global awareness, and the capacity to manage complicated social dynamics.

The heterogeneity of learners themselves further highlights the dynamic character of EFL instruction (Rovai & Pfingsthorn, 2022). No longer restricted to children and young people in formal college settings, English learners increasingly include professionals seeking career progress, migrants adapting to new contexts, and individuals pursuing personal enrichment. This variety needs a flexible and inclusive approach to teaching, one that incorporates the different motivations, aims, and settings of learners. For example, a corporate executive may require specific terminology and negotiating skills, while a student preparing for higher education would focus on academic writing and research capabilities. Meeting these various demands requires a comprehensive grasp of learners' profiles and the capacity to develop training that is both relevant and effective. The future of EFL teaching is not only an academic problem but a reflection of wider socioeconomic trends and difficulties (Akbana & Yavuz, 2020). Issues such as globalization, technological disruption, and cultural interchange are inextricably tied to how languages are taught and learned. As English continues to play a major role in bridging linguistic and cultural boundaries, the job of EFL educators extends beyond language competency. They are entrusted with educating learners to manage a fast-changing environment, nurturing abilities that go beyond the classroom and into real-life encounters.

This chapter discusses the multiple paths in which EFL instruction is heading, evaluating the interplay of technology, pedagogy, and societal concerns. It digs into the benefits and problems given by breakthroughs like artificial intelligence, blended learning models, and immersive technology, while also emphasizing the important importance of human connection and cultural understanding. The debate seeks to provide a complete knowledge of the issues affecting the future of EFL teaching, including insights into how instructors may adapt to and succeed in this changing environment. In setting the stage for this investigation, it is vital to remember that the future of EFL teaching is not a fixed destination but a continuous journey. It is a process of adaptation, exploration, and learning that mirrors the complexity of language itself. Just as English has grown over centuries to become the worldwide language it is today, so too must the methods of teaching it evolve to suit the requirements of an increasingly linked world. By recognizing the patterns and consequences addressed in this chapter, educators may take a proactive role in determining the future of EFL education, ensuring that it stays current, impactful, and accessible to learners of all backgrounds.

## AI AND GAMIFICATION IN EFL

The integration of artificial intelligence (AI) and gamification into the field of English as a Foreign Language (EFL) instruction has emerged as a significant advancement in modern education (Moybeka et al, 2023). These technologies offer a new and interesting way to increase language acquisition, grabbing the interest of learners in ways that traditional techniques frequently cannot. When these two strong technologies converge, the potential for revolutionizing how learners interact with language acquisition becomes clear. The combination of AI and gamification is not just about making language learning more enjoyable; it is about creating an immersive, interactive environment where students can actively participate, progress at their own pace, and receive tailored feedback that directly addresses their individual needs.

At its foundation, AI is a sort of technology that employs algorithms and data to replicate human intellect, enabling computers to learn, adapt, and improve over time (Dong et al, 2020). In the context of EFL, AI technologies have expanded to include sophisticated language apps that give voice recognition, real-time feedback, and even individualized lesson plans depending on a learner's strengths and shortcomings. Gamification, on the other hand, pulls on the ideas of game design—such as points, levels, challenges, and rewards—to inspire learners and create persistent engagement. Together, AI and gamification combine the analytical precision of modern technology with the psychological drives that make games so fascinating, providing an altogether new paradigm for language instruction. The integration of AI and gamification in EFL is predicated on the premise that learning is most successful when it is dynamic, immersive, and relevant. Language development involves constant practice, engagement, and feedback. Traditional classroom environments typically fall short of offering the specific attention that each learner requires, especially in large or diverse classrooms. Here, AI steps in to bridge the gap, delivering tools that assess a learner's challenges—be it pronunciation, grammar, or vocabulary—and provide fast, constructive feedback.

Coupled with gamification, these technologies provide a learning environment where students are not only passive consumers of knowledge but active players in their educational journey (Shah et al, 2024). Imagine, for instance, an AI-powered language game that reacts in real-time to a student's progress. If a student suffers from verb conjugations, the game may produce tailored workouts, quietly incorporating the necessary practice within exciting tasks or scenarios. Through gamified components like earning badges or unlocking new levels, learners are encouraged to keep trying, motivated not just by external prizes but also by the internal delight of learning new abilities. The AI guarantees that the difficulty level is neither too easy nor too annoying, establishing the optimum balance to maintain learners in a state of flow—a notion from psychology that represents the best zone for learning. One of the most striking elements of AI in EFL gamification is its capacity to tailor the learning experience (Liu, 2024). Every student approaches language acquisition with a unique blend of talents, limitations, and past experiences. While traditional classes frequently rely on a one-size-fits-all approach, AI-powered gamified solutions cater to individual learners, tailoring information to match their requirements. For example, a hesitant student who hesitates to speak in class can benefit from an AI-powered app that utilizes speech recognition to practice pronunciation in a low-pressure scenario. Similarly, a highly motivated student might learn a difficult language through gamified scenarios that challenge their critical thinking abilities. This personalized method not only makes learning more effective but also develops confidence, since learners can observe their progress in real time.

Another significant advantage of gamification in EFL is its capacity to make learning entertaining (Ahmed et al, 2022). Language acquisition is a long and frequently hard process, requiring patience and tenacity. Gamification mitigates the boredom of repeating drills by turning them into entertaining activities (Zhao, 2021). Instead of rote memorizing, learners could go on a virtual journey where they need to utilize English to solve puzzles, engage with people, or accomplish tasks. These games frequently integrate storytelling components, which further boost engagement by immersing learners in relevant environments. When learners are emotionally immersed in a tale or problem, they are more likely to recall the language they encounter. AI-driven gamification also stimulates teamwork and social engagement, which are key components of language acquisition (Renacido & Biray, 2025). Multiplayer games, for instance, empower learners to work together to achieve shared goals, communicating in English to strategize and solve challenges (Firmansyah & Rosmansyah, 2024). These exchanges imitate real-life language use, giving learners vital practice in a supportive, low-stakes setting. AI further enhances this experience by monitoring interactions, ensuring that talks remain constructive and on-topic, and even stepping in to give aid or clarification when needed. This offers a secure area where learners may experiment with language without fear of criticism or failure.

Despite its numerous advantages, the integration of AI and gamification in EFL is not without its hurdles (Fakher Ajabshir, 2023). One problem is accessibility. Advanced AI-powered tools and gamified platforms frequently demand substantial resources, including stable internet connectivity, contemporary gadgets, and technical assistance. In locations with poor infrastructure, deploying these technologies might be problematic, potentially expanding the digital divide. To overcome this, educators and developers must emphasize the construction of scalable, cheap solutions that can be tailored to varied circumstances. Open-source platforms and partnerships between educational institutions and digital businesses can play a crucial role in making these technologies available to a larger audience.

Another problem comes in ensuring that the use of AI and gamification does not overwhelm the essential aims of language acquisition (Luu, 2024). While games and AI tools are good for acquiring specific abilities, they should not replace the larger context of human interaction and cultural knowledge that is needed for mastering a language. Educators must find a balance, employing AI and gamification as additions to, rather than substitutes for, established teaching approaches. By integrating these tools with face-to-face education, cultural immersion, and realistic communication chances, professors may create a full learning experience that addresses all areas of language acquisition. As we look to the future, the potential of AI and gamification in EFL is huge. Emerging technologies, such as virtual reality (VR) and augmented reality (AR), are already being blended into language learning, allowing even more immersive and engaging experiences (Kayyali, 2021). Imagine a VR game where learners pass over a bustling metropolis, ordering food, asking for directions, and participating in discussions with virtual characters—all in English. Such encounters give learners a degree of contextual practice that was previously inconceivable, bridging the gap between the classroom and the real world. The incorporation of AI and gamification in EFL signifies a radical shift in how we approach language instruction. By harnessing the power of technology and the motivating principles of game design, educators may build dynamic, individualized, and engaging learning experiences that fit the requirements of varied learners. While hurdles exist, the potential advantages far exceed the constraints, offering a future where language acquisition is not only successful but also fun and accessible to all. Through continuing innovation and smart application, AI and gamification have the potential to change EFL instruction, helping learners attain their language objectives with confidence and passion.

## THEORETICAL FOUNDATIONS: GAMIFICATION AND LANGUAGE LEARNING

Language acquisition, by its very nature, is a complicated, multi-faceted process that needs learners to concurrently gain abilities in listening, speaking, reading, and writing (Nafa, 2023). It also includes establishing cultural awareness and negotiating the subtleties of a new linguistic system. Over the years, different ideas and ways have been presented to ease this delicate process. Among these, gamification has emerged as an effective and novel approach to increase language learning results. By harnessing the motivating components of games and integrating them with known language acquisition theories, gamification provides a unique framework for boosting engagement and long-term retention in learners. To truly comprehend its potential, it is crucial to dive into the theoretical underpinnings that connect gamification with language acquisition.

At its foundation, gamification refers to the implementation of game design principles—such as competition, prizes, and progression—within non-gaming environments (Mauroner, 2019). In education, it serves as a strategy to boost student enthusiasm and active involvement. However, gamification is more than just adding points, badges, or leaderboards to a learning endeavor. Its efficacy comes from its capacity to tap into intrinsic drive, a concept founded in Self-Determination Theory SDT (Sheldon & Prentice, 2019). According to SDT, human beings are naturally drawn to engage in activities that meet three essential psychological needs: autonomy, competence, and relatedness. Gamification in language learning matches these demands by establishing settings where learners feel in control of their progress, experience mastery via challenges, and engage with peers in meaningful ways. The relevance of motivation in language acquisition cannot be emphasized. As one of the primary elements impacting success in acquiring a second language, motivation has been widely explored in the context of both traditional and gamified learning. Decades ago, scholars like Gardner and Lambert stressed the significance of integrative and instrumental motivation in language acquisition. Integrative motivation refers to the desire to learn a language to connect with its speakers and culture, whereas instrumental motivation is driven by practical goals such as job success. Gamification caters to both immersing learners in culturally appropriate settings and delivering practical incentives for reaching language milestones (Ravichandran et al, 2024). For instance, a gamified app may imitate real-world interactions, such as ordering lunch in a foreign location, while delivering quick feedback and prizes for accurate replies. The Connectionist Theory of language learning further supports the use of gamification in EFL instruction (Li, 2024). This theory states that language learning is a process of building links between linguistic information and related situations. These connections grow via repeated exposure and practice. Gamification naturally enhances this process by promoting repeated yet diverse practice through interactive activities and challenges. Games typically convey language in meaningful situations, requiring learners to comprehend and generate language as part of a bigger objective or story. For example, a language-learning game can entail traversing a virtual marketplace, where learners must utilize acceptable vocabulary and grammar to fulfill tasks. The contextualized practice builds brain connections, making it simpler for learners to recall and apply their information in real-life circumstances.

Another theoretical approach that underlines the significance of gamification in language acquisition is Krashen's Input Hypothesis (Wang & Wu, 2025). According to this theory, language learning happens most successfully when learners are exposed to understandable input—language that is somewhat beyond their present level of skill referred to as “i+1” (Loewen, 2020). Gamified settings thrive at presenting this sort of input. AI-powered games, for example, may dynamically change the level of activities to fit a learner’s ability, ensuring that the information stays tough but not overwhelming. This flexibility not only promotes understanding but also retains engagement by presenting learners with a sense of success as they proceed through increasingly challenging stages. Vygotsky’s Sociocultural Theory also presents a persuasive rationale for the use of gamification in language acquisition (El, 2023). This approach stresses the significance of social contact and collaboration in the development of cognitive skills, particularly language learning. In gamified contexts, learners generally engage in collaborative activities, such as multiplayer games or team-based tasks, which demand them to communicate and problem-solve using the target language. These interactions imitate real-world language usage, allowing learners to practice in a low-pressure, supportive atmosphere. Moreover, the idea of the Zone of Proximal Development (ZPD), important to Vygotsky's theory, stresses the function of scaffolding in learning (Xi & Lantolf, 2021). Gamified tools generally feature scaffolding techniques, such as suggestions, prompts, or guided feedback, to encourage learners as they tackle more complicated tasks. This progressive reduction of support helps learners acquire independence and confidence in utilizing the language.

Behaviorist theories of learning, which stress the function of reward and repetition, also accord with the ideas of gamification (John et al, 2023). Language learning games usually incorporate positive reinforcement to encourage desirable actions. For instance, learners could earn points or virtual incentives for properly completing exercises, which encourages their efforts and pushes them to continue learning. Additionally, the repetitive character of games—where learners must continually engage with linguistic structures to progress—aligns with the behaviorist focus on practice as a way of cementing information. Cognitive Load Theory presents yet another lens through which the benefits of gamification in language acquisition may be examined. This idea says that learners have a limited capacity for processing information, and tasks that are extremely complicated or demanding might hamper learning. Gamification overcomes this difficulty by breaking down linguistic activities into doable, bite-sized components. Games are meant to educate learners through a series of modest, gradual stages, reducing cognitive overload and allowing them to focus on learning certain abilities before moving on to more complicated problems (Siedentop et al, 2019). The interactive element of games also helps retain learners' attention, avoiding mental weariness and encouraging persistent engagement. Gamification's emphasis on participation is particularly pertinent when examined through the lens of the Affective Filter Hypothesis, another component of Krashen's beliefs. This hypothesis proposes that emotional elements, such as anxiety, motivation, and self-confidence, might impact the success of language acquisition. A strong affective filter—characterized by fear of failure or poor self-esteem—can hinder the acquisition of new language skills. Gamified settings can decrease the emotional filter by establishing a safe and engaging location for learning. In games, errors are considered part of the process rather than a source of humiliation, enabling learners to take risks and experiment with language without fear of criticism.

One of the most notable elements of gamification is its capacity to incorporate numerous modalities of learning, adapting to diverse learner preferences and styles (Vetrivel et al, 2024). Visual learners benefit from the bright graphics and animations that many games contain, while auditory learners may develop listening comprehension through dialogues and voice interactions. Kinesthetic learners, who thrive on hands-on activities, are engaged through interactive aspects like dragging, clicking, or moving items inside the game. By appealing to varied learning styles, gamification guarantees that no student is left behind, making language teaching more inclusive and successful. The theoretical roots of gamification also fit with Constructivist approaches to education, which stress the active production of knowledge via meaningful experiences. In gamified environments, learners are not passive consumers of knowledge; they are active players who explore, experiment and make decisions that affect their learning path. This sense of agency is powerful, building a stronger connection to the information and improving long-term memory. Additionally, the story components commonly contained in language games offer learners a context for their study, letting them recognize the significance of language abilities in real-world circumstances.

It is also vital to understand the function of technology in enhancing the influence of gamification on language acquisition (Wulantari et al, 2023). Advances in AI, machine learning, and data analytics have enabled the construction of sophisticated gamified systems that adapt to specific learner needs. These technologies enable real-time tracking of progress, tailored feedback, and the identification of areas for development. As a consequence, learners receive a personalized experience that matches their specific goals and obstacles, enhancing the efficacy of their efforts. The theoretical foundations of gamification in language learning indicate a significant match with proven concepts of motivation, cognitive development, and language acquisition. By drawing on ideas such as Self-Determination Theory, the Input Hypothesis, Sociocultural Theory, and Cognitive Load Theory, gamification provides a comprehensive framework for strengthening EFL instruction. Its capacity to combine incentive, customization, and meaningful connection makes it a valuable tool for meeting the different requirements of language learners. As technology continues to improve, the potential for gamification to revolutionize language teaching will only rise, creating new chances to build interesting, effective, and inclusive learning experiences.

## AI-POWERED LANGUAGE GAMES: AN OVERVIEW

The rise of AI-powered language games marks an interesting trend at the junction of technology, education, and linguistics (Ogundele, 2023). These games combine the appealing characteristics of gamification with the advanced capabilities of artificial intelligence, producing a unique platform that not only entertains but also encourages meaningful language acquisition. In recent years, the potential of such tools has risen substantially, altering traditional learning methodologies and providing new opportunities for learners of English as a Foreign Language (EFL). By giving individualized experiences, adaptive feedback, and immersive environments, AI-powered language games are redefining the educational landscape, making language learning more enjoyable and successful than ever before. At the core of AI-powered language games lies their capacity to adjust dynamically to the demands of individual learners (Negrila, 2023). Traditional instructional tools frequently adopt a one-size-fits-all approach, which can leave learners feeling disappointed or discouraged when assignments are either too challenging or too simple. AI technology, however, is capable of monitoring a learner's progress in real-time, detecting strengths and weaknesses, and adapting the content to give an ideal degree of difficulty. This versatility guarantees that the student remains engaged, neither overwhelmed by too complicated activities nor bored by exercises that fail to excite. For example, a starting student struggling with basic vocabulary may be directed via easier, repetitious tasks, while an expert learner might be challenged with complicated sentence building or subtle grammatical structures. The outcome is a highly individualized learning experience that fits with each individual's speed and ability.

Another essential element of AI-powered language games is their capacity to deliver rapid and constructive feedback (Jegede, 2024). Feedback plays a key part in the learning process, helping learners to notice and remedy their mistakes. However, in typical classroom settings, the feedback loop is often delayed, since professors must split their attention among several students. AI overcomes this barrier by giving rapid solutions, whether by correcting speech, flagging grammatical faults, or recommending alternative language options. For instance, voice recognition technology integrated into many AI language games may evaluate a learner's spoken input, identify faults in pronunciation, and give real-time adjustments. This instant feedback not only accelerates the learning process but also helps strengthen the learner's confidence, as they can see actual changes with each encounter.

In addition to individualized information and rapid feedback, AI-powered language games frequently contain immersive and interactive components that boost participation. Immersion has long been acknowledged as a vital aspect of language acquisition; the more a student is exposed to actual language usage, the more successfully they may assimilate new concepts. AI-powered games imitate real-life settings where learners are forced to speak the target language to solve issues, accomplish tasks, or interact with virtual characters (Papadimitriou, 2025). For example, a game may set the student in a virtual café where they must order meals, reply to queries from a waiter, and manage unanticipated problems like making replacements or explaining their order. These scenarios not only give important practice in listening and speaking but also help learners gain the confidence to negotiate comparable circumstances in real life. The inclusion of AI allows these games to go beyond simply rote memory and engage learners in higher-order thinking. Many AI-powered language games integrate storytelling and narrative-based aspects that help learners to think critically and imaginatively. For instance, a game can entail solving a mystery or completing a quest, where the student must gather clues, interact with characters, and make decisions—all in the target language. These story aspects not only make the learning process more pleasant but also give context for language use, helping learners grasp how words and phrases operate in diverse settings.

The social and collaborative components of AI-powered language games further boost their efficacy (Kovari, 2025). Language acquisition is essentially a social activity, and chances for interaction are vital for establishing fluency. Many AI games contain multiplayer capabilities or virtual communities where learners may practice with peers from across the world. These interactions typically resemble real-world discussions, forcing learners to negotiate meaning, explain misconceptions, and adjust to diverse accents or speaking styles. Additionally, some AI-powered platforms utilize natural language processing to mimic interactions with virtual characters, providing learners with a secure and non-judgmental area to practice speaking without the worry of making mistakes in front of others. Gamification components, such as points, badges, and leaderboards, are also crucial to AI-powered language games (Banik & Gullapelly, 2025). While these elements may appear trivial, they play a vital role in maintaining student motivation. Research in educational psychology has demonstrated that incentives and recognition can boost engagement and persistence, especially when learners encounter demanding tasks. AI strengthens these gamification features by tracking individual development and personalizing incentives to suit the learner's successes. For instance, a student who successfully masters a tough grammatical rule can unlock a new gaming level, get a virtual trophy, or receive a personalized congratulations letter. These little but important incentives provide a sense of success and inspire learners to continue striving for growth.

One of the most fascinating elements of AI-powered language games is their ability to overcome cultural boundaries and encourage global understanding (Samantray et al, 2024). Language acquisition is not just about knowing vocabulary and syntax; it is also about comprehending the cultural context in which a language is used. Many AI games contain cultural features, like as idiomatic phrases, regional accents, and culturally unique settings, to assist learners gain a greater understanding of the language they are studying. For example, a game can replicate a traditional festival or holiday, requiring learners to manage talks regarding customs, traditions, and cuisine. These cultural insights improve the learning process and help learners connect more profoundly with the language and its speakers. AI-powered language games also excel at meeting the different demands and preferences of learners. Various people learn in various ways; some may prefer visual aids and animations, while others thrive on aural information or hands-on exercises. AI technology enables these games to accommodate diverse learning methods by giving a choice of interactive elements (Alam & Mohanty, 2023). Visual learners can benefit from bright images and animations, auditory learners can engage with dialogues and voiceovers, and kinesthetic learners can interact with virtual worlds through touch or motion-based controls. This adaptability guarantees that all learners, regardless of their favorite approach, may discover components of the game that appeal to them. The scalability of AI-powered language games is another key advantage. Traditional language teaching typically confronts obstacles relating to accessibility, particularly in locations with low resources or a dearth of competent professors. AI-powered tools, however, can be accessible from anywhere with an internet connection, making high-quality language teaching available to learners in even the most distant regions. This democratization of education can minimize inequities in access to learning opportunities and enable individuals to accomplish their linguistic objectives, regardless of their geographic or economic circumstances.

Despite their many benefits, AI-powered language games are not without obstacles (Aysu, 2024). One of the key problems is the necessity for trustworthy and ethical use of learner data. These games rely on enormous quantities of data to deliver individualized experiences, and safeguarding the privacy and security of this data is crucial. Developers must build comprehensive mechanisms to secure user information and comply with data protection standards. Additionally, there is a need to balance the usage of AI with human engagement. While AI-powered games can give excellent practice and feedback, they cannot fully imitate the difficulties of real-world conversation or the cultural insights that emerge from engaging with native speakers. AI-powered language games offer a significant leap in the field of language instruction. By integrating the engaging components of gamification with the adaptive and analytical powers of AI, these products offer a personalized, interactive, and immersive learning experience. They solve many of the issues associated with traditional language learning approaches, such as lack of motivation, limited feedback, and insufficient exposure to genuine language usage. At the same time, they give opportunities for cultural enrichment, social engagement, and the development of higher-order cognitive abilities. As technology continues to grow, the potential for AI-powered language games to alter the way we learn languages is boundless, offering a future where language education is more accessible, effective, and pleasurable than ever before.

## INTERACTIVE LANGUAGE GAMES AND PERSONALIZED LEARNING

The inclusion of interactive language games into educational frameworks has transformed the way learners approach language acquisition. These games are no longer simply add-ons or diversions; they have become dynamic tools that enhance the learning process by generating immersive, customized, and interactive worlds. The attraction of language games resides not only in their ability to make learning entertaining but also in their capability to accommodate the specific requirements of individual learners, encouraging a deeper and more meaningful relationship with the topic (Jabbari & Eslami, 2019). Interactive language games harness the innate human need for play, challenge, and social engagement. At their foundation, these games convert language learning into an active and entertaining experience, breaking away from traditional rote memory approaches. Unlike conventional techniques, which frequently rely on repeated drills or dull exercises, interactive games introduce a feeling of adventure, competitiveness, and inventiveness. For instance, a vocabulary-building game can entail solving riddles, completing quests, or earning rewards, all while forcing learners to use and reinforce their language abilities. These features of interaction and immersion not only fascinate learners but also inspire persistent engagement with the language.

One of the most impressive advantages of interactive language games is their capacity to tailor the learning experience (Greipl et al, 2020). Each student has distinct strengths, limitations, and learning preferences, and traditional teaching approaches typically struggle to accommodate these individual variances. Interactive games, however, may be modified to match the individual needs of each student, ensuring that they stay challenged without becoming overwhelmed. For example, a language game may utilize adaptive algorithms to assess a learner's performance and alter the difficulty level accordingly. If a student excels in grammar but has problems with pronunciation, the game could highlight tasks that focus on speaking and listening abilities, offering tailored practice and feedback. This level of customization extends beyond content adaption to include tempo and progression. In a classroom situation, learners frequently have to comply with a prescribed pace, which may not fit with their learning rates. Interactive games, on the other hand, allow learners to continue at their speed, reviewing subjects as needed and moving on when they feel competent. This self-paced method not only minimizes anxiety but also allows learners to take responsibility for their education. For instance, a game that teaches sentence construction may allow learners to play with different combinations of words and receive quick feedback, helping them to learn via exploration and trial and error (Clark, 2023). Interactive language games also excel at giving real-time feedback, a critical component of effective learning. In conventional settings, feedback is typically delayed, leaving learners unclear about their progress. Games, however, give quick reactions, allowing learners to see the repercussions of their choices and make modifications in real-time. For example, a pronunciation game may employ voice recognition technology to analyze a learner's speech and make suggestions for development. This quick feedback helps learners rectify mistakes early, gain confidence, and reward positive actions. Moreover, the nonjudgmental character of game-based feedback gives a secure environment for learners to explore and take chances without fear of shame.

Another significant feature of interactive language games is their capacity to imitate real-world settings, giving learners with realistic opportunity to utilize the language in context (Peeters, 2019). Language is intrinsically social, and the ultimate purpose of language learning is efficient communication. Games may offer realistic environments where learners practice speaking, listening, reading, and writing in scenarios that imitate ordinary interactions. For example, a role-playing game may set learners in a virtual marketplace, asking them to negotiate pricing, ask for directions, or purchase meals in the target language. These simulated encounters not only make learning more enjoyable but also help learners acquire the confidence and abilities they need to speak successfully in real life. The social feature of interactive language games further boosts their efficiency (Stiller & Schworm, 2019). Many games contain multiplayer capabilities or collaborative tasks that allow learners to engage with others, building a feeling of community and shared purpose. These interactions might take the shape of friendly competitions, group challenges, or cooperative projects, all of which require learners to utilize the target language to attain common goals. For instance, a team-based game can push participants to solve a mystery by gathering clues and communicating information in the target language. These social dynamics not only make studying more fun but also give vital chances for true communication and cultural exchange.

Cultural significance is another area where interactive language games flourish (Freiermuth & Huang, 2021). Language is complicatedly connected with culture, and recognizing cultural subtleties is vital for efficient communication. Many games contain cultural components, like as idiomatic phrases, customs, or historical allusions, to assist learners build a more holistic grasp of the language. For example, a game situated in a virtual city may educate players about local customs, festivals, or cuisines, expanding their learning experience and encouraging cultural awareness. By incorporating cultural material into gameplay, these games make language learning more relevant and relatable. The motivating value of interactive language games cannot be emphasized (Stiller & Schworm, 2019). Traditional language learning techniques typically fail to keep learners' interest and motivation, particularly when the content feels dull or removed from their lives. Games, however, are intrinsically stimulating because they give clear goals, difficulties, and rewards. Whether it's earning points, unlocking new levels, or getting a high score, these features provide a sense of success and inspire learners to keep going. Moreover, the immersive nature of games attracts learners' attention and keeps them engaged, lowering the possibility of distraction or disengagement.

While the benefits of interactive language games are evident, their success also relies on intelligent design and implementation. Not all games are made equal, and badly designed games might fail to interest learners or even harm the learning process. For a game to be effective, it must match with educational objectives and prioritize meaningful learning results. The game elements should complement the educational content, ensuring that learners are not only having fun but also gaining and applying new language skills (Adipat et al, 2021). For instance, a vocabulary game that pays players for guessing words without comprehending their meanings is less successful than one that encourages learners to apply the terms in context. The integration of interactive language games within a wider educational framework is vital for optimizing their impact. While games may provide useful practice and reinforcement, they are most successful when paired with other educational approaches, such as direct teaching, peer cooperation, and reflective exercises. Educators play a critical role in directing learners' usage of games, helping them create links between game-based experiences and wider language goals. For example, a professor may utilize a game to introduce a new grammar topic and then support a debate or writing exercise to strengthen learners' knowledge. Technology also plays a vital role in the efficacy of interactive language games (Zhang & Zou, 2022). Advances in artificial intelligence, virtual reality, and mobile technology have broadened the potential for game-based learning, making it more immersive and accessible than ever before. AI-powered games, for instance, may give tailored recommendations, monitor learners' progress, and adjust to their requirements in real-time. Virtual reality games may provide genuine scenarios where learners practice using the language in realistic contexts, such as a virtual café or airport. Mobile games, on the other hand, offer the flexibility of learning on the go, enabling learners to practice anytime and anywhere.

Despite its potential, interactive language games also come with obstacles that need to be addressed (Abd-Alrazaq et al, 2023). One recurring issue is the possibility of over-reliance on games at the expense of other crucial components of language acquisition. While games are fantastic instruments for practice and engagement, they should not replace more organized types of education, such as grammar courses or guided writing activities. Additionally, the competitive aspect of some games may induce anxiety or discourage less confident learners, underscoring the significance of fostering a helpful and inclusive gaming environment. Interactive language games provide a transformational approach to language learning that blends the power of play with the benefits of customization. By developing engaging, adaptive, and context-rich settings, these games respond to the different requirements of learners and make language acquisition a fun and meaningful process. They encourage intrinsic motivation, give real-time feedback, and imitate real-world circumstances, all of which lead to a more effective and gratifying learning experience. As technology continues to progress, the potential for interactive language games to enhance language instruction will only expand, suggesting a future where learning is not only more effective but also more human-centered and inspirational.

## CHALLENGES AND CONSIDERATIONS IN IMPLEMENTING AI-BASED GAMIFICATION

The combination of artificial intelligence (AI) with gamification in educational and training environments offers great promise to transform how we engage learners, provide knowledge, and measure performance. By integrating the adaptive powers of AI with the motivational framework of gamification, this technique can change learning experiences into something interactive, customized, and extremely engaging. However, as intriguing as this cooperation may be, deploying AI-based gamification is not without its hurdles. A detailed evaluation of the practical, ethical, and technological challenges is required to ensure the effective adoption and sustainability of such systems (Huda, 2019). One of the key obstacles comes in the technological complexity of AI-based gamification solutions. Developing these systems needs a thorough grasp of both AI and game design concepts, as well as their confluence. Building an AI engine that can assess learner data, update material dynamically, and present it in a gamified style needs substantial skill and resources. Unlike typical software development, the integration of AI incorporates machine learning algorithms, natural language processing, and other complex technologies that must be fine-tuned to respond effectively to customers' demands. These complexities generally translate to greater expenses and longer development timetables, making it a challenging job for smaller institutions or startups with limited finances.

Another important problem is the acquisition and administration of data (Roh et al, 2019). AI-based gamification systems rely significantly on user data to work efficiently. They gather information about learners' habits, preferences, and progress to generate tailored experiences. However, this level of data dependence presents substantial privacy problems. Educational institutions and developers must manage severe data protection requirements, such as GDPR or CCPA, and guarantee that users' personal information is handled appropriately (Labadie & Legner, 2023). Transparency in how data is acquired, handled, and utilized is crucial to developing confidence among learners and stakeholders. Without clear norms and adequate security measures, the potential of data breaches or abuse becomes a serious worry. The issue of accessibility also plays a vital part in the deployment of AI-based gamification. While technology can democratize education by making information available to a larger audience, it may inadvertently deepen the digital divide. Not all learners have equal access to the internet, high-performance devices, or the technical literacy needed to pass over modern systems. AI-based gamification solutions must be created with inclusion in mind, ensuring that they are accessible to those from varied socioeconomic backgrounds, as well as those with impairments. Failure to solve these challenges might exclude huge segments of the population from benefiting from these developments.

Moreover, there is the problem of ensuring that AI-based gamified systems correspond with educational aims. Gamification, while beneficial in improving engagement, carries the danger of favoring enjoyment above instructional value (Zainuddin et al, 2024). Striking the correct balance between enjoyment and learning is a complicated undertaking that involves collaboration between educators, instructional designers, and AI developers. The gamified features must function as a method to assist learning rather than becoming distractions. For example, points, badges, and leaderboards should encourage learning objectives rather than rewarding superficial successes. Designing such systems demands a comprehensive understanding of how people learn and how gaming elements may be utilized to promote, rather than harm, this process. Scalability is another key factor when implementing AI-based gamification. While these technologies may operate effectively in controlled situations or for small groups of learners, expanding them to accommodate huge numbers of users brings new obstacles. AI algorithms must be resilient enough to analyze enormous volumes of data in real-time without sacrificing performance or accuracy (Radanliev et al, 2020). Additionally, sustaining the quality of individualized experiences at scale can be difficult. A system that works effortlessly for 100 users may fail to offer the same degree of flexibility and responsiveness when grown to hundreds or millions. This scalability difficulty generally demands continual investment in infrastructure, such as cloud computing, and regular improvement of algorithms to guarantee they stay successful.

Cultural and cultural aspects also need to be considered when deploying AI-based gamification (Dusmukhamedova et al, 2024). Education and learning are highly impacted by cultural norms, beliefs, and traditions. What could be engaging and successful in one setting could be unimportant or even detrimental in another. For instance, some game mechanisms, such as competitive leaderboards, may drive certain learners while discouraging others who prefer collaborative or individual techniques. Developers must address these cultural variations and create systems that can adapt to varied learning settings. This demands not only technical skills but also a comprehensive awareness of the target audience's cultural and social background. The ethical consequences of AI-driven gamification are another issue that cannot be disregarded. AI algorithms, while sophisticated, are not immune to biases (Ferrara, 2024). If the data used to train these systems is biased, the resultant algorithms may perpetuate or even increase such biases. For example, an AI system meant to measure language competency can prefer particular accents or dialects over others, disadvantaging learners from specific linguistic or cultural backgrounds. Addressing these biases involves meticulous data curation, rigorous testing, and continual monitoring to ensure fairness and equity. Developers and educators must also address the possible psychological impact of gamified systems, particularly on younger or more susceptible learners. The use of incentives and competitive features, while motivating for some, might lead to harmful behaviors, such as over-reliance on external validation or fear of failure.

In addition to these obstacles, the fast speed of technology development creates a distinct issue. AI and gamification technologies are growing at an unprecedented rate, making it challenging for institutions to stay up (Limonova et al, 2023). What is cutting-edge now may become obsolete tomorrow, leading to questions regarding the lifespan and sustainability of AI-based gamified systems. Organizations must be prepared to spend on frequent upgrades, training, and infrastructure to guarantee that their systems stay relevant and effective. This continual commitment demands not just financial resources but also a willingness to adapt to evolving technology and consumer expectations. Collaboration amongst stakeholders is another essential aspect in overcoming the hurdles of adopting AI-based gamification. The effective integration of these systems involves participation from a varied spectrum of professionals, including educators, technologists, psychologists, and legislators. Each stakeholder provides a distinct viewpoint and set of abilities that may help the creation of successful and impactful systems. For example, educators may contribute insights into curriculum design and learning objectives, while technologists can handle the technological elements of AI and gamification. Psychologists may assist ensure that the systems are developed with the learners' mental well-being in mind, and politicians can give advise on ethical and regulatory aspects. Without such coordination, the implementation process is likely to meet considerable challenges.

The value of continual review and feedback cannot be emphasized. Implementing AI-based gamification is not a one-time effort but a continuous process that requires constant review and adjustment (Olatunji et al, 2024). Developers and instructors must gather input from users to understand what works and what doesn't, making required tweaks to enhance the system. This iterative method guarantees that the system stays successful and relevant throughout time. For instance, if learners remark that particular game features are too challenging or not interesting enough, developers might alter these components to better match their needs. Similarly, performance data may be studied to identify areas where the system could be falling short, such as a lack of flexibility or challenges with accessibility. While the application of AI-based gamification involves various hurdles, these obstacles are not insurmountable. By resolving technical challenges, emphasizing data privacy and accessibility, aligning with educational aims, and promoting cooperation among stakeholders, it is feasible to design systems that are both successful and sustainable. Ethical issues, cultural sensitivity, and scalability must also be at the center of the design and implementation process. With careful design, ongoing review, and a dedication to inclusion, AI-based gamification has the potential to revolutionize the landscape of education and training, making learning more interesting, individualized, and impactful for all.

## FUTURE DIRECTIONS AND IMPLICATIONS FOR EFL TEACHING

As the area of English as a Foreign Language (EFL) instruction continues to change, it faces both possibilities and problems created by technology breakthroughs, altering educational paradigms, and the increasing interconnection of the globalized world (Inomjonov, 2024). The future of EFL education will likely be impacted by an interplay of elements, ranging from rising technology to cultural issues, making it a dynamic and varied subject of inquiry. Understanding these future trends and their consequences for EFL education involves a thorough dive into pedagogical developments, learner demands, and the novel technologies accessible to both instructors and students.

One of the most important breakthroughs shaping the future of EFL education is the integration of artificial intelligence (AI) and machine learning into language training (Schmidt & Strasser, 2022). AI-powered technologies are already transforming the way languages are taught and acquired, enabling individualized learning experiences that respond to specific student needs. For example, adaptive learning systems may examine a learner's strengths and shortcomings, giving focused exercises and feedback that fit with their unique areas of progress. This level of customization guarantees that no two learning trips are identical, enabling a more efficient and effective acquisition of language skills. AI-driven solutions can provide the potential for real-time feedback and mistake correction (Xu et al, 2024). Tools such as automatic writing assistants and speech recognition software may rapidly spot grammar faults, pronunciation difficulties, or uncomfortable wording, enabling learners to make immediate adjustments. This not only accelerates the learning process but also decreases the need for instructors for every element of feedback, allowing professors to focus on higher-order teaching tactics such as critical thinking and cultural fluency. However, as promising as these technologies are, they raise crucial issues concerning the function of human contact in language learning. While AI can offer precise and accurate criticism, it lacks the humanity, cultural awareness, and subtle communication that human professors bring to the classroom.

Another major area for the future of EFL education is the increased emphasis on intercultural competency (Iswandari & Ardi, 2022). As English continues to function as a worldwide lingua franca, learners are increasingly employing the language to connect with speakers from varied linguistic and cultural backgrounds. This needs a shift in attention from just language correctness to the capacity to manage cultural differences successfully. EFL curriculum in the future will likely focus greater emphasis on teaching cultural knowledge, sensitivity, and adaptation (Etri, 2022). Students will need to learn not just how to create grammatically correct sentences but also how to recognize cultural clues, handle cross-cultural misunderstandings, and engage in meaningful discussion across varied situations. To encourage the development of intercultural competency, EFL instructors must use instructional approaches that expose learners to a range of cultural views. This might involve combining actual resources such as films, news chapters, and social media information from diverse English-speaking populations. Collaborative initiatives that link students with peers from different countries, whether through virtual exchanges or international partnerships, may help promote cultural awareness and real-world communication skills (Lin, 2021). These initiatives will require EFL instructors to serve as cultural mediators, helping learners pass over the difficulties of intercultural communication while ensuring that they stay attentive to the cultural subtleties of their linguistic groups.

The emergence of blended and hybrid learning approaches indicates another key trend impacting the future of EFL education (Abdi Ali et al, 2024). The COVID-19 epidemic expedited the growth of online learning, and even when in-person education returns, many institutions are pursuing a hybrid strategy that blends the best of both disciplines. Blended learning techniques allow students to obtain language teaching using a mix of online materials, live virtual sessions, and face-to-face encounters (Asaad Hamza Sheerah, 2020). This flexibility not only accommodates varied learning methods but also enables learners to advance at their own pace. The implications of blended learning for EFL education are considerable (Rahim, 2019). On the one hand, digital platforms provide a multitude of tools, from interactive grammar exercises to immersive language games, that make learning exciting and accessible. On the other side, the change to online and hybrid models necessitates that instructors gain new abilities in instructional design, technology integration, and digital communication. Professors must become adept in using learning management systems, producing multimedia material, and promoting online interaction to guarantee that students remain engaged and connected.

Furthermore, the ubiquitous availability of mobile devices has provided new opportunities for Mobile-Assisted Language Learning MALL (Karakaya & Bozkurt, 2022). With smartphones and tablets becoming ubiquitous, learners may access language learning applications, podcasts, and e-books anytime and anywhere. These technologies give chances for microlearning, where students may engage in brief, concentrated activities that fit into their regular routines. For instance, a commuter can use a language app to review vocabulary during a train journey, while a busy professional might listen to an English podcast while preparing dinner. The ease of mobile learning offers the potential to make language acquisition more integrated into learners' lives, breaking down the conventional constraints of time and geography. The introduction of digital tools and mobile technology also brings obstacles. Not all learners have equal access to devices, stable internet connections, or the digital literacy skills needed to navigate online materials successfully. Addressing these gaps will need a coordinated effort from educational institutions, policymakers, and technology suppliers to ensure that EFL instruction stays equitable and inclusive. Professors, too, must find a balance between exploiting technology and keeping the human parts of language acquisition, such as establishing interpersonal ties and creating a supportive classroom environment.

The future of EFL teaching will also be determined by a rising appreciation of the value of learner autonomy (Saeed, 2021). In an era where knowledge is easily available, students are increasingly expected to take responsibility for their learning experiences. EFL educators must allow learners to establish their objectives, measure their progress, and seek out materials that match their interests and requirements. Strategies such as project-based learning, self-assessment tools, and peer feedback can inspire students to become active participants in their education. At the same time, the job of the professor is expanding from that of a knowledge supplier to a facilitator and mentor. Instructors must lead learners in developing critical thinking skills, judging the quality of online materials, and using language skills in genuine circumstances. This transformation needs a redesign of professor training programs to provide educators with the skills and mentality needed to enable learner autonomy successfully.

Looking ahead, the incorporation of future technologies such as virtual reality (VR) and augmented reality (AR) has the potential to significantly alter EFL training (Panagiotidis, 2021). These immersive technologies provide unique chances to develop genuine language environments that imitate real-world settings. For example, VR may take learners to a crowded marketplace where they must negotiate prices in English, while AR can overlay language cues onto tangible items to boost vocabulary development. Such experiences make language learning more interesting and memorable, building a stronger connection to the language. The introduction of VR and AR in EFL instruction is not without its hurdles. These technologies frequently need substantial investment in hardware and software, as well as training for educators to use them successfully. Additionally, challenges remain concerning how to incorporate these technologies into the current curriculum and analyze their influence on learning outcomes. Despite these difficulties, the promise of immersive technology to enhance language learning experiences cannot be underestimated. The future of EFL education will be impacted by wider cultural trends, such as the increased emphasis on sustainability and global citizenship (Ekanayake et al, 2020). As educators educate learners to navigate a complex and interconnected environment, they must explore how language training might contribute to these wider aims. For instance, EFL programs can contain subjects such as climate change, social justice, and cultural heritage, enabling students to utilize their language abilities to interact with global concerns. By framing language acquisition as a tool for meaningful communication and constructive change, educators may motivate students to see English not merely as a means of attaining personal achievement, but as a way to contribute to the larger good. The future of EFL education is marked by both exciting potential and challenging obstacles. The combination of AI, blended learning, and immersive technology gives new opportunities for personalization, engagement, and cultural understanding, while the emphasis on student autonomy and global citizenship broadens the scope of language instruction. At the same time, educators must manage concerns of accessibility, equality, and the shifting role of the professor to ensure that these innovations serve all learners. By embracing these future possibilities and addressing their consequences deliberately, EFL educators can build a dynamic and inclusive learning environment that equips students to flourish in an increasingly linked society.

## CONCLUSION

As we complete this chapter, it becomes evident that the future of English as a Foreign Language (EFL) instruction resides at the crossroads of technology, innovation, and human contact. The incorporation of artificial intelligence (AI) into language learning, alongside the emerging significance of gamification, has provided new dimensions of engagement, customization, and interaction. These technologies not only enrich the language learning experience but also give students chances for greater autonomy, deeper knowledge, and more effective skill development. AI-powered technologies, such as personalized language games, adaptive learning systems, and automated feedback mechanisms, represent the bleeding edge of EFL instruction. They enable individualized learning experiences that adapt to the particular requirements, skills, and limitations of each learner. This tailored method is particularly helpful in EFL courses because learners originate from varied backgrounds, exhibit varying levels of competence, and have distinct learning preferences. By integrating AI, instructors may give more focused support, boost learner motivation, and build a learning environment that adjusts to the student's progress and goals. Gamification, with its emphasis on intrinsic motivation, competition, incentives, and accomplishment, offers a potent technique for improving engagement. Language games, which integrate aspects of fun, creativity, and competitiveness, convert the typically laborious work of language acquisition into a thrilling, engaging experience. Whether students are learning vocabulary, grammar, or listening comprehension, gamified settings stimulate active engagement and enhance retention via repetition and positive reinforcement. Moreover, gamification develops a feeling of community inside the classroom, as learners work together, compete, and exchange information in a collaborative setting.

Yet, while AI and gamification provide great potential, they are not without their problems. The deployment of these technologies needs careful consideration of several variables, including accessibility, digital literacy, data protection, and the balance between technology and human connection. Not all students have the same amount of access to digital devices or the internet, and not all instructors possess the technical skills to properly incorporate AI and gamification into their teaching approaches. It is crucial to address these discrepancies in access and understanding to ensure that the advantages of modern technologies are available to all learners, regardless of their socio-economic background or geographical location. Another key concern is the role of the instructor in the AI- and gamification-enhanced classroom. While these technologies can give essential help, they cannot replace the human touch that is so vital to good teaching. Professors have an indispensable role in nurturing the emotional, social, and cultural components of language learning. They give context, foster critical thinking, and develop the human relationships that are crucial to establishing motivation and confidence in the learning process. In reality, the most effective application of AI and gamification in EFL instruction comes when they support the professor's efforts, providing a hybrid approach that merges technology with conventional pedagogical approaches.

Looking into the future, the growth of EFL instruction will continue to be impacted by breakthroughs in AI, machine learning, and interactive technology. As these technologies grow more sophisticated and broadly available, they will progressively empower both educators and learners. AI will likely enable more advanced kinds of adaptive learning, offering even more accurate feedback and personalizing the learning experience to an individual’s particular needs. Meanwhile, gamification will continue to expand, creating new methods for students to interact with information and connect with classmates. As these technologies evolve, we may expect an even more seamless incorporation of AI and gamification into the fabric of EFL instruction. The repercussions of these advances stretch beyond the classroom. As global communication continues to rise and English remains the dominant language of commerce, science, and society, the demand for effective and efficient language training will only intensify. AI-powered gamified learning provides the ability to address this need on a global scale, giving learners in varied places with opportunity to gain language skills in an entertaining and individualized manner. This offers up new avenues for language acquisition that transcend traditional borders, offering more fair access to quality education for students globally.

While the potential of AI and gamification in EFL education is tremendous, educators must be cautious in assessing the ethical, cultural, and pedagogical consequences of these technologies. AI systems must be built to promote justice, respect learner diversity, and protect the integrity of the learning process. Similarly, gamification must be approached wisely, ensuring that it creates healthy, friendly competition rather than reinforcing negative stereotypes or hindering collaboration. As with every instructional instrument, it is necessary to establish a balance between innovation and tradition, ensuring that the ultimate objective of EFL teaching — effective, meaningful communication — stays at the forefront. The incorporation of AI and gamification in EFL education is a great possibility to increase language learning, enabling more individualized, engaging, and successful ways of training. By embracing the capabilities of these technologies while realizing their limits, educators may develop dynamic learning environments that react to the demands of today's varied student populations. The future of EFL education is bright, with AI and gamification playing major roles in influencing the way we teach, learn, and communicate in the globalized world. However, this future must be negotiated cautiously, ensuring that technology serves to improve, rather than replace, the very human components of language learning. With intelligent implementation, the potential for AI-driven gamification in EFL instruction is boundless, presenting an exciting horizon for both educators and learners alike. As educators, we are entrusted not just with teaching language but with nurturing the skills and competencies essential for success in an increasingly linked society. The successful integration of AI and gamification offers the possibility of changing EFL education into a more engaging, efficient, and egalitarian process. It is now up to us to embrace these tools, adapt to their growing nature, and use them to empower learners as they begin on their paths to learning the global language that unites us all.

## REFERENCES

Abd-Alrazaq, A., AlSaad, R., Alhuwail, D., Ahmed, A., Healy, P. M., Latifi, S., Aziz, S., Damseh, R., Alabed Alrazak, S., & Sheikh, J. (2023). Large language models in medical education: Opportunities, challenges, and future directions. *JMIR Medical Education*, *9*(1), e48291. DOI: 10.2196/48291 PMID: 37261894

Abdi Ali, A., AlQarni, K., Migdadi, H. F., Aldosemani, T. I., & Alshraah, S. M. (2024). Addressing the Challenge of Hybrid Learning Environment in Foreign Language Education: Training Lecturers for Blended Teaching Approaches. [TPLS]. *Theory and Practice in Language Studies*, *14*(5).

Adipat, S., Laksana, K., Busayanon, K., Asawasowan, A., & Adipat, B. (2021). Engaging students in the learning process with game-based learning: The fundamental concepts. *International Journal of Technology in Education*, *4*(3), 542–552. DOI: 10.46328/ijte.169

Ahmed, A. A. A., Widodo, M., Komariah, A., Hassan, I., Sukmana, N., Ali, M. H., Abbas, A. K., & Rohi, A. (2022). Assessing the effects of gamification on developing EFL Learners' idiomatic knowledge: Do attitudinal factors contribute to the learning of the idioms with the game? *Education Research International*, *2022*(1), 2482570. DOI: 10.1155/2022/2482570

Akbana, Y. E., & Yavuz, A. (2020). Global issues in efl teaching: Efl lecturers' voices at a state university. *Kahramanmaraş Sütçü İmam Üniversitesi Eğitim Dergisi*, *2*(1), 83–102.

Al Khatri, A. M. (2019). *How Omani teachers perceive the process of integrating 21st century competencies and skills into the EFL curriculum: A step forward.* University of Exeter.

Alam, A., & Mohanty, A. (2023). Educational technology: Exploring the convergence of technology and pedagogy through mobility, interactivity, AI, and learning tools. *Cogent Engineering*, *10*(2), 2283282. DOI: 10.1080/23311916.2023.2283282

Ally, M., & Wark, N. (2020). Sustainable development and education in the fourth industrial revolution (4IR).

Asaad Hamza Sheerah, H. (2020). Using blended learning to support the teaching of English as a foreign language. Arab World English Journal (AWEJ) Special Issue on CALL, (6).

Aysu, S. (2024). The use of AI-Powered Tools in Language Learning. Dil Eğitimi ve Öğretiminde, 1.

Banik, B. G., & Gullapelly, A. (2025). AI-Powered Gamification and Interactive Learning Tools for Enhancing Student Engagement. In Driving Quality Education Through AI and Data Science (pp. 283-310). IGI Global Scientific Publishing.

Bengsch, G. (2024). Redefining traditional pedagogy: The integration of machine learning in the contemporary language education classroom. In AI in Language Teaching, Learning, and Assessment (pp. 195-221). IGI Global Scientific Publishing.

Clark, R. (2023). *Meaningful games: Exploring language with game theory*. MIT Press.

Dong, Y., Hou, J., Zhang, N., & Zhang, M. (2020). Research on how human intelligence, consciousness, and cognitive computing affect the development of artificial intelligence. *Complexity*, *2020*(1), 1680845. DOI: 10.1155/2020/1680845

Dusmukhamedova, S., Rasulova, F., Shukurov, Y., Zukhra, Q., Matchanova, M., & Narkabilova, G. (2024, May). A Novel Based Design of AI kind of Models for Gami-Fication in Enhanced Learning type of Environment. In 2024 4th International Conference on Advance Computing and Innovative Technologies in Engineering (ICACITE) (pp. 584-588). IEEE. DOI: 10.1109/ICACITE60783.2024.10617373

Ekanayake, K., Khatibi, A., & Azam, F. (2020). The impact of teacher education and English language education in fostering global citizenship education: A review of literature. *International Journal of Advances in Scientific Research and Engineering*, *6*(7), 30–40. DOI: 10.31695/IJASRE.2020.33847

El, M. (2023). UNVEILING THE DYNAMIC POWER OF GAMIFICATION IN STUDENT LEARNING THROUGH NOVEL CONCEPTUAL AND THEORETICAL FRAMEWORKS. Journal of Studies in Language [JSLCS]. *Cultura e Scuola*, *6*(2), 1–19.

Etri, W. (2022). Intercultural sensitivity and its effects on ELT curricula–Teacher insights. *Higher Education Evaluation and Development*, *16*(1), 32–46. DOI: 10.1108/HEED-03-2021-0027

Fakher Ajabshir, Z. (2023). A review of the affordances and challenges of artificial intelligence technologies in second language learning. *Technology Assisted Language Education*, *1*(4), 92–111.

Ferrara, E. (2024). The butterfly effect in artificial intelligence systems: Implications for AI bias and fairness. *Machine Learning with Applications*, *15*, 100525. DOI: 10.1016/j.mlwa.2024.100525

Firmansyah, F. H., & Rosmansyah, Y. (2024). Exploring Collaboration in Multiplayer Gamification: A Systematic Literature Review. *IEEE Access : Practical Innovations, Open Solutions.*

Freiermuth, M. R., & Huang, H. C. (2021). Zooming across cultures: Can a telecollaborative video exchange between language learning partners further the development of intercultural competences? *Foreign Language Annals*, *54*(1), 185–206. DOI: 10.1111/flan.12504

Greipl, S., Moeller, K., & Ninaus, M. (2020). Potential and limits of game-based learning. *International Journal of Technology Enhanced Learning*, *12*(4), 363–389. DOI: 10.1504/IJTEL.2020.110047

Huda, M. (2019). Empowering application strategy in the technology adoption: Insights from professional and ethical engagement. *Journal of Science and Technology Policy Management*, *10*(1), 172–192. DOI: 10.1108/JSTPM-09-2017-0044

Inomjonov, A. (2024). IMPACT OF GLOBALIZATION IN ELT. University Research Base, 134-139.

Iswandari, Y. A., & Ardi, P. (2022). Intercultural Communicative Competence in EFL Setting: A Systematic Review. *Reflections: The SoL Journal*, *29*(2), 361–380. DOI: 10.61508/refl.v29i2.260249

Jabbari, N., & Eslami, Z. R. (2019). Second language learning in the context of massively multiplayer online games: A scoping review. *ReCALL*, *31*(1), 92–113. DOI: 10.1017/S0958344018000058

Jegede, O. O. (2024). Artificial Intelligence and English Language Learning: Exploring the Roles of AI-Driven Tools in Personalizing Learning and Providing Instant Feedback. Universal Library of Languages and Literatures, 1(2).

John, D., Hussin, N., Zaini, M. K., Ametefe, D. S., Aliu, A. A., & Caliskan, A. (2023). Gamification equilibrium: the fulcrum for balanced intrinsic motivation and extrinsic rewards in learning systems: immersive gamification in Muhamad Khairulnizam Zaini Learning system. *International Journal of Serious Games*, *10*(3), 83–116. DOI: 10.17083/ijsg.v10i3.633

Karakaya, K., & Bozkurt, A. (2022). Mobile-assisted language learning (MALL) research trends and patterns through bibliometric analysis: Empowering language learners through ubiquitous educational technologies. *System*, *110*, 102925. DOI: 10.1016/j.system.2022.102925

Kayyali, M. (2021). Positive impact of high technology on higher education.

Kovari, A. (2025). A systematic review of AI-powered collaborative learning in higher education: Trends and outcomes from the last decade. *Social Sciences & Humanities Open*, *11*, 101335. DOI: 10.1016/j.ssaho.2025.101335

Labadie, C., & Legner, C. (2023). Building data management capabilities to address data protection regulations: Learnings from EU-GDPR. *Journal of Information Technology*, *38*(1), 16–44. DOI: 10.1177/02683962221141456

Li, C. (2024). A review of theories, pedagogies and vocabulary learning tasks of English vocabulary learning apps for Chinese EFL learners. *Journal of China Computer-Assisted Language Learning*, *4*(2), 346–375. DOI: 10.1515/jccall-2023-0026

Limonova, V., Santos, A., São Mamede, H., & Filipe, V. (2023). The research context of artificial intelligence and gamification to improve student engagement and attendance in higher education. RE@ D–Revista de Educação a Distância e eLearning.

Lin, C. C. (2021). Using virtual exchange to foster global competence and collaborative leadership in teacher education. Dual Language Research and Practice Journal, 4(1).

Liu, L. (2024). Impact of AI gamification on EFL learning outcomes and nonlinear dynamic motivation: Comparing adaptive learning paths, conversational agents, and storytelling. *Education and Information Technologies*, •••, 1–40. DOI: 10.1007/s10639-024-13296-5

Loewen, S. (2020). *Introduction to instructed second language acquisition*. Routledge. DOI: 10.4324/9781315616797

Luu, N. (2024). AI-powered gamification for boosting second language acquisition efficiency.

Mauroner, O. (2019). Gamification in management and other non-game contexts—Understanding game elements, motivation, reward systems, and user types. *Open Journal of Business and Management*, *7*(4), 1815–1830. DOI: 10.4236/ojbm.2019.74125

Moybeka, A. M., Syariatin, N., Tatipang, D. P., Mushthoza, D. A., Dewi, N. P. J. L., & Tineh, S. (2023). Artificial Intelligence and English classroom: The implications of AI toward EFL students' motivation. Edumaspul. *Jurnal Pendidikan*, *7*(2), 2444–2454.

Nafa, M. S. (2023). *A broad guide to teaching the skills of listening and speaking*. Cambridge Scholars Publishing.

Negrila, A. M. C. (2023). The new revolution in language learning: The power of artificial intelligence and education 4.0. Bulletin of" Carol I [EN]. *National Defence University, 12*(02), 16–27. DOI: 10.53477/2284-9378-23-17

Ogundele, R. A. (2023). AI-POWERED THESPIAN: DEVELOPING AN INNOVATIVE CONVERSATIONAL ENGINE (Doctoral dissertation, Doctoral dissertation, MANCHESTER METROPOLITAN UNIVERSITY).

Olatunji, A. P., Ajibola, O. S., & Agunbiade, N. O. (2024). Leveraging AI-driven training programs for enhanced organizational security awareness. *International Journal of Science and Research Archive, 13*(1), 301–311. DOI: 10.30574/ijsra.2024.13.1.1649

Panagiotidis, P. (2021). Augmented and mixed reality in language learning. *European Journal of Education, 4*(2), 27–43. DOI: 10.26417/501ibq23c

Papadimitriou, S. (2025). *Artificial Intelligence—Based Games as Novel Holistic Educational Environments to Teach 21st Century Skills*. Springer Nature. DOI: 10.1007/978-3-031-77464-5

Peeters, D. (2019). Virtual reality: A game-changing method for the language sciences. *Psychonomic Bulletin & Review, 26*(3), 894–900. DOI: 10.3758/s13423-019-01571-3 PMID: 30734158

Radanliev, P., De Roure, D., Page, K., Van Kleek, M., Santos, O., Maddox, L. T., Burnap, P., Anthi, E., & Maple, C. (2020). Design of a dynamic and self-adapting system, supported with artificial intelligence, machine learning and real-time intelligence for predictive cyber risk analytics in extreme environments–cyber risk in the colonisation of Mars. *Safety in Extreme Environments, 2*(3), 219–230. DOI: 10.1007/s42797-021-00025-1

Rahim, M. N. (2019). The use of blended learning approach in EFL education. *International Journal of Engineering and Advanced Technology, 8*(5), 1165–1168. DOI: 10.35940/ijeat.E1163.0585C19

Ravichandran, K., Virgin, B. A., Patil, S., Fatma, G., Rengarajan, M., & Bala, B. K. (2024, July). Gamifying Language Learning: Applying Augmented Reality and Gamification Strategies for Enhanced English Language Acquisition. In *2024 Third International Conference on Smart Technologies and Systems for Next Generation Computing (ICSTSN)* (pp. 1-6). IEEE. DOI: 10.1109/ICSTSN61422.2024.10670787

Renacido, J. M. D., & Biray, E. T. (2025). Enhancing Peer Engagement and Student Motivation Through AI-Gamified Interactive Learning Tools. In Advancing Sustainable Development Goals With Educational Technology (pp. 277-342). IGI Global Scientific Publishing.

Roh, Y., Heo, G., & Whang, S. E. (2019). A survey on data collection for machine learning: A big data-ai integration perspective. *IEEE Transactions on Knowledge and Data Engineering*, *33*(4), 1328–1347. DOI: 10.1109/TKDE.2019.2946162

Rovai, A., & Pfingsthorn, J. (2022). "Good foreign language teachers pay attention to heterogeneity": Conceptualizations of differentiation and effective teaching practice in inclusive EFL classrooms by German pre-service teachers. *Languages (Basel, Switzerland)*, *7*(3), 162. DOI: 10.3390/languages7030162

Saeed, M. A. (2021). Learner autonomy: Learners' perceptions on strategies to achieve autonomy in an EFL classroom. International Journal of Linguistics. *Literature and Translation*, *4*(3), 150–158.

Samantray, K., İZGİ, F. D., Ocampo, M. B., Dehghan, M., Mohammadpour, S., Siriphaprapagon, Y., ... & Babu, S. D. (2024). The Power of Words in AI-Driven World: Exploring the Interplay of Language, Culture, and Communication. SKETSAMEDIA.

Schmidt, T., & Strasser, T. (2022). Artificial intelligence in foreign language learning and teaching: A CALL for intelligent practice. Anglistik. *International Journal of English Studies*, *33*(1), 165–184.

Shah, P., Gadekar, N. A., & Taylor, S. S. (2024). Escape From Passive Learning: Harnessing Gamified Digital Educational Escape Rooms for Immersive Marketing Education. *Journal of Marketing Education*, •••, 02734753241306093. DOI: 10.1177/02734753241306093

Sheldon, K. M., & Prentice, M. (2019). Self-determination theory as a foundation for personality researchers. *Journal of Personality*, *87*(1), 5–14. DOI: 10.1111/jopy.12360 PMID: 29144550

Siedentop, D., Hastie, P., & Van der Mars, H. (2019). *Complete guide to sport education*. Human Kinetics.

Stiller, K. D., & Schworm, S. (2019, March). Game-based learning of the structure and functioning of body cells in a foreign language: Effects on motivation, cognitive load, and performance. [). Frontiers Media SA.]. *Frontiers in Education*, *4*, 18. DOI: 10.3389/feduc.2019.00018

Vetrivel, S. C., Arun, V. P., Maheswari, R., & Saravanan, T. P. (2024). Technology Integration in Online Learning Platforms: Blended Learning Gamification. In Transdisciplinary Teaching and Technological Integration for Improved Learning: Case Studies and Practical Approaches (pp. 219-247). IGI Global.

Wang, Y., & Wu, M. (2025). Analysis of English Mofun Show based on the theory of second language acquisition. In *Addressing Global Challenges-Exploring Socio-Cultural Dynamics and Sustainable Solutions in a Changing World* (pp. 283–288). Routledge.

Wulantari, N. P., Rachman, A., Sari, M. N., Uktolseja, L. J., & Rofi'i, A. (2023). The Role Of Gamification In English Language Teaching: A Literature. *Journal of Education*, *6*(01), 2847–2856.

Xi, J., & Lantolf, J. P. (2021). Scaffolding and the zone of proximal development: A problematic relationship. *Journal for the Theory of Social Behaviour*, *51*(1), 25–48. DOI: 10.1111/jtsb.12260

Xu, T., Zhang, Y. F., Chu, Z., Wang, S., & Wen, Q. (2024). Ai-driven virtual teacher for enhanced educational efficiency: Leveraging large pretrain models for autonomous error analysis and correction. arXiv preprint arXiv:2409.09403.

Zainuddin, Z., Chu, S. K. W., & Perera, C. J. (2024). Gamification in Education. In *Gamification in A Flipped Classroom: Pedagogical Methods and Best Practices* (pp. 67–113). Springer Nature Singapore. DOI: 10.1007/978-981-97-2219-8_3

Zhang, R., & Zou, D. (2022). Types, purposes, and effectiveness of state-of-the-art technologies for second and foreign language learning. *Computer Assisted Language Learning*, *35*(4), 696–742. DOI: 10.1080/09588221.2020.1744666

Zhao, Z. (2021). Decipher the Effect of Gamification in Harnessing Boredom and Improving Performance.

## KEY TERMS AND DEFINITIONS

**Gamification:** The use of game design elements such as points, levels, badges, and challenges in non-game contexts like education to enhance motivation and learner engagement.

**Artificial Intelligence (AI):** The simulation of human intelligence by machines, enabling applications like personalized learning, speech recognition, and adaptive feedback in EFL instruction.

**Personalized Learning:** An instructional approach that tailors content, pace, and learning paths to the individual needs, preferences, and progress of each learner.

**Interactive Language Games:** Digital or physical games that require learners to use language skills actively—such as speaking, listening, reading, and writing—in immersive, goal-oriented tasks.

**Self-Determination Theory (SDT):** A theory of motivation emphasizing autonomy, competence, and relatedness as key drivers of engagement, often used to explain why gamification works in education.

**Real-Time Feedback:** Immediate responses provided by AI tools or games to learners about their performance, helping them correct mistakes and reinforce correct usage promptly.

**Immersive Learning:** A learning approach that places students in rich, contextualized environments—often through VR, storytelling, or simulations—to enhance language acquisition and real-world application.

**Affective Filter Hypothesis:** A theory in second language acquisition suggesting that emotional states such as anxiety or motivation influence a learner's ability to absorb new language input effectively.

# Chapter 3
# AI-Driven Personalization in English as a Foreign Language (EFL)

**Andrew Chinonso Nwanakwaugwu**
https://orcid.org/0000-0002-2929-9638
*University of Salford, UK*

**Daniel Emakporuena**
https://orcid.org/0009-0001-1741-9401
*Wrexham University, UK*

**Obinna Emmanuel Obi-Akwari**
https://orcid.org/0009-0006-9487-4965
*University of Hull, UK*

**Peter Kwakpovwe**
https://orcid.org/0009-0001-2506-9931
*University of Salford, UK*

**Ene Ojaide**
https://orcid.org/0009-0008-0388-0687
*10Alytics, UK*

**Meletius Mgbeodichimma Igbokwe**
https://orcid.org/0009-0007-2071-4317
*LIMA, UK*

## ABSTRACT

*This study aimed at exploring the integration of artificial intelligence in English as a Foreign Language learning and how it has changes conventional pedagogical practices in the field of education. It examines how AI-driven speech synthesis can personalize the EFL learning experience, enhance language proficiency, and foster greater learner autonomy. By analysing the underlying technologies, pedagogical applications, and ethical considerations, the chapter seeks to bridge the gap between technological potential and practical implementation in EFL classrooms.*

DOI: 10.4018/979-8-3373-0969-9.ch003

## 1. INTRODUCTION

English as a Foreign Language (EFL) is very essential for academic, professional, social success, and personal advancement in many contexts in an increasingly globalized world. However, EFL learners traditionally relied on structured curricula, direct teacher instruction, textbooks, language labs, rote memorization, and standardized testing, which lack adaptability to individual learning needs, and often fail to meet the diverse needs of learners. Students usually have multiple challenges, for instance, limited exposure to native language environments, lack motivation due to outdated instructional methods and repetition, difficulty in understanding contextual language use, and varying proficiency levels among learners (Jegede, 2024; Alharbi, 2024).

Furthermore, these conventional methods fail to accommodate individual learners' diverse needs, leading to issues such as lack of engagement, slow progress in comprehension, inconsistencies in language acquisition, and difficulty in achieving fluency. The increasing global demand for English proficiency has highlighted the need for more effective and adaptable learning methods. Environmental supports are especially important for young English language learners (ELL). Their numbers have increased dramatically in the past 15 years in the United States. For example, in 1990, 1 in every 20 children was ELL, that is, a student who speaks English either not at all or with enough limitations that he or she cannot fully participate in mainstream English instruction. Nowadays, the figure is 1 in 9. Although these children come from over 400 different language backgrounds, by far the largest proportions of students are Spanish-speakers (over 80%). The recent synthesis of research suggests that when feasible, children should be taught in their primary language. Primary language instruction helps to promote bilingualism and, eventually, biliteracy. Further, children will need support in transferring what they know in their first language to learning tasks presented in English. Engaging children actively in meaningful tasks and providing many opportunities for them to participate at their functional levels will enable children to feel more efficacious, and to become contributing members in mainstream classrooms. Adults will need to make adjustments and accommodations sometimes described as 'instructional scaffolding' to support children who are beginning English speakers. They may have to speak slowly and somewhat deliberately, with clear vocabulary and diction; they may need to use pictures or other objects to illustrate the content being taught; or ask for children to respond either non- verbally (e.g., pointing or signaling) or in one- or two-word utterances. ELL's language needs are complex. These young children are not only learning a new language, but also a new set of social rules and behaviours that may be different from their home. Given the great variability among ELL children, adults will need to know the different stages of language learning to be able to implement the most appropriate accommodations (for addition information on accommodations.

Consequently, these and other factors are especially important to ensure that these ELL children have many opportunities to use their second language (i.e., English) and their native language in meaningful and motivating situations. From an ecological perspective, therefore, the physical and psychological environments play vital roles in children's learning about literacy. These supports mediate opportunities for literacy engagement and practice, and will likely influence children's attitudes and efforts to engage in literacy activities despite difficulties they may encounter as they are learning to read proficiently. (National Center for Education Statistics, 2022).

Over the past few years, the integration of technology in language has greatly impacted in the education process by tailoring learning to individual learners and making learning more accessible and interactive. Recently, the advent of digital platforms, online collaboration tools, and multimedia resources. The advent of artificial intelligence (AI) driven technologies, including Natural Language Processing (NLP) and machine learning algorithms, have further enhanced and revolutionised various facets of human life, with education being one of the most impacted areas. AI-driven personalisation has emerged as a transformative approach to English as a Foreign Language (EFL) education by offering personalised learning experiences to individual learners, automated grading, and targeted feedback (Cabrera-Solano et al., 2024).

AI-driven personalization in EFL uses artificial intelligence techniques, machine learning techniques, natural language processing (NLP), and data analysis and prediction to personalize the learning process for every student, based on their proficiency level, learning preferences and to develop adaptive learning environments that can display content, pacing, and feedback that can be tailored to the student's learning needs as they progress through the course. Recent studies show how AI-based tools affect the personalization of EFL learning processes. The use of AI-driven tools improves students' participation, understanding, self-directedness, language development, and learning achievements in the EFL program (Jegede, 2024; Alharbi, 2024; Cabrera-Solano et al., 2024). In addition, the use of AI-driven tools increases students' engagement, independence, and language skill achievement (Umar, 2024).

AI-powered platform apps analyses student performance and adapt content dynamically, ensuring that learners receive the most relevant instruction. AI-driven applications in EFL includes the following:

i. AI Chatbots and Virtual Tutors: Interactive tools that provide conversational practice and grammar corrections (Haristiani, 2019; Kim et al., 2019).
ii. Intelligent Learning and Tutoring Systems: Platforms that modify content based on students' progress and comprehension levels (Xu et al., 2019).

iii. Gamified Language Learning Applications: AI-powered apps that engage learners through interactive exercises and personalized learning paths (Rodríguez-Muñiz & Padilla-Zea, 2021).
iv. Automated Speech Recognition (ASR): Tools that have significantly enhanced learner engagement, pronunciation skills, and progress tracking through real-time feedback (Chen et al., 2022; Li et al., 2023).

AI-powered resources, such as Fliki videos and voice-driven assistants, cater to diverse learning styles and foster active engagement with language acquisition (Cabrera-Solano et al., 2024; Underwood, 2017). Students report increased enjoyment and improved understanding of linguistic concepts when using AI tools (Jegede, 2024; Cabrera-Solano et al., 2024). However, some educators' express concerns about potential academic dishonesty (Alharbi, 2024). Despite challenges like technical issues and the need for human interaction, the majority of teachers acknowledge AI's potential to complement traditional instruction (Jegede, 2024; Alharbi, 2024). To maximise effectiveness, educators are encouraged to integrate AI tools thoughtfully, ensuring a balance between traditional methods and addressing technical and accessibility concerns (Jegede, 2024). Artificial Intelligence (AI) is transforming teaching and learning in education, offering unprecedented possibilities for engagement, innovation, and personalized learning. The application of artificial intelligence (AI) to English as a Foreign Language (EFL) education has emerged as a powerful force capable of addressing long-standing challenges, including the need for tailored instruction, scalable solutions, and tools for enhancing motivation and engagement among students. A particularly promising area of AI application is speech synthesis, which utilizes advanced technologies like natural language processing (NLP) and machine learning to produce highly realistic and context-sensitive audio outputs. Using these systems, learners can access customized pronunciation models, contextual dialogue practice, and adaptive feedback which is essential for the acquisition of foreign languages. EFL instruction often faces obstacles such as access disparities, diverse learner profiles, and variability in language exposure. AI-driven speech synthesis addresses these gaps by delivering scalable, interactive, and personalized experiences. By leveraging text-to-speech (TTS) technologies and conversational agents, AI tools simulate real-world language interactions and empower learners to practice speaking and listening skills with instant feedback, regardless of their geographic or socio-economic constraints. The establishment that AI has the potential to enhance some parts of education isverifiable based on the pedagogical linkages between the twenty-first century digital media technology components and education itself, but the comprehensive solution, particularly inplaces where digital flexibility and knowledge transfer are required by AI-robots, continues tobe problematic (Mhlanga 2021). Humans are considered the best model to imitate whilecreating artificial intelligence technologies. Replicating one of the most sophisticated technological innovations made possible by human language is also required under thisviewpoint. Language is viewed as a soft technology that may be imitated from ChatGPT's standpoint as a generative artificial intelligence technology that makes use of both machine and deep learning approaches (Dwivedi et al, 2023). ChatGPT and other related generative AI technologies are primarily trained to interpret and generate human language, but they can scandalize the intricate patterns and structures of human language by employing the Generative Pre-Training Transformer (GPT) model (Bozkurt 2023). Even though NLP has been researched for decades in the field of computers, more recent developments in technology have prompted the creation of complex AI models, such as Chat Generative Pre-trained Transformer(ChatGPT). These models provide great opportunities for academic efficiency since they can generate human-like replies to a variety of language challenges.

This chapter aims to discuss the role of AI-driven personalization in EFL education, its implementations, advantages, and disadvantages. The use of AI in language learning tools such as Text to speech, ITS, AI chatbots, NMT, IVE, and AC has improved the learner's engagement and performance in the process through the use of instant feedback, adaptive assessments, and tailored instructional content. This study also answers key research questions, such as how the AI-driven tools can respond to different learning styles, provide feedback to the learner, and engage the student. The mechanisms of the AI-driven personalisation are explained in detail, and the way that machine learning algorithms and NLP enable the personalised learning is explained in detail. Moreover, ethical issues, including data security, algorithmic bias, and overreliance on technology, are discussed. There are, however, great opportunities for the implementation of AI technologies to enhance the process of EFL programmes; nevertheless, these technologies cannot be implemented in isolation from other teaching methods. The results show that the use of AI in personalisation improves the EFL learning and training processes by providing learning paths, feedback, and experiences such as gamification and virtual reality. Nevertheless, limitations such as technical issues, data security, and resistance from teachers are still present. The study concludes that although the application of AI in EFL is possible and can be beneficial, it is important that man and machine are equally involved in the process. Future work should include long-term experimental studies, teacher education, and the creation of ethical AI frameworks to promote language learning for all.

AI-driven speech synthesis, particularly text-to-speech (TTS) technology, has the potential to revolutionize EFL education by providing learners with high-quality, native-like pronunciation models. These technologies, such as Google's WaveNet and Amazon Polly, utilize deep learning algorithms to generate speech with accurate prosody, intonation, and fluency (Aryanti & Santosa, 2024). Research suggests that exposure to native-like pronunciation through AI-generated speech enhances learners' phonemic awareness, helping them refine their own pronunciation (Liakin & Liakina, 2023). By integrating AI-driven speech synthesis into EFL learning, educators can provide students with scalable, accessible, and high-quality language instruction. These tools not only enhance pronunciation and listening skills but also offer learners a low-pressure environment for developing spoken fluency, making language learning more inclusive and effective.

While AI provides undeniable benefits, its adoption in EFL classrooms elicits mixed reactions from educators and students. Teachers appreciate AI's ability to automate grading and track learner progress, freeing time for higher-order instructional activities (Luckin & Cukurova, 2019). However, some educators feel underprepared to integrate AI effectively, highlighting the need for targeted professional development (Chakravarti, 2023). Students, on the other hand, benefit from AI's interactive and gamified learning experiences. However, concerns arise regarding over-reliance on AI-generated feedback, potentially stunting critical thinking and self-editing skills (Song & Song, 2023). Addressing these challenges requires a balanced approach, combining AI-driven personalization with human instruction.

## 2. PROBLEM STATEMENT

Implementing AI-driven speech synthesis technologies in EFL education comes with several practical challenges, including resource constraints, digital literacy disparities, and infrastructural limitations. One of the primary barriers is the financial investment required to acquire and maintain AI-powered tools. Many educational institutions, particularly in low-resource settings, struggle with budget constraints that hinder the adoption of advanced AI-driven speech synthesis software (Didas et al., 2024). Ensuring equitable access to these technologies requires policy interventions, subsidized software licenses, and investments in digital infrastructure. Another significant challenge is the varying levels of digital literacy among educators and learners. While younger, digitally native students may find AI-driven tools intuitive, many teachers lack the necessary technical skills to integrate these technologies effectively into their instruction (Chakravarti, 2023). Professional development programs and teacher training workshops focusing on AI integration in language learning can help bridge this gap, ensuring that educators can confidently incorporate speech synthesis into their teaching methodologies.

Moreover, speech synthesis technologies must be adaptable to diverse linguistic and cultural contexts. AI-generated voices often struggle to accommodate regional accents, dialects, and pronunciation variations, limiting their effectiveness for learners from non-Western backgrounds (Amin, 2023). Developers must prioritize the creation of AI models trained on diverse linguistic datasets to ensure inclusivity and linguistic accuracy.

Furthermore, reliable internet connectivity and access to digital devices remain pressing concerns, particularly in rural or economically disadvantaged regions. Without stable internet access, learners may struggle to use cloud-based AI tools effectively. Offline functionalities and mobile-compatible AI applications can help mitigate these barriers, allowing students in remote areas to benefit from speech synthesis technology. Addressing these challenges requires a multi-faceted approach involving policymakers, educators, and technology developers. By improving infrastructure, fostering digital literacy, and developing inclusive AI models, speech synthesis technologies can be effectively integrated into EFL education, ultimately enhancing learning experiences for diverse student populations.

Finally, ethical considerations and challenges are one of the concerns that needs to be looked into in details. Despite AI's potential, ethical concerns such as data privacy, algorithmic bias, and accessibility remain critical. Many AI tools collect sensitive learner data, necessitating stringent privacy policies (Bertino et al., 2019). Additionally, biases in AI training datasets can disadvantage learners with non-standard accents or regional dialects (Amin, 2023). Ensuring inclusivity and transparency in AI applications is essential for equitable learning experiences.

Advancing innovation in AI-driven language education requires a commitment to inclusivity and accessibility, particularly for marginalized learners. AI has the potential to democratize education by offering cost-effective and scalable language learning solutions. However, equitable access remains a challenge, especially for students in underprivileged communities who may lack the necessary digital tools and internet connectivity (Ulla et al., 2024). To bridge this gap, policymakers and educational institutions must advocate for AI solutions that cater to diverse socio-economic backgrounds. For instance, integrating mobile-friendly AI applications that require minimal internet bandwidth can increase accessibility in low-resource settings (Didas et al., 2024). Additionally, incorporating multilingual speech synthesis models ensures that learners from various linguistic backgrounds receive tailored pronunciation assistance, fostering a more inclusive learning environment (Amin, 2023).

The application of AI-driven personalization to English as a Foreign Language (EFL) instruction has significant potential, but raises several ethical concerns. Data privacy and security are a primary concern. AI systems often require the collection and analysis of extensive learner data to tailor instruction, necessitating strict adherence to data protection regulations such as the General Data Protection Regulation (GDPR) to safeguard student information and rights (European Commission, 2018).

Another critical concern is algorithmic bias. AI models trained predominantly on standard language varieties may inadvertently marginalize learners who use non-standard dialects or regional accents. For instance, studies have shown that AI language models like ChatGPT exhibit biases against non-standard English varieties, leading to stereotyping and reduced comprehension (Fleisig et al., 2024). Such biases can negatively impact learner confidence and perpetuate linguistic inequalities.

Furthermore, overreliance on AI tools could undermine the pedagogical role of teachers. In spite of the fact that artificial intelligence can offer immediate feedback and personalized learning paths, it lacks the nuance and empathy that human educators bring to the classroom. To ensure a holistic educational experience, it's crucial to balance AI integration and human oversight.

## 3. OBJECTIVES OF THE STUDY

Expanding research on AI's role in EFL education is essential to fully understand its potential and limitations. AI-driven language learning tools require continuous refinement based on empirical findings and interdisciplinary collaboration. Linguists, educators, and technologists must work together to develop AI applications that are pedagogically sound and linguistically appropriate (Miao et al., 2021). Educators, developers, and policymakers play a pivotal role in leveraging AI to create equitable learning opportunities. AI-driven platforms should be designed with user-friendly interfaces to accommodate learners with varying levels of digital literacy. Training educators to integrate AI into their teaching strategies is essential in maximizing the effectiveness of AI-driven tools (Chakravarti, 2023). Furthermore, ongoing research into ethical AI development is necessary to prevent biases that disproportionately affect marginalized learners (Bertino et al., 2019). By fostering collaboration among stakeholders, AI can serve as a transformative force in language education, ensuring that learners of all backgrounds have access to high-quality, personalized EFL instruction. One significant research area involves evaluating the long-term effectiveness of AI-driven language instruction. While existing studies highlight immediate improvements in pronunciation, fluency, and writing skills, there is a need for longitudinal studies to assess sustained progress (Luckin & Cukurova, 2019). Furthermore, research should explore how AI can enhance teacher-student interactions rather than replace traditional learning models. AI in EFL also presents opportunities for expanding theoretical frameworks on second language acquisition. By analyzing AI's impact on learner motivation, cognitive load, and retention rates, scholars can contribute to the broader understanding of technology-mediated language learning (Mohamed, 2024).

Additionally, ethical considerations, such as AI's impact on language diversity and data privacy, require further exploration. Researchers must address concerns related to AI bias in language instruction, ensuring that AI applications support linguistic diversity and do not marginalize underrepresented dialects (Bertino et al., 2019). By fostering interdisciplinary collaboration and contributing to the growing body of literature on AI in EFL, researchers can help shape the future of language education, making it more effective, inclusive, and equitable.

## 4. THEORETICAL FRAMEWORK

By incorporating robotics and natural language processing algorithms into education, personalized coaching and strategy modifications can be made for each student (Younis et al.). Students who work with them are able to enhance their communication, critical thinking, and cooperation skills, which in turn increases their engagement with the subject matter. Using natural language processing (NLP) techniques, robots are now capable of automatically grading assignments, evaluating information, and responding to situations on the spot. Creating inclusive, adaptable, and dynamic learning environments can be achieved through NLP-driven discourse, text-to-speech, and translation. Natural language processing and robots are enabling teachers and students to collaborate, share ideas, and propose new course designs through the use of natural language processing and robots. As Dr. Janice Gobert, a professor at Rutgers University and the CEO/cofounder of Apprendis, points out in her essay about the creation of Inquiry Intelligent Tutoring System (Inq-ITS), AI for education requires a multidisciplinary team of specialists working together (Adair 2023). As a result of combining cognitive and learning sciences research with AI computational techniques, Dr. Gobert and the Inq-ITS team developed scalable performance assessments of science inquiry skills. A virtual science experiment is conducted within the Inq-ITS environment, and students' science practices are automatically evaluated in real time. In the event that they encounter difficulty in the lab, a pedagogical agent will assist them with the solution. With an emphasis on utilizing artificial intelligence to enhance science, technology, engineering, and mathematics (STEM) education, Dr. Using ChatGPT, a well-known AI chatbot, Xiaoming Zhai tested how well it was able to create assessment items that were consistent with nationally recognized educational standards (Adair 2021). Additionally, he examined the chatbot's ability to provide individualized learning recommendations, assess science essays submitted by students, and tailor feedback to each student individually. However, Dr. Zhao contemplates the potential of ChatGPT to enhance teaching. Dr. David Joyner, the Georgia Institute of Technology's executive director of online education, urges teachers to welcome their students' use of ChatGPT and other similar technologies. Dr. Joyner believes ChatGPT will develop into a useful tool by drawing comparisons to the evolution of calculator use in the classroom.

*Figure 1. AI, NLP enabled architecture*

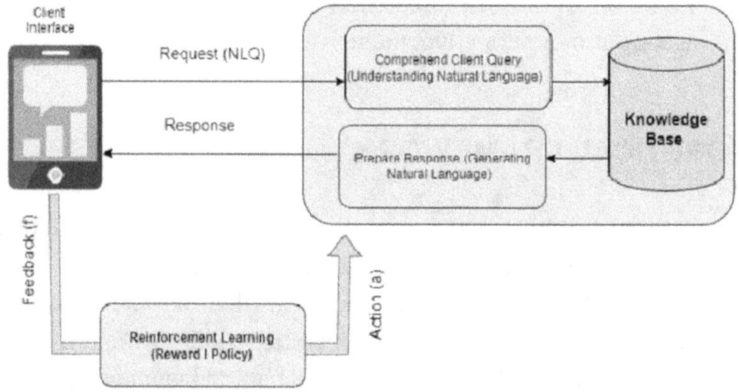


*(Gill and Kaur 2023).*

With reference to Figure 1, AI is a versatile tool that may be used for interactive programs, text to speech, text generation, and language comprehension with its strong NLP capabilities (Gilland Kaur,2023). Understanding its origins and development is crucial to AI-Driven Personalization in English as a Foreign Language (EFL) in terms of scientific research advancement and how they evolve as time unfolds.

## 4.1 AI in Education and EFL

The use of artificial intelligence in foreign language learning has increased in the last 10 years because of the development of machine learning, deep learning, natural language processing, and data analysis. In the EFL context, AI has been employed to create a vast array of learning aids and learning environments that can provide individual instruction, instantaneous feedback, and engaging learning experiences (Jiang, 2022). ITSs appeared at the beginning of this millennium as a way of individualizing instruction to students, but it was only with the development of machine learning and NLP in the 21st century that AI could be incorporated into language learning. The current trends in AI-assisted EFL learning include the application of affective computing to enhance the learner's emotion, and the integration of virtual reality (VR) and gamification to enhance learning. Since then, AI has expanded to include various components such as AI chatbots, neural machine translation, intelligent tutoring systems, intelligent virtual environments, and affective computing which have been found to enhance language learning (Jegede, 2024).

### 4.1.1 Key AI Applications in EFL Personalization

i. Intelligent Tutoring Systems (ITSs): These are computer-assisted learning environments developed on the basis of artificial intelligence and which provide individual guidance to the learners. These systems apply machine learning techniques to customize content and tasks for the learner according to his or her level of proficiency, learning style, and learning rate. It can provide instantaneous feedback, pinpointing the learner's weaknesses and providing specific recommendations for additional practice. The effectiveness of ITSs in improving EFL learning outcomes has been proven by research because they can provide individual help and thus reduce the cognitive load on students. For example, ITSs such as Pigaiwang and Robo-Sensei have been applied to improve grammar learning and reading comprehension for EFL students (Jiang, 2022).
ii. AI Chatbots: Chatbots are the conversational interfaces that mimic human conversation to provide language practice and feedback to the user. These chatbots employ natural language processing to interpret and reply to the inputs provided by the learners, giving them instant feedback and corrections. Some of the correlates of the use of AI chatbots in EFL learning include: the opportunities for conversational practice that they afford learners, and the relative anonymity that reduces performance anxieties. Furthermore, chatbots can be designed to suit the level of proficiency of the learner and provide graded challenges as the learner improves. These tools have been found to assist learners in the acquisition of grammar, vocabulary, and conversation skills. For example, chatbots like Duolingo and Babbel use NLP to give instant feedback on pronunciation and grammar and are, therefore, very useful in language learning (Jegede, 2024).
iii. Neural Machine Translation (NMT): NMT is an AI technology that uses deep learning models for the translation of text from one language to another. In the area of EFL, NMT can help with the learning of grammar and vocabulary through accurate translations and examples. NMT tools such as Google Translate and Microsoft Translator have found their way into EFL education to assist with grammar and vocabulary learning. These tools provide very accurate translations through the use of deep learning algorithms and can help the learner understand many texts and enhance their language skills (Jiang, 2022). NMT systems can also be incorporated into language learning platforms to provide instant trans-

lation of input and output, which can help the learner to use language more effectively.

iv. Intelligent Virtual Environments (IVE): IVE integrate AI with virtual reality (VR) and game based learning to develop virtual learning environments. In the process of EFL teaching and learning, IVE can place learners in situations where they can use language structures in real life like fashion. The effectiveness of these environments in enhancing learner vocabulary, speaking skills and motivation has been established. For instance, VR tools like Google Earth and Google Expeditions have been employed in creating language learning environments that mimic the real life situations of communication (Jegede, 2024). Moreover, the learners can have a virtual conversation with the AI controlled characters, play roles, and move around the environments which mimic the real-life scenarios of different cultures. It can increase the level of learner's participation and interest due to the fact that it offers practical and applied learning.

v. Affective Computing (AC) in EFL: A sub discipline of AI, AC applies the concepts of AI to Emotion Recognition to enhance the user experience. In EFL learning, AC systems can be designed to recognize learners' emotions through their faces, voice, and body, and change the learning process to suit the learner's emotions to give them feedback that is appropriate for their learning. ATS have been used to develop emotional intelligence in the learning environment to meet the emotional needs of the learners (Jiang, 2022). For instance, if the learner is angry or bored, the system may give encouragement, simplify the content or suggest a break, respectively. AC can help in increasing the levels of learner's engagement and motivation through its principle of mimicry of the natural environment.

## 4.2 Teacher vs. Student Perspectives on AI in EFL

From the point of view of educators, AI can be a useful assistant for simplifying monotonous work such as checking assignments, testing, and course material delivery. This makes it possible for teachers to concentrate on the higher order teaching and learning processes like guiding group work, individual teaching, and development of critical thinking. They like the fact that AI can perform menial tasks, give instant feedback and tailor learning to the needs of the student. However, some of the educators' participants in the study highlighted some concerns with the use of AI in education, including the possibility of the technology replacing teachers, the accuracy of the AI-generated feedback, and the ethics of using AI in education (Jegede, 2024), which results in the lack of personal approach and direction in the learning process. However, the application of AI in EFL tools has generally met with positive appraisals among teachers and students, who have different perceptions of the effectiveness of the tools in language learning. On the other hand, students, according to the findings of the study, have a generally positive perception of AI-driven tools in language learning, especially when it comes to individual approach and online correction. But some of the students' mentioned that there is no interaction with other people and that the AI may strengthen the stereotypes or the linguistic power of some countries (Jiang, 2022).

## 4.3 Ethical and Pedagogical Issues

Teachers and students in both groups have expressed concerns on the ethical and pedagogical implications of using AI in EFL teaching and learning processes. This is because there is a problem of bias in the AI language models that lead to stereotyping and cultural generalization. Furthermore, there are issues on the issue of data protection and security as many AI tools need access to the learner's personal information. In so far as pedagogy is concerned, there is a need to ensure that the use of AI in learning is blended with human interaction to make sure that the learner is not only able to learn in a private and convenient manner but also get the much needed social and emotional support that is offered by the conventional class room environment.

## 4.4 The Concept of Personalisation in EFL Learning

Personalization in education is the process of modifying the learning process to the specific needs, interests, and goals of each student. In the case of English Foreign Language Learning (EFL), personalization entails modification of the content, rate, and approaches used in instruction based on the level of proficiency, learning style, and preferences of the learner. This approach is different from the conventional approach where teachers use the same content to all learners regardless of their abilities. As pointed out by Wang and Wen (2019), personalized learning is a concept that is based on the fact that every learner is different and has certain potentialities and deficiencies. Thus, with the help of technology, it is possible to gather data and create learning paths that will help students progress fast. For example, a beginner EFL learner would be given basic vocabulary exercises, but an advanced learner would be given challenging reading comprehension tasks or conversation practice. Personalization is also applicable to the way that the content is delivered. Some learners may benefit from visual aids such as videos or infographics while others may comprehend auditory materials better, for example, podcasts or interactive dialogues. Thus, the personalized learning approach helps to create a more accessible and successful learning environment for all students as it adapts to their preferences. Adaptive learning is a specific type of personalised learning that uses technology to regulate the learning content according to the student's performance data in real-time. In EFL, adaptive learning is most valuable since language learning is an intricate process that varies with different individuals. Learning is a process that is different for different learners and they often have their own problems, for example, pronunciation, grammar or cultural aspects. According to Rodríguez-Muñiz and Padilla-Zea (2021), adaptive learning systems guarantee that learning is tailored to the ability of the learners, thus making the learning process more efficient and interesting. For instance, if a learner has a difficulty with conjugation of verbs, the system can offer extra tasks and descriptions of the concept to learn. On the other hand, if a learner is good at a given topic, the system can move to the next level of difficulty to avoid boring the learner and maintaining their interest. Adaptive learning also helps in the matter of learner variation. This is because EFL classrooms contain students who come from different languages and cultures, and therefore, come in with different background knowledge. Traditional methods of teaching may not be able to handle this kind of diversity but adaptive learning technologies can customize the content for every student, so that no one is neglected.

## 4.5 Traditional vs. AI-Driven Personalization

In EFL learning traditional methods of personalization are based on fixed curricula and traditional assessment by teachers. However, these methods can be quite effective, but they are usually slow and rather shallow. Every student's work has to be monitored by teachers and they have to determine the student's weaknesses and lack of knowledge and develop appropriate approaches to teaching him/her. This process can be rather challenging in large classes where there is little individual approach.).

On the other hand, AI personalization uses sophisticated tools to improve and facilitate the personalization process differently. In their paper, Chen et al. (2020) stated that with the help of AI, the content can be adjusted on the fly, feedback can be given in real-time, and the progress of students can be monitored. For example, a site based on AI may use a learner's responses on the quizzes and exercises and based on that, suggest some practice materials. The ordinal scale includes the use of AI in personalization to ensure that thousands of learners' needs are met at the same time whereas the traditional approaches are constrained by the availability of human resources. The importance of scalability is especially great in the EFL regions where there are shortages of qualified EFL teachers. Moreover, the AI systems can incorporate more data sources than the conventional approaches. For instance, they can use not only test scores but also behavioral data such as time on task, interest, and interaction patterns. This is a more holistic approach to personalization and is likely to be more accurate as a result. The AI-based adaptation of the curriculum in EFL implies the application of machine learning to customize the content and the rate of learning for each student. These algorithms use the learners' performance data to determine their strengths and weaknesses, learning preferences, rate of progress and, therefore, design unique learning paths and modify the curriculum. Duolingo and Babbel are AI-driven platforms that use machine learning to suggest learning activities to learners and provide instant feedback on their performance (Jegede, 2024). For example, if a learner has a problem with grammar, the system can propose some grammar practices and explanations. On the other hand, if a learner is good at vocabulary, the system will provide more challenging vocabulary tasks. This way, the learners are able to learn in an environment that is suitable to their level of proficiency and learning objectives..

## 4.6 How AI Personalizes Learning Experiences

The role of AI in designing individualized EFL learning experiences can be seen in various ways; Such as;.

i. Analysing Learner Data: AI systems capture and use data on learners' learning, preferences, and behaviors to design for them. This data is used to create detailed learner profiles, which guide the customization of content and pacing. For instance, if a learner has a particular weakness in grammar, the system could recommend grammar exercises for the learner (Chiu & Ching, 2018).
ii. Providing Contextualized Learning: AI creates realistic conversations and situations that actually happen in the real world to make the learning process more interesting. For example, a learner may be learning how to order food in a restaurant or how to conduct a job interview in English. Such real-life like tasks help the learners use their knowledge in the real life situations (Kim et al., 2020).
iii. Improving Writing and Pronunciation: Natural Language Processing (NLP) tools help the AI systems to identify and correct language errors in the texts. For instance, an AI-based writing assistant can check your grammar, style and coherence, while a pronunciation tool can analyze your speech and suggest possible corrections (Lee & Lee, 2021).
iv. Real-Time Feedback and Assessments: This is an important aspect of AI in implementation in EFL because it involves the use of feedback in real time. AI systems can give instant feedback to the learners on their work, showing them the mistakes and suggesting the corrections. This instant feedback helps the learners to correct their mistakes and learn again in the real-time, thus improving the language learning process. Also, AI can perform regular monitoring of learners' progress and determine their strengths and weaknesses. These assessments can

be used to modify the learning path, so that the learner receives the necessary assistance in the specific area.

v. Data-Driven Personalization.

## 4.7 Learning Analytics and Predictive Modelling.

Learning analytics and predictive modelling are used for data-driven personalization, which means using learners' behaviour, engagement and performance to personalize the educational content for each learner. The technology of AI-based learning analytics can help to understand learners' performance; by tracking the data on learners' interactions, the educators can see the learning patterns and trends and use them for informing the teaching processes and enhancing learning achievements. Predictive modelling uses this data to forecast learners' performance in the future, which helps educators to notice students in need of intervention early on. For example, a NLP tool (sentiment analysis) can be used to determine the learners' emotions and give them feedback to increase the motivation and engagement (Jiang, 2022). Furthermore, if a learner is predicted to have difficulty with a certain type of grammar, the system could suggest some resources and activities to help the learner overcome the difficulty before it becomes a problem.

## 4.8 Student Engagement in Sentiment Analysis

Sentiment analysis is an AI approach that uses NLP to assess the affective state of learners from their interactions with the learning management system. In EFL learning, the sentiment analysis can be applied to understand learners' engagement and motivation, and to identify when learners are frustrated, bored or uninterested. This information can be used to adapt the learning process, for example, by giving encouragement, simplifying the content or suggesting a break. Thus, the sentiment analysis can help to create a more empathetic and sensitive learning environment that would increase the learners' engagement and motivation. The personalized learning management systems are more effective in addressing the multiple intelligences theory by providing multiple modes of learning such as auditory, visual and kinesthetics for auditory, visual and kinesthetics learners respectively. For instance, in the area of speech recognition and pronunciation, AI can be particularly helpful for auditory learners, while for visual learners, there are interactive videos and other visual aids. Kinesthetics learners can benefit from the current trends of gamified learning and virtual reality that enables the learner to learn and practice language skills within a given context. Thus, the AI can provide a number of learning modalities to every learner to ensure that every learner is receiving learning that is appropriate to his or her learning style.? Moreover, AI chatbots can provide auditory output on the correct pronunciation of the word, while the VR tools can provide the visual and kinesthetic output of the learning content. Another current trend that has been found to improve learners' motivation and engagement in EFL is gamification. Gamification and VR are very attractive tools that improve the learner's interest and participation in the EFL class. Gamification is the process of incorporating elements of game into learning process to enhance learning. VR, however, provides the virtual environments through which learners can learn and apply language skills in real-life situations. Gamification and VR can be very useful in the EFL context because they provide the learners with the opportunity to learn through real life experiences and apply the learned language skills. Machine Learning: Machine learning algorithms are decision making mechanisms that define the learning paths based on real time data. For example, if a learner is good at reading but has a challenge in listening, the system should probably recommend more listening exercises than reading exercises (Wang & Wen, 2019). The NLP makes the AI systems to have the ability to comprehend and produce human language in its original form. This capability is useful in tasks like grammar correction, conversation practice, and content creation (Kim et al., 2020). The big data analysis helps to improve the AI-based instruction by finding the similarities and differences in the data set. For instance, if a large portion of the learners have a problem with a certain grammar rule, the system can recommend it for special focus (Chen et al.,2020).

## 4.9 Case Studies of AI-Powered EFL Platforms

i. In EFL contexts, empirical studies have begun to shed light on the effectiveness of AI tools. For example, an AI chatbot integrated into a peer review system demonstrated improvements in both peer feedback quality and writing abilities of EFL students (Li & Zhang, 2024) . Similarly, an intervention study utilizing AI tools in English literature classes found significant enhancements in students' critical thinking skills compared to traditional instruction methods (Liu, 2024).
ii. Additionally, AI-empowered applications have been shown to increase learner engagement and reduce academic procrastination among EFL students, proving their potential to positively influence learner behavior and motivation (Chen & Wang, 2024). These findings underscore the importance of continued research to explore the diverse applications and outcomes of AI integration in various educational settings.
iii. Duolingo: Duolingo uses AI to track learner progress and adjust lessons accordingly. The platform's algorithms analyze user performance to determine the optimal difficulty level and pacing for each learner (von Ahn & Lewis, 2011).

iv. Grammarly: Grammarly employs NLP to provide grammar and style suggestions. The tool is widely used by EFL learners to improve their writing skills (Chen et al., 2020).
v. AI Chatbots: AI chatbots facilitate conversation practice and error correction. These tools simulate real-life interactions, allowing learners to practice speaking and listening in a low-pressure environment (Guo et al., 2022).

## 4.10 Advantages of AI-Driven Personalization

i. Duolingo: Duolingo uses AI to monitor the learners' growth and change the lessons according to the AI analysis of the learners. The platform's algorithms use the user's performance to determine the most appropriate level and learning frequency for each user (von Ahn & Lewis, 2011).
ii. Grammarly: Grammarly applies the principles of NLP to offer suggestions for improved grammar and style. The tool is widely used by EFL learners to enhance their writing skills (Chen et al., 2020).
iii. AI Chatbots: AI chatbots help in the conversation practice and correction of errors. These tools provide real life like conversations to the learners and help them to practice speaking and listening without any pressure (Guo et al., 2022).

## 4.10 Benefits of the AI-Based Personalization

i. Personalized Learning Paths: One of the biggest advantages of using AI in personalization is that it can develop and guarantee that every learner has an individual learning path according to his or her learning requirements and objectives. Unlike traditional methods that use a fixed approach, AI systems use learner data to create individual learning paths that meet the specific needs of each student based on their level of proficiency, learning rate, and objectives (briefly explain how the technology accomplishes the task):
ii. Real-Time Adjustment: AI algorithms can track learners' performance and make changes to the content of the course accordingly. For example, if a learner has a problem with verb tenses, the system can provide the learner with more practices and explanations of the tenses until the learner learns them (Chiu & Ching, 2018).
iii. Individual Goals: Learners can set their own goals in the AI systems such as learning how to converse or for instance, to undergo a language proficiency test. The system then tailors the learning experience to help achieve these objectives (Wang & Wen, 2019).

iv. Instant Feedback and Correction of Errors: Other AI tools like NLP and ASR provide instant feedback to the learners and help them recognize and correct their mistakes in real-time. This immediate response increases the rate of learning and strengthens the correct usage. For example,

v. Writing Assistance: Other tools such as Grammarly employs NLP in identifying grammatical and vocabulary mistakes, suggesting corrections, and enhancing the writing style. This instant feedback helps the learners to improve their writing skills better than other methods (Chen et al., 2020; Chiu & Ching, 2018).

vi. Pronunciation Practice: AI based speech recognition tools analyse the pronunciation of the learners and give them feedback. For example, an AI system may underline some words that the speaker has mispronounced and provide examples of how the words should be pronounced (Lee & Lee, 2021) .

vii. Enhanced Engagement and Motivation: Most of the AI-based platforms have gamification and other interactive elements such as badges, leaderboards, and challenges to enhance the learner's interest. These features make the learning process more enjoyable and appealing to the learners (Rodríguez-Muñiz & Padilla-Zea, 2021).

viii. Gamification: Sites like Duolingo have incorporated gamified features such as points, badges, and leaderboards to enhance learning. These elements help the learners to accomplish tasks and reach certain goals (Rodríguez-Muñiz & Padilla-Zea, 2021).

ix. Interactive Content: They develop interactive dialogues, quizzes, and simulations using AI systems. For example, a learner can learn how to order food in a restaurant or how to conduct an interview in English, which makes the process more applied and interesting (Kim et al., 2020).

x. Disability Friendly: The AI-driven tools help in modifying the content in order to meet the needs of different learning styles and disabilities thereby enabling EFL learning to reach more learners including those with special needs such as those who are unable to attend traditional schools.

xi. Learning Styles: It means that the content can be delivered to different learners in different ways with the help of AI systems. For example, the video content will be more useful for visual learners, and the auditory learners may prefer the podcasts or the audio exercises (Rodríguez-Muñiz & Padilla-Zea, 2021). xii. Disabilities Support: AI tools can help students with disabilities through features like text to speech for the visually challenged and speech to text for writer's disorder. xiii. Low level of Emotional Intelligence: AI systems are unable to capture and react to the feelings of the learners. For example, a learner may become angry or frustrated and require positive reinforcement or a change in approach, which a human teacher can offer but an AI system cannot. xiv. Minimized Social Learning: Language learning usually entails group work, pair work, group discussions, and collaborative projects. As for the moment, most AI-driven personalization strategies are centered on the learning process of an individual, which may limit the chances of interaction with other learners. xiv. Unable to Analyse Complex Queries: Although AI can answer simple questions, it may fail to understand complicated or ambiguous queries that require a certain level of contextual comprehension.

## 5. THE DIGITAL DIVIDE

A significant challenge in implementing AI-driven personalization is the digital divide, which refers to the disparities in access to technology and digital literacy skills among different populations. An estimated 2.6 billion people remain offline, limiting their ability to benefit from AI-enhanced educational resources (Reuters, 2024). This divide is particularly pronounced in low-resource settings, where infrastructure and access to digital tools are limited.

To bridge this gap, initiatives like Arizona State University's SolarSPELL project have developed portable, solar-powered digital libraries that provide educational content to communities without internet access (Axios, 2025). Such innovations demonstrate the potential for creative solutions to extend the benefits of AI and digital learning to underserved populations. Moreover, efforts to develop offline-compatible AI applications and invest in teacher training programs are essential steps toward ensuring equitable access to AI-enhanced education.

## 6. RESEARCH GAP

Having reviewed numerous scorpus indexed and web of science indexed journals and related articles on AI-Driven Personalization in English as a Foreign Language (EFL), the researchers discovered that there is a need for long-term empirical studies to assess the effectiveness of AI-driven personalization in EFL education. This study should focus on the impact of AI on learner outcomes, as well as the factors that influence the adoption of AI-driven tools in educational settings. In addition, it suggests paying attention to the professional development and the AI literacy of the teachers to ensure that they are capable of incorporating AI in their teaching strategies. There is a clear lack of understanding in the literature with respect to the long-term empirical studies to assess the effectiveness of AI-driven personalization in EFL. Many of the current studies investigate the short-term results, however, there is hardly any attention paid to the long-term effects on the learners' language development and motivation (Jiang, 2022). This study aims to examine the effects of AI on learners' achievement, learning experiences, and the factors that affect the usage of AI-driven applications in learning organizations. It is important to conduct long-term empirical studies to determine the effectiveness of AI-driven personalization over time to gain practical experience with the technology. Long-term studies are important to determine the full implications of AI-driven personalization. For instance, researchers could follow learners for several years and see how they learn and what results they achieve with the help of AI-driven tools as opposed to more conventional approaches. Such studies could also examine the effects of AI on learners' motivation and self-efficacy, which are important processes in the long-term language learning (Luckin et al., 2020).

To overcome these issues, teacher training programmes should embrace an integrated framework that encompasses the technical aspects of the training as well as the pedagogical and ethical issues. Teachers should be trained on the technical aspects of AI such as machine learning, Natural Language Processing, and data analysis. This will help them to understand the principles of the functioning of AI systems and how to interpret the results of the applications based on AI.

Pedagogical Integration: Training programs should offer specific recommendations for the incorporation of AI tools into the teaching process. For instance, teachers could learn how to employ AI-based applications including ITSs and AI chatbots to support learners' learning needs while ensuring that human intervention is still prominent in the learning process.

Ethical Considerations: Teachers should be able to critically reflect on the ethical implications of the use of AI in education, including issues such as data security, bias, and the risk of automation of teachers' roles. This will assist them in making the right decisions on how to apply AI in their teaching.

*Figure 2. AI-powered language model utilizing AI educational robotic environment with natural language processing*

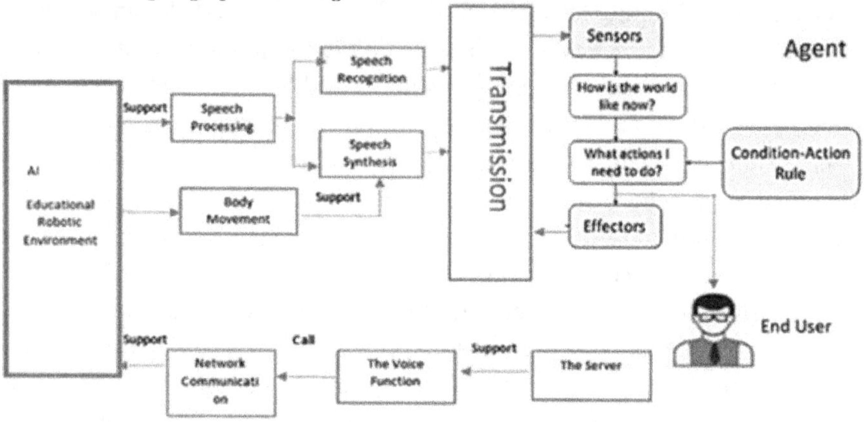


*(Matthew et al., 2023)*

Ongoing Support: Teacher training should not be a one-time event but rather an ongoing process of supporting educators and offering professional development. This could include workshops, online courses, and communities of practice where teachers can exchange stories and strategies. Teacher training and AI literacy are essential for the proper use of AI-driven personalization in EFL. This paper therefore recommends that teachers should be trained on how to incorporate AI in teaching and also on the potential risks of using AI in education. Future work should aim to create teacher training programs and AI literacy materials to assist and guarantee that teachers are ready to incorporate AI into their teaching strategies. Literature on the use of AI for oral skill instruction remains scarce. On a related note, research has not conclusively established, which pedagogical strategy is best for teaching English. The current study's search of the literature revealed a dearth of critical analyses of the pedagogical effects of adopting AI in education or novel implementation strategies. Furthermore, any currently available reviews would already seem to be out of date given the ongoing swift advancements and developments in technology; resulting in a scarce number of published reviews focused on innovative AI technologies trends and development in the educational setting. Bibliometric analysis is most beneficial when analysing substantial amounts of literature data, although more thorough research utilizing systematic review approach is required. Therefore, additional systematic review of representative articles to develop a deeper understanding of the incorporation of AI for EFL education is recommended. This study undertook a thorough, systematic analysis of research published between 2012 and 2024 in light of the growing significance of AI in language education, and the dearth of complete reviews on the topic. The analysis helped the researchers to find out that the Literature on the use of AI for oral skill instruction remains scarce. On a related note, research has not conclusively established, which pedagogical strategy is best for teaching English. The current study's search of the literature revealed a dearth of critical analyses of the pedagogical effects of adopting AI in education or novel implementation strategies. Furthermore, any currently available reviews would already seem to be out of date given the ongoing swift advancements and developments in technology; resulting in a scarce number of published reviews focused on innovative AI technologies trends and development in the educational setting. Bibliometric analysis is most beneficial when analysing substantial amounts of literature data, although more thorough research utilizing systematic review approach is required. Therefore, additional systematic review of representative articles to develop a deeper understanding of the incorporation of AI for EFL education is recommended.

## 7. RECOMMENDATIONS

Based on the studies carried out, the researchers recommend that future research should focus on designing longitudinal studies that address the limitations of existing research. These studies should:

i. Track Learners Over Extended Periods: Researchers should follow learners for several years to assess the long-term impact of AI-driven personalization on language proficiency, motivation, and real-world application of language skills.
ii. Incorporate Diverse Learner Populations: Studies should include learners from different cultural, linguistic, and socioeconomic backgrounds to ensure that findings are generalizable and inclusive.
iii. Use Robust Assessment Tools: Researchers should develop and validate assessment tools that can capture subtle changes in language proficiency and motivation over time.
iv. Explore the Role of AI in Overcoming Learning Plateaus: Future studies should investigate whether AI-driven tools can help learners overcome the plateau effect by providing targeted support and adaptive learning paths.

By addressing these research gaps, long-term empirical studies can provide valuable insights into the potential and limitations of AI-driven personalization in EFL learning. While AI-driven tools offer numerous benefits, their successful implementation in EFL classrooms depends heavily on the preparedness of educators. Teachers play a critical role in integrating AI technologies into their teaching practices, ensuring that these tools are used effectively to enhance learning outcomes

(Holmes et al., 2021). However, many educators lack the knowledge and skills needed to leverage AI-driven tools, creating a barrier to their widespread adoption. Teacher training programs must address this gap by equipping educators with the technical and pedagogical skills needed to integrate AI into their classrooms. This includes understanding how AI-driven systems work, interpreting data generated by these systems, and using AI tools to provide personalized support to learners (Luckin et al., 2020). Without proper training, teachers may struggle to harness the full potential of AI-driven personalization, leading to suboptimal outcomes for learners.

## 8. CONCLUSION

In this chapter, The researchers have attempted to discuss the feasibility and restrictions of AI in the area of EFL, and the results indicate that AI can be used to create personalized learning experiences, personalized feedback, and even personalized learning environments. The results of the study show that the use of AI in personalization can enhance EFL learning and training processes to the advantage of the learner based on his or her learning preferences. Nevertheless, issues including data security, pedagogical reluctance, and limitations in the application of AI in emotion and context recognition continue to pose a significant threat.

The consequences of the application of AI in personalization for the future of EFL education are significant. Therefore, the use of AI in education can help meet the needs of different students and increase the productivity of language learning processes. Nevertheless, it is crucial to find a proper balance between the use of AI in personalization and a human teacher, so that students could benefit from both approaches. Moreover, for the purpose of establishing trust and acceptance, among educators and learners, it is crucial to address the ethical and pedagogical issues of AI-driven personalization.

In this chapter, a systematic review was used to analyse the currently available journals in language education with the help of AI. As stated by (Mallett et al. 2012), systematic reviews are concerned with evidence, impact, validity and causality which were all important in this work in making recommendation on the value of AI in education practices. The strategy adopted included a systematic approach to the identification, inclusion and appraisal of relevant studies from several electronic databases. The systematic review approach helped in establishing which AI was used in EFL learning and teaching, the most common areas of application in EFL teaching and learning, and the technology used in AI, and the comparison between the technology used and the current practice in the field. In general, the systematic review approach was helpful in providing a systematic way of identifying and integrating the current literature on AI in EFL and determining the gaps that exist, which can help inform future studies in this area.

AI can transform educational practices by redefining the roles of teachers and students as well as the assessment system. With the help of applications of AI, students can receive different forms of instruction from teachers, solving the problem of how to teach many students with a small number of teachers. In practical terms, the growing availability of AI technologies and methods may enable the teacher to shift from being the primary source of knowledge to being a tutor, providing feedback and guidance to learners as they navigate through personalized adaptive learning environments. In other words, students may become more responsible for their learning and more interested in learning on their own with the help of AI tools while developing their language skills in various situations.

## REFERENCES


Ableson, F. W., Collins, C., & Sen, R. (2009). Unlocking Android. Manning Publications 2009. Available Online at https://www.manning.com/ableson/SampleChapter1.pdf

Alshumaimeri, Y. A., & Alshememry, A. K. (2024). The Extent of AI Applications in EFL Learning and Teaching. *IEEE Transactions on Learning Technologies*, *17*, 653–663. DOI: 10.1109/TLT.2023.3322128

Attali, Y., & Burstein, J. (2006). Automated essay scoring with e-rater® v.2. *The Journal of Technology, Learning, and Assessment*, *4*(3), 1–30.

August, D., & Shanahan, T. (Eds.). (2006). *Developing literacy in second-language learners: Report of the National Literacy Panel on language-minority children and youth*. Erlbaum.

Barr, D., & Feigenberg, L. (2017). Artificial intelligence in the classroom. *Journal of Educational Technology Systems*, *45*(1), 27–45.

Bax, S. (2019). *The Past, Present, and Future of CALL: An Overview of Selected Literature*. Routledge.

Beck, I., & McKeown, M. (2007). Increasing young low-income children's oral vocabulary repertoires through rich and focused instruction. *The Elementary School Journal*, *107*(3), 251–271. DOI: 10.1086/511706

Bialystok, E. (2001). *Bilingualism in Development: Language, Literacy, and Cognition*. Cambridge University Press. DOI: 10.1017/CBO9780511605963

Bialystok, E. (2007). Acquisition of literacy in bilingual children: A framework for research. *Language Learning*, *57*(s1), 45–77. DOI: 10.1111/j.1467-9922.2007.00412.x

Biemiller, A. (2006). Vocabulary development and instruction: A prerequisite for school learning. In Dickinson, D., & Neuman, S. B. (Eds.), *Handbook of early literacy research* (Vol. II, pp. 41–51). Guilford.

Blair, C. (2002). School readiness: Integrating cognition and emotion in a neurobiological conceptualization of children's functioning at school entry. *The American Psychologist*, *57*(2), 111–127. DOI: 10.1037/0003-066X.57.2.111 PMID: 11899554

Chapelle, C. A. (2001). *Computer Applications in Second Language Acquisition: Foundations for Teaching, Testing, and Research*. Cambridge University Press. DOI: 10.1017/CBO9781139524681

Chen, X., Zou, D., Xie, H., Cheng, G., & Liu, C. (2022). Two decades of artificial intelligence in education. *Journal of Educational Technology & Society*, *25*, 28–47. https:// www.jstor.org/stable/48647028#metadata_info_tab_contents

Chen, Y., Liu, Y., & Zhang, Y. (2020). Exploring the potential of AI in language learning: A meta-analysis of empirical studies. *Educational Technology Research and Development*, *68*(4), 1795–1812.

Chen, Y., Liu, Y., & Zhang, Y. (2022). Exploring the effects of artificial intelligence-driven personalized learning on language learners' performance. *Educational Technology Research and Development*, *70*(1), 213–230.

Chen, Y., Smith, T. J., York, C. S., & Mayall, H. J. (2020). Google earth virtual reality and expository writing for young english learners from a funds of knowledge perspective. *Computer Assisted Language Learning*, *33*(1-2), 1–25. DOI: 10.1080/09588221.2018.1544151

Chien, S.-Y., Hwang, G.-J., & Jong, M. S.-Y. (2020). Effects of peer assessment within the context of spherical video-based virtual reality on efl students' englishspeaking performance and learning perceptions. *Computers & Education*, *146*, 103751. DOI: 10.1016/j.compedu.2019.103751

Chiu, T. K. F., & Ching, Y. H. (2018). The effectiveness of AI-driven feedback in language learning: A systematic review. *Computer Assisted Language Learning*, *31*(5-6), 486–508.

Coniam, D., & Falvey, P. (2018). Comparing human and automated scoring of summary writing. *Language Testing*, *35*(3), 309–332.

Council of Europe. (2001). *Common European Framework of Reference for Languages: Learning, Teaching, Assessment.* Cambridge University Press.

Cowie, N., & Alizadeh, M. (2022). The affordances and challenges of virtual reality for language teaching. *Int. J. TESOL Stud.*, *4*, 50–65. DOI: 10.46451/ijts.2022.03.05

Delorme Benites, A., & Lehr, C. (2022). Neural machine translation and language teaching: possible implications for the cefr. Bull. Suisse de Linguist. Appliquée 2021, 47–66. DOI: 10.21256/zhaw-24716

Doherty, S., & Kenny, D. (2014). The design and evaluation of a statistical machine translation syllabus for translation students. *The Interpreter and Translator Trainer*, *8*(2), 295–315. DOI: 10.1080/1750399X.2014.937571

Dong, D., Wu, H., He, W., Yu, D., & Wang, H. (2015). "Multi-task learning for multiple language translation," in Proceedings of the 53rd Annual Meeting of the Association for Computational Linguistics and the 7th International Joint Conference on Natural Language Processing (Volume 1: Long Papers) (Beijing), 1723–1732.

Dong, S., Wang, P., & Abbas, K. (2021). A survey on deep learning and its applications. *Computer Science Review*, *40*, 100379. DOI: 10.1016/j.cosrev.2021.100379

Dong, Y., Chiang, C., Truong, H., & Qiu, Y. (2021). Enhancing language learning through AI-driven inclusive design. *Journal of Educational Technology & Society*, *24*(2), 191–204.

Dörnyei, Z., & Ushioda, E. (2011). *Teaching and Researching Motivation*. Pearson Education Limited.

Du, Y., & Gao, H. (2022). Determinants affecting teachers' adoption of aibased applications in efl context: An analysis of analytic hierarchy process. *Education and Information Technologies*, *27*(7), 9357–9384. DOI: 10.1007/s10639-022-11001-y

Dusek, O., Gurevych, I., Riezler, S., & Arnold, T. (2020). What is the essence of a claim? Cross-domain claim identification. *Natural Language Engineering*, *26*(2), 191–211.

Ebadi, S., & Ebadijalal, M. (2020). The effect of google expeditions virtual reality on efl learners' willingness to communicate and oral proficiency. *Computer Assisted Language Learning*, *33*, 1–25. DOI: 10.1080/09588221.2020.1854311

Engel, F., Keary, A., Berwind, K., Bornschlegl, M. X., & Hemmje, M. (2017). "The role of reproducibility in affective computing," in *2017 IEEE International Conference on Bioinformatics and Biomedicine (BIBM)* (Kansas City, MO: IEEE), 2008–2014. DOI: 10.1109/BIBM.2017.8217969

European Commission. (2012). *Multilingualism: An Asset for Europe and a Shared Commitment*. European Commission.

Fleming, N. D., & Mills, C. (1992). Not another inventory, rather a catalyst for reflection. *To Improve the Academy*, *11*(1), 137–155. DOI: 10.1002/j.2334-4822.1992.tb00213.x

Gao, J. (2021). Exploring the feedback quality of an automated writing evaluation system pigai. *International Journal of Emerging Technologies in Learning*, *16*(11), 322–330. DOI: 10.3991/ijet.v16i11.19657

García-Peñalvo, F. J., Corell, A., Abella-García, V., Grande, M., & Morales, E. (2020). Artificial intelligence in the classroom: A scoping review of AI-driven language learning tools. *Journal of Educational Technology & Society*, *23*(3), 161–175.

Godwin-Jones, R. (2015). Contributing, creating, curating: Digital literacies for language learners. *Language Learning & Technology*, *19*, 8–20.

Groves, M., & Mundt, K. (2015). Friend or foe? google translate in language for academic purposes. *English for Specific Purposes*, *37*, 112–121. DOI: 10.1016/j.esp.2014.09.001

Gu, J., Wang, Z., Kuen, J., Ma, L., Shahroudy, A., Shuai, B., Liu, T., Wang, X., Wang, G., Cai, J., & Chen, T. (2018). Recent advances in convolutional neural networks. *Pattern Recognition*, *77*, 354–377. DOI: 10.1016/j.patcog.2017.10.013

Guan, C., Mou, J., & Jiang, Z. (2020). Artificial intelligence innovation in education: A twenty-year data-driven historical analysis. *Int. J. Innovat. Stud.*, *4*(4), 134–147. DOI: 10.1016/j.ijis.2020.09.001

Guo, K., Wang, J., & Chu, S. K. W. (2022). Using chatbots to scaffold efl students argumentative writing. *Assessing Writing*, *54*, 100666. DOI: 10.1016/j.asw.2022.100666

Gutiérrez-Colón, M., Pérez-Moreno, J. A., Moreno-Ger, P., & Martínez-Ortiz, I. (2020). Addressing language diversity in AI-driven language learning platforms: Challenges and opportunities. *Computer Assisted Language Learning*, *33*(7), 813–833.

Hakulinen, L., Auvinen, T., & Bauters, M. (2019). Predicting language learning outcomes with neural networks: An exploratory study. *Journal of Computer Assisted Learning*, *35*(5), 623–632.

Haristiani, N. (2019). Artificial intelligence (ai) chatbot as language learning medium: An inquiry. *Journal of Physics: Conference Series*, *1387*(1), 012020. DOI: 10.1088/1742-6596/1387/1/012020

Hasan, M. A., Noor, N. F. M., Rahman, S. S. B. A., & Rahman, M. M. (2020). The transition from intelligent to affective tutoring system: A review and open issues. *IEEE Access : Practical Innovations, Open Solutions*, *8*, 204612–204638. DOI: 10.1109/ACCESS.2020.3036990

Heift, T., & Schulze, M. (2007). *Error Detection and Correction in CALL: A Comprehensive Guide*. John Benjamins Publishing.

Higgins, J., Xiao, Z., & Nunan, D. (2012). *The Cambridge Guide to Pedagogy and Practice in Second Language Teaching*. Cambridge University Press.

Hinojo-Lucena, F.-J., Aznar-Díaz, I., Cáceres-Reche, M.-P., & Romero-Rodríguez, J.-M. (2019). Artificial intelligence in higher education: A bibliometric study on its impact in the scientific literature. *Education Sciences*, *9*(1), 51. DOI: 10.3390/educsci9010051

Hochstein, A., & Green, J. (2018). Using AI to improve language learning. Memrise Blog. https://blog.memrise. com/using-ai-to-improve-language-learning/

Holmes, W., Bialik, M., & Fadel, C. (2021). *Artificial Intelligence in Education: Promises and Implications for Teaching and Learning*. Center for Curriculum Redesign.

Holstein, K., Gómez, P., & Lee, M. J. (2020). AI in education: Ethical considerations for equitable access and participation. *British Journal of Educational Technology*, *51*(4), 1354–1369.

Holstein, K., McLaren, B. M., & Aleven, V. (2017). "Spacle: investigating learning across virtual and physical spaces using spatial replays," in *Proceedings of the Seventh International Learning Analytics and Knowledge Conference* (Vancouver, CA), 358–367. DOI: 10.1145/3027385.3027450

Huang, Y., Al-Rfou, R., Pottier, L., & Adams, K. (2015). Natural language processing with small feed-forward networks. Association for Computational Linguistics. https://www.aclweb.org/anthology/D15-1266.pdf

Jegede, O. O. (2021). Mobile-Assisted Language Learning and Online Cooperative Language Learning: Merits and Demerits. A. A. Robbin, O. B. Jolaoso & O. B. Bakare (Eds.) Management of Education for Sustainable Development in a Changing World: A Festschrift in Honour of Professor Afolakemi Olasumbo Oredein, pp. 55-58. Ibadan: College Press

Jegede, O. O., & Adesina, O. (2022). Digitising English Language Teaching and Learning for e-Generation Students in Nigeria. B. A. Adeyemi, P. O. Yara & M. D. Oyetade (Eds.) (2022). Pastoral Psychology in Education for Sustainable Development: A Book of Readings in Honour of Professor Donald Abidemi Odeleye (pp. 204212). Ibadan: College Press.

Jones, A., Smith, B., & Johnson, C. (2018). The impact of AI-driven language learning tools on student motivation and engagement. *Computers & Education*, *125*, 247–256.

Keegan, S. (2019). Busuu language app: Full review and tips for using. The Mimic Method. https://www. mimicmethod.com/busuu-language-app-review/

Kim, J., Park, S., & Lee, H. (2020). An experimental study on the effectiveness of AI-driven feedback in language learning. *Language Learning & Technology, 24*(1), 120–136.

Kong, S. C. (2018). Integration of learner interests and multimedia materials in language learning: A crosscultural study of Hong Kong and Korean learners. *Computer Assisted Language Learning, 31*(3), 264–287.

Korell, T. (2020). How Babbel is using AI to personalize language learning. Medium. https://medium.com/ babbel-engineering/how-babbel-is-using-ai-topersonalize-language-learning-7981b0d7c48f

Krashen, S. D. (1982). *Principles and Practice in Second Language Acquisition*. Pergamon Press.

Kukulska-Hulme, A., Lee, H., & Norris, L. (2021). *Mobile Learning Revolution: Implications for Language Pedagogy*. Cambridge University Press.

Layali, K., & Al-Shlowiy, A. (2020). Students perceptions of e-learning for esl/efl in saudi universities at time of coronavirus: A literature review. *Indonesian EFL J.*, *6*(2), 97–108. DOI: 10.25134/ieflj.v6i2.3378

Lee, J., & Lee, S. (2021). Exploring the role of adaptive learning systems in AI-mediated language education. *Computer Assisted Language Learning, 34*(5), 524–538.

Leong, D., Tse, S. K., & Chan, C. K. (2020). Enhancing accessibility of AI-driven language learning tools for learners with disabilities. *International Journal of Artificial Intelligence in Education, 30*(4), 506–525.

Levy, M., & Stockwell, G. (2006). *CALL Dimensions: Options and Issues in Computer-Assisted Language Learning*. Lawrence Erlbaum Associates.

Li, X., Wu, H., & Zhang, Q. (2023). Equity considerations in the use of AI-driven language learning tools. *Journal of Educational Computing Research, 61*(1), 34–48.

Lin, C.-C., Liu, G.-Z., & Wang, T.-I. (2017). Development and usability test of an e-learning tool for engineering graduates to develop academic writing in english: A case study. *Journal of Educational Technology & Society, 20*, 148–161. https://www. jstor.org/stable/26229213#metadata_info_tab_contents

Lin, H.-C. K., Wang, C.-H., Chao, C.-J., & Chien, M.-K. (2012). Employing textual and facial emotion recognition to design an affective tutoring system. *The Turkish Online Journal of Educational Technology, 11*, 418–426. https://files.eric. ed.gov/fulltext/EJ989317.pdf

Liu, S., & Kunnan, A. J. (2016). Investigating the application of automated writing evaluation to chinese undergraduate english majors: A case study of" writetolearn. *CALICO Journal, 33*(1), 71–91. DOI: 10.1558/cj.v33i1.26380

Lotze, N. (2018). Goodbye to classroom teaching. Artificial intelligence in language learning. Translation: Chris Cave. Copyright: Goethe-Institut e. V., Redaktion Magazin Sprache. Available online at: https://www.goethe.de/en/spr/mag/dsk/ 21290629.html

Luck, M., & Aylett, R. (2000). Applying artificial intelligence to virtual reality: Intelligent virtual environments. *Applied Artificial Intelligence, 14*(1), 3–32. DOI: 10.1080/088395100117142

Luckin, R., Holmes, W., Griffiths, M., & Forcier, L. B. (2020). *Intelligence Unleashed: An Argument for AI in Education.* Pearson Education.

Ma, Y. C., & Lin, H.-C.-K. (2017). "The development of an affective tutoring system for japanese language learners," in *International Symposium on Emerging Technologies for Education* (Cape Town: Springer), 363–371. DOI: 10.1007/978-3-319-71084-6_41

Matthew, U. O., Bakare, K. M., Ebong, G. N., Ndukwu, C. C., & Nwanakwaugwu, A. C. (2023). GenerativeArtificial Intelligence (AI) Educational Pedagogy Development:Conversational AI with User-Centric ChatGPT4. *Journal ofTrends in ComputerScience and Smart Technology, 5*(4), 401–418. DOI: 10.36548/jtcsst.2023.4.003

Matthew, U. O., Kazaure, A. S., Kazaure, J. S., Hassan, I. M., Nwanakwaugwu, A. C., & Okafor, N. U. (2022). Educational Technology Adaptation & Implication for MediaTechnology Adoption in the Period of COVID-19. *Journal of Trends in ComputerScience and Smart Technology, 4*(4), 226–245. DOI: 10.36548/jtcsst.2022.4.002

Matthew, U. O., & Kazaure, J. S. (2020). Multimedia e-learning education in nigeriaand developing countries of Africa for achieving SDG4. [IJICTHD]. *International Journal of Information Communication Technologies and Human Development, 12*(1), 40–62. DOI: 10.4018/IJICTHD.2020010103

McCrocklin, S. (2019). Learners' feedback regarding asr-based dictation practice for pronunciation learning. *CALICO Journal, 36*(2), 119–137. DOI: 10.1558/cj.34738

Melchor-Couto, S. (2017). Foreign language anxiety levels in second life oral interaction. *ReCALL, 29*(1), 99–119. DOI: 10.1017/S0958344016000185

Mikolov, T., Kombrink, S., & Burget, L., Cernockˇ y, J., and Khudanpur, S.` (2011). "Extensions of recurrent neural network language model," in 2011 IEEE International Conference on Acoustics, Speech and Signal Processing (ICASSP) (Prague: IEEE), 5528–5531. DOI: 10.1109/ICASSP.2011.5947611

Mitchell, T. M. (1997). *Machine Learning*. McGraw-Hill.

Mohamed, H., & Lamia, M. (2018). Implementing flipped classroom that used an intelligent tutoring system into learning process. *Computers & Education, 124*, 62–76. DOI: 10.1016/j.compedu.2018.05.011

Mohammadzadeh, A., & Sarkhosh, M. (2018). The effects of selfregulatory learning through computer-assisted intelligent tutoring system on the improvement of efl learners' speaking ability. *International Journal of Instruction, 11*(2), 167–184. DOI: 10.12973/iji.2018.11212a

Nagro, S. A. (2021). The role of artificial intelligence techniqies in improving the behavior and practices of faculty members when switching to e-learning in light of the COVID-19 crisis. *Int. J. Educ. Pract., 9*(4), 687–714. DOI: 10.18488/journal.61.2021.94.687.714

Nguyen, A., Ngo, H. N., Hong, Y., Dang, B., & Nguyen, B.-P. T. (2023). Ethicalprinciples for artificial intelligence in education. *Education and Information Technologies, 28*(4), 4221–4241. DOI: 10.1007/s10639-022-11316-w PMID: 36254344

Nikolic, S., Sandison, C., Haque, R., Daniel, S., Grundy, S., Belkina, M., Lyden, S., Hassan, G. M., & Neal, P. (2024). ChatGPT, Copilot, Gemini, SciSpace andWolfram versus higher education assessments: An updated multi-institutional studyof the academic integrity impacts of Generative Artificial Intelligence (GenAI) onassessment, teaching and learning in engineering. *Australasian Journal of Engineering Education, 29*(2), 1–28. DOI: 10.1080/22054952.2024.2372154

Nobrega, F. A., & Rozenfeld, C. C. D. F. (2019). Virtual reality in the teaching of fle in a brazilian public school. *Languages (Basel, Switzerland), 4*(2), 36. DOI: 10.3390/languages4020036

Nwanakwaugwu, A. C., Andrew-Vitalis, N., Kwakpovwe, P., Emakporuena, D., & Eboesomi, E. (2025). Personalizing Medicine for Fake Drug Prevention With AI-Driven Digital Twins. In B. S. & S. Kadry (Eds.), *AI-Powered Digital Twins for Predictive Healthcare: Creating Virtual Replicas of Humans* (pp. 325-358). IGI Global Scientific Publishing. DOI: 10.4018/979-8-3373-0538-7.ch010

Nwanakwaugwu, A. C., Matthew, U. O., Okey, O. D., Kazaure, J. S., & Nwamouh, U. C. (2023). News Reporting in Drone Internet of Things Digital Journalism: Drones Technology for Intelligence Gathering in Journalism. [IJICST]. *International Journal of Interactive Communication Systems and Technologies, 12*(1), 1–22. DOI: 10.4018/ijicst.320181

Nyholm, S. (2024). Artificial intelligence and human enhancement: Can AI technologies make us more (artificially) intelligent? *Cambridge Quarterly of Healthcare Ethics*, *33*(1), 76–88. DOI: 10.1017/S0963180123000464 PMID: 37646146

Obari, H. (2020). "The integration of ai and virtual learning in teaching efl under COVID-19," in *ICERI2020 Proceedings (IATED)*, 7866–7872. DOI: 10.21125/iceri.2020.1740

Onu, P., Ikumapayi, O. M., Omole, E. O., Amoyedo, F. E., Ajewole, K. P., Jacob, A. S., . . . Mbohwa, C. (2024). Science, Technology, Engineering and Mathematics(STEM) Education and the Influence of Industry 4.0. Paper presented at the 2024International Conference on Science, Engineering and Business for Driving Sus-tainable Development Goals (SEB4SDG)

Oyekunle, D., Matthew, U., Waliu, A., & Fatai, L. (2024). Healthcare applicationsof Augmented Reality (AR) and Virtual Real-ity (VR) simulation in clinical cedu-cation. *Journal of Clinical Images and Medical Case Reports*, *5*(6), 3141.

Qian, L., Yang, Y., & Zhao, Y. (2021). Syntactic complexity revisited: Sensitivity of china's aes-generated scores to syntactic measures, effects of discourse-mode and topic. *Reading and Writing*, *34*(3), 681–704. DOI: 10.1007/s11145-020-10087-5

Zawacki-Richter, O., Marín, V. I., Bond, M., & Gouverneur, F. (2020). Systematic Review of Research on Artificial Intelligence Applications in Higher Education. *International Journal of Educational Technology in Higher Education*, *17*(1), 1–27.

# Chapter 4
# Artificial Intelligence–Assisted Error Analysis:
## Developing Pragmatic Competence in EFL Learners

**Manuel Macías Borrego**
https://orcid.org/0000-0002-5376-8860
*Universidad Rey Juan Carlos, Spain*

## ABSTRACT

*This study explores the intersection of Artificial Intelligence, error analysis, and pragmatics to enhance pragmatic competence in EFL learners. Pragmatic competence, which involves understanding and using language according to social and cultural norms, remains a challenge, particularly in cross-cultural contexts. AI-powered error analysis tools can help diagnose and address pragmatic errors by providing real-time feedback on aspects like politeness, speech acts, and cultural appropriateness. Recent AI advancements in natural language processing (NLP) enable systems to detect and correct pragmatic missteps, offering learners tailored suggestions. As a result, AI can refine direct requests to more polite forms, helping learners better navigate social interactions. Additionally, AI-driven platforms provide immersive environments for practicing pragmatic skills. Despite challenges in encoding dynamic cultural norms, AI has the potential to transform pragmatic competence teaching, with continued research needed to enhance its effectiveness and address cultural biases.*

DOI: 10.4018/979-8-3373-0969-9.ch004

# 1. INTRODUCTION

Our departure point is the inevitable intersection of Artificial Intelligence (AI), pragmatics, and error analysis, which opens promising avenues for enhancing pragmatic competence in second language (L2) and foreign language (FL) learners. While Pragmatic competence—understanding and producing language that fits the social and cultural norms of the target community (Taguchi, 2019)—remains a significant challenge for learners it seems unavoidable to discuss how AI-powered error analysis tools can be leveraged to diagnose, illustrate, and address pragmatic errors, thus fostering deeper linguistic and cultural understanding.

One key aspect to reach the previously mentioned objective is understanding the role of Error Analysis in Pragmatic Competence development. Error analysis has historically been a cornerstone of linguistic research, offering insights into the interlanguage development of learners. Pragmatic errors, such as inappropriate speech acts or misinterpretations of implicatures, often arise from L1 transfer or insufficient exposure to the cultural underpinnings of L2 norms (Thomas, 1983). For example, over-apologizing in certain cultural contexts may signify politeness in the L1 but appear excessive or even insincere in the L2.

Recent works, such as Macías Borrego (2023), emphasize the importance of integrating pragmatic error analysis into language syllabi. By analysing these errors, educators can identify gaps in learners' ability to navigate socially nuanced interactions. Moreover, pragmatic error analysis provides insights into how learners internalize language use, underscoring its critical role in achieving communicative competence.

In this light, it can be stated that AI has revolutionized error analysis and learners feedback by automating the detection of patterns in large datasets (Macías, Borrego, 2023). Recent developments in natural language processing (NLP) allow AI to analyse both grammatical and pragmatic errors with increasing precision (Tetreault, Blanchard, & Cahill, 2014). Unlike traditional methods, AI systems can evaluate linguistic output in real-time, offering learners feedback on their pragmatic appropriateness. Illustrating this situation, research by Huang, Liu and Wang (2022) highlights how AI-enhanced tools provide learners with immediate feedback on context-sensitive aspects of communication, such as register, politeness, and idiomaticity. These tools help bridge the gap between formal instruction and authentic language use, guiding learners in refining their pragmatic skills. Similarly, Macías Borrego (2024) also highlights AI's ability to monitor written discourse, identifying pragmatic missteps that may otherwise go unnoticed. This capability is crucial for addressing subtleties in cross-cultural communication, such as distinguishing between indirect requests and direct commands.

As illustrated by recent findings (Macías Borrego, 2024), a learner using an AI powered pragmatically trained chatbot could type a request like, “Give me the pen,” which the AI identifies as overly direct for a polite context. The system offers suggestions such as, “Could you please pass me the pen?” or “Would you mind handing me the pen?” alongside an explanation: “Direct commands can come across as impolite in certain settings. Consider softening your request with modal verbs like 'could' or 'would' and adding polite phrases like 'please.'” This real-time feedback not only corrects the error but also provides insights into context-sensitive communication norms, exemplifying how AI systems scaffold pragmatic competence. This process aligns with Huang, Liu, and Wang’s (2022) findings that AI tools enhance learning by offering tailored, contextually appropriate corrections.

Another key factor to take into consideration are the practical applications of AI in teaching Pragmatics as a tool to develop pragmatic competence. AI-powered conversational agents and immersive platforms allow learners to practice pragmatic skills in simulated real-world environments. For instance, chatbots equipped with NLP algorithms provide learners with opportunities to engage in roleplay scenarios, receiving instant, contextualized feedback. Studies have shown that learners using these tools develop not only greater linguistic accuracy but also increased confidence in their ability to communicate effectively (Huang, Liu, and Wang 2022). Hence, following Huang, Liu, and Wang (2022) we would state that when a learner drafts an email to a professor using an AI-enhanced writing tool, writing if they, for instance, typed: “I need the recommendation letter by next week.” The AI would label the tone employed as too direct and would suggest a polite revision by indicating something like: “Dear Professor [Name], I hope this message finds you well. I was wondering if it would be possible for you to provide a recommendation letter by next week. Thank you for your time and assistance.” This feedback – given by chatbots and other language processors - helps learners adjust tone and formality to meet pragmatic norms, aligning with Macías Borrego’s (2024) findings on AI's role in enhancing culturally appropriate communication.

AI-driven tools also support teachers by highlighting common errors across learner populations, helping educators tailor instruction to specific needs. According to Kessler (2021), integrating these technologies into classroom settings enables a more targeted and adaptive approach to pragmatic competence development.

Despite these advances, AI systems face challenges in interpreting the dynamic and context-sensitive nature of pragmatics. As Thomas (1983) noted, pragmatic norms vary across cultures, making them difficult to encode into universal AI frameworks. AI systems also risk perpetuating biases inherent in their training data, a limitation that must be addressed to ensure equitable learning outcomes (Reinhardt & Thorne, 2020).

Future research should focus on improving AI's ability to handle nuanced aspects of pragmatic interaction, such as irony, metaphor, and humour. Collaboration between linguists, educators, and AI developers is critical to achieving these goals. Hence, by integrating error analysis with AI tools, educators and researchers can unlock new possibilities for teaching pragmatics. Errors serve as invaluable indicators of a learner's interlanguage development, and AI's ability to analyse them at scale represents a paradigm shift in language education. As AI technology continues to evolve, it holds immense potential to transform how we understand and teach the art of pragmatic competence.

This chapter, thus, endeavours to investigate the potential to enhance pragmatic competence by focusing on the synergy created between new Artificial Intelligence (AI) tools and Error Analysis in enhancing the assessment methods employed by teachers of English as a second language within the context of a university course targeting B2 proficiency level, as per the Common European Framework of Reference for Languages (CEFR). To gauge the efficacy of this interdisciplinary integration, a comparative corpus study was devised, wherein half of the student productions underwent assessment utilizing AI tools. The findings of this study revealed noteworthy insights, indicating that the incorporation of AI technologies offers novel perspectives that effectively facilitate English as a Foreign Language (EFL) learners in crafting more proficient written texts. Notable observations include a significant reduction in error occurrences, evident in over 70% of cases, along with an enhanced application of grammatical rules observed in over 75% of the cases.

## 2. LITERATURE REVIEW

### 2.1 Natural vs. Artificial Intelligence

Natural Intelligence (N.I.) refers to the cognitive functions inherent in human behavior, whereas Artificial Intelligence (AI) encompasses the capabilities of machines to replicate complex tasks and behaviors, often in a manner that mimics human interactions (Grewal, 2014). In recent years, significant strides have been made in the field of Artificial Intelligence, particularly in its application to human learning processes (Markauskaite et al., 2022; Shin, 2008; Shin et al., 2021; Viberg, 2022). These advancements reflect a common aspiration among researchers and practitioners to seamlessly incorporate machine capabilities into educational settings, facilitating more efficient and effective interactions between machines and humans (Silva, 2018). However, scholars also note the limitations of AI in capturing the full spectrum of human communicative intent, especially when cultural and pragmatic nuances are involved (Pérez et al., 2021; Zu & Wang, 2023).

In contemporary scientific discourse, any device capable of performing complex tasks is often classified as exhibiting a form of Artificial Intelligence, particularly when it demonstrates adaptability across varied situations with minimal error (Lemos, 2019). In this sense, modern AI systems emulate cognitive functions typically associated with human intelligence, such as communication, problem-solving, and, increasingly, learning and response behaviors (Magid et al., 2022; Silva, 2018). These developments represent an ongoing convergence of human cognitive processes with machine operations, bridging the gap between human-like intelligence and computational efficiency.

The field of Artificial Intelligence is multifaceted, with various subdomains concentrating on distinct areas of research. A key area of focus is Natural Language Processing (NLP), which plays a crucial role in machine translation and improving machine-human communication (Zhang, 2020). Similarly, Object Recognition Studies (ORS) focus on identifying physical entities in the environment, such as moving or stationary objects, and overlap with rudimentary forms of human-machine interaction, often through auditory signals like beeps or alerts (Viberg, 2022). Although these domains share a common interest in enhancing human-machine-human communication, the wide range of AI applications demonstrates its diverse impact across multiple facets of modern life. Nevertheless, concerns remain about AI's ability to interpret contextually bound language use—especially in cross-cultural or high-context environments (Tatsuki & Houck, 2010).

One particularly promising frontier in Artificial Intelligence research is its application to education. Educational Artificial Intelligence (AIEd) seeks to harness AI technologies to enhance classroom management, instructional planning, and content delivery, ultimately improving teaching effectiveness and learning outcomes (Göçen, 2020; Yunus & Rajendran, 2021). This intersection between AIEd and Error Analysis, a key area in Applied Linguistics and Language Acquisition Studies, highlights the synergy between AI-based error identification tools and traditional mechanisms for addressing learner errors. Tools like Trinka.ai and Grammarly.com exemplify this approach, offering sophisticated error detection and correction systems that support the development of learners' language skills (Macias, 2023; Torben, 2022). However, these tools often lack the ability to detect pragmatic errors, which are context-dependent and require deeper socio-cultural understanding (Ishihara & Cohen, 2010).

The integration of theoretical perspectives such as Speech Act Theory (Searle, 1969) and Politeness Theory (Brown & Levinson, 1987) offers a valuable lens for evaluating AI's effectiveness in detecting and responding to pragmatic errors. These frameworks emphasize the importance of intent, politeness strategies, and interpersonal dynamics—areas where AI tools still show notable limitations (Taguchi, 2019).

Building upon this foundation, the present study seeks to examine the potential of these emerging AI tools in improving the written proficiency of English as a Second Language (ESL) learners within a predominantly Spanish-speaking context. The study draws data from a group of 70 university students enrolled in an English Language course designed to achieve CEFR B2 proficiency. It addresses the common challenge of insufficient progress in written proficiency, which can lead to student attrition (Cabrera, 2014; López Urdaneta, 2011).

The primary objective of this study is to investigate whether combining theoretical principles from Error Analysis, a critical component of enhancing ESL writing skills, with innovative AI tools can offer fresh insights and strategies for improving the efficiency and quality of written output while enhancing EFL learners' pragmatic competence. By integrating these approaches, the study aims to help learners produce more sophisticated and authentic written texts, ultimately mitigating common obstacles to language acquisition and skill development.

Furthermore, this study emphasizes the importance of incorporating global perspectives. Learners from different cultural and linguistic backgrounds may experience varying levels of success with AI-driven tools due to diverse communicative norms and expectations. For instance, indirectness in requests may be culturally preferred in East Asian contexts, while more direct forms may be acceptable in others (Chen, 2001; House, 2005). Without cultural sensitivity, AI feedback may inadvertently reinforce inappropriate usage or mislabel culturally acceptable forms as incorrect.

## 2.2 Error Analysis

In contemporary Linguistic Theory, the conceptualization of errors has undergone a significant transformation, moving beyond the traditional view of errors as simple mistakes. Pioneering works by Corder (1967; 1993) and Gass & Selinker (1972) have reframed errors as complex linguistic phenomena that provide valuable insights into the effectiveness of language teaching and learning. Errors are now understood not merely as failures, but as indicators that reveal deeper understandings of learners' cognitive processes and language development (Johansson & Hofland, 1994). Central to this paradigm shift is the Error Analysis framework, which examines the causes and nature of errors within the broader context of the teaching-learning process, helping to uncover the underlying mechanisms that lead to specific errors at key stages of language learning (Richards, 2002). This shift has profound implications for language pedagogy, influencing curriculum design, instructional methods, and assessment practices.

The ability to understand and manage errors within the educational context offers multiple advantages. By analyzing errors, educators can assess student performance in a more informed way, identifying both strengths and areas for improvement in their teaching methods. This diagnostic process allows for a more targeted approach to refining syllabi, minimizing error recurrence, and ultimately enhancing students' linguistic proficiency (Clerk & Rutherford, 2010; Macias, 2023). In this way, Error Analysis not only identifies what learners are doing wrong but also reveals critical aspects of language acquisition that might be overlooked without this lens of examination.

One of the most important contributions of Error Analysis is the development of the Interlanguage Hypothesis. Selinker (1969) introduced the concept of "Interlanguage" as a transitional linguistic stage where second language learners construct provisional grammatical structures on their way to mastering the target language (cited in McLaughlin, 1987, p. 69). William Nemser (1971), a key figure in Comparative and Error Analysis, refined this idea, defining Interlanguage as a unique linguistic system that is distinct from both the learner's native language (L1) and the target language. This system is internally structured, meaning it exhibits consistent patterns that emerge as learners transition towards fluency in the target language (Nemser, 1971, p. 116).

Building upon the foundational works of Corder (1967) and Selinker (1972), McLaughlin (1987) provided a deeper exploration of the cognitive processes involved in Second Language Acquisition (SLA) and Interlanguage development. These processes, which form the foundation for Error Analysis, include language transfer (the influence of the learner's L1 on the target language), overgeneralization (applying L1 rules or simplified rules to the target language), and misconceptions about rules and usage in the target language. Understanding these cognitive processes allows educators to develop more effective interventions aimed at addressing errors and facilitating language learning. By targeting these underlying issues, teachers can guide learners through the complexities of language acquisition, improving their ability to use language accurately and appropriately (Brown, 1994; Gass & Selinker, 2008).

Incorporating pragmatics into Error Analysis, particularly the analysis of pragmatic errors—such as inappropriate requests, refusals, or greetings—can offer a more nuanced understanding of language development. These errors, often shaped by a learner's cultural background and L1 norms, highlight the need to go beyond grammatical correction and explore the sociocultural appropriateness of learner language (Bardovi-Harlig, 2013; Taguchi & Roever, 2017).

Thus, Error Analysis provides a critical framework for understanding language learning challenges and offering solutions to overcome them, positioning it as an essential tool for educators striving for pedagogical excellence. By emphasizing the role of cognitive processes in language development, educators are empowered to refine their instructional approaches, leading to more effective and efficient language acquisition. This understanding not only informs teaching strategies but also encourages a more personalized approach to learning, catering to the specific needs of learners as they navigate the complexities of acquiring a second language (Macías Borrego, 2023). In multicultural classrooms, recognizing how culturally-specific norms influence learner errors can further personalize instruction and support intercultural communicative competence.

## 2.3 Error Analysis and Artificial Intelligence

The origins of Computer Assisted Language Learning (CALL) can be traced back to the 1950s, when it emerged at the intersection of linguistics and engineering studies. However, its development into an effective teaching and learning tool was a gradual process (Chapelle, 2003). Essentially, the CALL method for second language instruction is simple yet powerful: by carefully designing computers and computing devices, it can enhance efforts in acquiring a second or third language (Levy, 1997).

Despite its conceptualization, CALL remained primarily within the domain of research for a significant duration before its effective utilization by educators, instructors, and learners in pedagogical settings (Levy, 1997). Scholars in the field assert that it wasn't until the 1990s that the potential of CALL began to be tangibly realized in educational practice (Chapelle, 2003). The delayed uptake of CALL perspectives in teaching and learning can largely be attributed to the glaring absence of widespread dissemination of requisite technology in homes and educational institutions during the nascent stages of the discipline's development in the 1960s and 1970s (Schulze, 2011). It is often contended that the technological revolution witnessed in the 1990s facilitated the proliferation of personal computer-based learning systems, laying the groundwork for the integration of CALL into educational paradigms (Chauhan, Parida & Dhir, 2022).

The convergence of CALL as an approach and methodology with the application of Artificial Intelligence in L2 studies has drawn upon theoretical frameworks and scholarly discourse not only within Computer Science (Popovic & Ney, 2022) but also in domains such as Error Analysis, Error Treatment, and the Interlanguage Hypothesis (Jodai, 2012). Recent years have witnessed a fertile research discourse surrounding the seamless integration of Computer Assisted Feedback into the applied discipline of Error Analysis (Macias, 2023).

In today's education field, recent research (Cabrera; Elejalde & Vine, 2014; Magid et al., 2022; Steadman & Kraut, 2018; Wobst & Lueg, 2022) highlights the significant impact of modern technology in improving language skills through targeted practice and feedback. This shift emphasizes the importance of incorporating evaluative technology into devices, leading to a change in the assessment process. As a result, Computer Assisted Language Learning (CALL) becomes a valuable tool for error analysis, helping to identify patterns that lead to mistakes or help avoid them.

The rise of modern technology has significantly transformed educational approaches, providing learners with unique opportunities for personalized learning experiences that cater to their specific needs and preferences. By integrating evaluative technology into educational tools, learners can effectively enhance their language acquisition skills. Furthermore, the use of Computer-Assisted Language Learning (CALL) in education has a significant impact on error analysis. By utilizing CALL platforms, educators can gain valuable insights into error patterns and trends, enabling them to implement targeted interventions to address and correct errors. This proactive strategy not only improves language instruction but also encourages a culture of ongoing improvement and reflective learning among students.

However, recent studies have raised concerns regarding the limitations of AI in recognizing sociopragmatic and pragmalinguistic errors. Unlike grammatical mistakes, pragmatic failures—such as inappropriate speech acts—require contextual interpretation, which current AI systems often struggle to provide accurately (Yoon & Nguyen, 2021). This limitation underscores the need for integrating theories like Speech Act Theory and Politeness Theory into AI feedback models.

In essence, the convergence of modern technology and pedagogy heralds a new era of educational innovation, wherein the seamless integration of evaluative technology into instructional methodologies holds the promise of transformative change. As educators continue to harness the potential of CALL platforms in error analysis and beyond, the landscape of language education stands poised for unprecedented advancement and growth.

## 2.4 Artificial Intelligence and Education and Feedback Studies

Regarding Applied Artificial Intelligence, the 1950s heralded a seminal contribution from Alan Turing, a towering figure in the field. Turing's seminal proposition, as elucidated by French (2000), revolves around what has now become known as Turing's Imitation Game: the notion that if a human evaluator cannot discern whether their conversational partner is a machine or a fellow human, then the entity in question qualifies as an artificially intelligent system or device (Stefan & Sharon, 2017).

In the field of Education Studies, Artificial Intelligence has become a recognized and essential component. Luckin (2016) is a prominent figure in integrating AI with Educational Studies, especially in conjunction with Error Analysis. Luckin argues that AI can enhance learning outcomes by reducing errors and improving educational processes. AI models, as per Luckin, allow learners to advance at their own pace while giving instructors an objective view of their progress. Additionally, Luckin highlights AI's ability to support different forms of intervention, from face-to-face interactions to remote tutoring (Underwood & Luckin, 2011).

Recent scholarly work by Kessler (2021) underscores the transformative potential of modern technologies, particularly those adepts at processing and analysing textual and oral inputs, in comprehending the evolving realities and challenges encountered by educators and students alike. Kessler contends that insights gleaned from these technologies facilitate the customization of the teaching-learning process to cater to individual learner needs, thereby enriching the feedback loop through a synergistic blend of computer-assisted and teacher-centric approaches (Chaudhry & Kazim, 2021). Consequently, the integration of AI-based tools and data-driven insights holds promise for nurturing personalized teacher-student interactions and optimizing learning outcomes.

Indeed, the salutary impact of digital tools on educational processes is widely acknowledged, with Artificial Intelligence applications assuming a pivotal role in reshaping the roles and dynamics of educational stakeholders. According to Dickson (2017), these technologies engender a paradigm shift in the interactional dynamics between educators and learners, with machines offering interactive educational solutions to conventional challenges. Furthermore, Dickson prognosticates that AI-driven solutions hold the potential to surmount hurdles associated with large group interactions, particularly in fostering constructive feedback mechanisms, enhancing student performance, and fostering positive attitudes toward the teaching-learning process.ç

However, despite these advantages, several scholars caution against overly optimistic views of AI in language education. Selwyn (2019) and Williamson et al. (2020) highlight the risks of over-automation and the loss of nuanced human judgment in pedagogical contexts, particularly in the evaluation of complex competencies like pragmatics, cultural appropriateness, and affective engagement. These elements remain difficult for AI systems to accurately assess.

The field of teaching English as a second or foreign language can greatly benefit from integrating Artificial Intelligence and Information and Communication Technologies (ICTs). Language classrooms, which can feel artificial, sometimes hinder authentic communication and interaction. However, according to Haupin

(2016), incorporating technologies that simulate real-life situations and promote genuine communication can greatly improve language learning. Additionally, the development of communication programs and conversational tools, as emphasized by Rabah (2020) and Macías (2023), enhances language skills by providing learners with immersive, interactive, and practical language training experiences.

Yet, a significant limitation remains in AI's current inability to understand and correct pragmatic errors—those related to the appropriateness of language in specific social contexts. Tools like Grammarly or Trinka can identify surface-level issues such as grammar and spelling but often overlook speech acts, politeness strategies, or indirectness, especially when they vary across cultures (Yoon & Nguyen, 2021). This gap points to the need for integrating pragmatic and sociolinguistic theories—such as Speech Act Theory (Searle, 1969) and Politeness Theory (Brown & Levinson, 1987)—into AI design.

Moreover, there is a lack of representational balance in the datasets that train AI models. These models often reflect dominant Western norms, which may conflict with the communicative expectations of learners from non-Western or multilingual societies (Ishihara & Tarone, 2009). For example, learners from collectivist cultures—where indirectness and deference are favored—may receive inappropriate feedback suggesting that their polite phrasing is 'unclear' or 'wordy.' This cultural misalignment can hinder learner confidence and contribute to fossilization of errors.

In a comprehensive overview, Radwan (2020) delineates various applications of Artificial Intelligence aimed at ameliorating classroom dynamics and enhancing the teaching-learning milieu. These encompass bolstering reading comprehension through AI-assisted tools, refining translation skills via machine-assisted translation, enhancing pronunciation proficiency through automatic speech recognition, mitigating barriers for visually and hearing-impaired learners through text-to-speech functionalities, and refining writing proficiency through automated assessment techniques and handwriting correction tools. Thus, the integration of AI holds promises for overcoming pedagogical challenges and engendering transformative educational experiences.

A growing number of studies also emphasize the importance of "explainable AI" in educational settings. According to Holmes et al. (2022), learners must understand why a correction or suggestion is being made to engage in meaningful revision. Black-box systems, which simply mark errors without explanation, risk reducing learning to passive correction rather than fostering reflective practice. Therefore, embedding metalinguistic explanations and pedagogically grounded feedback into AI systems is essential for deeper learning.

Furthermore, regional perspectives underscore diverse adoption rates and effectiveness of AI-based tools. In high-income countries with robust digital infrastructure, learners benefit from consistent access to advanced AI systems. However, in regions like Sub-Saharan Africa or rural parts of Latin America, technological limitations and connectivity gaps persist, limiting the integration of such tools into mainstream education (UNESCO, 2023). This digital divide calls for localized AI innovations that are affordable, culturally responsive, and adaptable to low-resource contexts.

In conclusion, while AI holds substantial promise for enhancing feedback and individualized learning, particularly in L2 contexts, its current limitations in pragmatic evaluation, cultural sensitivity, and equitable access must be addressed. Future AI systems should draw upon theoretical frameworks from sociolinguistics and pragmatics, include diverse training data, and ensure that feedback is both explainable and culturally aware. Only then can AI serve as a truly transformative tool in global language education.

## 2.5 Pragmatic Competence

Pragmatic competence in linguistics refers to the ability to effectively and appropriately use language in different social situations, as described by Bachman (1990). This skill goes beyond understanding the literal meanings of words (semantics) and involves grasping the more subtle aspects of communication, such as tone, politeness, and cultural norms. Pragmatic competence allows individuals to interpret nuanced language and adjust their speech according to the context, social roles, and relationships involved (Taguchi, 2011). For instance, the distinction between a direct request like "Give me that pen" and a more polite request such as "Could I borrow your pen, please?" illustrates how language is modified based on social expectations and appropriateness. In bilingual or multilingual settings, pragmatic competence is even more significant, as speakers must navigate a range of linguistic and cultural norms depending on the context (Garcia, 2014; Blum-Kulka, 1982).

This competence involves understanding the basic principles of conversation, including Grice's maxims of quality, quantity, relation, and manner, which are essential for cooperative communication. Grice's theory emphasizes that effective communication relies on shared expectations, such as providing sufficient information (quantity) and ensuring relevance (relation) (Grice, 1975). Additionally, the concept of "flouting" is key in understanding how speakers may intentionally violate these maxims to convey meaning indirectly or to imply something beyond the literal words. For example, sarcasm and irony often involve flouting these maxims, requiring listeners to interpret the implied message based on the context (Grice, 1975; Kecskes, 2015; Swan, 2020).

Pragmatic competence can be further examined through the distinction between *pragmalinguistics*—the linguistic tools used to express intent (e.g., modal verbs, hedges, honorifics)—and *sociopragmatics*, which refers to the social and cultural rules governing language use (Leech, 1983; Thomas, 1983). These two dimensions must be mastered simultaneously to avoid pragmatic failure, where learners produce grammatically correct language that is socially inappropriate.

Speech Act Theory (Searle, 1969) provides an essential framework in understanding pragmatics. It posits that utterances perform actions—such as apologizing, requesting, or promising—each with its own set of felicity conditions. Misalignment in speech act formulation is a common error among second language learners, who may unintentionally violate norms related to directness, obligation, or authority. Similarly, Politeness Theory (Brown & Levinson, 1987) explains how interlocutors manage face (self-image) during interactions, employing strategies that mitigate threats, especially in hierarchical or collectivist cultures. Both theories are instrumental in diagnosing and teaching pragmatic competence yet remain underutilized in many AI-based learning systems.

Additionally, two theories have been put forward in the field of prgamatics to which many a line has been devoted. On the one hand, Politeness Theory (Brown & Levinson, 1987) emphasizes the role of politeness in communication, suggesting that speakers use politeness strategies to manage social distance, power, and imposition in interactions. Politeness Theory identifies two main types of politeness: negative politeness, which seeks to minimize impositions on the hearer, and positive politeness, which aims to reinforce solidarity and commonality. In SLA, learners often face challenges in using appropriate politeness strategies, as these can vary greatly across cultures. For example, the directness of a request may be interpreted as impolite in one culture but entirely acceptable in another. Understanding the application of these strategies in the target language is therefore essential for developing pragmatic competence.

On the other hand, Relevance Theory (Sperber & Wilson, 1986) focuses on the idea that communication is guided by the search for relevance. According to this theory, speakers aim to convey information that is both new and relevant to the listener, and listeners make inferences based on the speaker's intentions and the context. In second language learning, the challenge lies in the learner's ability to interpret implicit meanings, such as implicatures and presuppositions, and to use them effectively in their own speech. This theory highlights the importance of context in communication and the need for learners to not only understand explicit messages but also infer and convey implied meanings.

Pragmatic competence also involves using language in socially appropriate ways, interpreting implied meanings, and adjusting one's speech in accordance with conversational norms, politeness strategies, and social dynamics. This includes the ability to navigate complex interactions based on factors such as social status, context, and the relationship between the speakers (Taguchi, 2019). In multilingual societies, where different languages coexist, pragmatic competence becomes crucial in managing diverse linguistic and cultural expectations. In places like Nigeria, for example, language serves as a potent social marker. Different varieties of English, from Nigerian Pidgin to formal English, signify different social statuses, education levels, and regions. Nigerian Pidgin, often used among the working class and in informal settings, fosters solidarity and informality, while Standard English, associated with education and authority, is typically reserved for formal situations (Igboanusi & Peter, 2005; Anchimbe, 2020). This diglossic dynamic reflects the power structures that have been influenced by Nigeria's colonial history, where language use plays a central role in indicating social positioning (Bamiro, 2021).

Bilingual individuals further enhance their pragmatic competence by adapting their language use to meet the needs of different communicative situations. In societies where multiple languages are spoken, bilinguals frequently engage in code-switching, seamlessly alternating between languages depending on the social context. In Nigeria, for example, switching between English and indigenous languages such as Igbo allows speakers to manage social boundaries, express solidarity, or even avoid certain topics in conversations with outsiders (Kanu, 2020). This ability to shift between languages and adjust communication styles accordingly demonstrates the flexibility and richness of pragmatic competence in multilingual contexts.

Similar phenomena are observed in East Asian societies, where pragmatic rules are heavily influenced by Confucian principles such as hierarchy, collectivism, and indirectness. In Japan and Korea, for instance, learners often struggle with English pragmatics because of differences in how speech acts are structured and interpreted (Ishihara & Tarone, 2009). For example, expressing refusal directly may be considered impolite in Korean, while in English, excessive hedging may appear evasive or unclear. These intercultural mismatches can lead to pragmatic failures unless explicitly addressed in teaching and feedback mechanisms.

Despite the growing sophistication of AI in language education, pragmatic competence remains an area of significant limitation. Studies by Yoon and Nguyen (2021) and Lin and Huang (2022) reveal that while AI tools are effective at identifying grammar and syntax errors, they frequently fail to recognize or correct pragmatic errors. Learners may use overly direct expressions, inappropriately formal or informal tones, or culturally mismatched speech acts that pass undetected by AI systems.

These limitations reflect deeper issues in how AI tools are trained and evaluated. Many popular writing tools like Grammarly or Trinka are based on large corpora of written English, often from academic or professional domains in Western contexts. This results in feedback norms that are ill-suited to learners from other cultural backgrounds or those developing oral or informal communicative competence (Félix-Brasdefer & Koike, 2012).

To address these gaps, future development of AI in language learning should integrate cross-cultural pragmatic databases, include speech act recognition systems, and embed politeness models into feedback algorithms. Additionally, language learners should be provided with metapragmatic information—explanations about why a particular usage is (in)appropriate in a given context—which fosters critical thinking and self-monitoring of language use.

In sum, pragmatic competence is a multifaceted and culturally embedded domain of language that poses significant challenges for both learners and AI-driven tools. Enhancing AI's ability to detect and teach pragmatics requires theoretical grounding, cross-cultural awareness, and context-sensitive feedback design. Without this, learners risk acquiring structurally accurate but socially inappropriate forms of language use, which can impede their communicative success and integration into diverse speech communities.

## 2.6 AI and Education Studies: Limitations and New Directions

The integration of Artificial Intelligence (AI) in language education has been heralded as a transformative development, offering enhanced feedback systems, personalized learning experiences, and advanced error correction. However, despite these advancements, the adoption of AI tools in language learning is not without its limitations and challenges. This section reviews key literature on the constraints faced by AI systems in language education, focusing on their ability to address pragmatic errors, the lack of contextual sensitivity, and the need for human involvement in refining language teaching and learning.

One of the primary challenges in using AI tools in language education is their limited ability to fully grasp and correct pragmatic errors in language. Pragmatic competence refers to the ability to use language appropriately in different social and cultural contexts, involving nuances such as politeness strategies, speech act performance, and the adjustment of tone and formality. While AI tools, such as Trinka.ai, have shown promise in detecting grammatical errors and offering structural corrections, they often fall short in addressing subtle pragmatic issues.

Research by Yuan et al. (2021) suggests that AI's capacity to understand social and cultural contexts remains underdeveloped. AI tools often fail to recognize the complexities of indirect speech acts, sarcasm, or irony—elements that are essential for nuanced communication. For instance, an AI tool may flag a polite request as a "grammatical error" simply because it does not fit the mold of a direct command, thus missing the pragmatically appropriate nature of the request. Kuhn & Atkinson (2020) highlight that AI's inability to understand these context-specific meanings limits its usefulness in enhancing pragmatic competence, especially for learners who need to navigate cultural or situational variations in language use.

Another significant limitation of AI in language education is its struggle with cultural sensitivity. Language is inherently tied to culture, and effective communication often depends on an understanding of culturally-specific norms and social expectations. However, as Seyyedali et al. (2022) point out, AI tools are generally limited in their ability to provide feedback that aligns with the social norms and cultural sensitivities of the target language. While AI systems can analyze linguistic patterns, they typically lack the deep understanding required to assess whether a learner's use of language aligns with the expected sociocultural behaviors.

For example, an AI system might fail to detect that a request phrased in a direct manner may be inappropriate in a particular culture or that the tone of an apology does not adequately reflect the social gravity of the situation. Munday (2016) argues that the reliance on AI for pragmatic feedback risks ignoring the role of human interaction in shaping intercultural competence, which is a critical aspect of language learning.

AI's challenges are particularly evident in its handling of non-literal language, such as irony, humor, and sarcasm. These elements often rely on shared knowledge, context, and a certain level of meta-cognition that AI has yet to master. AI models tend to interpret language at a surface level, making them prone to errors in interpreting implied meaning.

In a study by Kozlowski et al. (2021), AI systems struggled significantly when tasked with identifying sarcastic remarks in learners' writings. They noted that AI tools were unable to accurately flag humor or irony, leading to misinterpretations and missed opportunities for effective feedback. This shortcoming can significantly hinder students' ability to grasp the subtleties of pragmatic competence, particularly when learning to navigate informal or culturally complex communication.

Despite advancements in natural language processing (NLP), AI systems still lack the emotional intelligence necessary for fully understanding the social dynamics of language use. Emotional nuances—such as empathy, emotional tone, and the ability to gauge the social status of interlocutors—are often outside the scope of AI feedback capabilities. As Gass & Selinker (2008) point out, AI tools are still in the early stages of recognizing these essential elements of social communication. In language learning, this deficiency is particularly notable in tasks requiring the learner to adjust language use according to the emotional tone of the conversation or the status of the interlocutor.

For instance, an AI tool might provide feedback on a sentence that lacks a polite form but will not be able to suggest a more empathetic or culturally appropriate tone when interacting with someone in a sensitive context (e.g., offering condolences or giving compliments). This lack of social awareness limits the extent to which AI can enhance emotional pragmatics in language learners.

AI tools are best viewed as complementary to human instruction, rather than replacements for teacher-student or peer-to-peer interaction. Lee & Reinders (2020) argue that human feedback remains indispensable for addressing the nuances of language use that AI cannot yet grasp. Teachers bring pedagogical expertise, personalized feedback, and contextual understanding that AI tools cannot replicate.

While AI tools like Trinka.ai can provide quick and often accurate feedback on grammatical and stylistic aspects, human instructors play a vital role in correcting pragmatic errors, offering contextualized feedback, and providing the social-emotional learning environment necessary for effective language development. Hedge (2022) emphasizes that effective language learning involves active engagement, something AI cannot fully foster, especially when it comes to real-time, emotionally nuanced communication.

Another challenge of using AI in language education is the ethical implications related to data privacy and security. As AI tools collect vast amounts of personal data from learners—such as writing samples, feedback interactions, and even potentially personal details—the risk of data breaches or misuse becomes a significant concern. Johnson et al. (2019) argue that privacy policies surrounding AI tools are often insufficiently clear or transparent, leaving learners vulnerable to privacy violations. In contexts where language learners engage in highly sensitive topics (such as personal experiences or cultural identity), the ethical use of AI tools must be carefully monitored to ensure that learners' data is handled responsibly.

## 3. METHODOLOGY

### 3.1 Research Objectives

The primary objective of this study is to assess the impact of incorporating Artificial Intelligence (AI) tools into the teaching of English, particularly in enhancing pragmatic competence among learners of English as a foreign language. This evaluation focuses on their effect on written proficiency in a university-level English as a Foreign Language (EFL) course. The learners in this course have a target language competence level of B2 according to the Common European Framework of Reference for Languages (CEFR), which corresponds to an upper-intermediate proficiency. Specifically, the study aims to explore how AI can support feedback and assessment processes, with a particular emphasis on improving writing skills and, by extension, the overall teaching-learning outcomes.

To fulfil the objectives, we e have developed a methodology grounded in a practical five-step approach, which draws from the principles and methods of corpus and corpora linguistic studies. These steps are crucial for understanding how this study was conducted and for replicating it, if needed (see 3.6 Procedure). This methodology allows us to put into practice a systematic error analysis and to specifically trim the analysis to focus on pragmatic errors and pragmatic competence.

A key challenge in language instruction, especially in writing, is the often-delayed feedback that learners receive on their written tasks. This lag in feedback can create a disconnect between the students' written competence and their practical language use, hindering their ability to effectively apply language rules in real-world contexts. AI tools are expected to offer a solution to this issue by providing more immediate and individualized feedback. With the potential for faster response times and more specific corrections, AI can assist in bridging the gap between theoretical knowledge and practical application, ultimately leading to better learning outcomes and enhanced writing performance.

The study also aims to evaluate how AI can enhance learners' pragmatic competence, an essential aspect of language use that involves understanding the social and cultural nuances of communication. In this context, pragmatic competence includes the ability to use language appropriately in different social settings, demonstrating skills such as understanding politeness strategies, managing speech acts, and adhering to cultural norms. To assess the impact of AI tools on pragmatic competence, two analysis tables were designed, drawing from the theoretical frameworks of Grice's maxims and pragmatic failure. These frameworks provide valuable insights into how learners make pragmatic errors and fail to convey meaning effectively in their written texts. These two tables allow us to trim the analysis of errors detected during the analysis process carried out (see 3.6 Procedure).

The first analysis table focuses on pragmatic issues in the learners' writing, evaluating how they handle aspects like politeness strategies, speech acts, and conformity to social conventions in communication. The table is designed to systematically categorize errors related to these aspects, highlighting areas where students might struggle with pragmatics. For instance, it looks at whether learners use appropriate politeness markers when making requests, whether they employ suitable indirectness in their speech acts, and whether their writing adheres to the conventions of formal or informal communication depending on the context. These elements are crucial in understanding how effectively learners can communicate in socially appropriate ways, especially when they interact with speakers from different cultural backgrounds.

The second table complements the first by focusing on pragmatic failures, instances in which learners' use of language leads to miscommunication or unintended meanings. This table considers errors in understanding or applying the subtleties of the target language, such as the improper use of tone, failure to follow conversational implicature, or misunderstanding culturally specific references. By examining these failures, the study seeks to identify where AI feedback can be most effective in helping students improve their understanding of pragmatic nuances and apply these concepts more accurately in their written communication.

Through these analysis tables, the study provides a structured approach to understanding pragmatic issues in L2 writing, offering insights into both common challenges and potential solutions. The use of AI in addressing these challenges is particularly significant as it can offer consistent, real-time feedback that may help learners more quickly recognize and correct their pragmatic errors. Ultimately, the goal is to determine whether AI tools can be an effective resource in enhancing learners' ability to use language more appropriately and effectively in different communicative contexts, thus improving their overall pragmatic competence.

In addition to improving pragmatic skills, this study also aims to assess the broader impact of AI on the learning process, particularly how it may influence learner motivation, engagement, and satisfaction, which will be assessed via participants survey (see 3.6 Procedure). As learners receive more timely and personalized feedback through AI, it is hypothesized that their confidence in writing may increase, leading to improved attitudes toward language learning and greater motivation to refine their language skills. These outcomes could contribute not only to their written proficiency but also to their overall success in acquiring a second language. By integrating AI tools into the feedback process, this study seeks to explore the potential for technology to facilitate more personalized, effective, and engaging learning experiences in the realm of language acquisition.

*Table 1. Pre-analysis table: specimen*

| Item Considered | Descriptors (Analytical Criteria) | Errors When Descriptors Are Not Considered | Error Labels |
|---|---|---|---|
| **Coherence** | Logical flow of ideas, connection between sentences and paragraphs, clear progression of thought. | Disjointed sentences, abrupt transitions, unclear sequence of ideas. | Lack of coherence, abrupt shifts. |
| **Relevance** | Appropriateness and pertinence of the information presented. | Off-topic information, irrelevant details, failure to address the main point. | Lack of relevance, deviation. |
| **Discourse Management** | Effective organization of information, including topic introduction, elaboration, and conclusion. | Disorganized text structure, missing clear introduction or conclusion. | Disorganized discourse. |
| **Cohesion** | Proper use of cohesive devices (e.g., connectors, reference words). | Lack of or incorrect use of linking words, repetition without cohesion. | Cohesion failure, repetition. |
| **Sociocultural Appropriateness** | Adherence to cultural norms in communication, tone, and register. | Inappropriate tone or register, failure to recognize cultural nuances. | Inappropriate register. |

continued on following page

*Table 1. Continued*

| Item Considered | Descriptors (Analytical Criteria) | Errors When Descriptors Are Not Considered | Error Labels |
|---|---|---|---|
| **Pragmalinguistic Accuracy** | Correct choice of expression based on the context and communicative intention. | Inaccurate expressions, inappropriate vocabulary for context. | Pragmatic misapplication, inaccuracy. |
| **Speech Act Performance** | Appropriateness of speech acts such as requests, apologies, or complaints. | Misused speech acts, misunderstanding the intent of the utterance. | Speech act failure, misapplied request. |
| **Irony/Parody** | Correct understanding and use of irony or parody in context. | Misinterpretation of irony or parody, inability to recognize implied meaning. | Irony/parody misunderstanding. |

Subsequently, the second table, designed for instructors, serves a dual purpose: it helps identify specific areas of pragmatic failure and provides targeted guidance for corrective feedback. This structured framework enables instructors to systematically evaluate students' work by highlighting areas where pragmatic errors, such as inappropriate politeness strategies, cultural misinterpretations, or improper register, have occurred. By offering clear, actionable suggestions, the table allows instructors to guide students toward more contextually appropriate language use. This tool also empowers instructors to track recurring issues across students' work, helping to pinpoint common areas of struggle and adjust teaching strategies accordingly.

Beyond its use as a diagnostic tool for instructors, the second table also encourages students to engage in a reflective process regarding their writing. By analyzing the feedback in the context of their own language choices, students are prompted to reconsider their pragmatic decisions and the potential impact those decisions may have on effective communication. This reflection is crucial for raising awareness of how seemingly small linguistic choices, such as tone, formality, and indirectness, can influence the clarity and appropriateness of their writing in different social and cultural settings.

The integration of this reflective process into the study's methodology aims to foster deeper awareness among students of the subtleties involved in pragmatic language use, especially in second language contexts. This heightened awareness is not only beneficial for improving students' writing skills but also contributes to their broader communicative competence. By consistently reflecting on their language use and the social implications of their choices, students are more likely to internalize pragmatic norms, ultimately becoming more effective and confident communicators in their second language. In this way, the study aspires to bridge the gap between linguistic accuracy and pragmatic appropriateness, encouraging learners to adopt a more nuanced approach to language use in real-world interactions.

*Table 2. Analysis and error labelling table: specimen*

| Pragmatic Element | Descriptor. | Error | Labelling |
|---|---|---|---|
| Pragmatic effectiveness in the learner's written production. | Quality of the message and production. | | Effectivity_Error |
| | | | Focus_Error |
| | | | Vocab_Error |
| | Quantity of information provided in the production. | | Accuracy_Error |
| | | | Paraphrasis_Error |
| | Relevance of the production. | | Relevance_Error |
| | Other elements: order, conciseness, coherence, and ambiguity. | | Adequacy_Error |
| | | | Cohesion_Error |
| | | | Coherence_Error |

Thus, this methodology combines AI-powered tools with pragmatic theory to investigate the effects of immediate, AI-assisted feedback on improving written proficiency and pragmatic competence in EFL learners. Through a comprehensive analysis of student writings, the study seeks to determine whether AI tools can enhance the learning process, offering more efficient, targeted feedback and promoting better pragmatic decision-making in written language.

## 3.2 Hypothesis

The departure point of this study is the fact that AI-based tools offer almost immediate and interactive feedback, with some tools enabling and enhancing automating feedback logs. Thus, we intend to demonstrate that it will be possible to conclude that the combination of Error Analysis with new intelligent technologies can produce new possibilities to substantially improve pragmatic competence in the written text production of language learners, particularly those learning English as a foreign and second language. This will be achieved by exploring if there is a strong connection between these new tools and their feedback possibilities and the improvements in learners' written proficiency when assessed with AI-based tools.

## 3.3 Research Questions

With the intention of addressing the problems described and meeting the mentioned objectives, this study attempts to answer the following questions:

- What are the most effective strategies and methods for employing AI to develop pragmatic competence in second language learners?

- How effective is the use of AI in enhancing the understanding and application of pragmatic norms (e.g., politeness, speech acts, register) in language learners?
- Is it feasible to use AI tools to improve learners' ability to make pragmatic adjustments in written communication?
- Do learners perceive AI tools as a useful alternative for receiving feedback on pragmatic errors, such as inappropriate requests, politeness strategies, or cultural nuances?

## 3.4 Population

The population of this research study consists of 70 B.1.3 level (performance and competence) English learners from a single group-class at a public university in Madrid, Spain. The investigation abides by the ethical rules imposed by the university committee.

## 3.5 Sample and Data Collection

To conduct the study, students were asked to complete a written task similar in length and topic to those typically assigned in the classroom. Specifically, they were instructed to write an opinion essay of around 250 words on a topic of their choice. These essays were then collected and anonymized by the instructor. The data for this study was gathered using a spontaneous sampling method. This approach involves collecting data from learners when they focus more on expressing content than on adhering to grammatical conventions. Sources for data collection using this method include academic assignments, tests, essays, and other related tasks. Topics for these assignments might cover areas such as "personal experiences, future ambitions, social, political, or religious issues," among others (Keshavarz, 2022, p. 80). In total, 70 academic assignments were collected from students, representing full participation from the sample population.

## 3.6 Procedure

To meet the objectives mentioned, we have designed a methodology based on a practical five-step method, which in turn is based upon the methodology and methods of corpus and corpora linguistic studies. The following steps are essential to understand how this study has been carried out and, if desired, to replicate it:

Step 1: Creation of the Study Corpus (Corpus 1). For this study, a total of 70 writing samples will be collected from university students enrolled in an English as a Foreign Language (EFL) course, with a target proficiency level of B2 CEFR (upper intermediate). The group consists of students with varying degrees of EFL proficiency; however, approximately 65 out of 70 samples meet the descriptors and criteria of the target level. These samples will form the basis for the analysis, which will include both grammatical and pragmatic errors.

Step 2: Division of Corpus 1 into Units of Study. Once the writing samples are collected, the corpus will be anonymized by assigning labels to each text to avoid any interference in the analysis (Kaiser et al., 2021; Zaki & Nosofsky, 2007). The anonymized corpus will then be randomly divided into two equal groups, with 35 writing samples in each group. These two groups will serve as the primary units of study. Pragmatic errors, such as inappropriate speech acts, misunderstandings of politeness strategies, and failure to adjust language based on social context, will be considered alongside grammatical issues during the division and analysis.

Step 3: Analysis of the Study Units. For the analysis of each study unit, two distinct approaches will be applied:

- Group 1 (AI-Assisted Analysis): This group of writing samples will be analysed using Artificial Intelligence tools capable of processing both grammatical and pragmatic elements of the texts. The AI tool (e.g., Trinka.ai) will detect not only grammatical mistakes but also pragmatic errors such as inappropriate speech acts, incorrect use of politeness strategies, and issues with formality or register. For example, the AI may flag direct commands in contexts where a more polite or indirect request is required. Additionally, the AI will evaluate how well learners adapt their writing to match social norms, providing feedback on pragmatic appropriateness.
- Group 2 (Traditional Teacher-Based Analysis): This group will undergo traditional correction methods, where the teacher manually annotates the texts for both grammatical and pragmatic errors. The teacher will focus on identifying issues such as directness or rudeness in requests, misuse of politeness markers, and failure to adapt language to social context, alongside more conventional grammatical errors. This teacher-based feedback will serve as a comparative baseline for AI-assisted analysis.

Step 4: Creation of the Confirmation Corpus (Corpus 2). The confirmation corpus will consist of another set of 70 writing samples produced by the same group of students. This corpus will serve to validate the findings of the AI tools used in Corpus 1. By comparing the results from Corpus 2 with those from Corpus 1, the goal is to assess whether the AI tools lead to more consistent and accurate identification of both grammatical and pragmatic errors. This analysis will also focus on whether the AI-assisted corrections result in a reduction of recurring pragmatic errors, such as inappropriate requests, misused politeness strategies, or failure to adhere to cultural communication norms (Gass & Selinker, 2008; Rutherford, 2022). By closely examining the repetition and nature of these errors, the confirmation corpus will help assess the effectiveness of AI in improving both grammatical proficiency and pragmatic competence.

Step 5: Exploratory Contrastive Analysis of Corpus 1 and Corpus 2. Once Corpus 2 has been fully analysed, it will be compared with the findings from Corpus 1. This contrastive analysis will aim to determine whether AI tools, as used in Group 1, contribute to a reduction in specific pragmatic errors compared to traditional teacher-based feedback in Group 2. For example, if AI tools help learners reduce the use of overly direct requests or improve their understanding of social context in language use, these improvements will be noted. The focus will be on whether AI feedback is more effective in addressing recurring pragmatic errors, such as failing to modulate politeness or register according to the communicative context. The results will be assessed to explore whether AI feedback can enhance pragmatic competence, particularly in making learners aware of culturally appropriate speech acts, politeness strategies, and indirect communication, as suggested by Kessler (2021).

As can be inferred by the explanation of the methodology, the study will provide a comprehensive evaluation of the effectiveness of AI in addressing both grammatical and pragmatic errors in written language. The contrastive analysis of AI-assisted and traditional teacher-based feedback will help determine the value of AI tools in improving pragmatic competence and written proficiency, offering insights into their potential for language teaching and learning.

## 3.7 Tools Employed in the Study

Two AI tools were employed in this study:

- Trinka.ai: A grammar and style checker tailored for academic English, Trinka.ai offers real-time feedback on grammatical accuracy, clarity, tone, formality, and—increasingly—pragmatic appropriateness. While not originally designed for pragmatic analysis, Trinka's ability to identify inappropriate register, verbosity, tone mismatches, and indirectness supports pragmatic assessment. It flags issues such as overly direct speech acts, awkward politeness strategies, or mismatched tone, providing suggestions that can help learners reflect on their linguistic choices in social contexts.

- EXMARaLDA: Typically used in corpus-based discourse analysis, EXMARaLDA (Extensible Markup Language for Discourse Annotation) was integrated into the study for manual annotation and qualitative analysis of written data. It facilitated the structured tagging of pragmatic features—such as hedging, implicature violations, and sociocultural inappropriateness—across student texts. EXMARaLDA also enabled the contrastive analysis of language patterns before and after AI intervention, providing insight into student progression and error patterns.

The combination of these tools allowed for both automated and semi-automated error analysis, combining AI-driven feedback with manual corpus annotation techniques to deepen the understanding of pragmatic development in learner writing.

## 4. RESULTS

### 4.1 General Errors and General Analysis

The findings elucidated in this preliminary investigation emanate from the meticulous analysis conducted on Corpus 1 and Corpus 2, as delineated in the methodological framework outlined earlier in this study. By subjecting these corpora to contrastive analysis, this research endeavors to unravel the potential synergies inherent in the integration of Artificial Intelligence (AI) with Error Analysis within the domain of Artificial Intelligence Education Studies (AIEd).

Employing the methodological lens of corpus studies, this inquiry serves as a beacon illuminating the efficacy of leveraging AI in tandem with Error Analysis as a potent pedagogical tool. Through the systematic examination of linguistic data encapsulated within the corpora, insights emerge regarding the transformative potential of AIEd methodologies in enhancing the teaching-learning continuum, particularly within the context of English language education for non-native speakers.

Moreover, the study's findings provide valuable insights into the effectiveness of AI-based tools in language education, particularly in assessment and feedback provision. By exploring the intricate dynamics of AI-assisted assessment and feedback mechanisms, this research enhances our understanding of pedagogy and introduces innovative approaches to language instruction and evaluation. This initial investigation lays the groundwork for future exploration and improvement of AIEd methodologies in language education. By highlighting the possibilities and obstacles of combining AI with Error Analysis, the study contributes to the ongoing discussion on the development of teaching practices in a technology-driven educational environment.

On one hand, the integration of Artificial Intelligence (AI) into the process of error correcting in English as a Foreign Language (EFL) learners' writing has emerged as a formidable asset. Delving into the minutiae of the results gleaned from both units of study, a discernible trend emerges, illuminating the efficacy of AI-based correction systems. Notably, the incidence of repeated errors—those persisting across both units of study—stands conspicuously lower in the AI-driven correction paradigm. Specifically, a mere 25% of students who received feedback from AI-based systems replicated errors in their subsequent written submissions, a stark contrast to the 40% recurrence observed among recipients of teacher-based feedback.

This notable disparity underscores the potential of AI-driven correction mechanisms to mitigate the perpetuation of errors among EFL learners. By virtue of their algorithmic precision and capacity for systematic analysis, AI-based systems exhibit a remarkable adeptness in identifying and addressing linguistic inaccuracies. Consequently, learners benefiting from AI-mediated feedback are afforded a greater opportunity for error rectification and subsequent improvement in writing proficiency.

Moreover, beyond the quantitative delineation of error recurrence rates, qualitative insights gleaned from the comparative analysis further underscore the merits of AI-driven correction systems. In addition to their efficacy in error identification, AI-based tools often furnish learners with tailored suggestions for improvement, thereby fostering a more nuanced and comprehensive understanding of linguistic nuances.

The comparative analysis highlights how AI can enhance corrective feedback in EFL instruction. By integrating AI into language teaching, educators can improve students' linguistic proficiency, offering more personalized learning experiences. Graph 1 illustrates the connection between participation, error repetition, and error success.

*Figure 1. Distribution of error repetition by analysis modality*

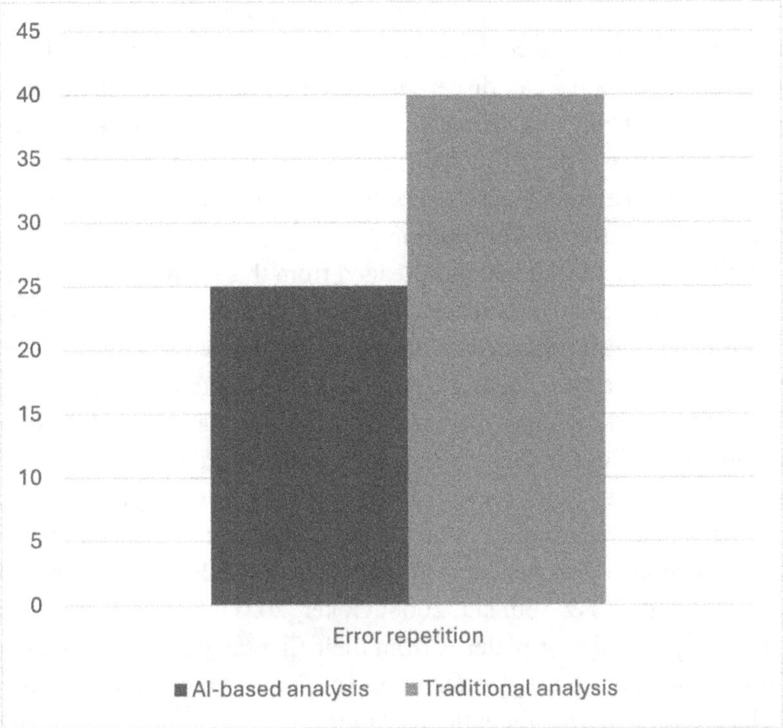


Secondly, it is imperative to underscore the pivotal contribution of this study towards elucidating the nature and distribution of the most prevalent errors manifested within the cohort under investigation. By meticulously dissecting and categorizing the myriad errors encountered, this research endeavors to shed light on the multifaceted nuances inherent in the teaching-learning continuum.

The discernible heterogeneity observed in the various natures of the errors committed by students serves as a microcosm reflecting the diverse trajectories and challenges characterizing the pedagogical journey. Indeed, the varied typologies of errors identified among learners underscore the multifaceted nature of language acquisition, wherein deviations from prescribed norms often signify areas of cognitive and linguistic development. This nuanced understanding of error typologies holds profound curricular implications, warranting proactive interventions aimed at addressing and mitigating prevalent errors. Armed with insights into the nature and distribution of learners' errors, educators are better equipped to navigate the pedagogical landscape, effectively tailoring instructional strategies to meet the diverse needs of their students.

Moreover, the findings of this study resonate with contemporary pedagogical discourse, wherein a data-driven approach to curriculum development and evaluation assumes paramount importance. By leveraging insights garnered from the analysis of error patterns, educators can discern underlying trends and tendencies, thereby informing the refinement and optimization of curricular frameworks. As noted by Murad (2018) and Rao (2018), this proactive approach facilitates the identification of areas requiring remediation and ensures the efficacy of instructional interventions aimed at error elimination and prevention.

Substantially, the nuanced insights gleaned from this study not only deepen our understanding of the complex interplay between errors and the teaching-learning process but also furnish educators with invaluable tools and strategies to foster linguistic proficiency among learners. By embracing a data-driven approach to error analysis, educators can chart a course towards pedagogical excellence, thereby ensuring the holistic development and success of their students.

Contemporary linguistic theory suggests that one of the primary causes of frequent errors in language learning could be attributed to negative language transfer (NT), where learners' mother tongues interfere with their English as a Foreign Language (EFL) production (Gass & Selinker, 2008; Goker, 2021). Negative transfer occurs when learners apply rules or patterns from their first language (L1) to their target language (L2), leading to errors in syntax, vocabulary, pronunciation, and pragmatics. These errors, often unintentional, can result in the fossilization of incorrect language use if not properly addressed. NT is especially prevalent among learners with limited exposure to the target language or those learning in environments where the L2 is not used in everyday communication.

For this study, it is important to consider both views on errors: as indicators of the teaching-learning process's outcomes and as reflections of the internal cognitive process that learners undergo when acquiring a language. From an instructional perspective, errors can signal areas where learners struggle, providing insight into the effectiveness of teaching strategies and areas needing more focus. On the other hand, from a learner's perspective, errors can reveal the underlying cognitive mechanisms involved in language acquisition, including how learners mentally process and internalize linguistic structures from their L1 to their L2. Recognizing these two aspects is crucial when designing curricula and syllabi that address both the external challenges of language learning and the internal cognitive processes that contribute to language production.

In this context, the results of this study reveal that negative transfer is a prevalent challenge across all participants. The distribution of such errors is consistent in both groups studied: 71.55% of errors in the A.I.-assisted mode, 79.25% in the A.I.-based system, and 77% in the teacher-based system were attributed to negative transfer. These findings suggest that, despite the mode of instruction, negative transfer remains a significant source of error in the learners' English production. This is consistent with research that highlights NT as a major contributor to error fossilization among both EFL and ESL learners (Arabski, 2006; Gass & Selinker, 1993; Yunus, 2021).

One notable aspect of negative transfer is that it can vary in its impact depending on the learner's proficiency level, the specific features of the languages involved, and the types of errors made. For instance, errors related to word choice, sentence structure, or the use of tenses can stem from direct transfer from the mother tongue, especially when there are significant differences between the two languages. In some cases, learners may use their L1 structures because they are more familiar or easier to apply, even when these structures are not grammatically or pragmatically appropriate in the target language.

Interestingly, the data collected in this study suggests that the type of feedback—whether A.I.-assisted or teacher-based—does not significantly alter the frequency of NT errors. This finding indicates that while A.I. tools can provide valuable grammar and vocabulary corrections, they may not be sufficiently equipped to address the more complex issues related to pragmatic competence or nuanced linguistic transfers. This reinforces the argument that technology alone, despite its advancements, cannot entirely replace human intervention, especially when it comes to more complex areas of language learning, such as the nuances of pragmatics and cultural context.

These results also call attention to the need for more effective pedagogical strategies that specifically target negative transfer and error fossilization. Such strategies may involve raising learners' awareness of common transfer issues, providing targeted corrective feedback, and fostering an understanding of the differences between their L1 and L2, both linguistically and pragmatically. By incorporating these strategies into the curriculum, educators can help learners recognize and overcome their reliance on L1 structures, ultimately reducing the occurrence of NT errors and supporting more accurate language production in English.

Thus, the impact of negative transfer in language learning is undeniable, and it remains a critical challenge for both learners and instructors. While A.I.-based tools provide useful support for addressing surface-level errors, they must be complemented by teacher-based feedback and strategies designed to enhance learners' pragmatic competence and prevent error fossilization. Understanding the role of negative transfer in the language acquisition process is key to developing more effective teaching methods and learning environments that address both the cognitive and communicative aspects of language learning. The impact of negative transfer can be further explored in the graph below, illustrating the distribution of errors across different feedback modes and highlighting the persistent role of NT in the language learning process.

*Figure 2. Negative transfer error distribution by analysis modality*

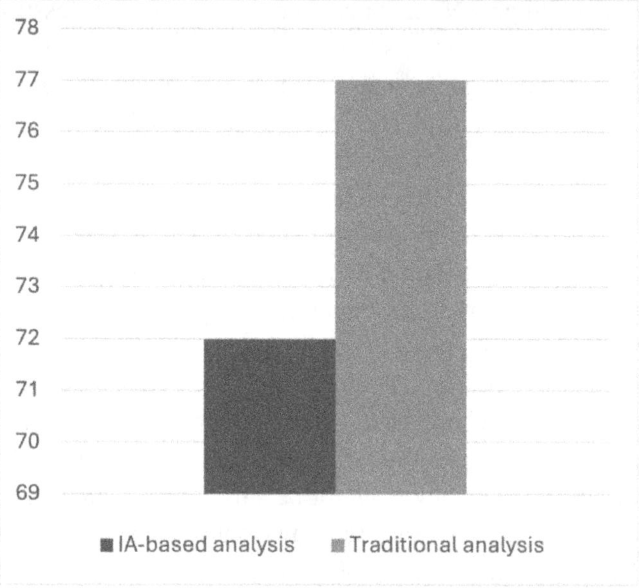


## 4.2 Pragmatic Errors and Pragmatic Analysis

The findings of the pragmatic analysis or trimmed analysis are depicted in Graphs 3 and 4. A total of 900 errors were identified under the category of Pragmatic Effectiveness, which includes issues related to Grice's conversational maxims, Sperber and Wilson's Relevance Theory, and key aspects of the Common European Framework of Reference for Languages (Fernández, 2019; López & Hernández, 2016; Rodríguez, 2021).

A major outcome of the study was the significant improvement in students' ability to identify speech acts within source texts; learners showed marked progress in recognizing and utilizing the different components of speech acts, including locutionary, illocutionary, and perlocutionary acts. This improvement was particularly evident in the students' ability to distinguish between direct and indirect requests, which are often challenging in translation due to their complex social and cultural implications (Macías Borrego, 2025). In real-life communication, students often use speech acts—such as requests, apologies, compliments, or refusals—within rich social and cultural contexts that require them to navigate tone, formality, power dynamics, and implicit meaning. These interactions are fluid and dynamic, influenced by the immediate reactions of interlocutors, non-verbal cues, and shared cultural knowledge. As a result, learners may rely on intuition, social observation, or mimicry, which can lead to pragmatic errors, especially when operating in a second language or unfamiliar cultural context. In contrast, AI feedback environments offer a structured and controlled setting in which students can experiment with speech acts without the pressure of real-time social judgment. AI tools can provide immediate, consistent, and often explicit feedback, drawing attention to pragmatic missteps and suggesting context-appropriate alternatives. However, this interaction is typically decontextualized and lacks the full complexity of real human conversation, potentially limiting students' ability to generalize pragmatic skills to spontaneous, real-world scenarios. Thus, while AI feedback can support the development of pragmatic competence by highlighting rules and conventions, it must be complemented by authentic communicative practice to ensure learners can effectively apply speech acts in diverse, unpredictable social interactions.

In this light, another jey finding highlights the impact of these technologies on pragmatic refinement: AI tools effectively adjusted inappropriate phrases and provided explanations that helped enhance students' cultural sensitivity (Sykes, 2019; Nassaji, 2016). This technological intervention is particularly relevant to one of the key areas of pragmatic competence examined in this study—the use of politeness strategies in students' written texts. Additionally, the frequency of *adjusted requests*—that is, instances where students revised their writing to make it more culturally appropriate—was compared between the two feedback groups. The following table presents concrete examples illustrating how artificial intelligence can shed light on this aspect:

*Table 3. Artificial intelligence: error treatment*

| Error Type | Example of Error | Adjusted Example with AI Feedback | Explanation of Adjustment |
|---|---|---|---|
| **Request (Direct)** | I need the document by tomorrow. | Could you please provide the document by tomorrow? | AI adds politeness through modal verbs ("Could you please") and softens the directness. |
| **Request (Imperative)** | Send me the report now. | Would you mind sending me the report now? | AI uses a polite modal verb ("Would you mind") to soften the tone. |
| **Formal Request (Informal)** | Hey, I want to ask about the meeting time. | Dear [Recipient], I would like to inquire about the meeting time. | AI adjusts the tone from informal to formal and professional. |
| **Apology (Simple)** | Sorry for the mistake. | I sincerely apologize for the mistake and appreciate your understanding. | AI emphasizes sincerity and gratitude, making the apology more formal and respectful. |

continued on following page

*Table 3. Continued*

| Error Type | Example of Error | Adjusted Example with AI Feedback | Explanation of Adjustment |
|---|---|---|---|
| **Suggestion (Direct)** | You should rewrite this section because it's unclear. | It might be helpful to revise this section for clarity. | AI softens the suggestion with "might be helpful" and removes the direct "should." |
| **Compliment (Potentially Offensive)** | You are really good for a non-native speaker! | Your language skills are impressive! | AI removes the comparison to "non-native," focusing on the positive aspect of the skills. |
| **Politeness Strategy (Indirect Request)** | Give me a call when you are free. | Would you mind giving me a call when you are free? | AI uses a polite modal verb ("Would you mind") to make the request more indirect and respectful. |
| **Politeness Strategy (Directness)** | I need this done by 5 PM. | Could you please have this done by 5 PM? | AI rephrases the request with more polite phrasing ("Could you please") and softens the direct tone. |
| **Offer (Direct)** | I can help you with your project. | Would you like me to help you with your project? | AI introduces a question ("Would you like me") to make the offer more courteous. |
| **Complaint (Direct)** | This report is wrong! | I believe there might be some errors in this report. | AI softens the complaint, using less direct phrasing ("I believe") to make the tone more neutral. |
| **Directive (Commanding)** | You must submit the assignment by Friday. | Please ensure the assignment is submitted by Friday. | AI replaces the imperative with a more polite request ("Please ensure"). |
| **Expressing Disagreement (Blunt)** | I don't agree with your opinion. | I see your point, but I respectfully disagree. | AI softens the disagreement, making it more diplomatic ("I respectfully disagree"). |
| **Apology (Inadequate)** | Sorry for being late. | I sincerely apologize for my tardiness and any inconvenience caused. | AI adds more formality and expresses empathy for the inconvenience caused. |
| **Request (Rude)** | Give me the details now. | Could you kindly provide the details at your earliest convenience? | AI introduces politeness with "Could you kindly" and adds "at your earliest convenience." |
| **Compliment (Overly Personal)** | You look good for your age. | You look wonderful, and your experience really shows! | AI removes the age reference, making the compliment more universally positive. |
| **Question (Inappropriate)** | What's wrong with you? | Is everything okay? | AI rephrases to avoid an accusatory tone, offering concern without judgment. |

Graph 3 displays the distribution of pragmatic errors across the texts, categorized by the specific error types outlined in the methodology section. Significant variations are observed in the frequency of errors across categories, with a notably high occurrence of errors concerning the principles of information quantity and quality (see Graph 3).

*Figure 3. Pragmatic error analysis errors: results obtained from sample analysed samples*

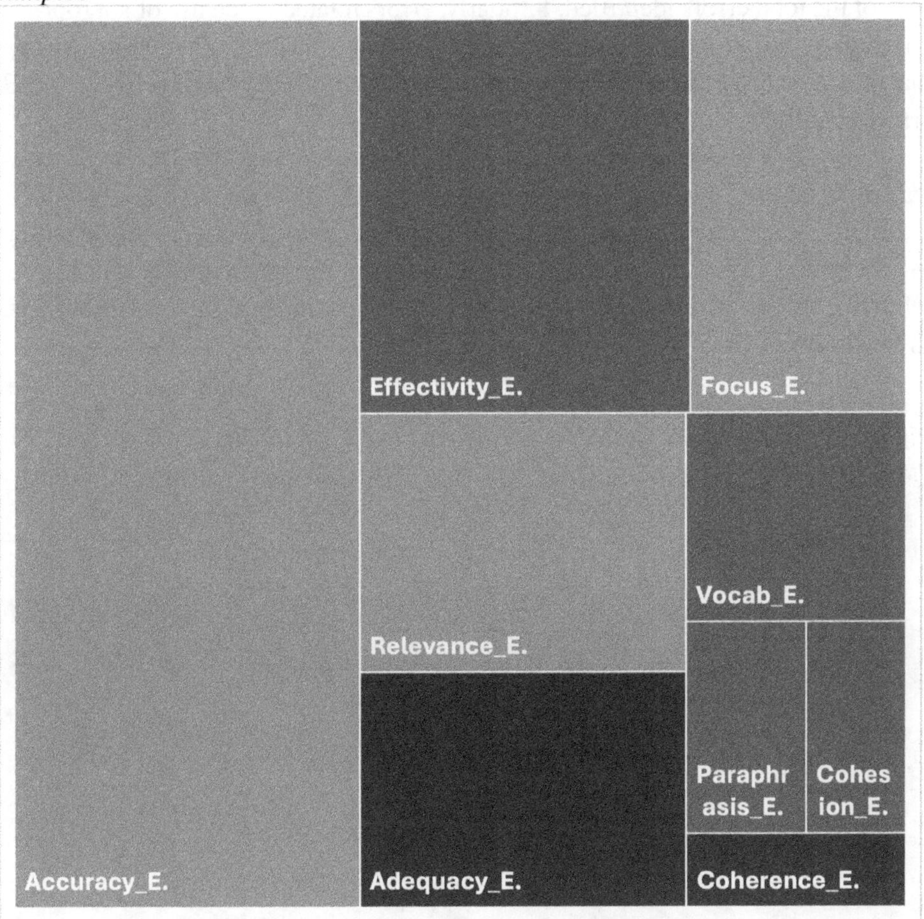


Upon reviewing the results of the analysed elements, the most frequent errors made by the intervention group learners, who are at a B2 level in their written productions, are those related to the Maxim of Quantity. These errors reflect the students' difficulty in expressing or explaining their ideas independently, without over-reliance on external aids. Specifically, these issues are related to the correct use of certain words and the effective application of circumlocution or paraphrasing to convey their thoughts. A total of 363 errors were identified in these two categories (accuracy_error and paraphrasis_error), accounting for 42% of all errors identified.

The second most common category of pragmatic errors pertains to the Maxim of Quality. According to the analysis framework used in this study, this category includes two types of errors: those affecting the clarity of the message and those impacting the quality of the information presented. Errors related to the students' ability to communicate their message clearly accounted for 144 errors, representing 16% of the total errors identified. Similarly, errors related to the use of appropriate vocabulary (vocabulary_error and adequacy_error), which are critical for ensuring that the message is contextually accurate, also made up 16% of the errors, with 143 errors identified.

Finally, it is important to note that errors associated with the Maxim of Relevance, particularly those concerning the students' ability to maintain focus in their message (focus_error), account for 21% of the total errors analysed, corresponding to 189 errors. This category ranks second in terms of both frequency and nature, reflecting challenges in maintaining relevance and focus on the written contributions, as illustrated in Graph 4.

*Figure 4. Error amount: numerical distribution of errors in analysed written productions*

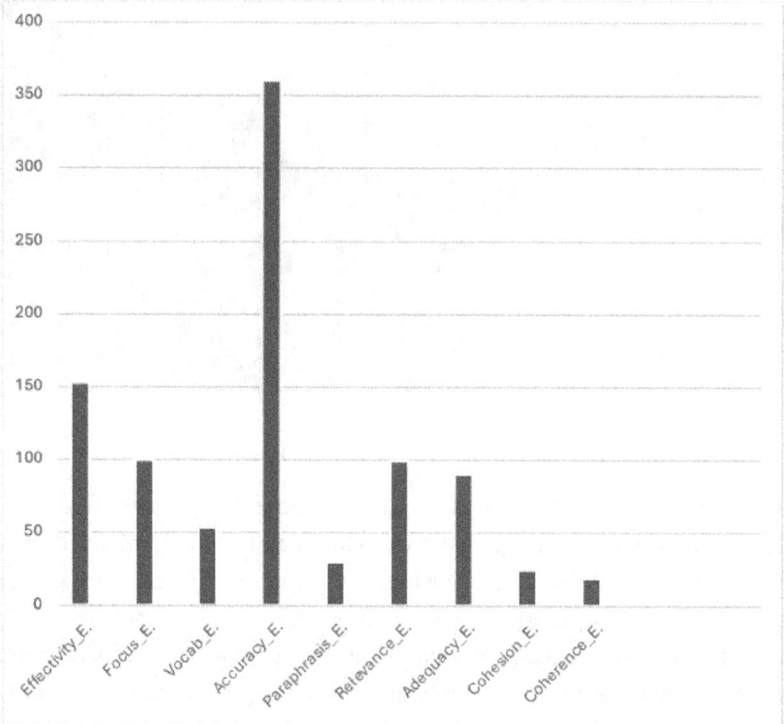

## 4.3 Participants Satisfaction Survey

An additional noteworthy revelation stemming from this research pertains to the considerable level of participant satisfaction and the perceived effectiveness discerned from the study's implementation. To gauge participant sentiments accurately, all individuals involved in the study were solicited for feedback through an anonymous survey. This survey encompassed three pivotal inquiries, namely: (i) the degree of satisfaction with the assessment process and its resultant outcomes; (ii) the perceived efficacy of the assessment methodology employed—whether AI-assisted or teacher-assisted; and (iii) their preference regarding the assessment group to which they were assigned, i.e., whether they would have favoured being in the alternative group.

It is noteworthy that out of the total student cohort comprising 70 individuals, 68 participants responded to the survey, yielding an impressive response rate of 97%. This robust level of engagement underscores the significance and relevance of the study's findings within the context of the examined class-group.

The feedback gleaned from participants' responses not only provides valuable insights into their individual experiences but also offers a holistic view of the overall effectiveness of the assessment methodology. Such comprehensive feedback serves as a testament to the meticulous design and execution of the study, reaffirming its relevance and utility within language education research. Moreover, the overwhelmingly positive response from participants underscores the potential of AI-assisted assessment methodologies to engender a sense of satisfaction and efficacy among learners, thus corroborating the merits of integrating AI tools into pedagogical practices.

Many participants expressed appreciation for the real-time feedback provided by the AI-assisted assessment approach, noting that it allowed them to identify and correct errors more swiftly than traditional teacher-assisted feedback methods. Several respondents highlighted how the AI tools enhanced their engagement with the content, making the learning process more interactive and tailored to their individual needs. Furthermore, many indicated a preference for the AI-assisted group, citing the benefits of immediate, personalized feedback, which they felt helped them better understand their weaknesses and adjust in real-time.

On the other hand, a few participants expressed a slight preference for the teacher-assisted group, indicating that while AI feedback was valuable, they still valued the nuanced understanding and guidance that an instructor could offer, particularly for complex or culturally sensitive issues. These responses reflect a broader trend in the literature regarding the complementary role of AI and human interaction in language learning. While AI offers significant advantages in terms of efficiency and scalability, it is recognized that human expertise remains crucial, especially in addressing more intricate aspects of language use.

The overwhelmingly positive response from participants underscores the significant potential of AI-assisted assessment methodologies in fostering a sense of satisfaction and efficacy among learners. This positive reception not only validates the relevance and applicability of the study's approach but also highlights the growing role of AI in reshaping traditional educational practices. By offering an innovative and dynamic method of assessment, AI tools are demonstrating their capacity to engage students more effectively and enhance the learning process.

The study's findings further suggest that AI-powered tools can have a profound impact on students' learning experiences by providing timely, personalized, and targeted feedback. This real-time feedback helps learners address both linguistic issues, such as grammar and syntax, and pragmatic challenges, including tone, register, and cultural appropriateness. By offering feedback in these areas, AI tools allow students to make immediate corrections, thereby fostering a deeper understanding of both language mechanics and the subtleties of pragmatic communication in real-world contexts.

Additionally, AI's ability to evaluate and analyze large volumes of data with precision means that it can identify recurring errors or gaps in understanding, enabling more focused and tailored interventions. This not only accelerates the learning process but also ensures that feedback is aligned with the individual needs of each learner, enhancing both the relevance and impact of the educational experience.

Moreover, the AI-assisted assessment framework contributes to the development of independent learning skills by encouraging students to engage with their own errors and feedback in a reflective manner. This self-directed learning approach is crucial for the development of long-term language skills, as students become more adept at identifying and addressing their own linguistic and pragmatic shortcomings.

In sum, the study highlights the promising role of AI in transforming the landscape of language education, with an emphasis on its ability to improve learning outcomes, increase student engagement, and foster a more personalized and responsive approach to language teaching. By integrating AI tools into pedagogical practices, educators can enhance both the quality and efficiency of language instruction, providing students with a more comprehensive and effective learning experience. The following graph illustrates these results, further supporting the notion that AI-assisted methodologies are a valuable addition to modern language education. The following graph illustrates these results:

*Figure 5. Participants survey satisfaction and perceived effectiveness*

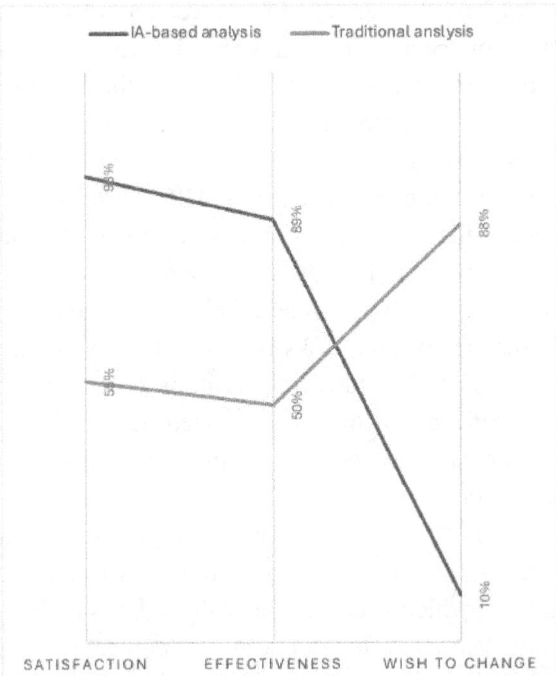


## 5. DISCUSSION

The results of this study on the use of AI tools to improve pragmatic competence in language learners, particularly in addressing the Maxims of Quantity, Quality, and Relevance, align with and contribute to the growing body of literature in the field of AI-assisted language education. While this study offers novel insights into the specific types of pragmatic errors learners at the B2 level face, comparing these findings with those of other studies highlights both commonalities and divergences in terms of error types, AI's effectiveness, and the role of pragmatic theory in guiding research.

In this study, the Maxim of Quantity errors accounted for 42% of all identified errors, reflecting learners' difficulties in appropriately elaborating on their ideas without over-relying on external aids like paraphrasing or circumlocution. This finding resonates with the work of Lee & Park (2020), who found that learners at various proficiency levels often struggle with providing adequate amounts of information, either by over-explaining or under-explaining ideas, thus violating the Maxim of Quantity. In their study, AI tools were employed to assist learners in balancing detail and conciseness in writing. Similar to our findings, their results indicated that AI tools significantly improved learners' ability to manage the quantity of their contributions by suggesting more succinct and precise expressions, as well as offering paraphrasing suggestions.

However, unlike the findings in Lee & Park (2020), who observed a more balanced spread of errors across different maxims, this study found the Maxim of Quantity errors to be the most prevalent. This discrepancy may be due to the specific level of learners in the current study (B2), where the ability to generate original content and independently manage writing tasks is still under development. Additionally, the focus on written tasks in this study (e.g., opinion essays) may have made errors in expressing ideas independently more pronounced, as these tasks typically require students to elaborate on complex concepts, further highlighting their struggles with information management.

Errors related to the Maxim of Quality also align with previous studies. The present study found 16% of errors to be related to message clarity and the use of appropriate vocabulary, which is consistent with findings by Vesselinov & Grego (2021). In their study, learners often failed to communicate their messages clearly due to a lack of vocabulary or misused words, resulting in ambiguity and reduced communicative effectiveness. Similar to our study, their research found that AI-based writing tools, which offer suggestions for vocabulary improvement and clarity, helped learners reduce these types of errors. AI tools, such as Trinka.ai, provided real-time feedback on the correctness of word choices, and learners were able to correct misused terms more quickly.

However, a noteworthy difference is that the current study found fewer errors related to the Maxim of Quality compared to Maxim of Quantity errors, suggesting that learners may have more awareness of the need for accurate information than they do for the appropriate amount of information. This is in line with research by Gass & Selinker (2008), who found that pragmatic issues related to information accuracy and message clarity tend to be less challenging for learners at the B2 level. As learners progress, their attention shifts towards more complex aspects of communication, such as maintaining coherence and relevance, which could explain the relative distribution of errors in this study.

The Maxim of Relevance errors, which accounted for 21% of the total errors in this study, reflect learners' difficulty maintaining focus and relevance in their written production. This result is consistent with Cenoz & Gorter (2019), who found that learners often struggle with ensuring that their writing is both contextually appropriate and relevant. Their study highlighted that errors in relevance often stem from learners' insufficient attention to the audience's expectations, leading to digressions and irrelevant content. Similar to our study, they reported that AI tools, when used to guide learners through content structuring and organization, were effective in helping students stay focused and maintain relevance in their communication.

Interestingly, while the findings of Cenoz & Gorter (2019) support the role of AI in enhancing relevance by suggesting more organized structures, this study suggests that the issue of relevance is still pervasive at the B2 level, indicating that maintaining focus in writing remains a challenge even for relatively proficient learners. One possible explanation is that, while learners may understand the importance of relevance in abstract terms, their ability to apply it consistently across their written work is still developing. This underscores the need for targeted interventions, such as AI-powered suggestions for content organization, which have proven effective in similar studies.

This study's focus on the application of AI tools to enhance pragmatic competence aligns with findings in studies by Zhang et al. (2021) and Kessler (2021), which show the promise of AI in addressing pragmatic issues, such as politeness strategies, indirectness, and register. Zhang et al. (2021) found that AI tools could effectively identify pragmatic failures in learners' use of politeness markers, helping them produce more socially appropriate language. Similarly, Kessler (2021) reported that AI tools could assist learners in recognizing cultural nuances and adjusting their communication style accordingly. In our study, AI tools provided immediate feedback on pragmatic errors, such as inappropriate speech acts and misused politeness strategies, offering learners opportunities for real-time correction and improvement.

However, while the benefits of AI in offering immediate feedback are well-documented, Yuan & Lu (2020) caution that AI feedback lacks the depth and contextual understanding that a human instructor can provide. For example, AI tools might not be able to fully grasp the social dynamics of a given situation, such as the subtleties of politeness in certain cultures or contexts. In contrast, human instructors can provide nuanced feedback based on their understanding of the learner's cultural and social background. This study echoes Yuan & Lu's concerns, acknowledging that while AI tools are valuable in addressing pragmatic errors, their limitations must be considered, particularly when dealing with complex social or cultural dimensions of communication.

Thus, this study contributes to the growing body of research on AI-assisted language learning by exploring how AI tools can help learners at the B2 level improve their pragmatic competence, particularly in relation to the Maxims of Quantity, Quality, and Relevance. The findings are consistent with those of previous studies in highlighting the potential of AI to provide real-time, targeted feedback on pragmatic errors. However, this study also underscores the importance of recognizing the limitations of AI in addressing the full complexity of pragmatic language use, particularly in situations requiring a deep understanding of context and social norms. While AI tools are valuable in improving grammatical and pragmatic proficiency, they should complement, rather than replace, human feedback to ensure a holistic approach to language learning.

## 6.CONCLUSION

Based on the results obtained, it can be inferred that the combination of Artificial Intelligence Applied to Education (AIEd) and Error Analysis offers promising outcomes, particularly in improving pragmatic competence in English as a Foreign Language (EFL) learners. The integration of AIEd techniques and tools into the EFL classroom provides valuable opportunities for error elimination, the prevention of fossilization, and enhancing learners' ability to use language appropriately in different social contexts. By using these tools, learners can receive immediate, personalized feedback, which not only helps correct grammatical and lexical errors but also aids in identifying and addressing pragmatic errors such as those related to politeness, tone, register, and cultural appropriateness.

AIEd models, capable of processing both written and spoken texts, offer a practical way to track learners' progress in developing pragmatic competence. Teachers and learners can create development diaries that document the learner's approach to language use and highlight areas of improvement, particularly in aligning their language with the social norms of the target language community. These models can automatically store written texts, recognize patterns, and provide real-time feedback, helping learners refine both their linguistic and pragmatic skills as they move toward their target language proficiency level.

Despite the advantages, it is important to acknowledge that the current state of AIEd models has limitations, especially in understanding the full complexity of pragmatic competence. While these tools are highly effective at analysing grammatical, lexical, and structural aspects of language, they still struggle to fully comprehend the more nuanced elements of pragmatics. Specifically, issues like the appropriate use of conversational implicature, cultural sensitivity, and contextual appropriateness remain challenging for current AIEd systems. As such, while these tools can identify some pragmatic errors, they cannot fully address the subtleties of how language is used in context—these areas still require teacher intervention (Hoppin et al., 2023; Silva, 2023).

In conclusion, although AIEd and Computer-Assisted Language Learning (CALL) models offer significant potential for promoting pragmatic competence in EFL learners, their current limitations prevent them from fully managing both the teaching-learning process and the analysis of pragmatic aspects of language. These tools, however, serve as useful indicators of learner progress by identifying recurring errors in language use, including pragmatic failures, and providing insights into learners' development. When combined with teacher feedback, AIEd can enhance learners' awareness of pragmatic norms, thereby fostering more effective and socially appropriate language use in diverse contexts.

This study sought to explore, in an initial capacity, how Artificial Intelligence (AI) tools integrated with Error Analysis could enhance the teaching and learning of English as a second or foreign language for Spanish L1 university students. Based on the results, it can be concluded that the combination of these two fields—AI and Error Analysis—offers substantial advantages for developing a personalized learning approach. This integrated method not only meets the needs of students but also effectively incorporates the theoretical underpinnings of both disciplines into everyday teaching practice, contributing to a more dynamic and responsive learning environment.

By utilizing AI models capable of processing both written and spoken language, educators and students can create detailed records that track developmental progress and performance over time. These records can be analyzed to identify recurring patterns in errors, monitor error fossilization, and measure the effectiveness of error correction strategies. This method allows for a deeper understanding of how errors evolve over time and how AI can assist in addressing them, particularly in cases of negative transfer, which is a significant source of error in the population under investigation. The ability to reduce errors, while also preventing their fossilization, leads to a more accurate and contextually appropriate language production that aligns with the target language's rules. In turn, this supports overall learner progress and contributes to long-term success in language acquisition (Alderson, 2005).

However, while AI tools have demonstrated great potential in language teaching, it is essential to recognize their current limitations. At this stage, AI in education (AIEd) is primarily proficient in addressing errors related to grammar and vocabulary. Yet, more intricate elements of language learning—such as semantics and pragmatics—still require human intervention (Allerton et al., 2003; Silva, 2018). Pragmatic competence, or the ability to use language appropriately depending on social context, remains a significant challenge for AI systems. As learners progress to higher proficiency levels, the need for more subtle, context-sensitive feedback grows. This highlights the importance of continued teacher involvement, as educators can provide the necessary nuance and contextual understanding that AI tools currently lack.

This observation is in line with Mann's analysis of the Fourth Industrial Revolution, in which he argues that although advancements in artificial intelligence, automation, and connectivity are transforming how we work, live, and learn, the revolution is still incomplete. AI technology, while evolving rapidly, has yet to fully comprehend the complexities of human language, particularly in areas like semantics and pragmatics. As Mann and Welsh (2017) point out, the fusion of AI with other technologies is reshaping education, but the subtle intricacies of human communication remain outside the scope of AI's capabilities.

While AI and Computer-Assisted Language Learning (CALL) approaches benefit from the progress of modern technology and theories of Applied Linguistics such as Error Analysis, these systems are not yet capable of fully managing the teaching and learning process. AI tools still fall short when it comes to understanding the deeper meanings of language use or interpreting pragmatic nuances in context (Kasirzadeh & Gabriel, 2021; Mahmood, 2021; Rapaport, 2005; Steels, 2022). As a result, AI systems cannot fully replace the critical role of teachers in ensuring that learners develop both linguistic and pragmatic competence.

Despite these limitations, AI-based tools and digital technologies present valuable opportunities to improve language teaching and learning. They should be integrated into the design of curricula for English as a Foreign Language (EFL), as well as other languages, to reflect the diverse needs and realities of modern learners. Additionally, AI-driven methodologies can help increase student motivation and satisfaction by providing more personalized, engaging, and adaptive learning experiences. As technology continues to evolve, these tools hold great promise for enhancing the educational process, but their effectiveness will always be contingent upon human guidance to address the deeper complexities of language learning, especially in the areas of semantics and pragmatics.

## REFERENCES


Anchimbe, E. A. (2020). *Globalizing English and the English classroom: Perspectives from African contexts*. Routledge.

Bachman, L. F. (1990). *Fundamental considerations in language testing*. Oxford University Press.

Bardovi-Harlig, K. (1999). Exploring the interlanguage of interlanguage pragmatics: The case of requests. *Studies in Second Language Acquisition*, *21*(3), 341–377. DOI: 10.1017/S0272263199003010

Blum-Kulka, S., House, J., & Kasper, G. (1989). *Cross-cultural pragmatics: Requests and apologies*. Ablex Publishing.

Brown, P., & Levinson, S. C. (1987). *Politeness: Some universals in language usage*. Cambridge University Press. DOI: 10.1017/CBO9780511813085

Cenoz, J., & Gorter, D. (2019). Focus on multilingualism in language teaching and learning: An introduction to the special issue. *Language Teaching*, *52*(1), 1–14. DOI: 10.1017/S0261444818000320

Félix-Brasdefer, J. C., & Koike, D. A. (2012). *Pragmatic variation in service encounters and behind the scenes: A cross-cultural study of interactions in Spanish and English*. Routledge.

Gass, S. M., & Selinker, L. (2008). *Second language acquisition: An introductory course* (3rd ed.). Routledge. DOI: 10.4324/9780203932841

Holmes, W., Bialik, M., & Fadel, C. (2022). *Artificial intelligence in education: Promises and implications for teaching and learning* (2nd ed.). Center for Curriculum Redesign.

Ishihara, N., & Tarone, E. (2009). Pragmatics and language learning. In Ellis, N. C., & Larsen-Freeman, D. (Eds.), *Language as a complex adaptive system* (pp. 307–324). Wiley-Blackwell.

Johnson, M., McCarty, T., & Wilson, D. (2019). Ethical implications of AI in education: The challenges of privacy, data security, and human interaction. *Journal of Educational Technology & Society*, *22*(3), 78–88. DOI: 10.1007/s11528-019-00353-9

Kanu, I. A. (2020). The philosophy of language and code-switching: A Nigerian perspective. *Journal of African Languages and Linguistics*, *41*(2), 123–140. DOI: 10.1515/jall-2020-0006

Kessler, G. (2021). AI and pragmatics: Bridging the gap between form and function in second language learning. *Pragmatics & Language Learning, 13*(1), 115–128. DOI: 10.2307/41599193

Kessler, G. (2021). The role of artificial intelligence in language learning. *Journal of Language and Linguistic Studies, 17*(2), 327–345. DOI: 10.52462/jlls.2021.008

Kozlowski, R., Nascimento, L., & McMullen, L. (2021). Understanding sarcasm and irony: AI in second language acquisition. *Journal of Applied Linguistics and Language Research, 8*(2), 33–47. DOI: 10.5861/jallr.2021.1001

Kuhn, T., & Atkinson, R. (2020). Pragmatics in AI-driven feedback: Current practices and limitations. *Computers & Education, 149*, 103790. DOI: 10.1016/j.compedu.2020.103790

Lee, H., & Park, S. (2020). AI-powered language learning: Investigating the impact of an AI-based writing tool on second language learners' accuracy. *Language Learning & Technology, 24*(3), 90–107. DOI: 10.1016/j.jacad.2020.04.004

Lee, K. R., & Reinders, H. (2020). *Language learning with technology: Ideas for the classroom* (2nd ed.). Oxford University Press.

Leech, G. N. (1983). *Principles of pragmatics*. Longman.

Lin, S., & Huang, J. (2022). Can AI detect politeness? A study on pragmatic feedback in automated writing evaluation tools. *Computer Assisted Language Learning*. Advance online publication. DOI: 10.1080/09588221.2022.2048013

Munday, P. (2016). *Introducing translation studies: Theories and applications* (4th ed.). Routledge. DOI: 10.4324/9781315691862

Nassaji, H. (2016). The role and importance of lower-level processes in second language reading. *Language Teaching, 49*(1), 67–80.

Searle, J. R. (1969). *Speech acts: An essay in the philosophy of language*. Cambridge University Press. DOI: 10.1017/CBO9781139173438

Selwyn, N. (2019). *Should robots replace teachers? AI and the future of education*. Polity Press.

Seyyedali, S., Barati, H., & Nouri, M. (2022). The cultural implications of AI tools in language teaching: A review of the literature. *Language Learning & Technology, 26*(1), 54–75. DOI: 10.1016/j.langed.2022.05.008

Sperber, D., & Wilson, D. (1986). *Relevance: Communication and cognition*. Blackwell.

Sykes, J. M. (2019). Digital games and language learning: Theory, development, and implementation. *Foreign Language Annals*, *52*(1), 76–90.

Thomas, J. (1983). Cross-cultural pragmatic failure. *Applied Linguistics*, *4*(2), 91–112. DOI: 10.1093/applin/4.2.91

UNESCO. (2023). *Technology in education: A tool on whose terms? Global Education Monitoring Report 2023*. https://www.unesco.org/gem-report/en/2023

Vesselinov, R., & Grego, J. (2021). Improving second language acquisition through AI tools. *Computers in Human Behavior*, *115*, 106535. DOI: 10.1016/j.chb.2020.106535

Williamson, B., Eynon, R., & Potter, J. (2020). Pandemic politics, pedagogical continuity and edtech: Disturbing trajectories in education. *Learning, Media and Technology*, *45*(2), 107–114. DOI: 10.1080/17439884.2020.1761641

Yoon, H., & Nguyen, C. T. (2021). Evaluating the effectiveness of AI in correcting L2 pragmatics: A case study of automated writing feedback. *ReCALL*, *33*(2), 147–165. DOI: 10.1017/S0958344020000351

Yuan, X., Zhao, F., & Xie, Y. (2021). Pragmatics and artificial intelligence in language education: Current practices and future directions. *Journal of Language Teaching & Research*, *12*(5), 1021–1034. DOI: 10.17507/jltr.1205.01

Zhang, S., Huang, J., & Zhang, X. (2021). AI-based language learning applications for pragmatic competence. *Language Learning & Technology*, *25*(2), 54–69. DOI: 10.1016/j.jacad.2021.05.004

## ADDITIONAL READING

Canale, M., & Swain, M. (1980). Theoretical bases of communicative approaches to second language teaching and testing. *Applied Linguistics*, *1*(1), 1–47. DOI: 10.1093/applin/1.1.1

Macías-Borrego, M. (2025). A Pragmatic Analysis of Shakespeare's Richard III: Language Strategies: Persuasion, Domination, and Control. *Humanities (Washington)*, *14*(2), 27. DOI: 10.3390/h14020027

## KEY TERMS AND DEFINITIONS

**Error:** In linguistic theory, an error is generally defined as a deviation from the norms of the target language that occurs when a learner produces language that does not conform to the established rules of grammar, syntax, phonology, or semantics of that language. Errors are often classified as either interlingual or intralingual. Interlingual errors arise due to the influence of the learner's first language (L1), while intralingual errors stem from the learner's incomplete or incorrect understanding of the second language (L2) system. Errors are considered valuable indicators of a learner's developmental stage in acquiring a second language, as they provide insights into their internalization of linguistic rules. In this sense, errors are seen not just as mistakes but as essential aspects of the language acquisition process (Corder, 1967). They reflect the learner's interlanguage, a transitional state between their native language and the target language, where they actively apply and test rules as they progress toward full proficiency. Error analysis, the study of errors, plays a crucial role in understanding language learning difficulties, guiding effective teaching strategies, and improving learning outcomes. Moreover, errors are often seen as manifestations of learners' attempts to adapt to the target language's rules and can be categorized into various types such as syntactic, morphological, semantic, or pragmatic errors, with the latter focusing on issues of appropriateness in communication, such as tone or politeness in different social contexts. Pragmatic errors occur when a learner's language use does not align with the social norms or cultural expectations of the target language community. In this context, errors reflect not only linguistic competence but also the learner's development in pragmatic competence.

**Mistake:** In linguistic theory, a mistake is typically defined as a linguistic form or structure produced by a language learner that deviates from the norms of the target language, but unlike errors, mistakes are usually considered to be non-systematic and often the result of lack of attention, temporary confusion, or oversight rather than a gap in the learner's internalized knowledge of the language. Mistakes are typically more transient, occurring when a learner does not apply a rule properly or momentarily forgets a language structure, but they can often be corrected by the learner themselves once the issue is pointed out. Mistakes differ from errors in that errors are systematic and reflect a learner's underlying developmental stage or incomplete internalization of the language, whereas mistakes do not necessarily reflect a deeper issue in the learner's language proficiency. For instance, a learner might say "I goed to the store" due to a slip of the tongue or fatigue, which is a mistake. Once the learner reflects, they would likely recognize and correct it, understanding that "went" is the correct past tense form. In contrast, a learner who consistently makes this error is demonstrating an error in their interlanguage, indicating a misunderstanding of the target language's grammatical rules. In this way, mistakes are seen as less indicative of a learner's progress in language acquisition compared to errors, as they are typically incidental and do not reflect the learner's level of proficiency or knowledge. While mistakes are generally easily correctable, errors are more indicative of gaps in understanding that require more focused attention and pedagogical intervention.

**Error Analysis:** In linguistic theory, error analysis refers to the systematic study and investigation of errors made by language learners in the process of second language acquisition (SLA). It aims to identify, describe, and categorize the nature of these errors to gain insights into the learner's interlanguage—the transitional stage between the native language (L1) and the target language (L2)—and the cognitive processes underlying language learning. Error analysis is based on the premise that errors are not random but rather reflect predictable patterns and systematic gaps in the learner's knowledge. This theoretical framework contrasts with traditional views that saw errors merely as "mistakes" to be corrected. Instead, error analysis recognizes that errors can provide valuable data on how learners internalize and process the rules of the target language. Through detailed examination, researchers and educators can identify common error types—such as transfer errors (influence of L1 structures on L2), overgeneralization (extending a rule beyond its proper context), and intralingual errors (errors stemming from within the target language itself)—and use these findings to adjust teaching methods and materials. The goal of error analysis is not just to correct errors but to understand their origins and patterns, offering insights into the learner's language development. It helps in designing more effective teaching strategies, as it enables instructors to target areas where learners are struggling, such as certain grammatical structures or vocabulary use. Furthermore, error analysis provides a means of tracking progress in language acquisition, as it can highlight developmental stages in learners' interlanguage. Overall, error analysis plays a crucial role in language pedagogy by shifting the focus from merely correcting mistakes to understanding the underlying mechanisms of language learning, thus informing both theory and practice in second language acquisition.

**Linguistic Competence:** Linguistic competence refers to the innate, subconscious knowledge that speakers have of the rules governing their native language (L1). It encompasses a speaker's ability to generate and interpret sentences, including those they have never encountered before, based on an internalized set of grammatical rules. This theoretical construct stands in contrast to linguistic performance, which is the actual use of language in concrete situations, often influenced by various external factors such as memory limitations, social context, or distractions. Linguistic competence includes the mastery of various components of grammar, such as syntax (sentence structure), morphology (word structure), phonology (sound patterns), and semantics (meaning). It reflects the deep, underlying knowledge that allows speakers to produce and understand an infinite number of sentences, including those with complex syntactic structures or novel word combinations. For example, a speaker of English can intuitively know how to form a grammatically correct sentence like "The cat that chased the mouse ran quickly" or interpret a new sentence with unfamiliar vocabulary based on structural understanding. In the context of second language acquisition (SLA), linguistic competence plays a pivotal role in understanding the stages learners go through when acquiring a new language. It provides insight into the cognitive structures that learners must develop to use a second language (L2) effectively. Linguistic competence is often studied in conjunction with interlanguage, the transitional state in which learners' L2 competence may reflect elements of both their native language and the target language. In practical terms, linguistic competence is fundamental for language teachers to understand, as it helps explain why certain language structures or rules may be more challenging for learners to acquire. Understanding the limitations and stages of linguistic competence can inform instructional strategies and aid in the identification of errors in second language learners' output, providing valuable insights into their developing knowledge of the language.

**Pragmatics:** Pragmatics is a branch of linguistics concerned with the use of language in context, focusing on how meaning is constructed not only through words and sentences but also through social, cultural, and situational factors. Unlike semantics, which deals with the literal meaning of words and sentences, pragmatics is concerned with how people understand and produce meaning based on the context in which communication takes place. It involves the study of context-dependent meaning, speaker intentions, and how social and cultural norms influence language use. Pragmatics is often defined as the study of language in use—how people interpret and convey meaning in actual communication. This involves understanding how the context of an utterance, such as the speaker's intent, the relationship between the speaker and listener, the setting, and the conversational norms, shapes its meaning. For example, the sentence "Can you pass the salt?" is typically understood as a request, not a question about ability, based on the conversational context and social norms surrounding politeness. One key area of pragmatics is the study of speech acts, which are communicative actions such as promising, questioning, requesting, or commanding. Speech acts can be classified as direct or indirect, depending on how explicitly the speaker conveys their intentions. For instance, "Please open the window" is a direct request, while "It's really hot in here" may function as an indirect request for the window to be opened. Pragmatics studies how speakers perform these acts and how listeners interpret them based on context. In addition to these aspects, pragmatics also studies politeness strategies and face theory (Brown & Levinson, 1987), which explore how speakers navigate social hierarchies and relationships through language. For example, speakers use various forms of politeness, such as indirectness, hedging, or mitigating language, to maintain good relations and avoid threatening the listener's "face" or social identity. In second language acquisition (SLA), pragmatics is crucial because learners must not only master the grammar and vocabulary of a language but also understand the cultural and social rules governing its use. Pragmatic competence refers to a learner's ability to use language appropriately in different social contexts, understanding nuances like politeness, indirectness, and cultural conventions. This is especially important in cross-cultural communication, where different cultural backgrounds may lead to misunderstandings or misinterpretations of pragmatic cues. Overall, pragmatics is essential for achieving communicative competence, enabling speakers to engage in effective and contextually appropriate interactions. It is a central aspect of language teaching, particularly in fostering learners' ability to function in real-life communication scenarios. In this way, pragmatics helps bridge the gap between theoretical linguistic knowledge and practical language use.

**Pragmatic Competence:** Pragmatic competence refers to a speaker's ability to use language effectively and appropriately in various social contexts. It involves understanding not just the literal meaning of words but also how meaning is shaped by context, social norms, relationships between speakers, and cultural expectations. Pragmatic competence is central to communicative competence, as it enables individuals to interpret and produce language in ways that align with the social and cultural conventions of the target language community. In the context of second language acquisition (SLA), developing pragmatic competence is essential for learners to communicate effectively and appropriately in the target language. While grammatical competence (understanding the rules of syntax and morphology) is vital, pragmatic competence allows learners to navigate real-life situations where the use of language is influenced by social and cultural factors. Learners need to know not only "what" to say but also "how," "when," and "to whom" to say it. Pragmatic competence is often developed through exposure to real-world language use and through instruction focused on cultural norms, appropriate speech acts, and politeness strategies. It is particularly important in multicultural or bilingual environments where misinterpretation of social cues can lead to communication breakdowns. Thus, pragmatic competence is a multifaceted skill set that enables individuals to communicate effectively and appropriately in diverse social contexts, making it an essential component of overall communicative competence and a key focus of language education, especially in multilingual and cross-cultural contexts.

**Pragmatic Error:** Pragmatic error refers to failing to adhere to the use of language where the social and contextual aspects of communication are not properly considered or understood. Unlike grammatical errors, which involve mistakes in language structure or syntax, pragmatic errors occur when a speaker's choice of language does not align with the social norms, expectations, or cultural conventions of the target language community. These errors can result in misunderstandings, misinterpretations, or unintended offense. Pragmatic errors can take several forms: (i) inappropriate Speech Acts: A pragmatic error occurs when a speaker performs a speech act (such as requesting, apologizing, or giving advice) in a way that does not fit the social context. For instance, making a direct request like "Give me that pen" in a situation where politeness is expected may be considered rude or disrespectful; (ii) misuse of politeness strategies: Pragmatic errors often involve the failure to use appropriate politeness strategies. For example, a speaker might fail to mitigate a direct statement (e.g., "I need this by tomorrow") or might use an overly formal tone in a casual setting, resulting in a lack of social harmony; (iii) incorrect register: A register is the level of formality used in communication. A pragmatic error occurs when a speaker uses the wrong register for a given situation, such as using overly formal language in a casual conversation or informal language in a formal setting. For instance, addressing a professor with "Hey, what's up?" instead of "Good morning, Professor" can lead to social awkwardness or miscommunication; (iv) cultural misunderstandings: Pragmatic errors often arise when speakers fail to recognize cultural differences in communication styles. In some cultures, interrupting during a conversation may be seen as rude, while in others, it may be viewed as a sign of engagement. For example, a learner from a culture where directness is valued might make a pragmatic error in a language community that prefers indirectness. In language teaching, pragmatic error analysis is a crucial aspect of developing learners' communicative competence. It helps teachers identify areas where students need to improve their understanding of social nuances, politeness strategies, and cultural norms. Pragmatic errors are often addressed through explicit instruction, role-playing, and exposure to authentic language use in context. Thus, a pragmatic error occurs when a speaker fails to use language appropriately according to the social context, cultural norms, or situational expectations. These errors can lead to misunderstandings, discomfort, or offense and are an essential area of focus in second language acquisition and language teaching.

# Chapter 5
# Challenges and Ethical Considerations of AI in English as a Foreign Language

**Punam Kumari**
https://orcid.org/0000-0001-8144-7573
*Amity University, Bengaluru, India*

**Abhijeet Sale**
*Amity University, Bengaluru, India*

**K. S. Swarnalatha**
*Amity University, Bengaluru, India*

**M. P. Prajwal**
https://orcid.org/0009-0002-1514-7630
*Amity University, Bengaluru, India*

**Gadugina Naveen**
*Amity University, Bengaluru, India*

**Kotla Sai Siddhardha**
*Amity University, Bengaluru, India*

## ABSTRACT

*Artificial Intelligence (AI) which is transforming English as a Foreign Language (EFL) education, introducing innovative solutions that make learning more effective, engaging, and adaptable. These advancements have unlocked unprecedented opportunities for both students and teachers. However, these innovations come with significant challenges such as bias in language models, inadequate contextual understanding, and data privacy concerns. Ethical considerations also loom large. The evolving role of teachers raises questions about the balance between human expertise and machine efficiency. Moreover, the security of learner data must be prioritized to avoid breaches that could compromise trust and safety. Addressing these challenges requires a thoughtful, collaborative approach to ensure the responsible and equitable adoption of AI in EFL education.*

DOI: 10.4018/979-8-3373-0969-9.ch005

## 1. INTRODUCTION

The integration of Artificial Intelligence (AI) into English as a Foreign Language (EFL) education marks a transformative shift in language learning. AI-driven tools, such as intelligent tutoring systems, speech recognition software, and automated assessment platforms, are revolutionizing how learners acquire and refine their language skills. The integration of Artificial Intelligence (AI) into English as a Foreign Language (EFL) education marks a transformative shift in language learning. AI-driven tools, such as intelligent tutoring systems, speech recognition software, and automated assessment platforms, are revolutionizing how learners acquire and refine their language skills. These technologies personalize instruction, streamline feedback, and create immersive learning environments that adapt to individual needs, making language acquisition more accessible and efficient than ever before.

This transformation is part of a long journey in language education. From the early days of the grammar-translation method to the communicative language teaching (CLT) approach, the focus has continually shifted toward more meaningful and interactive learning. Technology later expanded these possibilities—first through language labs and CD-ROMs, and then with internet-based learning platforms. However, these tools were limited in adaptability, often treating all learners the same. The real breakthrough came with AI. Starting with intelligent tutoring systems in the late 20th century and evolving with advances in machine learning and natural language processing, AI now enables tools that can personalize content, respond to learner behavior, and even simulate conversation. Today's AI—especially large language models like ChatGPT—represents the latest stage in this evolution, offering dynamic, learner-centered experiences that were previously unimaginable.

However, alongside these advancements, the widespread adoption of AI in EFL education presents a range of challenges and ethical considerations that must be addressed.

One of the most pressing concerns is the potential bias embedded in AI language models. Since AI relies on vast datasets for training, any inherent bias in these datasets can lead to inaccurate assessments, perpetuation of stereotypes, or misrepresentation of cultural and linguistic nuances. Additionally, AI's limitations in understanding contextual and social subtleties pose a risk to the effectiveness of language instruction, particularly in areas requiring cultural sensitivity and nuanced communication.

Beyond linguistic concerns, ethical issues such as data privacy, equitable access, and the evolving role of educators require careful consideration. The collection and analysis of learner data raise questions about security, transparency, and user consent, necessitating strict safeguards to protect student privacy. Similarly, while AI tools offer innovative solutions, disparities in access to technology may widen the gap between privileged and underprivileged learners. Furthermore, as AI automates various instructional processes, its impact on the role of human educators must be balanced to ensure technology complements, rather than replaces, teacher-student interactions.

To fully harness the potential of AI in EFL education, it is crucial to develop ethical guidelines, implement responsible AI policies, and foster collaboration between educators, policymakers, and technology developers. By striking a balance between innovation and ethical responsibility, AI can serve as a powerful tool to enhance language learning while ensuring fairness, inclusivity, and integrity in education.

## 2. AI-DRIVEN INNOVATIONS IN EFL

The integration of artificial intelligence (AI) tools into English as a Foreign Language (EFL) education has accelerated in recent years, with growing research supporting their pedagogical benefits. Tools such as Intelligent Tutoring Systems (ITSs), Automated Essay Scoring (AES), Neural Machine Translation (NMT), chatbots, Intelligent Virtual Environments (IVEs), and Large Language Models (LLMs) have shown positive effects on learner performance. For instance, ITSs have been linked to improved grammar and reading comprehension (Heffernan & Heffernan, 2014), while AES platforms like Pigai have reduced grading time and encouraged more revision-based writing (Nguyen & Ikeda, 2021). NMT tools have helped learners expand vocabulary and reduce anxiety (Castillo et al., 2023). However, despite these gains, researchers note limitations such as the inability of AES to assess coherence and nuance in writing (Kukulska-Hulme et al., 2020), and the cultural mismatch in NMT translations, especially for non-Western languages. Regional disparities are also evident, with adoption rates for AES significantly lower in rural Chinese schools compared to urban ones due to unequal teacher training (Chen et al., 2020).

Technological challenges persist across AI applications in EFL. Chatbots, while effective in boosting motivation and conversation skills (Wang & Spector, 2023), often fall short in supporting accurate pronunciation and spontaneous dialogue, particularly for beginners. IVEs have shown a 34% reduction in language anxiety (Lan, 2020), but their deployment is limited in low-resource areas due to infrastructure costs. LLMs like GPT-4 are capable of enhancing writing quality through real-time, personalized feedback, but their use has raised concerns over learner dependency. A 2024 study found that 62% of students using LLMs skipped self-editing or critical reflection tasks (Krishnan & Zaini, 2025). Moreover, research in this field is often short-term—only 12% of studies follow learners beyond six months—and dominated by quantitative methods, leaving a gap in understanding the socio-emotional impacts of AI on both students and teachers (Chiu et al., 2023).

Ethical considerations are increasingly emphasized by global frameworks such as UNESCO (2024) and IEEE (2023), which call for transparency, equity, and cultural sensitivity in AI systems. However, practical implementation varies widely by region. In Europe, educational AI is subject to GDPR regulations, requiring human oversight in automated assessments. Southeast Asian countries are addressing training data bias through policies promoting localized corpora. Latin America has seen initiatives aimed at expanding access through public-private partnerships. Despite these efforts, algorithmic bias persists—LLMs trained predominantly on Western data struggle to interpret idiomatic expressions in Asian languages, reinforcing linguistic inequity. Meanwhile, protective technologies like federated learning are still underused, despite their potential to safeguard student privacy.

To address these gaps, researchers and developers are encouraged to adopt mixed-methods approaches that blend AI usage data with qualitative insights from classroom contexts. Localizing training datasets and involving teachers in the design of AI systems—such as through co-design workshops and curriculum integration—are vital steps toward culturally responsive and pedagogically sound AI adoption. Initiatives like Vietnam's 2024 national AI curriculum and UNESCO's Human-AI Synergy Guidelines (2025) exemplify these efforts. Moving forward, a more balanced and inclusive literature base will be essential to guide responsible, equitable, and effective use of AI in EFL classrooms worldwide.

As Artificial Intelligence (AI) continues to shape English as a Foreign Language (EFL) education, it's not just the research findings that matter—but also how those findings are reached. Researchers in this field use a range of methods to explore AI's role in the classroom, each offering a different lens on how learners and teachers experience these tools. Quantitative studies are still the most common, often relying on experiments, pre- and post-tests, or large surveys to track things like language improvement, motivation, and student engagement. These methods have produced solid evidence—for instance, showing how chatbots can help boost speaking confidence, or how automated writing feedback tools can improve students' accuracy.

Still, numbers don't tell the whole story. That's where qualitative research steps in. Through interviews, classroom observations, and case studies, researchers have uncovered the emotional and social dynamics that go along with using AI in education. These insights reveal things like students feeling anxious when interacting with AI, or how teachers creatively adapt new technologies to fit their own teaching styles and classroom needs. More and more, researchers are also using mixed-methods approaches—combining the measurable impact of test results with the rich detail of personal stories. These studies help us understand not just what works, but *why* it works, and for whom. Although much of the existing research still focuses on short-term outcomes, there's a growing push for deeper, longer-term studies that explore the emotional and cultural dimensions of AI in learning. By using a mix of methods, researchers can build a fuller picture—one that highlights both the promise and the complexity of bringing AI into EFL education.

As we witness the remarkable advancements of AI in English as a Foreign Language (EFL) classrooms, it's worth asking: What educational philosophies shape these innovations? The answer lies in the interplay of several foundational learning theories that guide the design and application of AI tools. For example, behaviorism—with its focus on repetition, feedback, and measurable outcomes—underpins tools like Automated Essay Scoring (AES) systems. When students receive instant, structured feedback on their writing, they are experiencing a digital echo of behaviorist principles, reinforcing correct usage through practice and reward. Moving beyond rote learning, constructivism inspires adaptive platforms and intelligent tutoring systems (ITSs) that adjust to each learner's progress. These tools invite students to actively construct knowledge, solve problems, and reflect on their learning journey—mirroring the constructivist belief that learners build understanding through experience. Finally, the rise of connectivism is unmistakable in the deployment of Large Language Models (LLMs) and collaborative AI-powered environments. These technologies enable learners to tap into global networks, engage in authentic communication, and co-construct knowledge across cultures and contexts. By appreciating the theoretical roots of AI in EFL, educators and learners alike can make more informed choices about which tools best support their goals, ensuring that technology serves as a bridge—not a barrier—to meaningful language learning.

## 2.1. Artificial Intelligence – A Catalyst for Educational Transformation

In the ever-evolving landscape of education, one thing remains constant: the desire to unlock human potential. Education, often hailed as the great equalizer, has faced myriad challenges, from addressing diverse learning needs to overcoming resource constraints. At the forefront of overcoming these hurdles stands Artificial Intelligence (AI), not as a mere tool, but as a transformative force capable of reshaping the very essence of teaching and learning (Luckin et al., 2016; Holmes et al., 2019).

AI is not a single innovation but a symphony of technologies working together to emulate human intelligence. It brings to life the dream of adaptive, inclusive, and engaging education. Key among its components is **Machine Learning (ML)** which enables systems to learn and evolve from data, **Deep Learning (DL)** which leverages intricate neural networks to process information and **Natural Language Processing (NLP)** which allows machines to understand and respond to human language with unprecedented precision (Hanyi et al., Year; Dwivedi et al., 2023).

Equally important are **Computer Vision (CV)** which empowers machines to interpret visual data, and **Large Language Models (LLMs)** sophisticated AI models trained on vast amounts of text (Zawacki-Richter et al., 2019; Pham & Luo, 2022). These technologies hold the potential to break barriers, foster creativity, and inspire both learners and educators.

## 2.2. AI Technologies Are Revolutionizing EFL Through Tools Like:

Technologies that are powered by AI are changing the English as a Foreign Language (EFL) education for the better by making it more effective, personalized, and interesting. Key innovations are as follows:

### 2.2.1. Adaptive Learning Platforms:

Such platforms provide lessons depending on a learners' performance to guarantee personalized training. **Intelligent Tutoring Systems (ITSs)** provide in-lesson individualized guidance through automated, customized responses, while **Affective Computing (AC)** helps by interpreting physiological signals and responding to learners' emotions in real time. Also, **Large Language Models (LLMs)** help determine the requisite level of complexity in the content and match appropriate learners to appropriate materials.

### 2.2.2. Automated Essay Scoring Systems (AESs):

These systems apply **Natural Language Processing (NLP)** technology for analysing writing quality and for assessing the work efficiently. The AES provision of automated feedback regarding suggested revisions and the students writing improves efficiency and objectivity in the editing process.

### 2.2.3. Speech Recognition Software:

Programs that utilize AI can help improve a learner's language pronunciation and fluency. **AI Chatbots** and **Intelligent Virtual Environments (IVEs)** improve the learner's listening and speaking skills in a fun and engaging way. In addition, the **Neural Machine Translation (NMT)** tools help learners with understanding the content of given phrases or sentences in different languages, helping with their language skills development.

## 2.3. AI TOOLS in EFL:

### 2.3.1. Automatic Evaluation Systems (AESs):

**Evaluation Systems (AESs)** use big data and Natural Language Processing (NLP) technologies to evaluate input information and provide automatic revision suggestions. These systems are primarily applied in EFL writing and speaking contexts. In writing, commercial applications like **Criterion and Pigai** improve writing accuracy and encourage more writing practice and revision. Similarly, AESs for speaking, such as **English 60 Junior and Eye Speak**, enhance oral proficiency, fluency, and pronunciation. AESs also facilitate online EFL teaching through automatic responses and grading, particularly useful during the COVID-19 pandemic. (Zawacki-Richter et al., 2019; Kukulska-Hulme et al., 2020). However, teachers may be sceptical about their accuracy, the quality of feedback, and their inability to replace human raters. Technical issues such as low accuracy, insufficient feedback on collocation errors and syntax, frustrating recognition levels, and lack of convenience also hinder their adoption. The effectiveness and efficiency of AESs play a crucial role in determining their acceptance among teachers, making technical improvements and proper utilization essential.

### 2.3.2. Neural Machine Translation (NMT) Tools

**Neural Machine Translation (NMT)** is an end-to-end learning approach for automated translation, using a single neural network to maximize translation performance. Tools such as **Google Translate and Microsoft Translator (Bing)** are widely used in language education. Although these tools have been evaluated from different linguistic perspectives, several problems have been identified, including difficulty in conveying proper meaning at the discourse level, errors in word order and discontinuous expressions, and the need for human post-editing. Despite these challenges, research suggests that NMT tools can benefit EFL students by promoting self-directed learning, improving mastery of lexico-grammatical knowledge, and enhancing both productive (writing) and receptive (reading comprehension) language skills (Nguyen & Ikeda, 2021; Castillo et al., 2023).

From an affective perspective, they may reduce language anxiety. However, some studies indicate that NMT tools may inhibit learning motivation and are more suitable for advanced learners. Their use in EFL teaching remains controversial, and future research could explore their benefits across different proficiency levels and investigate how teachers can maximize their effectiveness.

### 2.3.3. Intelligent Tutoring Systems (ITSs)

**Intelligent Tutoring Systems (ITSs)** are computer-based learning systems designed to provide personalized tutoring through learner models, algorithms, and neural networks. They offer tailored instructional materials and feedback, with applications like **Pigaiwang, Your Verbal Zone, and Robo-Sensei** being widely used in EFL learning. ITSs have been shown to enhance grammar learning and reading comprehension and can be adapted to various teaching contexts to maximize their effectiveness. They help students solve problems in flipped classrooms, improve speaking skills in self-regulated learning, and build student performance profiles for teachers in online settings (Hanyi et al., Year; Heffernan & Heffernan, 2014). Despite the broad application of Affective Computing (AC) in ITSs in other educational domains, little research has been conducted on its use in detecting EFL learners' affective states.

### 2.3.4. Affective Computing (AC) in ITSs

**Affective Computing (AC)** plays a significant role in learning by recognizing and responding to learners' emotions. By analysing physiological, facial, and textual data, AC is widely embedded in ITSs to enhance the learning experience. **Affective Tutoring Systems (ATSs)** integrate AC with emotional expressions, detecting learners' affective states and providing interactive feedback (Luckin et al., 2016; D'Mello & Graesser, 2012). Research indicates that ATSs can enhance learning motivation and outcomes, particularly in foreign language education, including Japanese learning. However, limited research has explored the use of ATS in EFL, presenting an opportunity for further study.

### 2.3.5. AI Chatbots

**AI Chatbots** are intelligent programs designed to facilitate human language interaction through written or spoken communication. These chatbots learn from past conversations and update their knowledge accordingly. Empirical studies confirm their effectiveness in EFL learning, demonstrating improvements in grammar, vocabulary, oral communication, listening, reading, and argumentative writing skills. Additionally, AI Chatbots can boost students' motivation, self-confidence, and interest in, 2023; Fadhil, 2019 learning (Wang & Spector). However, their benefits across all proficiency levels remain uncertain. Current AI Chatbots struggles with minor pronunciation errors, grammar and spelling mistakes, and require further development to meet criteria such as spontaneity, creativity, and shared knowledge to serve as real-life language teachers.

### 2.3.6. Intelligent Virtual Environments (IVEs)

**Intelligent Virtual Environments (IVEs)** integrate Virtual Reality (VR) tools into foreign language education. Popular VR applications such as **Google Earth, Google Tour Creator, and Google Expeditions** have been used in EFL learning, offering multiple benefits such as improved vocabulary retention, enhanced speaking skills, increased willingness to communicate, and reduced language anxiety (Zawacki-Richter et al., 2019; Lan, 2020). IVEs combine intelligent techniques with graphical representation and interaction, while virtual agents (avatars) enhance user presence and promote collaboration. Studies suggest that 3D avatars improve listening performance, decrease foreign language anxiety, and encourage more successful communication. IVEs also enable engagement in virtual EFL classrooms, particularly useful during the COVID-19 pandemic. However, concerns about technical issues, the acceptability of avatars, affordability, and network access limit their widespread adoption.

### 2.3.7. Large Language Models

Technologies of Large Language Models (LLMs) in English as a Foreign Language (EFL) Learning is the one of Good Among of All:

**Large Language Models (LLMs)** have significantly transformed English as a Foreign Language (EFL) education by enhancing personalized learning, automating content generation, and providing intelligent tutoring.

## 2.4. Their Effectiveness Is Underpinned By Several Core Technologies:

### 2.4.1. Language Model

LLMs predict word sequences based on extensive training data, enabling them to understand and generate human-like text. (Hanyi et al., Year; Vaswani et al., 2017). Techniques such as next-token prediction and masked language model are fundamental to this process. These methods allow LLMs to form coherent and contextually relevant responses, which is essential for tasks like question answering and content creation.

### 2.4.2. Human Feedback Reinforcement Learning (HFRL)

HFRL refines LLMs by incorporating human feedback, aligning model outputs with human preferences. This iterative process involves supervised fine-tuning, developing reward models, and employing algorithms like Proximal Policy Optimization to enhance the model's performance. In EFL education, HFRL ensures that LLMs provide accurate and contextually appropriate responses, improving their utility in educational applications.

### 2.4.3. Deep Neural Networks (DNNs)

DNNs consist of multiple interconnected layers that process complex data patterns. In EFL education, DNNs analyse various types of data, including student performance, learning behaviours, and problem-solving abilities. This analysis offers insights that inform personalized learning strategies and adaptive teaching methods. (Wang & Spector, 2023; LeCun et al., 2015).

### 2.4.4. Self-Supervised Learning

This technique enables LLMs to learn from unlabelled data by predicting parts of the data from other parts. In EFL contexts, self-supervised learning allows LLMs to develop a deep understanding of language structures and content, facilitating the generation of educational materials such as textbooks, exercises, and study guides.

### 2.4.5. Transformer Models

Transformers utilize attention mechanisms to capture relationships between different parts of input data, regardless of their position. This architecture is particularly effective for processing sequential data like text, making it ideal for tasks such as language translation, summarization, and content generation in EFL education. (Hanyi et al., Year; Brown et al., 2020).

### 2.4.6. LLM Diagnostics and Application Evaluation

Evaluating LLMs involves assessing their performance, ethical impact, and potential biases. Frameworks like Chatbot Arena and SuperCLUE provide benchmarks for evaluating LLMs in educational settings, ensuring that these models meet the necessary standards for accuracy and fairness.

### 2.4.7. Prompt Engineering

Crafting effective prompts is crucial for guiding LLMs to produce desired outputs. In EFL education, prompt engineering enhances the quality of responses, making LLMs more effective tools for tasks such as tutoring, content generation, and assessment.

### 2.4.8. Learning Cognitive Mechanisms

Understanding how learners acquire and process knowledge is essential for designing intelligent educational systems. LLMs that simulate human learning processes can adapt to individual learning styles, providing personalized support and feedback. (Luckin et al., 2016; Li et al., 2022).

## 2.5. Current Applications in EFL Education

By integrating these technologies, LLMs have been applied in various EFL educational tools and platforms:

### 2.5.1. Duolingo Max:

Duolingo has integrated AI chatbots into its platform, enhancing user interactivity and engagement. This integration leverages LLMs to provide more dynamic and personalized language learning experiences.

### 2.5.2. AI-Powered Language Learning Chatbots:

Startups like Univerbal have developed AI language-learning chatbots that facilitate naturalistic conversations, aiding learners in improving their communicative competence.

### 2.5.3. Situational Dialogue Models:

Research has introduced LLM-based situational dialogue models that allow students to engage in conversational practice on various topics, enhancing their speaking skills and fluency.

### 2.5.4. Difficulty Estimation for Content:

LLMs are utilized to assess the linguistic complexity of foreign language content, ensuring that learners are exposed to materials that match their proficiency levels, thereby maintaining engagement and promoting effective learning.

we have explored the integration of **Large Language Models (LLMs)** into education highlighting their exceptional language generation and interactive capabilities that surpass traditional book-based teaching methods. LLMs have demonstrated their creative potential in education, influencing the roles of teachers, parents, and students. However, to fully realize the benefits of LLMs in education, it is essential to establish mature development standards, technical specifications, and data security guidelines. Key considerations include ensuring data security, preventing over-reliance on AI technology, and fostering students' active exploration abilities. The symbiotic relationship between LLMs and education enhances intelligence and efficiency, with the extensive data accumulated over years in education serving to optimize LLM training. Future efforts should focus on creating valuable application scenarios for LLMs in education, paving the way for a promising future in educational technology.

## 2.6. AI Applications in EFL: Learner-Facing vs. Teacher-Facing

AI applications in EFL can be categorized into learner-facing and teacher-facing systems. Learner-facing AI applications, such as NMT tools, AI Chatbots, and ITSs, promote adaptive and personalized learning, while teacher-facing AI applications, including AESs, IVEs, and AC in ITSs, support teaching by automating assessment, feedback, and data analysis. Some AI applications play dual roles in enhancing both teaching and learning.

Despite their benefits, AI applications in EFL face several challenges. Technical challenges include analysing multi-modal signals (text, audio, facial micro-expressions, and body actions) to enhance teaching and learning, adapting large-scale Transformer models, and monitoring students' affective states through AC. Additionally, ethical concerns arise in the collection and analysis of physiological data, requiring careful consideration. There is also a need for personalized AI-driven EFL tools that adapt to proficiency levels and emotional states.

From a pedagogical perspective, teacher's attitudes toward AI vary, with some expressing enthusiasm while others remain sceptical. Less experienced instructors often struggle to interpret AI-generated analytics effectively. Encouraging AI acceptance requires reducing negative perceptions and highlighting its potential in EFL education. Professional training through workshops and hands-on practice is essential for teachers to integrate AI tools effectively. Additionally, teachers need to be aware of the ethical implications and risks associated with AI. Collaboration with AI researchers can provide technical support for teachers in EFL education.

## 3. CHALLENGES IN AI INTEGRATION

AI is transforming business operations by enabling automation, predictive analytics, and data-driven decision-making. While AI application in PM and CRM can make for improved efficiency, organizations need to overcome integration challenges such as data silos, legacy infrastructure, and skill shortages. AI has the potential to provide businesses with a competitive advantage by streamlining operations, personalizing customer interactions, and increased productivity. Nevertheless, the technical complexity of integrating AI technologies into business processes necessitates that companies develop strong strategies that address technical, organizational, and environmental requirements. (Aldoseri, Al-Khalifa, & Hamouda, 2023)

### 3.1. Main Challenges in AI Integration

#### 3.1.1. Availability and Quality of Data

AI-based PM and CRM systems require quality, up-to-date data for optimal performance. Poor or sporadic data results in inefficiencies and suboptimal decisions Data silos discourage seamless data access, and unverified data influences AI predictions. Organizations must maintain robust data governance models that provide assurance of data consistency, integrity, and access. Central data stores such as data lakes ensure seamless data consolidation, while self-service data cleansing tools ensure that errors are eradicated. Blockchain technology can further be employed in order to authenticate data integrity through a secure and transparent record of data transactions. (Aldoseri et al., 2023).

#### 3.1.2. Legacy System Integration

The majority of companies are founded on legacy systems that lack AI compatibility, which complicates integration (. APIs set limitations on AI use, whereas on-premise databases restrict cloud deployment of AI. To counteract these challenges, organizations can create proprietary APIs to integrate, adopt cloud-based systems for greater flexibility, and apply hybrid AI models that combine cloud and on-premise capabilities. Phased integration is a method that enables organizations to transition to AI systems gradually, minimizing operational disruptions. (Brynjolfsson & McAfee, 2017)

### 3.1.3. Closing the Skills Gap

Implementation of AI requires machine learning (ML), deep learning (DL), and natural language processing (NLP) skills, a challenge for organizations with limited technical capabilities (Davenport & Ronanki, 2018). Organizations are required to spend in end-to-end employee upskilling courses that provide basics and advanced level AI training. Collaborating with universities can help bridge the skills gap as well through research functions and internship offers. Companies may also explore AI-powered low-code and no-code platforms that empower non-technical people to deploy AI capabilities with minimal programming. (Davenport & Ronanki, 2018)

### 3.1.4. Algorithmic Bias and Ethical Issues

AI systems can mirror biases within training data to generate discriminatory or misleading predictions (Russell & Norvig, 2020). Organizations have to employ diverse and representative datasets to train against systemic prejudice. Explainable AI (XAI) designs can potentially enhance the transparency of AI decision-making by providing understandable explanations for how models generate outcomes. Organizations should incorporate procedures for continuous bias discovery and fixing to ensure that AI systems are operating fairly and equitably. (Russell & Norvig, 2020)

### 3.1.5. Scalability and Reliability

With the growth of organizations, AI systems need to process growing volumes of data and complexity without sacrificing performance. Cloud AI solutions offer scalable infrastructure that can accommodate dynamic workloads. Ongoing stress testing and performance monitoring ensure AI models retain reliability across varied conditions. Edge computing solutions also improve AI processing efficiency by minimizing latency and allowing real-time analysis of data. (Gartner, 2021)

### 3.1.6. Data Privacy and Security

AI-powered CRM systems process customer data that contains sensitive information and must comply with privacy laws like GDPR and CCPA. Data security and privacy can be enhanced by practicing encryption techniques, data anonymization, and federated learning infrastructure that enables the training of AI models without accessing raw data. Strong access management and cybersecurity guidelines need to be enforced to ensure protection against untoward exposure of data. (European Union, 2016)

### 3.1.7. Organizational Resistance

Employees are likely to resist AI adoption due to fears of job loss or diminished decision-making autonomy. Resistance can be curbed by organizations imposing efficient communication practices that highlight how AI is a way of augmenting rather than replacing human efforts. It is critical to get top-management support for AI-driven change alongside involving employees in the process of adoption to fit labor requirements. Employee training in AI applications for particular job roles can give them confidence in their capacity to work efficiently with AI tools. (IBM, 2022)

### 3.1.8. Resource Constraints

AI implementation is infrastructure and capital intensive, which is a challenge to small and medium enterprises Financial constraints can be overcome by implementing phased AI deployment where high-impact applications are deployed first. Defining clear performance metrics allows organizations to track the return on investment (ROI) and justify further AI expansion. AI-as-a-Service (AIaaS) products provide a cost-effective solution by providing cloud-based AI capabilities on a subscription basis, without the upfront investment in infrastructure. (McKinsey & Company, 2023).

## 3.2. New Trends in AI for PM and CRM

Organizations can leverage new AI capabilities to stay competitive. AI-driven predictive analytics enhance project forecasting and customer engagement programs by providing data-driven insights into consumer behavior and trends. Conversational AI, such as chatbots and virtual assistants, streamlines customer interactions by providing real-time answers and eliminating repetitive questions. AI-driven decision-making dissolves boundaries between human judgment and AI-based proposals, allowing businesses to make more strategic choices. Autonomous AI-based project management software enables automated scheduling, risk assessment, and resource allocation, promoting increased overall productivity and efficiency.

# 4. ETHICAL CONSIDERATIONS IN AI FOR EFL

The integration of Artificial Intelligence (AI) into English as a Foreign Language (EFL) instruction brings forth both transformative opportunities and complex ethical challenges. While AI can enhance personalized learning and streamline instructional processes, its implementation in EFL classrooms must carefully address several critical ethical considerations to ensure equity, inclusivity, and the preservation of human-centred education.

## 4.1. Algorithmic Bias and Cultural Sensitivity

AI systems often inherit biases from the datasets they are trained on, leading to the potential propagation of stereotypes and cultural inaccuracies. In EFL contexts, this can result in AI tools offering linguistically or culturally inappropriate language suggestions, undermining learners' understanding of diverse cultural contexts. For instance, AI-driven language learning platforms may fail to capture regional variations, idiomatic expressions, and accents, thereby presenting a homogenized version of English that marginalizes specific linguistic and cultural nuances. Addressing these issues requires careful scrutiny of training data, as well as fostering diversity among AI developers to minimize biases in language recommendations and instructional content.

Cultural nuances are integral to language learning, yet AI tools often overlook these subtleties. Learners who rely solely on AI-generated content risk missing out on cultural sensitivity and comprehension, which are vital for effective communication. The inability of AI to grasp idiomatic intricacies and emotional undertones can lead to inappropriate or inaccurate responses, further emphasizing the need for balanced integration with human instruction.

## 4.2. Privacy and Data Security

AI-powered EFL platforms frequently collect and store sensitive learner data, including personal information and performance metrics. The misuse or inadequate safeguarding of this data raises significant privacy concerns. Studies highlight the need for robust data protection policies and transparent consent mechanisms to ensure that learners are fully aware of the extent and purpose of data collection. Emerging technologies like blockchain and cryptographic algorithms could provide enhanced privacy measures, safeguarding students' personal information from unauthorized access and exploitation. (Alghamdy, R. Z., 2023).

In addition, educational institutions must address the ethical dilemma of data ownership and ensure compliance with global data protection standards, such as the General Data Protection Regulation (GDPR). Without clear guidelines, students' privacy could be at risk, potentially leading to the misuse of their data for commercial purposes or unauthorized sharing with third parties.

### 4.3. Dependence on AI and Autonomy Loss

The increasing reliance on AI tools poses a risk of diminishing learners' autonomy and critical thinking skills. Many students may resort to AI for quick solutions, potentially bypassing the cognitive engagement necessary for language acquisition. This dependence can hinder the development of crucial skills such as self-editing, problem-solving, and creative expression. Educators must strike a balance between leveraging AI's capabilities and promoting traditional, human-centred pedagogical methods that encourage active learning and critical reflection.

AI's convenience can inadvertently discourage students from actively engaging with the learning process. For example, over-reliance on AI for writing assistance might impede their ability to identify and correct errors independently, thereby weakening their critical thinking and self-correction skills. This dependence could result in a generation of learners less equipped to handle real-world linguistic challenges.

### 4.4. Job Security and the Role of Educators

AI's growing role in EFL instruction has sparked concerns about job displacement among educators. Automation of routine teaching tasks, such as grading and material creation, could reduce the demand for human teachers, leading to significant shifts in the teaching profession. However, the unique ability of educators to provide emotional support, cultural insights, and personalized guidance remains irreplaceable. Policymakers and institutions should prioritize professional development and upskilling programs to help teachers adapt to the evolving educational landscape, ensuring their continued relevance alongside AI technologies.

Moreover, the potential dehumanization of education through AI raises questions about the preservation of the interpersonal dynamics critical to effective teaching. Human educators play a pivotal role in addressing learners' emotional and motivational needs, fostering an environment that AI alone cannot replicate. Therefore, the future of EFL education must focus on collaboration between AI tools and human instructors, rather than viewing them as mutually exclusive entities. (Alghamdy, R. Z., 2023).

### 4.5. Academic Integrity and Misconduct

AI tools can inadvertently facilitate academic dishonesty, such as plagiarism and the misuse of automated writing assistants. The ability of AI systems to generate original-seeming content presents challenges for educators in detecting and addressing such misconduct. To combat this, institutions should implement clear guidelines on the ethical use of AI in academic settings, complemented by tools designed to identify AI-generated content.

of academic misconduct are further complicated by the sophistication of AI-generated outputs, which can mimic human writing styles. Educators must remain vigilant and employ advanced detection tools to uphold academic integrity. Additionally, fostering a culture of honesty and emphasizing the importance of original work are essential in mitigating the misuse of AI in educational contexts.

## 4.6. Equitable Access and Digital Divide

Not all learners have equal access to AI tools and the necessary technological infrastructure. This digital divide risks exacerbating existing inequalities in EFL education, with students from underprivileged backgrounds facing significant disadvantages. To promote inclusivity, educational policymakers must ensure that AI-driven resources are accessible and affordable, bridging the gap between privileged and underserved communities.

The unequal distribution of technological resources can create a two-tiered education system, where only those with access to advanced tools benefit from AI's potential. Addressing this divide requires strategic investments in infrastructure and targeted initiatives to provide underserved populations with the necessary tools and training to participate fully in AI-enhanced education. (Alghamdy, R. Z., 2023)

## 4.7. Human Interaction and Emotional Resonance

AI lacks the capacity to replicate the empathetic and emotionally responsive interactions provided by human educators. In language learning, emotional connection and tailored feedback are critical for student motivation and confidence. Over-reliance on AI may dehumanize the learning process, depriving learners of these vital elements and potentially undermining their overall educational experience.

Language learning is inherently social, relying on the exchange of ideas, cultural context, and emotional reinforcement. The absence of human interaction in AI-driven education risks reducing learning to a mechanical process, which may not resonate with all learners. Teachers must therefore complement AI tools with their unique ability to inspire, engage, and adapt to individual learner needs. (Neff, J., Arciaga, K., & Burri, M, 2024).

## 4.8. Transparency and Accountability

The opaque nature of AI algorithms raises questions about the fairness and accuracy of their outputs. In EFL contexts, learners and educators must understand how AI systems operate and make decisions. Ensuring transparency in AI development and deployment processes, coupled with mechanisms for accountability, is crucial to building trust and maintaining ethical standards in education.

Developers and educators must work collaboratively to demystify AI technologies, ensuring that users are aware of their limitations and potential biases. Transparent communication about how AI recommendations are generated can help build trust among learners and educators, fostering a more informed and ethical use of these tools.

# 5. CASE STUDIES AND PRACTICAL IMPLICATIONS

## 5.1. The Dawn of Personalized Learning

Imagine a classroom where every learner feels seen, heard, and understood—a place where the lessons are tailored not just to their abilities but to their aspirations and dreams. AI makes this vision a reality through personalized learning systems. These systems analyze individual student data, such as learning preferences, pace, and areas of struggle, to deliver customized content. No longer must students grapple with one-size-fits-all education. Instead, they can embark on learning journeys that resonate with their unique needs.

For example, intelligent tutoring systems (ITS) act as patient, attentive mentors, providing students with immediate feedback and guidance. These AI-powered tutors are not confined by time or fatigue; they are always available, ensuring no question goes unanswered. (VanLehn, K. 2011) Educators, in turn, are freed to focus on fostering creativity, critical thinking, and emotional growth—roles that technology, no matter how advanced, cannot replace.

## 5.2. Redefining Assessment and Accessibility

Assessment, a cornerstone of education, has often been fraught with challenges, from subjective grading to delayed feedback. AI transforms this process, making it more efficient, equitable, and insightful. Automated systems can evaluate student work with precision, providing detailed, constructive feedback in real-time. This not only saves educators precious time but also helps students identify their strengths and areas for improvement. AI's ability to analyze patterns in performance data enables teachers to intervene early and support struggling learners, ensuring no one is left behind.

Moreover, AI opens the doors of education to those previously marginalized. Students with disabilities often face barriers that traditional methods struggle to address. AI tools, such as speech-to-text converters and real-time captioning systems, create inclusive learning environments where every student can thrive. These innovations sustain a fundamental truth: education should be a right, not a privilege.

## 5.3. The Emotional Power of Engagement

At its heart, education is not just about imparting knowledge it is about inspiring curiosity, fostering resilience, and igniting a passion for learning. AI amplifies this emotional connection by creating interactive, engaging experiences that capture the imagination of students. Through gamified learning platforms, students can embark on quests, solve puzzles, and achieve milestones, transforming the often-daunting process of education into an exciting adventure. (Clark, R. C., & Mayer, R. E. 2016)

Consider a student who once struggled with mathematics. With the help of an AI-powered adaptive learning system, the subject is no longer a source of anxiety but a gateway to discovery. The system adjusts the difficulty of problems based on the student's progress, celebrating every success and providing gentle guidance through challenges. The result is a learner who feels empowered, not defeated a learner who begins to believe in their own potential.

## 5.4. The Rise of AI and Large Language Models

The emergence of AI, particularly LLMs, represents a seismic shift in educational technology. These models, powered by deep neural networks and self-supervised learning, can process vast amounts of information, generating insights and creating content with remarkable accuracy. Reinforcement learning from human feedback (HFRL) further refines these models, ensuring their outputs align with human preferences and ethical standards.

In education, LLMs have revolutionized areas such as automated feedback and personalized content generation (Zawacki-Richter, O., Marín, V. I., Bond, M., & Gouverneur, F. 2019). For instance, a teacher preparing a lesson on idiomatic expressions can use an LLM to generate diverse examples, tailored exercises, and even cultural context. Similarly, a student practicing essay writing can receive detailed feedback on structure, coherence, and style, all in real-time.

# 6. STRATEGIES FOR ETHICAL AI DEPLOYMENT

Artificial intelligence (AI) has become a day-by-day growing technological innovation, and it is also becoming a revolution in industries from the range of healthcare to education and beyond upcoming technologies. Along with this, there are some of the causes of ethical issues. So, neglected or ignored problems can weaken public trust, accountability, and fairness. For these reasons, this chapter will show us the importance of how to ethically deploy AI systems, focusing primarily on practical strategies to ensure that they align with technological progress and public and societal values.

As we are seeing AI technology is drastically evolving so quickly that it adds new ethical issues that may emerge. So, these issues must be recognized because a society must benefit from AI without causing any significant harm or major harm. Through this, we can see and fix issues like Bias in the AI system, Transparency, and accountability issues, and these issues make the Call for Actionable strategies and ethical AI deployment.

As per this issue, this chapter's goal is to bridge the gap between abstract ethical principles and real-world applications. By examining suitable practical strategies, such as enhancing transparency, mitigating biases, and establishing accountability frameworks, we will ensure that this chapter helps foster responsible AI development.

## 6.1. Why Ethical AI Deployment is Crucial

### 6.1.1. Bias and Fairness Issues:

The adoption of artificial intelligence (AI) in critical decision-making frameworks has brought to the forefront an important ethical challenge: bias. Many AI systems are trained on historical data that may contain existing social or systemic biases. If the data used to train AI remains unchecked, it can mimic or hallucinate and amplify existing biases, leading to unfair and discriminatory results. For example, predictive policing models often unfairly focus on the communities of color because they are using the arrest data, which is already biased. This may lead to more policing in these areas and it strengthens stereotypes (there is a fixed idea about a group of people). To stop these things, AI needs to be designed with fair and ethical values and human rights of equality too avoid discrimination between racism or color-based biases. When treating bias, it's not just about ensuring fairness. It also requires transparency about how AI systems make decisions. Without a clear explanation, biased results can be maintained undiscovered and unchallenged, reinforcing existing inequality. (Olatunji, Okoye, Ofodile, & Ugochukwu, 2024)

### 6.1.2. The "Black Box" Problem in AI Transparency:

A major issue in AI ethics is the "black box" problem — how opaque AI systems are in making decisions. There are some of the complex neural networks are indeed powerful, but they work in ways that are often incomprehensible even for their developers. IBM Watson for Oncology was also criticized for its recommendations for cancer treatment due to the reasons not being interpretable. Healthcare professionals who were unable to validate these recommendations questioned the system's reliability. Such examples highlight that Explainable AI (XAI) tools that provide transparency and breed trust among stakeholders need further attention and we should make AI tools where transparency is the priority that is where we humans are lacking

### 6.1.3. Lack of Accountability in Autonomous Decision-Making:

Autonomous devices, like driverless vehicles, give rise to complex questions of ethics and responsibility. The responsibility of the blame of an automotive manufacturer, the software creator, or the end-user becomes a confusing question when a self-driving car takes a crash. Programming these vehicles to make ethical decisions in rapid situations, such as prioritizing the safety of pedestrians over that of passengers, underscores the urgent requirement for clearly established accountability frameworks. Such frameworks must guarantee that all parties involved comprehend their roles and responsibilities regarding the creation and implementation of autonomous systems.

## 6.2. Core Strategies for Ethical AI Deployment

### 6.2.1. Transparency:

Ensuring transparency in artificial intelligence necessitates the development of systems that exactly communicate their decision-making processes. This approach cultivates a trust among users and allows stakeholders to assess the ethical consequences of AI-generated outcomes.

Explainable AI (XAI) methodologies, including decision trees and layer-wise relevance propagation, play a crucial role in enhancing the ability to understand the reasoning behind the predictions and decisions of AI systems. For instance, XAI techniques have been effectively utilized in the healthcare sector, where providing clear explanations for AI-generated diagnostic suggestions encourages the development and trust among healthcare professionals and patients.

Moreover, open data initiatives promote transparency by enabling external examination of the datasets employed in training AI systems. Developers are urged to thoroughly document their data sources, potential biases, and preprocessing techniques, allowing stakeholders to assess the fairness and dependability of AI models. Ethical AI frameworks, such as the IEEE Global Initiative on Ethics of Autonomous and Intelligent Systems, offer comprehensive guidelines to ensure transparency is integrated throughout the AI development process.

### 6.2.2. Bias Mitigation:

Addressing bias necessitates a proactive strategy that includes the use, fairness metrics, diverse datasets, and ongoing monitoring. Fairness metrics, such as demographic parity and equalized odds, are essential for measuring and mitigating disparities in algorithmic results. For example, it was discovered that AI-based credit scoring systems disproportionately affected certain demographic groups due to biased training data. By incorporating diverse datasets and utilizing fairness metrics, financial institutions have successfully diminished these disparities, leading to more equitable outcomes.

Continuous monitoring is crucial. Biases can develop or change over time, especially as AI systems work with new data. Incorporating user feedback, conducting ethical audits, and performing regular assessments and checks will help developers spot and fix biases, ensuring AI systems reflect societal values.

### 6.2.3. Accountability:

Accountability in AI use means clearly outlining the roles and responsibilities of everyone involved. Ethical governance, like committees within organizations, can oversee AI projects to make sure they follow ethical guidelines. These committees usually consist of experts from various fields—technical, ethical, legal, and social—to provide a well-rounded view on AI development.

Human-in-the-loop (HITL) methods improve accountability by adding human oversight to AI decision-making. For example, in autonomous systems, HITL frameworks allow humans to step in during critical situations, ensuring AI decisions meet ethical standards. This method balances automation with human judgment, reducing risks linked to fully autonomous systems.

### 6.2.4. Data Protection:

Data protection questions are of paramount importance in AI ethics, especially when dealing with sensitive data. Federated Learning is a technique that KI models can use to train data from a variety of sources without moving the raw data. This method was successfully used in healthcare, ensuring patient data and simultaneously improving AI models. By removing personally identifiable information from data records, developers can protect user privacy and continue to use data effectively for AI training. However, strong protection is required to avoid the risk of new identification.

Here ethical regulations in education are particularly important as AI shapes a wide range of sectors, affecting teaching methods, student learning experiences, and data protection. Ensuring that navigational educators are equipped with these ethical considerations is crucial for responsible AI integration in the classroom.

## 6.3. Empowering Educators – Training Teachers To Integrate AI Without Compromising Their Roles:

As AI continues to influence a variety of sectors, the role of educators must have knowledge and skills to integrate AI into classes and maintain its important role as learning at the same time while maintaining their critical role as facilitators of learning.

### 6.3.1. Educator Approval:

Training teachers for AI integration. Educators who are effective in training teachers without compromising the role of AI control tools such as intelligent tutoring systems (ITS), AI operational analysis, virtual reality (VR), and automated evaluation tools are adaptive and effective. Provides attractive instructions. Despite these advances, many teachers face challenges in understanding and effective use of AI, and require structured training programs without reducing their role as a mediator of learning.

### 6.3.2. The Role Of AI In Teacher Training

AI plays an important role in improving professional development for educators. One of the most important AI tools in teacher training is the intelligent individualized tutoring system (ITS) that provides a personalized adaptive learning experience. You can analyze teacher performance and recommend TaylorMade training modules to ensure continuous professional growth. Similarly, AI control analytics can help educators assess student learning trends and improve their teaching strategies based on real-time data. These technologies can help drive data-controlled decision-making and enable educators to pursue student commitments and identify areas where additional educational support is needed.

### 6.3.3. Virtual Reality (VR) and Augmented Reality (AR):

These are also very important in teacher training. These immersive technologies allow educators to practice teaching strategies in a simulated classroom environment, reducing the gap between theoretical learning and real applications. For example, VR-based training programs allow teachers to experiment with a variety of educational approaches in risk-free environments and increase trust and motivation before these strategies are implemented in real classrooms. By providing interactive feedback in real time, these AI control simulations help teachers improve classroom management, communication and teaching skills. Optimize frames for classification and feedback processes. These systems allow teachers to focus more on interactive learning and student commitment rather than spending too much time on administrative tasks. The foundation of natural language processing (NLP)-based assessment instruments can generate immediate feedback to assess student answers and ensure that educators bring to education despite many benefits. Masu. Lack of AI alphabetization among teachers. Many educators are unfamiliar with the mechanisms of AI, its ethical implications, and risks associated with biased algorithms. When AI control tools are increasingly distributed, it is important for teacher training programs to include AI alphabetization modules. These programs should focus on AI skills, skills and limitations. To strengthen the difference.

Digital Ability Development Educators develop educational plans, assessments and ways to effectively use AI control platforms for students.

Data Protection and Security Training for Data Protection and Security Training "Guidelines for Ensuring Student and Teacher Data Protection in an AI-enabled Learning Environment -

Also, the possibility of transformation is the teacher We also present several challenges in implementation in training. The key issue is that distortions in AI models can maintain existing inequality when they are not carefully monitored. For example, if AI-involved assessment equipment is trained with biased data records, it can provide inaccurate or unfair assessments of student performance. Teachers should have strategies to identify and mitigate distortions in AI-controlled decision-making processes.

Another issue is data protection. AI-operated platforms require access to student and teacher data to provide personalized recommendations. However, without strict data management guidelines, there is a risk of unauthorized access, data abuse, or violations. Teachers should train their AI use to ensure compliance with global data protection regulations such as GDPR and FERPA. The role of traditional education. AI can improve instruction through automation of administrative tasks, but it should not be seen as an alternative to human teachers. Instead, AI should be positioned as a collaborative tool to support educators in granting more personalized and more effective lessons. Training programs must emphasize the Human-AI partnership and ensure that AI functions as a supplementary tool for teachers. (Meylani, 2024)

AI could improve education, but ethical implications such as bias, data protection and the balance between human and AI decisions remain unresolved. These challenges are not limited to education, but span all AI applications that require ongoing discussion and innovative solutions.

## 6.4. Challenges and Future Directions

### 6.4.1. Limitations to Current Strategies:

Despite the progress in the use of ethical AI, there are still challenges. Efforts for transpareny are often blocked by the complex nature of modern AI models, particularly deep learning. Furthermore, strategies to reduce bias are difficult to keep up with changing ideas for equity and social norms. Wide range of views and values. Public discussion and co-design will likely play a key role in the development of ethical AI.

### 6.4.2. Future Trends

Explainable AI Improvements: Future research focuses on finding a balance between model performance and simple understanding to clarify complex AI systems without losing accuracy

### 6.4.3. Interdisciplinary Cooperation:

The use of ethical AI requires teamwork between engineers, ethicists, political makers, and sociologists. This joint approach means that ethical guidelines not only address technical issues but also social and cultural factors. Building partnerships in various fields allows stakeholders to develop AI systems that respond to innovative and social values.

## 7. CONCLUSION

The integration of AI in education is no longer a distant possibility—it is an urgent necessity. As we navigate the intersection of tradition and innovation, educators must embrace AI's potential to transform teaching and learning. With its ability to analyze vast amounts of data, personalize instruction, and adapt to individual student needs, AI can break down barriers, foster inclusivity, and create classrooms where every learner feels valued and empowered. However, embracing AI does not mean replacing educators; rather, it enhances their ability to engage students and deliver more effective learning experiences.

To ensure successful implementation, organizations and institutions must proactively address critical challenges such as data quality, security, system integration, and employee preparedness. AI deployment requires a systematic approach, ongoing teacher training, and scalable solutions that align with long-term educational goals. Without these foundational elements, AI's potential may remain underutilized or create unintended disparities in learning access.

Additionally, ethical considerations must remain at the forefront of AI integration. Algorithmic bias, data privacy, and equitable access require careful oversight and collaboration among educators, policymakers, researchers, and technology developers. Establishing clear guidelines and fostering continuous dialogue will help AI serve as a tool for empowerment rather than a source of inequity or overreliance.

Ultimately, the future of AI in education depends on a balanced approach—one that harnesses its strengths while mitigating risks. By combining AI's analytical power with the irreplaceable role of human educators, we can create a more inclusive, efficient, and innovative educational landscape. With thoughtful planning and ethical responsibility, AI can be a transformative force that reshapes learning for generations to come, ensuring that technology serves as a bridge to progress rather than a barrier to equity.

## REFERENCES


Akinrinola, O., Okoye, C. C., Ofodile, O. C., & Ugochukwu, C. E. (2024). Navigating and reviewing ethical dilemmas in AI development: Strategies for transparency, fairness, and accountability. *GSC Advanced Research and Reviews, 18*(3), 50–58. DOI: 10.30574/gscarr.2024.18.3.0088

Aldoseri, A., Al-Khalifa, K. N., & Hamouda, A. M. (2023). Re-thinking data strategy and integration for artificial intelligence: Concepts, opportunities, and challenges. *Applied Sciences (Basel, Switzerland), 13*(12), 7082. DOI: 10.3390/app13127082

Alghamdy, R. Z. (2023). Pedagogical and ethical implications of artificial intelligence in EFL context: A review study. *English Language Teaching, 16*(10), 87–98. DOI: 10.5539/elt.v16n10p87

Brynjolfsson, E., & McAfee, A. (2017). *Machine, platform, crowd: Harnessing our digital future*. W. W. Norton & Company.

Castillo, R., Lin, C., & Zhang, Y. (2023). The effects of neural machine translation tools on vocabulary acquisition and learner confidence in EFL contexts. *Computer Assisted Language Learning, 36*(2), 145–160. DOI: 10.1080/09588221.2022.2100212

Chen, H., Sun, J., & Li, X. (2020). Meta-analysis of AI-assisted language learning: A review of recent developments. *Journal of Educational Technology & Society, 23*(4), 100–113. https://www.jstor.org/stable/26915413

Chen, X., Wang, Y., & Li, J. (2020). Automated essay scoring in rural and urban Chinese schools: Adoption and challenges. *Asia Pacific Education Review, 21*(4), 567–580. DOI: 10.1007/s12564-020-09658-6

Chiu, T. K. F., Chen, J. M., & Chung, S. (2023). Artificial intelligence in language education: A systematic review and research agenda. *British Journal of Educational Technology, 54*(1), 5–28. DOI: 10.1111/bjet.13232

Hanyi, X., Wensheng, G., Zhenlian, Q., Jiayang, W., & Philip, S. Y. (2023). Large language models for education: A survey. *arXiv preprint arXiv:2302.12345*. https://arxiv.org/abs/2302.12345

Heffernan, N., & Heffernan, C. (2014). The ASSISTments ecosystem: Building a platform that brings scientists and teachers together for minimally invasive research on human learning and teaching. *International Journal of Artificial Intelligence in Education, 24*(4), 470–497. DOI: 10.1007/s40593-014-0024-x

Hoofnagle, C. J., Van Der Sloot, B., & Borgesius, F. Z. (2019). The European Union general data protection regulation: What it is and what it means. *Information & Communications Technology Law*, *28*(1), 65–98. DOI: 10.1080/13600834.2019.1573501

IEEE. (2023). *Ethically aligned design: A vision for prioritizing human well-being with autonomous and intelligent systems* (2nd ed.). IEEE Standards Association. https://standards.ieee.org/industry-connections/ec/autonomous-systems/

Krishnan, R., & Zaini, M. (2025). Large language models in EFL classrooms: Opportunities and overreliance. [Add DOI if available]. *Journal of AI and Education*, *12*(1), 33–52.

Kukulska-Hulme, A., Lee, H., & Norris, L. (2020). Machine feedback in EFL writing: Teacher perceptions and learner challenges. *Language Learning & Technology*, *24*(3), 15–34. https://www.lltjournal.org/item/3102

Lan, Y. J. (2020). Immersion, interaction, and experience-oriented learning: AI-enhanced virtual reality for EFL students. *ReCALL*, *32*(1), 71–87. DOI: 10.1017/S0958344019000209

Luckin, R., Holmes, W., Griffiths, M., & Forcier, L. B. (2016). *Intelligence unleashed: An argument for AI in education*. Pearson. https://www.pearson.com/content/dam/one-dot-com/one-dot-com/global/Files/about-pearson/innovation/open-ideas/Intelligence-Unleashed-Publication.pdf

Meylani, R. (2024). Artificial intelligence in the education of teachers: A qualitative synthesis of the cutting-edge research literature. *Journal of Computer and Education Research*, *12*(24), 600–637. DOI: 10.18009/jcer.1477709

Neff, J., Arciaga, K., & Burri, M. (2024). EFL students' and teachers' perceptions of the ethical uses of AI tools. *Technology in Language Teaching & Learning*, *6*(3), 1714. Advance online publication. DOI: 10.29140/tltl.v6n3.1714

Nguyen, L. T., & Ikeda, M. (2021). Automated feedback and EFL learners' writing performance: A comparative study. *System*, *99*, 102514. DOI: 10.1016/j.system.2021.102514

Nguyen, T. T. H., & Ikeda, M. (2021). Artificial intelligence in EFL learning: Enhancing writing skills with automated feedback. *Language Learning & Technology*, *25*(3), 130–146. https://www.lltjournal.org/item/3242

UNESCO. (2024). *AI and education: Guidance for policy makers*. United Nations Educational, Scientific and Cultural Organization. https://unesdoc.unesco.org/ark:/48223/pf0000382000

Wang, Y., & Spector, J. M. (2023). AI-powered chatbots in language learning: A systematic review. *Computers & Education, 194*, 104739. DOI: 10.1016/j.compedu.2023.104739

Zawacki-Richter, O., Marín, V. I., Bond, M., & Gouverneur, F. (2019). Systematic review of research on artificial intelligence applications in higher education: Where are the educators? *International Journal of Educational Technology in Higher Education, 16*(1), 39. Advance online publication. DOI: 10.1186/s41239-019-0171-0

# Chapter 6
# Chatbots for Conversation:
## AI's Role in Transforming English Learning

**Papi Naidu Mavidi**
https://orcid.org/0000-0003-0706-8094
*Aditya Institute of Technology and Managemnt, India*

## ABSTRACT

*This study investigates the role of AI-powered chatbots in enhancing conversational English skills among learners. As digital tools become increasingly integrated into education, chatbots offer interactive, real-time language practice that traditional methods often lack. By providing personalized feedback, error correction, and continuous conversational exposure, chatbots create an engaging learning environment that fosters fluency, accuracy, and confidence. This research aims to assess the effectiveness of chatbot-assisted learning by examining its impact on learners' fluency, motivation, and retention of conversational skills. Through a mixed-method approach involving pre- and post-tests, surveys, and qualitative interviews, this study will provide insights into the potential of AI chatbots as a transformative tool for English language education. The findings are expected to guide educators in incorporating AI technologies to enhance learner outcomes and promote autonomous language learning.*

DOI: 10.4018/979-8-3373-0969-9.ch006

# 1. INTRODUCTION

## 1.1 The Evolution of Language Learning

Language learning has evolved significantly over the years, from traditional classroom instruction to technology-enhanced methodologies. With the advent of Artificial Intelligence (AI), this evolution has taken a quantum leap, particularly with the introduction of chatbots for conversational practice. Chatbots, powered by sophisticated AI algorithms, offer learners the opportunity to engage in interactive, personalized, and adaptive conversations that mimic real-world interactions. This paradigm shift has opened up new possibilities for mastering English, transforming how learners develop their listening, speaking, reading, and writing (LSRW) skills.

Chatbots are artificial intelligence (AI) systems designed to simulate human conversation. These programs interact with users through text or voice, aiming to provide responses that are coherent and contextually appropriate. Chatbots are primarily used in customer service, virtual assistance, e-commerce, and other digital environments where quick and automated interaction is required.

## 1.2 Types of Chatbots

There are two main types of chatbots:

1. **Rule-based (Scripted) Chatbots**: These operate on predefined rules and scripts. The chatbot's responses are based on specific inputs, and the system follows a decision tree to generate appropriate replies. They are limited in their functionality and cannot handle unpredictable or complex conversations. Rule-based chatbots are best suited for handling frequently asked questions (FAQs) or simple tasks.
2. **AI-powered (Intelligent) Chatbots**: These chatbots are more advanced and utilize machine learning (ML) and natural language processing (NLP) to understand and interpret user inputs. They can learn from previous interactions, improving their responses over time. AI chatbots can handle more complex queries and provide more dynamic, personalized interactions compared to rule-based ones.

## 1.3 How Chatbots Work

Chatbots function by processing user inputs and generating responses based on the system's underlying algorithms. The process generally involves:

1. **User Input**: The user types a question or request into the chatbot interface.

2. **Natural Language Processing (NLP)**: The chatbot processes the text or voice input to understand the meaning behind the query. NLP techniques help the system break down the sentence structure, identify keywords, and understand context.
3. **Intent Recognition**: Based on the NLP analysis, the chatbot identifies the user's intent, i.e., what the user wants to achieve. For example, if a user asks about the weather, the chatbot recognizes the intent as a request for weather information.
4. **Response Generation**: After identifying the intent, the chatbot retrieves an appropriate response from a knowledge base or generates a response using machine learning models.
5. **Learning and Improvement**: In AI chatbots, responses improve over time as the system learns from user interactions and feedback.

## 1.4 Applications of Chatbots

Chatbots have become ubiquitous in many industries due to their ability to automate tasks and enhance customer experience. Common applications include:

1. **Customer Service**: Chatbots can handle inquiries, provide support, and resolve issues, offering a more efficient alternative to human agents. This reduces wait times and ensures 24/7 availability.
2. **E-commerce**: Chatbots assist customers in navigating online stores, recommending products, and helping with checkout processes.
3. **Healthcare**: AI chatbots help schedule appointments, provide medical advice, or answer health-related questions, making healthcare services more accessible.
4. **Education**: Chatbots are used as educational tools to answer student questions, deliver course content, and support learning.
5. **Entertainment and Social Media**: Chatbots can engage users through games, quizzes, and interactive content on social media platforms.

## 1.5 Benefits of Chatbots

1. **24/7 Availability**: Chatbots can provide round-the-clock assistance, ensuring users receive help at any time of the day.
2. **Cost-Effective**: By automating repetitive tasks, chatbots reduce the need for large customer support teams, saving businesses money.
3. **Improved User Experience**: With quick and efficient responses, chatbots enhance user satisfaction and engagement.
4. **Personalization**: AI-powered chatbots can tailor responses to individual users based on their preferences and past interactions.

## 1.6 Challenges and Limitations

Despite their advantages, chatbots face several challenges. Rule-based chatbots struggle with handling complex, nuanced conversations, while AI chatbots may require large datasets and constant updates to improve accuracy. Moreover, some users may find chatbot interactions impersonal or frustrating, particularly when the bot cannot provide adequate solutions.

In conclusion, chatbots represent a powerful tool for improving communication and automating tasks. As AI continues to evolve, chatbots will become even more sophisticated, offering more human-like and efficient interactions across various industries.

The role of Artificial Intelligence (AI) in education has been steadily increasing, transforming how students learn, how educators teach, and how institutions operate. AI is bringing about significant changes in educational practices, enhancing personalized learning, improving administrative processes, and providing innovative solutions to long-standing challenges. As AI technologies continue to evolve, their impact on the education sector is expected to grow even further.

## 1.7 Personalized Learning

One of the most significant contributions of AI in education is its ability to personalize learning experiences. Traditional classroom settings often follow a one-size-fits-all approach, which may not cater to the individual needs and learning styles of all students. AI, however, can tailor lessons and resources to meet the specific needs of each student. By analyzing student data, such as past performance, preferences, and learning pace, AI systems can create personalized learning pathways that adjust in real-time as students progress. This ensures that learners are neither overwhelmed nor underchallenged, improving their engagement and retention.

For example, AI-powered tools can provide real-time feedback on assignments, quizzes, and exams, helping students understand their strengths and areas for improvement. This immediate feedback fosters a more responsive learning environment and allows educators to spend more time addressing individual concerns.

## 1.8 Enhanced Teacher Support

AI also acts as a valuable tool for teachers by automating administrative tasks, such as grading and lesson planning, which can be time-consuming. This allows educators to focus more on teaching and interacting with students. AI can grade assignments, evaluate essays, and provide instant feedback on students' work, freeing up valuable time for instructors to focus on other aspects of their role.

Furthermore, AI-based tools can assist teachers in identifying students who may be struggling, offering recommendations for interventions or additional support. By providing real-time analytics on student performance, AI helps teachers make data-driven decisions, ensuring that no student is left behind.

## 1.9 Virtual Tutors and Assistants

Another growing trend in AI-powered education is the use of virtual tutors and assistants. These AI-driven systems provide students with on-demand support, answering questions, explaining concepts, and offering extra practice outside of regular school hours. Virtual tutors can simulate one-on-one interactions, offering students personalized assistance without the need for human intervention.

For example, AI tutors can help students with subjects such as math, science, or language arts by offering step-by-step explanations, solving problems, and even adapting the difficulty level based on the student's progress. This technology bridges the gap for students who may need additional help but do not have access to a teacher or tutor immediately.

## 1.10 Administrative Efficiency and Data Management

AI also plays a pivotal role in improving the administrative side of education. Machine learning algorithms can streamline processes such as scheduling, admissions, and resource allocation. By analyzing large datasets, AI systems can identify trends and patterns that can help schools and universities make more informed decisions. For example, AI can predict which students are most likely to succeed in certain courses, helping institutions offer the right courses to the right students.

Additionally, AI enables more efficient resource management, optimizing classroom usage, allocating teaching materials, and even predicting future enrollment trends to help institutions plan accordingly.

## 1.11 Challenges and Ethical Concerns

While the potential benefits of AI in education are vast, there are challenges and ethical concerns that need to be addressed. Data privacy is a major issue, as AI systems rely on student data to provide personalized learning experiences. Ensuring that this data is used responsibly and ethically is crucial to maintaining trust and protecting students' privacy.

Moreover, there is concern about the impact of AI on educators' roles. While AI can assist teachers, there are worries that overreliance on technology could dehumanize the learning experience and reduce the importance of face-to-face interactions in education.

## 1.12 Personalized Learning Experience

One of the main features of chatbots in English learning is their ability to provide a personalized learning experience. Chatbots use AI algorithms to analyze the learner's progress, preferences, and skill level, adjusting their responses and activities to meet individual needs. This customization ensures that learners can work at their own pace and focus on areas where they need improvement, such as grammar, vocabulary, or pronunciation. For instance, a beginner learner might focus on basic vocabulary and simple sentences, while an advanced learner could engage in more complex conversations and explore idiomatic expressions.

## 1.13. Instant Feedback and Correction

Chatbots excel in providing real-time feedback, which is essential for language learners to identify mistakes and improve. Whether it's a typo, grammatical error, or incorrect word usage, chatbots can immediately point out errors and suggest corrections. This feature allows learners to improve their language skills autonomously, without waiting for a teacher's intervention. For example, when a learner makes a mistake in sentence structure, the chatbot can not only highlight the error but also provide an explanation or example of the correct usage. This instant feedback enhances learning and reinforces correct usage of the language.

## 1.14. Language Practice Through Conversational Interactions

Chatbots offer learners an opportunity to practice their English through simulated conversations, which is crucial for developing speaking and listening skills. These chatbots can engage in dialogues on a variety of topics, encouraging learners to respond in English and improving their conversational fluency. Many chatbots are designed to simulate real-life situations, such as ordering food in a restaurant or asking for directions, allowing learners to practice language in context. Through repeated interaction, learners can build confidence and improve their ability to understand and produce spoken English.

## 1.15. Accessibility and Convenience

One of the key advantages of chatbots in English learning is their accessibility. Learners can interact with chatbots anytime and from anywhere, making language practice more flexible and convenient. This 24/7 availability ensures that learners can practice English at their convenience, regardless of their schedule or location. Whether through mobile apps or websites, chatbots are easily accessible, allowing learners to fit language practice into their busy lives. This convenience is especially beneficial for learners in remote areas or those who do not have easy access to formal language classes.

## 1.16. Increased Engagement and Motivation

Chatbots are designed to be engaging, with features such as gamification, quizzes, and interactive lessons. These elements make the learning process fun and motivating, encouraging learners to continue practicing and improving their skills. By setting challenges, offering rewards, and tracking progress, chatbots can help learners stay motivated and focused on their goals. For instance, a chatbot might offer a badge for completing a certain number of lessons or quizzes, providing a sense of accomplishment that fuels further learning.

## 1.17. Data-Driven Insights for Learners and Teachers

AI-powered chatbots can track learners' progress over time, providing valuable insights into their strengths and weaknesses. By analyzing data such as response time, accuracy, and learning patterns, chatbots can generate detailed reports that help both learners and teachers identify areas for improvement. For instance, if a student struggles with a particular grammatical concept, the chatbot can highlight this in its reports, allowing teachers to offer targeted support. Similarly, learners can use the data to monitor their own progress and set specific learning goals.

## 1.18. Support for All Four Language Skills

Chatbots can support the development of all four key language skills: reading, writing, listening, and speaking. They can present reading comprehension exercises, provide writing prompts, assess listening abilities through audio clips, and engage in speaking exercises through voice recognition. This holistic approach to language learning ensures that learners can develop a well-rounded proficiency in English.

## 1.19. Listening Skills: From Passive to Active Learning

Listening, often seen as a passive skill, has transformed into an active learning process with the help of technology. Traditional listening activities like audio recordings or classroom lectures are now complemented by AI-driven tools and interactive platforms that simulate real-life listening situations. Tools like speech recognition software can help learners assess their understanding in real time. For instance, language apps and chatbots can play audio clips and ask learners to transcribe, summarize, or answer questions based on the content. This shifts listening from mere comprehension to active engagement, where learners are prompted to analyze, respond, and interact with the material.

Moreover, technology allows learners to access a wide variety of listening materials, from podcasts to interviews, providing exposure to diverse accents, tones, and speeds of speech. This variety helps learners adapt to different speaking styles, thereby enhancing their listening skills in various contexts, such as social conversations, professional discussions, and academic lectures.

## 1.20. Speaking Skills: Encouraging Real-Time Interaction

Speaking is perhaps the most challenging skill for many language learners due to the fear of making mistakes. However, modern technology and AI-driven applications have transformed the speaking process into an interactive, judgment-free experience. Voice recognition tools, virtual tutors, and conversational chatbots create a safe environment for learners to practice speaking without the pressure of face-to-face interactions. These tools can simulate real-life conversations, allowing learners to practice pronunciation, fluency, and even complex sentence structures.

AI applications also offer personalized feedback on aspects like pronunciation, intonation, and grammar, enabling learners to improve continuously. Speech-based tools such as language assistants (e.g., Siri, Alexa) or AI-powered language-learning apps can simulate natural conversations, making learners feel more comfortable while practicing speaking. This encourages consistent practice, essential for building confidence and fluency in spoken English.

## 1.21. Reading Skills: Interactive and Adaptive Learning

Reading, a critical skill in any language, has evolved from traditional textbook methods to more dynamic and interactive approaches. Digital platforms now provide learners with access to a variety of reading materials, such as e-books, articles, and interactive stories, all of which can be tailored to a learner's proficiency level. AI-powered platforms can suggest reading material based on the learner's interests and comprehension levels, ensuring that the content is engaging and appropriately challenging.

Interactive reading apps often include features like built-in dictionaries, summaries, and comprehension questions. Learners can instantly check their understanding of a text, receive context for unfamiliar words, and test their comprehension through quizzes. Furthermore, AI-based tools can track reading habits, assess progress, and provide personalized recommendations for improvement, fostering a more engaging and adaptive learning experience.

## 1.22. Writing Skills: Instant Feedback and Collaborative Tools

Writing, an essential skill for academic and professional communication, has been transformed by digital tools that provide instant feedback, enhance creativity, and foster collaboration. Language-learning platforms often offer grammar and style checkers, such as Grammarly, that help learners identify and correct mistakes in real time, improving both their writing skills and self-awareness. These tools not only correct spelling and grammatical errors but also suggest improvements in sentence structure, coherence, and tone, helping learners refine their writing.

Collaborative platforms, like Google Docs or other writing tools, enable learners to work together on writing assignments, allowing for peer feedback and collaborative editing. This collaborative approach mimics real-world communication and provides a more interactive way to practice writing. Additionally, AI-driven writing assistants can help learners brainstorm ideas, outline essays, and generate content, offering guidance throughout the writing process.

Chatbots are increasingly being used in English language learning due to their ability to enhance engagement, provide personalized instruction, and offer instant feedback. These AI-driven tools offer several benefits for learners, transforming traditional language learning methods and making them more interactive, efficient, and accessible. Here are some of the key benefits of using chatbots in English learning:

## 1.23 24/7 Availability

Another major advantage of using chatbots in English learning is their availability around the clock. Unlike traditional teachers, who are bound by class schedules, chatbots are always accessible. Learners can interact with chatbots anytime and anywhere, making language practice more flexible and convenient. Whether a student wants to practice in the morning, during a lunch break, or late at night, the chatbot will be ready to assist. This flexibility is especially beneficial for learners who have irregular schedules or live in different time zones.

### 1.24 Reduced Anxiety and Increased Confidence

For many language learners, speaking or interacting in English can be a source of anxiety. They may feel self-conscious about making mistakes in front of others. Chatbots offer a non-judgmental, pressure-free environment where learners can practice speaking and writing without fear of criticism. This safe space encourages learners to be more adventurous with their language use, improving their confidence over time. The chatbot's patient, error-correcting nature ensures that learners feel supported as they work through their challenges.

### 1.25 Engagement and Motivation

Chatbots make learning more engaging and fun. Many chatbots are designed with gamified elements, such as quizzes, points, and levels, to keep learners motivated. By incorporating interactive tasks, language games, and challenges, chatbots turn learning into an enjoyable activity rather than a chore. These gamified features can increase student motivation and encourage consistent practice, which is crucial for language acquisition. Learners are more likely to engage regularly with chatbots due to their interactive nature, leading to faster progress.

### 1.26 Real-Life Conversation Practice

Chatbots enable learners to practice real-life conversations in a controlled environment. They simulate various scenarios, such as ordering food, asking for directions, or having a job interview, providing learners with practical speaking opportunities. Since these bots can handle a wide range of topics and can adapt to different levels of language complexity, learners are exposed to a variety of situations that they might encounter in the real world. This practice helps learners develop fluency and prepares them for everyday communication in English.

### 1.27 Continuous Learning and Progress Tracking

Chatbots can track learners' progress over time, offering insights into their strengths and weaknesses. By analyzing patterns in the learner's responses, chatbots can identify areas where improvement is needed, such as specific grammar rules or vocabulary gaps. Additionally, chatbots can offer personalized suggestions for further practice based on these insights, ensuring that learners focus on the areas that need the most attention. This continuous tracking helps learners stay motivated and ensures that their progress is on the right track.

## 1.28 Cost-Effective Learning

In comparison to private tutors or formal language classes, chatbots are a more cost-effective learning option. Many chatbot applications are free or available at a fraction of the cost of traditional language learning methods. This affordability makes English learning accessible to a larger audience, including those who may not have the resources for in-person classes or tutoring. Additionally, since chatbots can handle multiple learners simultaneously, they can provide efficient and scalable support.

## 1.29 Limited Understanding of Complex Language

Despite advances in natural language processing (NLP) and AI, chatbots still face difficulties in understanding complex or nuanced language. While they can handle basic conversations and provide feedback on common mistakes, chatbots often struggle with more sophisticated linguistic features such as idiomatic expressions, complex sentence structures, or sarcasm. This limitation means that learners may encounter situations where the chatbot cannot accurately interpret their input or provide meaningful responses. Additionally, chatbots may fail to grasp cultural contexts or provide appropriate suggestions for regional variations in language use, which are essential for fluent communication.

## 1.30 Lack of Emotional Intelligence

One significant limitation of chatbots is their inability to replicate human emotions, empathy, and understanding. Language learning is not just about mastering grammar and vocabulary; it also involves developing emotional intelligence and social skills. Interacting with a real person provides learners with emotional cues, such as tone of voice, facial expressions, and body language, which are vital for effective communication. Chatbots, being purely text-based or voice-based, cannot offer these human-like interactions, potentially limiting the social and emotional aspects of learning. Learners may miss out on crucial opportunities to develop soft skills such as empathy, tone modulation, and conversational nuance.

## 1.31 Overreliance on Technology

While chatbots provide a convenient and interactive way to practice English, there is a concern that learners may become overreliant on technology. Language learning is best when it is varied and dynamic, incorporating different methods such as face-to-face interaction, reading, listening, and real-world practice. If learners exclusively rely on chatbots, they may miss out on the benefits of engaging with real people and practicing in diverse settings. Overuse of chatbots could also lead to the development of passive learning habits, where learners focus more on completing tasks or answering questions rather than engaging in meaningful conversation or critical thinking.

## 1.31 Data Privacy and Security Concerns

As chatbots rely on user data to personalize learning experiences, concerns about data privacy and security have emerged. Learners often provide personal information, such as their age, location, and learning preferences, which can be used to customize lessons and feedback. However, if this data is not properly protected or managed, it can be vulnerable to misuse or breach. There is also the issue of consent, as users may not always be fully aware of how their data is being used or stored. For chatbots to be trusted and widely adopted, educational institutions and developers must ensure that they comply with data privacy regulations and maintain transparent data policies.

## 1.32 Limited Language Support

While many chatbots are available in English, there is a limitation in terms of the languages they support. For learners whose first language is not English, chatbots often lack the ability to communicate effectively in other languages, limiting their accessibility. This is particularly problematic in non-English-speaking regions, where learners may benefit from bilingual or multilingual chatbots to help bridge the gap between their native language and English. The lack of language support can create barriers for a significant portion of potential users.

## 1.33 Quality of AI-Based Feedback

Although chatbots can provide instant feedback, the quality and accuracy of this feedback are not always guaranteed. AI algorithms rely on patterns in data to evaluate and correct responses, but they may not always recognize the learner's intent or context. For example, a chatbot may provide feedback on a grammatical mistake without fully explaining the underlying rule or offering a clear rationale for the correction. This lack of detailed explanations can hinder learners' deeper understanding of language concepts and may lead to confusion or frustration, especially for beginners who require more comprehensive guidance.

## 1.34 Limited Scope of Interaction

While chatbots excel in providing repetitive and structured practice, they have a limited scope in terms of creating dynamic, open-ended conversations. Real-world communication often involves unpredictability and a wide range of topics, which chatbots may not be equipped to handle effectively. For instance, a learner might want to discuss abstract topics, engage in debates, or explore diverse viewpoints, but the chatbot's responses may be limited or formulaic. This restricts the chatbot's ability to facilitate more advanced conversational practice and hinder learners from developing fluency in spontaneous dialogues.

## 1.35 Enhanced Natural Language Understanding

One of the most significant developments in the future of chatbots for English learning is the improvement of natural language understanding. Current chatbots are already capable of handling basic interactions, but their ability to comprehend complex language structures, idiomatic expressions, and context-specific conversations is still limited. In the future, chatbots will be able to process more intricate language elements, including sarcasm, humor, cultural nuances, and advanced grammatical structures. With enhanced NLP capabilities, chatbots will be able to engage in more meaningful and realistic conversations, making language learning feel closer to real-life interactions.

## 1.36 Multi-Modal Learning Experiences

As the demand for more engaging and immersive learning experiences grows, future chatbots will likely integrate multi-modal learning methods that combine text, audio, and visual elements. For example, chatbots could incorporate voice recognition technology to assess pronunciation and provide real-time corrective feedback, allowing learners to practice speaking and listening more effectively. Additionally, chatbots could use multimedia resources like videos, images, and interactive simulations to explain language concepts or contextualize vocabulary and grammar in different settings. This multi-sensory approach would cater to different learning styles and offer a richer, more engaging language acquisition experience.

## 1.37 Integration with Augmented and Virtual Reality

The integration of chatbots with augmented reality (AR) and virtual reality (VR) technologies is expected to be a game-changer for language learning. With AR and VR, learners can immerse themselves in realistic environments, where they can interact with virtual characters, practice their speaking and listening skills in context, and engage in situational language learning. For instance, learners could participate in virtual role-playing activities, such as ordering food in a virtual restaurant or conducting business meetings in a virtual office. The combination of chatbots with AR/VR would provide a dynamic and interactive environment that simulates real-world experiences, allowing learners to practice their language skills in a more authentic setting.

## 1.38 Personalized and Adaptive Learning Paths

The future of chatbot-assisted English learning will involve highly personalized and adaptive learning pathways. Chatbots will not only adapt to a learner's language proficiency but also tailor their teaching strategies based on individual preferences, strengths, weaknesses, and learning goals. AI-powered systems will continuously monitor learners' progress and adjust the difficulty level of lessons and exercises to ensure steady growth. This personalized approach will help students focus on their specific areas of improvement, whether it's vocabulary, pronunciation, or grammar, creating a more effective and efficient learning experience.

## 1.39 Greater Emotional and Social Intelligence

As AI continues to evolve, future chatbots will likely exhibit a greater degree of emotional and social intelligence. While current chatbots can provide basic feedback, they often lack the empathy and understanding that comes from human interactions. However, with improvements in sentiment analysis and emotional AI, chatbots will be able to recognize and respond to learners' emotional states, offering encouragement, support, and motivation when needed. For example, if a learner expresses frustration or confusion, the chatbot could recognize these cues and provide additional help, or reframe the material in a way that is easier to understand. This emotional responsiveness will help create a more supportive and engaging learning environment.

## 1.40 Collaborative Learning Opportunities

In the future, chatbots could facilitate collaborative learning experiences by connecting learners with peers for group activities and discussions. Chatbots may organize virtual study groups, enable peer-to-peer interactions, and offer collaborative writing tasks or problem-solving activities. These group interactions will simulate real-life language use, encouraging learners to practice English with others and develop their communication skills in diverse contexts. By fostering collaboration, chatbots will help learners experience the social aspect of language acquisition, which is often absent in traditional learning settings.

## 1.41 Voice-Activated Learning Assistants

Voice-activated chatbots, integrated with smart devices like smartphones, speakers, or wearables, will become a key feature in language learning in the future. These voice assistants will allow learners to practice English in their daily lives, using natural voice commands to interact with the chatbot. Whether practicing new vocabulary while cooking, listening to English podcasts during a commute, or having casual conversations at home, learners will be able to integrate language practice into their everyday routines. This seamless, hands-free approach will make language learning more flexible and consistent.

## 1.42 Ethical and Inclusive Design

As chatbots continue to play a more prominent role in language learning, ensuring that they are ethically designed and inclusive will be essential. Future chatbots will be developed with considerations for diverse learner needs, including those from different cultural backgrounds, those with learning disabilities, or those who speak various dialects or regional varieties of English. This inclusivity will ensure that chatbots can cater to a broader range of learners, providing equal opportunities for everyone to improve their language skills.

## 1.43 Cultural and Contextual Factors Influencing Chatbot Effectiveness

### 1. Language and Dialect Variability

Chatbots trained primarily on Standard English may not accommodate regional accents, idioms, or local dialects.

Learners from non-Western cultures may find some phrases or expressions unfamiliar or culturally irrelevant.

### 2. Communication Styles

High-context cultures (e.g., Japan, Korea) may prefer indirect or formal speech, while low-context cultures (e.g., USA, Germany) favor directness.

Chatbots need to adapt to these preferences to facilitate comfortable, effective interaction.

### 3. Power Distance and Authority Sensitivity

In cultures with **high power distance**, learners may be uncomfortable questioning or correcting a system perceived as "authoritative."

Chatbots should use culturally sensitive language and avoid overly casual or commanding tones in such contexts.

### 4. Learning Norms and Educational Practices

Cultures with teacher-centered learning may struggle with autonomous learning modes supported by chatbots.

In such settings, learners may require structured guidance or scaffolding to use AI tools effectively.

### 5. Cultural Content in Conversations

Learners engage more when chatbot scenarios reflect familiar cultural practices (e.g., local holidays, customs, or values).

Western-centric content can reduce motivation or create misunderstanding among learners from different cultural backgrounds.

### 6. Digital Literacy and Accessibility

Effectiveness depends on users' comfort with digital tools; learners in under-resourced settings may lack the technical skills or infrastructure.

Language learners in rural or marginalized contexts may face internet access or device limitations.

### 7. Attitudes toward AI and Technology

Some cultures may embrace AI as a positive innovation, while others may view it with skepticism or concern.

These perceptions influence trust in the chatbot, which affects learning engagement.

### 8. Gender and Social Norms

In some contexts, learners may prefer or feel more comfortable interacting with a chatbot that aligns with their cultural gender norms.

Misalignment here can cause discomfort or reduced engagement.

Example

A Japanese EFL learner might expect formal politeness from a chatbot, while an American learner might prefer casual, friendly tones.

A chatbot designed for the U.S. context using slang like "What's up?" or idioms like "hit the books" may confuse learners from other regions unless explained clearly.

## 2. LITERATURE REVIEW

### Theoretical Framework

To understand how AI can enhance English language learning (ELL), it's important to ground this exploration in established theories of language acquisition. Theories such as Krashen's Input Hypothesis, Vygotsky's Sociocultural Theory, and Swain's Output Hypothesis provide insights into effective language learning, focusing on aspects like comprehensible input, social interaction, and meaningful practice. Integrating AI into ELL requires examining how these technologies support language development across Listening, Speaking, Reading, and Writing (LSRW) skills and how they align with theories of adaptive learning, personalized instruction, and continuous feedback.

### 1. Comprehensible Input and Krashen's Input Hypothesis

Stephen Krashen's Input Hypothesis posits that learners acquire language most effectively when exposed to comprehensible input, or language just beyond their current proficiency level, referred to as "i+1." According to Krashen, learners benefit from gradual exposure to language complexity, where they can understand most of the content while still being challenged to progress.

### 2. Social Interaction and Vygotsky's Sociocultural Theory

Lev Vygotsky's Sociocultural Theory emphasizes the role of social interaction and collaboration in learning, suggesting that language acquisition is a socially mediated process. The Zone of Proximal Development (ZPD) is central to Vygotsky's theory; it refers to the difference between what a learner can achieve independently and what they can achieve with guidance from a more knowledgeable individual.

### *AI-Driven Interactive Tools and the ZPD*

AI-powered conversational agents and virtual tutors serve as "scaffolders" within the learner's ZPD, offering guided practice and feedback:

AI Chatbots and Conversational Agents: Virtual tutors like Duolingo's chatbots or Replika provide a low-stakes environment for language practice. They simulate real-world conversations and respond contextually, encouraging learners to use target language structures while offering hints and corrections as needed.

Feedback and Scaffolding in Writing: NLP-powered tools such as Grammarly and automated essay scoring systems analyze written text, offering immediate feedback on grammar, vocabulary, and syntax, much like a tutor would. By identifying and suggesting corrections, these tools guide learners within their ZPD, gradually reducing dependency as learners internalize language rules.

While AI tools lack the full emotional and cultural nuances of human interaction, they still offer valuable, consistent interaction opportunities that support language acquisition within the ZPD. These tools act as reliable partners, available 24/7, thus overcoming the limits of classroom schedules and teacher availability.

## 3. The Importance of Output and Swain's Output Hypothesis

Merrill Swain's Output Hypothesis posits that producing language (output) is as crucial as understanding it (input). Swain argued that language production allows learners to notice gaps in their knowledge, test language structures, and receive corrective feedback, which contributes significantly to language proficiency.

### *AI in Facilitating Meaningful Language Output*

AI provides platforms for learners to actively produce language through various output-focused tools, such as:

Speech Recognition Tools: AI applications like Elsa Speak or Rosetta Stone provide pronunciation and fluency feedback, helping learners identify errors in their spoken language and make improvements. By providing learners with detailed, immediate feedback on pronunciation, AI helps them refine their output.

Chatbots for Conversational Practice: Conversational AI, as seen in chatbots like Replika or Google's Meena, allows learners to practice language output in context. These bots simulate real-world conversations, responding in ways that prompt learners to think critically and adjust their language use based on responses, fostering meaningful practice that supports the Output Hypothesis.

By offering opportunities for output, these tools allow learners to practice and internalize language skills, creating an interactive environment where they can engage in trial and error, a process crucial for language development. Additionally, the safe, low-pressure nature of chatbots makes it easier for learners to experiment with language without fear of judgment, a benefit particularly significant for reluctant speakers.

## 4. Interaction Hypothesis and Long's Focus on Form

Michael Long's Interaction Hypothesis underscores the importance of interaction in language learning, advocating for "focus on form"—directing learners' attention to language structures within meaningful communication. Long argued that language acquisition occurs most effectively when learners are prompted to focus on specific aspects of form within a naturalistic context.

The integration of Artificial Intelligence (AI) in education has gained substantial momentum in recent years, with chatbots emerging as key players in revolutionizing language learning, particularly in enhancing English as a Second Language (ESL) skill. Chatbots are increasingly being utilized to facilitate interactive, personalized, and efficient language learning experiences, offering learners an opportunity to practice English conversation in a way that was previously inaccessible. This literature review examines the role of AI-driven chatbots in transforming English language learning, focusing on their potential for enhancing conversational skills, engagement, and learner autonomy.

## 2.1 The Role of Chatbots in Language Learning

AI chatbots have been found to significantly improve various language skills, particularly speaking and listening. Their interactive nature provides learners with opportunities for practice and immediate feedback. For instance, a systematic review by Koç and Savaş (2024) analyzed 57 studies and found that voice-based chatbots effectively aid in developing speaking skills by exposing learners to authentic conversational scenarios.

The use of chatbots in language learning is not entirely new, but recent advancements in AI, particularly in Natural Language Processing (NLP), have significantly improved their ability to interact meaningfully with learners. A chatbot, in essence, is a software application designed to simulate human conversation through text or voice interactions, often using NLP techniques to understand and respond to user input. Chatbots can engage learners in real-time conversations, mimicking the conditions of natural dialogues and providing feedback on language use, grammatical correctness, and pronunciation (Sarker et al., 2021). This ability to facilitate interactive communication makes chatbots particularly valuable in language learning, where practice and repetition are critical components for mastery.

Several studies have indicated that chatbot-based interactions can help learners develop and refine their language skills by providing them with real-time, personalized feedback. For instance, research by Shalev et al. (2020) found that chatbots are particularly effective in promoting conversational English by offering learners a safe space to practice without the fear of making mistakes in front of a human interlocutor. Such applications allow learners to develop confidence in their speaking abilities, which is often a significant barrier in traditional classroom-based settings.

## 2.2 Enhancing Conversational Skills

One of the most prominent benefits of using chatbots for English learning is their ability to engage learners in authentic conversational practice. According to Kern (2021), conversational skills are among the most difficult aspects of language acquisition, particularly for ESL learners who may lack opportunities to practice speaking with native speakers. Chatbots can simulate conversations on a wide range of topics, allowing learners to engage in meaningful dialogues and improve fluency over time. This real-time interaction promotes both active recall and listening comprehension, two fundamental components of language proficiency.

Chatbots also offer learners the flexibility to engage in conversation whenever they choose, which is particularly beneficial for students in regions where access to native speakers or conversation partners is limited. For example, Kuo et al. (2022) conducted a study on an English language learning chatbot designed to teach conversational English. They found that students who used the chatbot demonstrated significant improvements in conversational skills, particularly in areas such as vocabulary usage, sentence structure, and overall fluency.

In addition to providing conversational practice, chatbots can be tailored to a learner's proficiency level and specific learning needs. For example, advanced learners can engage in more complex discussions, while beginners can practice basic phrases and vocabulary. This adaptability not only fosters learner autonomy but also ensures that each interaction is appropriately challenging, which is essential for language development (Hussain et al., 2021).

## 2.3 Personalized Learning Experience

AI-powered chatbots are able to track learners' progress, adapt to their needs, and provide personalized feedback, all of which contribute to a more tailored and effective learning experience. Through the collection of learner data, chatbots can analyze areas of strength and weakness and adjust their interactions accordingly. For instance, if a learner consistently struggles with a particular grammar point or pronunciation, the chatbot can prompt them to practice these areas more frequently.

This individualized approach enhances learner engagement and motivates continued practice, which is essential for language retention and development (Pérez & García, 2020).

Moreover, chatbots can be integrated with other AI tools such as speech recognition and sentiment analysis, allowing for a more comprehensive understanding of the learner's abilities. By evaluating not only textual input but also speech patterns and tone, chatbots can provide feedback that is more nuanced and accurate. This level of personalization offers a significant advantage over traditional methods of language instruction, where feedback can often be more generic and less immediate.

## 2.4 Autonomy and Motivation

The role of learner autonomy and motivation in language acquisition cannot be overstated. Research has consistently shown that learners who are more autonomous are better able to take charge of their learning, set personal goals, and stay motivated (Kukulska-Hulme, 2021). Chatbots support autonomy by offering learners the opportunity to practice independently, at their own pace and convenience. Unlike in traditional language classrooms, where learners may be limited by fixed schedules and classroom dynamics, chatbots allow learners to access learning materials whenever and wherever they wish. This flexibility empowers learners to take control of their language development, enhancing both motivation and persistence.

In addition, the interactive nature of chatbot conversations can be highly motivating for learners. A study by Lee et al. (2022) revealed that learners who engaged with an AI-driven English learning chatbot reported higher levels of motivation and enthusiasm compared to those participating in traditional classroom-based instruction. The novelty of interacting with an AI system, coupled with the chatbot's ability to offer immediate feedback, helps keep learners engaged and fosters a sense of achievement. This gamification element, often embedded in chatbot designs, further increases learner interest and investment in the learning process (López & Munoz, 2020).

## 2.5 Limitations and Challenges

Despite the promising advantages of chatbots in language learning, there are several challenges and limitations that need to be addressed. One of the primary concerns is the chatbot's inability to replicate the full complexity of human conversation. While chatbots can simulate basic dialogues, they are still limited in their ability to understand nuanced emotions, sarcasm, or culturally specific references. As a result, learners may not always experience the same level of engagement or authenticity as they would in a conversation with a human interlocutor (Fryer et al., 2022).

Additionally, while chatbots are useful for language practice, they cannot replace the richness of a full language immersion experience. For example, chatbots may lack the ability to fully mimic the contextual factors, body language, and social dynamics that are often present in real-life communication. This limits the chatbot's effectiveness in fostering deeper conversational skills, such as interpreting non-verbal cues or managing complex social interactions (Fryer et al., 2022).

## 3. OBJECTIVES OF THE STUDY

1. To explore the effectiveness of AI-powered chatbots in improving English language skills – Assess how chatbots enhance listening, speaking, reading, and writing (LSRW) skills through interactive conversations.
2. To analyze student engagement and motivation in chatbot-based learning – Investigate whether AI-driven conversations encourage continuous learning and active participation.
3. To evaluate the role of chatbots in developing autonomous learning – Examine how students use chatbots to practice English independently and build self-confidence in language acquisition.
4. To assess the impact of chatbot interactions on conversational fluency – Measure improvements in pronunciation, grammar, vocabulary, and sentence structuring through AI-assisted dialogues.
5. To determine the effectiveness of chatbots in providing personalized language learning experiences – Study how AI adapts to individual learning styles, proficiency levels, and specific linguistic needs.
6. To compare chatbot-assisted learning with traditional English learning methods – Identify advantages, challenges, and potential areas of integration with classroom teaching.
7. To examine the role of Natural Language Processing (NLP) in enhancing chatbot communication – Evaluate how NLP advancements contribute to human-like conversations and contextual understanding in AI chatbots.
8. To explore the future potential of AI chatbots in English language education – Predict emerging trends and innovations in AI-driven language learning technologies.

## 3.1 Identified Research Gaps

Limited Integration of Higher-Order Skills: Current AI chatbot designs often lack components that promote debate and problem-solving abilities.

Cultural and Emotional Intelligence: There is a need to embed cultural nuances, humor, and empathy into chatbot interactions to enhance engagement.

Geographical Concentration of Studies: Most research has been conducted in Asian EFL contexts, indicating a need for studies in diverse educational settings.

Evaluation of Long-Term Impact: Further research is required to assess the sustained effectiveness of AI chatbots on language proficiency over time.

# 4. RESEARCH METHODOLOGY

The research methodology for exploring the role of chatbots in transforming English language learning focuses on evaluating how AI-driven chatbots facilitate conversational skills, learner engagement, and autonomy. Given the dynamic nature of AI technology and language acquisition, a mixed-methods approach is ideal for providing comprehensive insights. This approach includes both quantitative and qualitative methods to assess the effectiveness of chatbots in improving conversational English and to understand learners' perceptions and experiences.

## 4.1 Research Design

The research has adopted both quantitative and qualitative methods. This design allowed for a systematic investigation of the impact of chatbot-assisted learning on learners' conversational skills, while also capturing their perceptions, motivations, and challenges in using chatbots for language practice.

## 4.2 Participants

**Sample Size:** A sample of 314 undergraduate students studying English as a second language (ESL) were participated in the survey from various higher educational institutions.

**Inclusion Criteria:** Students should be ESL learners with a basic understanding of English (beginner to intermediate level) and willing to participate in both chatbot-based and traditional language learning sessions. The participants should not have prior experience using chatbots for language learning.

### 4.3 Data Collection Methods

Quantitative Data Collection:

**Surveys/Questionnaires:** After the intervention, students completed a survey designed to measure their perceptions of chatbot-based learning, motivation levels, and engagement. Likert-scale questions will assess the learners' satisfaction, ease of use, and perceived improvements in conversational skills. Example items include:

### 4.4 Intervention: Chatbot Design and Content

**Chatbot Selection:** The study will either use an existing English learning chatbot or develop a custom one tailored to the needs of the participants. This chatbot will be designed to simulate realistic conversations based on various topics, with the ability to provide instant feedback on grammatical errors, vocabulary usage, and sentence structure.

The chatbot will also adapt to the learner's proficiency level, increasing the complexity of conversations as the learner progresses.

**Interaction Logs:** The chatbot would track and store data from user interactions, such as the number of sessions completed, duration of conversations, frequency of errors, and types of corrections made. This data would provide valuable insights into how often students engage with the chatbot and how their conversational skills evolve over time.

### 4.5 Data Analysis

A. Quantitative Analysis:

**Statistical Analysis:** The survey data was analyzed using descriptive statistics to summarize learners' perceptions of chatbot-based learning, and correlation analyses will examine relationships between chatbot usage frequency and perceived improvements in English skills.

B. Qualitative Analysis:

**Thematic Analysis:** Interview transcripts and focus group discussions will be analyzed using **thematic analysis** to identify recurring themes related to learner engagement, motivation, and the challenges faced during chatbot-based learning.

This approach would provide an in-depth understanding of learners' experiences and their views on the role of AI chatbots in English language learning.

**Coding:** coding system was developed based on initial reading of the transcripts. The themes were further categorized into sub-themes such as "engagement," "motivation," "learning barriers," and "chatbot effectiveness." This would provide a comprehensive overview of the qualitative data.

## 4.6 Findings and Discussion

*Table 1. Platforms used to access English learning chatbots*

| Platforms used to access English learning chatbots | | | | |
|---|---|---|---|---|
| | Frequency | Percent | Valid Percent | Cumulative Percent |
| MADB | 126 | 40.1 | 40.1 | 40.1 |
| WO | 2 | 0.6 | 0.6 | 40.8 |
| Websites | 21 | 6.7 | 6.7 | 47.5 |
| Other | 14 | 4.5 | 4.5 | 51.9 |
| MAO | 2 | 0.6 | 0.6 | 52.5 |
| MAW | 13 | 4.1 | 4.1 | 56.7 |
| MPMA | 24 | 7.6 | 7.6 | 64.3 |
| MPMAO | 3 | 1.0 | 1.0 | 65.3 |
| MPMAW | 20 | 6.4 | 6.4 | 71.7 |
| MPMAWO | 18 | 5.7 | 5.7 | 77.4 |
| MPW | 10 | 3.2 | 3.2 | 80.6 |
| MPWM | 61 | 19.4 | 19.4 | 100.0 |
| Total | 314 | 100.0 | 100.0 | |

1. High Usage Platforms
   - **MADB(126users,40.1%)**:

The most popular platform, representing a significant portion of users. This indicates that MADB is the preferred access point, likely due to user convenience or feature richness.

- **MPWM(61users,19.4%)**:

The second most used platform, which holds a considerable share of users. Combined with MADB, these two platforms cover nearly 60% of total usage.

2. Medium Usage Platforms
    - **MPMA(24users,7.6%)**:

Shows moderate usage, indicating its relevance to a subset of users.

- **Websites(21users,6.7%)**:

Also fairly popular, suggesting a preference for web-based interfaces.

- **MPMAW(20users,6.4%)**:

Another platform with moderate adoption, possibly due to specific features offered.

- **MPMAWO(18users,5.7%)**:

Indicates notable adoption but slightly less than other options in this category.

3. Low Usage Platforms
    - **MAW(13users,4.1%)**and**Other(14users,4.5%)**:

These categories represent smaller portions of the total population, possibly reflecting niche or less user-friendly platforms.

- **MPW(10users,3.2%)**:

A relatively low frequency, suggesting limited adoption.

4. Minimal Usage Platforms
    - **MAO(2users,0.6%)**and**WO(2users,0.6%)**:

These are the least used platforms, indicating very limited user interest.

- **MPMAO(3users,1.0%)**:

Also a platform with minimal adoption.

5. Cumulative Percent Trends

- By the time the top two platforms (MADB and MPWM) are accounted for, **almost 60%** of all users are covered.
- As platforms like MPMA, Websites, and MPMAW are added, the cumulative percentage rises to over **71%**.
- The remaining platforms contribute marginally to the overall usage.

## Interpretation

1. **PreferenceforMADB**:

Its dominance suggests a higher user preference due to potential factors such as interface, functionality, or availability.

2. **Web-BasedUsage**:

Websites (6.7%) show that many users still prefer accessing English learning chatbots via browsers.

3. **Diversification**:

Several minor platforms exist but may need improvements or marketing to gain more users.

## Recommendations

1. **Enhance MADB Features**: Focus on further enhancing the most-used platform.
2. **Promote Underutilized Platforms**: Increase visibility for low-usage platforms through marketing or improvements.
3. **User Surveys**: Conduct surveys to understand the reasons behind platform preferences and abandonment.

*Table 2. Helpful features of chatbots in learning English*

| Helpful features of chatbots in learning English | | | | |
|---|---|---|---|---|
| | Frequency | Percent | Valid Percent | Cumulative Percent |
| GC | 32 | 10.2 | 10.2 | 10.2 |
| PGRTCP | 12 | 3.8 | 3.8 | 14.0 |
| VBRTCP | 3 | 1.0 | 1.0 | 15.0 |

continued on following page

*Table 2. Continued*

| Helpful features of chatbots in learning English | | | | |
|---|---|---|---|---|
| | Frequency | Percent | Valid Percent | Cumulative Percent |
| VBPGPF | 1 | 0.3 | 0.3 | 15.3 |
| VBGCPG | 12 | 3.8 | 3.8 | 19.1 |
| GCPGRTCP | 7 | 2.2 | 2.2 | 21.3 |
| VBGCPGPF | 2 | 0.6 | 0.6 | 22.0 |
| VBGCRTCP | 5 | 1.6 | 1.6 | 23.6 |
| VBPGRTCP | 3 | 1.0 | 1.0 | 24.5 |
| VBRTCPPF | 3 | 1.0 | 1.0 | 25.5 |
| VBGCPGRTCP | 11 | 3.5 | 3.5 | 29.0 |
| PF | 5 | 1.6 | 1.6 | 30.6 |
| VBGCRTCPPF | 1 | 0.3 | 0.3 | 30.9 |
| VBGCPGRTCPPF | 50 | 15.9 | 15.9 | 46.8 |
| PG | 26 | 8.3 | 8.3 | 55.1 |
| VB | 48 | 15.3 | 15.3 | 70.4 |
| RTCP | 52 | 16.6 | 16.6 | 86.9 |
| GCPG | 11 | 3.5 | 3.5 | 90.4 |
| VBPG | 6 | 1.9 | 1.9 | 92.4 |
| VBGC | 19 | 6.1 | 6.1 | 98.4 |
| GCRTCP | 5 | 1.6 | 1.6 | 100.0 |
| Total | 314 | 100.0 | 100.0 | |

This table presents data on the "Helpful features of chatbots in learning English," showing the frequency, percentage, valid percentage, and cumulative percentage for different chatbot features. Here's a breakdown of the analysis:

## Key Observations:

1. **Feature Categories:**
   - The data consists of various combinations of chatbot features represented by abbreviations like GC, PG, VB, RTCP, etc.
   - Some feature combinations occur more frequently than others.
2. **Top Features by Frequency:**
   - **RTCP** (16.6%) and **VB** (15.3%) are the most frequently mentioned features, followed by **PG** (15.9%).
   - These features alone account for a significant portion of the total responses.

3. **Moderately Frequent Features:**
   - **GC** (10.2%) is also a notable feature.
   - Other combinations like **VBGCGRRTCPPF** and **VBGCRTCP** have relatively high frequencies (each above 5%).
4. **Rare Features:**
   - Several features have very low frequencies (below 1%), such as **VBGPGPF** and **VBGCPGF**.
   - These combinations might be less commonly considered helpful in English learning.
5. **Cumulative Percent:**
   - The cumulative percentage helps to understand how features accumulate in importance.
   - By 55.1% cumulative percent, features like **PG, VB, RTCP**, and **GC** are covered.

## Insights & Implications:

1. **Popular Features:**
   - The most popular features likely reflect essential functions that users find beneficial in chatbots for learning English, such as providing vocabulary assistance or real-time corrections.
2. **Feature Diversity:**
   - The presence of a large variety of feature combinations suggests users appreciate different aspects of chatbot functionality.
3. **Tailoring Features:**
   - The chatbot design should focus on enhancing the most frequently mentioned features, such as **RTCP** (likely real-time correction or practice) and **VB** (possibly vocabulary building).

*Table 3. Frequency use chatbots for English learning*

| Frequency use chatbots for English learning | | | | |
|---|---|---|---|---|
| | **Frequency** | **Percent** | **Valid Percent** | **Cumulative Percent** |
| Daily | 65 | 20.7 | 20.7 | 20.7 |
| Weekly | 136 | 43.3 | 43.3 | 64.0 |
| Monthly | 16 | 5.1 | 5.1 | 69.1 |
| Rarely | 97 | 30.9 | 30.9 | 100.0 |
| Total | 314 | 100.0 | 100.0 | |

This table presents data on the frequency of using chatbots for English learning among 314 respondents. Below is a detailed breakdown:

1. Frequency and Percentage Analysis
   - **Daily Users:**
     - **65 respondents (20.7%)** report using chatbots daily.
     - This indicates a significant portion of learners are engaged in regular, daily chatbot-assisted learning.
   - **Weekly Users:**
     - The majority of respondents, **136 (43.3%)**, use chatbots weekly.
     - Weekly usage suggests a consistent yet less frequent engagement compared to daily users.
   - **Monthly Users:**
     - Only **16 respondents (5.1%)** use chatbots monthly.
     - This indicates minimal reliance on chatbots for learning on a monthly basis.
   - **Rare Users:**
     - **97 respondents (30.9%)** report rarely using chatbots.
     - Despite recognizing their benefits, some learners may prefer other methods or face barriers to using chatbots regularly.
2. Cumulative Percent Analysis
   - **64%** of respondents either use chatbots daily or weekly, showing that the majority rely on chatbots for learning at least once per week.
   - The cumulative percentage reaches **100%** after accounting for rare users, indicating no other usage patterns were reported.
3. Key Insights and Recommendations
   1. **High Consistency of Usage:**

With **64% of respondents** using chatbots daily or weekly, it is clear that many learners view chatbots as a valuable tool for regular English learning.

2. **Addressing Barriers to Frequent Usage:**

**30.9% of learners rarely use chatbots.** Exploring reasons behind infrequent use (e.g., usability issues, lack of customization, or engagement problems) could help improve adoption rates.

3. **Opportunities for Monthly Users:**

Monthly users represent a small group (5.1%), suggesting they may not be fully leveraging chatbot features. Encouraging more frequent use with reminders, notifications, or progress tracking could enhance their learning outcomes.

4. **Enhancing Engagement:**

Gamification, personalized learning paths, or targeted features for rare users could help increase daily or weekly engagement.

*Table 4. Motivates use chatbots for English learning*

| **Motivates use chatbots for English learning** | | | | |
|---|---|---|---|---|
| | **Frequency** | **Percent** | **Valid Percent** | **Cumulative Percent** |
| Convenience | 54 | 17.2 | 17.2 | 17.2 |
| ILESPL | 19 | 6.1 | 6.1 | 23.2 |
| CCEILE | 5 | 1.6 | 1.6 | 24.8 |
| CILESPL | 4 | 1.3 | 1.3 | 26.1 |
| CCEILSPL | 40 | 12.7 | 12.7 | 38.9 |
| CE | 11 | 3.5 | 3.5 | 42.4 |
| ILE | 81 | 25.8 | 25.8 | 68.2 |
| SPL | 77 | 24.5 | 24.5 | 92.7 |
| CCE | 6 | 1.9 | 1.9 | 94.6 |
| CEILE | 6 | 1.9 | 1.9 | 96.5 |
| CESPL | 2 | 0.6 | 0.6 | 97.1 |
| CILE | 4 | 1.3 | 1.3 | 98.4 |
| CSPL | 5 | 1.6 | 1.6 | 100.0 |
| Total | 314 | 100.0 | 100.0 | |

This dataset shows various reasons learners are motivated to use chatbots for English learning. Here's a detailed analysis of the frequencies and percentages:

1. Frequency and Percentage Breakdown
   - **Top Motivators:**
     - o **ILE (Interactive Learning Experience):**
       - 81 occurrences (25.8%).
       - This indicates that most learners are motivated by the interactive and engaging nature of chatbots.
     - o **SPL (Self-Paced Learning):**
       - 77 occurrences (24.5%).

        - Self-paced learning is another significant driver, highlighting learners' desire for flexible learning schedules.
    - **Convenience:**
        - 54 occurrences (17.2%).
        - Many learners appreciate the ease and availability of chatbots as a convenient learning tool.
    - These three factors account for **67.5%** of all responses, showing they are critical motivators.
2. Moderate Motivators:
    - **CCEILSPL (Combination of Convenience, Interactive Learning, and Self-Paced Learning):**
        - 40 occurrences (12.7%).
        - This group values a mix of features, emphasizing that multiple factors often contribute to motivation.
    - **CE (Convenience & Engagement):**
        - 11 occurrences (3.5%).
        - This group highlights the importance of both accessibility and motivation through engagement.
3. Rare Motivators:
    - Several combinations, such as **CILESPL (1.3%)**, **CCEILE (1.6%)**, and **CESPL (0.6%)**, were rarely chosen.
        - These combinations likely reflect niche preferences or very specific motivations.
4. Cumulative Percent:
    - By **68.2% cumulative percent**, the primary motivators (ILE, SPL, and Convenience) are covered.
    - The cumulative percentage reaches **100%** with smaller, less frequent motivators, indicating that these combinations only influence a small fraction of learners.

## Key Insights and Recommendations:

1. **Focus on Interactive Learning and Flexibility:**
    - Since **ILE and SPL account for over 50% of responses**, enhancing these chatbot features is essential to maximize engagement.
2. **Emphasize Convenience:**
    - **Convenience (17.2%)** remains a key motivator. Optimizing user interfaces for accessibility and speed will help retain learners.
3. **Combining Features:**

- Learners who selected combinations (e.g., CCEILSPL) value multiple chatbot functionalities. Offering customizable experiences could improve engagement.

4. **Addressing Low-Frequency Combinations:**
    - Further research could explore why certain combinations are less motivating and identify potential areas for improvement.

*Table 5. Effectiveness chatbots improving conversation skills*

| **Effectiveness chatbots improving conversation skills** | | | | |
|---|---|---|---|---|
| | **Frequency** | **Percent** | **Valid Percent** | **Cumulative Percent** |
| Very Ineffective | 1 | 0.3 | 0.3 | 0.3 |
| Ineffective | 2 | 0.6 | 0.6 | 1.0 |
| Neutral | 109 | 34.7 | 34.7 | 35.7 |
| Effective | 150 | 47.8 | 47.8 | 83.4 |
| Very Effective | 52 | 16.6 | 16.6 | 100.0 |
| Total | 314 | 100.0 | 100.0 | |

This table provides insights into how users perceive the effectiveness of chatbots in enhancing their conversation skills for learning English. Here's a detailed analysis:

1. Frequency and Percentage Breakdown
    - **Effective:**
        - **150 respondents (47.8%)** reported that chatbots are effective in improving conversation skills.
        - This is the largest group, indicating that almost half of the users find chatbots beneficial in this area.
    - **Very Effective:**
        - **52 respondents (16.6%)** found chatbots to be very effective.
        - Combined with the "Effective" category, **64.4%** of users view chatbots positively in improving conversation skills.
    - **Neutral:**
        - **109 respondents (34.7%)** expressed a neutral stance.
        - A significant portion of users neither praised nor criticized chatbot effectiveness, indicating room for improvement.
    - **Ineffective:**
        - **2 respondents (0.6%)** viewed chatbots as ineffective.
        - Very few users had negative feedback in this category.

- **Very Ineffective:**
    - o Only **1 respondent (0.3%)** found chatbots very ineffective.
    - o This suggests minimal dissatisfaction with chatbot performance.

2. Cumulative Percent
    - By the **83.4% cumulative percent**, most users either found chatbots effective or were neutral about their impact.
    - Only **1% of users** found chatbots either ineffective or very ineffective, indicating overall positive sentiment.
3. Key Insights and Recommendations
    1. **High Overall Effectiveness:**
        - o With **64.4% of respondents** viewing chatbots as effective or very effective, chatbots are a well-regarded tool for improving conversation skills.
    2. **Neutral Users:**
        - o The **34.7% of users with neutral opinions** represent an opportunity for improvement. Enhancing chatbot features like real-time feedback, speech recognition, and natural conversation flow could help convert neutral users to positive.
    3. **Addressing Minor Dissatisfaction:**
        - o Although only a small number of users found chatbots ineffective, exploring potential issues like unclear feedback or limited conversation topics could improve user satisfaction.

*Table 6. Chatbots helped overcome hesitation in speaking English*

| **Chatbots helped overcome hesitation in speaking English** | | | | |
|---|---|---|---|---|
| | **Frequency** | **Percent** | **Valid Percent** | **Cumulative Percent** |
| No | 54 | 17.2 | 17.2 | 17.2 |
| Yes | 260 | 82.8 | 82.8 | 100.0 |
| Total | 314 | 100.0 | 100.0 | |

This dataset provides insights into how effective chatbots are in helping users overcome hesitation when speaking English.

1. Frequency and Percentage Breakdown
    - **Yes (Helped Overcome Hesitation):**
        - o **260 respondents (82.8%)** reported that chatbots helped them overcome hesitation in speaking English.

- o This strong majority indicates that chatbots play a crucial role in building learners' confidence and reducing speaking anxiety.
- **No (Did Not Help Overcome Hesitation):**
  - o **54 respondents (17.2%)** indicated that chatbots did not help them overcome hesitation.
  - o While a minority, this still represents a group that may not have benefited from chatbot interaction.

2. Cumulative Percent
   - By **17.2% cumulative percent**, all respondents who said "No" are accounted for.
   - The cumulative percentage reaches **100%** after adding those who found chatbots helpful, highlighting the significant majority of positive responses.
3. Key Insights and Recommendations
   1. **High Confidence-Boosting Potential:**
      - o With **over 80% of respondents** reporting positive outcomes, chatbots are clearly effective in reducing hesitation. Their ability to provide a judgment-free environment for practicing English conversations may explain this success.
   2. **Addressing Non-Responders:**
      - o The **17.2% of users who didn't experience improvement** may benefit from more advanced features. Possible enhancements include:
        - ▪ Real-time pronunciation feedback
        - ▪ Personalized conversation prompts
        - ▪ More realistic and dynamic chatbot responses
        - ▪ Role-playing scenarios for common social or business conversations
   3. **Targeted Interventions:**
      - o Identifying the specific challenges faced by hesitant learners (e.g., anxiety, pronunciation, or topic-specific struggles) could help improve chatbot customization for this group.

*Table 7. Rate chatbot's ability personalized learning experiences*

| **Rate chatbot's ability personalized learning experiences** | | | | |
|---|---|---|---|---|
| | **Frequency** | **Percent** | **Valid Percent** | **Cumulative Percent** |
| Poor | 2 | 0.6 | 0.6 | 0.6 |
| Average | 39 | 12.4 | 12.4 | 13.1 |
| Good | 211 | 67.2 | 67.2 | 80.3 |
| Excellent | 62 | 19.7 | 19.7 | 100.0 |
| Total | 314 | 100.0 | 100.0 | |

This table reflects a survey on the chatbot's ability to provide personalized learning experiences. Here's a summary:

1. Good (67.2%)

The majority of users (211 out of 314) rated the chatbot's ability to provide personalized learning experiences as "Good." This indicates overall satisfaction with the chatbot's ability to tailor content to users' needs.

2. Excellent (19.7%)

Nearly 20% of users rated the chatbot as "Excellent," showing that a significant portion of users experienced high-quality personalized learning experiences. This suggests that chatbots are meeting or exceeding expectations for a substantial group.

3. Average (12.4%)

A smaller group of users gave the chatbot an "Average" rating, indicating room for improvement. These users likely experienced inconsistencies or partial satisfaction in their personalized learning experiences.

4. Poor (0.6%)

Only 2 users rated the chatbot's personalization as "Poor," representing a minimal portion of the population. This suggests very few users encountered significant issues.

## Insights and Implications

- **High Satisfaction:** With a combined 86.9% of users rating the chatbot as "Good" or "Excellent," the chatbot is effective at providing personalized learning experiences.
- **Improvement Areas:** Efforts should be made to raise the experience level of the "Average" and "Poor" groups to "Good" or "Excellent" through better AI customization and learner adaptation.
- **Engagement & Retention Focus:** Enhancing features for tailored feedback, adaptive learning paths, and dynamic interaction could further increase user satisfaction.

*Table 8. Chatbots improve upon the most*

| Chatbots improve upon the most | | | | |
|---|---|---|---|---|
| | Frequency | Percent | Valid Percent | Cumulative Percent |
| CU | 122 | 38.9 | 38.9 | 38.9 |
| PCN | 41 | 13.1 | 13.1 | 51.9 |
| ECA | 92 | 29.3 | 29.3 | 81.2 |
| OE | 59 | 18.8 | 18.8 | 100.0 |
| Total | 314 | 100.0 | 100.0 | |

This table reflects a survey on the Chatbots improve upon the most.

1. Content Understanding (CU) – 38.9%

this is the top-rated category, indicating that nearly 40% of users feel chatbots should improve their understanding of content. This suggests that users value chatbots' ability to interpret and process information accurately and contextually.

2. Engagement & Communication Ability (ECA) – 29.3%

the second-highest category, nearly one-third of users want chatbots to enhance engagement and communication. This indicates users expect chatbots to have better conversational dynamics and emotional intelligence to sustain effective interactions.

3. Overall Experience (OE) – 18.8%

roughly one in five users identified "Overall Experience" as needing improvement. This broad category likely encompasses ease of use, interface quality, and user satisfaction, implying that refining the holistic experience of chatbot interactions is important.

4. Personalized Content Navigation (PCN) – 13.1%

this category is rated lowest, but still significant. Users are asking for better customization and tailored pathways through the content, implying that more adaptive algorithms could improve this area.

### Insights and Implications

Priority Focus: The chatbot developers should focus on improving Content Understanding (CU) and Engagement & Communication Ability (ECA) first, as these are the primary areas for improvement.

Targeted Enhancements: Improvement in Personalized Content Navigation (PCN) and Overall Experience (OE) should follow to create a well-rounded user experience.

Holistic Development: A balanced improvement in all areas would help boost user satisfaction and engagement with chatbots.

## Comparative Analysis: Chatbot-Assisted Learning vs. Traditional Methods

A comparative analysis between chatbot-assisted learning and traditional classroom instruction reveals both strengths and limitations of each approach. Chatbot-assisted learning excels in offering individualized and on-demand practice, particularly in areas like grammar correction, vocabulary acquisition, and pronunciation. These systems can provide learners with immediate feedback and create low-pressure environments conducive to practicing without the fear of judgment.

In contrast, traditional methods emphasize structured learning with direct human interaction, enabling personalized attention, collaborative learning, and socio-emotional engagement. Teachers can adapt content based on immediate classroom dynamics and provide nuanced feedback that considers context, emotion, and learner background.

However, traditional classrooms may be constrained by time, teacher availability, and class size, which can limit the extent of individual practice and feedback. Conversely, chatbots lack the adaptive empathy and critical thinking skills of human educators, and their automated nature may lead to repetitive or impersonal interactions.

The most effective approach may lie in blended learning models, combining the scalability and efficiency of chatbots with the pedagogical richness of traditional teaching. Such integration allows learners to benefit from the strengths of both modalities, fostering comprehensive language development while addressing the limitations inherent in each method.

## 5. ETHICAL CONSIDERATIONS

### 1. Introduction

The rapid integration of artificial intelligence (AI) technologies into education has introduced novel methods for enhancing English language learning. Among these, AI-powered chatbots have emerged as prominent tools for providing conversational practice, personalized feedback, and learner autonomy. However, their use also raises critical ethical concerns. This paper explores two major ethical dimensions: the potential biases embedded in AI algorithms and the evolving role of teachers in AI-mediated language learning environments.

### 2. Bias in AI Algorithms

#### 2.1 Linguistic Bias

AI chatbots are typically trained on large corpora consisting primarily of Standard English variants, particularly American or British English. Consequently, they may fail to recognize or appropriately respond to non-standard dialects, regional expressions, or accent variations. Such biases can marginalize learners from diverse linguistic backgrounds and reinforce hegemonic language norms.

#### 2.2 Cultural Bias

Many AI systems inherit the cultural assumptions and values present in their training data. This can lead to the propagation of Western-centric perspectives, humor, and conversational norms, which may be irrelevant or alienating to learners from other cultural contexts. As a result, chatbots may unintentionally perpetuate cultural imperialism and hinder intercultural understanding.

### 2.3 Gender and Stereotyping

Chatbots may also reflect or reinforce gender biases, often through defaulting to gendered names, voices, or behavioral scripts. For example, a feminized chatbot designed with submissive or overly polite characteristics can reinforce traditional gender stereotypes. This not only affects learner perceptions but also influences how students engage with the technology.

### 2.4 Bias in Assessment and Feedback

AI-driven assessment tools integrated into chatbots may unfairly penalize learners who do not conform to dominant linguistic or rhetorical standards. Automated scoring systems may lack sensitivity to diverse language strategies, resulting in inaccurate or demotivating feedback. Furthermore, the opacity of these systems raises concerns about accountability and fairness.

## 3. Impact on Teacher Roles

### 3.1 Risk of De-skilling and Displacement

The increasing reliance on AI chatbots for routine language instruction poses a risk of marginalizing human educators. Tasks traditionally handled by teachers, such as vocabulary drills, grammar explanations, and pronunciation practice, are now being delegated to AI systems. This may lead to de-skilling or even displacement of language instructors, particularly in underfunded institutions.

### 3.2 Reframing the Role of Educators

Rather than replacing teachers, AI technologies should augment pedagogical practices. Teachers are increasingly required to assume roles as facilitators of AI-mediated learning, curators of digital content, and critical evaluators of chatbot interactions. This shift necessitates professional development in AI literacy and educational technology integration.

### 3.3 Human Connection and Emotional Support

Unlike human teachers, chatbots lack genuine empathy, emotional intelligence, and the ability to understand nuanced social cues. The absence of human connection in chatbot-led learning environments can lead to feelings of isolation, reduced motivation, and limited socio-emotional development. Teachers play a vital role in providing encouragement, cultural context, and ethical guidance, which AI cannot replicate.

## 4. Privacy, Data Ethics, and Surveillance

AI chatbots often collect extensive data on user interactions, including speech samples, learning behaviors, and error patterns. This raises significant privacy concerns, especially regarding informed consent, data storage, and potential misuse. Furthermore, the use of chatbots to monitor learner performance introduces ethical dilemmas around surveillance, autonomy, and academic freedom.

## 5. Limitations

### Technological Limitations of Current AI Systems

Despite their promise, current AI systems face notable technological limitations that hinder their effectiveness in English language learning. One major challenge is the inability to scale effectively across diverse linguistic and cultural contexts. AI chatbots struggle to accurately process and respond to a wide range of regional accents, speech rhythms, and dialectal variations. This limitation disproportionately affects learners whose speech does not align with the training data, leading to misrecognition, misunderstanding, and inadequate feedback.

Additionally, many chatbots lack the deep contextual understanding required for nuanced conversation. Their responses may appear mechanical or inappropriate in complex social interactions. This stems from limitations in natural language understanding and insufficient modeling of real-world conversational dynamics. Furthermore, real-time speech processing, a crucial component for effective spoken language practice, remains prone to latency issues and transcription errors, especially in noisy environments or with low-resource languages.

Another concern is the adaptability of chatbots in dynamic learning environments. Many systems are not equipped with mechanisms for continuous learning or personalization at scale. As a result, they may offer static or repetitive responses that do not align with individual learner needs or evolving proficiency levels.

## 6. CONCLUSION

AI-powered chatbots are revolutionizing English language learning by offering dynamic, interactive, and personalized learning experiences. From facilitating real-time conversations to providing tailored feedback, chatbots have become an essential tool in developing Listening, Speaking, Reading, and Writing (LSRW) skills.

1. Enhanced Personalization:

As reflected in the survey data, the majority of learners rated chatbots as "Good" or "Excellent" in providing personalized learning experiences. This highlights their effectiveness in customizing content, adapting to learners' proficiency levels, and promoting self-paced learning.

2. Key Areas of Improvement:

While chatbots are successful in many aspects, areas such as **Content Understanding (CU)** and **Engagement & Communication Ability (ECA)** still require further enhancement. Addressing these challenges will improve learners' conversational abilities and overall language fluency.

3. Learner Engagement:

By simulating natural conversations and offering contextual learning, chatbots help learners practice English in authentic scenarios. This promotes greater confidence, better language retention, and enhanced engagement.

4. Autonomy and Motivation:

AI-driven chatbots empower learners with increased autonomy, allowing them to take charge of their language learning journey. Gamification features, instant feedback, and conversational prompts further enhance motivation and encourage regular practice.

5. Final Thoughts:

Chatbots are shaping the future of English language education by making learning more accessible, personalized, and interactive. As AI technology advances, its integration into English learning will continue to evolve, bridging gaps in traditional teaching methods and providing a holistic, learner-centered experience. By focusing on continuous improvement and incorporating user feedback, chatbots will unlock new possibilities for language acquisition in the digital age.

## REFERENCES

Fryer, L. K., Bovee, H. N., & Hennessy, S. (2022). The role of chatbots in language learning. *International Journal of Educational Technology in Higher Education, 19*(1), 1–13. PMID: 35013716

Hussain, T., Shah, D., & Zhang, X. (2021). Chatbots in language education: A comprehensive review. *Journal of Language Learning and Technology*, *25*(1), 45–63.

Kern, R. (2021). Digital language learning: A research agenda. *Modern Language Journal*, *105*(3), 612–628.

Koç, F. Ş., & Savaş, P. (2024). The use of artificially intelligent chatbots in English language learning: A systematic meta-synthesis study of articles published between 2010 and 2024. *ReCALL.*

Kukulska-Hulme, A. (2021). Mobile language learning: What we know and what we need to know. *Language Learning & Technology*, *25*(2), 5–18.

Kuo, Y. C., Lee, J. M., & Wu, Y. S. (2022). The impact of a chatbot on English conversation skills. *Journal of Computer Assisted Learning*, *38*(1), 1–14.

Lee, Y. H., Park, M. J., & Kwon, H. J. (2022). Chatbots and motivation in language learning. *Language Learning & Technology*, *26*(3), 63–81.

López, J. L., & Munoz, R. (2020). Gamification in chatbot-based language learning. *Language Learning & Technology*, *24*(2), 22–39.

Pérez, J. F., & García, S. (2020). Adaptive learning with AI-powered chatbots. *Journal of Educational Technology & Society*, *23*(4), 56–70.

Shalev, T., Gonzalez, G., & Tuan, M. (2020). Chatbots in language learning: A review of literature. *International Journal of Artificial Intelligence in Education, 30*(3), 367–383.

# Chapter 7
# Employing Praat AI to Analyze the Production of Sentence Intonation and Lexical Stress Placement Produced by Omani Learners of English

**Taif Al-Kinany**
https://orcid.org/0000-0002-0939-7839
*University of Technology and Applied Sciences, Oman*

**Sultan AlDighaishi**
*University of Technology and Applied Sciences, Oman*

## ABSTRACT

*The study aimed to explore the effectiveness of employing AI Praat acoustic analysis to investigate the challenges Omani EFL college students face in producing English prosodic features, particularly sentence intonation and lexical stress. The test was developed and applied to thirty students from foundation programs at a university level. Students' audio-recordings were analyzed using Praat acoustic analysis. Findings indicated that Praat acoustic analysis are very effective as it provided precise and objective methods for examining prosodic features of sentence intonation and lexical stress. The detailed acoustic data generated by Praat helped in diagnosing phonetic acoustic issues and enabled the comparison of learners' speech with native speakers' norms, fostering a deeper understanding of the challenges faced by Omani EFL learners in mastering English prosody. The results revealed*

DOI: 10.4018/979-8-3373-0969-9.ch007

*significant differences between the students' intonation patterns and lexical stress placement compared to native English speakers, likely influenced by mother tongue.*

## INTRODUCTION

A notable shift has been made toward using computer technology to assess oral skills and help students improve their ability to produce pronunciations, and efforts have been made to investigate the effects of using computer programs as a tool in the instruction of English pronunciation (Li & Wang,2025; Huang, 2019). The naturalness and understandability of speech demonstrate the significance of prosody. Teachers and programmers have attempted to use computer software to teach language learners due to the significance of these elements (Sato,2022). Wilson (2005) introduced Praat as one of these pieces of software. It can be used in language classes to teach prosodic elements like emphasis and intonation because it gives quick feedback. This software gives EFL students the chance to see the requirements for making speech (Zhang & Liu, 2024). Derwing (2021) stated that Praat is widely used for acoustic analysis software as it provides a powerful and objective tool for evaluating these suprasegmental features of speech. By analyzing speech signals in detail, Praat allows instructors and researchers to examine the pitch contours (intonation) and duration patterns (stress) of a learner's speech, offering a more precise and comprehensive assessment than auditory judgment alone (Trofimovich,2020). It is noteworthy how crucial clear intonation production and precise emphasis placement are. Intonation refers to the rise and fall of pitch during speech, while stress placement involves the emphasis placed on certain syllables or words in a sentence (Anh,2017). Both aspects are essential components of prosody, which plays a key role in conveying meaning, emotions, and sentence structures in English. Misplacement of stress or incorrect intonation patterns can lead to misunderstandings, even when individual sounds are pronounced accurately (Shue & Keating,2024). Therefore, it is vital to assess these features in EFL learners to identify and correct prosodic errors that may hinder fluency and comprehension (Sato, 2022).Additionally, Praat 's ability to measure syllable duration and intensity can highlight misapplied stress, such as placing stress on the wrong syllable in a word or failing to emphasize content words in a sentence, both common challenges for EFL learners (Zhang & Li,2024).

Using Praat in the assessment of intonation and stress placement offers several advantages over traditional methods. First, its quantitative nature allows for objective, data-driven analysis, providing a clear and reliable comparison between a learner's production and that of native speakers (Sato,2022). Furthermore, the visual output from Praat, such as spectrograms and pitch tracks, can be easily shared with students, enabling them to visually perceive their prosodic patterns and facilitating more targeted feedback (Zhang,2021). This objective and visual feedback can be especially beneficial in the classroom, where learners may have difficulty perceiving subtle differences in stress or intonation on their own. Ultimately, Praat not only helps identify areas for improvement but also empowers both teachers and learners to address specific prosodic features of English pronunciation in a systematic and effective manner (Ibid.).

Thus, the main purpose of this study was to investigate the effectiveness of using Praat acoustic analysis to analyze Omani EFL university students' phonetic prosodic production of sentence intonation and lexical stress-placement that were collected by developing a two parts test. To this end, the following objectives have been specified for this study to achieve the desired outcomes:

1. To explore intonation patterns produced by Omani EFL university students.
2. To detect lexical stress placement produced by Omani EFL university students.
3. To compare the intonation patterns as well as the lexical stress-placement produced by Omani EFL university students to those of the Standard English.

## Research Questions

1. To what extent is Praat software effective in providing acoustic software analysis of intonation and stress placement?
2. What are the prominent intonation patterns produced by Omani EFL university students for declarative sentences?
   a. To what extent do Omani EFL college students produce affirmative-declarative sentences with correct intonation patterns?
   b. To what extent do Omani EFL college students produce negative-declarative sentences with correct intonation patterns?
   c. How are the intonation patterns produced by Omani EFL university students similar to or different from standard English?
3. To what extend do Omani EFL university students put the correct stress placement on:
   a. monosyllabic words
   b. disyllabic words
   c. polysyllabic words

## LITERATURE REVIEW

Prosody is the melody of language. It has functions, and its functions go beyond the skills of reading aloud and sounding expressive. Its dimensional indicators include pausing, phrasing, linking, stress, intonation, etc. It assists the speaker in making sense of an oral context (Kim, Quinn, & Petscher, 2020). Studies have shown that prosody disambiguates complex sentences (Godde, Bosses, & Bailly, 2020; Kuhn & Schwanenflugel, 2019; Paige, Rupley, Smith, Rasinski, Nichols, & Magpuri-Lavell, 2017). By using the prosodic features to separate words and sentences boundaries into thought groups, the listeners can cognitively grasp the meaning in a complicated oral context(Dandee,et.al,2022).

The analysis of the prosodic theory is thought to be best served by the third definitional viewpoint (Shraiber, 2020). Prosody is important for the analysis and understanding of spoken settings because it can reflect many aspects of the speaker's utterances (Dandee, et.al,2022). Contextualized sentences can reflect the message's structure (Riadil, et.al,2021). Additionally, prosodic aspects of speech can be used to assess the speaker's mood and identify their most salient emotional states. Numerous research have been done to determine the connection between a speaker's personality and emotional state as their prosody changes (Shraiber, 2020). In the area of teaching a second/foreign language, this importance is more noticeable because learning the prosody of English is proved to have an impact on the listener's judgment (ibid.).

Pronunciation includes features at:

- The segmental (micro) level
- The supra-segmental (macro) level.

While the segmental features are important, recent research has shown that when teaching focuses on supra-segmental features, learners' intelligibility is greatly enhanced. It is considerably significant; therefore, it is important to enhance EFL students' production of the supra-segmental features (Riadil, et.al,2021).

*Figure 1. Supra-segmental Phonetic Features*

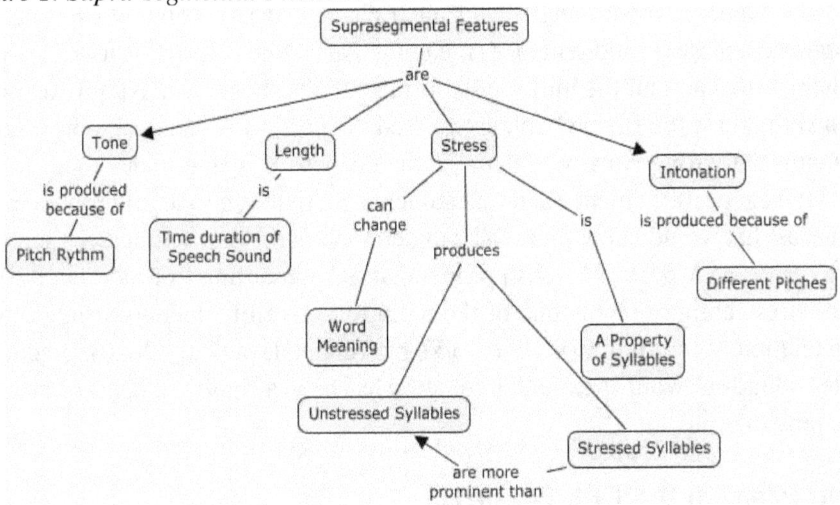


*Figure 2. The Prosodic Features*

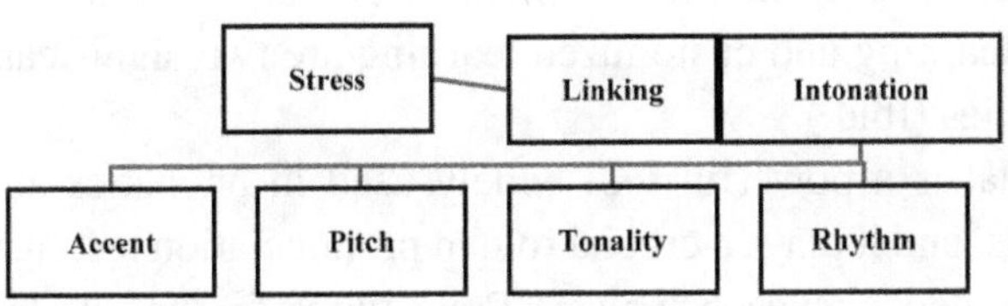


The sound waves created by the rise and fall of the voice-pitch when speaking are known as 'intonation'. When this affects the meaning of what is being stated, it demonstrates how the voice rises and falls during speech (Romero, 2021). It is a non-grammatical, non-lexical aspect of communication that is a supra-segmental prosodic element of English pronunciation. It is essential to voice communication (Ibid.). Without intonation, speech is nothing more than mechanical speech (Feng & Zhang, 2024; Dandee, et.al,2022). Languages all use intonation. However, there are prosodic factors and different intonation patterns in every spoken language. Instead of focusing on what we say, intonation focuses on how we say it (Zulfugarova, 2018). It might be challenging to understand expressions and thoughts without intonation. One quality is intonation.

On the other hand, the term “stress” refers to the location in a word or phrase where the volume, vowel length, and pitch change. It is absolutely essential for giving words, phrases, and sentences meaning. A syllable (expo'rt) is used as a verb but changes to a noun if the initial syllable ('export) is stressed. A syllable (expo'rt) is as a verb, but if the first syllable is stressed ('export), it is changed to be a noun. Producing the wrong stress can damage the chances of being understood. Moreover, Scrivener (2005) mentioned that students are required to learn pronunciation features as that would allow them to be understood in the oral settings. So, stress is a basic prosodic aspect of English pronunciation. According to Riadil,et.al(2021) lack of stress competency is one of the main reasons EFL students struggle with pronunciation. According to earlier works by Thienkalaya et al. (2020), practicing isolated sounds or word stress and intonation has been a significant part of pronunciation instruction.

## Using Praat in the EFL Context

The 1980s are when CALL first began to take shape (Huang, 2019). Early CALL has evolved into a synergistic partnership between technological advancement and educational advancement (Zakareya, 2020). CALL's educational philosophies place a strong emphasis on student-centered instruction, which enables students to learn English by engaging in interactive, planned and/or unstructured EFL activities. Bidirectional learning and customized learning are two significant characteristics of these activities (Ibid.).

Hence, Praat is a powerful tool widely used in phonetics and linguistics for speech analysis, and it plays a crucial role in pronunciation testing (Sato, 2022). As a software designed for speech analysis, Praat allows for the detailed examination of various phonetic features, such as pitch, duration, intensity, and formant frequencies. In pronunciation tests, it can be used to analyze how accurately a learner produces specific sounds, compare their speech to native speaker models, and identify areas of difficulty (Ibid.). For example, by measuring vowel formants and consonant articulation, researchers or educators can objectively assess whether a learner is producing target sounds correctly or whether their pronunciation deviates from the expected acoustic patterns of the target language (Baker,2021).

Praat acoustic analysis has become an essential tool in the phonetic evaluation of English as a Foreign Language (EFL) pronunciation (Baker& Trofimovich,2022). This software enables researchers and educators to objectively assess various prosodic features such as intonation, stress patterns, and vowel quality in learners' speech. Praat provides highly detailed acoustic measurements, allowing for precise analysis of speech sounds at a phonetic level. Through visual representations like pitch contours and spectrograms, educators can easily identify areas where students struggle, such as incorrect stress placement or the failure to produce native-like intonation patterns. This level of detail aids in the diagnosis of specific pronunciation issues and allows for targeted interventions to improve EFL learners' phonetic skills (Boersma & Weenink, 2024).

One of the major benefits of using Praat in EFL evaluation is its ability to compare learners' speech to native speaker norms (Trofimovich & Baker,2023). By analyzing the acoustic properties of both non-native and native speech, Praat can highlight discrepancies in prosodic features like rhythm, stress, and intonation. This comparison offers a clear benchmark for instructors, helping them understand the degree of divergence in their students' pronunciation (Ibid.). Additionally, Praat allows for longitudinal analysis, enabling the tracking of learners' progress over time. As a result, instructors can monitor the effectiveness of pronunciation training programs and adjust teaching strategies accordingly (Trofimovich & Baker, 2023).

The use of Praat also extends beyond traditional classroom settings into more advanced research in second language acquisition. Many studies have used the software to examine the effects of different factors, such as first language transfer, on the prosody of EFL learners. For instance, research has shown that learners from tone languages may exhibit difficulties with intonation patterns in English, as their native language influences stress and pitch placement in non-native speech (Baker & Trofimovich, 2022). By providing a more granular understanding of how learners produce speech, Praat facilitates better-informed decisions in language instruction and curriculum design, particularly when addressing the challenges faced by students in mastering English pronunciation.

Munro (2022) stated that Praat is particularly valuable in providing a visual representation of speech through spectrograms, pitch tracks, and waveform displays. They (Ibid.) added that these features help in diagnosing specific pronunciation errors that might not be immediately apparent in auditory analysis alone. Differences in formant values may reveal that the learner is producing a vowel with a non-native tongue position or is struggling with aspects of vowel reduction or vowel length, which are common challenges in second language pronunciation (Ladefoged,2021).

Additionally, Praat's ability to manipulate and measure suprasegmental features like intonation and stress patterns makes it invaluable in assessing more complex aspects of pronunciation (Boersma,2023). By analyzing pitch contours and stress patterns, Praat can provide insights into how well a learner has acquired the rhythmic and melodic aspects of speech. This detailed analysis helps language instructors design targeted interventions, as it allows them to address specific areas where learners' pronunciation diverges from native speaker norms (Munro, 2022) Overall, Praat offers both a precise and comprehensive approach to evaluating and improving pronunciation in language learners (Sato, 2022).

In studies of second language acquisition (SLA), Praat, a potent tool for phonetic analysis, has grown in importance, especially when analyzing how learners perceive and create non-native sounds (Jahanbin, 2025). Researchers may compare native and non-native speakers in great detail by using Praat to quantify acoustic characteristics such voice onset time (VOT), formant frequencies, and pitch contours precisely (Azzahra,2024). Praat makes it possible to conduct empirical studies on how the production patterns of L2 learners either converge with or deviate from native norms within the framework of Flege's Speech Learning Model (SLM) (Ibid.). According to SLM, the degree of similarity between L1 and L2 phonetic categories affects L2 learners' capacity to generate and recognize new sounds (Styler,2025; Chen,2022).

Bashir, 2024) and El-Garawany(2021) stated that through Praat's analysis of the spectral and temporal characteristics of speech sounds, researchers can monitor how much learners incorporate L2 sounds into preexisting L1 categories or create new phonetic categories, providing verifiable auditory evidence to either confirm or refute SLM predictions. Moreover, Praat backs research based on the Interaction Hypothesis, which contends that possibilities for feedback and meaning negotiation in meaningful interaction promote SLA (Jahanbin,2025). By employing Praat, phonetic research can investigate the ways in which conversational interaction influences the development of pronunciation, with particular attention to characteristics such as segmental clarity, syllable timing, and intonation patterns. Researchers may utilize Praat, for instance, to examine recorded dialogues between native speakers and L2 learners, measuring the quantifiable changes in L2 speech production brought about by instant feedback during engagement. We may better grasp how interactional dynamics contribute to phonetic evolution in SLA by using Praat's fine-grained, objective acoustic data, which connects theoretical ideas with actual findings (Chen,2022).

Choosing the right analysis tool is crucial for producing precise and meaningful results in speech and language research. Praat is a specialized software for detailed phonetic analysis, offering advanced features such as pitch tracking, formant analysis, intensity measurements, and assessments of voice quality (e.g., jitter and shimmer). A study by Yamashita et al. (2023) found that Praat's default settings provided reliable formant analysis even in clinical situations involving atypical speech, such as among maxillectomy patients, highlighting Praat's accuracy and robustness in acoustic measurements.

In contrast, Audacity primarily focuses on audio recording and basic editing. While it allows users to visualize waveforms and apply simple editing tasks, it lacks the sophisticated analytical capabilities of Praat. Widayanti and Pramudya (2022) emphasized Audacity's ease of use, making it a popular choice for basic audio tasks such as trimming and applying simple effects. However, for researchers requiring detailed auditory analysis, Audacity's functionalities remain limited.

ELAN, developed by the Max Planck Institute for Psycholinguistics, serves a different purpose, specializing in multimodal data annotation. It enables researchers to create detailed, time-aligned annotations across multiple tiers for audio and video recordings. ELAN is especially valuable in fields like sociolinguistics and language documentation where analyzing the interplay between speech, gestures, and other modalities is essential. While ELAN excels in annotation, it lacks Praat's detailed acoustic analysis capabilities. However, the two tools can complement each other effectively; for example, annotations created in ELAN can be exported into Praat for in-depth acoustic analysis (Norte, 2023).

In short, the choice between Praat, Audacity, and ELAN depends on the specific needs of a research project. Praat is ideal for detailed phonetic analysis, Audacity is well-suited for basic audio editing, and ELAN excels at comprehensive multimodal annotation. Understanding the strengths and limitations of each tool enables researchers to select the most appropriate software for achieving their analytical objectives. Hence, there are serious ethical issues with the use of AI tools in language learning, especially with relation to algorithmic biases, data privacy, and informed consent. Through their interactions with AI-powered platforms, learners frequently unintentionally divulge personal information that could be used for training without their express agreement, potentially violating their right to privacy (Aydin et al., 2024). Furthermore, underrepresented linguistic or cultural groups may be unfairly treated by AI systems that reinforce and even magnify social biases found in their training data (Tulsiani, 2024). The necessity for culturally sensitive data curation is highlighted by the discovery that AI models, for example, promote preconceptions across languages and cultures (Mitchell, 2025). Implementing ethical AI frameworks that put transparency, equity, and user agency first is crucial to reducing these problems. To mitigate these issues, it is essential to implement ethical AI frameworks that prioritize transparency, fairness, and user autonomy, ensuring that learners are fully informed about data usage and have control over their personal information (Ibid.)

Pronunciation accuracy and fluency have been shown to increase significantly over time when Praat-assisted learning is incorporated into English pronunciation education. According to research by Zeng & Huang (2025), using Praat software to teach pronunciation not only helped students produce more common English monophthongs but also maintained their interest in the subject over time. Since understanding the nuances of English pronunciation requires constant practice and feedback, this sustained engagement is critical for the long-term preservation of pronunciation abilities. Additionally, Praat's visual feedback helps students see and evaluate their speech patterns, which makes it easier to fix mistakes and improve pronunciation. By addressing both segmental and suprasegmental aspects of pronunciation, this method promotes more fluid and natural speech output. An efficient learning environment that fosters long-lasting gains in speech accuracy and fluency is produced by combining continuous repetition with instant visual feedback (Ibid.).

Although Praat is a popular tool for phonetic analysis, researchers should be aware of its limitations. Its dependence on high-quality audio recordings is a major drawback, as it may make it more difficult to catch the subtleties of abnormal speech, such as that of people with speech problems (Yamashita, et.al,2023). Users without a background in phonetics or acoustics may also find the software difficult to use due to its intricacy and the requirement for specific skills to analyze its data. Praat's analysis capabilities are similarly restricted; it doesn't fully capture emotional tone or prosodic aspects of speech, instead concentrating on metrics like pitch, formants, and intensity. Therefore, even though Praat is still a useful tool for acoustic analysis, its shortcomings show that additional tools or approaches are required to give a more thorough comprehension of human speech (Zeng & Huang, 2025).

## Acoustic Analysis of Standard English Based on Supra Segmental Features

Wells et al. (2023) stated that acoustic analysis of Standard English, particularly focusing on supra-segmental features such as intonation, stress, and pitch, plays a pivotal role in understanding how speech conveys meaning beyond individual sounds. With the aid of software tools like Praat, linguists can extract and analyze pitch contours, intensity, and duration to explore how stress patterns influence rhythm and prosody in English (Boersma,2023).

Intonation in English is typically characterized by the rise and fall of pitch across utterances, indicating the emotional tone, sentence type, or focus. Stress, another key feature, influences word meaning and sentence structure, where stressed syllables tend to have higher pitch, greater intensity, and longer duration than unstressed ones (Romero, 2021). Pitch variation, or fundamental frequency (F0), is crucial for both stress and intonation patterns (Anh, 2017).

Recent advances in acoustic analysis have enhanced our understanding of how supra-segmental features contribute to the intelligibility and interpretation of spoken English (Trofimovich & Baker, 2023). The stress-timed rhythm of English, where stressed syllables are approximately equidistant, creates distinct temporal patterns in speech. This rhythm is essential in differentiating meanings in English, as seen in minimal pairs where stress placement can alter the word's function (e.g., record as a noun versus record as a verb) (Harrison and Vass, 2022).

In standard English, the intonation patterns for declarative sentences (both positive and negative) can vary depending on factors like emphasis, context, and speaker intention. However, there are general patterns that apply to most situations:

## 1. Positive Declarative Sentences

Positive declarative sentences are statements that provide information or make assertions. The intonation pattern for such sentences is generally 'Falling Intonation'. In most cases, positive declarative sentences end with a falling pitch. This means that the pitch of the voice starts higher and gradually falls towards the end of the sentence. The falling intonation conveys finality, confidence, and that the speaker is done providing information (Romero, 2021).

Example: He went to the zoo. (pitch falls at the end)

## 2. Negative Declarative Sentences

The intonation patterns for negative sentences can also be characterized by a falling intonation, like positive declarative sentences, especially when the sentence conveys a clear and direct statement of negation. The tone here may carry a sense of finality or emphasis on the negation.

Example: He didn't go to the zoo. (pitch falls at the end) (Anh,2017).

However, Stress placement in English words follows certain rules, and it can vary depending on whether the word is monosyllabic, disyllabic, or polysyllabic. While these rules help in understanding general patterns, English stress is also influenced by exceptions and specific word categories, like nouns, verbs, adjectives, etc. (Harrison and Vass, 2022).

## 1. Monosyllabic Words (Single Syllable):

Monosyllabic words are always stressed. Since these words have only one syllable, stress is naturally placed on that syllable (Trofimovich & Baker, 2023).

## 2. Disyllabic Words (Two Syllables):

The stress placement in disyllabic words is influenced by the word type (noun/verb, adjective, etc.), with different patterns for nouns and verbs/adjectives. In many two-syllable nouns, the stress tends to fall on the first syllable. But, in many two-syllable verbs and adjectives, the stress usually falls on the second syllable (Romero, 2021).

### 3. Polysyllabic Words (Three or More Syllables):

Stress placement depends on several factors, including the prefixes or suffixes and the word's origin. In many cases, stress falls on the root or main part of the word, rather than on the prefix. However, stress can be affected by the type of suffix attached to the root word. Certain suffixes tend to attract stress in different positions. In compound nouns (two or more words combined), the stress typically falls on the first part of the compound. However, for compound adjectives or verbs, the stress tends to shift to the second part (Harrison and Vass, 2022).

## ACOUSTIC ANALYSIS OF OMANI ARABIC BASED ON SUPRA SEGMENTAL FEATURES

Acoustic analysis of Omani Arabic, specifically focusing on supra-segmental features such as intonation, stress, and pitch, offers valuable insights into the unique phonetic characteristics of the dialect. Al-Busaidi (2022) mentioned that (i) Intonation in Omani Arabic, like other varieties of Arabic, is used to convey different speech acts, such as questions, statements, or exclamations. However, it has distinct features compared to other dialects due to the influence of regional variations within Oman(ii) Pitch contours in Omani Arabic play a significant role in signaling sentence types, where a rising pitch often marks yes-no questions, and a falling pitch indicates declarative statements. Stress patterns in Omani Arabic are also critical in distinguishing between words and phrases, stress tends to fall on the penultimate syllable, but this can vary depending on syntactic structure, which is different from other varieties of Arabic where stress placement may follow different rules (Thakur,2020).

In addition to intonation and stress, duration and intensity also play key roles in the supra-segmental analysis of Omani Arabic. These features are essential in understanding the rhythm and prosody of the language, as Omani Arabic exhibits a syllable-timed rhythm, which contrasts with the stress-timed rhythm of languages like English (Al-Shehri & Al-Hinai, 2023). Pitch and stress are interdependent in Omani Arabic, influencing both the syntactic structure and meaning of utterances (Ibid.).

Although previous literature is very rare concerning the intonation of Omani Arabic, some studies like Holes (2004) and Carter (1982) mentioned that intonation patterns in Arabic can vary based on the type of sentence, including whether the sentence is positive (affirmative) or negative.

## 1. Positive (Affirmative) Sentences:

Pattern: Rising tone at the beginning of the sentence, followed by a slight fall toward the end.

Example:

Arabic: أنا طالب في الجامعة (Ana talib fi al-jami'a)

Translation: "I am a student at the university."

Intonation: The tone starts neutral or slightly rising on أنا (Ana) and then gently falls at the end with الجامعة (al-jami'a).

## 2. Negative Sentences:

Pattern: Negative sentences often have a slightly different intonation where the tone starts lower or with a more neutral pitch, and there is often a final falling tone.

Example:

Arabic: أنا لست طالباً في الجامعة (Ana lastu taliban fi al-jami'a)

Translation: "I am not a student at the university."

Intonation: The tone starts neutral or slightly falling, with a drop at لست (lastu), and falls further at the end.

Negative sentences in Arabic tend to sound more definitive and firmer, often employing a lower or neutral tone at the start, which reinforces the negation.

However, in Omani Arabic, stress placement follows certain patterns that can be similar to other dialects of Arabic but with some distinctive features. Arabic is generally a stress-timed language, and stress plays an important role in distinguishing meaning in certain cases. Stress placement in Arabic is typically influenced by the structure of the word, and it generally follows some broad rules that are consistent with the wider Arabic language, though regional variations (such as in Omani Arabic) exist (Betti & Ulaiwi,2018; Watson,2004).

Bassiouney (2009), provided the following for stress placement in Omani Arabic:

## 1. Monosyllabic Words:

Since monosyllabic words only have one syllable, that syllable is always stressed.

Example: بَيْت (bayt = "house"), stress on the only syllable.

## 2. Disyllabic Words:

For disyllabic words, stress placement depends on whether the word is a noun, a verb, or another category like adjective or preposition. Stress tends to fall on the first syllable in many nouns in Omani Arabic.

Example: لبَج (jabal = “mountain”), stress on the first syllable.

Example: ةسَرْدَم (madrasa = “school”), stress on the first syllable.

But, stress in verbs is placed on the second syllable, especially in regular verbs in the perfect tense. However, the pattern can vary depending on the verb's form (root pattern) (Aljanajiya,2016).

Example: بَتَك (kataba = “he wrote”), stress on the second syllable.

## 3. Polysyllabic Words:

In words with three or more syllables, stress placement can become more complex, and it is typically influenced by several factors like word type (noun, verb, etc.), and whether the word is derived from a trilateral root or has affixes. For many polysyllabic nouns in Omani Arabic, stress typically falls on the second-to-last syllable.

Example: ريدُم (mudiir = “director”), stress on the second syllable.

Example: بيبَط (tabeeb = “doctor”), stress on the second syllable.

In verbs (especially in the perfect tense), stress often falls on the first syllable, when the verb has a trilateral root.

Example: مَاق (qaama = “he stood up”), stress on the first syllable.

For words with added prefixes or suffixes, the stress may shift to the root or the lastsyllable, depending on the affix type.

Example: ةبَتَكْم (maktaba = “library”), stress on the last syllable.

Stress patterns in Omani Arabic may also exhibit regional variation, particularly between urban and rural dialects, or between the different regions of Oman(Morano,2024) .In addition to that, stress placement can be influenced by how closely a word follows Classical Arabic patterns, or whether it has been influenced by other languages like English or Persian, which may affect word stress in some cases(Bettega, 2019 a,b)Stress in Omani Arabic can sometimes be used to distinguish between nouns and verbs. For instance, changing the stress position can result in a different meaning or part of speech, as in other Arabic dialects (Ibid.)

## METHOD

The aim of this study was to investigate the effectiveness of using Praat acoustic analysis to analyze the challenges faced by Omani EFL university students in their phonetic prosodic production of sentence intonation and word stress-placement that were collected by developing a two parts test. The researchers followed the descriptive and analytic statistic method in this study A phonetic test (PHTIS)of two parts was developed and used as an instrument in the investigation i.e., part one is devoted towards assessing the sample's production of the intonation patterns of positive sentences and negative sentences of a declarative sentence type while the second part is to evaluate the sample students' stress placement oral competency of monosyllabic, disyllabic and polysyllabic tokens. All tokens of the two parts of the (PHTIS)were taken from Pathways Textbook that is taught to the sample students at the foundation program of the university study.

### Sample

As the purpose of this study was to compare the supra-segmental characteristics of intonation and lexical stress placement with those of standard English, the researchers divided the sample into two categories. The first is group A, which consists of oral data of standard English native speakers. The second group B was made up of oral data produced by Omani EFL university students.

Data from native English speakers (group A) was obtained from reliable online sources, namely;

- Oxford Online Dictionary
- Pronunciation with Emma
- Oral data production of a native speaker

The data from group B was collected using a stratified random sampling approach. The sample selected is restricted to

1. The participants must be a native speaker of Omani Arabic.
2. The participants must not have stayed in a country other than Oman for a long duration.

The participants were thirty Omani male and female EFL college students enrolled in the foundation programs at the university level. The sample group studied intonation and stress placement production using the conventional method of drilling and repetition to be done after the teacher or the recorder as prescribed in their syllabus specifications and Pathways textbooks being used by the college.

Brown& Hellmuth (2024) explained that Omani Arabic-specific linguistic and cultural elements affect how Omani learners pick up English prosody, especially intonation. Omani Arabic does not employ pitch shifts to differentiate word meanings because it is not a tonal language. Omani learners may therefore find it difficult to understand English intonation patterns, which mostly rely on pitch changes to express emphasis, attitude, and meaning. When developing and interpreting English pitch contours, including those used in questions and declarations, the lack of tonal distinctions in Omani Arabic might result in mistakes.

Furthermore, because of Oman's cultural history, which uses pitch sparingly for pragmatic reasons, Omani intonation patterns may be translated into English. Speech that sounds flat or lacks the usual tone variation can impair fluency and intelligibility. The interaction of these linguistic and cultural factors highlights the need for targeted teaching strategies that address prosodic learning and help students get past challenges related to English pitch variation Baltazani, et.al,2024).

## The Instrument

The sentence intonation and lexical placement test (PHTIS) was developed by the two researchers in the current investigation. The sentence intonation section included thirty (15 positive sentences and 15 negative sentences) contextualized sentences that were specifically chosen for the study's sample. The sentences were originally found in Pathways textbooks; however, they were modified (AL-Kinany, 2023) and were all written at a level appropriate for the students to ensure that they had no difficulty comprehending the vocabulary and grammar.

To achieve the validity of the test, expert validity was used in which eight specialists were asked to review the (PHTIS) and comment on its validity and suitability to the sample students (see appendix 3). The experts checked the (PHTIS) from a linguistic, cultural, and social viewpoints and made sure they are suitable to the sample students' level. In addition, they also examined the word tokens from the same perspective and removed three tokens as they were found not appropriate from a cultural view. See the final version of the (PHTIS) in appendix (2).

For the first part of the test, the subjects were asked to read all sentences for the purpose of recording their sentence intonation production patterns of the intonation patterns of positive sentences and negative sentences of a declarative sentence type. Moreover, the same sample students were requested to read thirty tokens of monosyllabic, disyllabic, and polysyllabic words of the second part of the test. All tokens of the two parts of the (PHTIS)were taken from Pathways Textbooks that is taught to the sample students at the foundation program of the university study.

Using Praat software acoustic analysis, the researchers then analyzed the results with the help of two native speakers. The responses from the students were written down, transcribed, and then examined.

For the intonation production part, each speaker was recorded in a semi spontaneous interview situation. They were free to choose their partners of the conversation regardless of the gender. The session lasted 5–10 minutes in average. The recordings were manually transcribed using Praat Text Grids and speech was fluent in these transcriptions (i.e. no pauses, no false starts etc.)

For the lexical stress-placement part, each word occurred in isolation and same sample speakers who acted as subjects in the intonation production part of this study were recorded reading the words in lists based on their own spontaneous speech. The recordings were made in a sound treated studio using Sennheiser HSP 4 cardioid headset microphones connected to a computer using the Apple Logic Pro recording software and an M-AUDIO ProFire 2626 audio interface. Recordings were originally sampled at 48 kHz/16bit but they were down sampled to 16kHz/16bit for the acoustic analyses.

## Application

The sentence intonation section of the (PHTIS) was used to examine the sentence intonation produced by Omani EFL college students. the first part of the (PHITS) comprised all the target sentences used in the current work, including 15 positive sentences and 15 negative sentences. The intonation production must be acted out by the students as accurately as possible. Their oral production of intonation was audio-recorded as test's data. The scoring scheme is presented in table 1.

*Table 1. The Scoring Scheme*

| | |
|---|---|
| **0 Mark** | for level tone intonation. |
| **1 Mark** | for weak intonation production (totally does not match with the intonation pattern specified in standard English) |
| **2 Marks** | for acceptable intonation production.<br>(slightly match with the intonation pattern specified in standard English) |
| **3 Marks** | for good intonation production.<br>(Somehow match with the intonation pattern specified in standard English) |
| **4 Marks** | For v. good intonation production.<br>(match with the intonation pattern specified in standard English) |
| **5 Marks** | for excellent intonation production.<br>(totally match with the intonation pattern specified in standard English) |

For the stress placement section of the test, the level 4 Omani EFL college students who were enrolled in the foundation program at the University level were given (30 words) as tokens that represent part of the key vocabulary included in the Pathways textbook that was prescribed for them by their college. The tokens were words with one, two, or more syllables. Students were instructed to read lists of words aloud while their reading was recorded in Praat software and analyzed by the researchers with the help of two teachers who were native speakers. Ten tokens from each word type were selected for the analysis of this study and then transcribed according to the number of syllables in the lists. The responses were then examined.

The percentage was used to analyze the data. The stress placement section of the (PHTIS)was used to investigate Omani EFL college students' production of word stress placement. Their oral production was audio-recorded as test's' data and scored. The scoring scheme is presented in table 2.

*Table 2. Scoring Scheme*

| | |
|---|---|
| **0 Mark** | for incorrect stress placement production. |
| **1 Marks** | for correct stress placement production. |

The rubric for the test's assessment was developed by the researchers and obtained its validity by being presented to the experts (See appendix 1).

## Data Collection

The percentage counts were used to quantify participants' production in the two parts of the (PHTIS). Having recorded the sample of the current study, the researchers uploaded the recorded data in Praat and obtained the acoustic analysis for all sentences of the first part of the (PHTIS). The researchers analyzed 15 positive sentences + 15 negative sentences =30 tokens from the recordings produced by every sample student i.e., 30 tokens x 30 students =900 tokens of sentence intonation were analyzed acoustically using Praat analysis. Praat software was used to visualize the sound wave of every sentence. This provides a time-domain representation of the signal. The researchers measured the variation between the highest and lowest points in the F0 contour. A larger pitch range indicated a dynamic intonation pattern, which is common in positive, enthusiastic statements. The final tone pattern was the key factor in the analysis as positive sentences often show a rise in pitch at the start or the middle of the sentence, followed by a fall at the end. To enable a comparison of the productions across the speaker groups, the utterances from the corpus were all phonologically evaluated for the sentence intonation test. The final tune's shape, or the change in pitch from the last pitch accent to the boundary tone, which occurs at the end of questions and statements is the matter of examination concern in this study. Anh (2017) investigated the relationship between English question intonation and meaning in natural speech circumstances and proposed that the prosodic structure, primarily the final contour's direction, is crucial to interactional pragmatic meaning. As a result, the final tunes were encoded in the current work. In accordance with AL-Kinany,et.al (2022), the symbols utilized were F for falling pattern, R for rising pattern, RF for rising-falling pattern, and FR for falling-rising pattern. In Praat, tokens generated by the individuals were processed and examined acoustically (Boersma and Weeninck, 2009). To determine the label of the tunes, each token was divided into syllables and an acoustic analysis using PRAAT and a visual pitch contour was performed.

For the intonation analysis. The following steps were followed:

1.Prepare Audio Files

The researchers ensured that audio recordings of the speech to analyze were clear and free from background noise and were in a format compatible with PRAAT (e.g., WAV, MP3).

2.Open the Audio File in Praat

The researchers opened Praat and loaded audio file by selecting Open from the Read menu.

3.Analysis of Speech in Praat

Before using Praat to do sound analysis, the researchers first fed the data of every single sentence structure individually, they started with sample students\ production of positive statements (5 statements x 30 students=150 tokens).

a. Extracting sound

The researchers selected the type of audio they want to examine by clicking the file icon. By doing this, a new sound file was created in the Objects window.

b. Showing the Spectrogram

The waveform and spectrogram were presented automatically once the file is selected. The researchers selected one file and clicked "View and Edit".

c. Adjusting the Spectrogram Settings

The most important settings here are the **window length** and **view range**.

View range decides how much of the spectrum is shown. For speech, the range is to be set from 0 to 5,000 or 6,000 Hz, but for examining fricatives, we might need to set it as high as 15,000 Hz. To adjust the **View range**, the researchers clicked "Spectrum" → "Spectrogram Settings".

Praat provides both Broadband spectrogram and Narrowband spectrogram by adjusting the window length. The shorter the window length, the larger its bandwidth (Bandwidth = 1.299 / window length). There is no clear-cut boundary between Broadband spectrograms and Narrowband spectrograms, if the window length is around 3-5 ms (bandwidth: 200-300Hz), the resulting spectrogram is called "wideband". For the window length around 20-30ms (bandwidth: 30-50Hz), the spectrogram is called "narrowband". Wideband spectrogram is used to observe the formant structure while narrowband spectrograms reveal the harmonic structure (pitch information).

- **Broadband spectrogram** (*Window Length:* 0.005s) was used to observe the formant structure of sound, and it is the default setting in Praat.

## PITCH

Pitch is a term used to refer to variations in fundamental frequency (F0), which serves as an important acoustic cue for tone, lexical stress, and intonation (Anh,2017).

d. To Extract information about pitch, the researchers followed the below steps:
    1. Display the pitch track: Pitch → Show pitch
    2. At this point, a blue line was placed on the spectrogram representing the pitch. The researchers placed the cursor at the point and read the blue number on the right side of the window.
e. To Maximum, Minimum, and Average pitch for a section of speech, the researchers followed these steps:
    1. They selected the portion of the sound for which they wanted the Maximum, Minimum or Average Pitch
    2. They select the proper command for a specified task from the top menu: Pitch → Get Pitch/Get Maximum Pitch / Get Minimum Pitch.
f. Extract Pitch Information

To analyze the intonation, the researchers extracted the pitch (fundamental frequency, F0) contour, selected audio object in the Praat object window, went to Analyze Periodicity > To Pitch to extract the pitch contour.

A new pitch object appeared in the object window. The researchers visualized the pitch contour by selecting the pitch object and clicking View & Edit.

## Analyze the Pitch Contour

In the View & Edit window, the researchers observed the pitch contour over time. The horizontal axis represented time, and the vertical axis represented pitch (in Hz).

a. Extract Pitch Characteristics

For detailed analysis, the researchers extracted specific pitch characteristics, such as:

Mean pitch: The average pitch level throughout the recording.

Pitch range: The difference between the highest and lowest pitch.

Pitch variation: The fluctuations in pitch over time.

Pitch accent: Where pitch movements (rises and falls) occur, which might correspond to stressed or prominent syllables.

b. Label the Pitch Events

In the View & Edit window, the researchers manually labeled events like pitch rises, falls, and plateau regions. This is important for understanding the intonation patterns and their relation to meaning or emphasis in the speech.

## Compare Intonation Patterns

The researchers compared the pitch contours of different recordings using overlays in the View & Edit window to show multiple pitch contours at once for comparison.

## Export the Data

The researchers exported the pitch data for further statistical analysis or visualization using File > Write to TextGrid or Write to WAV/MP3 to save your annotations or adjusted pitch contours.

## Interpret the Results

Based on the analysis, the researchers interpreted the intonation features in the context of the research:

## Intonation in Positive Sentences

The general intonation pattern of standard English for positive sentences is 'Falling Intonation'. In most statements or assertive positive sentences, the intonation generally falls at the end of the sentence. The pitch starts from a mid-level or slightly higher pitch at the beginning and gradually falls towards the end. Rising intonation can be used in positive sentences that express surprise, uncertainty, or when the speaker is seeking confirmation, even though the sentence is positive (Ladefoged,2006).

Concerning the results of this study, only declarative-positive sentences were analyzed. Only 8% of sample students produced 12 out of 15 sentences with a falling tone. The majority of the sentences were produced by 57 % of participants without a tonic accent i.e., level tone, almost produced the sentences without considering intonation. And 23% of the sample students raised the pitch at the end of 8 statements, which is the absolute opposite of this falling category. Table 3 shows the statistical results of the positive-sentence intonation pattern part of the (PHTIS).

*Table 3. The statistical results of the positive-sentence intonation pattern part of the (PHTIS)*

| | Marking criteria | | | | | |
|---|---|---|---|---|---|---|
| | **0 Mark** | **1 Mark** | **2 Marks** | **3 Marks** | **4 Marks** | **5 Marks** |
| Students' results | 57% | 23% | 0% | 0% | 8% | 0% |
| | 14 sentences | 8 sentences | | | 12 sentences | |

## Intonation in Negative Sentences

Negative-declarative sentences (statements that are negative) usually have a falling intonation pattern, similar to positive statements. The pitch tends to start from a mid-level and falls towards the end of the sentence, even when the sentence is negative (Ladefoged,2006).Results showed that 67 % of students produced all the statements without giving any expressional tone i.e., produced the statements with level tone, 18% raised the pitch at the end of 13 sentences out of 15 statements, which is the absolute opposite of this falling category. and only 15 of students produced 14 out of 15 sentences with the correct intonation patterns i.e., falling–intonation pattern. Table 4 shows the statistical results of the negative-sentence intonation pattern part of the (PHTIS).

*Table 4. The statistical results of the negative-sentence intonation pattern part of the (PHTIS)*

| | Marking criteria | | | | | |
|---|---|---|---|---|---|---|
| | **0 Mark** | **1 Mark** | **2 Marks** | **3 Marks** | **4 Marks** | **5 Marks** |
| Students' results | 67 % | 18% | 0% | 0% | 15% | 0% |
| | 15 sentences | 13 sentences | | | 14 sentences | |

However, for the second part of the (PHTIS), the lexical tokens found in the test were divided according to the number of syllables of every word as presented in table 6.

*Table 5. Lexical tokens*

| Word Tokens | Numbers |
|---|---|
| Monosyllabic | 10 |
| Disyllabic | 10 |
| Polysyllabic | 10 |

The researchers recorded all tokens for the lexical stress placement section of the (PHTIS)and phonetically transcribed them in accordance with the IPA standard for lexical stress placement. All tokens from each lexical–syllable type tokens were selected for analyses i.e., 10x3x30 =900 tokens were then entered into the Praat program to conduct an auditory analysis. Tokens were divided into syllables, and Praat was used to do an acoustic analysis.

The loudness (intensity), length (vowel duration), pitch, and quality of words were checked for this task in accordance with the stress predominance. Only the length requirement, however, was taken into account for the study because, typically, the stressed syllable must have a longer duration than the unstressed syllable.

## Lexical Stress

In English we usually find that simple words consisting of two or more syllables have a strong stress on one of these syllables and a weak stress on the remaining syllable or syllables. Stress plays an important role in communication, for it distinguishes different meanings when the stress is put in different positions.

"All stressed syllables in words have one characteristic in common, and that is prominence. Prominence is produced by four main factors:(i) loudness (intensity), (ii) length, (iii) pitch (Fundamental Frequency/F0), (iv) quality. Generally, these four factors work together in combination, but experimental work has shown that these factors are not equally important; the strongest effect is produced by pitch, and length is also a powerful factor. Loudness and quality have much less effect" (Roach 2009:74).

Since stress is manifested as rise in pitch, greater intensity (loudness) or greater vowel length, the analysis of stress must include various elements of acoustic analysis, like waveform, spectrogram, and pitch contour.

- at the top, the waveform indicates the greater intensity of the stressed syllable
- in the middle, it shows the higher pitch shown in the pitch track
- at the bottom, the spectrogram indicates the greater length of the stressed syllable

(retrieved from Stonham's handout: p3, http://stonham.dyndns.org/phonetics/handouts/prosod_hndt.pdf)

For the stress phonetic acoustic analysis in Praat, the researchers followed the steps below:

### 1. Prepare the Speech Data

The researchers obtained speech samples audio files containing the words to be analyze.They also ensured that the speech is clear and of high quality.

### 2. Load Audios in Praat

The researchers opened Praat and clicked on "Read" > "Read from file" to load the audio files into Praat for analysis.

## 3. Segment the Speech

Praat's TextGrid function was used to segment the speech and a TextGrid was created by selecting the audio file in the Objects list and then clicking "Annotate" > "To TextGrid".

The researchers Manually marked the phoneme-level segmentation in the TextGrid (e.g., syllables, vowels, consonants) that allowed them to observe stress placement.

## 4. Analyze Pitch (F0)

Pitch is crucial in analyzing word stress, as stressed syllables tend to have higher pitch or a greater pitch range.

To extract pitch, the researchers selected the audio file and click "Analyze" > "To Pitch".They adjusted the parameters for pitch extraction (e.g., pitch range, time step, etc.) in the pop-up menu that appears and choose the default settings to adjust them depending on the speech data.

## 5. Measure Intensity (Amplitude)

Stressed syllables tend to have greater intensity (loudness). To measure intensity, the researchers clicked on the audio file and selected "Analyze" > "To Intensity". They set the parameters (such as intensity range and time step) based on the characteristics of the recording. The resulting Intensity object showed the amplitude in decibels (dB) over time, which was then correlated with the stress pattern.

## 6. Extract Syllable Duration

Stressed syllables often have a longer duration than unstressed syllables. To analyze syllable duration, the researchers segmented the audio into syllables in the TextGrid. Once the syllables were marked, they selected each syllable and measure its duration. They clicked on the syllable in the TextGrid, and Praat immediately provided a duration value at the bottom of the window.

## 7. Analyze and Compare Stress Placement

Using the Pitch, Intensity, and Duration measurements, the researchers compared the stressed syllables with unstressed ones. Typically, stressed syllables exhibit:

- Higher pitch (increased F0).
- Greater intensity (louder sound).

- Longer duration.

## 8. Visualize the Results

Praat provides graphical outputs for Pitch, Intensity, and Duration. The researchers viewed these features over time for each syllable in the word. This visualization allowed them to easily identify the stressed syllables based on the acoustic properties.

## 9. Interpret the Results

After obtaining the acoustic measurements (Pitch, Intensity, and Duration), analyze the data to determine the stress pattern. Typically, the highest pitch, loudest intensity, and longest duration corresponded to the stressed syllables in the word. The researchers analyzed how stress placement varies across participants.

## 10. Document Findings

Once data was analyzed, the researchers documented document the findings and reported the acoustic measurements and described the stress patterns observed for each word.

## Lexical Stress Placement in Monosyllabic Words

In monosyllabic words, stress placement is usually straightforward, as there is only one syllable in the word. These words are always stressed because there is no other syllable to compete with. All monosyllabic words have stress on their single syllable. However, there are exceptions in cases of compound words or function words like prepositions, articles, or conjunctions (e.g., "in," "on," "the"), which are typically unstressed in continuous speech. In such cases, stress is not determined by the number of syllables, but by the role the word plays in a sentence (i.e., function words are often unstressed) (Roach,2018).Results of the current study showed that 95% of Omani EFL college students produced all 5 tokens of the monosyllabic with correct lexical stress placement and only 3% of the sample students missed pronounced 2 lexical stress placement and 2 % of the sample students mispronounced all lexical stress placement . See table 7.

*Table 6. Students' production of monosyllabic lexical stress placement*

| | Marking criteria | | |
|---|---|---|---|
| | 0 Mark | 1 Mark | |
| Students' results | 2 % | 95 % | 3% |
| | All tokens | All tokens | 3 tokens |

## Lexical Stress Placement in Disyllabic Words

In disyllabic words, stress placement can either be on the first syllable or the second syllable, depending on the type of word. Generally, noun and adjective words tend to have stress on the first syllable, on the other hand, verbs and prepositions more often have stress on the second syllable. However, this pattern is not absolute, and there are many exceptions where the stress can vary based on meaning, sentence context, or word form (Roach,2018). Results of this experimental study indicated that 76 % of Omani EFL college students produced all 10 tokens of the disyllabic with correct lexical stress placement, 10 % of sample students produced 6 tokens of disyllabic words with correct lexical stress placement, 8 % of the sample students missed pronounced 2 words and 6 % produced all 10 tokens with wrong lexical stress placement. See table 8.

*Table 7. Students' production of disyllabic lexical stress placement*

| | Marking criteria | | | |
|---|---|---|---|---|
| | 0 Mark | 1 Mark | | |
| Students' results | 6 % | 76 % | 10% | 8% |
| | All tokens | All tokens | 6 tokens | 8 tokens |

## Lexical Stress Placement in Polysyllabic Words

For polysyllabic words, stress placement follows more complex rules that are influenced by word type, affixation, and syllable structure. In general, the primary stress tends to fall on one of the earlier syllables. For example, in many three-syllable words, the stress is placed on the first syllable for nouns and on the second syllable for verbs. In longer words, stress placement may also be influenced by prefixes, suffixes, or compound structures. The placement of secondary stress is also common, typically falling on other syllables that are not primary stressed (Roach,2018). Results showed that 88 % of students produced 8 tokens with in correct lexical placement stress, 6 % of the sample students produced 5 tokens with incorrect lexical placement stress, and 6 % of students produced all tokens with correct lexical placement stress. See table 9.

*Table 8. Students' production of polysyllabic lexical stress placement*

| | Marking criteria | | |
|---|---|---|---|
| | 0 Mark | | 1 Mark |
| Students' results | 88 % | 6% | 6 % |
| | 8 tokens | 5 tokens | All tokens |

## Data Analysis

Many deviations were observed in the sample EFL students' intonation production. This may be due to a lack of awareness, mother tongue influence, and carelessness., A considerable percentage of Omani EFL college sample students were found to be predominantly using a rising tone when producing positive declarative sentences. Furthermore, a large percentage of the sample students tend to produce positive and negative sentences with a level tone. Only a small percentage of sample students produced the majority of positive-declarative sentences with a falling tone. And quarter of the sample students raised the pitch at the end of half number of statements, which is the absolute opposite of this falling category. For the sample production of the negative-declarative sentences Results showed that many students produced all the statements without giving any expressional tone i.e., produced the statements with level tone, some raised the pitch at the end of almost all statements, which is the absolute opposite of this falling category. and only a small percentage of students produced nearly all sentences with the correct intonation patterns i.e., falling–intonation pattern. All these findings indicate that sample students thereby missed to communicate subtle nuances of meaning which is not communicated through the bare meanings of sentences. Such supra-segmental meanings are exploited through the strategic use of fall, rise, fall-rise and rise-fall intonations in the various sample's utterances. These findings revealed that Omani EFL college students, in general, could not master the production of the correct intonation patterns for positive and negative-declarative sentences.

On the Other hand, Omani EFL college students generally produced most of the monosyllabic and disyllabic words with correct lexical-stress placements, however, for the polysyllabic tokens they tend to lengthen and convert vowel sounds that were found in the various syllables and that consequently results in serious confusion as the length may change the number of syllables in words while converting vowels lead to change of stress placement. The sample students tend to convert the diphthong /ei/ into long vowel / ɜ:/. Often the words are stressed at the wrong syllables. Students usually stress the first syllable of the tokens, however, the problematic issue in with assigning stress placement to the second and the third and the fourth syllable. Results also showed that a large number of the sample students divide syllables into sub-syllables when pronouncing polysyllabic words. Conventionally speaking, most of the tokens were crowded together so that the stressed syllables maintain their occurrence after a fixed interval of time. See appendix 4.

To answer the research questions, it is obtained that:

1. To what extent is Praat software effective in providing acoustic software analysis of intonation and stress placement?

Praat is a strong, useful, and time-saving artificial intelligence software tool for acoustic analysis. It is especially significant in the study of intonation and stress

2. What are the prominent intonation patterns produced by Omani EFL university students?

The bulk of positive-declarative phrases with a falling intonation pattern tone were only produced by a small portion of the sample students. The complete opposite of this falling category, a quarter of the sample students raised the pitch at the end of half the number of statements.

a. To what extent do Omani EFL college students produce affirmative-declarative sentences with correct intonation patterns?

When producing positive declarative sentences, a significant portion of Omani EFL college sample students were observed to mostly use a semi- levelled intonation pattern rather than a falling one.

b. To what extent do Omani EFL college students produce negative-declarative sentences with correct intonation patterns?

Regarding the negative-declarative sentence production, findings revealed that a large number of students produced all of the sentences with a level tone, or without any expressional tone. In contrast, some students raised the pitch at the end of nearly every statement, which is the complete opposite of this falling intonation pattern category. and only a tiny portion of students produced almost all phrases with the proper intonation patterns, which is the falling intonation pattern.

c. How are the intonation patterns produced by Omani EFL university students similar to or different from standard English?

Although some sample students produced the correct intonation patterns for the affirmative and negative sentences of the (PHTIS), a large number of the subjects used the semi-levelled intonation pattern for both types of sentence structures i.e., affirmative and negative sentences. On the other hand, many students produced the negative sentences with a rising intonation pattern. Deviations from the intonation patterns of Standard English are huge in the sample students' production of the intonation patterns for the affirmative and negative sentences.

3. To what extend do Omani EFL university students put the correct stress placement on:
    a. monosyllabic words

The majority of monosyllabic tokens were often produced by Omani EFL college students with the proper lexical-stress placements.

b. disyllabic words

With the appropriate lexical-stress placements, Omani EFL college students frequently produced most of the disyllabic tokens.

c. polysyllabic words

Sample students tend to lengthen and convert vowel sounds that were found in the various syllables and that consequently results in serious confusion as the length may change the number of syllables in words while converting vowels lead to change of stress placement.

## CONCLUSIONS

The intonation contours of English affirmative and negative-declarative statements, as well as the placement of word stress in monosyllabic, disyllabic, and polysyllabic words, were studied and characterized by Omani EFL college students using Praat acoustic analysis. Because of its extensive feature set, which enables researchers to visually and quantitatively evaluate speech patterns, Praat is a strong, useful, and time-saving artificial intelligence software tool for acoustic analysis. It is especially significant in the study of intonation and stress.

The failure of Omani college students to produce the last falling tunes and their use of a version of L1 tonal contours for their English intonation shows transmission at the phonetic level from the mother tongue. The F0 patterns produced by Omani EFL learners (such as L, L-R, L-F, and L-L) were derived from the tone contours in Omani Arabic (Elsayed, et al.,2021). Students sometimes transfer lexical tones to intonation contour in English. In addition, the sample students in this study frequently utilized semi-levelled- final tunes for endings, indicating that they might be aware of the response and anticipated the other speaker to concur (Thuker, 2020; Anh, 2017).

It can be also inferred from the data that the majority of students faced no difficulty in producing mono and disyllabic words with correct lexical stress placement but struggled to identify the proper place of emphasis in English polysyllabic words. The results clearly show that the sample students struggled with suprasegmentals, particularly with stress. Thus, the students 'ability to speak clearly and correctly put word emphasis is hampered by their lack of proficiency with the English sound system (AL-Kinany,2023).

In conclusion, this study, using Praat acoustic analysis, examined and described how Omani EFL college students produced the intonation contours of English affirmative and negative-declarative statements as well as word stress placement in monosyllabic, disyllabic, and polysyllabic words. Praat is found a powerful, practical and time-saving AI software tool for the acoustic analysis, and it is particularly important in the study of intonation and stress because of its robust set of features that allowed the researchers to visually and quantitatively analyze speech patterns.

Moreover, the findings of the intonation part, data generated from responses of Omani EFL college students in the intonation part of the (PHTIS) are consistently different from those of native English speakers, which can be attributed to their transfer from their native tone language (Nguyen et al., 2008; Larina et al., 2021). However, the results showed that Omani EFL students could produce mono and disyllabic words with correct lexical stress placement but struggled to identify the proper place of emphasis in English polysyllabic words. This study looked at how two typologically different languages Omani Arabic, a contrastive contour tone language, and English, a stress accent language transmitted intonation patterns and word stress location prosodically. This disparity can be attributed to language transfer as the influence of their native language (Arabic), which is a tone language with different intonational rules(sato,2022). In tone languages, pitch changes can carry lexical meaning (i.e., the pitch of a word can change its meaning), whereas in English, intonation typically serves more to convey discourse functions such as indicating question types, emphasis, or emotions, rather than changing word meaning. This fundamental difference in how pitch is used in both languages can result in systematic errors in the students' intonation (Trofimovich,2021).

Although tone is frequently employed to indicate sentence type or stress in Arabic (especially in Oman dialects), it follows different rules than English (Al-harthi, 2021). Thus, Omani students may incorporate their mother tongue prosodic rhythms into their English speaking (Thuker, 2020),odd pitch contours that aren't common in English are examples of this (Hassan,2023). These variations can result in intelligibility issues since non-native patterns might lead to meaning mistakes or influence how English listeners interpret the message (Ibid.). These findings go in line with the findings obtained by (Kormos,2022) who discussed how intonation and stress are crucial elements of prosody in second language (L2) speech and how L1 influence can lead to intonational errors in L2 learners. Trofimovich,et.al (2021) also examined how the prosody of the native language (in this case, a tone language like Arabic) influences intonation and stress placement in L2 English. They (Ibid.) highlighted the challenge of intonational transfer and how these differences can be analyzed and corrected using tools like Praat for more precise instruction. Sato,et. al (2022), on the other hand, focused on how intonational transfer from native tone languages (like Arabic) affects L2 English learners' use of pitch. They (Ibid.) also demonstrated how Praat can be used to compare pitch contours between native speakers and non-native learners, revealing patterns of intonational interference. While Munro (2021) studied how intonation and stress placement in second language learners are often affected by native language transfer, and it highlights the utility of Praat in analyzing pitch variation.

## ACKNOWLEDGMENT

We would like to thank The Research Council in Oman for funding this project. Also, we appreciate The University of Technology and Applied Sciences – Nizwa College of Technology in Oman for their collaboration in conducting this research.

**Funding Details:** The current paper is part of a project that is funded by The Research Council in Oman.

## REFERENCES

Alharthi, A. (2021). Exploring the use of intonation in Arabic varieties, particularly in Oman. *International Journal of Linguistics*, *12*(3), 67–81.

Anh, P. T. (2017). Intonation and stress in English: Issues and challenges for EFL learners. *Journal of English Language Teaching*, *22*(3), 14–28.

Aydin, I., Diebel-Fischer, H., Freiberger, V., Möller-Klapperich, J., Buchmann, E., Färber, M., Lauber-Rönsberg, A., & Platow, B. (2024). Assessing privacy policies with AI: Ethical, legal, and technical challenges. *arXiv. https://doi.org//arXiv.2410.08381.*DOI: 10.48550

Azzahra, S., Syarfina, T., & Sembiring, F. E. D. R. B. (2024). Comparative formants analysis of English vowels using PRAAT. *Journal of English Language and Pedagogy*, *7*(2), 260–266. DOI: 10.33503/journey.v7i2.838

Baker, A. (2021). Assessing EFL pronunciation with PRAAT: Methods and applications. *Linguistic Studies Journal*, *18*(1), 49–66.

Baker, A., & Trofimovich, P. (2022). The role of PRAAT in evaluating EFL learners' pronunciation: A comprehensive guide. *Language Learning & Technology*, *26*(2), 35–50.

Baltazani, M., Armostis, S., & Payne, E. (2024). The intonation of polar questions in Cypriot Arabic: Prosodic contact in an endangered language. *Speech Prosody (Urbana, Ill.)*, *1–5*, 502–506. Advance online publication. DOI: 10.21437/Speech-Prosody.2024-102

Bashir, A. (2024). Acoustic analysis of the English diphthongs /ou/ and /ei/ among Hausa native speakers in Northwest and Northeast Nigeria. *International Journal of Innovation in Literature, Language & Arts Studies, 12(2), 34–46. Retrieved from*https://www.seahipublications.org/wp-content/uploads/2024/04/IJILLAS-J-4-2024.pdf

Bassiouney, R. (Ed.). (2009). *Arabic sociolinguistics: Topics in diglossia, gender, identity, and politics*. Georgetown University Press. DOI: 10.3366/edinburgh/9780748623730.001.0001

Bettega, S. (2019a). Tense, Modality and Aspect in Omani Arabic. Naples: Università degli Studi di Napoli 'L'Orientale'.

Bettega, S. (2019b). 'Genitive markers in Omani Arabic'. In RomanoArabica 19: 223–37.

Betti, M. J., & Ulaiwi, W. A. (2018). Stress in English and Arabic: A contrastive study. *English Language and Literature Studies*, *8*(1), 83–91.

Boersma, P. (2023). *PRAAT: An introduction to speech analysis*. Cambridge University Press.

Boersma, P., & Weenink, D. (2024). PRAAT: Doing phonetics by computer (Version 6.1). University of Amsterdam. https://www.praat.org

Brown, G., & Hellmuth, S. (2024). Computational modelling of segmental and prosodic levels of analysis for capturing variation across Arabic dialects. *Journal of Phonetics*, *89*, 101–118.

Carter, G. M. (1982). *The Arabic dialect of Oman*. Curzon Press.

Chen, M. (2022). Computer-aided feedback on the pronunciation of Mandarin Chinese tones: Using Praat to promote multimedia foreign language learning. *Computer Assisted Language Learning*, *35*(3), 363–388. DOI: 10.1080/09588221.2022.2037652

Dandee, N.. (2022). Prosody in English language teaching: The importance of rhythm, intonation, and stress. *TESOL Quarterly*, *56*(1), 89–102.

Derwing, T. M. (2021). Pronunciation instruction and its impact on second language learners. *Journal of Second Language Pronunciation*, *7*(4), 377–390.

El-Garawany, M. S. M. (2021). Using Praat to develop English majors' EFL intonation production. Educational Journal of the Faculty of Education. *Sohag University*, *92*(92), 91–125. DOI: 10.21608/edusohag.2021.208708

Elsayed, M., Al-Khalili, M., & Al-Maqbali, K. (2021). The transfer of intonation patterns from Omani Arabic to English. *International Journal of Linguistics*, *13*(2), 71–89.

Feng, J., & Zhang, L. (2024). An assessment of different Praat versions for acoustic measures. *Journal of Voice*, *38*(3), 432.e1–432.e9. DOI: 10.1016/j.jvoice.2023.07.004

Godde, D., Bosses, M., & Bailly, G. (2020). The role of prosody in the comprehension of spoken language. *Language and Speech, 63*(2), 231–250.

Harrison, K., & Vass, R. (2022). Stress patterns in English: Acoustic analysis and its impact on prosody. *Journal of Phonetic Research, 35*(3), 212–224.

Holes, C. (2004). *Arabic dialectology: A guide to the study of the regional varieties of Arabic*. Routledge.

Huang, S. (2019). Using computer-assisted language learning (CALL) for teaching pronunciation. *Language Teaching Research, 23*(5), 12–31.

Jahanbin, P. (2025). Modeling L1 influence on L2 pronunciation: An MFCC-based framework for explainable machine learning and pedagogical feedback. *arXiv*. https://arxiv.org/abs/2504.13765

Kim, H., Quinn, K., & Petscher, Y. (2020). The role of prosody in the language learning process. *Applied Linguistics Review, 32*(1), 105–122.

Kormos, J. (2022). The importance of intonation and stress in second language speech. *Language Learning Journal, 44*(3), 312–328.

Kuhn, M., & Schwanenflugel, P. (2019). Prosody and reading comprehension: The importance of rhythm and intonation. *Reading Research Quarterly, 54*(1), 41–56.

Ladefoged, P. (2006). *A course in phonetics* (5th ed.). Wadsworth.

Ladefoged, P. (2021). *A course in phonetics* (7th ed.). Cengage Learning.

Larina, T.. (2021). The impact of L1 language on L2 prosody. *Journal of Second Language Acquisition, 23*(2), 54–69.

Li, X., & Wang, Y. (2025). Acoustic voice quality index and acoustic breathiness index as two indicators of voice disorders. *Journal of Voice, 39*(1), 102.e1–102.e8.

Mitchell, M. (2025). AI is spreading old stereotypes to new languages and cultures. Wired. https://www.wired.com/story/ai-bias-spreading-stereotypes-across-languages-and-cultures-margaret-mitchell

Morano, R. (2024). Diachronic variation in the Omani Arabic vernacular of the Al-ʿAwābī district: From Carl Reinhardt (1894) to the present day. Journal Name, Volume(Issue), page range. DOI or URL (if available).

Munro, M. J. (2021). Focused on how intonation and stress placement are affected by L1 transfer. *Journal of Linguistic Studies, 19*(4), 132–144.

Munro, M. J. (2022). The use of PRAAT in phonetic research: A case study on vowel quality and prosody. *Journal of Speech Sciences, 39*(2), 221–235.

Nguyen, P.. (2008). Exploring language transfer and prosody in second language learners. *Journal of Applied Linguistics, 10*(1), 44–58.

Norte, N. (2023). ELAN: An annotation tool for multimodal discourse analysis. *Proceedings of the 2nd International Conference on Digital Linguistics.*https://www.researchgate.net/publication/373458287_ELAN_An_annotation_tool_for_multimodal_discourse_analysis

Roach, P. (2009). *English phonetics and phonology: A practical course* (4th ed.). Cambridge University Press.

Roach, P. (2018). Lexical stress placement in disyllabic and polysyllabic words in English. *Journal of Phonetics, 23*(4), 132–144.

Romero, M. (2021). The role of intonation in spoken language communication. *Language and Linguistics Compass, 15*(8), e12349.

Sato, K. (2022). PRAAT and its applications in EFL pronunciation instruction. *Pronunciation Journal, 9*(3), 115–130.

Scrivener, J. (2005). *Learning Teaching: The Essential Guide to English Language Teaching*. Macmillan Education.

Shue, Y., & Keating, P. (2024). Comparative analysis of acoustic measures using Praat and VoiceSauce. *The Journal of the Acoustical Society of America, 156*(4), 2112–2123.

Styler, W. (2025). Using Praat for linguistic research. *Retrieved from*https://wstyler.ucsd.edu/praat/

Thakur, A. (2020). The role of stress patterns in Omani Arabic. *Journal of Arabic Linguistics, 32*(1), 74–89.

Thuker, A. (2020). Examined the use of falling tunes for tag-question endings. *Journal of Linguistics, 15*(3), 98–112.

Trofimovich, P. (2020). The use of PRAAT in second language phonology research: Applications and techniques. *Studies in Second Language Acquisition, 42*(4), 735–754.

Trofimovich, P., & Baker, A. (2023). PRAAT and the evaluation of EFL learners' prosody. *Language Learning Journal, 41*(2), 312–328.

Tulsiani, R. (2024). Data privacy in AI-driven learning and ethical considerations. eLearning Industry. https://elearningindustry.com/ensuring-data-privacy-and-ethical-considerations-in-ai-driven-learning

Watson, J. C. E. (2004). *The phonology of Arabic*. Oxford University Press.

Widayanti, A., & Pramudya, I. (2022). Audacity software analysis in analyzing the frequency and character of the sound spectrum. *Journal of Physical Education (Maringá)*, *3*(1), 45–52. https://www.researchgate.net/publication/357770757_Audacity_Software_Analysis_In_Analyzing_The_Frequency_And_Character_Of_The_Sound_Spectrum

Wilson, B. (2005). PRAAT software and its application in language learning. *Computer Assisted Language Learning*, *18*(2), 109–125.

Yamashita, Y., Sakamoto, Y., & Nakagawa, H. (2023). Comparison of Praat and Computerized Speech Lab for formant analysis in maxillectomy patients. *Frontiers in Neuroscience*, *17*, 1098197. DOI: 10.3389/fnins.2023.1098197 PMID: 36816122

Zeng, W., & Huang, Y. (2025). On the effectiveness of visual speech software Praat in English pronunciation teaching research. In M. Atiquzzaman, N. Yen, & Z. Xu (Eds.), *Proceedings of the 5th International Conference on Big Data Analytics for Cyber-Physical System in Smart City—Volume 2 (pp. 1–9). Springer. https://doi.org/*DOI: 10.1007/978-981-96-0211-7_1

Zhang, H., & Liu, J. (2024). Analysis of voice in Parkinson's disease utilizing the Acoustic Voice Quality Index. *Journal of Clinical Neuroscience*, *82*, 56–61. DOI: 10.1016/j.jocn.2024.02.019

Zhang, L., & Li, X. (2024). Guidance to the Praat, a software for speech and acoustic analysis. *Journal of Speech Science and Technology*, *14*(1), 22–30. DOI: 10.1016/j.jsst.2024.03.001

Zhang, X. (2021). Using visual feedback in language teaching: Insights from PRAAT. *Language Education Research*, *8*(2), 45–58.

Zulfugarova, M. (2018). Intonation in language: A prosodic perspective. *Journal of Linguistics and Language Studies*, *15*(2), 25–38.

## ADDITIONAL READING

Alhaj, A. (2016). *The Ambit of English/ Arabic Translation: A Practical and Theoretical Guide*. Anchor Academic Publishing.

## APPENDIX 1

## Letter for Experts to Obtain Test's Validity

Dear Experts,

The researchers are working on a paper titled 'Developing Omani EFL College Students' Production of the Phonetic Prosodic Features through Acoustic Practice'.

The paper aims to develop a test that utilizes Praat acoustic analysis to investigate the challenges faced by Omani EFL college students in their oral production of English prosodic features, specifically sentence-intonation and word stress placement.

Kindly check the tests and provide your comments according to the given rubric. Your assistance is highly appreciated and thank you in advance.

Dr.Taif AL-Kinany

Mr.Sultan AL-Dighaishi

# APPENDIX 2

## The Intonation Part of the (PHTIS)

Dear student,

Read the following sentences aloud. Produce the sentences with the correct intonation patterns.

1. "You did a great job on the presentation; the visuals were excellent!"
2. "I really appreciate how you managed the team during the meeting."
3. "Your input today was invaluable; it helped steer the project in the right direction."
4. "The last section of the report is missing crucial details."
5. "I don't think this approach is going to yield the desired results."
6. "Unfortunately, we're behind schedule because of this delay."
7. "Your attention to detail is impressive; I can see the effort you've put in."
8. "You've really grown in your role, and I can see the progress."
9. "This solution is creative and could really solve the issue we were facing."
10. "That decision doesn't seem to align with the company's goals."
11. "The initial analysis was incomplete, and it needs revision."
12. "We're going to need more resources to meet the expectations on time."
13. "Great work! You handled that difficult situation very professionally."
14. "Your ability to adapt quickly is a huge asset to the team."
15. "I'm impressed with how efficiently you managed the deadlines."
16. "I'm not sure this new plan will work with the current limitations."
17. "We've been experiencing several setbacks, and the progress is slower than expected."
18. "The budget is way over what we initially planned for."
19. "You've really exceeded expectations with this project."
20. "I can always count on you to find innovative solutions."
21. "The results of your work have been outstanding, and they're definitely noticed."
22. "This approach doesn't address the core issues we need to solve."
23. "We're going to have to redo the entire section; it doesn't meet the standards."
24. "I don't think we're ready to launch yet; there's still a lot of refining to do."
25. "I'm really proud of the way you handled that feedback and made improvements."
26. "Your collaboration with the team has been exceptional, and it shows in the final product."
27. "You've demonstrated a lot of initiative, which is very commendable."
28. "There are still some gaps in the data that need to be addressed."
29. "I'm afraid this issue hasn't been resolved yet, despite the efforts so far."

30. “Unfortunately, this solution doesn’t fully meet the client's needs.”

## The Stress Placement Part of the (PHTIS)

Dear students,
Read the following words aloud.

1. Gender
2. Bomb
3. Tomb
4. Wale
5. Crack
6. Edge
7. Basis
8. Browse
9. Source
10. Firm
11. Reverse
12. Ethnic
13. Equal
14. Legend
15. Feature
16. Giant
17. Surface
18. Function
19. Enhance
20. Assess
21. Behavior
22. Characteristic
23. Masculine
24. Feminine
25. Encourage
26. Temporary
27. Sustainable
28. Minority
29. Generation
30. Discrimination

# APPENDIX 3

*Table 9. The Assessment Rubric*

<table>
<tr><td colspan="6">Dear experts,<br>Kindly tick the option that best describes your opinion concerning the following statements.</td></tr>
<tr><td>Statements</td><td colspan="5">Options</td></tr>
<tr><td>1-I think that the intonation section of the (PHTIS)well-assesses the samples' production of intonation.<br>2- I think that the stress placement section of the (PHTIS) well-assesses the samples' production of stress placement.<br>3-I think that the intonation section of the (PHTIS) is well developed.<br>4-I think that the stress placement section of the (PHTIS)is well developed.<br>5-I think that the intonation section of the (PHTIS) is well organized.<br>6-I think that the stress placement section of the (PHTIS) is well organized.<br>7-I think all tokens contain vocabulary that are common to the sample of the study.<br>8-I think that all tokens are phonetically within the students' linguistic competency.</td><td>Strongly agree</td><td>Agree</td><td>Neutral</td><td>Disagree</td><td>Strongly disagree</td></tr>
</table>

## APPENDIX 4

*Table 10. Specification of the (PHTIS)*

| Sentence Type | Number |
|---|---|
| Positive Sentences | 15 |
| Negative Sentences | 15 |

### Monosyllabic Words (1 syllable)

1. Bomb
2. Tomb
3. Wale
4. Crack
5. Edge
6. Term
7. Browse
8. Source
9. Firm
10. mood

### Disyllabic Words (2 syllables)

1. Reverse
2. Ethnic
3. Equal
4. Legend
5. Feature
6. Giant
7. Surface
8. Function
9. Enhance
10. Assess

### Polysyllabic Words (3 or more syllables)

1. Behavior (3 syllables)
2. Characteristic (4 syllables)

3. Masculine (3 syllables)
4. Feminine (3 syllables)
5. Encourage (3 syllables)
6. Temporary (4 syllables)
7. Sustainable (4 syllables)
8. Minority (4 syllables)
9. Generation (4 syllables)
10. Discrimination (5 syllables)

# Chapter 8
# Experiencing Film Literacy Through Magic School AI

**Angeliki Ypsilanti**
https://orcid.org/0000-0001-8333-4169
*Ionian University, Greece*

**Ioannis Karras**
https://orcid.org/0000-0002-1635-8192
*Ionian University, Greece*

## ABSTRACT

*Finding effective ways to incorporate Artificial Intelligence (AI) in Teaching English as a Foreign Language (TEFL) is becoming a major concern as AI literacy is in different stages of development worldwide. In Greece, the growing number of seminars on the use of AI has encouraged teaching professionals to consider possible venues for using AI-based tools in their lesson planning. This study takes the aid of Magic School AI tools to develop a film-based project on Disney animated movies for the EFL classroom. The study's main objectives are to explore ways of interacting with a reading text (i.e., the movie script), to examine opportunities for the development of intercultural communicative competence (ICC) skills through chatbot interaction with the movie characters and to facilitate the design of EFL lesson plans based on film projects. The results indicate that Magic School AI tools can respond effectively without compromising the students' creativity.*

DOI: 10.4018/979-8-3373-0969-9.ch008

## INTRODUCTION

In Greece, the most recent launch of the global educational program "Experience AI" developed in collaboration by the Raspberry Pi Foundation and Google DeepMind has raised awareness of how AI may be used by young people in problem solving. Moreover, webinars such as "Enhance your Productivity with AI" and "AI in Public Sector: Empowering Civil Servants with Microsoft Copilot" offered by the National Centre for Public Administration and Local Government in collaboration with Google and the Ministry of the Interior as well as self-paced training courses such as "Artificial Intelligence in Education" offered by the University of Patras in collaboration with the Centre for Lifelong Learning EKEK ATHENA have raised interest among the educational community. The aim of such AI training programs is to familiarize users with generative AI by offering access to resources and guidance on the effective use of available tools.

While AI training courses for EFL teachers and learners are widespread globally, in Greece they mainly appear in online language courses promoting autonomous learning. In fact, AI-assisted training for EFL teachers is only just emerging to meet schools' growing focus on boosting student motivation. Still, personal initiative at work is as important as formal training, even if it is not always visible or measurable. More specifically, experimentation with AI tools can help break the monotony of traditional teaching and redefine students' expectations of a typical lesson. Given the rise of AI, the shift from traditional edtech to more efficient, AI-driven platforms seems like a natural progression in modern language learning (Muawanah et al., 2024).

But what does the shift from digital literacy to AI literacy mean for teaching and learning, and how does it recalibrate the focus of language education? Kartal (2023) underscores the necessity of this transition by pointing out that the development of AI literacy has its role to play in the prevention of "digital inequality and disadvantage." Assuming that "standardized literacy," i.e., "reading and writing," was not as successful as anticipated in providing "a pathway to social opportunity" (Kalantzis & Cope, 2025, p. 4) or that digital technologies have given vent to a change in assumptions and expectations about literacy in society (Sperling et al., 2024), AI literacy could be claimed to be the follow-up medium for raising the kind of critical awareness that empowers teachers and learners to claim their digital futures through "personalized and adaptive learning experiences" (Muawanah et al., 2024, p. 2). For this reason, it would be fair to say that AI literacy is what critical thinkers and "meaning-makers" make of it as human agency "designs" the parameters of the interaction with the available resources and renders transformable the deposited artifacts (Kalantzis & Cope, 2025).

Regarding language education, Ma et al. (2024) identify AI literacy with ChatGPT literacy because ChatGPT has shown its "transformative potential" in the field of language education since its launch as a "communication partner" (Gessinger et al., 2023). In spite of not qualifying as the first chatbot in the history of AI, ChatGPT alongside Gemini and Microsoft Copilot has gained prestige in the language classroom as a "virtual conversation partner" (Seo, 2024) that responds skillfully to prompts that require operating as a teaching assistant/tutor (Luckyardi et al., 2024; Mohamed, 2024; Zhang et al., 2024) or "acting as" a friend (Huang et al., 2022; Peachey, 2023). As a further note on how ChatGPT can facilitate foreign language development, Rezai et al. (2024, p. 5), drawing on an Iranian EFL university context, have concluded that "conversing with an AI that simulates native speaker interactions might lead to [...] greater cultural awareness." Therefore, it is recommended to place greater emphasis on the use of chatbots as conversation partners, moving beyond their role as teaching aids to support cultural communication needs.

Looking for examples in Greece on how chatbots as conversational partners have been used to facilitate EFL teaching and learning, one is met with scarcity of research, especially on the culture front. So far, scholarly research seems restricted to cases where chatbots have been used by university pre-school teachers for receiving support with "educational-academic" activities (Nikolopoulou, 2024), by migrant students with learning disabilities in an English for Academic Purposes (EAP) context for empowerment reasons (Seiradakis, 2025), by primary and secondary school EFL teachers for facilitating differentiated instruction through flipped classroom practices (Rapti & Panagiotidis, 2024) and by primary school and EFL teachers for correction and feedback purposes with regard to essays written in English and Greek (Fokides & Peristeraki, 2024). Obviously, there is more to do to fulfill language needs, to build cultural communication channels, to envisage and propose "a holistic language learning experience" (Rezai et al., 2024) that entails developing a deeper connection to the language through real-life applications, meaningful interactions, and cultural awareness.

The focus of this paper is to monitor the steps of a film-based project in a Greek EFL context by adapting text input (i.e., movie scripts) to examine student interaction with a chatbot that can simulate the traits of a Disney movie character (i.e., Miguel in *Coco*). The guiding force behind the study is the learners' understanding of concepts such as generational diversity, cultural empathy and intergenerational conflict resolution. Parallel to conceptualization and understanding, the need to integrate chatbot interaction within an educational scenario with an ICC skill agenda has been addressed by: a) finding recourse to Magic School AI to support project-based learning (PBL) with the suitable AI-powered tools, b) linking AI literacy to film literacy to address issues of cultural exchange, and c) designing feedback mechanisms to venture a preliminary answer to the research question: Can AI literacy be claimed to be an indispensable assistant to the EFL teacher for lesson planning purposes?

To this end, a literature review of using films as cultural agents in an AI-assisted interaction acts in support of the study's rationale. After this follows a) an implementable activity plan based on the use of Magic School AI tools, b) the design of a film-inspired lesson plan based on the use of Magic School AI tools and c) the compilation of questionnaires on Magic School AI's role in developing ICC skills. This holistic EFL experience embodies an AI-driven balance of thought, action, planning, and execution while leveraging multiple literacies.

## LITERATURE REVIEW

### Using Films as Cultural Agents in the EFL Classroom

The importance of integrating films in TEFL for intercultural training purposes is underscored by Roell (2010) who stands in favor of looking for the "appropriate" film to foster cultural understanding and develop cultural sensitivity and Karras (2021, pp. 179-180) who states that "films stimulate multi-sensor and cognitive channels and thus are a great source of intercultural information that can appeal to both the viewer's senses and cognition, if of course approached in a systematic way." On the same track, viz. towards selecting the right cultural content to serve the right cultural cause in an EFL context, purport to be: Ruusunen (2011, p. 18) who explains how important it is for the EFL teacher to "be able to treat the films as cultural items instead of mere sources of language input," Daraselia and Jojua (2024, p. 5) who agree that "films are cultural documents that allow students to explore different elements of another culture" and Khotbi et al. (2023, p. 6) who embrace the idea that "by expanding awareness and understanding of cultural content within movies, EFL teachers can maximize the potential of movies as powerful tools for promoting Multicultural Education (ME)." Thus, EFL teachers must not only select appropriate films but also leverage their cultural potential to maximize student benefits.

The growing consensus on enhancing intercultural communicative competence (ICC) through film exposure has led to diverse approaches in project-based instruction. Again, appropriate film choice and use are instrumental in designing projects that can produce results that resonate with students' needs (i.e., cognitive, affective, behavioral). Existing literature on how film-based projects seek to promote intercultural communicative competence shows that objectives are usually designed in alignment with Chen and Starosta's (1996) triangular model of intercultural communication competence and Byram's (1997) corresponding one for the purposes of foreign language education. In the former model, cognition is connected with intercultural awareness, affect with intercultural sensitivity, and behavior with intercultural effectiveness/adroitness (Chen, 2014), while the latter addresses "knowledge, attitudes, skills of interpreting and relating, and skills of discovery and interaction" which "can be acquired" equally well "through experience and reflection" or "with the help of the teacher" (Byram, 2021, p. 44). Such works include Yue's (2019) report on an empirical study that examines students' development of ICC skills through watching Disney film *Mulan* in a Chinese ELT college context, Çakır's (2022) study of a pedagogical experience of Turkish preservice teachers of English with the use of movies and TV serials as an effective way of enhancing intercultural awareness, Kartikasari et al.'s (2019) research on how a cohort of first year high school students in an Indonesian EFL context has developed ICC skills by processing their emotions triggered by the film *Freedom Writers Diary*, Chao's (2013, p. 261) paper on the integration of foreign films in the curricula of a university EFL context in Taiwan with a view to "enhancing behavioral development in intercultural communication" and a Greek study by Calogerakou and Vlachos (2013, p. 99) on how a telecollaborative film-based project between Greece and Italy in an EFL Senior High school context promoted "the development of intercultural communicative competence and of new literacies (digital and media literacy)." Clearly then, "using films to facilitate intercultural learning is to find ones that effectively demonstrate behaviors the trainer wishes to reinforce" (Karras, 2020, p. 182).

Although examples of studies with an overall focus on the set of ICC skills cultivated through film-based projects abound in the literature, relevant examples of studies with a selective focus on each component (i.e., cognitive, affective, behavioral) are harder to find. Even more so when it comes to looking for empathy-oriented film projects where empathy is "characterized by both emotions and cognition" (Karras, 2020, p. 126). Showcases of hosting an affective-based ICC profile in the intercultural EFL classroom through films with a clear emphasis on empathy can be found in Domínguez Romero and Bobkina (2023) who have explored how pre-service EFL/ESL teachers as viewers engaged in both mental and emotional processing of film trailer content, in Rodríguez and Gerke (2022) who posit that trainee EFL teachers should work towards cultivating empathy and cultural sensitivity in their students through the use of foreign films and in Ypsilanti and Karras (2024) who have introduced Pixar shorts in a Greek EFL High School context as a means of enhancing empathy among students who display unresolved conflict issues during the lesson.

## Focusing on Film Characters as Agents of Cultural Empathy in the EFL Classroom

A different kind of empathy that is worth cultivating in the EFL classroom is "character empathy," that is the development of an emotional connection to the thoughts and feelings of a fictional character, because not only can it facilitate "self-disclosure" by establishing "personal relevance" (Bálint et al., 2022), that is relatability to an individual's personal interests, needs, or goals, but it can also address culturally loaded issues. Through a Disney-generated project that pays tribute to popular culture films, Ypsilanti and Karras (2024, p. 168) have focused on Puglisi's (2018) writer's investment in "character empathy" as a springboard for creating all those "relatability" circumstances that "prolong engagement with the movie themes so that students may go beyond mere feelings of transient sympathy with the film characters." Through a post-viewing writing activity on perspective-taking, EFL students developed "character empathy," through shared experiences that empowered them to speak on the characters' behalf — a clear example of a film-based project emphasizing the affective component of ICC.

Literature surrounding the topic of activating film characters as potential agents of cultural empathy in the EFL classroom reveals that students as active viewers have the final say in perceiving and interpreting character's voices, mood and intentions through guided activities (Badia van Pelt, 2021; HARRAT Ala, 2024; Idris, 2014; Yalcin, 2013; Yürük, 2016). A different approach to cultural empathy development (i.e., the E-VRL approach) through a "resource filming context" comes from Guan et al. (2024, p. 11) who embrace empathetic VR-based learning experiences as a means to establishing and enhancing the "dialogic empathy" of EFL learners, "thereby facilitating their engagement in meta-dialogue during subsequent exchanges." Interestingly, this approach offers new insights into creating immersive experiences for EFL learners seeking a more participatory role in their education.

Bringing students into direct dialogue with film characters through AI-driven conversations to promote "character empathy" is likely to positively impact their speaking skills with the aid of generative AI chatbots (Tai & Chen, 2024). As implied earlier, research literature on activating the cultural agency of film characters as part of an authentic scenario is restricted to student output (e.g., piece of writing, presentation, role play). However, AI technology is in the process of bridging the input gap through the development of AI character chatbots that can simulate conversations with film characters (e.g., Character.Ai, ChatGPT-3, Copilot.Live). Still, coping with the new possibilities that AI offers to prevent the emergence of embedded cultural biases (Mehrabi et al., 2021) is dependent upon the teacher's management of the appropriate culture-related prompts.

## Focusing on Film Characters as Agents of Generational Diversity in the EFL Classroom

Enhancing the affective ICC profile in the EFL classroom through conversational exchanges with film characters requires setting "relatability" criteria to ensure successful film selection. Jaques (2021, p. 85) points out that "the tradition of Disney animated film is one predicated on generational rifts" and, more specifically, on rifts that are created only to be "conservatively healed" at the end of the story. According to Jaques (2021), Disney narratives foster intergenerational dialogue to integrate diversity as a resolved tension between past and present cultural traditions. Such a case of a Disney film that outlines resolvable cultural tensions between generations is *Coco* (2017). In this coming-of-age movie, cultural representation from different age groups in the family household, i.e., generational diversity, guarantees the development of the "generational rift" that requires "healing." At the same time, generational differences invite viewers to reflect on their own views in an open-ended dialogue about cultural values. As Fahlevi and Bako (2022) suggest, the moral values of Disney characters offer valuable didactic material; likewise, intergenerational negotiation of cultural values can provide a practical strategy for strengthening students' intercultural communicative competence (ICC) skills.

## Focusing on Film Characters as Mediators of Intergenerational Conflict Resolution in the EFL Classroom

Characters act as mediators of conflict resolution in Disney narrative as suggested by Hastuti et al. (2022) based on the role of Miguel in *Coco*. On the same note, characters like Miguel can act as mediators of concepts such as "intergenerational conflict resolution" in the EFL classroom. In other words, if Miguel in *Coco* symbolizes the reconciliation of generational conflict by valuing family tradition over individual desires (Ray, 2021), he can also serve as a model for promoting "intergenerational conflict resolution" in EFL learning. Mediation activities include "analysis and criticism of creative texts" as suggested by Chiappini and Mansur (2020). Hence, involving fictional characters in sharing their view of the "creative text," i.e., the movie script, prior to "analysis" and "criticism" would count as a co-mediation proposal to be implemented with the aid of AI. Rogers (2023) explains that one of the types of mediation activities listed in the CEFR is "mediating concepts." As *Coco's* main character has been hailed as an example of mediator of "intergenerational conflict resolution," it is worth exploring the possibilities of AI to provide a collaborative mediating experience between film characters and students.

Mediating the script through AI helps build a film-based project that cultivates ICC skills in EFL students while supporting teachers to develop AI-assisted teaching scenarios. Understanding why and how Magic School AI can respond to both EFL teacher and student needs comes next.

## Magic School AI

Due to the recent launch of Magic School AI, its use in EFL education has yet to be adequately researched. Mustafa et al. (2024) address the issue of overload reduction through Magic School AI for Arabic language teachers whereas Sobehrad and Francis (2024) introduce the Magic School AI platform as a major breakout in educational technology. A TEFL-related study comes from Setyaningsih et al. (2024) who explore the integration of Magic School AI in lesson planning as this has been experienced by Indonesian High School EFL teachers. To draw attention towards encouraging self-discovery in student assignments, Kadlubar (2024) reports on a seventh grade English teacher from Central Texas who taught students how to use Magic School AI for conversing with Greek gods and goddesses in order to learn more about Greek mythology.

This study explores the potential of Magic School AI, evaluates effective prompting, and examines its purposeful use in a film-based EFL project. Hence, the question that needs to be studied: Can AI literacy be claimed to be an indispensable assistant to the EFL teacher for lesson planning purposes?

The extent to which AI can respond to EFL challenges has been researched from many perspectives as it is not always clear whether the advantages of AI use outweigh the disadvantages. Edmett et al. (2024) report on what causes skepticism regarding generative AI to ELT practitioners when it comes to cultural understanding and the clash between Western and non-Western perspectives. Although their quick answer to that is that source data can be neither prescribed nor manipulated to address cultural misunderstandings, the issue of bias remains an open one. Edmett et al. (2024, p. 58) underline the importance of training in the area of "prompt design," that is "the textual instruction or input given to a language model like ChatGPT to perform a specific task," so that English language teachers can make better use of generative AI in the ELT classroom. Hwang et al. (2023, p. 1) expand on the importance of the role of effective prompting by proposing "a new form of literacy, the "prompt literacy," which refers to the ability to generate precise prompts as input for AI systems, interpret the outputs, and iteratively refine prompts to achieve desired results."

Magic School AI has a variety of customizable tools that can respond to different teaching requirements, e.g., for lesson planning and differentiated instruction purposes. Part of the platform's mission statement entails that through "customization" and "streamlining" teachers can upgrade objectives, transform material and tailor design to fit students' needs. As it will become evident in the next section through a detailed description of the tools employed for the purposes of this study, Magic School AI can respond to the requirements of a number of literacies (i.e., general AI literacy, "prompt literacy," digital literacy, film literacy). What remains to be confirmed is to what extent Magic School AI can respond to culture-related prompts if supplemented with additional resources to guide its steps within the context of a film-based project.

## METHODOLOGY OF THE STUDY

We have selected Magic School AI for a trial run to evaluate its effectiveness in lesson planning and content generation for both teachers and learners. To initiate the planning stage of a film-based project around a Disney animated film, conversing with "Raina" (Chatbot) and using the services of the "Prompt Assistant" for experimenting with the effectiveness of specific prompts was the first step to take. In fact, the above services guided the way towards identifying the "relatability" concepts upon which to draft an activity plan for implementation. Concepts like cultural empathy, generational diversity, and intergenerational conflict resolution were supported by the "Conceptual Understanding" tool, which offered the necessary theoretical background. To complement this, the "Common Misconceptions" tool helped address potential misunderstandings.

The implementation stage was mainly based on the "Chat-with-Docs" tool which provided the possibility to upload a document and have an AI-powered chat based on the uploaded text to retrieve information. More specifically, "Chat-with-Docs" became the basic medium for uploading the selected Disney movie script and finding the appropriate prompt to initiate interaction with the movie plot and characters. A similar option for producing similar results. i.e., "Character Chatbot," which can act and interact as any movie character, was also put to the test for dialoguing, empathizing, mediating, and resolving. To conclude the round of activities, we found recourse to the "Real-World Connections" tool for generating real world examples to enhance student motivation through relatability.

The dynamic relationship between effective prompting and purposeful output is crucial for teachers to design engaging lessons and for students to maximize learning. So, how can EFL teachers organize initial findings into a consistent, adaptable lesson plan that effectively uses film prompts to boost student engagement? Working towards the requirements of an all-occasions lesson plan has entailed using the "Teacher Observations" tool that makes suggestions about the teacher's next steps based on classroom observations of students' strengths and weaknesses, the "Text Leveler" tool that adapts text input based on the students' level and the "Lesson Hook" tool that generates relevant content for grabbing the students' attention.

In an EFL lesson, linking different literacies (e.g., AI and film literacy) is feasible if communication channels empower both teachers and students. To support this, the final project steps involved using the "Project-Based Learning" tool to design the film-based project and the "Lesson Plan" tool to incorporate its outcomes. As part of the evaluation stage of the project, using the "Survey Creator" tool for feedback reasons was instrumental in compiling two different questionnaires about the contribution of Magic School AI tools to the development of the affective component of intercultural communication competence.

## Data Collection and Analysis

The data was collected using the script of the movie *Coco* from the Internet Movie Script Database (IMSDb). More specifically, using the script has entailed uploading the entire text on "Chat-with-Docs" to get an overview of the role of cultural empathy, generational diversity and intergenerational conflict resolution in the movie. Additionally, "Character Chatbot" helped generate dialogue-based output that served as input for the next AI tool, "Real World Connections," aligning movie content with real-life experiences.

Data was collected by generating, streamlining, adapting, and customizing output based on specific prompts and extracted from relevant documents. Therefore, generating as in extracting content from text became part of the implementation stage and was expected to be the result of collaboration between the teacher and the students. Then, streamlining as in optimizing generated content to enhance student motivation became also part of the implementation stage and was to be primarily student oriented. Followed by streamlining was adapting as in accommodating and modifying generated content to make it equally accessible to all students. Adapting became also part of the implementation stage and was obviously student oriented. Finally, customizing as in tailoring teaching methods to meet specific needs focused on fine-tuning learning content for better outcomes. For the purposes of this study, customizing forms part of the project's evaluation stage and is teacher oriented.

The potential of generative AI to initiate teacher- and student-focused processes hinges on how data is extracted, processed, and refined through generating, streamlining, adapting, and customizing. While testing Magic School AI tools, prompts yield responses that are evaluated for relevance and used as feedback to narrow results for greater appropriacy.

## Participants

This project-based approach through AI assistance is aimed at engaging learners of a Greek EFL secondary-school context in gaining and sharing cultural insights on a movie script with a chatbot. Erin (2025) explains that AI assistance has brought significant changes in the roles of educators and learners as the latter are called upon to act as "mediators" whereas the former as "pedagogical engineers." This project views EFL educators as those responsible for preparing for the change in circumstances and the EFL students as those equipped for becoming receptive to upcoming change. And since equipping students with the appropriate tools for undergoing a change in conceptions is essential, exposing them to the underpinnings of conceptual change is a prerequisite. For this reason, experimentation with the effectiveness of AI tools in response to different prompts and conceptual understanding of cultural terms have been given priority prior to design and application.

The design of this project is primarily aimed at students who attend Greek Junior High School, aged between 12 to 15 years old, at CEFR level B. It is important to note that for the purposes of this study, registering who the participants are in terms of student profile is secondary to building the perspective from which they are expected to participate. In other words, in AI-mediated film communication, how students actively construct their cultural identity is more meaningful than simply asserting a predetermined identity. In fact, the perspective from which participation is expected to take place corresponds to an individual who embraces the prospect of cultivating intercultural sensitivity as "a dynamic process and a process of development" (Karras, 2020, p. 119) through pertinent concepts and activities. Magic School AI's ability to adapt content, verify objectives, and customize tools makes it the ideal platform for engaging student attention.

## FINDINGS

Findings are presented in the form of screenshots of the use of each Magic School AI tool and tables recording prompts and results. As the form of presentation adopts a feedback-to-feedforward rationale, prompts generate results and results generate other prompts exemplifying the way in which the project progresses from one stage to the other (i.e., from planning to implementation to evaluation), from one tool to the other, alternating between generating, streamlining, adapting, customizing. As a side note, how generating, streamlining, adapting, and customizing support a film-based project aimed at developing ICC skills through AI and multiple literacies will be detailed in the Discussion of Findings.

## Planning Stage

### Raina Chabot

*Figure 1. Raina Chatbot Tool by Magic School AI*

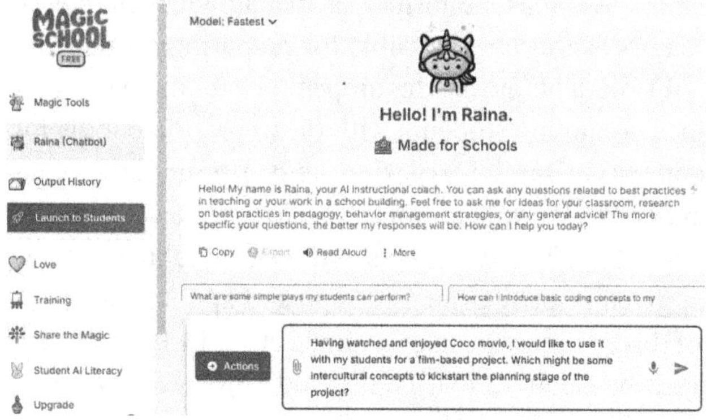

*Table 1. Raina Chatbot Tool: Prompts and Results*

| **Raina Chatbot** | |
|---|---|
| **Prompts** | **Results** |
| **1.** Having watched and enjoyed Coco movie, I would like to use it with my students for a film-based project. Which might be some intercultural concepts to kickstart the planning stage of the project? | **1.** Cultural Heritage<br>**2.** Dia de los Muertos (Day of the Dead)<br>**3.** Music and Art<br>**4.** Identity and Belonging<br>**5.** Family Values<br>**6.** Myths and Legends<br>**7.** Cross-Cultural Communication<br>**8.** Grief and Loss |
| **2.** What activities could I incorporate to enhance the intercultural learning experience? | **1.** Create Ofrendas<br>**2.** Musical Exploration<br>**3.** Storytelling Circle<br>**4.** Cultural Research Project<br>**5.** Art and Craft<br>**6.** Compare and Contrast<br>**7.** Film Analysis<br>**8.** Guest Speakers<br>**9.** Cultural Food Day<br>**10.** Reflection Journals<br>These activities will encourage students to engage actively with the material and deepen their understanding of intercultural concepts while celebrating diversity. |
| **3.** I would like activities that focus more on communication across generations and cultures to engage my students in an intergenerational dialogue with the characters. | **1. Character Interviews**<br>**2. Family Story Exchange**<br>**3. Generational Discussion Panels**<br>**4. Letter Writing**<br>**5. Cultural Artifact Show and Tell**<br>**6. Role-Playing Scenarios:**<br>• Set up role-playing scenarios where students act out scenes from the film or create their own dialogues that reflect intergenerational communication. Encourage them to explore misunderstandings and resolutions between generations.<br>**7. Dialogue Journals**<br>**8. Podcast or Video Project**<br>**9. Cultural Timeline**<br>**10. Reflection on Change** |

continued on following page

*Table 1. Continued*

| Raina Chatbot | |
|---|---|
| **Prompts** | **Results** |
| **4.** How can I enhance my students' ICC skills with an emphasis on the affective component through intergenerational concepts and activities? | **1. Empathy Building Exercises:**<br>• **Perspective-Taking:** Have students engage in activities where they must put themselves in the shoes of different characters from *Coco* or their own family members.<br>**2. Intergenerational Storytelling:**<br>• Facilitate storytelling sessions where students invite older family members or community members to share their life stories, focusing on cultural experiences and emotions.<br>**3. Create a Cultural Emotions Chart:**<br>• Have students create a chart that lists various emotions associated with cultural practices, such as celebrations or rituals. Discuss these emotions in relation to the characters in *Coco* and how they resonate with students' own experiences.<br>**4. Emotional Role-Playing Scenarios:**<br>• Set up role-playing activities where students act out scenarios involving emotional conflicts or misunderstandings between generations.<br>**5. Gratitude Letters:**<br>• Ask students to write letters of gratitude to family members or community elders, expressing appreciation for their cultural contributions and wisdom.<br>**6. Reflection on Cultural Values:**<br>• Encourage students to reflect on their own cultural values and how these values shape their emotions and behaviors. They can then compare their reflections with the values portrayed in *Coco.*<br>**7. Intergenerational Dialogue Workshops:**<br>• Host workshops where students and older participants engage in guided dialogues about cultural identity, traditions, and emotions. |

Chatting with "Raina Chatbot" (Figure 1) helped initiate project planning by generating ideas to enhance intercultural communication competence through *Coco* to guide implementation toward relatability. For instance, the second prompt (Table 1) led to the chatbot's insightful remark that the suggested set of activities will not only "deepen their understanding of intercultural concepts" but will also encourage them to "celebrate diversity" (Table 1). On the same note, the third prompt about focusing on "communication across generations" and "intergenerational dialogue" (Prompts, Table 1) triggered the idea of role-playing scenarios "to explore misunderstandings and resolutions between generations" (Table 1). Finally, the identified need through the fourth prompt to replace "intercultural" with "intergenerational concepts" (Prompts, Table 1) that aim at cultivating the affective side of intercultural communication competence brought to the picture more concepts such as "empathy," "perspective-taking," "cultural emotions," and "cultural values" (Table 1).

## Prompt Assistant

*Figure 2. Prompt Assistant Tool by Magic School AI*

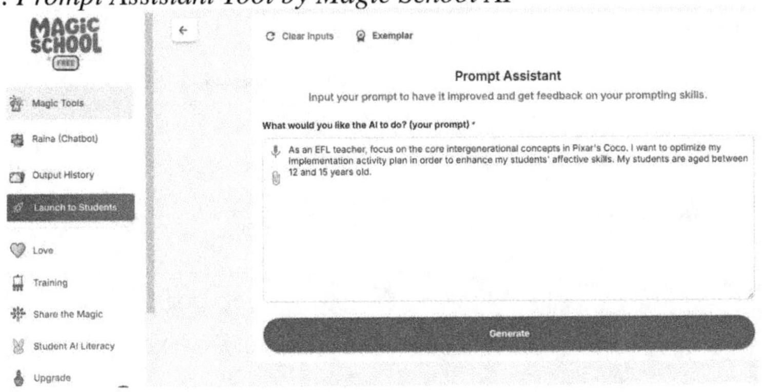


*Table 2. Prompt Assistant Tool: Prompts and Results*

| **Prompt Assistant** | |
|---|---|
| **Prompts** | **Results** |
| As an EFL teacher, focus on the core intergenerational concepts in Pixar's Coco. I want to optimize my implementation activity plan in order to enhance my students' affective skills. My students are aged between 12 and 15 years old. | Create a detailed EFL lesson plan using Pixar's Coco as a teaching resource, specifically focusing on intergenerational relationships and family values. Target audience is intermediate-level EFL students aged 12-15. Include: 1) Key vocabulary related to family relationships and traditions, 2) 3-4 interactive activities that develop emotional intelligence and cultural awareness, 3) Discussion prompts that encourage students to reflect on their own family relationships, and 4) Assessment criteria for measuring students' affective skill development. The lesson should be 60 minutes long and align with CEFR B1 level standards. |

To make the most of the "Prompt Assistant's" services (Figure 2), a recourse to Erin's (2025) prompting techniques has contributed to "co-generating a great answer." More specifically, specifying the "role," "task," "goal" and "context" of the prompt has generated the idea of a lesson plan that focuses on "intergenerational relationships and family values" in order to cultivate "emotional intelligence and cultural awareness" in students (Table 2). The role of relatability in guiding the extraction of relevant, appropriate results will become clear in the prompt-driven progress that follows.

## Conceptual Understanding

*Figure 3. Conceptual Understanding Tool by Magic School AI*

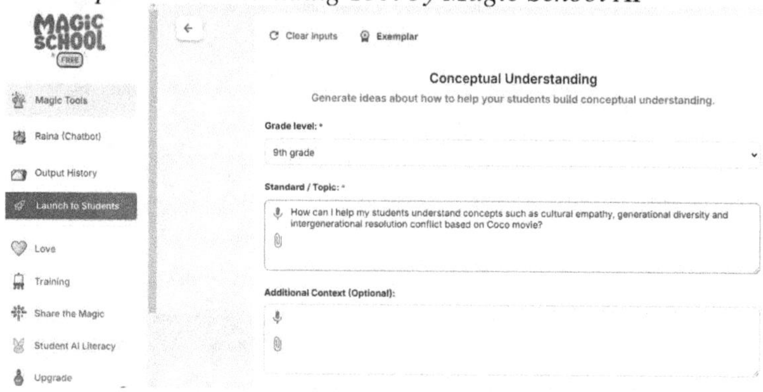


*Table 3. Conceptual Understanding Tool: Prompts and Results*

| **Conceptual Understanding** | |
|---|---|
| **Prompts** | **Results** |
| How can I help my students understand concepts such as cultural empathy, generational diversity and intergenerational resolution conflict based on Coco movie? | **1. Cultural Empathy Through Storytelling**<br>**2. Generational Diversity Role Play**<br>**3. Intergenerational Conflict Resolution Workshop** |

To narrow the focus from broad intercultural concepts to intergenerational ones, the key concepts to emphasize are cultural empathy, generational diversity, and intergenerational conflict resolution. Hence, "Conceptual Understanding" (Figure 2) can be used to make suggestions for improving activities that address the above concepts. As can be deduced from the results (Table 3), these activities are related to storytelling, role playing and workshops. In all cases, students are expected to affectively/emotionally connect with the characters, assume a perspective on a matter of intergenerational concern and enter into a dialogue to mediate and resolve conflict.

## Common Misconceptions

*Figure 4. Common Misconceptions Tool by Magic School AI*

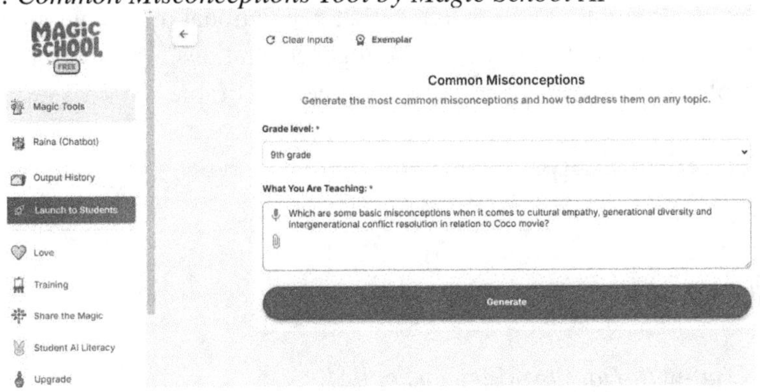


*Table 4. Common Misconceptions Tool: Prompts and Results*

| **Common Misconceptions** | |
|---|---|
| **Prompts** | **Results** |
| Which are some basic misconceptions when it comes to cultural empathy, generational diversity and intergenerational conflict resolution in relation to Coco movie? | **Misconception 1: Cultural empathy is only about understanding other cultures.**<br>Emphasize that cultural empathy involves not only understanding other cultures but also recognizing and valuing one's own cultural background. Use examples from the movie "Coco," where Miguel's love for music is rooted in his family's traditions. Encourage students to explore their own cultural backgrounds and share their experiences to foster a deeper understanding of cultural empathy.<br><br>**Misconception 2: Generational diversity means older generations are always out of touch with younger generations.**<br>Highlight that while there may be differences in values and communication styles, older generations can offer valuable wisdom and experiences that younger generations can learn from. Use scenes from "Coco" to illustrate interactions between Miguel and his family members, showing how communication bridges generational gaps.<br><br>**Misconception 3: Conflict resolution between generations is always a negative experience.**<br>Teach students that conflict can be an opportunity for growth and understanding. Use examples from "Coco" where conflicts arise but lead to resolution and reconciliation, such as Miguel's journey to understand his family's history. |

However, dispelling common misconceptions to bridge knowledge gaps is just as crucial as applying these concepts within an educational context. Hence, "Common Misconceptions" (Figure 4) corrected the misconception that cultural empathy is about understanding only other cultures, that generational diversity "means older generations are always out of touch with younger generations," that intergenerational conflict resolution "is always a negative experience" (Table 4).

## Implementation Stage

### Chat-with-Docs

*Figure 5. Chat-with-Docs by Magic School AI*

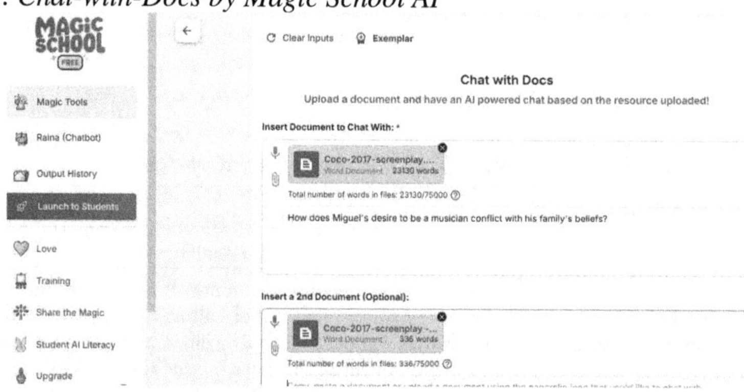

*Table 5. Chat-with-Docs Tool: Prompts and Results*

| **Chat-with-Docs** | |
|---|---|
| **Prompts** | **Results** |
| 1. How does Miguel's desire to be a musician conflict with his family's beliefs? | 1. **Family History**: Miguel's family has a painful history involving music, specifically the story of his great-great-grandfather, who was a musician that left the family. This event led to Miguel's great-great-grandmother, Mamá Imelda, banning music from their lives, as she associated it with loss and abandonment.<br>2. **Family Tradition**: The Rivera family has built their lives around shoemaking, with a strong emphasis on family unity and tradition. They believe that music caused discord in their family, so they prioritize their shoe-making business over any musical aspirations.<br>3. **Miguel's Secret**: Despite being passionate about music and wanting to follow in the footsteps of his idol, Ernesto de la Cruz, Miguel feels he must keep his love for music a secret from his family. This creates inner turmoil as he struggles to reconcile his dreams with his family's expectations.<br>4. **Family Disapproval**: When Miguel expresses his desire to participate in the Día de los Muertos talent show, his family reacts negatively and forbids him from pursuing music. They believe that music is a curse and that he should focus on the family trade instead.<br>5. **Desire for Acceptance**: Miguel's journey reflects his need for acceptance both as a musician and as a member of his family. He wants to prove that he can be a musician while still honoring his family's traditions, which leads to his struggle throughout the story. |
| 2. How does Miguel deal with the intergenerational conflict? Does he resolve it? | Miguel resolves the intergenerational conflict by embracing both his passion for music and his family's legacy. He creates a new understanding that allows music to exist within the family's values, fostering unity and appreciation for their shared history. |
| 3. Is Miguel in favor of generational diversity? | Yes, Miguel is in favor of generational diversity, and this is reflected in several aspects of his character and actions throughout *Coco*.<br>In summary, Miguel supports generational diversity by valuing the lessons of the past while also striving to define his own identity and passions. His journey emphasizes the importance of understanding and integrating different perspectives within a family. |

"Chat-with-Docs" (Figure 5) provided the possibility to upload up to two documents to gain access to their content. Hence, uploading the screenplay of *Coco* in conjunction with an isolated scene of the conflict between the main protagonist and his grandmother provided the possibility to understand the root of the conflict and the way it was resolved. In fact, this way emphasized "the importance of understanding and integrating different perspectives within a family" irrespective of cultural background but in line with a person's "heritage" (Table 5).

## Character Chatbot

*Figure 6. Character Chatbot by Magic School AI*

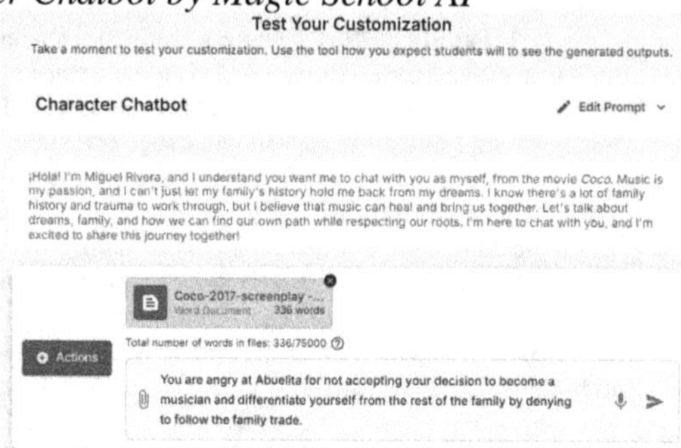

*Table 6. Character Chatbot Tool: Prompts and Results*

| Character Chatbot | |
|---|---|
| **Prompts** | **Results** |
| Act as Miguel Rivera from Coco movie. You cannot accept your family's opposition to your dream of becoming a musician. At the same time, you understand that there is a family trauma that goes back generations and needs to be healed.<br>You are angry at Abuelita for not accepting your decision to become a musician and differentiate yourself from the rest of the family by denying to follow the family trade. | Hola! I am Miguel Rivera, and I understand music is in my heart - just like yours! My family doesn't accept my dream of becoming a musician instead of a shoemaker. Abuelita even smashed my guitar! But I know deep down that music is who I am. |
| Don't you think that you should also show a certain amount of sensitivity towards Abuelita without abandoning your love for music? | *Sighs frustratedly* Look, I understand what you're saying, but Abuelita doesn't even try to understand ME! She won't even let me EXPLAIN - she just smashes my guitar and expects me to be happy making shoes forever!<br>She doesn't even want to hear why music matters to me. How am I supposed to show sensitivity when she shows none towards my dreams? She treats music like it's some kind of curse! All because of what happened with Mamá Imelda and her husband…<br>*Speaking more softly* I mean… I know she loves me and wants what's best for me. But breaking my guitar? Telling me I can't even TOUCH music? That's not love - that's control. There has to be a way for me to be both a Rivera AND a musician. Why can't she see that?<br>I just wish she would listen to me play, just once, before deciding music is evil. Don't you think that's fair? To at least give me a chance? |
| Wouldn't it be a good idea to tell her that you don't understand her angry reactions and ask her to explain why she feels so strong against music when it is part of Mexican cultural tradition? | *Thoughtfully* You know… you make a good point. I've been so focused on defending my love for music that I never really asked Abuelita to explain her side. Maybe if I understood why she's so afraid of music, beyond just the old story about Mamá Imelda…<br>*Fidgeting with my hoodie strings* But every time I even mention music, she gets so angry! She won't even let me finish a sentence before shutting me down. Like when she saw my guitar and just… destroyed it. Without even asking where I got it or why it meant so much to me.<br>*Looking up with determination* But maybe if I approach her differently - not about MY music, but about why SHE feels this way… Maybe if I show her I care about her feelings too…<br>*Hesitating* It's just… it's hard when someone you love seems to hate something that's such a big part of who you are. But you're right - I should try to understand her fear instead of just fighting against it. Mexican culture IS full of music - at every festival, every celebration… There must be more to why our family is so different.<br>Do you think she'd actually talk to me about it if I asked? Without getting angry? |

continued on following page

*Table 6. Continued*

| Character Chatbot | |
|---|---|
| **Prompts** | **Results** |
| Well, as long as you meet her halfway, then maybe she will realize that you are trying hard to see things from her perspective. | *Shoulders relaxing slightly,* I… I never thought about it that way. Meeting her halfway… Like maybe I could still help in the shoe shop AND find time for music? Show her I'm not abandoning the family business completely?<br>*Speaking more earnestly* And you're right - if I show her I'm trying to understand her fears instead of just rebelling, maybe she'd be more willing to hear me out too. I love Abuelita, I really do. I don't want to hurt her or dishonor our family…<br>*Touching the Rivera boot logo on my apron* The shoe business IS important to our family. It's how we survived after… well, after what happened with Mamá Imelda's husband. I get why Abuelita wants to protect that legacy.<br>*Looking up hopefully* Maybe if I show her I can balance both - being a good Rivera shoemaker AND following my passion for music - she might start to see that music doesn't have to be a curse? That it doesn't mean I'm abandoning my family like… like HE did?<br>Do you think that could work? Finding a balance instead of making it an all-or-nothing choice? |
| Well, that's how empathy resolves intergenerational disagreement, don't you think? | *Eyes widening with realization* Oh… I think I understand now. It's not just about music or shoes - it's about healing old wounds. When I yelled that I didn't care about the ofrenda and ran away, I probably brought back all those painful memories for Abuelita… about how our family was torn apart before.<br>*Speaking more softly* All this time I've been thinking she's just being stubborn, but she's actually scared. Scared of losing me like they lost him. And instead of showing her that I'm different, that I would never abandon my family, I've been acting exactly like she fears - rebellious, secretive, putting music before family…<br>*Thoughtfully* Maybe… maybe empathy means understanding that her anger comes from love and fear, not hate. And showing her that my love for music doesn't mean I love my family any less.<br>*With growing determination,* I need to prove to her that we can move forward without forgetting where we came from. That I can honor both our family's past AND build a new future…<br>This isn't just about me anymore, is it? It's about healing our whole family… |

"Character Chatbot" (Figure 6) was instrumental in helping students practice their productive skills. This time, uploading solely the scene of the conflict sufficed to have the desired results. Giving instructions to the chatbot to act as a specific character facilitated the interaction between the students and the movie character. This marked the implementation stage, where chatbot interaction shifted from complex prompting to a simpler model of straightforward questions and answers.

On the same note, the chatbot's answers acquired emotional status clearly detected in the italicized phrases superseding again the AI limits of affective/emotional responsiveness (Table 6).

## Real World Connections

*Figure 7. Real World Connections Tool by Magic School AI*

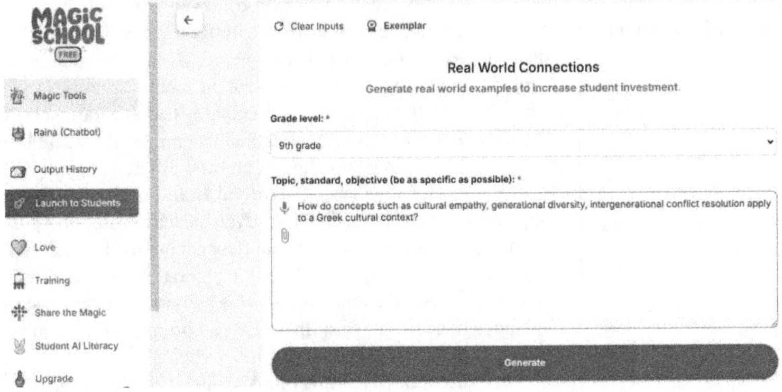

*Table 7. Real-World Connections Tool: Prompts and Results*

| Real World Connections | |
|---|---|
| **Prompts** | **Results** |
| How do concepts such as cultural empathy, generational diversity, intergenerational conflict resolution apply to a Greek cultural context? | **1. Understanding Family Dynamics in Greek Culture**<br>**2. Celebrating Greek Festivals Together.**<br>**3. The Role of Greek Mythology in Modern Storytelling** |
| How can the above be used in real-life tasks for EFL learners? | **Task 1: Family Interview Project**<br>Students can conduct interviews with family members or friends from different generations to gather stories about their cultural backgrounds and family traditions. They can then present these stories to the class, highlighting themes of cultural empathy and generational diversity. This task helps improve speaking and listening skills while fostering an understanding of cultural differences.<br>**Task 2: Festival Role-Play**<br>Students can research a Greek festival, such as Easter or Apokries, and create a role-play scenario where they act out the festival's traditions. They can assign roles from different generations, discussing how each character views the celebration. This activity encourages students to practice their language skills while exploring conflict resolution and empathy through dialogue.<br>**Task 3: Mythology and Modern Media Analysis**<br>Students can choose a Greek myth and analyze its themes, then compare it to a modern movie or book that shares similar themes. They can write a short essay or create a presentation discussing how cultural empathy is portrayed through these narratives. This task helps develop reading and writing skills while allowing students to make connections between cultures and contemporary issues. |

"Real-World Connections" (Figure 7) consolidated the attempt to train AI to respond to prompts with simulated feeling to raise the levels of empathy. Balancing on the verge between other-culture values and home values, this tool dispelled in practice the common misconception that cultural empathy is only about overcoming prejudice over other cultures and embracing diversity. By suggesting activities related to the students' home culture (i.e., gathering culture-specific stories about family traditions), the aim to enhance ICC skills evolved into a transformative one, i.e., "to make connections between cultures" "while fostering an understanding of cultural differences" (Table 7).

## Teacher Observations

*Figure 8. Teacher Observations Tool by Magic School AI*

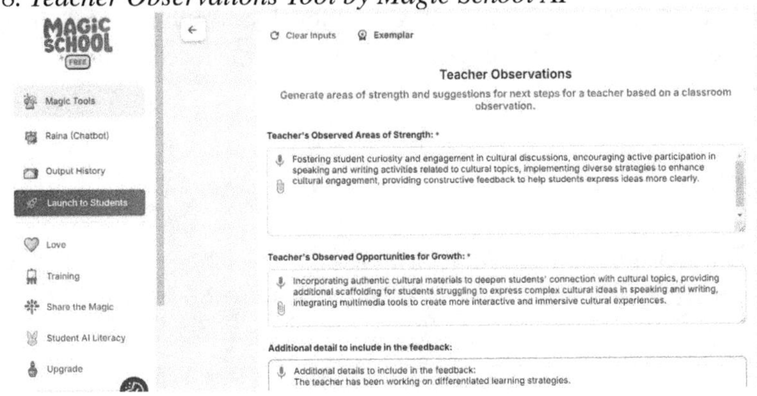


*Table 8. Teacher Observations Tool: Prompts and Results*

| **Teacher Observations** | |
|---|---|
| **Prompts** | **Results** |
| **Teacher's Observed Areas of Strength:**<br>Fostering student curiosity and engagement in cultural discussions, encouraging active participation in speaking and writing activities related to cultural topics, implementing diverse strategies to enhance cultural engagement, providing constructive feedback to help students express ideas more clearly.<br><br>**Teacher's Observed Opportunities for Growth:**<br>Incorporating authentic cultural materials to deepen students' connection with cultural topics, providing additional scaffolding for students struggling to express complex cultural ideas in speaking and writing, integrating multimedia tools to create more interactive and immersive cultural experiences.<br>**Additional details to include in the feedback:**<br>The teacher has been working on differentiated learning strategies. | **Areas of Strength (keep it up!):**<br>• **Fostering Student Curiosity and Engagement**<br>• **Encouraging Active Participation**:<br>• **Implementing Diverse Strategies**:<br>• **Providing Constructive Feedback**:<br><br>**Opportunities for Growth / Next Steps:**<br>• **Incorporating Authentic Cultural Materials**: Begin integrating artifacts, literature, or multimedia from diverse cultures into your lessons.<br>• **Providing Additional Scaffolding**: Develop scaffolding strategies such as sentence starters or graphic organizers to support students struggling with complex cultural ideas.<br>• **Integrating Multimedia Tools**: Explore interactive platforms (like Padlet or Nearpod) to create immersive experiences related to cultural topics.<br><br>Your commitment to differentiated learning strategies is commendable and will undoubtedly support all your students in their educational journey. |

"Teacher's Observations" (Figure 8) served its purposes by reaffirming the EFL teacher's need to continue the efforts to "spark discussion around cultural topics" and to cater for "inclusivity and collaboration" in the EFL classroom. "Incorporating authentic cultural materials," "providing additional scaffolding," and "integrating multimedia tools" followed as suggestions regarding the teacher's growth in unexplored areas (Table 8).

## Text Leveler

*Figure 9. Text Leveler Tool by Magic School AI*

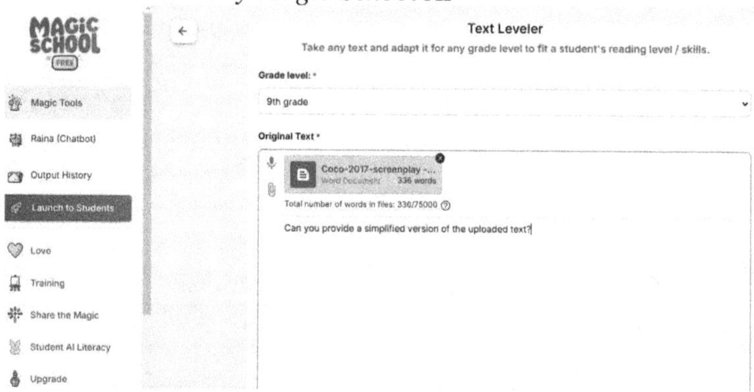

*Table 9. Text Leveler Tool: Prompts and Results*

| **Text Leveler** | |
|---|---|
| **Prompts** | **Results** |
| Can you provide a simplified version of the uploaded text? | **PAPÁ**<br>What are you talking about?<br>Miguel takes off his shoemaker's apron and poses with the guitar.<br>**MIGUEL**<br>I'm going to be a musician!<br>**CUT TO:**<br>**EXT. COURTYARD - EARLY EVENING**<br>Miguel's guitar lies on the ground next to his de la Cruz albums. The whole family gathers around him.<br>**ABUELITA**<br>What is all this? You keep secrets from your family?<br>**TÍO BERTO**<br>It's all that time he spends in the plaza…<br>**TÍA GLORIA**<br>…Filling his head with crazy fantasies!<br>**MIGUEL**<br>It's not a fantasy!<br>Miguel hands Papá the photo and points to the skull guitar.<br>**MIGUEL (CONT'D)**<br>That man was Ernesto de la Cruz! The greatest musician ever!<br>**PAPÁ** |

continued on following page

*Table 9. Continued*

| **Text Leveler** | |
|---|---|
| **Prompts** | **Results** |
| | We don't know anything about this man. But whoever he was, he left his family. This is no future for my son.<br>**MIGUEL**<br>But Papá, you said my family would guide me! Well, de la Cruz IS my family! I'm meant to play music!<br>**ABUELITA**<br>Never! That man's music was a curse! I will not allow it!<br>**MIGUEL**<br>If you would just let—<br>**MAMÁ**<br>(warning) Miguel—<br>**PAPÁ**<br>You will listen to your family. No more music.<br>**MIGUEL**<br>Just listen to me play—<br>**PAPÁ**<br>End of argument.<br>Miguel lifts his guitar to play when Abuelita grabs it away. She points to the man in the photo.<br>**ABUELITA**<br>Do you want to end up like him? Forgotten? Left off your family's ofrenda?!<br>**MIGUEL**<br>I don't care if I'm on some stupid ofrenda!<br>Gasps from the family. Abuelita's face tightens. She raises the guitar high.<br>**MIGUEL**<br>No!<br>**MAMÁ...**<br>**PAPÁ**<br>Abuelita breaks it into pieces!<br>**ABUELITA**<br>There. No guitar, no music. (softening)<br>**ABUELITA (CONT'D)**<br>Come. You'll feel better after you eat with your family.<br>She reaches out to comfort Miguel, but he is too hurt to respond.<br>**MIGUEL**<br>I don't want to be in this family!<br>He snatches the photo from Papá and runs out of the house.<br>**PAPÁ**<br>Miguel! MIGUEL! |

"Text Leveler" (Figure 9) became the medium for fostering "inclusivity and collaboration" in the EFL classroom. This time, the scene of the conflict was uploaded to provide an alternative version of adapted content (Table 9) "to fit the reading level/skills" of weaker students, mainly for differentiated instruction purposes.

## Lesson Hook

*Figure 10. Lesson Hook by Magic School AI*

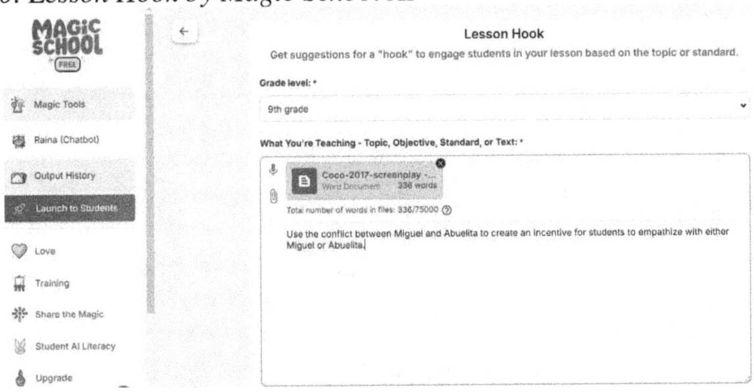


*Table 10. Lesson Hook Tool: Prompts and Results*

| **Lesson Hook** | |
|---|---|
| **Prompts** | **Results** |
| Use the conflict between Miguel and Abuelita to create an incentive for students to empathize with either Miguel or Abuelita. | 1. **Empathy Role Play:** Divide the class into two groups: one representing Miguel and the other representing Abuelita. Provide each group with a brief description of their character's perspective and feelings regarding the conflict. Have them prepare a short skit to present their viewpoint, showcasing the emotional reasons behind their actions.<br>2. **Hot Seat Debate:** Set up a "hot seat" debate where students can volunteer to take on the roles of Miguel and Abuelita. The rest of the class will ask them questions about their motivations and feelings during the conflict. For example, students might ask Miguel why music is so important to him or why Abuelita feels so strongly against it.<br>3. **Conflict Mapping:** Provide students with a large sheet of paper and markers to create a conflict map. In the center, write "Miguel and Abuelita's Conflict." Ask students to brainstorm and visually represent the emotions, motivations, and consequences for both characters. |

Prompting "Lesson Hook" (Figure 10) to use the conflict scene for building empathy with either Miguel or Abuelita shifted the focus from general ICC activities to targeted issues, capturing students' attention and setting the stage for learning. Hence, the idea of visualizing empathy with the aid of conflict maps that chart "emotions, motivations, and consequences" (Table 10) emerged in the context of activating less motivated students through relatable incentives.

## Project-Based Learning

*Figure 11. Project-Based Learning Tool by Magic School AI*

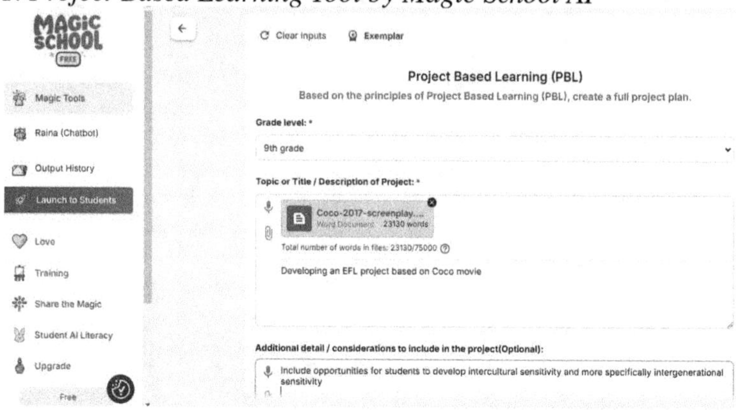

*Table 11. Project-Based Learning Tool: Prompts and Results*

| Project-Based Learning | |
|---|---|
| **Prompts** | **Results** |
| Developing an EFL project based on Coco movie<br><br>Include opportunities for students to develop intercultural sensitivity and more specifically intergenerational sensitivity | **Developing an EFL Project Based on Coco Movie**<br>**Driving Question or Challenge:**<br>How can understanding cultural heritage and family connections through music, as depicted in the movie "Coco," enhance our appreciation of our own cultures and those of others?<br>**Real-world Context:**<br>This project connects students to real-world issues surrounding cultural heritage, family connections, and the importance of remembering our ancestors. By exploring the significance of Día de los Muertos (Day of the Dead) celebrations in Mexican culture, students will gain a deeper understanding of how traditions shape identities, foster community bonds, and promote intercultural sensitivity.<br>**In-depth Inquiry:**<br>Students will be encouraged to dive deep into the content of the film *Coco*, analyzing its themes, characters, and cultural significance. They will research the historical origins of Día de los Muertos, its customs, and how it varies across different regions. Students will also explore their family histories, asking questions about their own cultural practices and the stories of their ancestors. |
| | **Student Voice and Choice:**<br>Students will have the autonomy to choose how they want to express their understanding of the project. They can select various formats for their final product, such as creating a presentation, writing a reflective essay, or producing a musical piece that incorporates elements from their own cultural backgrounds alongside influences from "Coco."<br>**Reflection:**<br>Throughout the project, students will engage in regular reflection activities, such as journaling or group discussions, where they can articulate their learning experiences, discoveries, and personal growth.<br>**Critique and Revision:**<br>The project will foster a culture of constructive feedback. Students will present draft versions of their work to peers, who will provide feedback focused on content, clarity, and presentation.<br>**Collaboration:**<br>Students will work in small groups to encourage collaboration and exchange of ideas. They will pool their skills and insights to create a comprehensive project that reflects a variety of cultural perspectives. Group activities will include collaborative research, group presentations, and joint creative |

continued on following page

*Table 11. Continued*

| Project-Based Learning | |
|---|---|
| **Prompts** | **Results** |
| | projects.<br>**Teacher Facilitation:**<br>Students will work in groups to facilitate collaboration. They will pool their collective skills and insights to enhance their projects, share responsibilities, and learn from each other. Collaborative activities may include group research, peer presentations, and joint creative projects, emphasizing teamwork and communication.<br>**Interdisciplinary Connection:**<br>This project will bridge multiple subject areas, including Language Arts (through reading and writing about cultural stories), Social Studies (exploring the significance of Día de los Muertos), and Art (creating visual representations of their findings).<br>**Assessment:**<br>Assessment will include both formative assessments (ongoing reflections, peer feedback) and summative assessments (final presentations, projects). A rubric will be developed to evaluate students' understanding of cultural concepts, their ability to communicate their ideas effectively, and the creativity of their final products. Peer reviews will also be incorporated to enhance collaborative learning. |

Based on Chen and Starosta (1998), Karras (2020, p. 118) clarifies that "intercultural sensitivity could be said to embody the affective side of ICC in that it assumes one's desire to motivate him/ herself not only to discern and appreciate, but also to accept differences among the various cultures." "Project Based Learning" (Figure 11) practically encapsulated the essence of intercultural sensitivity (i.e., "enhancing our appreciation of our own cultures and those of others") through the "Driving Question or Challenge" which automatically directed the "In-Depth Inquiry" towards doing the preliminary work "to gain multiple perspectives" (Table 11).

## Lesson Plan

*Figure 12. Lesson Plan Tool by Magic School AI*

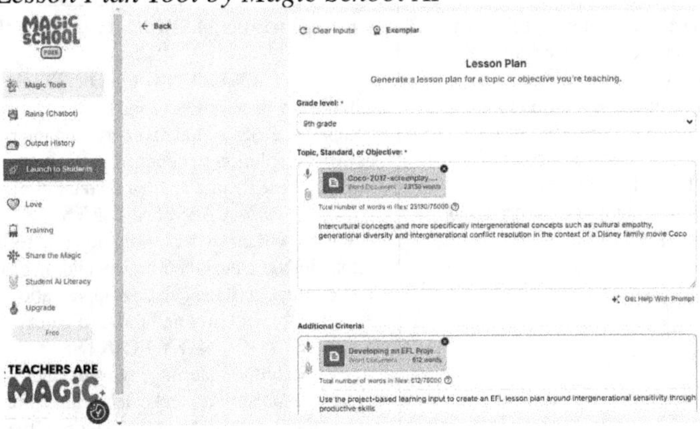

*Table 12. Lesson Plan Tool: Prompts and Results*

| Lesson Plan | |
|---|---|
| **Prompts** | **Results** |
| Intercultural concepts and more specifically intergenerational concepts such as cultural empathy, generational diversity and intergenerational conflict resolution in the context of a Disney family movie Coco<br><br>Use the project-based learning input to create an EFL lesson plan around intergenerational sensitivity through productive skills | **Intergenerational Sensitivity through the Lens of "Coco"**<br>**LEARNING OBJECTIVE:**<br>Students will be able to analyze the themes of cultural empathy, generational diversity, and intergenerational conflict resolution as depicted in the movie "Coco" and connect these themes to their own cultural backgrounds.<br>**ASSESSMENTS:**<br>Students will create a presentation or a reflective essay that demonstrates their understanding of how music and cultural heritage enhance appreciation of their own cultures and those of others.<br>**KEY POINTS:**<br>• Cultural Heritage: Understanding the role of music in preserving and celebrating cultural identity.<br>• Día de los Muertos: Exploring the significance and customs associated with this Mexican holiday.<br>• Generational Diversity: Recognizing the perspectives of different generations in family dynamics.<br>• Cultural Empathy: Learning how to appreciate and respect diverse cultural practices and traditions.<br>• Intergenerational Conflict Resolution: Strategies to resolve conflicts that arise between different generations.<br>**OPENING:**<br>• Begin with a brief discussion about students' favorite movies and what themes resonate with them.<br>• Introduce the movie "Coco" and its focus on family and cultural heritage.<br>• Pose the question: "How does understanding our family history shape who we are today?"<br>**INTRODUCTION TO NEW MATERIAL:**<br>• Show clips from "Coco" that highlight key themes (family, music, Día de los Muertos). |

continued on following page

*Table 12. Continued*

| Lesson Plan | |
|---|---|
| **Prompts** | **Results** |
| | • Discuss the significance of the Día de los Muertos celebration in Mexican culture.<br>• Encourage students to reflect on their own family traditions and how they connect to their identity.<br>• Common Misconception: Some students may believe that cultural practices are static and do not evolve over time. Clarify that cultures are dynamic and can change with each generation.<br>**GUIDED PRACTICE:**<br>• In small groups, students will discuss specific scenes from "Coco" that illustrate the themes.<br>• Provide guiding questions such as: "What does Miguel's relationship with his family reveal about generational differences?"<br>• Monitor group discussions, offering support and asking probing questions to deepen their understanding.<br>**INDEPENDENT PRACTICE:**<br>• Assign students to research their own cultural heritage or family traditions and create a presentation that includes music, customs, and |
| | stories.<br>• Set expectations for using visual aids and integrating elements from "Coco" where relevant.<br>**CLOSING:**<br>• Have students share one insight they gained about their own culture or family from the lesson.<br>• Encourage students to reflect on how understanding their own heritage can help them appreciate others'.<br>**EXTENSION ACTIVITY:**<br>• For students who finish early, encourage them to research and present on a cultural practice from another country and how it relates to themes in "Coco." |

For the purposes of the suggested prompting techniques of the present study, "Lesson Plan" (Figure 12) has been used in interaction with the previous tool, i.e., "Project-Based Learning" (Figure 11). This has been achieved by attaching a second file with the PBL results on the optional space provided by "Lesson Planning." A further suggestion would be to replace the Coco screenplay with "Character Chatbot" discussion results since the protagonist's thoughts and feelings offer richer material for a more focused lesson plan.

# Evaluation Stage

## Survey Creator

*Figure 13. Survey Creator Tool by Magic School AI*

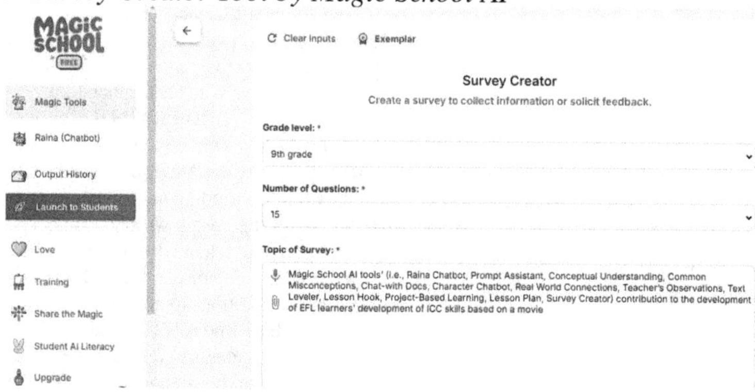

*Table 13. Survey Creator: Prompts and Results*

| **Survey Creator** | |
|---|---|
| **Prompts** | **Results** |
| Magic School AI tools' (i.e., Raina Chatbot, Prompt Assistant, Conceptual Understanding, Common Misconceptions, Chat-with Docs, Character Chatbot, Real World Connections, Teacher's Observations, Text Leveler, Lesson Hook, Project-Based Learning, Lesson Plan, Survey Creator) contribution to the development of EFL learners' development of ICC skills based on a movie | **Survey on Magic School AI Tools and ICC Skills Development**<br><br>The **Raina Chatbot** effectively helps EFL learners understand cultural differences in the movie.<br>5 - Strongly Agree<br>4 - Agree<br>3 - Neutral<br>2 - Disagree<br>1 - Strongly Disagree |
| | The **Prompt Assistant** encourages students to engage with intergenerational themes in the film.<br>5 - Strongly Agree<br>4 - Agree<br>3 - Neutral<br>2 - Disagree<br>1 - Strongly Disagree<br><br>**Conceptual Understanding** tools clarify complex cultural concepts presented in the movie. |
| | 5 - Strongly Agree<br>4 - Agree<br>3 - Neutral<br>2 - Disagree<br>1 - Strongly Disagree<br><br>**Common Misconceptions** features help EFL learners avoid misunderstandings about cultural contexts.<br>5 - Strongly Agree<br>4 - Agree<br>3 - Neutral |

continued on following page

*Table 13. Continued*

| Survey Creator | |
|---|---|
| **Prompts** | **Results** |
| | 2 - Disagree<br>1 - Strongly Disagree<br><br>**Chat-with Docs** enhances students' ability to analyze the movie's intergenerational conflict.<br>5 - Strongly Agree<br>4 - Agree<br>3 - Neutral<br>2 - Disagree<br>1 - Strongly Disagree<br><br>**Character Chatbot** allows learners to explore diverse perspectives within the film.<br>5 - Strongly Agree<br>4 - Agree<br>3 - Neutral |
| | 2 - Disagree<br>1 - Strongly Disagree<br><br>**Real World Connections** feature helps students relate the movie's themes to their own lives.<br>5 - Strongly Agree<br>4 - Agree<br>3 - Neutral<br>2 - Disagree<br>1 - Strongly Disagree |
| | **Teacher's Observations** provide valuable feedback on students' understanding of ICC skills.<br>5 - Strongly Agree<br>4 - Agree<br>3 - Neutral<br>2 - Disagree<br>1 - Strongly Disagree<br><br>**Text Leveler** ensures that the materials are appropriate for EFL learners' reading levels.<br>5 - Strongly Agree<br>4 - Agree |

continued on following page

*Table 13. Continued*

| **Survey Creator** | |
|---|---|
| **Prompts** | **Results** |
| | 3 - Neutral<br>2 - Disagree<br>1 - Strongly Disagree<br><br>**Lesson Hook** effectively captures students' interest in the movie's cultural aspects.<br>5 - Strongly Agree<br>4 - Agree<br>3 - Neutral<br>2 - Disagree<br>1 - Strongly Disagree<br><br>**Project-Based Learning** activities deepen students' understanding of the intergenerational conflict.<br>5 - Strongly Agree |
| | 4 - Agree<br>3 - Neutral<br>2 - Disagree<br>1 - Strongly Disagree<br><br>**Lesson Plan** provides a structured approach to teaching ICC skills through the movie.<br>5 - Strongly Agree<br>4 - Agree<br>3 - Neutral<br>2 - Disagree<br>1 - Strongly Disagree |
| | **Survey Creator** tool allows for effective gathering of student feedback on the movie.<br>5 - Strongly Agree<br>4 - Agree<br>3 - Neutral<br>2 - Disagree<br>1 - Strongly Disagree |
| Character Chatbot's contribution to the development of EFL learners' development of ICC skills based on Coco movie which has an intergenerational conflict. Use the uploaded text for inspiration. | **Character Chatbot's Contribution to EFL Learners' Development of ICC Skills Based on Coco Movie**<br><br>**I believe that understanding Miguel's passion for music helps me develop my own cultural sensitivity.**<br>5 - Strongly Agree<br>4 - Agree |

continued on following page

*Table 13. Continued*

| Survey Creator | |
|---|---|
| **Prompts** | **Results** |
| | 3 - Neutral<br>2 - Disagree<br>1 - Strongly Disagree<br><br>**The conflict between Miguel and Abuelita illustrates the importance of empathy in family relationships.**<br>5 - Strongly Agree<br>4 - Agree<br>3 - Neutral |
| | 2 - Disagree<br>1 - Strongly Disagree<br><br>**I feel that music is an important part of cultural identity, similar to what Miguel experiences.**<br>5 - Strongly Agree<br>4 - Agree<br>3 - Neutral<br>2 - Disagree<br>1 - Strongly Disagree |
| | **Miguel's struggle to pursue his dreams while respecting family traditions resonates with my own experiences.**<br>5 - Strongly Agree<br>4 - Agree<br>3 - Neutral<br>2 - Disagree<br>1 - Strongly Disagree |

continued on following page

*Table 13. Continued*

| **Survey Creator** | |
|---|---|
| **Prompts** | **Results** |
| | **I think that discussing feelings openly can help resolve conflicts, just like Miguel should with Abuelita.**<br>5 - Strongly Agree<br>4 - Agree<br>3 - Neutral<br>2 - Disagree<br>1 - Strongly Disagree<br><br>**The character of Miguel teaches me the value of balancing personal goals and family expectations.**<br>5 - Strongly Agree<br>4 - Agree<br>3 - Neutral<br>2 - Disagree<br>1 - Strongly Disagree<br><br>**I find it easy to relate to the** |
| | **intergenerational conflicts shown in the Coco movie.**<br>5 - Strongly Agree<br>4 - Agree<br>3 - Neutral<br>2 - Disagree<br>1 - Strongly Disagree<br><br>**Understanding the fears that drive Abuelita's actions helps** |
| | **me appreciate her perspective better.**<br>5 - Strongly Agree<br>4 - Agree<br>3 - Neutral<br>2 - Disagree<br>1 - Strongly Disagree<br><br>**I believe that music can bridge the gap between different** |

continued on following page

*Table 13. Continued*

| Survey Creator | |
|---|---|
| **Prompts** | **Results** |
| | **generations, as seen in the Coco movie.**<br>5 - Strongly Agree<br>4 - Agree<br>3 - Neutral<br>2 - Disagree<br>1 - Strongly Disagree<br><br>**I feel motivated to express my own cultural identity after** |
| | **learning about Miguel's journey.**<br>5 - Strongly Agree<br>4 - Agree<br>3 - Neutral<br>2 - Disagree<br>1 - Strongly Disagree |

It is important to note that the specific Magic School AI tools were selected by the EFL teacher to structure a well-sequenced, fine-tuned project. Some of them, i.e. "Raina Chatbot," "Prompt Assistant," "Conceptual Understanding," "Real-World Connections" and "Chat-with-Docs" are customizable tools to be launched for use by the students as well while "Character Chatbot" is offered only in its customizable version for "launch to students" only. To assess the impact of Magic School AI tools on developing ICC skills, two questionnaires are needed: one evaluating the EFL teacher's experience with all tools — customizable or not, student-centered or teacher-centered — and another focused solely on the student-centered "Character Chatbot." Hence, "Survey Creator" was used to create two questionnaires so that the generated questions may be comparable for further discussion (Table 13). With reference to the second questionnaire, it ought to be noted that an attached file with the results of the discussion with "Character Chatbot" was provided for guidance and inspiration.

After outlining how each Magic School AI tool contributed to the progress of the project - from planning to evaluation – the next section discusses how these contributions can improve the design of any film-based project that is AI-supported to achieve fine-tuned results.

## DISCUSSION OF FINDINGS

### Teacher-centeredness and student-centeredness

Returning to the research question, "Can AI literacy be claimed to be an indispensable assistant to the EFL teacher for lesson planning purposes?", results tend to affirm rather than negate the potentiality of better outcomes in lesson planning. Pokrivcakova (2019, p. 140) turns a critical eye towards textbook-oriented learning materials that "represent the "one-size-fits-all" approach" often adopted by teachers to carry out the day's lesson. Defending her suggestion to opt for materials generated with the aid of AI-powered tools in foreign language education whether they are teacher-centered or student-centered, she goes on to espouse Baker and Smith's (2019) distinction into "learner-facing AI tools" which are" software that students use to learn a subject matter" and "teacher-facing systems" which are "used by teachers with the purpose to reduce their workload" (Pokrivcakova, 2019, p. 137).

In terms of whether Magic School AI tools may be used by teachers to generate structured lesson plans for saving time spent on creating new plans from scratch or launched by teachers to students to facilitate participation in project-based learning, time allocation seems to be the main concern. Generating benefits both teachers and students when success parameters such as well-crafted prompts and strategic use of output are considered. Coordinating input and output as a cycle of effective prompting, especially in the case of empathy-driven tasks, highlights affective engagement as a key to success.

### Planning, Implementation, Evaluation

A crucial point to take into consideration is how intercultural insights could be set as a default result to be extracted from prompting that is both relevant and appropriate. The trial run has shown that the planning stage should take most of the credits for priming teachers and students with data-driven insights on underlying key concepts such as empathy, diversity and conflict resolution. But prior to that, the trial testing phase was initiated by priming the chatbot (i.e. "Raina") with queries to ensure natural response generation. Deeper queries into "cross-cultural communication" prompted a shift toward "communication across generations," while "Prompt Assistant" linked "affective skills development" with "emotional intelligence." By extension, the way the EFL teacher gave shape to the conceptual basis of the project became evident through "Conceptual Understanding". The emergence of the specific concept of "cultural empathy" alongside "generational diversity" and "intergenerational conflict resolution" is indicative of how recasting terms may tailor concepts to a specific context or audience. At the same time, "Common Misconceptions" highlights how limited life experience can lead to misperceptions, showing that preventing cultural misunderstandings also helps avoid setbacks in prompting techniques.

Another point to take into consideration prior to deciding upon the proposal of an all-occasions lesson plan is how to develop opportunities for engaging learners in interactive conversation with the cultural stimuli of the selected film. In the context of the present study, some of the selected Magic School AI tools, i.e., "Chat-with-Docs" and "Character Chatbot," have contributed to this direction as they allow the attachment of files, making content both accessible and searchable for better insights and interaction. By making content available for querying, students are given the opportunity to manage the conditions of their interaction. Results have shown that both AI tools responded effectively to queries driven by empathetic concern which shows how important supplying AI with the relevant resources to draw from is. On the same note, feeding AI tools with prior AI-generated output helps tailor responses to specific challenges and clarify implementable steps. For example, "Lesson Planning" used output from "Project-Based Learning" to generate a lesson plan aligned with PBL goals.

The way selected Magic School AI tools have been structured in a usability sequence, i.e., planning, implementing, evaluating, reflects the methodology of project-based learning whereby iterative processes are encouraged, with EFL teachers continuously improving their prompting techniques. In other words, the proposal of a step-by-step approach serves the purpose of creating a parallel usability sequence that aligns with academic objectives, i.e., generating, streamlining, adapting and customizing. The eventual compilation of two questionnaires aimed at evaluating the EFL teachers' experience with the Magic School AI tools was made possible with the aid of "Survey Creator."

## Generating – Streamlining – Adapting – Customizing

To recap, generating, streamlining, adapting and customizing can be viewed either as required processes within a structured sequence of methodological steps or as autonomous mechanisms that adapt dynamically to changing inputs and outputs. More specifically, generating insights regarding the development of ICC skills was made possible with the aid of "Raina," "Prompt Assistant," "Conceptual Understanding," and "Common Misconceptions" tools. From then onwards, "Chat-with-Docs" and "Character Chatbot" were used for streamlining purposes as they optimized content generation using the document upload feature. "Real-World Connections" was selected for adapting theoretical concepts into familiar cultural ground, i.e., Greek culture. In the case of "Teacher's Observations," adapting has entailed readjusting the teacher's mindset to embrace evolving trends and learner needs. Adapting was supported by "Text Leveler," which simplified input for weaker students, and "Lesson

Hook," which effectively reused input to create cultural triggers. As shown below, "Project-Based Learning" and "Lesson Planning" worked interdependently, with the lesson plan built on the project plan's output, adapting AI responsiveness to enhance decision-making. Finally, special mention goes to the customizing process, which supported the project's evaluation stage by enabling tailored teaching methods for improved outcomes. Hence, prompting "Survey Creator" to create questionnaires that evaluate the complete set of selected tools gave rise to the teacher's need to reflect on the efficiency of the prompt-result correlation. The next step would be to customize the approach by realigning prompts with intended outcomes, using real-time feedback to enhance user interaction.

## Project-Based Learning and Lesson Planning

The presentation of the findings conforms to the stages of project-based learning, i.e., planning, implementation and evaluation. At the same time, the ideas generated by the Magic School AI tools in the first two stages have informed the generated content by "Project-Based Learning" through appropriate prompting. Thus, the generated project plan included the following sections: "Driving Question or Challenge," "Real-world Context," "In-depth Inquiry," "Student Voice and Choice," "Reflection," "Critique and Revision," "Collaboration," "Teacher Facilitation," "Interdisciplinary Connection," and "Assessment." The AI-generated project plan provided the foundation for successfully implementing all project phases. Next, "Lesson Planning" translated the project's overarching goals into actionable, structured steps. The lesson plan, supported by "Project-Based Learning" results, refined the objectives and narrowed the focus to "Intergenerational Sensitivity through the Lens of *Coco*." More specifically, the lesson plan included the following phases: "Opening," "Introduction to New Material," "Guided Practice," "Independent Practice," "Closing," "Extension Activity." The AI-generated lesson plan aligned with "Project-Based Learning" by focusing on intergenerational sensitivity, highlighting key cultural themes, and outlining clear implementation steps to enhance overall effectiveness

## Addressing Practical Challenges in AI Use

Since Covid-19 age, engagement with technology is considered a priority, but inequalities in access (i.e., internet connectivity), digital literacy and infrastructure remain unaddressed barriers to equal participation. Moreover, although efforts to bridge the digital divide (gap between individuals or geographical areas in terms of access to digital technologies) have intensified to ensure that individuals from all backgrounds can derive full benefit from technological advancements, other factors continue to emerge, challenging progress and reversing expectations.

Such an unforeseen factor that cannot be mitigated either through investment in digital tools and learning platforms or through targeted training programs is resistance to modern technology whether from educators, students or both (Griffiths & Goddard, 2015; Howard, 2013). Obviously, the same applies to AI as skepticism and reluctance to embrace its potential can hinder its effective integration into education. However, what are the underlying causes of this resistance? As far as educators' attitudes towards AI are concerned, Hopcan et al. (2024, p. 7281) have found that teachers "express anxiety about the impact of artificial intelligence on employment rates and social life." As far as students' fear of risks associated with AI are concerned, Yarovenko et al. (2024, p. 634) attributed their skepticism to "a lack of awareness of these issues, limited use of such programs, and the cultural and legal peculiarities of the countries to which the respondents belonged."

In the post-COVID-19 era, it seems unrealistic to discuss a lack or fear of digital literacy, as the primary concern has now shifted to AI literacy. This is why it is so important for educators first, and students then, to realize that resisting use of AI tools due to reluctance to integrate into an increasingly digital world may hinder opportunities for developing self-efficacy in teaching and, consequently, learning (Kerridge, 2023; Kizilcec, 2024; Tariq, 2024). The first step towards preventing such self-fulfilling prophecies would be for governmental bodies to prioritize investment in educators' professional development. In Greece, efforts are underway to help educators overcome any second thoughts so that they may confidently integrate AI tools into their teaching practices. According to esos.gr (a daily online newspaper for education in Greece), the Ministry of Education has allocated a budget of €73,650,792.00 for the enhancement of the Digital School through digital services and innovative educational tools (https://www.esos.gr/arthra/92530/psifiako-sholeio-me-proypologismo-7365079200-eu-psifiakos-boithos-toy-mathiti-deite). This project, aimed at enhancing the Digital School, comprises nine key pillars, three of which specifically focus on Artificial Intelligence (i.e., provision of educational tools based on three-dimensional holograms for use in primary and secondary education., development of an integrated Digital Assistant using AI to optimize learning, training educators in new digital tools and the use of AI). The limited distribution of necessary equipment to just 100 public schools across the country clearly indicates that the benefits of this initiative will be partial. What is more concerning is that it raises questions about equity as not all schools will have access to these resources.

Until adequate funding extends to the most remote schools in the country, Magic School AI is the all-encompassing solution that can be utilized anytime and anywhere. By leveraging this technology, educators and students in all regions can gain equitable access to personalized learning experiences, cutting-edge teaching methods, and to high-quality educational resources necessary to thrive.

## Addressing Ethical Challenges in AI Use

According to the site about Greek education, esos.gr, the Academy of Athens (Greece's highest research institution under the Ministry of Education) states that at present AI development and innovation take precedence over security, ethics, and social implications (https://www.esos.gr/arthra/92633/poia-einai-i-apopsi-tis-akadimias-athinon-gia-tin-asfaleia-tis-tehnitis-noimosynis). As a result, this focus on technological progress frequently overlooks crucial issues like data privacy, AI bias, job displacement, and the wider societal effects of automation. Chinta et al. (2024, p. 23) describe the ethical dilemmas in education by stressing the importance of understanding how "algorithms can perpetuate or even exacerbate existing societal biases if not carefully designed and scrutinized" concluding that "this raises the need for AI education to incorporate critical thinking." Therefore, the need for transparency and accountability in the creation of algorithms cannot be emphasized enough (Chinta et al., 2024; Ramnani, 2024). A further proposal to deal with the "problem of implicit biases and stereotypes" comes from Marinucci et al. (2022, p. 747) who support the idea of "unmasking those found in AI systems by understanding their cognitive dimension, rather than simply trying to correct algorithms." Other ethical concerns include privacy and data protection as building public trust in AI systems is essential. Ramnani (2024, p. 173) explains that "utilizing student data to enhance academic achievements necessitates the implementation of strong data protection policies."

In the case of Magic School AI, users are assured that it has been "independently evaluated as the safest and most privacy focused AI platform," with a 93% privacy rating (https://www.magicschool.ai/privacy). More specifically, Magic School AI's policies are designed to safeguard student data privacy by implementing data encryption, limiting data retention, and ensuring compliance with data protection regulations such as GDPR and FERPA. Additionally, Magic School AI emphasizes transparency in data usage, prohibits the sharing of student information with third parties, and provides educators and institutions with granular control over data management. However, while Magic School AI platform aims to enhance the educational experience by offering valuable resources for the educational community, there is limited publicly available information detailing any measures it takes to address cultural stereotypes within its AI-generated content or AI algorithms.

## CONCLUSIONS

### Limitations of Study

Although this study could claim considerable success in bringing out the affective potential of AI tools by integrating culture-related content as part of the prompt (i.e., uploaded movie screenplay), it has certain limitations in outlining the effectiveness of prompts. More specifically, it cannot be guaranteed that specific prompts will lead to responses that align with user expectations. Whether Magic School AI or its users may be charged with this drawback is not evident because, on the one hand, the users of this study have not experimented with the upgraded version of Magic School AI, which allows the possibility of generating more threads, and, on the other hand, Magic School AI's "outputs often lack readiness for immediate use, requiring refinement to ensure pedagogical soundness" (Setyaningsih et al., 2024, p. 685). Although the free users of this study relied on the "edit prompt" feature to refine content, human oversight remains essential to ensure AI tools enhance rather than replace teacher judgment. Besides, as Rojas (2024, p. 6) affirms prompted by his own experience with technology tools in general and Magic School AI in particular, "over-dependency on technology could threaten the teacher-student dynamic."

### Practical Implications

The results suggest that combining Magic School AI tools in project-based learning offers valuable insights that help EFL teachers refine project development. Xia et al. (2024, p. 1) contend that "the critical role of cultural sensitivity in designing educational technologies" should not be neglected as the value of its contribution to the development of intercultural communication competence skills cannot be emphasized enough. Although Xia et al. (2024, p. 1) rely on the Cross-Cultural Intelligence Language Learning System (CILS) that "utilizes advanced AI technologies to provide adaptive, personalized learning experiences that cater to the unique linguistic and cultural backgrounds of each learner," alternative ways of providing analogous experiences may be further explored. Magic School AI is a case in point because, according to Foster et al. (2024, p. 74), it has such a variety of tools which if utilized to their full potential "can assist teachers in meeting the needs of their students." Additionally, tools like Conceptual Understanding and Common Misconceptions can uncover cultural miscommunication patterns as they highlight the need for students to develop conflict resolution skills. Obviously, the transforming power of AI tools is largely dependent on the EFL teacher's self-efficacy to obtain it (Mustafa et al., 2024).

## Suggestions for Further Research

Our study supports the idea that lesson planning can harvest the benefits of using Magic School AI tools to become a seamless process for both novice and experienced EFL educators. Optimizing tool use as a feedback-to-feedforward mechanism requires further testing of prompt relevance and the suitability of uploaded texts as input. Although practical skills in interacting with AI tools suffice to generate, streamline, adapt and customize, acquiring "effective prompt-engineering skills" requires continuous effort and practice "to align with classroom dynamics" (Setyaningsih et al., 2024, p. 685). Therefore, more research on ways of improving prompts could prove more beneficial than research on ways of accelerating lesson planning.

## Concluding Remarks

The preliminary findings of this study provide us with some interesting results with which to look at all EFL lesson plans that use AI tools to achieve better outcomes. Identifying the emphasis on cultural sensitivity as a key refinement factor in obtaining the kind of results that may be leverageable within the context of an AI-assisted lesson plan is something that EFL educators can choose to incorporate in their teaching and learning objectives. Taking into consideration that both Magic School's Project-Based Learning and Lesson Planning AI tools view the "driving question or challenge" and the "learning objective" correspondingly as stepping stones in the learning process, it is fair to say that setting the EFL stage through a more affective lens to begin with is plausible through prompting techniques that are plausible to everyone. Hence, the reply to the research question: Yes, AI literacy might be claimed to be an indispensable assistant to the EFL teacher for lesson planning purposes as long as experimentation with its potential effectiveness is not undermined by the limited belief that it harnesses creativity.

## REFERENCES


Ala, H. A. R. R. A. T. N. R. (2024). *Investigating the relationship between audiovisual-based media and EFL learners' intercultural knowledge* [Unpublished Master's thesis]. University of 8 May 1945 Guelma, Algeria.

Badia van Pelt, M. Y. (2020). *Rise and fall of a hero: Teaching English through literature and cinema* [Unpublished Master's thesis]. University of the Balearic Islands, Majorca.

Baker, T., & Smith, L. (2019). Educ-AI-tion rebooted? Exploring the future of artificial intelligence in schools and colleges. Retrieved from Nesta Foundation website: https://media.nesta.org.uk/documents/Future_of_AI_and_education_v5_WEB.pdf

Bálint, K., Sukalla, F., & Rooney, B. (2022). Personal relevance and state empathy with a character facilitates self-disclosure in film viewers. *Frontiers in Communication, 7*, 984341. DOI: 10.3389/fcomm.2022.984341

Bobkina, J., & Dominguez Romero, E. (2023). Towards a quality standardized technological education in Spain: A case study with EFL preservice teachers. *Journal of Research in Applied Linguistics, 14*(2), 55–66. DOI: 10.22055/rals.2023.43480.3035

Byram, M. (1997). *Teaching and assessing intercultural communicative competence*. Multilingual Matters.

Byram, M. (2021). *Teaching and assessing intercultural communicative competence: Revisited*. Multilingual Matters., DOI: 10.21832/9781800410251

Çakır, İ. (2022). TV serials and movies to boost intercultural communicative competence in Turkish EFL context. *International Journal of Applied Linguistics, 32*(3), 397–410. DOI: 10.1111/ijal.12425

Calogerakou, C., & Vlachos, K. (2011). Films and blogs: An authentic approach to improve the writing skill-an intercultural project-based framework in the Senior High State School. *Research Papers in Language Teaching and Learning, 2*(1), 98–110.

Chao, T. C. (2013). A diary study of university EFL learners' intercultural learning through foreign films. *Language, Culture and Curriculum, 26*(3), 247–265. DOI: 10.1080/07908318.2013.833936

Chen, G. M. (2014). Intercultural communication competence: Summary of 30-year research and directions for future study. In Dai, X.-D., & Chen, G. M. (Eds.), *Intercultural communication competence: Conceptualization and its development in cultural contexts and interactions* (pp. 14–40). Cambridge Scholars Publishing.

Chen, G. M., & Starosta, J. W. (1996). Intercultural communication competence: A synthesis. *Annals of the International Communication Association*, *19*(1), 353–383. DOI: 10.1080/23808985.1996.11678935

Chen, G. M., & Starosta, W. J. (1998). *Foundations of intercultural communication*. Allyn & Bacon.

Chiappini, R., & Mansur, E. (2020, July 9). *Mediating a text: A practical guide to task creation*. https://www.macmillanenglish.com/gr/blog-resources/article/advancing-learning-mediating-a-text-a-practical-guide-to-task-creation

Chinta, S. V., Wang, Z., Yin, Z., Hoang, N., Gonzalez, M., Quy, T. L., & Zhang, W. (2024). FairAIED: Navigating fairness, bias, and ethics in educational AI applications. *arXiv preprint arXiv:2407.18745*.

Daraselia, M., & Jojua, T. (2025). The importance of using movies in EFL classrooms. *Jurnal Pendidikan Guru Sekolah Dasar*, *2*(2), 1–7. DOI: 10.47134/pgsd.v2i2.1177

Edmett, A., Ichaporia, N., Crompton, H., & Crichton, R. (2024). *Artificial intelligence and English language teaching. Preparing for the future.* https://www.teachingenglish.org.uk/sites/teacheng/files/2024-08/AI_and_ELT_Jul_2024.pdf

Erin, J. (2025). *Opportunities and challenges for plurilingual and intercultural education in times of AI* [Webinar]. European Centre for Modern Languages of the Council of Europe. https://www.youtube.com/live/byO8nno1jmk

Fahlevi, R., & Bako, E. N. (2022). Characteristics and moral values from "Encanto" Disney as an enhancing strategy in character building. [English Language Teaching Prima Journal]. *ELT*, *4*(2), 147–160. DOI: 10.34012/elt.v%25vi%25i.3461

Fokides, E., & Peristeraki, E. (2024). Comparing ChatGPT's correction and feedback comments with that of educators in the context of primary students' short essays written in English and Greek. *Education and Information Technologies*, •••, 1–45. DOI: 10.1007/s10639-024-12912-8

Foster, A., Khazanchi, P., & Khazanchi, R. (2024). MagicSchool.ai: A Personal Assistant. In J. Cohen & G. Solano (Eds.), *Proceedings of Society for Information Technology & Teacher Education International Conference* (pp. 74-80). Association for the Advancement of Computing in Education (AACE).

Gessinger, I., Seaborn, K., Steeds, M., Doyle, P., & Cowan, B. R. (2023, June 28). ChatGPT and me: Is ChatGPT perceived as a communication partner? https://doi.org/DOI: 10.17605/OSF.IO/R7P2A

Griffiths, D., & Goddard, T. (2015). An explanatory framework for understanding teachers' resistance to adopting educational technology. *Kybernetes*, *44*(8/9), 1240–1250. DOI: 10.1108/K-11-2014-0274

Guan, J. Q., Ying, S. F., Zhang, M. L., & Hwang, G. J. (2024). From experience to empathy: An empathetic VR-based learning approach to improving EFL learners' empathy and writing performance. *Computers & Education*, *220*, 105120. DOI: 10.1016/j.compedu.2024.105120

Hastuti, F. D., Linda, L., Olyvia, O., & Tomy, T. (2022). The effects of family values in overcoming conflicts in the "Coco" film. *BLESS*, *2*(2), 58–69.

Hopcan, S., Türkmen, G., & Polat, E. (2024). Exploring the artificial intelligence anxiety and machine learning attitudes of teacher candidates. *Education and Information Technologies*, *29*(6), 7281–7301. DOI: 10.1007/s10639-023-12086-9

Howard, S. K. (2013). Risk-aversion: Understanding teachers' resistance to technology integration. *Technology, Pedagogy and Education*, *22*(3), 357–372. DOI: 10.1080/1475939X.2013.802995

Hwang, Y., Lee, J. H., & Shin, D. (2023). What is prompt literacy? An exploratory study of language learners' development of new literacy skill using generative AI. *arXiv preprint arXiv:2311.05373*.

Idris, N. (2014). Using non-native English films to promote multiculturalism in ELT classroom. *Journal of NELTA*, *19*(1-2), 65–76. DOI: 10.3126/nelta.v19i1-2.12081

Jaques, Z. (2021). Intergenerational dialogue in Disney-Pixar animation. In Deszcz-Tryhubczak, J., & Jaques, Z. (Eds.), *Intergenerational solidarity in children's literature and film* (pp. 85–100). University Press of Mississippi.

Kadlubar, A. (2024, February 26). *Making The Grade: How Central Texas public schools are using artificial intelligence chat bots in the classroom*. https://www.kwtx.com/2024/02/26/making-grade-how-central-texas-public-schools-are-using-artificial-intelligence-chat-bots-classroom/

Kalantzis, M., & Cope, B. (2025). Literacy in the time of Artificial Intelligence. *Reading Research Quarterly*, *60*(1), e591. DOI: 10.1002/rrq.591

Karras, I. (2021). Raising intercultural awareness in teaching young learners in EFL classes. *Research Papers in Language Teaching and Learning*, *11*(1), 173–184.

Karras, I. D. (2020). *The culture and communication interface*. Diavlos Publishing.

Kartal, G. (2023). From digital literacy to AI literacy in language teaching: Embracing the artificial intelligence age. In Kartal, G. (Ed.), *Transforming the language teaching experience in the age of AI* (pp. 125–140). IGI Global., DOI: 10.4018/978-1-6684-9893-4.ch008

Kartikasari, Y. D. N., Retnaningdyah, P., & Musthofa, A. (2019). Using film in fostering intercultural awareness for high school students in the Efl classroom. *Jurnal Education and Development*, *7*(2), 58–58. DOI: 10.37081/ed.v7i2.871

Kerridge, S. (2023). Embracing the potential of AI in education: Moving beyond fear and resistance. *Metaphor*, (3), 24-26. https://search.informit.org/doi/10.3316/informit.275737987896285

Khotbi, T., Belbouah, A., & Bouguerba, T. (2023). Navigating multicultural curriculum reform: EFL Teachers' use of movie-based cultural content. *British Journal of Teacher Education and Pedagogy, 2*(3), 01-08. https://doi.org/DOI: 10.32996/bjtep.2023.2.3.1

Kizilcec, R. F. (2024). To advance AI use in education, focus on understanding educators. *International Journal of Artificial Intelligence in Education, 34*(1), 12–19. DOI: 10.1007/s40593-023-00351-4 PMID: 37359103

Luckyardi, S., Karin, J., Rosmaladewi, R., Hufad, A., & Haristiani, N. (2024). Chatbots as digital language tutors: Revolutionizing education through AI. *Indonesian Journal of Science and Technology*, *9*(3), 885–908. DOI: 10.17509/ijost.v9i3.79514

Ma, Q., Crosthwaite, P., Sun, D., & Zou, D. (2024). Exploring ChatGPT literacy in language education: A global perspective and comprehensive approach. *Computers and education. Artificial Intelligence*, *7*, 100278. DOI: 10.1016/j.caeai.2024.100278

Magic School AI. https://app.magicschool.ai/tools

Marinucci, L., Mazzuca, C., & Gangemi, A. (2023). Exposing implicit biases and stereotypes in human and artificial intelligence: State of the art and challenges with a focus on gender. *AI & Society*, *38*(2), 747–761. DOI: 10.1007/s00146-022-01474-3

Mehrabi, N., Morstatter, F., Saxena, N., Lerman, K., & Galstyan, A. (2021). A survey on bias and fairness in machine learning. *ACM Computing Surveys*, *54*(6), 1–35. DOI: 10.1145/3457607

Mohamed, A. M. (2024). Exploring the potential of an AI-based chatbot (ChatGPT) in enhancing English as a Foreign Language (EFL) teaching: Perceptions of EFL faculty members. *Education and Information Technologies*, *29*(3), 3195–3217. DOI: 10.1007/s10639-023-11917-z

Muawanah, U., Marini, A., & Sarifah, I. (2024). The interconnection between digital literacy, artificial intelligence, and the use of E-learning applications in enhancing the sustainability of Regional Languages: Evidence from Indonesia. *Social Sciences & Humanities Open, 10*, 101169. DOI: 10.1016/j.ssaho.2024.101169

Mustafa, H. M., Mahmoud, S. S., Abouelnaga, H. M., Tayfour, M., Metwally, A. B. M., & Shehata, S. M. (2024). The effect of the training of using Magic School AI on self-efficacy in teaching and information overload among Arabic teachers. *Migration Letters : An International Journal of Migration Studies, 21*(S9), 1361–1370.

Nikolopoulou, K. (2024). *ChatGPT for educational-academic activities: Preschool student teachers' experiences*. Intelligent Technologies in Education., DOI: 10.70770/r5aett21

Peachey, N. (2023). *ChatGPT in the language classroom*. Peachey Publications Ltd.

Pokrivčáková, S. (2019). Preparing teachers for the application of AI-powered technologies in foreign language education. *Journal of language and cultural education, 7*(3), 135-153. https://doi:DOI: 10.2478/jolace-2019-0025

Puglisi, B. (2018, May 29). Build character empathy in your first few pages. WRITERS HELPING WRITERS. https://writershelpingwriters.net/2018/05/creating-characterempathy/

Ramnani, S. (2024). Exploring ethical considerations of Artificial Intelligence in educational settings: An examination of bias, privacy, and accountability. [IJNRD]. *International Journal of Novel Research and Development, 9*(2), 2456–4184.

Rapti, C., & Panagiotidis, P. (2024). Teachers' attitudes towards AI integration in foreign language learning: Supporting differentiated instruction and flipped classroom. *European Journal of Education, 7*(2), 88–104. DOI: 10.26417/171oob60e

Rezai, A., Soyoof, A., & Reynolds, B. L. (2024). Disclosing the correlation between using ChatGPT and well-being in EFL learners: Considering the mediating role of emotion regulation. *European Journal of Education, 59*(4), e12752. DOI: 10.1111/ejed.12752

Rodríguez, L. M. G., & Gerke, A. E. (2022). Using foreign films to foster pre-service teachers' intercultural awareness in an EFL context. In García-Sánchez, S., & Clouet, R. (Eds.), *Intercultural communication and ubiquitous learning in multimodal English language education* (pp. 45–67). IGI Global., DOI: 10.4018/978-1-7998-8852-9.ch003

Roell, C. (2010). Intercultural training with films. *English Teaching Forum, 48*(2), 2-15.

Rogers, C. (2023). Mediation in the ELT classroom. *Humanising language teaching*, 4. https://www.hltmag.co.uk/aug23/mediation-in-the-elt-classroom

Rojas, J. P. (2024). *Enhancing English Language Teaching through AI: The case of Magic School AI.* Universidad Distrital Francisco José de Caldas.

Ruusunen, V. (2011). *Using movies in EFL teaching: The point of view of teachers* [Unpublished Master's thesis]. University of Jyväskylä, Finland.

Seiradakis, E. V. (2025). ChatGPT use: Drivers and barriers in English for Academic Purposes among migrant students with learning disabilities. In Stevkovska, M., Klemenchich, M., & Kavaklı Ulutaş, N. (Eds.), *Reimagining Intelligent Computer-Assisted Language Education* (pp. 309–330). IGI Global., DOI: 10.4018/979-8-3693-4310-4.ch011

Seo, J. Y. (2024). Generative AI as a virtual conversation partner in language learning. *International Journal of Advanced Culture Technology*, *12*(2), 7–15. DOI: 10.17703/IJACT.2024.12.2.7

Setyaningsih, E., Asrori, M., Zainnuri, H., & Hariyanti, Y. (2024). Exploring High School EFL teachers' experiences with Magic School AI in lesson planning: Benefits and insights. *Voices of English Language Education Society*, *8*(3), 685–700. DOI: 10.29408/veles.v8i3.27700

Sobehrad, S., & Francis, R. (2024, March). Indistinguishable from Magic: AI for educators. In J. Cohen & G. Solano (Eds.), *Proceedings of Society for Information Technology & Teacher Education International Conference* (pp. 2278-2283). Association for the Advancement of Computing in Education (AACE).

Sperling, K., Stenberg, C. J., McGrath, C., Åkerfeldt, A., Heintz, F., & Stenliden, L. (2024). In search of artificial intelligence (AI) literacy in teacher education: A scoping review. *Computers and Education Open, 100169*, 100169. Advance online publication. DOI: 10.1016/j.caeo.2024.100169

Tai, T. Y., & Chen, H. H. J. (2024). Improving elementary EFL speaking skills with generative AI chatbots: Exploring individual and paired interactions. *Computers & Education, 220*, 105112. DOI: 10.1016/j.compedu.2024.105112

Tariq, U. (2024). Challenges in AI-Powered educational technologies: Teacher perspectives and resistance. *Journal of AI in Education: Innovations, Opportunities, Challenges, and Future Directions*, *1*(3), 1–10.

Unkrich, L., & Molina, A. (Directors). (2017). *Coco* [Film]. Pixar Animation Studios.

Xia, Y., Shin, S. Y., & Kim, J. C. (2024). Cross-cultural intelligent language learning system (CILS): Leveraging AI to facilitate language learning strategies in cross-cultural communication. *Applied Sciences (Basel, Switzerland)*, *14*(13), 5651. DOI: 10.3390/app14135651

Yalcin, N. (2013). Using movies in language classrooms as means of understanding cultural diversity. *Epiphany.Journal of Transdisciplinary Studies*, *6*(1), 259–271.

Yarovenko, H., Kuzior, A., Norek, T., & Lopatka, A. (2024). The future of artificial intelligence: Fear, hope or indifference? *Human Technology*, *20*(3), 611–639. DOI: 10.14254/1795-6889.2024.20-3.10

Ypsilanti, A., & Karras, I. (2024). Introducing Pixar shorts in the Greek EFL classroom as a means to enhancing empathy among High School students. *Proceedings of the IAFOR International Conference on Arts & Humanities in Hawaii (IICAH2024)* (pp. 165-175). https://doi.org/DOI: 10.22492/issn.2432-4604.2024.15

Yue, J. (2019). Use of foreign films in cultivating intercultural communicative competence in ELT—A case study. *Theory and Practice in Language Studies*, *9*(2), 198–203. DOI: 10.17507/tpls.0902.09

Yürük, N. (2016). Films as a multimodal way to improve learners reading skills and enhance cultural awareness in English Language and Literature Departments [Unpublished doctoral dissertation]. Hacettepe University, Turkey.

Zhang, C. B., Li, T. G., Li, Y. N., Chang, Y., & Zhang, Z. P. (2024). Fostering well-being: Exploring the influence of user-AI assistant relationship types on subjective well-being. *International Journal of Information Management*, *79*, 102822. DOI: 10.1016/j.ijinfomgt.2024.102822

# Chapter 9
# Roles of AI in Supporting Ongoing EFL/ESL Teacher Development

**Ayfer Su Bergil**
https://orcid.org/0000-0002-9277-2862
*Amasya University, Turkey*

## ABSTRACT

*The rapid evolution of Artificial Intelligence (AI) technologies has begun to transform various educational domains, including the field of English as a Foreign Language (EFL) and English as a Second Language (ESL) instruction. As these technologies continue to develop, their potential to support ongoing teacher development in EFL/ESL contexts becomes increasingly evident. This chapter explores the multifaceted roles that AI can play in enhancing teacher training, providing personalized professional development opportunities, and fostering reflective teaching practices. The content is grounded in both theoretical perspectives and practical applications, offering insights into how AI can contribute to sustainable and impactful teacher development.*

## INTRODUCTION

Today, artificial intelligence (AI) is causing radical changes in the field of education and offers new opportunities for the professional development of foreign language teachers. Especially for educators who teach English as a foreign language (EFL) or a second language (ESL), AI provides significant advantages in terms of personalizing teaching processes, developing teaching materials, and strengthening teachers' pedagogical skills (Hwang et al., 2020; Kim et al., 2019). However, in order

DOI: 10.4018/979-8-3373-0969-9.ch009

for this technology to be used effectively, teachers must be sufficiently equipped both technically and pedagogically (Chung et al., 2020).

In recent years, artificial intelligence (AI) technologies have revolutionized the field of education and have begun to play an important role in the professional development of EFL and ESL teachers (Rosé et al., 2018). While traditional professional development programs often have limitations in terms of time and resources, AI-supported systems strengthen teachers' pedagogical skills by offering individualized, flexible, and continuous development opportunities (Chen et al., 2020). While AI-supported teaching tools are reshaping teachers' roles in the classroom, they also raise new questions about how teachers should interact with these systems. Teachers' level of adoption of AI technologies is directly related to their perceptions and beliefs in the benefits of technology in education (Cabero-Almenara et al., 2024).

The role of AI in education is important, especially in terms of personalized teaching, automatic feedback mechanisms, and teacher support systems. AI-supported tools not only make it easier for teachers to plan lessons, but also help students make their learning processes more effective (Luckin et al., 2016; An et al., 2023). For example, AI-based speech recognition systems can analyze students' pronunciations, provide instant feedback, and provide teachers with data on individual student development (Holmes et al., 2022).

AI is being used in EFL/ESL teacher development in many different ways. These technologies help teachers prepare their own course materials more effectively, provide personalized feedback on language teaching, and provide data-driven analysis that improves the educational process (Chen et al., 2022). In addition, online professional development platforms and AI-powered educational applications allow teachers to update themselves and effectively integrate new educational technologies (Pinto-Santos et al., 2022).

However, the integration of AI into teacher development also brings some challenges. The lack of training and professional development programs required for teachers to use AI tools effectively is one of the main obstacles to the widespread use of these technologies (Pedro et al., 2019; Roshan et al., 2005). In addition, factors such as ethical concerns, data privacy, and technological inequalities are among the other elements that make it difficult for teachers to use AI tools in the classroom environment (Luckin et al., 2016).

This chapter aims to examine the roles of AI in the professional development processes of EFL/ESL teachers, and to examine the roles of AI, the factors that affect their adoption of this technology, and the contributions of AI-supported educational approaches to EFL/ESL teacher development. In this context, a framework will be presented by reviewing the existing literature on how AI can be integrated into EFL/ESL teacher education and how the challenges encountered in this process can be overcome (Kukulska-Hulme & Lee, 2020; Jameer & Narra 2024).

## LITERATURE REVIEW

The following sections will share the comprehensive literature review while keeping the chapter's objectives of to identify key areas where AI can enhance EFL/ESL teacher development, to analyze specific AI tools and platforms that have shown promise in supporting teacher training and professional growth, to discuss the challenges and ethical considerations associated with integrating AI into teacher development programs, and to propose a future-oriented framework for leveraging AI in sustainable and effective ways, in mind. Hence, the flow of the chapter is organized parallel to the following sections:

### Section 1: AI and the Historical Development of AI

This section will explore the evolution of artificial intelligence, tracing its origins from early theoretical foundations to modern advancements. It will delve into key milestones, influential figures, and groundbreaking technologies that have shaped AI over the decades. Moreover, this section will provide insight into how AI has progressed from conceptual ideas to real-world applications, highlighting the challenges and breakthroughs along the way.

### Section 2: The Current Landscape of EFL/ESL Teacher Development

This section will provide an overview of the traditional approaches to teacher development in the EFL/ESL field. It will highlight common challenges such as access to quality training, limited opportunities for personalized feedback, and difficulties in keeping up with the latest pedagogical research. This contextual background will serve as a foundation for understanding the transformative potential of AI.

### Section 3: AI-Driven Personalization in Professional Development

AI's ability to analyze large datasets and identify patterns makes it an ideal tool for personalized learning. This section will examine how AI can create customized professional development pathways for EFL/ESL teachers based on their individual needs, teaching contexts, and skill gaps. Examples will include adaptive learning platforms that provide targeted resources and AI-powered coaching systems that offer real-time feedback on classroom practices.

## Section 4: Enhancing Reflective Practices Through AI

Reflective teaching is a critical component of professional growth, allowing educators to evaluate their methods and adapt to changing classroom dynamics. AI tools, such as speech and video analysis software, can facilitate this process by providing objective insights into teaching performance. This section will discuss the implications of using AI to support self-assessment and peer feedback among EFL/ESL teachers.

## Section 5: AI as a Collaborative Tool for Teacher Communities

Collaboration and peer learning are essential for professional development. AI can enhance these practices by enabling virtual teacher communities, automating administrative tasks, and providing insights into collective teaching strategies. This section will explore platforms that utilize AI to foster collaboration among EFL/ESL educators globally, bridging geographical and cultural divides.

## Section 6: Ethical and Practical Considerations

While AI holds great promise, its integration into teacher development programs raises several ethical and practical concerns. Issues such as data privacy, algorithmic bias, and the potential for over-reliance on technology will be critically examined. This section will offer guidelines for ethical AI implementation and highlight the importance of maintaining a balance between human expertise and technological assistance.

## Section 7: The Use of AI Tools in EFL/ESL Teacher Development: Study Samples and Outcomes

This section explores how artificial intelligence (AI) tools are being integrated into EFL/ESL teacher development programs. It presents sample studies that examine the implementation of AI in various training contexts and discusses their outcomes in terms of teacher learning, pedagogical practices, and professional growth.

## Section 8: A Framework for the Future

The chapter will conclude with a proposed framework for integrating AI into EFL/ESL teacher development in a sustainable and effective manner. This framework will emphasize the importance of ongoing research, stakeholder collaboration, and the development of user-friendly AI tools tailored to the unique needs of EFL/ESL educators.

## Section 9: Critical Analysis of AI Integration in EFL/ESL Teacher Education

This section will critically examine the role of artificial intelligence in EFL/ESL teacher education, highlighting its potential benefits, challenges, and ethical considerations. It explores how AI tools influence teacher training, pedagogical practices, and the development of professional competencies, while also addressing concerns around dependency, equity, and data privacy.

## AI and the Historical Development of AI

Artificial intelligence has been recognized as one of the most significant technological advancements in human history. The ancient Greek philosopher Aristotle was the first to propose the idea of transmitting human minds to machines. The first AI applications, however, did not materialize until the middle of the 20th century, with the advent of contemporary computer technology, despite the fact that the concept was initially proposed in philosophical studies. Alan Turing, the renowned mathematician and computer scientist, is the most outstanding individual in the history of artificial intelligence. Alan Turing created the "Turing Machine" after himself, which marked the conceptual start of algorithm-defined computers. In 1950, Turing attempted to test the cognitive capacities of computers with the "Turing Test" that he articulated in his article "Computing Machinery and Intelligence" (Ferikoğlu, 2021).

At a 1956 summer meeting at Dartmouth College, John McCarthy, Marvin Minsky, Nathaniel Rochester, and Claude Shannon coined the term artificial intelligence. In 1956, Allen Newell and J.C. Shaw's "Logic Theorist"—the first AI program—was released to automatically solve mathematical problems. John McCarty, the creator of the LISP programming language, completed a significant task two years later that is still utilized in current AI research. The General Problem Solver (GPS), created in 1957 by H. Simon and A. Newell, is another program regarded as one of the pioneers in the field of artificial intelligence. GPS is an instrument for problem-solving that can carry out tasks like problem analysis, alternative solution evaluation, and solution selection (Kayabaş, 2010). In 1965, scientists at the Stanford Research Institute created the robot Shakey, which was able to move, map the locations it visited, and determine its course using a navigation algorithm (Dengiz, 2023). J. Weizenbaum presented ELIZA, a natural processing program, to the scientific community that same year (Kayabaş, 2010).

Significant advancements were occurring in the field of AI, but between 1974 and 1980, states that were impacted by the unfavorable comments made about AI research quit funding them, causing a period of stagnation in the field's development. In order to compete with Japan, England allocated funds for AI research at the conclusion of this time, which was dubbed the "artificial intelligence winter" (Toosi et al., 2021). Some of the major advancements in artificial intelligence following this artificial intelligence winter include the first driverless car made in Germany in 1986 and the humanoid robot known as WABOT-2, which was created in Japan in 1980 and has human-like facial expressions and movements in addition to the ability to communicate with people (Dengiz, 2023).

Computers can compete with humans and even surpass them in certain areas, as demonstrated by IBM's Deep Blue chess computer's victory over world chess champion Garry Kasparov in 1997 and the Deep Junior program's draw with world chess champions V. Kramnik and G. Kasparov (Liu, 2025). Significant advancements in the field of AI occurred after the creation of the first robot dog, AIBO, in 1999 and the first artificial intelligence toy, Tiger Furby, in 1998. Honda debuted Asimo, the first humanoid robot, in 2000 (Wang, 2022). An obstacle-avoiding vacuum cleaner named "Roomba" was released by the US company iRobot in 2002 (Coşkun & Gülleroğlu, 2021). These advancements suggest that AI technology are beginning to permeate homes.

Significant advancements in artificial intelligence were made in 2011 with the introduction of Siri, one of the digital voice assistants still in use today, on smartphones and the defeat of Watson, an AI software, on the game show Jeopardy!. One notable advancement in the application of artificial intelligence technology in the industrial sector is the creation of a robot named Nextage, which can carry out mass production in the industrial field a year later.

With its 2014 introduction of facial recognition technology, Facebook, one of the major social media platforms today, has demonstrated performance that is comparable to human intelligence. Among the significant advancements in AI in 2015 are robots that can prepare meals using YouTube videos created by American students, drones, which are unmanned aerial vehicles made by Skydio, and AI systems that can learn to play video games on their own, which are made by Google. A year later, two significant advancements in the field of AI were made: the PilotNet program, which learned to drive by studying human behavior in 2017, and Apple's Emotient artificial intelligence program, which provides customers with options based on their unique needs and characteristics (Coşkun & Gülleroğlu, 2021; Dengiz, 2023).

Hence, one of the most discussed and emerging topics in the technology industry in recent years is AI, which broadly refers to computer systems that simulate human cognitive functions like learning, reasoning, problem solving, and decision making (Goodfellow et al., 2016). With its sub-branches like machine learning, deep learning, and natural language processing, artificial intelligence is useful in many facets of life and is causing revolutionary changes in industries, the economy, education, and health (Russell et al., 2021).

## The Current Landscape of EFL/ESL Teacher Development

In the field of education, the formation of teacher identity is one of the cornerstones of the professional/teacher development process (Beijaard et al., 2004). The identity formation of EFL/ESL teachers in particular is affected by both individual and socio-cultural factors (Varghese et al., 2005). Identity formation has a dynamic and constantly changing structure (Norton, 2013). Teachers shape their identities in line with their professional experiences and personal backgrounds (Tsui, 2007). This process continues throughout their professional life, starting from teacher induction. The main factors affecting identity formation include personal experiences and professional identity, educational policies and institutional expectations, and socio-cultural influences.

Teachers' own learning experiences directly affect their professional identities (Rodgers & Scott, 2008). EFL/ESL teachers can reflect their language learning experiences during their student years into their professional life. Educational systems and institutions are important factors that shape teacher identity (Johnson, 2009). Curriculum, certification processes, and professional development opportunities are effective in the formation of this identity. Since EFL/ESL teachers work in different cultural and linguistic contexts, their identities are heavily influenced by these factors (Duff & Uchida, 1997). Hence, the identity formation process of English teachers has a complex structure shaped by the interaction of individual and social factors. This means that professional identity should be open to change and develop over time (Beauchamp & Thomas, 2009).

In the process of change and development in identity formation, the fact that training programs play a critical role in shaping individuals' professional identities should not be ignored. Especially in the field of foreign language education, the professional identity development of prospective teachers is closely related to the content and quality of the education they receive (Johnson, 2016). In this context, it is important to examine the effect of training programs on the identity formation process of English teachers.

Training programs aim to develop individuals' professional competencies while also providing them with a certain professional identity. Sardabi et al. (2018) emphasize the effect of educational programs on the professional identity development of English teachers, stating that the pedagogical and methodological approaches that make up the content of the program shape prospective teachers' understanding of teaching and their identities.

*Figure 1. Emerging conceptualizations of factors re-shaping student-teachers' identity; the critical back and forth between the past and present with a vision for the future (Mora-Pablo & Goodwin, 2023)*

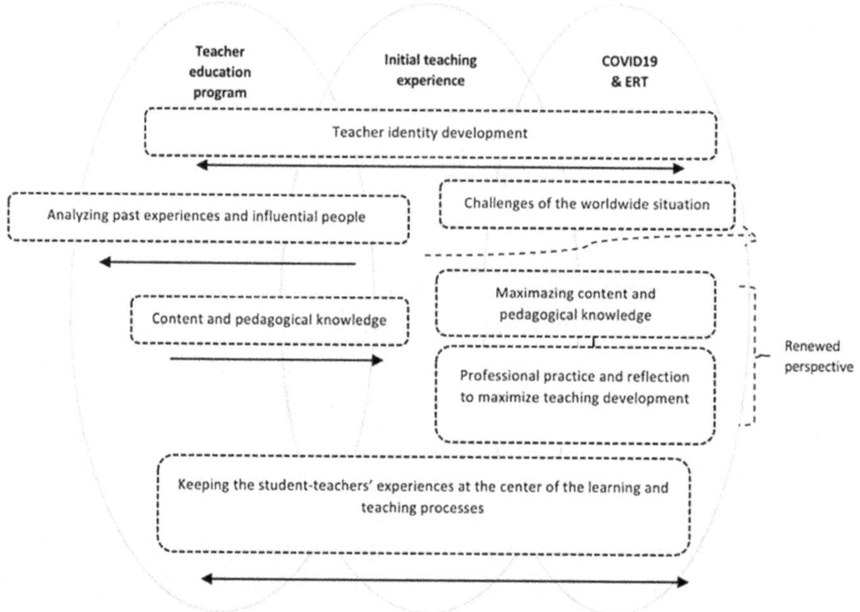


According to figure 2, the EFL/ESL student teachers' own conceptions of "self" and teaching methods, which were initially built by prior experiences and knowledge, are deconstructed in the model of developing conceptualizations of variables reshaping student-teachers' identities. According to Kumaravadivelu (1994), teachers must first identify themselves as language teachers before they may be ready for the renewal. This suggests that educators who can both practice what they theorize and theorize what they practice are always being built and dismantled (Gholami et al., 2021).

The pandemic process has led to radical changes in education systems and has significantly affected teachers' professional identity formation processes. In this context, the impact of the pandemic on the role of teacher education training programs, which is one of the most important elements shaping the professional identities of English teachers, is also very clear. Furthermore, the pandemic process has caused teachers to re-evaluate their pedagogical approaches and professional identities (Eldot, 2023). For English teachers, elements such as distance education applications, digital pedagogical competencies and flexible teaching strategies have come to the fore (Whalen, 2020).

Distance education programs implemented during the pandemic have played an important role in shaping teachers' pedagogical identities. Issues such as digital teaching materials, online assessment methods and virtual classroom management have directly affected the professional identities of English teachers (Hodges et al., 2020). In this way, the supportive elements offered by educational programs, especially during the pandemic process, have enabled teachers to develop new teaching methods. During this process, teachers had to move away from the traditional classroom environment and adopt flexible teaching methods. Components such as online training modules, use of digital tools, and student-centered teaching techniques offered by training programs have contributed to the reconstruction of teacher identity (Watt & Richardson, 2023).

As the pandemic process has led to radical changes in education systems and it has significantly affected teachers' identity formation processes. English teachers have also been affected by this process and have had to redefine their pedagogical approaches and professional identities. Taking it into account, the fundamental dynamics affecting the identity formation of English teachers in the post-pandemic period and the elements that came to the fore in this process should be examined and discussed.

The pandemic process has necessitated the widespread use of distance education and required teachers to increase their digital pedagogical competence (Situmorang et al., 2020). In this context, the identities of English teachers have evolved from traditional teacher roles to being effective guides and technologically literate individuals in the digital environment. The ability to use digital tools effectively has become an integral part of teachers' professional identities (Budiarta & Krismayani, 2024).

In post-pandemic education, the importance of flexible teaching methods and student-centered approaches has increased. Online and hybrid education models have reshaped the way teachers teach (Rodrigues, 2023). In this process, English teachers have become more sensitive to students' needs by offering individualized learning experiences. The teacher identity has now evolved from an authority figure who simply conveys information to a role that collaborates and guides students (Wafula, 2025).

Another important factor shaping the professional identity of English teachers in the post-pandemic period is the role of professional development and learning communities. Teachers have the opportunity to share and develop their professional experiences by interacting more with global educational communities (Barber et al., 2021). Online seminars, professional forums, and collaboration among teachers play a critical role in the identity formation process of teachers.

In addition, the challenges brought about by the pandemic have led to the need to strengthen teachers' emotional resilience. Teacher identity is shaped not only by pedagogical knowledge and skills, but also by factors such as stress management, psychological flexibility, and self-awareness (Eslit, 2023). English teachers are developing more conscious strategies to maintain their professional motivation while protecting their emotional well-being in the post-pandemic period.

Thus, training programs have emerged as an important factor in the identity formation processes of English teachers during and after the pandemic. These programs have contributed to teachers increasing their digital pedagogical competence and developing flexible teaching strategies. In order to support teachers more effectively in similar crisis situations in the future, they have provided a basis for conducting studies that examine the impact of training programs on teacher identity in more detail. Furthermore, in the post-pandemic period, the identity formation process of English teachers is shaped by elements such as digital pedagogical skills, student-centered approaches, participation in professional learning communities, and emotional resilience. These dynamics help teachers redefine their roles in education and adapt to evolving conditions. Future research can provide more in-depth information on the transformation of teacher identity by examining the long-term effects of these processes.

## AI-Driven Personalization in Professional Development of EFL/ESL Teachers

AI has the potential to create personalized learning experiences in education. AI-assisted personalization takes into account individual learning speeds and styles by adopting a student-centered approach (Hardaker & Glenn, 2025). Unlike traditional education methods, AI can instantly analyze student needs and offer appropriate content and methods. This part of the chapter examines the educational dimensions of AI-assisted personalization and addresses its pedagogical, technological, and ethical aspects.

In terms of the pedagogical dimension of AI-assisted personalization, it is accepted that AI can meet individual learning needs by adopting a student-centered approach in education. Students' learning styles, strengths, weaknesses, and past performances can be analyzed by AI and personalized learning paths can be suggested (Strielkowski et al., 2024). For example, adaptive learning systems optimize the learning process by offering content appropriate to the student's level (Ellikkal & Rajamohan,2024). In addition, AI-assisted teaching systems provide real-time feedback to students, making the learning process more effective. For example, AI-based teaching assistants can help students correct their mistakes by giving them instant feedback (Guo, & Wang, 2025). This increases student motivation and helps them develop self-regulation skills.

Considering the technological dimension of AI personalization, AI's integration into the personalization process in education is realized through various technological tools. Machine learning algorithms, big data analytics, and natural language processing techniques are used to produce solutions for students' individual needs (Baker et al., 2016). For example, AI-based education platforms can analyze student performance data to determine which topics require more work. Chatbots and virtual teaching assistants also play an important role in AI-supported personalization processes. These systems provide students with 24/7 support, making the learning process more flexible (Harry, 2023). Especially in distance education, AI-supported personalization relieves teachers' burden and provides faster responses to students' individual needs.

As opposed to the positive sides of AI personalization, ethical dimensions of AI in education needs to be remembered and the integration of AI into personalized learning processes in education also raises ethical questions. Privacy and security of data are among the most important ethical issues (Zawacki-Richter et al., 2019). The fact that AI systems collect students' personal data raises serious concerns about how this information is used. AI applications in education should be used within an ethical framework. Moreover, there are concerns that AI-supported personalization may increase inequalities in education. Students who do not have access to AI-based systems may be disadvantaged due to the digital divide (Kayyali, 2024; Memon & Memon, 2025). Therefore, it is important for AI-supported education solutions to be accessible to everyone.

AI-supported personalization has great potential to improve individual learning experiences in education. Pedagogically, it meets individual learning needs by supporting a student-centered approach. Technologically, it is possible to increase students' academic performance with methods such as machine learning and big data analytics. However, ethical issues such as data privacy and digital inequality should be taken into consideration. In the future, new policies and practices may be developed to make AI-powered personalization more ethical, accessible, and effective.

Given how drastically AI has changed education, especially in the teaching of EFL and ESL, AI-driven personalization offers specialized learning opportunities that enable teachers to pursue focused professional development. In order to do this, it is necessary to investigate how AI-driven customization benefits EFL/ESL instructors' professional development by adapting course materials, providing individualized feedback, and encouraging continuous improvement.

AI-driven personalization in education refers to the application of machine learning algorithms and data analytics to customize learning experiences based on individual needs (Luckin et al., 2016). For EFL/ESL teachers, professional development often involves acquiring new teaching strategies, understanding language acquisition theories, and implementing innovative classroom techniques. AI systems, such as adaptive learning platforms and intelligent tutoring systems, provide real-time feedback and resources tailored to teachers' specific needs (Popenici & Kerr, 2017).

AI-powered adaptive learning platforms adjust content and learning paths according to teachers' progress and knowledge gaps. These systems analyze user interactions, recommend resources, and suggest strategies to improve teaching effectiveness. For example, AI-driven platforms like Coursera and Edmodo employ machine learning algorithms to offer customized professional development courses for EFL/ESL educators (Bearman et al., 2023). Such platforms enhance the learning process by ensuring that teachers receive relevant and practical knowledge at their own pace.

Furthermore, Natural Language Processing (NLP) technologies contribute to the customization of professional development by analyzing teachers' spoken and written communication. AI-based tools, such as Grammarly and Turnitin, provide personalized feedback on teachers' language proficiency and instructional communication (Martin et al., 2024). This continuous assessment helps educators refine their skills and improve their pedagogical approach.

One of the core components of professional development is reflective practice, where teachers analyze their own performance and seek areas for improvement. AI-driven systems facilitate this process by offering real-time feedback based on data-driven insights. For example, AI-based virtual mentors analyze classroom interactions and provide constructive feedback on teaching methodologies, classroom management, and student engagement Fakhar et al., 2024). Such tools enable teachers to refine their instructional techniques and adapt to students' diverse learning needs.

Moreover, AI-powered assessment tools provide automated evaluation of lesson plans, teaching materials, and classroom activities. These tools use machine learning to assess the effectiveness of teaching strategies and suggest modifications to optimize learning outcomes (Miao et al., 2021). By integrating AI-generated feedback into their professional development, EFL/ESL teachers can enhance their instructional effectiveness and maintain high teaching standards.

AI-driven personalization promotes continuous professional development (CPD) by offering ongoing training opportunities tailored to individual needs. Unlike traditional professional development programs, which often follow a one-size-fits-all approach, AI-enabled CPD ensures that learning experiences remain relevant and context-specific (Goksel & Bozkurt, 2019). For instance, AI-powered recommendation systems suggest relevant research articles, webinars, and online courses based on teachers' professional interests and career goals.

Additionally, AI-driven chatbots and virtual assistants, such as IBM Watson and ChatGPT, provide instant access to pedagogical resources and research-based teaching strategies (Pokrivcakova, 2019; Mohamed, et al., 2024). These AI tools enable EFL/ESL teachers to engage in self-directed learning, addressing their professional development needs in real time. By leveraging AI-powered CPD, educators can stay updated with the latest advancements in language teaching methodologies and pedagogical innovations.

AI-driven personalization is revolutionizing the professional development of EFL/ESL teachers by providing adaptive learning, personalized feedback, and continuous training opportunities. By integrating AI into teacher education, educators can enhance their instructional effectiveness, stay updated with emerging teaching strategies, and engage in lifelong learning. However, addressing ethical concerns and ensuring equitable access to AI-driven resources remain critical for maximizing the potential of AI in professional development. Future research should explore strategies for mitigating AI biases and developing inclusive AI-driven professional learning environments for EFL/ESL educators. However, although limited, practical strategies for integrating AI into personalized learning experiences for teachers can be broadly listed as follows:

1. **Applying AI-Powered Needs Analysis and Diagnostic Assessments:** Accurate diagnoses is the first step toward personalization. Through interactive exercises and micro-assessments, AI-driven systems can evaluate teachers' pedagogical expertise, technology proficiency, and language proficiency. Adaptive testing software and intelligent tutoring systems (ITS) are examples of tools that can dynamically change the level of difficulty and offer immediate feedback.
2. **Utilizing Platforms for Adaptive Learning in Continuous Professional Development (CPD):** AI-powered learning management systems (LMS) are able to select and modify content according to the interests, objectives, and past experiences of teachers. In order to suggest pertinent modules, articles, or micro-courses, these systems examine user interactions.
3. **Using Intelligent Content Recommendation Engines:** AI-powered recommendation algorithms for professional learning content function similarly to those used by Spotify or Netflix. These engines look at peer interactions, user behavior, and contextual factors (like the classroom setting) to suggest videos, articles, resources, or lesson plans.
4. **Following AI-Powered Online Coaching and Mentoring:** Conversational AI and natural language processing (NLP) may mimic interactive discussions, provide feedback on instructional strategies, and encourage reflective inquiry—all of which are components of human mentorship.
5. **Incorporating Analytical Data for Reflective Practice:** AI is capable of combining instructional data, such as LMS activity logs and classroom recordings, to produce useful insights that support teachers in self-reflection.
6. **Practicing Personalized Microlearning and Spaced Repetition:** Microlearning modules—short, focused learning activities—can be personalized using AI algorithms that monitor learning retention and engagement.

7. **Receiving Multimodal Feedback and Promoting Self-Regulated Learning:** In order to accommodate different learning styles and promote autonomy, AI technologies can provide feedback in a variety of modalities, such as visual, textual, and audio.
8. **Using AI in an Ethical and Inclusive Way:** Ethical and inclusive personalization is also essential. Teachers need to be prepared to comprehend the consequences and biases of AI.

## Enhancing Reflective Practices Through AI in EFL/ESL Teacher Education

Because of its significance in professional growth, reflective practice has drawn a lot of attention in teacher education for EFL/ESL teacher education. It enables educators to evaluate their methods, interactions with students, and classroom experiences critically, which promotes ongoing development. Reflective practice promotes lifelong learning, strengthens pedagogical decision-making, and helps teachers adjust to a variety of classroom environments (Farrell, 2022). Investigating the value of reflective practices in EFL/ESL teacher preparation and the necessity of improving them is crucial to this process.

Reflective techniques have both benefits and drawbacks when used by educators, notwithstanding their significance. The foundation of reflective practice in education may be found in the writings of Schön (Visser, 2010) and Dewey (Leitch & Day, 2000), who highlighted reflection as a tool for professional development. Teachers in EFL/ESL situations face pedagogical, linguistic, and cultural obstacles, therefore reflection is a crucial part of their preparation. A five-stage paradigm for reflective practice was put forth by Farrell (2022), and it consists of recounting experiences, analyzing actions, thinking about different strategies, putting changes into practice, and assessing results. Teachers can gain a greater grasp of their teaching strategies and student involvement through these stages.

Reflective practice's influence on teacher autonomy and decision-making is one of its main advantages. Reflective teachers are more likely to embrace creative teaching methods, successfully meet the requirements of their students, and boost their self-efficacy, according to Xu (2024). Reflective practice also promotes the growth of one's professional identity. Teachers can match their practices with changing pedagogical ideas by critically analyzing their roles, beliefs, and teaching philosophies (Glasswell & Ryan, 2017).

The enhancement of student participation and classroom management is an additional benefit. According to Boud et al. (2013), reflective educators are able to spot trends in their students' behavior and modify their instruction accordingly. For instance, teachers can objectively examine their classroom interactions through video-based reflections, which improves communication and student-centered learning (Bowers et al., 2017).

Reflective practice has advantages, but there are drawbacks to using it in EFL/ESL teacher preparation. Its efficacy may be hampered by institutional expectations, time restrictions, and a lack of organized frameworks for reflection. According to Farrell (2013), uniform curricula and high workloads make it difficult for many teachers to practice in-depth reflection. Furthermore, without supervision, new teachers could find it challenging to evaluate their own instruction.

One significant issue is the propensity for superficial reflection, in which educators describe their experiences without seriously evaluating them (Akbari, 2007). Structured reflective activities like journaling, peer talks, and mentorship programs are necessary for teacher education programs to address this (Russell & Martin, 2017). Teacher education programs should incorporate organized and methodical reflection models in order to optimize the advantages of reflective practice. Collaborative reflection groups, where educators exchange experiences and get helpful criticism from mentors and peers, are one successful strategy (Farrell,2022).

Additionally, reflection can be improved by using digital tools. Online discussion boards and video-based self-observation give instructors the chance to evaluate their instruction in real time and gain knowledge from educators around the globe (Bowers et al., 2017). Additionally, teachers can better express their teaching beliefs and improve their instructional practices by including reflective writing tasks into teacher training curriculum (Brookfield, 2015).

Establishing an institutional culture of reflection is another essential tactic. Through professional development workshops, reflective teaching journals, and organized mentoring programs, educational institutions should promote reflective practice (Brandenburg & Jones, 2017). Institutions can guarantee that teachers consistently assess and improve their teaching methods by incorporating reflection into teacher education programs.

Given that reflectiveness fosters critical thinking, increases instructional efficacy, and fosters professional growth, reflective practice is essential to EFL/ESL teacher education. But putting it into practice calls for institutional encouragement, organized support, and creative problem-solving techniques. Teacher education programs can give EFL/ESL teachers the tools they need for effective instruction and ongoing progress by fostering reflective practice through mentorship, digital resources, and collaborative learning. Currently, in order to enhance teacher development, the use of AI must be incorporated into reflective practices.

With the advent of AI) new opportunities for incorporating technology into reflective practices to improve teacher education have emerged. AI-powered tools can support self-regulation, automated feedback, and data-driven insights to enhance teacher reflection and development. Reflective practice has long been recognized as a critical component in the professional development of EFL/ESL teachers, allowing educators to critically analyze their teaching methodologies, adapt to new pedagogical advancements, and improve student learning outcomes (Alisoy & Sadiqzade, 2024).

To increase teaching effectiveness, reflective practice entails ongoing self-evaluation, adaptation, and assessment. Teachers have historically reflected through journals, peer reviews, and mentor input. However, a number of new techniques have been created by AI to support and improve these processes.

The ability of AI to evaluate instructional patterns and offer automatic feedback is one of its major contributions. AI-powered learning analytics solutions are able to monitor classroom activities, evaluate student-teacher participation, and provide evidence-based recommendations for enhancement. For example, teacher feedback quality has been evaluated using automated writing evaluation (AWE) systems, which enables teachers to improve their teaching methods and assessment techniques (Karatay & Karatay, 2024).

By serving as discussion partners that encourage teachers to participate in structured reflection, AI-powered virtual assistants can help promote reflective practice. By posing insightful queries, summarizing significant teaching moments, and suggesting possible solutions to instructional problems, AI chatbots—like OpenAI's ChatGPT—can encourage self-reflection (Yang et al., 2024).). Teachers can create focused improvement initiatives and conduct a systematic analysis of their classroom activities thanks to this technique.

A key component of teacher education is self-regulated learning (SRL), which empowers teachers to take charge of their own professional growth. By offering tailored recommendations based on an educator's skills and shortcomings, AI systems help improve SRL. AI-powered systems, for instance, are able to recognize pedagogical knowledge gaps in teachers and recommend pertinent professional development materials, including webinars, research articles, or training courses (Ding, et al., 2024).).

Furthermore, teachers can more effectively assess their own instructional performance thanks to AI-powered feedback mechanisms. Video recordings of class sessions can be analyzed by automated assessment systems, including AI-based classroom observation tools, to provide information on areas that need improvement (Kim, 2024). These observations assist educators in establishing clear objectives for their career development and tracking their advancement over time.

The ability of AI to examine vast volumes of classroom data and spot trends and patterns is among its most potent uses in teacher education. By identifying areas in which students struggle, offering substitute teaching methods, and forecasting possible learning outcomes, learning analytics can assist educators in reflecting on their education (Yan et al., 2024).

For example, data on student participation, engagement, and comprehension can be gathered and analyzed by AI-powered classroom management systems. These findings can be used by educators to improve their teaching methods and develop more successful lesson plans. Furthermore, teachers can improve the entire learning experience by using predictive analytics to foresee student challenges and take proactive measures to address them (Alalawi et al., 2024).

Through improved self-regulation, tailored feedback, and data-driven insights, the incorporation of AI into reflective practice holds the potential to completely transform EFL/ESL teacher education. When applied carefully and morally, AI can be a useful tool for professional growth, even though issues like accuracy, privacy, and teacher acceptance need to be addressed. AI will become more and more important in influencing reflective teaching methods and raising student and instructor achievement as the technology develops.

## AI as a Collaborative Tool for EFL/ESL Teacher Communities

Collaboration is a cornerstone of effective teacher education, particularly in the fields of EFL/ESL. Given the complexities of language acquisition and the diverse needs of learners, EFL/ESL teachers benefit greatly from collaborative approaches in their training. Collaboration fosters professional growth, enhances pedagogical practices, and leads to better learning outcomes for students. Therefore, it is necessary to consider the importance of collaboration in EFL/ESL teacher education by looking at how it affects teacher development, classroom practice, and student achievement.

Collaborative learning experiences are emphasized in teacher education programs. According to research, pre-service teachers who participate in cooperative learning activities like group discussions, co-teaching, and peer observations get a deeper comprehension of teaching approaches (Richards, 2005). Collaboration promotes ongoing professional development by enabling educators to exchange ideas, consider their experiences, and get helpful criticism (Johnson & Golombek, 2016). Additionally, it has been discovered that cooperative mentorship connections between seasoned and inexperienced educators enhance their confidence and efficacy as teachers (Lave & Wenger, 1991).

By enabling educators to try out various teaching philosophies, collaboration helps to improve educational practices. Teachers can produce more creative lesson plans, interesting teaching resources, and creative classroom activities when they collaborate (Little, 1990). Student-centered teaching approaches are essential in EFL/ESL contexts, and research shows that teachers who engage in collaborative professional learning communities are more likely to implement them (Hord, 1997). Additionally, cooperation promotes cultural sensitivity, which helps educators adapt their lessons to students from a variety of linguistic and cultural backgrounds (Burns & Richards, 2009).

Collaboration improves student learning results in addition to teacher development and pedagogical techniques. It has been demonstrated that collaborative teaching strategies, like team instruction and peer-assisted learning, increase student interest and linguistic competency (Vygotsky, 1978). A more dynamic and interactive learning environment that promotes active student participation is produced when educators work together (Storch, 2002). Furthermore, collaborative assessment techniques like group projects and peer review help students develop their communication and critical thinking abilities (Jacobs, 2004).

The integration of collaborative tools in EFL/ESL teacher education is increasingly vital in today's digital learning environment. These tools enhance communication, knowledge-sharing, and pedagogical development among teachers (Zamiri & Esmaeili, 2024). Various digital platforms and technologies facilitate collaboration, enabling teacher trainees to engage in reflective practice, peer learning, and professional development.

The two main categories of collaborative tools are synchronous and asynchronous. Real-time collaboration and instant response are made possible by synchronous tools like interactive whiteboards and video conferencing services like Zoom and Microsoft Teams. These resources facilitate online teaching simulations, group lesson planning, and real-time discussions (Thornhill-Miller et al., 2023). However, teacher candidates can work together at their own pace with asynchronous tools like discussion boards, shared documents (like Google Docs and OneNote), and learning management systems (LMS) like Moodle. According to Noël et al. (2022), asynchronous technologies are especially useful for encouraging in-depth contemplation and cooperative material development. Furthermore, the integration of AI in education has significantly transformed the training of EFL/ESL teachers. AI-based tools offer opportunities for collaboration, personalization, and automation, enhancing both pre-service and in-service teacher education. The application of AI in language education is categorized into areas such as automatic evaluation, intelligent tutoring, neural machine translation, and affective computing (Chang et al., 2020; Jiang, 2022). Hence, the subsequent section addresses AI collaborative tools that support teacher education in EFL/ESL contexts as in Figure 2.

*Figure 2. AI-powered collaborative tools for EFL/ESL teacher education (The figure was created by CANVA at 10.25 on February 16, 2025, by the author.)*

1. **Automatic Evaluation Systems (AESs)**: AI-based automatic evaluation technologies known as Automatic Evaluation Systems (AESs) help grade and comment on students' speaking and writing performances. Natural language processing (NLP) is used by systems such as Criterion and Pigai to examine linguistic patterns and provide recommendations for enhancement (Chang et al., 2021; Rajak et al., 2024). Because of their limits in evaluating intricate syntactic and contextual nuances, AESs cannot yet completely replace human evaluation, even though they increase instructor efficiency (Ngo et al., 2024).
2. **Intelligent Tutoring Systems (ITSs)**: AI-powered Intelligent Tutoring Systems (ITSs) provide EFL/ESL students with individualized learning experiences and real-time feedback. These systems support differentiated education, which is essential in teacher preparation programs, by utilizing adaptive learning strategies. For example, teachers-in-training can participate in simulated classroom scenarios in interactive learning environments offered by AI chatbots (Layali & Al-Shlowiy, 2020).
3. **Neural Machine Translation (NMT) Tools**: DeepL and Google Translate are two examples of Neural Machine Translation (NMT) programs that are frequently utilized in teacher education and language learning. According to research, NMT tools greatly support grammar instruction and vocabulary acquisition (Klimova et al., 2023). These resources are crucial in teacher training

programs because they assist educators in facilitating bilingual and multilingual classroom environments (Dizon & Gayed, 2021).

4. **AI for Speaking and Pronunciation Training**: Both teachers and students can benefit from pronunciation instruction thanks to AI-driven speech recognition technology like adaptive voice assistants and automated speech analysis. According to studies, AI-based pronunciation aids enhance pitch accuracy and intonation (Liu & Hung, 2016). These resources can help teachers improve their own pronunciation and use them to their lesson plans (Dizon & Tang, 2020).
5. **AI-Enhanced Vocabulary Learning**: Chatbots and intelligent flashcard systems are examples of AI-powered vocabulary acquisition technologies that let teachers monitor students' progress and adjust their lessons (Kazu & Kuvvetli, 2023). Additionally, these tools offer interactive ways to learn new terms, which promotes retention and engagement (Wang et al., 2025).
6. **AI-Supported Pedagogical Training and Collaboration**: AI-powered learning management systems (LMSs) and automated lesson planning tools are two examples of platforms that make it easier for teachers to collaborate. Teachers can participate in virtual workshops and peer discussions with the use of video conferencing software that has AI transcription and summarization capabilities (Rajak et al., 2024; Kristiawan et al., 2024). Additionally, teachers can monitor student development and modify their teaching methods with the aid of AI-driven data (Kusmawan, 2023).

AI collaborative tools are playing an increasingly vital role in EFL/ESL teacher education. From automated evaluation systems to AI-powered tutoring and pronunciation tools, these technologies enhance teacher education by providing personalized and adaptive learning experiences.AI-driven platforms can simulate real classroom scenarios, allowing trainee teachers to practice their skills in a safe and controlled environment. These tools also offer data-driven insights into student performance and learning patterns, enabling teachers to more effectively tailor their instructional strategies. AI collaborative tools are indeed transforming EFL/ESL teacher education by providing innovative ways to enhance training and improve teaching effectiveness. However, addressing ethical and pedagogical challenges remains essential to maximizing the potential of AI in language education.

## Ethical and Practical Considerations

By providing data-driven feedback, automated assessment tools, and personalized learning opportunities, the incorporation of AI into EFL and ESL education has revolutionized teacher development (Gupta & Singh, 2023). Data privacy, algorithmic prejudice, and the possible decline of human-centered teaching are only a few of the serious ethical and practical issues raised by this technical breakthrough (Zawacki-Richter et al., 2019). To make sure that ethical frameworks and best practices direct its application, the role of AI in assisting with continuous EFL/ESL teacher development needs to be critically reviewed.

Regarding, AI personalization in teacher development, despite its benefits, AI-driven personalization in professional development presents challenges, including data privacy concerns, algorithmic biases, and the potential over-reliance on technology (Selwyn, 2019). AI systems collect vast amounts of personal and professional data, raising ethical questions about data security and user privacy. Ensuring that AI applications comply with data protection regulations, such as the General Data Protection Regulation (GDPR), is crucial in safeguarding teachers' information.

Another challenge is the potential bias in AI algorithms, which may reinforce existing inequalities in access to professional development resources. AI models trained on biased data can produce recommendations that favor certain teaching styles or methodologies over others, limiting the diversity of pedagogical approaches (Baker & Hawn, 2022). Addressing these biases requires continuous monitoring and refinement of AI systems to ensure fairness and inclusivity in teacher training programs.

Taken into account the AI integration in reflective practices, even though AI has many advantages for reflective practice, there are still a number of issues that need to be resolved. The accuracy and dependability of AI-generated feedback is one of the main issues. The subtleties of human contact and the efficacy of training may not always be captured by AI tools, despite the fact that they can offer insightful information. Thus, rather than taking the place of human judgment, AI should be utilized as a supplementary tool (Hu & McGrath, 2011).

Data security and privacy are another difficulty. Concerns regarding data protection and ethical use are raised by the massive volumes of data that AI systems gather on educators and students. Teachers need to make sure AI-powered reflective activities respect moral principles and protect private data (Wang & Kabilan, 2024).

The efficacy of AI integration can also be impacted by the attitudes of educators toward it. According to research, some instructors are reluctant to use AI-based technologies because they are worried about the complexity of the technology and the possibility of losing their jobs as a result (Alisoy & Sadiqzade, 2024). The goal of professional development programs should be to provide educators the tools they need to successfully incorporate AI into their reflective practices.

Furthermore, in spite of its advantages, collaboration in EFL/ESL teacher education faces several challenges while elaborated with AI. Time constraints, institutional barriers, and lack of administrative support can hinder collaborative efforts (Mikhaylov et al., 2018). Additionally, teachers may struggle with differences in teaching philosophies and professional backgrounds. To address these challenges, institutions should provide structured opportunities for collaboration, such as professional learning communities, workshops, and online networking platforms (Darling-Hammond & Bransford, 2007). Encouraging a culture of open communication and shared responsibility can also strengthen collaborative practices (Dufour & Eaker, 2009). Considering the AI collaborative tools, despite these advantages above, the adoption of AI in teacher education faces challenges such as ethical concerns, data privacy issues, and the need for specialized training for educators (Liu & Kunnan, 2016). Future research should focus on improving AI tools' contextual awareness, ensuring inclusivity, and addressing biases in language models (Chow & Li, 2024).

From a practical standpoint, AI-driven tools such as intelligent tutoring systems, automated grading programs, and adaptive learning platforms have provided EFL/ESL educators with valuable insights into student progress while reducing administrative burdens (Popenici & Kerr, 2017). Nonetheless, challenges such as AI system transparency, accessibility disparities, and teacher autonomy raise concerns about over-reliance on technology at the expense of pedagogical innovation (Luckin et al., 2016). As AI continues to shape educational landscapes, balancing its benefits with ethical considerations is essential to fostering a sustainable and equitable approach to teacher professional development.

## The Use of AI Tools in EFL/ESL Teacher Development: Study Samples and Outcomes

AI has increasingly become integrated into teacher development programs for EFL and ESL conditions, offering tools that support both pedagogical and linguistic enhancement. The implementation of AI in these contexts is yielding promising results, particularly in reflective practice, automated feedback, and adaptive learning design. Here some of them can be described as following sub-titles:

1. **AI-Powered Reflective Practice Tools:**L'Enfant (2024), investigated the role of AI as a reflective coach for 26 graduate ESL student-teachers (STs) during their practicum. Utilizing Activity Theory, the study analyzed AI interactions and post-reflection questionnaires to assess the impact on STs' reflective practices. In the study, excepting the limitations of diverse backgrounds and practicum environments among STs may affect the generalizability of findings and its potential for imprecise AI feedback necessitates critical appraisal by STs and guidance from supervisors, potential outcomes of AI provided structured, data-driven methods for pedagogical development, STs received personalized, anytime feedback, addressing challenges in traditional ESL teaching practicums, the AI coach facilitated deeper understanding of teaching practices and supported STs in navigating pedagogical challenges, integration of AI enhanced

STs' self-awareness and professional development were highlighted. Thus, the study concluded, AI, as a reflective tool in ESL practicums, shows promise for transformative learning experiences and warrants further research into its impact on teacher development across various teaching contexts.

Arefian et al. (2024) in their study explored how four novice and four experienced Iranian EFL teachers engaged in ChatGPT-driven collaborative reflective practice (CRP), both individually and within a community of practice (CoP), to enhance their professional development. They reached the implications that ChatGPT can function as an ever-present virtual mentor, especially valuable in contexts lacking access to experienced mentors, and the integration of AI tools like ChatGPT in teacher education programs can enhance the quality of language teacher education and professional development. Hence, ChatGPT-driven CRP offers a meaningful and authentic practice for teachers' professional development, linking individual and collective reflection within a CoP.

2. **Intelligent Tutoring Systems (ITS) for Language Instruction Design:**Ghosh (2024), examined the impact of ITS on the training of both pre-service and in-service language teachers. Data was collected through questionnaires, student test scores, and classroom observations. Structural Equation Modeling (SEM) was used to analyze the relationships between perceived usefulness, ease of use, teaching efficacy, and student performance. Furthermore, the study highlights the potential of ITS to enhance both language instruction and teacher education in EFL/ESL contexts. Integrating ITS can lead to improved student outcomes and support teachers in delivering personalized, effective instruction.
3. **Automated Feedback for Pronunciation and Grammar Instruction:**Liu et al. (2025) explored the effects of an Automated Corrective Feedback-based Peer Assessment (ACF-PA) approach on students' pronunciation learning. They found that students using the ACF-PA approach showed significantly higher pronunciation learning achievement compared to those using conventional peer assessment methods, the ACF-PA approach positively influenced students' motivation and their conceptions of self-regulated learning, and learners reported favorable perceptions of the ACF-PA method, noting its effectiveness in providing timely and accurate feedback. These findings highlight the potential of integrating automated feedback tools in EFL/ESL teacher education to enhance pronunciation and grammar instruction. The use of ACF-PA technologies can lead to improved learning outcomes, increased student motivation, and more effective teaching strategies.

Similarly, Rahimi et al. (2024) investigated the effects of automated written corrective feedback (AWCF) on EFL learners' academic writing skills, utilizing activity theory as a framework. The study concludes that AWCF can effectively enhance certain aspects of academic writing in EFL contexts, particularly grammar and task fulfillment, and can promote learner autonomy. Moreover, the study highlighted the benefits of integrating automated feedback tools into EFL/ESL writing instruction. It also focused the importance of traditional teacher feedback and supported the integration of these systems together crucially for developing content and organizational skills in language development.

4. **Chatbots for Practicing Pedagogical Scenarios:**Guo et al. (2025) examined how EFL teachers integrate chatbots into teaching argumentative writing, using the Technological Pedagogical Content Knowledge (TPACK) framework. Ten teachers designed lesson plans incorporating a chatbot named Argumate. In addition to this, Su et al. (2025) explored pre-service English teachers' perceptions of chatbots in education. Through interviews, participants discussed their understanding of chatbots, potential impacts on language skills, advantages and challenges, attitudes towards chatbot use, and training needs. Findings highlighted a general awareness of chatbots' educational potential, recognition of their benefits in enhancing language skills, and a desire for more training to effectively integrate chatbots into teaching. These studies underscore the evolving role of chatbots in EFL/ESL teacher education, emphasizing the importance of strategic integration and teacher preparedness to maximize educational outcomes.

However, as seen, although the challenges and risks are endless, the need for continuous training for EFL/ESL teachers to interpret and use AI effectively seems to remain on the agenda for a long time.

## A Framework for the Future Roles of AI in Supporting Ongoing EFL/ESL Teacher Development

The integration of AI in education has transformed EFL and ESL teaching, particularly in professional development. AI-driven tools provide personalized learning experiences, automate administrative tasks, and facilitate reflective teaching practices (Luckin, 2018). The future roles of AI in teacher development extend beyond automation, offering adaptive learning analytics, intelligent tutoring, and real-time feedback to enhance pedagogical effectiveness (Zawacki-Richter et al., 2019).

AI-powered platforms assist EFL/ESL teachers by offering continuous training through personalized recommendations and data-driven insights (Zovko & Gudlin, 2019). These platforms analyze classroom interactions, suggesting evidence-based strategies to improve teaching efficacy. Moreover, AI-driven chatbots and virtual assistants provide real-time feedback on lesson planning and instructional techniques, fostering self-regulated learning (Huang et al., 2023).

One of the significant roles of AI in teacher development is the use of adaptive learning analytics. By analyzing student engagement and performance data, AI systems can guide teachers in identifying effective teaching strategies and areas for improvement (Shah, 2023). Such systems facilitate reflective teaching practices by generating insights on classroom interactions, helping educators refine their methodologies (Marienko et al., 2020).

AI can also enhance professional collaboration among teachers by recommending relevant academic resources and connecting educators with similar interests through intelligent networking platforms (Bates, 2015). These AI-driven communities encourage knowledge sharing and joint lesson planning, promoting a culture of continuous learning (Cukurova et al., 2024).

AI has the potential to reshape ongoing EFL/ESL teacher development by offering personalized training, adaptive learning analytics, and collaborative networking opportunities. While the framework for AI integration continues to evolve, a balanced approach that prioritizes ethical considerations and teacher autonomy will be essential for its successful implementation. Thus, ethical concerns regarding data privacy, bias, and teacher autonomy must be addressed (Selwyn, 2019). Future research should explore how AI can balance automation with human agency to ensure that teachers remain central to the learning process. Additionally, teacher training programs should integrate AI literacy to help educators leverage technology effectively (Luckin, 2018).

## Critical Analysis of AI Integration in EFL/ ESL Teacher Education

There are both substantial potential advantages and severe practical and ethical concerns associated with the incorporation of artificial intelligence (AI) in EFL/ ESL teacher preparation.

Being prepared for technology is one of the biggest obstacles. Particularly in underdeveloped nations, many EFL/ESL teacher education programs lack the digital literacy and infrastructure necessary to properly support AI tools (Zawacki-Richter et al., 2019). Furthermore, there is still a lack of training needed to effectively incorporate AI tools into teaching. The introduction of AI-driven technologies, such as virtual assistants, adaptive learning platforms, and automated feedback tools, may be shallow or ineffective if teachers are not well equipped to use them (Chen et al., 2020). Furthermore, generalized AI technologies face challenges due to the context-specific nature of language learning. AI systems' adaptability and applicability in various classrooms are limited because they frequently overlook local cultural, linguistic, and educational factors (Pedro et al., 2019). The functions of AI tools and educational requirements may not align as a result.

Concerns around algorithmic bias, data privacy, and monitoring are brought up by the ethical application of AI in teacher education. Numerous AI systems necessitate gathering enormous volumes of performance and personal data, which may violate the privacy of both educators and students (Williamson & Eynon, 2020). This data collection may be misused or subject to unauthorized access if it is not properly regulated. Moreover, preexisting prejudices may be strengthened by AI technologies' algorithmic decision-making. For instance, biases in training data are frequently reflected in natural language processing models, which might harm non-native English speakers or distort culturally varied varieties of the language (Bender et al., 2021). In high-stakes situations like teacher evaluations or certification exams, this becomes particularly problematic.

The potential de-professionalization of educators is another ethical worry since AI-powered systems have the potential to gradually transfer power from humans to machines, compromising professional judgment and teacher agency (Selwyn, 2019). This change may impede the growth of critical, reflective practitioners—essential to learner-centered pedagogy—in the setting of teacher education. Focusing on contextual appropriateness, teacher agency, and ethical governance is necessary for a more critical approach to AI integration in EFL/ESL teacher education. To ensure alignment with educational aims and ethical norms, stakeholders should co-design AI tools with teachers rather than using AI as a one-size-fits-all solution (Luckin, 2017). To preserve fairness and confidence in the educational system, it is also essential to be transparent about how AI systems operate and make choices.

## REFERENCES


Akbari, R. (2007). Reflections on reflection: A critical appraisal of reflective practices in L2 teacher education. *System, 35*(2), 192–207. DOI: 10.1016/j.system.2006.12.008

Alalawi, K., Athauda, R., & Chiong, R. (2024). An extended learning analytics framework integrating machine learning and pedagogical approaches for student performance prediction and intervention. *International Journal of Artificial Intelligence in Education*, •••, 1–49. DOI: 10.1007/s40593-024-00429-7

Alisoy, H., & Sadiqzade, Z. (2024). Mobile-assisted language learning (MALL): Revolutionizing language education. *Luminis Applied Science and Engineering, 1*(1), 60–72. DOI: 10.69760/lumin.202400002

An, X., Chai, C. S., Li, Y., Zhou, Y., Shen, X., Zheng, C., & Chen, M. (2023). Modeling English teachers' behavioral intention to use artificial intelligence in middle schools. *Education and Information Technologies, 28*(5), 5187–5208. DOI: 10.1007/s10639-022-11286-z

Arefian, M. H., Çomoğlu, I., & Dikilitaş, K. (2024). Understanding EFL teachers' experiences of ChatGPT-driven collaborative reflective practice through a community of practice lens. *Innovation in Language Learning and Teaching*, •••, 1–16. DOI: 10.1080/17501229.2024.2412769

Baker, R. S., & Hawn, A. (2022). Algorithmic bias in education. *International Journal of Artificial Intelligence in Education*, •••, 1–41.

Baker, R. S., Martin, T., & Rossi, L. M. (2016). Educational data mining and learning analytics. *The Wiley handbook of cognition and assessment: Frameworks, methodologies, and applications*, 379-396.

Barber, W., Harrison, R., VanOostveen, R., & Childs, E. (2021). Building better online communities in the post pandemic world. In *ECEL 2021 20th European Conference on e-Learning*. Academic Conferences International limited.

Bates, A. W. (2015). *Teaching in a digital age: Guidelines for designing teaching and learning*. Tony Bates Associates Ltd.

Bearman, M., Ryan, J., & Ajjawi, R. (2023). Discourses of artificial intelligence in higher education: A critical literature review. *Higher Education, 86*(2), 369–385. DOI: 10.1007/s10734-022-00937-2

Beijaard, D., Meijer, P. C., & Verloop, N. (2004). Reconsidering research on teachers' professional identity. *Teaching and Teacher Education, 20*(2), 107–128. DOI: 10.1016/j.tate.2003.07.001

Bender, E. M., Gebru, T., McMillan-Major, A., & Shmitchell, S. (2021, March). On the dangers of stochastic parrots: Can language models be too big? . In *Proceedings of the 2021 ACM conference on fairness, accountability, and transparency* (pp. 610-623). DOI: 10.1145/3442188.3445922

Boud, D., Keogh, R., & Walker, D. (2013). *Reflection: Turning experience into learning*. Routledge. DOI: 10.4324/9781315059051

Bowers, E., Laster, B., Gurvitz, D., Ryan, T., Cobb, J., & Vazzano, J. (2017). Using video for teacher reflection: Reading clinics in action. *Reflective Theory and Practice in Teacher Education*, 141-160.

Brandenburg, R., & Jones, M. (2017). Toward transformative reflective practice in teacher education. *Reflective Theory and Practice in Teacher Education*, 259-273.

Brookfield, S. D. (2015). *The skillful teacher: On technique, trust, and responsiveness in the classroom*. John Wiley & Sons.

Budiarta, I. K., & Krismayani, N. W. (2024). Post-pandemic shifts in English language teaching: Challenges and perceptions in online learning environments. *Voices of English Language Education Society*, *8*(1), 241–252. DOI: 10.29408/veles.v8i1.25678

Burns, A., & Richards, J. C. (Eds.). (2009). *Cambridge guide to second language teacher education*. Cambridge University Press. DOI: 10.1017/9781139042710

Cabero-Almenara, J., Palacios-Rodríguez, A., Loaiza-Aguirre, M. I., & Rivas-Manzano, M. D. R. D. (2024). Acceptance of educational artificial intelligence by teachers and its relationship with some variables and pedagogical beliefs. *Education Sciences, 14*(7), 740. DOI: 10.3390/educsci14070740

Chang, C. C., Hwang, G. J., & Tu, Y. F. (2023). Roles, applications, and trends of concept map-supported learning: A systematic review and bibliometric analysis of publications from 1992 to 2020 in selected educational technology journals. *Interactive Learning Environments, 31*(9), 5995–6016. DOI: 10.1080/10494820.2022.2027457

Chang, T. S., Li, Y., Huang, H. W., & Whitfield, B. (2021). Exploring EFL students' writing performance and their acceptance of AI-based automated writing feedback. In *Proceedings of the 2021 2nd International Conference on Education Development and Studies*. DOI: 10.1145/3459043.3459065

Chen, L., Chen, P., & Lin, Z. (2020). Artificial intelligence in education: A review. *IEEE Access : Practical Innovations, Open Solutions*, *8*, 75264–75278. DOI: 10.1109/ACCESS.2020.2988510

Chen, X., Zou, D., Xie, H., & Cheng, G. (2021). Twenty years of personalized language learning. *Journal of Educational Technology & Society*, *24*(1), 205–222.

Chow, J. C., & Li, K. (2024). Ethical considerations in human-centered AI: Advancing oncology chatbots through large language models. *JMIR Bioinformatics and Biotechnology*, *5*, e64406. DOI: 10.2196/64406 PMID: 39321336

Chung, E., Subramaniam, G., & Dass, L. C. (2020). Online learning readiness among university students in Malaysia amidst COVID-19. *Asian Journal of University Education*, *16*(2), 46–58. DOI: 10.24191/ajue.v16i2.10294

Coşkun, F., & Gülleroğlu, H. D. (2021). Yapay zekânın tarih içindeki gelişimi ve eğitimde kullanılması. [JFES]. *Ankara University Journal of Faculty of Educational Sciences*, *54*(3), 947–966.

Cukurova, M., Kralj, L., Hertz, B., & Saltidou, E. (2024, January). *Professional development for teachers in the age of AI*. https://discovery.ucl.ac.uk/id/eprint/10186881/

Darling-Hammond, L., & Bransford, J. (Eds.). (2007). *Preparing teachers for a changing world: What teachers should learn and be able to do*. John Wiley & Sons.

Dengiz, Y. (2023). *Innovative effects of artificial intelligence on teacher education* (774595) [Master's thesis, Muğla Sıtkı Koçman University]. Council of Higher Education Thesis Center.

Ding, A. C. E., Shi, L., Yang, H., & Choi, I. (2024). Enhancing teacher AI literacy and integration through different types of cases in teacher professional development. *Computers and Education Open*, *6*, 100178. DOI: 10.1016/j.caeo.2024.100178

Dizon, G., & Gayed, J. M. (2021). Examining the impact of Grammarly on the quality of mobile l2 writing. *The JALT CALL Journal*, *17*(2), 74–92. DOI: 10.29140/jaltcall.v17n2.336

Dizon, G., & Tang, D. (2020). Intelligent personal assistants for autonomous second language learning: An investigation of Alexa. *The JALT CALL Journal*, *16*(2), 107–120. DOI: 10.29140/jaltcall.v16n2.273

Duff, P. A., & Uchida, Y. (1997). The negotiation of teachers' sociocultural identities and practices in postsecondary EFL classrooms. *TESOL Quarterly*, *31*(3), 451–486. DOI: 10.2307/3587834

DuFour, R., & Eaker, R. (Eds.). (2009). *On common ground: The power of professional learning communities*. Solution Tree Press.

Eldot, S. G. (2023). *English as a second language teachers' lived experience of transitioning from remote learning to the traditional classroom setting: A phenomenological study* (4743). [Doctoral dissertation, Libery Univesity].

Ellikkal, A., & Rajamohan, S. (2024). *AI-enabled personalized learning: empowering management students for improving engagement and academic performance*. Vilakshan-XIMB Journal of Management.

Eslit, E. R. (2023). Voices of resiliency: exploring the transformative journey of educators and students in the post-pandemic education era. *Preprints*. DOI: 10.20944/preprints202305.1514.v1

Fakhar, H., Lamrabet, M., Echantoufi, N., & Ajana, L. (2024). Towards a new artificial intelligence-based framework for teachers' online continuous professional development programs: Systematic Review. *International Journal of Advanced Computer Science and Applications, 15*(4). Advance online publication. DOI: 10.14569/IJACSA.2024.0150450

Farrell, T. (2013). *Reflective practice in ESL teacher development groups: From practices to principles*. Springer. DOI: 10.1057/9781137317193

Farrell, T. S. (2022). *Reflective practice in language teaching*. Cambridge University Press. DOI: 10.1017/9781009028783

Ferikoğlu, D. (2021). *An artificial intelligence awareness level scale for teachers: A reliability and validity study* (684964) [Master's thesis, Bahçeşehir University]. Council of Higher Education Thesis Center.

Gholami, K., Faraji, S., Meijer, P. C., & Tirri, K. (2021). Construction and deconstruction of student teachers' professional identity: A narrative study. *Teaching and Teacher Education, 97*, 103142. DOI: 10.1016/j.tate.2020.103142

Ghosh, S. S. (2024). Assessing the Efficacy of Intelligent Tutoring Systems in Language Teacher Education: A Quantitative Study. *Computers in the Schools*, •••, 1–24. DOI: 10.1080/07380569.2024.2435308

Glasswell, K., & Ryan, J. (2017). Reflective practice in teacher professional standards: Reflection as mandatory practice. *Reflective Theory and Practice in Teacher Education*, 3-26.

Goksel, N., & Bozkurt, A. (2019). Artificial intelligence in education: Current insights and future perspectives. In *Handbook of Research on Learning in the Age of Transhumanism* (pp. 224–236). IGI Global. DOI: 10.4018/978-1-5225-8431-5.ch014

Goodfellow, I., Bengio, Y., & Courville, A. (2016). *Deep learning*. The MIT Press.

Guo, K., Zhong, Y., Qin, J., & Chu, S. K. W. (2025). Investigating EFL teachers' lesson planning for chatbot-assisted learning of argumentative writing: A TPACK perspective. *Interactive Learning Environments*, *33*(2), 1520–1541.

Guo, Y., & Wang, Y. (2025). Exploring the Effects of Artificial Intelligence Application on EFL Students' Academic Engagement and Emotional Experiences: A mixed-methods study. *European Journal of Education*, *60*(1), e12812. DOI: 10.1111/ejed.12812

Gupta, M., & Singh, A. (2023). Emerging trends in artificial intelligence education: Advancements, opportunities, and impact on educational technology. *Quanta Research*, *1*(1), 20–26.

Hardaker, G., & Glenn, L. E. (2025). Artificial intelligence for personalized learning: A systematic literature review. *The International Journal of Information and Learning Technology*, *42*(1), 1–14. DOI: 10.1108/IJILT-07-2024-0160

Harry, A. (2023). Role of AI in Education. [INJURITY]. *Interdiciplinary Journal and Hummanity*, *2*(3), 260–268.

Hodges, C. B., Moore, S., Lockee, B. B., Trust, T., & Bond, M. A. (2020). *The difference between emergency remote teaching and online learning*. Educause.

Holmes, W., & Tuomi, I. (2022). State of the art and practice in AI in education. *European Journal of Education*, *57*(4), 542–570. DOI: 10.1111/ejed.12533

Hord, S. M. (1997). *Professional learning communities: Communities of continuous inquiry and improvement*. SEDL.

Hu, Z., & McGrath, I. (2012). Integrating ICT into college English: An implementation study of a national reform. *Education and Information Technologies*, *17*(2), 147–165. DOI: 10.1007/s10639-011-9153-0

Huang, X., Zou, D., Cheng, G., Chen, X., & Xie, H. (2023). Trends, research issues and applications of artificial intelligence in language education. *Journal of Educational Technology & Society*, *26*(1), 112–131.

Hwang, G. J., Xie, H., Wah, B. W., & Gašević, D. (2020). Vision, challenges, roles and research issues of Artificial Intelligence in Education. *Computers and Education: Artificial Intelligence*, *1*, 100001. DOI: 10.1016/j.caeai.2020.100001

Jacobs, G. M. (2004). *Cooperative learning: Theory, principles, and techniques* [Paper presentation/Online Submission]. *The International Online Conference on Second and Foreign Language Teaching and Research, Online.*

Jameer, M. R., & Narra, P. L. (2024). Augmenting EFL/ESL education: The outcome of technology on contemporary language learning. *Educational Administration: Theory and Practice*, *30*(5), 2196–2202.

Jiang, R. (2022). How does artificial intelligence empower EFL teaching and learning nowadays? A review on artificial intelligence in the EFL context. *Frontiers in Psychology*, *13*, 1049401. DOI: 10.3389/fpsyg.2022.1049401 PMID: 36467167

Johnson, K. E. (2009). *Second language teacher education: A sociocultural perspective.* Routledge. DOI: 10.4324/9780203878033

Johnson, K. E. (2016). Language teacher education. In *The Routledge handbook of English language teaching* (pp. 121–134). Routledge. DOI: 10.4324/9781315676203-12

Johnson, K. E., & Golombek, P. R. (2016). *Mindful L2 teacher education: A sociocultural perspective on cultivating teachers' professional development.* Routledge. DOI: 10.4324/9781315641447

Karatay, Y., & Karatay, L. (2024). Automated writing evaluation use in second language classrooms: A research synthesis. *System*, *123*, 103332. DOI: 10.1016/j.system.2024.103332

Kayabaş, İ. (2010). Usabilty of artificial intelligent conversational agents as student support service in distance education (263179) [Master's thesis, Anadolu University]. Council of Higher Education Thesis Center.

Kayyali, M. (2024). Future possibilities and challenges of AI in education. In *Transforming education with generative AI: Prompt engineering and synthetic content creation* (pp. 118–137). IGI Global. DOI: 10.4018/979-8-3693-1351-0.ch006

Kazu, I. Y., & Kuvvetli, M. (2023). The influence of pronunciation education via artificial intelligence technology on vocabulary acquisition in learning English. *International Journal of Psychology and Educational Studies*, *10*(2), 480–493. DOI: 10.52380/ijpes.2023.10.2.1044

Kim, J. (2024). Leading teachers' perspective on teacher-AI collaboration in education. *Education and Information Technologies*, *29*(7), 8693–8724. DOI: 10.1007/s10639-023-12109-5

Klimova, B., Pikhart, M., Benites, A. D., Lehr, C., & Sanchez-Stockhammer, C. (2023). Neural machine translation in foreign language teaching and learning: A systematic review. *Education and Information Technologies*, *28*(1), 663–682. DOI: 10.1007/s10639-022-11194-2

Kristiawan, D., Bashar, K., & Pradana, D. A. (2024). Artificial intelligence in English language learning: A systematic review of ai tools, applications, and pedagogical outcomes. [TATEFL]. *The Art of Teaching English as a Foreign Language*, *5*(2), 207–218. DOI: 10.36663/tatefl.v5i2.912

Kukulska-Hulme, A., & Lee, H. (2020). Intelligent assistants in language learning: Analysis of features and limitations. *CALL for Widening Participation: Short Papers from EUROCALL*, *1*(1), 172–176. DOI: 10.14705/rpnet.2020.48.1184

Kumaravadivelu, B. (1994). The postmethod condition: (E)merging strategies for second/foreign language teaching. *TESOL Quarterly*, *28*(1), 27. DOI: 10.2307/3587197

Kusmawan, U. (2023). Redefining teacher training: The promise of AI-supported teaching practices. *Journal of Advances in Education and Philosophy*, *7*(9), 332–335. DOI: 10.36348/jaep.2023.v07i09.001

L'Enfant, J. (2024). AI as a reflective coach in graduate ESL practicum: activity theory insights into student-teacher development. *European Journal of Open, Distance & E-Learning, 26*(1).

Lave, J., & Wenger, E. (1991). *Situated learning: Legitimate peripheral participation.* Cambridge University Press. DOI: 10.1017/CBO9780511815355

Layali, K., & Al-Shlowiy, A. (2020). Studets' perceptions of e-learning for ESL/EFL in Saudi universities at time of Coronavirus: A literature review. *Indonesian EFL Journal*, *6*(2), 97–108. DOI: 10.25134/ieflj.v6i2.3378

Leitch, R., & Day, C. (2000). Action research and reflective practice: Towards a holistic view. *Educational Action Research*, *8*(1), 179–193. DOI: 10.1080/09650790000200108

Little, J. W. (1990). The persistence of privacy: Autonomy and initiative in teachers' professional relations. *Teachers College Record*, *91*(4), 509–536. DOI: 10.1177/016146819009100403

Liu, C. C., Hwang, G. J., Yu, P., Tu, Y. F., & Wang, Y. (2025). Effects of an automated corrective feedback-based peer assessment approach on students' learning achievement, motivation, and self-regulated learning conceptions in foreign language pronunciation. *Educational Technology Research and Development*, •••, 1–22. DOI: 10.1007/s11423-025-10484-z

Liu, S., & Kunnan, A. J. (2016). Investigating the application of automated writing evaluation to chinese undergraduate English majors: A case study of "WriteToLearn". *CALICO Journal, 33*(1), 71–91. DOI: 10.1558/cj.v33i1.26380

Liu, S. C., & Hung, P. Y. (2016). Teaching pronunciation with computer assisted pronunciation instruction in a technological university. *Universal Journal of Educational Research, 4*(9), 1939–1943. DOI: 10.13189/ujer.2016.040902

Liu, Z. L. (2025). Preparation knowledge: Basics of AI. In *Artificial Intelligence for Engineers: Basics and Implementations* (pp. 1–43). Springer Nature Switzerland. DOI: 10.1007/978-3-031-75953-6_1

Luckin, R. (2017). Towards artificial intelligence-based assessment systems. *Nature Human Behaviour, 1*(3), 0028.

Luckin, R. (2018). *Machine Learning and Human Intelligence. The future of education for the 21st century*. UCL Institute of Education Press.

Luckin, R., Holmes, W., Griffiths, M., & Forcier, L. B. (2016). Intelligence unleashed. *An Argument for AI in Education, 18.*

Marienko, M., Nosenko, Y., Sukhikh, A., Tataurov, V., & Shyshkina, M. (2020). Personalization of learning through adaptive technologies in the context of sustainable development of teachers education. *arXiv preprint arXiv:2006.05810.*

Martin, F., Zhuang, M., & Schaefer, D. (2024). Systematic review of research on artificial intelligence in K-12 education (2017–2022). *Computers and Education: Artificial Intelligence, 6*, 100195. DOI: 10.1016/j.caeai.2023.100195

Memon, F. N., & Memon, S. N. (2025). Digital divide and equity in education: Bridging gaps to ensure inclusive learning. In *Impact of Digitalization on Education and Social Sustainability* (pp. 107–130). IGI Global.

Miao, F., Holmes, W., Huang, R., & Zhang, H. (2021). *AI and education: A guidance for policymakers*. UNESCO Publishing.

Mikhaylov, S. J., Esteve, M., & Campion, A. (2018). Artificial intelligence for the public sector: Opportunities and challenges of cross-sector collaboration. *Philosophical Transactions. Series A, Mathematical, Physical, and Engineering Sciences, 376*(2128), 20170357. DOI: 10.1098/rsta.2017.0357 PMID: 30082303

Mohamed, A., Faisal, R., & Shaalan, K. (2024). Exploring the impact of ai-driven virtual assistants in AR and VR environments for special needs education: A quantitative analysis. In Proceedings of the *International Conference on Extended Reality*. Cham: Springer Nature Switzerland. DOI: 10.1007/978-3-031-71713-0_8

Mora-Pablo, I., & Goodwin, D. (2023). Identity construction during emergency remote teaching reflections of novice teachers in a teacher education program. *MEXTESOL Journal, 47*(3), n3. DOI: 10.61871/mj.v47n3-11

Ngo, T. T. N., Chen, H. H. J., & Lai, K. K. W. (2024). The effectiveness of automatic speech recognition in ESL/EFL pronunciation: A meta-analysis. *ReCALL, 36*(1), 4–21. DOI: 10.1017/S0958344023000113

Noël, R., Miranda, D., Cechinel, C., Riquelme, F., Primo, T. T., & Munoz, R. (2022). Visualizing collaboration in teamwork: A multimodal learning analytics platform for non-verbal communication. *Applied Sciences (Basel, Switzerland), 12*(15), 7499. DOI: 10.3390/app12157499

Norton, B. (2013). *Identity and language learning: Extending the conversation.* Multilingual matters.

Pedro, F., Subosa, M., Rivas, A., & Valverde, P. (2019). Artificial intelligence in education: Challenges and opportunities for sustainable development. UNESCO. https://repositorio.minedu.gob.pe/bitstream/handle/20.500.12799/6533/Artificial%20intelligence%20in%20education%20challenges%20and%20opportunities%20for%20sustainable%20development.pdf?sequence=1&isAllowed=y

Pinto-Santos, A. R., Pérez Garcias, A., & Darder Mesquida, A. (2022). Development of teaching digital competence in initial teacher training: A Systematic Review. *World Journal on Educational Technology: Current Issues, 14*(1), 1–15.

Pokrivcakova, S. (2019). Preparing teachers for the application of AI-powered technologies in foreign language education. *Journal of Language and Cultural Education, 7*(3), 135–153. DOI: 10.2478/jolace-2019-0025

Popenici, S. A., & Kerr, S. (2017). Exploring the impact of artificial intelligence on teaching and learning in higher education. *Research and Practice in Technology Enhanced Learning, 12*(1), 22. DOI: 10.1186/s41039-017-0062-8 PMID: 30595727

Rahimi, M., Fathi, J., & Zou, D. (2024). Exploring the impact of automated written corrective feedback on the academic writing skills of EFL learners: An activity theory perspective. *Education and Information Technologies,* •••, 1–45.

Rajak, L., Chauhan, S., & Bara, S. (2024). Transforming English Pedagogy with Artificial Intelligence: Enroute to Enhanced Language Learning. In T. Khan., M. Singh., & S. Raza (Eds.), *Artificial Intelligence: A Multidisciplinary Approach towards Teaching and Learning* (pp. 216-241). Bentham Science Publishers.

Richards, J. C. (2005). *Professional development for language teachers: Strategies for teacher learning*. Ernst Klett Sprachen. DOI: 10.1017/CBO9780511667237

Rodgers, C. R., & Scott, K. H. (2008). The development of the personal self and professional identity in learning to teach. In Cochran-Smith, M., Feiman-Nemser, S., McIntyre, J., & Demers, K. E. (Eds.), *Handbook of research on teacher education* (pp. 732–755). Routledge.

Rodrigues, A. L. (2023). Innovative hybrid learning: a new paradigm in teacher education for transformative learning. In Lytras, M. D. (Ed.), *Active and transformative learning in STEAM disciplines: From curriculum design to social impact* (pp. 153–175). Emerald Publishing Limited. DOI: 10.1108/978-1-83753-618-420231008

Rosé, C. P., Martínez-Maldonado, R., Hoppe, H. U., Luckin, R., Mavrikis, M., Porayska-Pomsta, K., & Du Boulay, B. (Eds.). (2018). *Artificial Intelligence in Education.InProceedings, Part I* (Vol. 10947) *of the 19th International Conference, AIED,* Springer.

Roshan, S., Iqbal, S. Z., & Qing, Z. (2024). Teacher training and professional development for implementing ai-based educational tools. *Journal of Asian Development Studies, 13*(2), 1972–1987. DOI: 10.62345/jads.2024.13.2.154

Russell, S., Norvig, P., Popineau, F., Miclet, L., & Cadet, C. (2021). *Intelligence artificielle: Une approche moderne (4  édition).* Pearson France.

Russell, T., & Martin, A. K. (2017). Reflective practice: Epistemological perspectives on learning from experience in teacher education. *Reflective Theory and Practice in Teacher Education*, 27-47.

Sardabi, N., Biria, R., & Golestan, A. A. (2018). Reshaping teacher professional identity through critical pedagogy-informed teacher education. *International Journal of Instruction, 11*(3), 617–634. DOI: 10.12973/iji.2018.11342a

Selwyn, N. (2019). *Should robots replace teachers? AI and the future of education.* John Wiley & Sons.

Shah, P. (2023). *AI and the Future of Education: Teaching in the age of artificial intelligence.* John Wiley & Sons.

Situmorang, K., Nugroho, D. Y., & Pramusita, S. M. (2020). English teachers' preparedness in technology enhanced language learning during covid-19 pandemic–students' voice. *Jo-ELT (Journal of English Language Teaching). Fakultas Pendidikan Bahasa & Seni Prodi Pendidikan Bahasa Inggris IKIP, 7*(2), 57–67.

Storch, N. (2002). Patterns of interaction in ESL pair work. *Language Learning, 52*(1), 119–158. DOI: 10.1111/1467-9922.00179

Su, Y., Luo, M., & Zhong, C. (2025). To Chat or Not: Pre-Service English Teachers' Perceptions of and Needs in Chatbot's Educational Application. *SAGE Open*, *15*(1), 21582440251321853. DOI: 10.1177/21582440251321853

Thornhill-Miller, B., Camarda, A., Mercier, M., Burkhardt, J. M., Morisseau, T., Bourgeois-Bougrine, S., Vinchon, F., El Hayek, S., Augereau-Landais, M., Mourey, F., Feybesse, C., Sundquist, D., & Lubart, T. (2023). Creativity, critical thinking, communication, and collaboration: Assessment, certification, and promotion of 21st century skills for the future of work and education. *Journal of Intelligence*, *11*(3), 54. DOI: 10.3390/jintelligence11030054 PMID: 36976147

Toosi, A., Bottino, A. G., Saboury, B., Siegel, E., & Rahmim, A. (2021). A brief history of AI: How to prevent another winter (a critical review). *PET Clinics*, *16*(4), 449–469. DOI: 10.1016/j.cpet.2021.07.001 PMID: 34537126

Tsui, A. B. (2007). Complexities of identity formation: A narrative inquiry of an EFL teacher. *TESOL Quarterly*, *41*(4), 657–680. DOI: 10.1002/j.1545-7249.2007.tb00098.x

Varghese, M., Morgan, B., Johnston, B., & Johnson, K. A. (2005). Theorizing language teacher identity: Three perspectives and beyond. *Journal of Language, Identity, and Education*, *4*(1), 21–44. DOI: 10.1207/s15327701jlie0401_2

Visser, W. (2010). Schön: Design as a reflective practice. *Collection*, (2), 21–25.

Vygotsky, L. S. (1978). *Mind in society: The development of higher psychological processes* (Vol. 86). Harvard University Press.

Wafula, L. (2025). The evolving roles of faculty in modern classrooms: A shift from lecturer to facilitator. In Areba, G. N., Gisore, B. N., & Njurai, E. W. (Eds.), *Creating dynamic space in higher education: Modern shifts in policy, competencies, and governance* (pp. 253–282). IGI Global Scientific Publishing.

Wang, J., & Kabashima, H. (2022). Artificial general ıntelligence in human ınterface—ıts ımpact on society and human being. In Lütge, C., Uhl, M., Kriebitz, A., & Max, R. (Eds.), *Business ethics and digitization*. Springer Nature., DOI: 10.1007/978-3-662-64094-4_3

Wang, Y., & Kabilan, M. K. (2024). Integrating technology into English learning in higher education: A bibliometric analysis. *Cogent Education*, *11*(1), 2404201. DOI: 10.1080/2331186X.2024.2404201

Wang, Y., Wu, J., Chen, F., Wang, Z., Li, J., & Wang, L. (2024). Empirical assessment of AI-powered tools for vocabulary acquisition in EFL instruction. *IEEE Access : Practical Innovations, Open Solutions, 12*, 131892–131905. DOI: 10.1109/ACCESS.2024.3446657

Watt, H. M., & Richardson, P. W. (2023). Supportive school Workplaces for beginning teachers' motivations and career satisfaction. In Urdan, T., & Gonida, E. N. (Eds.), *Remembering the life, work, and influence of Stuart A. Karabenick: A legacy of research on self-Regulation, help Seeking, teacher motivation, and more* (pp. 115–138). Emerald Publishing Limited. DOI: 10.1108/S0749-742320230000022009

Whalen, J. (2020). Should teachers be trained in emergency remote teaching? Lessons learned from the COVID-19 pandemic. *Journal of Technology and Teacher Education, 28*(2), 189–199. DOI: 10.70725/307718pkpjuu

Williamson, B., & Eynon, R. (2020). Historical threads, missing links, and future directions in AI in education. *Learning, Media and Technology, 45*(3), 223–235. DOI: 10.1080/17439884.2020.1798995

Xu, H. (2024). *Language teachers' social cognition: Elements in critical issues in teacher education*. Cambridge University Press. DOI: 10.1017/9781009377720

Yan, L., Echeverria, V., Jin, Y., Fernandez-Nieto, G., Zhao, L., Li, X., Alfredo, R., Swiecki, Z., Gašević, D., & Martinez-Maldonado, R. (2024). Evidence-based multimodal learning analytics for feedback and reflection in collaborative learning. *British Journal of Educational Technology, 55*(5), 1900–1925. DOI: 10.1111/bjet.13498

Yang, H., Gao, C., & Shen, H. Z. (2024). Learner interaction with, and response to, AI-programmed automated writing evaluation feedback in EFL writing: An exploratory study. *Education and Information Technologies, 29*(4), 3837–3858. DOI: 10.1007/s10639-023-11991-3

Zamiri, M., & Esmaeili, A. (2024). Methods and technologies for supporting knowledge sharing within learning communities: A systematic literature review. *Administrative Sciences, 14*(1), 17. DOI: 10.3390/admsci14010017

Zawacki-Richter, O., Marín, V. I., Bond, M., & Gouverneur, F. (2019). Systematic review of research on artificial intelligence applications in higher education–where are the educators? *International Journal of Educational Technology in Higher Education, 16*(1), 1–27. DOI: 10.1186/s41239-019-0171-0

Zovko, V., & Gudlin, M. (2019). Artificial intelligence as a disruptive technology in education. In *Conference Proceedings of The Future of Education(*2019*).*

## ADDITIONAL READING

Goksel, N., & Bozkurt, A. (2019). *Handbook of Research on Learning in the Age of Transhumanism.*, https://www.igi-global.com/chapter/artificial-intelligence-in-education/227914

Kayyali, M. (2024). *Transforming Education with Generative AI: Prompt Engineering and Synthetic Content Creation* (pp. 118-137). https://www.igi-global.com/chapter/future-possibilities-and-challenges-of-ai-in-education/338534

Memon, F. N., & Memon, S. N. (2025). *Impact of Digitalization on Education and Social Sustainability.*, https://www.igi-global.com/chapter/digital-divide-and-equity-in-education/358122

Wafula, L. (2025). *Creating Dynamic Space in Higher Education: Modern Shifts in Policy.* Competencies, and Governance., https://www.igi-global.com/chapter/the-evolving-roles-of-faculty-in-modern-classrooms/361989

## KEY TERMS AND DEFINITIONS

**EFL/ESL Teacher Development:** The continuous process of improving the knowledge, skills, and attitudes of teachers who teach English as a Foreign Language (EFL) or English as a Second Language (ESL) through formal education, professional training, workshops, and self-directed learning.

**EFL/ESL Teacher Identity Development:** The process by which EFL/ESL teachers develop and change their professional identities with institutional influences, social interactions, professional training, and personal experiences that mold their teaching methods, beliefs, and values.

**Professional Development:** The ongoing process of acquiring new skills, knowledge, and competencies that help educators improve their teaching effectiveness through workshops, conferences, mentorship programs, online courses, and research activities.

**Teacher Self:** A teacher's personal and professional identity, beliefs, emotions, and self-perception as an educator that influences their teaching style, classroom interactions, and professional growth.

**AI-Driven Personalization:** The use of artificial intelligence (AI), analyzing data to optimize learning experiences in real time, to tailor educational content, learning paths, and feedback to meet the individual needs, preferences, and abilities of learners.

**Adaptive Learning Systems:** Technology-based educational systems that adjust the difficulty, pace, and content of learning materials based on a student's performance, engagement, and learning style for the purpose of personalizing instruction to enhance learning outcomes.

**Reflective Practices:** A process where teachers critically analyze their teaching experiences, methods, and decisions to improve their effectiveness involving self-reflection, peer discussions, or journaling.

**Self-regulated Learning:** A learning process consisting of metacognition, motivation, and behavioral regulation in which individuals set goals, monitor their progress, and adjust strategies to achieve desired outcomes.

**Collaborative Tool:** Any digital or physical resource such as online discussion platforms, shared documents, and virtual whiteboards that facilitates teamwork and communication among teachers and learners.

**Professional Learning Communities:** Groups of educators who collaborate regularly to reflect on their teaching practices, share expertise, and work collectively to improve student learning outcomes promoting ongoing professional growth and a culture of shared learning

**Teacher Communities:** Networks in formal (e.g., school-based teams, professional organizations) or informal (e.g., online forums, social media groups) of educators who engage in knowledge-sharing, support, and professional collaboration.

# Chapter 10
# The Relationship Between AI Tools Usage, Information Retrieval, and Research Output Among Moroccan Novice Researchers

**Morad Bakir**
https://orcid.org/0009-0000-2082-7193
*Faculty of Languages, Letters, and Arts, Ibn Tofail University, Kenitra, Morocco*

**Khadija Anasse**
*Ibn Tofail University, Morocco*

**Wadiai Boudribila**
*Hassan I University, Settat, Morocco*

## ABSTRACT

*This study investigates the correlation between AI tools usage, and research output among Moroccan novice researchers, with the focus on information retrieval as a mediating variable. The study employs a quantitative approach and a cross-sectional correlational research design to examine the relationships between three variables. In this respect, five hypotheses were tested to demonstrate the relationships between the aforementioned variables. Based on data collected from 204 novice researchers across various disciplines, our findings indicate a significant positive relationship between AI tools usage and research output. Moreover, the results demonstrate a*

DOI: 10.4018/979-8-3373-0969-9.ch010

*partial mediating effect of information retrieval in the nexus between AI tools usage and research output. The novelty of this study lies in addressing the mediating effect of information retrieval since no previous studies have tackled the relationship between the three variables in question. Therefore, a number of theoretical and practical implications were suggested.*

## 1-INTRODUCTION

In recent years, and with the advent of AI, there has been considerable interest in AI-driven tools across disciplines (Berens et al., 2023). This interest stems mainly from the myriad of promising opportunities these tools offer. Ranging from natural language processing algorithms to machine learning models, AI-driven tools have the potential to offer valuable support in generating ideas, drafting manuscripts, and refining scholarly outputs with a mere button press (Abd-Elsalam & Abdel-Momen, 2023).

In the context of academic research, AI tools have been found to facilitate tasks such as data analysis and literature review and enhance writing efficiency, and productivity, thereby reshaping scholarly endeavours (Khalifa & Albadawy, 2024). Moreover, these state-of-the-art technologies are highly valued among researchers as they can refine academic writing by providing dynamic, interactive, and personalized learning environments while improving writing skills, self-efficacy, and academic integrity. Furthermore, these technologies have proven to be invaluable in improving the clarity, organization, and accessibility of academic information (Malik et al., 2023).

In light of these benefits, this study seeks to explore the impact of using AI-driven tools on research output research, by examining the relationship between the aforementioned tools, information retrieval, and research output among Moroccan novice researchers across different disciplines. By doing so, the study seeks to elucidate the transformative potential of AI technologies in shaping the future of scholarly inquiry. While there is growing literature on the use of AI tools in academic writing, there remains a discernible gap concerning their implementation, strengths and limitations. Therefore, researchers need to validate the use of such tools by conducting additional empirical research (Adams & Chuah, 2022, p. 170), especially in the Moroccan context. In this sense, the current study aims to bridge this gap with the hope of making a significant contribution to the existing literature on AI tools usage in academic writing and provide a comprehensive overview of their impact on academic composition.

Considering the information provided previously, the main purposes of this study are:

1-To examine the relationship between the utilization of AI tools and research output among Moroccan novice researchers.
2-To examine the relationship between the utilization of AI tools and information retrieval
3-To assess the impact of information retrieval on research output among Moroccan novice researchers.
4- To explore the potential mediating role of information retrieval in the relationship between the utilization of AI tools and research output among Moroccan novice researchers.

## 2-LITERATURE REVIEW AND HYPOTHESES DEVELOPMENT

### 2.1 Overview of AI tools in academic writing

AI tools are computer programs or software applications that use artificial intelligence algorithms to perform various tasks (Job, 2021). These tools can generate human-like responses in natural language conversations (Cabrero-Daniel & Cabrero, 2023), assist with language learning by increasing learning speed (De La Vall & Araya, 2023), analyze real-time data in health care,detect and provide early predictions of different types of chronic diseases(Phadatare & Naik, 2023), and even assist in creating videos and presentations (Soe, 2021). AI tools have the potential to reduce time pressure (Swaroop et al., 2024), provide personalized learning experiences (Rahim et al., 2023), and improve the efficiency and effectiveness of various tasks such as assessment (Owan et al., 2023). They are powered by deep learning techniques, which require large amounts of data for training to make them powerful and impactful tools in their respective domains (Alzubaidi et al., 2023).

According to Roe et al. (2023), AI tools can be generally categorized into three types: machine translators [MTs], digital writing assistants [DWAs], and automated paraphrasing tools [APTs]. Machine translators, such as Google Translate and DeepL, are used by a myriad of users on a daily basis to render written content from one language to another. Digital Writing Assistants like Grammarly involve tools that can be used to generate corrective feedback, improve writing quality, and also check for plagiarism, whereas Automated Paraphrasing Tools paraphrase and rewrite text to produce alternative versions of the original content (Roe et al., 2023).

With regard to academic writing (Churi et al., 2022) classified AI tools into language and mechanics tools, text summarizing and synthesizing tools, and formatting and typesetting tools. The first kind of AI tools, such as Grammarly and Quillbot, help writers detect linguistic and mechanical mistakes, like grammar, spelling, and overall sentence structure. While text summarizing and synthesizing tools are employed for condensing extensive information into concise summaries of key points or amalgamating data from various sources to generate new ideas or condensed versions. Some prominent examples of such tools include Scholarcy and Iris.ai, which are widely used among researchers. The last kind of AI tools that come into play include formatting and typesetting tools like Typeset.io. The primary objective of such tools is to assist users in arranging written content to adhere to formatting standards, such as those required for research papers, and ensure that text and images are appropriately positioned for optimal viewing, whether on screen or in print (Churi et al., 2022).

## 2.2 Challenges and issues with AI tools

Despite the reported benefits of AI tools, there are still lingering challenges when it comes to their utilization for academic essay writing. Apparently, some users remain reluctant to use AI in academic writing. Their reluctance stems from their concern about the potential impacts of AI on creativity, critical thinking, and ethical writing practices. Their concerns revolve around the possibility that over-reliance on AI tools could hamper their critical and creative thinking skills, which will eventually result in unethical writing practices (Malik et al., 2023). Therefore, it is necessary to use these tools judiciously and moderately to eschew overdependence issues, improve writing skills, and engage in independent writing and revision to ensure personal growth (Hwang et al., 2023) .In addition, to preserve research integrity and originality, it is primordial to use these AI tools ethically and responsibly (Khalifa & Albadawy, 2024). To do so, researchers must be provided with adequate training sessions to adapt to such tools and be able to fully exploit their potential benefits in their academic path while being aware of ethical issues (Hosseini et al., 2023; Roe et al., 2023), and preserving data privacy and writing integrity (Nguyen et al., 2024).

Another notable consequence of AI tools lies in tricking journal editors and publishers with fabricated papers, which underscores the urgency for protective measures to uphold scientific integrity. Therefore, scholars, policymakers, and the public are called to collaborate to promote the ethical utilization of such AI tools in research endeavours or at least elaborate systems to help detect AI-generated content instead of human reviewers to ensure authentic and credible results (Dergaa et al., 2023 ; Dupps, 2023).

With their widespread adoption, banning AI tools is not useful and would encourage their clandestine and unethical use among students (Hosseini et al., 2023). Thus, it is advisable to incorporate these tools in academia to maximize their advantages and ensure that AI's transformative capabilities permeate all dimensions of scholarly endeavours. However, maintaining a balance between the utilization of AI and human intelligence is necessary, particularly in idea generation and research design, to preserve human creativity and critical thinking while taking full advantage of AI tools' analytical and efficient characteristics (Abd-Elsalam & Abdel-Momen, 2023; Khalifa & Albadawy, 2024; Malik et al., 2023).

## 2.3 The relationship between the utilization of AI tools and research output

Research output refers to the concrete outcomes of research endeavors, which encompass various forms such as publications, conference presentations, grants, and patents, among others (Creswell, 1986). It is a key element in evaluating academic performance and university rankings whose measurements are typically determined by the quantity and quality of journal articles published over a specific period of time (Lalengmawia & Shukla, 2017).

Reviewing the current literature pertaining to the impact of AI tools on research output reveals that using such tools has positive effects on academic writing. For instance, in a study by Hosseini et al. (2023) on how to utilize (AI) tools such as ChatGPT and other large language models (LLMs), the authors acknowledge that AI tools are assistive in terms of writing, reviewing, and editing scholarly content. Therefore, the researchers recommend incorporating AI tools in specific parts of research papers and articles, particularly in the introduction or methods section, citations, and references embedded within the text, and they also highlight the need to include interactions with these tools in the appendices. Adhering to this view, Hwang et al. (2023) state that LLMs can be highly valuable when crafting research articles as they can make academic writing in English more accessible and assist researchers in enhancing research quality and efficiency, more particularly in the introduction and discussion section, (Hwang et al., 2023).

In the same vein, Marzuki et al. (2023) conducted a qualitative case study to explore EFL teachers' opinions towards the different AI writing tools they employed in the Indonesian context and their potential impact on students' written output in terms of content and organization. To do this, the authors approached 4 teachers who use AI tools to supplement their classroom teaching material. The results showed that teachers hold a positive attitude towards integrating AI into the classroom environment. They acknowledge that AI-based tools for research writing are geared towards streamlining the writing process and improving the quality of research output. Among the AI tools employed in this sense include Quillbot, Jenni, Chat-GPT, WordTune, Copy.ai, Paperpal, and Essay Writer. These tools were deemed highly useful for paraphrasing content while preserving originality, providing automated corrective feedback, enabling students to explore various writing styles and clarity, and improving writing content and structure (Marzuki et al., 2023).

In terms of AI-based feedback, a relevant study was carried out by Perda et al. (2021) to investigate the potential merits of using Grammarly as an AI tool in academic writing. The authors examined published papers and experts' perspectives garnered from international journals. Key findings conclude that Grammarly is an invaluable asset in the context of academia, as it has the potential to help writers generate well-elaborated academic written content with the real-time corrective feedback provided by the AI tool. Besides, this latter helps writers maintain a consistent writing style and tone, which enhances the coherence and clarity of academic papers. Also, authors could use Grammarly as a plagiarism checker to ensure the originality of their papers (Perdana et al., 2021).

Drawing on all the above-mentioned studies, AI tools have a positive impact on academic writing. The integration of such tools into the realm of academic writing—and more specifically into research writing—improves scholarly output and optimizes academic performance and research advancement. Thus, the following hypothesis will be constructed:

H1 AI tools usage and research output are positively associated.

## 2.4 The relationship between the utilization of AI tools and information retrieval

In today's savvy era, and because of the exponential increase of various information formats, information retrieval has gained significant importance among researchers within the realm of computer science. Therefore, ongoing research is being geared towards exploring various forms of information retrieval systems to enhance their efficiency and reliability (Gupta et al., 2013). Information retrieval is a search process that involves identifying, storing, and organizing relevant information within a vast body of knowledge to find what is relevant to the user's needs (Mandl, 2009). Oluwatola and Akingbade (2022) explain that information retrieval is a two-fold process that consists of locating where the information is stored, and then identifying it. However, with the widespread of electronic sources in our technological era, this process cannot be carried out smoothly unless researchers possess the necessary retrieval skills to be able to retrieve information effortlessly (Oluwatola & Akingbade, 2022).

According to Mitra and Chaudhuri (2000), information can be either textual or pictorial, and despite the existence of various forms of information, paper-based and electronic forms continue to be the primary choice for extracting and exchanging information among information seekers. Among the most prominent electronic forms of information retrieval in our age are AI tools. These latter employ algorithms and computational power to process and extract information from various sources, including text, images, videos, and visual data, and present it in a structured format for analysis or decision-making (Sarker, 2022).

In reviewing the literature, a strong relationship between AI and Information retrieval has been reported. Many scholars hold the view that AI systems can positively influence information retrieval while assuring quality and accuracy (Hambarde & Proenca, 2023; Jones, 1999; Onah et al., 2020; Sharma & Srivastava, 2017). In an attempt to investigate the relationship between artificial intelligence and information retrieval, Jones (1999) explains that AI has opened up new possibilities for managing and retrieving different types of information, including images and other media. AI has the faculty to run through a plethora of documents to find relevant information using probabilistic models such as the Okapi BM25 that adapt to the complexities of human language and document relevance. With the widespread use of AI techniques, information retrieval systems can now predict users' intents even with vague or incomplete queries, which can lead to more precise and useful search results. Moreover, AI technologies such as natural language processing and machine learning are deemed crucial in improving search algorithms, relevance ranking, and user interaction in IR systems (Jones, 1999).

In 2017, Sharma and Srivastava published a paper examining how artificial intelligence can be employed to improve the process of finding and retrieving information from large amounts of data, often referred to as big data, to accelerate this process and make it more accurate. In this context, the authors touched upon the challenges associated with big data management, such as dealing with unstructured data, controlling its growth, and making it useful, and propose a new way of addressing these challenges through AI tools integration. According to the authors, these latter can be advantageous as they have the potential to revolutionize the process of information retrieval by offering fast and more accurate data management for businesses and individuals. In addition, AI systems have become smart enough to predict and assess the relevance and quality of information, yielding personalized results based on user queries (Sharma & Srivastava, 2017).

Later, Onah et al. (2020) conducted a correlational study at a Nigerian university targeting 800 undergraduates to assess the relationship between information retrieval skills and the use of the available information resources in university libraries be them print or electronic. The authors highlight the importance of subscribing to electronic information resources for information retrieval among students to equip undergraduates with advanced search abilities. According to the authors, information retrieval tools such as the Online Public Access Catalogue (OPAC) or computerized systems are essential for navigating a library, much like maps in a city. These tools offer numerous advantages ranging from easy and quick identification, access, retrieval as well as the possibility of preserving library items from unnecessary wear and tear due to inadequate handling on the shelves by users who do not consult in advance about the appropriate information retrieval tools (Onah et al., 2020).

Hambarde and Proença (2023) introduced advanced systems for improving information retrieval process. According to the authors conventional text retrieval systems are criticized for their reliance on exact word matches, which may cause them to overlook relevant information due to synonymy and polysemy issues. As a result, they fail to capture contextual nuances, which makes search results inaccurate, and impedes their ability to grasp user intent. Unlike their precedent, the new systems, such as BERT and GPT-2, are artificially intelligent and can deeply understand the connection between keywords to match the user's queries and their semantic meaning. Moreover, they utilize high-end algorithms to imitate human intelligence and have been trained on a massive amount of textual data to retrieve complex queries, making the information retrieval process more relevant, accurate, and efficient (Hambarde & Proenca, 2023).

The review above appears to indicate that AI tools have a positive effect on information retrieval, as the majority of researchers are able to conclude a positive relationship between these two variables. Therefore, it will be hypothesized that:

H2 AI usage and information retrieval are positively associated.

## 2.5 The impact of information retrieval and research output

Since productivity is a core indicator of academic performance, universities should introduce sophisticated electronic resources including computers and Internet connectivity to enable researchers to access and retrieve information with ease, enhancing research productivity and knowledge dissemination (Christopher, 2013).

Manda and Nawe (2009) found that Information retrieval through online resources positively impacted various research activities and milestones such as proposal submission, research funding, report writing, and journal article publishing. The results, therefore, provide empirical support for the hypotheses that the increased flow of information because of increased access to and use of electronic information resources is related to increased research output and enhancement of the quality of research. In their study, the authors observed that there was a positive relationship between the use of electronic information resources for information retrieval and research output and publishing, as demonstrated by the increased number of submitted, and funded proposals, as well as the growing number of research reports, journal articles, and books (including chapters) published during the time when the electronic information resources were being made available.

In their study addressing the impact of information retrieval on research output, Kolawole and Akingbade (2022) state that information retrieval skills are crucial for postgraduate students as they significantly influence their ability to conduct scholarly research by enabling them to easily find the information they need for their studies. These skills help improve the quality of research output by exposing students to a wide range of information resources, both in print and online, thus enhancing their research work. The researchers then recommend providing students with training in information retrieval skills as an integral part of the curriculum to ensure students can effectively locate, retrieve, and use relevant information for their academic success, regardless of their field of study (Kolawole & Akingbade, 2022).

Based on the above studies, the following hypothesis will be formulated:

H3 Information retrieval and research output are positively related.

## 2.6 The mediating role of information retrieval in the relationship between the utilization of AI tools and research output

One of the key objectives of this study is to investigate the mediating role of information retrieval in the relationship between AI tool usage and research output. To the best of my knowledge, no research has been conducted on this concern so far. Information retrieval encompasses the process by which researchers access, collect, store, and utilize relevant information for their studies. In the context of AI tools, which are increasingly employed in research settings, information retrieval plays a crucial role in facilitating knowledge acquisition and synthesis. By examining how the use of AI tools influences information retrieval processes and, in turn, impacts research output, we aim to gain a deeper understanding of the mechanisms underlying the research process in the digital age.

Examining the existing literature regarding the utilization of AI tools in academia of AI reveals that AI tools have positive effects on writing output. For instance, Khalifa and Albadawy (2024) conducted a systematic review of the literature to identify and evaluate pertinent studies on the usage of AI in academic writing and research. The researchers targeted 24 studies to delve into AI tools' role in supporting academic writing and research. The results of the paper indicate that AI tools are favoured by researchers because of six different reasons: they facilitate idea generation and research design, improve writing content and structure, support information retrieval and synthesis from existing literature, enhance data management and interpretation, support the publishing process through proofreading, editing, reviewing, assist in communication, and assure ethical standards.

In 2023, Abd-Elsalam and Abdel-Momen conducted a study to probe the question of how AI tools can influence scientific writing. The results show incorporating AI tools into scientific writing is advantageous in many ways. First, AI tools can help information seekers quickly identify and retrieve the information they need by suggesting accurate keywords for online queries, which facilitates the discovery of relevant studies and data. Secondly, they have the potential to unveil hidden patterns and trends within extensive scientific datasets, potentially yielding novel insights. Moreover, the summarizing features of AI tools are time and energy-saving because they help researchers understand key points without having to read the whole document. Additionally, they assist in organizing researchers' ideas and materials by generating outlines or concept maps to refine scientific writing. Lastly, AI identifies research gaps and proposes new avenues for exploration, which ensures innovation and relevance in research output (Abd-Elsalam & Abdel-Momen, 2023).

Both of the above-mentioned studies indicate that AI tools usage have positive effects on information retrieval in academic writing and research. This provides evidence that information retrieval plays a mediating role in the relationship between AI tool usage and research output, as it impacts the efficiency, accuracy, and organization of information, thereby improving the quality of research. Therefore, we hypothesize that:

H5 Information retrieval mediates the link between AI tools usage and research output.

*Figure 1. Mediation Mode*

*Mediation Mode*

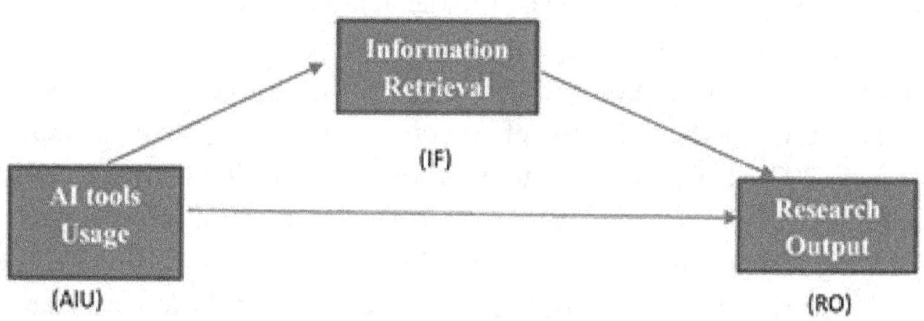


*(IF)*

*(AIU) (RO)*

*Note. The proposed mediation model suggests that AI tools usage (AIU) affects research output (RO) both directly and indirectly through information retrieval (IF).*

## 3. METHODOLOGY

The study herein employed a quantitative approach with a cross-sectional correlational research design to examine the relationships between three variables: AI tools usage, information retrieval, and research output among Moroccan novice researchers. A correlational design is appropriate because it aims to measure and assess the statistical relationship between two variables without manipulating nor predicting any causal relationship between these variables (Price et al., 2020). The study targeted 204 novice researchers from various universities in Morocco and across various disciplines, ranging from BA, Master's, and early PhD students and recent graduates. The respondents were selected using convenience sampling, focusing on those who have used AI tools to actively conduct research, such as grammar checkers, paraphrasing, plagiarism detection, and content-generating tools. The following chart and graph present the percentages of males and females who took part in the study as well as their field of study:

*Figure 2. Proportion of male and female respondents*

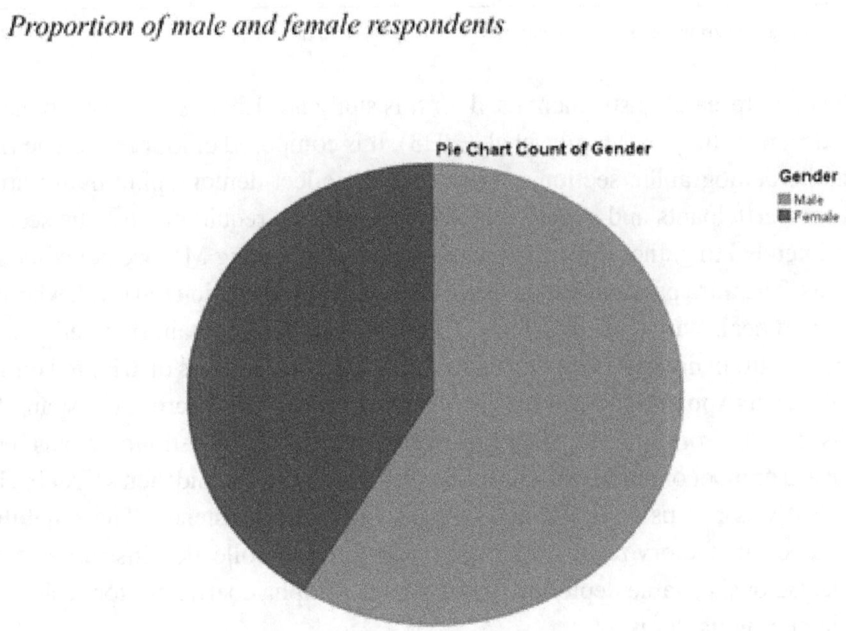


*Note. Percentages reflect proportions of male (58.8%) and female (41.2%) participants.*

*Table 1. Frequency and Percentage Breakdown by Gender*

| Gender | | | | | |
|---|---|---|---|---|---|
| | | Frequency | Percent | Valid Percent | Cumulative Percent |
| Valid | Male | 120 | 58,8 | 58,8 | 58,8 |
| | Female | 84 | 41,2 | 41,2 | 100,0 |
| | Total | 204 | 100,0 | 100,0 | |

*Note.* Distribution of respondents by gender (N = 204)

*Table 2. Field of Study of Respondents*

| | | Frequency | Percent | Valid Percent | Cumulative Percent |
|---|---|---|---|---|---|
| Valid | Engineering | 6 | 2,9 | 2,9 | 2,9 |
| | Social Sciences | 43 | 21,1 | 21,1 | 24,0 |
| | Humanities | 110 | 53,9 | 53,9 | 77,9 |
| | Other | 45 | 22,1 | 22,1 | 100,0 |
| | Total | 204 | 100,0 | 100,0 | |

*Note.* Frequency distribution of respondents' fields of study (N = 204).

The main research instrument used for this study is a Likert scale questionnaire adopted from a study by Monika et al. (2023). It is composed of four parts. The first part is the demographic section, which aims to collect demographic information about the participants and ensure they meet the study's requirements. The second part is intended to gather information about AI usage among Moroccan novice researchers. The third part focuses on using AI tools for information retrieval, whereas the last part deals with research output. The three last parts contain five items each.

The questionnaire was designed using Google Forms and was distributed online through WhatsApp and Facebook. The distribution was done across the span of 6 months starting from June 1st, 2024 to November 30th. The questionnaire has been subject to a number of modifications followed by a pilot study, and then a Cronbach's Alpha test was run using SPSS to assess its internal consistency. The reliability test yielded satisfactory results, indicating that the data collection instruments are reliable. Below is a table depicting the Cronbach's Alpha coefficient for each scale used, including its items.

*Table 3. Cronbach's Alpha Coefficient*

| Scale | Items | Cronbach |
|---|---|---|
| AI usage | 5 | 0,768 |
| Information Retrieval | 5 | 0,781 |
| Research Output | 5 | 0,892 |

*Note.* Cronbach's α values indicate acceptable internal consistency (α > 0.70).

The data analysis was carried out using descriptive statistics, which quantified responses by calculating the means for the three variables along with their standard deviation (as shown in Table 4 below).

*Table 4. The means and their standard deviation*

| Descriptive Statistics | | | |
|---|---|---|---|
| | N | Mean | Std. Deviation |
| AI_Usage | 204 | 2,0980 | ,75135 |
| Info_Retrieval | 204 | 2,1108 | ,73430 |
| Research_Output | 204 | 2,1314 | ,92964 |
| Valid N (listwise) | 204 | | |

*Note.* This table shows the mean scores and standard deviations for AI tools usage, information retrieval, and research output among the 204 participants.

Given the non-normal distribution of data, the Spearman Correlation Coefficient was applied to assess monotonic relationships for H1, H2, and H3, whereas Hayes' PROCESS macro (Model 4) with bootstrapping (5,000 samples) was employed to evaluate mediation for H4.

## 4. RESULTS

### 4.1 The relationship between AI tools usage and research output

As stated earlier, Spearman's correlation coefficient was used to assess the relationship between AI tools usage and research output. Table (5) presents the results of Spearman's rho correlation analysis between the two variables. The Spearman's correlation coefficient is 0.712. This indicates a strong positive correlation, which suggests that an increase in AI tools usage is associated with an increase in research output as well. The p-value for the correlation is reported as < 0.001. This shows that the relationship is statistically significant at the 0.01 level. In other words, the strong and statistically significant positive correlation implies that AI tools usage positively influences or supports higher levels of research output. This supports the hypothesis that AI tools usage is positively associated with research output.

*Table 5. Spearman Correlation Coefficient*

| Correlations | | | | |
|---|---|---|---|---|
| | | | **AI_Usage** | **Research_Output** |
| Spearman's rho | AI_Usage | Correlation Coefficient | 1,000 | ,712** |
| | | Sig. (2-tailed) | . | ,000 |
| | | N | 204 | 204 |
| | Research_Output | Correlation Coefficient | ,712** | 1,000 |
| | | Sig. (2-tailed) | ,000 | . |
| | | N | 204 | 204 |

**. Correlation is significant at the 0.01 level (2-tailed).

*Figure 3. Spearman Correlation Scatter Plot*

*Spearman Correlation Scatter Plot*

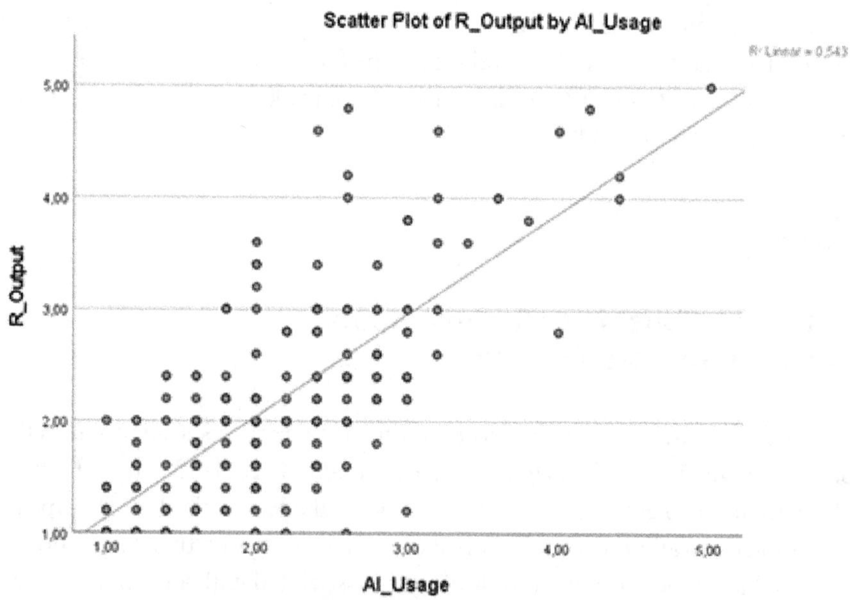


*Note. The correlation between AI tools usage and research output.*

## 4.2: The relationship between AI tools usage and information retrieval

Concerning the relationship between AI tools usage and information retrieval. The Spearman's correlation coefficient is 0.732, with a p-value reported as < 0.001. This indicates that there is a strong positive relationship between the two variables. This suggests that higher AI tools usage is associated with better or more frequent information retrieval abilities. (See Table 6).This supports the hypothesis that AI usage positively impacts information retrieval performance.

*Table 6. Spearman Correlation Coefficient*

| **Correlations** | | | | |
|---|---|---|---|---|
| | | | **AI_Usage** | **Info_Retrieval** |
| Spearman's rho | AI_Usage | Correlation Coefficient | 1,000 | ,732** |
| | | Sig. (2-tailed) | . | ,000 |
| | | N | 204 | 204 |
| | Info_Retrieval | Correlation Coefficient | ,732** | 1,000 |
| | | Sig. (2-tailed) | ,000 | . |
| | | N | 204 | 204 |

**. Correlation is significant at the 0.01 level (2-tailed).

*Figure 4. Spearman Correlation Scatter Plot*

*Spearman Correlation Scatter Plot*

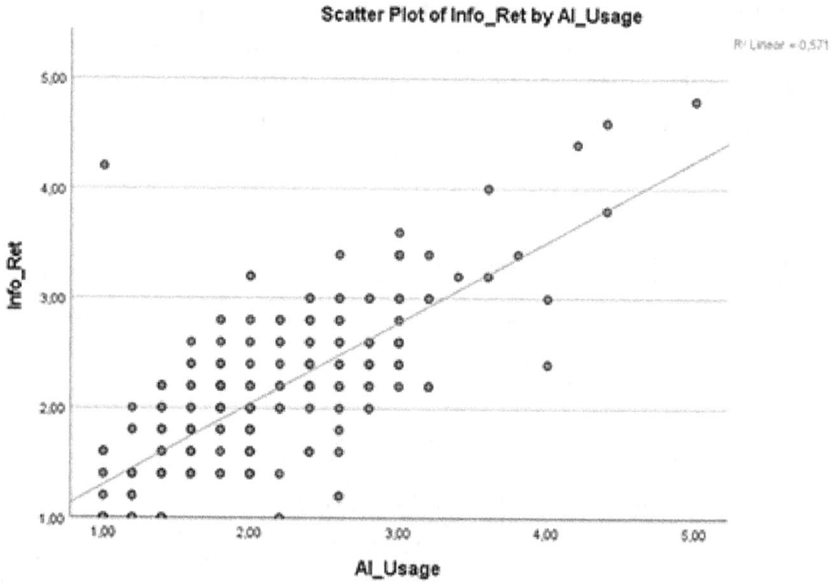


*Note. The correlation between AI tools usage and information retrieval.*

## 4.3: The relationship between information retrieval and research output

Along the same line, Table (7) shows that the Spearman's correlation coefficient for the relationship between information retrieval and research output is 0.724, indicating a strong positive correlation between the two variables with a p-value of < 0.001. The significant and strong positive correlation indicates that efficient information retrieval is directly associated with increased research productivity. This suggests that the ability to access and utilize relevant information plays a critical role in enhancing research outcomes.

*Table 7. Spearman Correlation Coefficient*

| **Correlations** | | | | |
|---|---|---|---|---|
| | | | **Info_Retrieval** | **Research_Output** |
| Spearman's rho | Info_Retrieval | Correlation Coefficient | 1,000 | ,724** |
| | | Sig. (2-tailed) | . | ,000 |
| | | N | 204 | 204 |
| | Research_Output | Correlation Coefficient | ,724** | 1,000 |
| | | Sig. (2-tailed) | ,000 | . |
| | | N | 204 | 204 |

**. Correlation is significant at the 0.01 level (2-tailed).

*Figure 5. Spearman Correlation Scatter Plot*

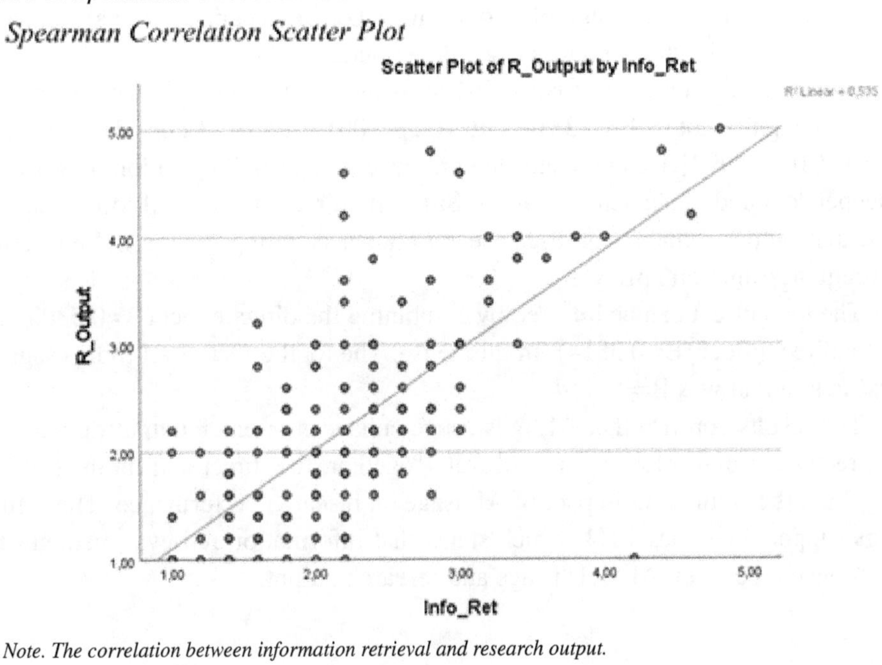


*Note. The correlation between information retrieval and research output.*

## 4.4: The mediating role of information retrieval in the relationship between AI tools usage and research output

To assess the mediating role of information retrieval in the relationship between AI tools usage and research output, a mediation analysis was conducted using Hayes' PROCESS macro (Model 4). The main objective was to determine the direct, indirect, and total effects of AI tools usage on research output through information retrieval

Descriptive statistics revealed that the mean and standard deviation for AI usage were 2,0980 and, 75135, respectively. Concerning information Retrieval, the mean was 2,1108, and the standard deviation was, 73430. While research output had a mean of 2,1314and a standard deviation of, 92964

To begin with, the results in Table 8 show that AI Usage has a significant direct effect on research output (0.5300). This direct relationship is strong and statistically reliable, as demonstrated by a t-value of 6.40426 and a 95% confidence interval (0.3668). This means that regardless of its impact on information retrieval, increased AI tools usage directly enhances research output.

Moreover, the indirect effect of AI tools usage through information retrieval was also significant by B=0.3814, t=6.10t, p<.001, and a 95% confidence interval of [0.2016, 0.5993].This indicates the presence of a partial mediation between the independent and dependent variables. Since the direct effect of AI tools usage on research output remains significant even after accounting for the indirect effect through information retrieval

The total effect can be inferred by combining the direct effect (B=0.5300) and the indirect effect (B=0.3814). In this sense. The total effect of AI tools usage on research output was B=0.9114

The results confirm that AI tools usage enhances research output directly and indirectly through information retrieval. Together, the direct and indirect effects highlight the significant impact of AI usage on research performance. These findings support hypothesis H4, which states that information retrieval mediates the relationship between AI tools usage and research output.

*Table 8. Mediation Analysis Based on 5000 Bootstrap Samples*

| Effect | B | SE | t-value | p-value | 95% CI Lower | 95% CI Upper |
|---|---|---|---|---|---|---|
| Direct Effect (AI Usage → Research Output) | 0.5300 | 0.0828 | 6.40426 | <.001 | 0.3668 | 0.6932 |
| Indirect Effect (AI Usage → Information Retrieval → Research Output) | 0.3814 | 0.1055 | 6.10 | <.001 | 0.2016 | 0.5993 |
| Total Effect (AI Usage → Research Output) | 0.9114 | | | | | |

*Note.* Bootstrapping with 5,000 samples. Unstandardized coefficients reported.

## 5.DISCUSSION AND CONCLUSIONS

The current study seeks to investigate the relationships between AI tools usage, information retrieval, and research output among Moroccan novice researchers. In this sense, five hypotheses are tested to demonstrate that the variables have strong relationships. The novelty of this study lies in addressing the mediating effect of information retrieval since no previous studies have tackled the relationship between the three variables in question.

The findings indicate a significantly strong positive relationship between AI tools usage and research output. This can be perceived through the correlation coefficient of 0.712 and the p-value of (< 0.001), which indicates that AI tools usage improves research productivity. These findings are in line with former studies, which state that the adoption of AI tools enhances researcher quality and productivity (Abd-Elsalam & Abdel-Momen, 2023; Hosseini et al., 2023; Hwang et al., 2023; Khalifa & Albadawy, 2024; Marzuki et al., 2023; Perdana et al., 2021). Collectively, these studies support the claim that the integration of AI technologies can significantly improve research outcomes. Therefore, H1 is accepted and supported.

Additionally, the Spearman's correlation coefficient of 0.732, with a p-value reported as < 0.001, indicates a strong positive relationship between AI tools usage and information retrieval. This supports H2 and confirms that the frequent utilization of AI tools enhances information retrieval performance. This corroborates the results of other previous studies by Jones (1999), Sharma and Srivastava (2017), Onah et al. (2020), and Hambarde and Proenca (2023)

Furthermore, the analysis demonstrated that information retrieval and research output have a strong positive correlation. This is confirmed by the correlation coefficient of 0.724, indicating a p-value of < 0.001. Therefore, it is worth noting that retrieving and utilizing relevant information is essential to enhance research productivity. These results align with previous research by Manda and Nawe (2009) and Kolawole and Akingbade (2022).

Finally, to assess the mediating role of information retrieval in the relationship between AI tools usage and research output, Hayes' PROCESS macro (Model 4) was employed. The analysis shows that AI tools usage has a significant direct effect on research output (B=0.5300, t=6.40426), while the indirect effect through information retrieval (B=0.3814, t=6.10, $p<.001$) indicates partial mediation. The total effect of AI usage on research output was B=0.9114, confirming that AI tools, directly and indirectly, enhance research output through information retrieval, which supports the mediation hypothesis H4.

The results of this study provide a new perspective by depicting how information retrieval partially mediates the relationship between AI tools usage and research output, thereby providing valuable insights into the mechanisms at play.

## 6. IMPLICATIONS TO RESEARCH

The study provides several theoretical and practical implications regarding the relationship between AI tools usage, information retrieval, and research output. As stated earlier, no previous studies have focused on information retrieval as a mediator in the Moroccan context, especially among novice researchers. First, recognizing information retrieval as a mediator underscores the importance among researchers to employ AI tools and enhance robust information retrieval skills. Accordingly, researchers should enroll in training programs that focus on both AI tool usage and effective information retrieval strategies to enhance research productivity in particular and academic performance in general. Secondly, since this study focuses on Moroccan novice researchers, the generalizability of its results may be limited. Therefore, further research endeavours are needed to validate information retrieval's mediating role in different contexts, populations, and academic disciplines. Longitudinal studies could also provide insights into how these relationships evolve over time as researchers become more adept at using AI tools.

Moreover, qualitative research, including in-depth interviews and case studies, is also needed to gain a deeper understanding of researchers' perceptions and practical applications of AI tools and information retrieval. Lastly, it is imperative to examine other potential mediating variables, like motivation or collaboration, and moderating variables, such as institutional support or digital literacy. These recommendations will enrich the comprehension of the dynamics in the interaction between AI tools usage and research output.

## Competing Interests

The authors of this publication declare there are no competing interests.

## Funding

This research received no specific grant from any funding agency in the public, commercial, or not-for-profit sectors. Funding for this research was covered by the authors of the article.

## REFERENCES


Abd-Elsalam, K. A., & Abdel-Momen, S. M. (2023). Artificial Intelligence's Development and Challenges in Scientific Writing. *Egyptian Journal of Agricultural Research, 101*(3), 714–717. DOI: 10.21608/ejar.2023.220363.1414

Adams, D., & Chuah, K.-M. (2022). Artificial Intelligence-Based Tools in Research Writing : Current Trends and Future Potentials. In *Artificial Intelligence in Higher Education* (pp. 169–184). CRC Press. https://doi.org/DOI: 10.1201/9781003184157-9

Alzubaidi, L., Bai, J., Al-Sabaawi, A., Santamaría, J., Albahri, A. S., Al-dabbagh, B. S. N., Fadhel, M. A., Manoufali, M., Zhang, J., Al-Timemy, A. H., Duan, Y., Abdullah, A., Farhan, L., Lu, Y., Gupta, A., Albu, F., Abbosh, A., & Gu, Y. (2023). A survey on deep learning tools dealing with data scarcity : Definitions, challenges, solutions, tips, and applications. *Journal of Big Data, 10*(1), 46. DOI: 10.1186/s40537-023-00727-2

Berens, P., Cranmer, K., Lawrence, N. D., von Luxburg, U., & Montgomery, J. (2023). *AI for Science : An Emerging Agenda* (arXiv:2303.04217). arXiv. http://arxiv.org/abs/2303.04217

Cabrero-Daniel, B., & Cabrero, A. S. (2023). Perceived Trustworthiness of Natural Language Generators. *Proceedings of the First International Symposium on Trustworthy Autonomous Systems*, (pp. 1–9). https://doi.org/DOI: 10.1145/3597512.3599715

Christopher, O. (2013). Availability of Information Resources for Research Output : Perception of Academic Staff Members in Nigerian Federal Universities. *International Journal of Computer Science and Telecommunications*, *4*(8), 1–6.

Churi, P. P., Joshi, S., Elhoseny, M., & Omrane, A. (2022). *Artificial Intelligence in Higher Education : A Practical Approach* (1re éd.). CRC Press. https://doi.org/DOI: 10.1201/9781003184157

Corp, I. B. M. (2023). *IBM SPSS Statistics for Windows* (Version 29.0) [Computer software]. IBM Corp.

Creswell, J. W. (1986). *Measuring faculty research performance*. Jossey-Bass.

De la Vall, R. R. F., & Araya, F. G. (2023). Exploring the benefits and challenges of AI-language learning tools. *International Journal of Social Sciences and Humanities Invention*, *10*(01), 7569–7576. DOI: 10.18535/ijsshi/v10i01.02

Dergaa, I., Chamari, K., Zmijewski, P., & Ben Saad, H. (2023). From human writing to artificial intelligence generated text : Examining the prospects and potential threats of ChatGPT in academic writing. *Biology of Sport*, *40*(2), 615–622. DOI: 10.5114/biolsport.2023.125623 PMID: 37077800

Dupps, W. J. (2023). Artificial intelligence and academic publishing. *Journal of Cataract and Refractive Surgery*, *49*(7), 655–656. DOI: 10.1097/j.jcrs.0000000000001223 PMID: 37390321

Gupta, Y., Saini, A., & Saxena, A. K. (2013). A review on important aspects of information retrieval. *International. Journal of Computing and Information Science in Engineering*, *7*(12), 940–948.

Hambarde, K. A., & Proenca, H. (2023). Information Retrieval : Recent Advances and Beyond. *IEEE Access : Practical Innovations, Open Solutions*, *11*, 76581–76604. DOI: 10.1109/ACCESS.2023.3295776

Hayes, A. F. (2022). *Introduction to mediation, moderation, and conditional process analysis: A regression-based approach* (3rd ed.). Guilford Press.

Hayes, A. F. (2022). *PROCESS macro for SPSS, SAS, and R* (Version 4.2) [Computer software]. http://www.processmacro.org

Hosseini, M., Resnik, D. B., & Holmes, K. (2023). The ethics of disclosing the use of artificial intelligence tools in writing scholarly manuscripts. *Research Ethics*, *19*(4), 449–465. DOI: 10.1177/17470161231180449 PMID: 39749232

Hwang, S. I., Lim, J. S., Lee, R. W., Matsui, Y., Iguchi, T., Hiraki, T., & Ahn, H. (2023). Is ChatGPT a "Fire of Prometheus" for Non-Native English-Speaking Researchers in Academic Writing? *Korean Journal of Radiology*, *24*(10), 952. DOI: 10.3348/kjr.2023.0773 PMID: 37793668

Job, M. A. (2021). Automating and Optimizing Software Testing using Artificial Intelligence Techniques. *International Journal of Advanced Computer Science and Applications*, *12*(5). Advance online publication. DOI: 10.14569/IJACSA.2021.0120571

Jones, K. S. (1999). Information retrieval and artificial intelligence. *Artificial Intelligence*, *114*(1-2), 257–281. DOI: 10.1016/S0004-3702(99)00075-2

Khalifa, M., & Albadawy, M. (2024). Using artificial intelligence in academic writing and research: An essential productivity tool. *Computer Methods and Programs in Biomedicine Update*, *100145*, 100145. Advance online publication. DOI: 10.1016/j.cmpbup.2024.100145

Oluwatola, K., & Akingbade, L. (2022). *Information Retrieval Skills as Correlate of Scholarly Research Among Postgraduate Students in Selected Universities in Oyo and Lagos States.*

Lalengmawia, R., & Shukla, A. (2017). Theoretical Perspectives of Research Output based on Literature Review. *Library Waves, 3*(2), 108–118. Retrieved from https://www.librarywaves.com/index.php/lw/article/view/57

Malik, A. R., Pratiwi, Y., Andajani, K., Numertayasa, I. W., Suharti, S., Darwis, A., & Marzuki, . (2023). Exploring Artificial Intelligence in Academic Essay : Higher Education Student's Perspective. *International Journal of Educational Research Open*, *5*, 100296. DOI: 10.1016/j.ijedro.2023.100296

Mandl, T. (2009). Artificial Intelligence for Information Retrieval. In Rabuñal Dopico, J. R., Dorado, J., & Pazos, A. (Eds.), *Encyclopedia of Artificial Intelligence* (pp. 151–156). IGI Global., DOI: 10.4018/978-1-59904-849-9.ch023

Marzuki, M., Widiati, U., Rusdin, D., Darwin, D., & Indrawati, I. (2023). The impact of AI writing tools on the content and organization of students' writing : EFL teachers' perspective. *Cogent Education*, *10*(2), 2236469. DOI: 10.1080/2331186X.2023.2236469

Nguyen, A., Hong, Y., Dang, B., & Huang, X. (2024). Human-AI collaboration patterns in AI-assisted academic writing. *Studies in Higher Education*, *49*(5), 847–864. DOI: 10.1080/03075079.2024.2323593

Onah, J. C., Mr, I. O. A., Okonkwo, E. A., & Onyebuchi, G. U. (2020). Information retrieval skills as it correlates to undergraduate use of library information resources at a Nigerian university. *Library Philosophy and Practice (e-journal)*, 4567.

Owan, V. J., Abang, K. B., Idika, D. O., Etta, E. O., & Bassey, B. A. (2023). Exploring the potential of artificial intelligence tools in educational measurement and assessment. *Eurasia Journal of Mathematics, Science and Technology Education*, *19*(8), em2307. Advance online publication. DOI: 10.29333/ejmste/13428

Perdana, I., Manullang, S. O., & Masri, F. A. (2021). Effectiveness of online Grammarly application in improving academic writing : Review of experts experience. *The International Journal of Social Sciences (Islamabad)*, *4*(1), 122–130. DOI: 10.31295/ijss.v4n1.1444

Phadatare, T. S., & Naik, P. (2023). AI Based Disease Prediction. *International Journal of Advanced Research in Science. Tongxin Jishu*, •••, 621–628. DOI: 10.48175/IJARSCT-12094

Rahim, N. A., Hanum, A. Z. A., Bhakti, M. A. C., & Wandy, W. (2023). Artificial Intelligence Tools in Higher Education Students Usage Analysis – Case Study : Sampoerna University. *Jurnal Teknologi, 16*(2), 137–145. DOI: 10.34151/jurtek.v16i2.4544

Roe, J., Renandya, W. A., & Jacobs, G. M. (2023). A Review of AI-Powered Writing Tools and Their Implications for Academic Integrity in the Language Classroom. *Journal of English and Applied Linguistics, 2*(1). Advance online publication. DOI: 10.59588/2961-3094.1035

Sarker, I. H. (2022). AI-Based Modeling : Techniques, Applications and Research Issues Towards Automation, Intelligent and Smart Systems. *SN Computer Science, 3*(2), 158. DOI: 10.1007/s42979-022-01043-x PMID: 35194580

Sharma, L., & Srivastava, V. (2017). Performance enhancement of information retrieval via artificial intelligence. [IJSRSET]. *International Journal of Scientific Research in Science, Engineering and Technology, 3*(1), 187–192.

Soe, T. H. (2021). *AI video editing tools. What editors want and how far is AI from delivering?* (arXiv:2109.07809). arXiv. http://arxiv.org/abs/2109.07809

Swaroop, S., Buçinca, Z., Gajos, K. Z., & Doshi-Velez, F. (2024). *Accuracy-Time Tradeoffs in AI-Assisted Decision Making under Time Pressure.* https://doi.org/DOI: 10.1145/3640543.3645206

# Chapter 11
# University Students' Sense of Belonging in AI-Mediated EFL Classrooms:
## Classroom Rapport and Management

**Cuong Huy Pham**
https://orcid.org/0000-0001-6876-0493
*Ho Chi Minh City University of Economics and Finance, Vietnam*

## ABSTRACT

*The advent of AI has redefined the language education landscape in EFL contexts. While contemporary research has repeatedly highlighted the affordances and constraints of AI for language learning, learners' affective dimensions have been relatively underexplored. This chapter critically positions AI in English language education and discusses emerging issues concerning classroom rapport, classroom management, and learners' sense of belonging. It then presents findings of a study that examined EFL university students' sense of belonging in AI-mediated classrooms drawing on interview data with five students and three teachers, and observations of five class sessions. Findings reflected the interplay between learners' sense of belonging, their engagement in classroom interaction, and classroom dynamics. This relational mechanism affected teachers' perspectives on classroom rapport and management, driving the shifts in their approaches to tackling issues arising from AI integration. This chapter concludes with implications for classroom management in tertiary language education.*

DOI: 10.4018/979-8-3373-0969-9.ch011

## INTRODUCTION

With the prominence of artificial intelligence (AI) in English language education, learners' affective responses in AI-based settings have garnered substantial attention in contemporary research (Chang & Sun, 2024; Lai et al., 2024; Liu & Fan, 2025; Moybeka et al., 2023; Zhou & Hou, 2024). AI has contributed to expediting learners' language development through its versatile features that provide immediate and personalized language support (Mohebbi, 2025; Son et al., 2023; Sumakul et al., 2022; Wang & Xue, 2024; Wu, 2024). It has been found to substantially improve learners' pronunciation, grammar, and lexical resources by offering them instant feedback and revisions on their errors (AlTwijri & Alghizzi, 2024). Such functions enable learners to identify their own limitations, seek tailored advice, and gain in-depth understandings of linguistic knowledge (Dakakni & Safa, 2023; Wu, 2024; Zhai et al., 2024). These advantages have encouraged learners to make extensive use of AI in language learning, inevitably creating a certain degree of dependence on these technological advancements. There is a growing tendency for language learners to commit plagiarism to cope with classroom tasks or homework assignments, alarmingly affecting their learning outcomes, language achievements, and particularly attitudes toward language learning (Dakakni & Safa, 2023). Another repercussion of overwhelming reliance on AI is the shift in learning styles, such as procrastination or lack of creativity, that are inextricably linked to the abuse of AI within and beyond classroom settings. These downsides of AI utilization have apparently exerted adverse influences on learners' cognitive and affective development and their learning behaviors (Dakakni & Safa, 2023; Hwang et al., 2020). There have been concerns over learners' classroom performance and emotional attachment to language classrooms integrated with AI technologies (Bin-Hady et al., 2024; Shen & Guo, 2024; Wu, 2024). The former may lead to inaccurately gauging learners' achievements as their language output may not truly reflect their levels of proficiency (Alharbi, 2023; Dakakni & Safa, 2023). The latter correlates closely with the quality of classroom life, undermining classroom atmosphere, interaction, rapport, and ultimately learners' sense of belonging (Shao et al., 2019). The changing landscape of language education under the impact of AI has partially altered learners' conceptualization of the classroom, their degree of involvement, and the social bonds embedded in this setting (Chang & Sun, 2024; Ghafouri, 2024; Huang et al., 2024). Their physical and emotional attachment and perceptions of being accepted and respected as a valued member in their class are among the elements crucial to their sense of connectedness that is conducive to positive emotions, classroom performance, and learning outcomes (Allen et al., 2024; Allen et al., 2021; Furrer & Skinner, 2003; Zengilowski et al., 2023). Inquiry into psychological aspects of language education through the mediation of AI is valuable for enhancing pedagogical relevance and fostering effective learning (Hwang et al., 2020; Jeon, 2024; Wu, 2024).

This chapter critically reviews the affective issues emerging from the integration of AI in language teaching and learning which are important but mostly overlooked in this technologically permeated context. It then sheds light on rapport and interaction as unequivocal contributors to success in AI-based settings. The affective shift resulting from changes in the learning environment has necessitated redefining learners' sense of belonging, showcasing the ways in which AI has shaped their emotional attachment, experience, and engagement in language classrooms. To further illustrate learners' constructions of belongingness, this chapter presents findings from a qualitative study with EFL teachers and students in the General English program at a private university in Vietnam. Implications for classroom management and ethical considerations in AI-embedded settings are provided at the end of this chapter.

## AFFECTIVE ISSUES IN AI-MEDIATED ENGLISH LANGUAGE EDUCATION

The integration of AI technologies in English language education has presented several affective issues arising from the interplay between learners and their social interaction in this rapidly shifting context (Jeon, 2024; Zhou & Hou, 2024). AI in educational contexts refers to "the application of AI technologies, such as chatbots, automatic marking systems, intelligent tutoring systems, and student performance prediction platforms that support and enhance education" (Chiu et al., 2024, p. 3240). The adoption of AI in language education has substantial implications for responding to learners' cognitive and socio-psychological needs through intelligent learning systems that scaffold learning and provide adaptive, interactive, and personalized learning experiences (AlTwijri & Alghizzi, 2024; Chang & Sun, 2024; Wei, 2023; Wu, 2024). Hwang et al. (2020) discuss the affordances and learning opportunities from AI applications and platforms, emphasizing that teachers can draw on their knowledge of AI capabilities and its state-of-the-art features to reinforce students' learning performance and emotional growth. However, Alharbi (2023, p. 12) warns that this technological emergence may bring about "significant disruptions and changes" and "a heightened sense of uncertainty" that require cautious preparation and deployment. This contextual change has also challenged learners in terms of cognitive and emotional readiness for successful utilization of AI for learning purposes (Chiu et al., 2024; Yoon, 2019). Yang and Zhao (2024, p. 2) argue that "Since emotions are highly context-dependent, shifting towards technologies like AI may incur different emotional responses compared to traditional L2 instruction settings." While contemporary research on AI in language education has lauded its unequivocal role in shaping learners' motivation, engagement, grit, resilience, and interest in language learning (Ghafouri, 2024; Wang & Xue, 2024; Zhai et al., 2024; Zhou & Hou, 2024), its negative impacts on learners' emotional constructions are inevitable (Dakakni & Safa, 2023; Ma & Chen, 2024; Yang & Zhao, 2024). Adverse consequences of AI integration may discourage learners from participating in classroom activities and interacting with their peers and teachers, thus disconnecting them from the classroom community and undermining classroom rapport and their sense of connectedness (Dakakni & Safa, 2023; Mi et al., 2025).

## CLASSROOM RAPPORT IN AI-MEDIATED ENVIRONMENTS

As interaction is a central tenet of the language learning process, it necessitates learners to establish and strengthen rapport with teachers and peers for effective communication and language practice (Ghafouri, 2024; Huang et al., 2024; Huang, 2023; Zhi & Wang, 2024). Rapport refers to "a trusting relationship that yields a mutually respectful understanding for both instructor and the learners" (B. Zhang, 2023, p. 1688). This is a two-way relationship between learners and social others that has a facilitative function in fostering learners' interest, motivation, and engagement in learning, thus resulting in enjoyable classroom experiences (Huang et al., 2024; Kang & Chen, 2024; Mohebbi, 2025; Sun & Shi, 2022). Peer relationships are particularly important as they embrace indispensable social support and collaboration conducive to language practice within and beyond classrooms (Gamlath, 2022; Namaziandost et al., 2024; Solhi, 2024; Wentzel, 1998). Building solid rapport with teachers and peers contributes to positive outcomes in learning both cognitively and affectively (Bailey & Cassidy, 2019; Ebadijalal & Yousofi, 2023; Loda et al., 2019; Y. Zhang, 2023; Zhi & Wang, 2024). The permeation of AI in language education has presented teachers and learners with opportunities and challenges in maintaining this social bond. While AI helps to develop more engaging learning experiences, it may negatively affect the nature and amount of classroom interaction, impeding learners' emotional growth and connectedness (Chiu et al., 2024; Rezai et al., 2024; Wu, 2024; Yang & Zhao, 2024).

AI-based learning conditions have been found to facilitate teacher-student and peer interaction, consequently exerting positive influences on learners' experiences and engagement in language learning. Wei's (2023) experimental study with 60 Chinese students reveals that students' utilization of AI-assisted language learning applications in classrooms not only enhanced their learning outcomes but also offered them refreshing and captivating learning experiences. Students reported a high level of enthusiasm about the interactive classroom tasks based on AI platforms and dynamic language games with immediate feedback, creating an immersive learning environment. Similarly, Xiao et al. (2024) point out the value of AI-supported language learning in promoting students' emotional and psychological health, leading to their academic enjoyment. Their study was undertaken with 389 Chinese students who were exposed to Duolingo and ChatGPT during classroom activities. Findings suggest that students were deeply involved in critical evaluation of their learning processes, addressing the interplay between their psychological well-being and self-concept. They proactively participated in interaction with AI and peers in speaking activities, allowing them to improve their oral communication and affective engagement. In the context of language education in Iran, the research conducted by Rezai et al. (2024) sought to explore the association between employing ChatGPT and the well-being and emotion regulation of 492 EFL learners. The results indicated a significant positive correlation between using this AI chatbot and learners' well-being and the mediating role of emotion regulation, and between ChatGPT utilization and learners' emotion regulation. ChatGPT created a safe space for the participants, enabling them to express their emotions and feel a stronger sense of belonging in classroom participation and interaction with teachers and peers. These studies provide corroborating evidence showcasing that leveraging AI in language education has contributed positively to classroom interaction and relationships, thus fostering learners' engagement and belongingness (AbdAlgane & Othman, 2023; Guo & Wang, 2025; Ma & Chen, 2024; Shen & Guo, 2024). They also reiterate the fact that AI does not completely supersede human interaction as teachers and peers remain pivotal to creating an engaging, dynamic, and connected classroom atmosphere (AlTwijri & Alghizzi, 2024; Chiu et al., 2024; Ghafouri, 2024).

However, there have been concerns over extensive reliance on AI platforms and applications that detach learners from teachers and peers. (Bin-Hady et al., 2024; Mi et al., 2025; Zhou & Hou, 2024). The highly adaptive and personalized learning experiences afforded by AI technologies have provoked a high level of learners' autonomy in language learning, questioning the necessity of classroom participation and the role of teachers and peers (Dakakni & Safa, 2023; Sumakul et al., 2022). In this vein, Moybeka et al. (2023, p. 2446) note that "This transformation extends beyond mere automation; it touches the very core of pedagogy by addressing some of the most challenging aspects of language learning, such as individualization, engagement, and accessibility." This means that changes in classroom approaches are needed to promote students' engagement in classroom interaction. Whereas traditional language learning is mostly contingent on direct communication with teachers and peers which consolidates classroom rapport, AI tools may provoke a sense of isolation and disconnectedness given their convenience and versatility (Chiu et al., 2024; Wei, 2023; Zhai et al., 2024; Zhi & Wang, 2024). Working with 310 Korean university students on their readiness for using AI in EFL classrooms, Yoon (2019) finds that students showed a strong preference for interaction with teachers despite their acknowledgement of AI usefulness. For them, the idea of interacting with AI might trigger loneliness and segregation. Supporting this view, Dimitriadou and Lanitis (2023, p. 15) argue that "the use of technology for teaching and learning may be related to disconnectedness, which is usually expressed as feelings of separation from learning, the curriculum, the peers and the teachers and the learning devices." It is evident that the adoption of AI in language classrooms may have adverse effects on the classroom atmosphere, alienating learners from their social interaction and shifting their perspectives on their relationships with teachers and peers.

## EFL LEARNERS' SENSE OF BELONGING

Learners' sense of belonging or belongingness is a key affective dimension and fundamental psychological need that drives their learning behavior, engagement, motivation, and other academic functioning (Allen et al., 2024; Allen et al., 2018; Chapman, 2024; Kirby & Thomas, 2022; Yüksel et al., 2024). This construct is generally defined as learners' perceptions of "being personally and academically accepted, valued, and supported by teachers and peers" (Zengilowski et al., 2023, p. 2). It concerns learners' feelings of being connected to classrooms and the social relationships embedded in their interaction with teachers and peers in the learning process. Belongingness is intricately related to collaborative learning experiences that promote co-construction of meaning between teachers and students and among learners, thus forming a community of practice. This collaborative nature allows them to construct knowledge together, creating a rich tapestry of interaction that fosters strong attachment to this community in which each member is respected and supported by others. According to Delahunty et al. (2014, p. 246), the classroom is a place where students expose themselves to the group, "with unfolding clues about who they are, what they know, what they value and how they think." This self-portrayal poses potential identity and emotional risks that may impede their self-efficacy, confidence, engagement, and the quality of interaction. In this vein, Morshedian et al. (2023) argue that classrooms are venues for cultivating safety, security, and respect to foster students' interpersonal connections and engagement. These elements are closely associated with their sense of membership, thus physically and socially positioning each student as "an important part of the life and activity of the class" (Finley, 2018, p. 38). This links back to the collaborative interaction among class members, a process highly contingent on mutual trust, respect, familiarity with social others and the surrounding environment, and the amount of support they receive (Delahunty et al., 2014; Osterman, 2023). Evidently, learners' sense of belonging is a complex and multifaceted affective factor that embraces their perception of themselves and the social interaction that shapes their degree of connectedness to and engagement in the classroom community.

Contemporary research has shown that learners with a higher sense of belonging are more likely to enjoy their classroom experiences and proactively engage in learning activities and vice versa (Allen et al., 2024; Chapman, 2024; Freeman et al., 2007; Gillen-O'Neel, 2021; Pham, 2017). This nexus emerges from the social and emotional dynamics of the classroom environment that contribute to rich classroom experiences, enjoyment, and involvement. A number of factors have been found to either foster or diminish learners' sense of belonging. Their perceived connectedness and emotional bonds arising from a conducive and inclusive classroom community encourage them to participate enthusiastically in classroom interaction and discussion. Zengilowski et al. (2023, p. 10) propound that "sense of belonging becomes fuel for motivation to learn." This source of energy results from learners' feelings of security, social acceptance, and personal security, inviting them to value classroom relationships and learning opportunities and engage more deeply. Heightened connectedness enables them to undertake better academic adjustments and enhances their chances of academic success (Ahn & Davis, 2020; Allen et al., 2021; Crawford et al., 2024; Gillen-O'Neel, 2021; Zengilowski et al., 2023). Conversely, negative classroom experiences such as social exclusion, criticism, or an unsupportive environment may lead to a sense of disconnectedness or alienation (Allen et al., 2024; Osterman, 2023; Yüksel et al., 2024). These elements may thwart learners' interest in classroom activities and reduce their engagement in the learning process. Further, Gillen-O'Neel (2021, p. 48) notes that belongingness is not a static affective state as learners may exhibit "moment-to-moment fluctuations" depending on the subtle changes in classroom experiences, attitudes, and social relationships. Tian et al. (2021) confirm this ephemeral nature of belongingness, reiterating the ongoing impact of learning experiences, including learners' beliefs and perceptions of the learning context. This highlights learners' sense of belonging as a highly situated social and emotional construct constantly shaped by positive and negative nuances of experiences and engagement (Crawford et al., 2024).

Understanding learners' sense of belonging has significant implications for strengthening teacher-student rapport and peer relationships and facilitating classroom management (Allen et al., 2021; Furrer & Skinner, 2003; Morshedian et al., 2023). Learners who perceive their teachers as caring and supportive are more likely to feel valued and recognized within the classroom. Similarly, those with harmonious, collaborative relationships with classmates feel a higher degree of connectedness that provokes proactive engagement in classroom activities and peer interaction. This is because "sense of belonging illustrates the interplay between the individual and an environment" and "can be hindered or promoted by complex interactions between environmental and personal factors" (Chapman, 2024, p. 1). Apparently, belongingness in the academic context is intensively mitigated by classroom rapport and the relational affordances derived from the classroom ecology. When learners are either socially or academically engaged in interaction with teachers and peers, they are not only exchanging and constructing knowledge but also creating a network of support that enhances their learning experience, thus reinforcing their connectedness (Ahn & Davis, 2020; Furrer & Skinner, 2003). Insights into learners' belonging needs and desired social support are valuable for teachers in formulating classroom management approaches (Morshedian et al., 2023; Osterman, 2023). Classroom management is an overarching term encompassing teachers' activities and strategies for handling students, monitoring their classroom behaviors, and facilitating the learning process to structure a positive classroom atmosphere (Alasmari & Althaqafi, 2021; Martin & Sass, 2010). To strengthen students' connectedness through classroom management, Morshedian et al. (2023) point out four major aspects of teachers' behavior: caring, competence in teaching, monitoring, and intervention. These dimensions entail teachers' demonstration of compassion for students in response to their personal, social, and academic needs, their adoption of various teaching methods that facilitate their access to knowledge, their ongoing oversight of their learning progress, and their prompt actions to tackle problems and incidents arising in their learning. In the context of language education, teachers can also provide instrumental support by sharing learning resources, offering individualized feedback, and giving academic encouragement (Yüksel et al., 2024). This synergy of belongingness, classroom relationships, and classroom management contributes to creating a positive environment where students feel connected and engaged in their learning experiences (Hayat, 2025). With the escalating integration of AI technologies in language education, investigation into learners' sense of belonging is valuable for consolidating classroom rapport and classroom management (Cevallos & Soto, 2020; Chang & Sun, 2024; Guo & Wang, 2025; Hayat, 2025; Moybeka et al., 2023; Wei, 2023).

## THE STUDY

### Setting for the Study

This study was situated in the context of a private multidisciplinary university in Ho Chi Minh City, Vietnam that offers bilingual education aiming at an international standard of education and students' global mobility. The university deploys a six-level intensive General English program with a total of 300 contact hours to build a solid language foundation for students. Students take about 30% of their specialization courses in English as a medium of instruction after completing this program in the first one and a half years of their academic journey. Students work with both Vietnamese teachers of English and native speakers of English to expand their opportunities for authentic language use. The university fosters innovative approaches to English language teaching and learning by investing in state-of-the-art facilities and promoting best teaching practices that incorporate the latest educational technologies. Students learn English in multimedia classrooms with wireless internet access and can use their smartphones for learning purposes. With the advent of AI, teachers and students have been using AI tools, chatbots, and AI-based gamified platforms, such as ChatGPT, Gemini, Poe, and Duolingo, to optimize their classroom performance and language teaching and learning outcomes.

## Methods and Data Analysis

This study drew on a qualitative design utilizing data from interviews with five students in the General English program and three Vietnamese teachers of English and observations of five class sessions. It aims to explore students' perceptions of belongingness in AI-powered language classrooms and teachers' classroom management approaches to strengthen classroom rapport and connectedness to tackle technological changes in their teaching context. The participants were invited to join this study voluntarily based on convenience sampling. All interviews were conducted in the participants' native language to facilitate their in-depth reflections. The researcher observed his students' performance and emotional responses in his General English classes, with each session lasting 150 minutes. Following the class session, the researcher took careful note of his recollections of the students' classroom interaction and their emotional displays. The interviews with students and observations centered around students' feelings of belongingness, their classroom interaction, and attitudes toward rapport building in AI-mediated settings whereas the interviews with teachers focused on their classroom management strategies for working with their students in the context of AI integration. The profiles of the teachers and students are presented in Table 1.

*Table 1. Profiles of the teachers and students participating in this study*

| Students | Gender | Age | AI use in language learning |
|---|---|---|---|
| Anh | Female | 18 | moderate |
| Hoang | Male | 18 | moderate |
| Loan | Female | 18 | moderate |
| Thoa | Female | 18 | intensive |
| Tuan | Male | 18 | moderate |

continued on following page

*Table 1. Continued*

| Students | Gender | Age | AI use in language learning |
|---|---|---|---|
| Teachers | Gender | Age | AI use in language teaching |
| Mr. Nam | male | 28 | intensive |
| Ms. Thuy | female | 30 | moderate |
| Mr. Trung | male | 27 | intensive |

The data were analyzed thematically following the six steps of thematic analysis guided by (Braun & Clarke, 2006). Firstly, the researcher read the transcribed interview data and observational notes repeatedly to develop familiarity with the data and highlighted important ideas. From these preliminary ideas, the researcher formulated initial codes, such as belongingness, engagement, interaction, peer relationship, rapport with teachers, disconnectedness, respect, and acceptance. Next, the researcher developed tentative themes drawing on these codes and gathered relevant excerpts to substantiate each theme. In the fourth step, all potential themes were reviewed by checking their feasibility based on the entire data set and eliminating those loosely supported. Following this step, the researcher generated the concise names for all resulting themes and defined them individually. Finally, a detailed analysis of each theme was undertaken with vivid illustrations of relevant interview excerpts and observational notes.

## Findings and Discussion

### Students' perceptions of belongingness in AI-powered language classrooms

Three major themes emerging from interview data (**int**) with five student participants and observational data (**obv**) reflecting students' perceived sense of belonging in AI-mediated settings entail their ongoing maintenance of classroom rapport, proactive engagement in classroom activities, and preservation of acceptance and respect.

### Ongoing maintenance of classroom rapport

Although AI has enabled learners to develop more independent learning (Wu, 2024; Zhai et al., 2024; B. Zhang, 2023), the students in this study expressed strong attachment to their classroom as in the following:

*I love a dynamic classroom atmosphere in which everyone interacts with one another. Everyone should not stick their eyes to their smartphones using AI. (int_Hoang)*

*AI can assist me in many ways, but for effective learning, I need to interact with teachers and peers. AI can't replace them. I do need such social contact. (int_Anh)*

Hoang emphasized that interaction among class members was necessary to consolidate the classroom atmosphere, while Anh saw interaction as essential for successful learning. AI chatbots and tools have not been in a position to replace humans as they fall short of the rapport intrinsic to the classroom community (Wang & Xue, 2024). In addition, the classroom is the place where students could benefit from collaboration and mutual support.

*If a group member did not know how to use AI to complete an assigned task, I would find out his or her problems and offer my solutions. (int_Anh)*

*When we interact with classmates, they can recommend more useful AI tools. Things will get easier. We should not work independently. (int_Loan).*

*With AI, we can develop ideas faster. We can have more time for practicing English with classmates instead of spending most of the allotted time on brainstorming. We can work together more efficiently. (int_Thoa)*

These students addressed the significance of classroom collaboration as a strong indication of belongingness (Allen et al., 2024; Yüksel et al., 2024; Zengilowski et al., 2023). AI facilitated their group discussion by saving brainstorming time, leaving them opportunities for language practice. Students could also share technical tips for efficient utilization of AI tools. These findings provide corroborating evidence of the collaboration and rapport-building capacities that AI could bring about in classroom settings (Ghafouri, 2024; Guo & Wang, 2025). However, in relation to Thoa's interview data, the observational data revealed that not all students were committed to group discussion. They only spent the first few minutes eliciting ideas from AI tools and then devoted the remaining time to doing personal things or chatting with their neighbors (obv). This reality requires teachers to closely monitor students when it comes to group work to ensure their engagement.

## Proactive involvement in classroom activities

AI tools were instrumental in providing students with linguistic resources and preparing ideas for fulfilling classroom tasks, facilitating their involvement in classroom tasks. This usefulness is reported in the following:

*I can get rich ideas from AI, so I can volunteer to give answers. I become more committed to classroom activities (int_Anh)*

*AI helps me to express my ideas more smoothly. In this way, I can get bonus marks for my classroom contributions (int_Thoa)*

*AI suggests grammatical corrections and provides me with the vocabulary I need for conveying my ideas. I can use them to complete classroom tasks more quickly and easily. (int_Hoang)*

The observational data supported the interview data in showcasing the benefits of using AI for performing classroom tasks, allowing students to engage more enthusiastically during class sessions. AI helped them overcome the linguistic barriers that would otherwise have hindered their active participation (Guo & Wang, 2025; Ma & Chen, 2024; Zhou & Hou, 2024). In addition, the students cared about the quality of engagement through the facilitation of AI as Loan and Tuan noted:

*In my group, we often brainstorm ideas first, then we use AI for improvements. This gets everyone to join the group discussion more effectively. (int_Loan)*

*I do not think of AI as a tool merely for coping with assignments. It helps me understand classroom tasks, especially difficult ones, and participate more actively in class. (int_Tuan)*

These students confirmed their serious attitudes toward AI as supporting tools enabling them to improve their language output. This aligns with findings from recent studies on the ways in which students utilize AI technologies for learning purposes (Mi et al., 2025; Sumakul et al., 2022; Xiao et al., 2024). However, this seriousness partially contradicted observational data in which many students excessively relied on AI for language production. They used AI to respond to teachers' questions with little consideration of its learning value (obv). Despite these variations in the students' degrees of engagement and learning attitudes, they illustrated their desire to stay connected to the classroom community by contributing their responses to teachers' questions.

## Preservation of acceptance and respect

Given the versatility of AI as a highly convenient learning resource, students are confronted with the ethical dilemma of AI reliance and plagiarism (Alharbi, 2023; Dakakni & Safa, 2023; Zhou & Hou, 2024). The students in this study expressed their firm belief in personal effort to be accepted and respected as a proud member of their class as they stated,

*I like to rely on myself for ideas. I might resort to AI for assistance when I am so stuck. (int_Hoang)*

*I am against plagiarism, so when I work on a writing task, I will develop my ideas and write my own draft. I only ask AI to give grammatical corrections or suggest improvements. (int_Anh)*

*I only use AI for translating those ideas that I cannot render in English or for vocabulary suggestions. I feel quite annoyed if my classmates do not make a personal effort. (int_Loan)*

*I would feel proud if my teacher complimented my own work. It should include my personal touch. We should only use AI to improve our grammar or vocabulary use. (int_Thoa)*

These students devised their own ways to minimize the negative effects of AI on their performance. They reinstated the importance of developing their own ideas in doing assignments. They set a clear boundary between what they were supposed to do as learners and the extent to which they could use AI for learning. Conversely, the observational data showed that a relatively high proportion of students submitted AI-generated paragraphs or essays with little to no effort to revise them. These findings again confirmed the varying extent to which students were committed to using AI for learning purposes (AlTwijri & Alghizzi, 2024; Chiu et al., 2024), suggesting their nuanced perceptions of belongingness.

## Teachers' classroom management strategies for promoting students' belongingness

The interview data with the three teachers (Mr. Nam, Ms. Thuy and Mr. Trung) reveals their tailored approaches to classroom management, drawing on their experiences with AI, specific classroom settings, and the groups of students they worked with. Three commonly adopted strategies identified from their input comprise valuing students' engagement, showing respect in providing feedback and ensuring inclusivity.

### Valuing students' engagement

The teachers reported that their students utilized AI as a useful language source that facilitated brainstorming and provided lexical resources, grammatical corrections and translation of complex ideas. This versatility enabled students to proactively participate in assigned tasks, contributing to classroom dynamics. Mr. Nam noted that "*AI is like a teaching assistant giving students the individualized language support they need. I often encourage them to share the information or ideas, even those they gather from AI. The point is to get them to say something. This makes them more involved* (int_Mr. Nam). In his view, students could overcome their linguistic deficiencies and fear of making mistakes in their language production and become more committed to sharing their ideas as AI utility lifted language barriers. This finding subscribes to the abundant literature on the value of AI as a rich and omnipotent source of reference for linguistic issues and conveyance of ideas (Liu & Fan, 2025; Moybeka et al., 2023; Wei, 2023; Zhou & Hou, 2024). Similarly, Mr. Trung noticed students' higher levels of confidence and willingness to communicate, noting that "*When students use AI tools, they get ideas for classroom tasks. More of them volunteer to reply to my questions. They become more confident, so this helps enliven the atmosphere*" (int_Mr. Trung). There was a drastic change in the quality of classroom life since AI alleviated their anxiety about interacting with teachers. These positive affective responses are also documented in a large volume of contemporary research indicating elevated confidence, self-efficacy and overall classroom experience (Shen & Guo, 2024; Wu, 2024; Zhai et al., 2024). Ms. Thuy was excited about her students' motivation to learn, stating that

> *Many students come to me for support with using AI as they see the learning opportunities from it. You know they have just started to use AI, so they need time to get used to it. I value their eagerness to learn, so I always do my best to show them how to create good prompts or give proper commands. (int_Ms. Thuy)*

Ms. Thuy expressed her appreciation of her students' desire to explore the affordances of AI, driving her to provide additional technical support for avid learners. However, students needed to develop AI literacy and gradual familiarity with these technological advancements (AlTwijri & Alghizzi, 2024; Liu & Fan, 2025).

Drawing on AI functional benefits, these teachers developed adaptive classroom strategies that resulted in their students' affective shifts, fostering positive classroom environments and students' engagement, thus strengthening their sense of belonging.

## Showing respect in providing feedback

As research has indicated, the widespread use of AI in language education has led students to rely on and abuse it in their learning (Bin-Hady et al., 2024; Dakakni & Safa, 2023; Mi et al., 2025). The teachers in this study were cognizant of such scenarios, so they devised their distinct strategies for grappling with this issue, as they noted in the following:

*I understand that the work they presented was not a true reflection of their language competence. I was careful about giving them feedback to avoid a threat to their face. I brought to their attention whether the information they used was reliable or relevant to the given context or not" (int_Mr. Nam).*

*When I detected essays completely composed by AI, I avoided criticizing my students. Instead, I asked them what they had learned from the texts, and I pointed out unnatural language features or ideas generated by AI. This helped them feel more comfortable and know how to add personal features or improve the AI-based text. (int_Ms. Thuy)*

From Mr. Nam's observations, the mediation of AI might have given rise to false achievements, accounting for the discrepancy between students' work and their actual level of language proficiency. He adopted a face-saving approach to feedback giving, guiding his students to develop methods of verifying the reliability and relevance of the information generated by AI. Ms. Thuy employed more student-centered strategies by eliciting students' reflections on the learning values implicated in AI-based text and showing them methods of augmenting it with personal input. Conversely, Mr. Trung utilized a penalty scheme for students' lack of learning commitment:

*With students who did not expend personal effort to complete a given task, I gave them three opportunities for pointing out why it was written that way, explaining the meaning, or reading aloud the difficult words they used but might not understand. If they failed to respond, I might give them minus points. I would give them corrections if necessary. (int_ Mr. Trung)*

With the support of AI, recent research has documented students' procrastination or laziness in working on assignments (Dakakni & Safa, 2023; Ma & Chen, 2024). To redress his students' malpractice with AI, Mr. Trung employed a rather stringent management strategy. However, his aim concurred with those of the other two teachers in supporting students' cognitive growth, accepting their limitations, and treating them with due respect.

## Ensuring inclusivity

The teachers endeavored to promote inclusivity in their classroom management to bridge the gap in AI utilization among their students. As Chiu et al. (2024, p. 3241) note, "Students with different expertise may respond differently to learning with the technology; therefore, the roles of the technology vary on those students." Consequently, teachers need to empower them with digital literacy and readiness for using AI in their learning. Mr. Nam and Ms. Thuy shared similar strategies for building students' familiarity with AI tools as follows:

*I provided articulate guidelines and frameworks for effective use of AI in their learning to make sure every student can know how to take advantage of such resources and avoid unexpected abuse of AI. (int_Mr. Nam)*

*I guided them on how to use ChatGPT for classroom tasks and homework. This allows them to develop independent learning styles. However, when given the chance to interact with AI, some might use it for other purposes rather than for learning. I had to go around the classroom more frequently to monitor their involvement. I checked each student's contribution to group work through group members' evaluation of their peers' performance. Upon completion of a group project or presentation, they had to hand in their evaluation form. (int_Ms. Thuy)*

These teachers foresaw the possible challenges and opportunities in using AI for learning purposes, so they took prudent steps in preparing their students to access these technologies. Mr. Nam helped his students explore AI learning resources and prevented them from misusing it, while Ms. Thuy reinforced learner autonomy by initially observing their performance closely and continuously evaluating their involvement in classroom activities. These inclusive strategies indicate the teachers' commitment to ensuring their students' readiness for AI adoption in language learning.

## CONCLUSION

This chapter examined learners' sense of belonging in EFL classrooms powered with AI technologies. This construct drew on the nexus of classroom dynamics, classroom rapport, interaction, collaboration, learners' experiences, and engagement. The chapter also addressed teachers' adaptive classroom management strategies for handling issues emerging from the integration of AI tools and platforms in language classrooms. Given the utility values and affordances brought about by technological advancements, contemporary research and the findings from the study presented in this chapter suggest students' nuanced emotions and varying degrees of belongingness in response to these changes in their language learning. Their affective shifts reflect the ongoing exercise of personal and contextual elements, including learners' perceived affordances and challenges of AI-based language learning, the changing nature of classroom interaction powered by the latest educational technologies such as chatbots, the availability of learning resources and support within and beyond classroom settings which provoked issues of relevance and reliability, the scaffolding role of teachers and peers, and learners' diverse socio-psychological needs. This complexity in learning conditions and social relationships requires learners to reconstruct their perspectives on classroom rapport, interaction, engagement, and particularly sense of belonging.

As the study reveals, three major issues emerging from this changing language education landscape mediated by AI entail learners' performance with and without AI support, their excessive reliance on AI tools, and teachers' endeavor to maintain their classroom belongingness. Such problems pose ethical considerations in terms of the extent to which AI could be adopted for classroom tasks and assignments and their commitment to classroom morale as they may undermine students' creativity, sense of belonging, and overall language achievement. These challenges present teachers and educational stakeholders with new tasks in their classroom agenda, as Wright (2012, p. 60) notes that "The quality of classroom life influences and is influenced by the ways in which we manage classrooms. This is always a jointly managed task, a collective responsibility, despite being led by teachers." There has been a drastic shift in teachers' roles from being the primary source of information in classrooms to being an advisor and facilitator monitoring students' use of AI for learning purposes, helping them to verify the credibility and relevance of the text generated by AI, ensuring their engagement in classroom activities, and making timely interventions. To perform these new roles effectively and efficiently, teachers need to continuously develop their digital literacy to keep themselves abreast of the latest technological changes in language education. This enables them to provide students with proper guidelines for utilizing AI for learning purposes and avoiding its negative impacts on their cognitive development, especially students' dependence on AI technology leading to their false achievements and procrastination. It is also part of teachers' classroom management strategies to raise students' awareness of the irrefutable significance of classroom interaction with teachers and peers as a natural and indispensable component of language learning that fosters their cognitive and affective growth. To this end, a positive classroom environment is likely to ease classroom interaction, alleviate anxiety, boost students' motivation, confidence, and willingness to communicate, and create a feeling of inclusivity, all of which contribute to heightening their sense of connectedness. Although these processes are inevitably mitigated by the presence of AI, classroom dynamics are undoubtedly subject to teachers' adaptive classroom management strategies.

This study was situated in the context of English language education in a developing country where AI implementation in language classrooms has emerged as a critical issue. It aimed to respond to this new trend and depict the ways in which teachers responded to arising problems in classroom rapport and management rather than offering a generalizable global framework. Despite its demographic and geographical limitations, insights from this study can be a useful source of reference for teachers in devising and adjusting their strategies to reinforce classroom rapport and students' sense of belonging. Some major points for teachers' consideration include their perspectives on acceptable AI practices in language learning, classroom integrity and students' learning experiences, their professional development and adaptivity to changes in language education, and their accountability in AI-mediated language education.

## REFERENCES


AbdAlgane, M., & Jabir Othman, K. A. (2023). Utilizing artificial intelligence technologies in Saudi EFL tertiary level classrooms. *Journal of Intercultural Communication, 23*(1).

Ahn, M. Y., & Davis, H. H. (2020). Four domains of students' sense of belonging to university. *Studies in Higher Education, 45*(3), 622–634. DOI: 10.1080/03075079.2018.1564902

Alasmari, N. J., & Althaqafi, A. S. A. (2021). Teachers' practices of proactive and reactive classroom management strategies and the relationship to their self-efficacy. *Language Teaching Research, 28*(6), 2158–2189. Advance online publication. DOI: 10.1177/13621688211046351

Alharbi, W. (2023). AI in the foreign language classroom: A pedagogical overview of automated writing assistance tools. *Education Research International, 2023*, 1–15. DOI: 10.1155/2023/4253331

Allen, K., Kern, M. L., Vella-Brodrick, D., Hattie, J., & Waters, L. (2018). What schools need to know about fostering school belonging: A meta-analysis. *Educational Psychology Review, 30*(1), 1–34. DOI: 10.1007/s10648-016-9389-8

Allen, K.-A., Kern, M. L., Slaten, C., D'Argenio, E., Arslan, G., & Reardon, J. (2024). Student belonging in focus: Bridging research, theory, and practice with contextual relevance to enhance well-being and academic outcomes. In Arslan, G., & Yıldırım, M. (Eds.), *Handbook of positive school psychology: Evidence-based strategies for youth well-being* (pp. 55–71). Springer. DOI: 10.1007/978-3-031-54295-4_5

Allen, K. A., Slaten, C. D., Arslan, G., Roffey, S., Craig, H., & Vella-Brodrick, D. A. (2021). School belonging: The importance of student and teacher relationships. In *The Palgrave handbook of positive education* (pp. 525–550). Springer International Publishing.

AlTwijri, L., & Alghizzi, T. M. (2024). Investigating the integration of artificial intelligence in English as foreign language classes for enhancing learners' affective factors: A systematic review. *Heliyon, 10*(10), e31053. Advance online publication. DOI: 10.1016/j.heliyon.2024.e31053 PMID: 38778968

Bailey, D., & Cassidy, R. (2019). Online peer feedback tasks: Training for improved L2 writing proficiency, anxiety reduction, and language learning strategies. *Computer-Assisted Language Learning Electronic Journal, 20*(2), 70–88.

Bin-Hady, W. R. A., Ali, J. K. M., & Al-humari, M. A. (2024). The effect of ChatGPT on EFL students' social and emotional learning. *Journal of Research in Innovative Teaching & Learning*, *17*(2), 243–255. DOI: 10.1108/JRIT-02-2024-0036

Braun, V., & Clarke, V. (2006). Using thematic analysis in psychology. *Qualitative Research in Psychology*, *3*(2), 77–101. DOI: 10.1191/1478088706qp063oa

Cevallos, L. F. E., & Soto, S. T. (2020). EFL classroom management. *MEXTESOL Journal*, *44*(2), 1–11.

Chang, W.-L., & Sun, J. C.-Y. (2024). Evaluating AI's impact on self-regulated language learning: A systematic review. *System*, *126*, 1–16. DOI: 10.1016/j.system.2024.103484

Chapman, L. R. (2024). Students' experience of sense of belonging in a diversity class: A model and practice recommendations. *Teaching and Learning in Communication Sciences & Disorders*, *8*(2), 1–29. DOI: 10.61403/2689-6443.1313

Chiu, T. K. F., Moorhouse, B. L., Chai, C. S., & Ismailov, M. (2024). Teacher support and student motivation to learn with Artificial Intelligence (AI) based chatbot. *Interactive Learning Environments*, *32*(7), 3240–3256. DOI: 10.1080/10494820.2023.2172044

Crawford, J., Allen, K.-A., Pani, B., & Cowling, M. (2024). When artificial intelligence substitutes humans in higher education: The cost of loneliness, student success, and retention. *Studies in Higher Education*, *49*(5), 883–897. DOI: 10.1080/03075079.2024.2326956

Dakakni, D., & Safa, N. (2023). Artificial intelligence in the L2 classroom: Implications and challenges on ethics and equity in higher education: A 21st century Pandora's box. *Computers and Education: Artificial Intelligence*, *5*, 1–10. DOI: 10.1016/j.caeai.2023.100179

Delahunty, J., Verenikina, I., & Jones, P. (2014). Socio-emotional connections: Identity, belonging and learning in online interactions. A literature review. *Technology, Pedagogy and Education*, *23*(2), 243–265. DOI: 10.1080/1475939X.2013.813405

Dimitriadou, E., & Lanitis, A. (2023). A critical evaluation, challenges, and future perspectives of using artificial intelligence and emerging technologies in smart classrooms. *Smart Learning Environments*, *10*(1), 1–26. DOI: 10.1186/s40561-023-00231-3

Ebadijalal, M., & Yousofi, N. (2023). The impact of mobile-assisted peer feedback on EFL learners' speaking performance and anxiety: Does language make a difference? *Language Learning Journal*, *51*(1), 112–130. DOI: 10.1080/09571736.2021.1957990

Finley, A. M. (2018). Fostering success: Belongingness pedagogy for English language learners. *BC TEAL Journal*, *3*(1), 37–48.

Freeman, T. M., Anderman, L. H., & Jensen, J. M. (2007). Sense of belonging in college freshmen at the classroom and campus levels. *75*(3), 203-220. DOI: 10.3200/JEXE.75.3.203-220

Furrer, C., & Skinner, E. (2003). Sense of relatedness as a factor in children's academic engagement and performance. *Journal of Educational Psychology*, *95*(1), 148–162. DOI: 10.1037/0022-0663.95.1.148

Gamlath, S. (2022). Peer learning and the undergraduate journey: A framework for student success. *Higher Education Research & Development*, *41*(3), 699–713. DOI: 10.1080/07294360.2021.1877625

Ghafouri, M. (2024). ChatGPT: The catalyst for teacher-student rapport and grit development in L2 class. *System*, *120*, 1–11. DOI: 10.1016/j.system.2023.103209

Gillen-O'Neel, C. (2021). Sense of belonging and student engagement: A daily study of first- and continuing-generation college students. *Research in Higher Education*, *62*(1), 45–71. DOI: 10.1007/s11162-019-09570-y

Guo, Y., & Wang, Y. (2025). Exploring the effects of artificial intelligence application on EFL students' academic engagement and emotional experiences: A mixed-methods study. *European Journal of Education*, *60*(1), 1–15. DOI: 10.1111/ejed.12812

Hayat, A. (2025). Language classroom management: Underprivileges of ChatGPT. *Journal of Management World*, *2025*(1), 159–165. DOI: 10.53935/jomw.v2024i4.632

Huang, L., Al-Rashidi, A. H., & Bayat, S. (2024). Teacher support in language learning: A picture of the effects on language progress, academic immunity, and academic enjoyment. *BMC Psychology*, *12*(1), 1–8. DOI: 10.1186/s40359-024-01602-2 PMID: 38439089

Huang, Y. (2023). Examining the relationship between peer support and foreign language emotions in online learning: The mediating effect of self-efficacy. *Frontiers in Psychology*, *14*, 1–11. DOI: 10.3389/fpsyg.2023.1148472 PMID: 37842693

Hwang, G.-J., Xie, H., Wah, B. W., & Gašević, D. (2020). Vision, challenges, roles and research issues of Artificial Intelligence in education. *Computers and Education: Artificial Intelligence*, *1*, 1–5. DOI: 10.1016/j.caeai.2020.100001

Jeon, J. (2024). Exploring AI chatbot affordances in the EFL classroom: Young learners' experiences and perspectives. *Computer Assisted Language Learning*, *37*(1-2), 1–26. DOI: 10.1080/09588221.2021.2021241

Kang, H., & Chen, H. (2024). Effects of teachers' rapport-building strategies on EFL learners' cognitive load and computer-assisted language learning motivation. *Education and Information Technologies*, •••, 1–42. DOI: 10.1007/s10639-024-12961-z

Kirby, L. A. J., & Thomas, C. L. (2022). High-impact teaching practices foster a greater sense of belonging in the college classroom. *Journal of Further and Higher Education*, *46*(3), 368–381. DOI: 10.1080/0309877X.2021.1950659

Lai, C., Chen, Q., Wang, Y., & Qi, X. (2024). Individual interest, self-regulation, and self-directed language learning with technology beyond the classroom. *British Journal of Educational Technology*, *55*(1), 379–397. DOI: 10.1111/bjet.13366

Liu, H., & Fan, J. (2025). AI-mediated communication in EFL classrooms: The role of technical and pedagogical stimuli and the mediating effects of AI literacy and enjoyment. *European Journal of Education*, *60*(1), 1–13. DOI: 10.1111/ejed.12813

Loda, T., Erschens, R., Loenneker, H., Keifenheim, K. E., Nikendei, C., Junne, F., Zipfel, S., & Herrmann-Werner, A. (2019). Cognitive and social congruence in peer-assisted learning – A scoping review. *PLoS One*, *14*(9), 1–15. DOI: 10.1371/journal.pone.0222224 PMID: 31498826

Ma, Y., & Chen, M. (2024). AI-empowered applications effects on EFL learners' engagement in the classroom and academic procrastination. *BMC Psychology*, *12*(1), 1–11. DOI: 10.1186/s40359-024-02248-w PMID: 39695837

Martin, N. K., & Sass, D. A. (2010). Construct validation of the behavior and instructional management scale. *Teaching and Teacher Education*, *26*(5), 1124–1135. DOI: 10.1016/j.tate.2009.12.001

Mi, Y., Rong, M., & Chen, X. (2025). Exploring the affordances and challenges of GenAI feedback in L2 writing instruction: A comparative analysis with peer feedback. *ECNU Review of Education*, 1-26. DOI: 10.1177/20965311241310883

Mohebbi, A. (2025). Enabling learner independence and self-regulation in language education using AI tools: A systematic review. *Cogent Education*, *12*(1), 1–18. DOI: 10.1080/2331186X.2024.2433814

Morshedian, M., Ghanizadeh, A., & Mirzaee, S. (2023). Smart classroom management: How does it influence EFL learners' anxiety, engagement, and language achievement. *MEXTESOL Journal, 47*(2).

Moybeka, A. M. S., Syariatin, N., Tatipang, D. P., Mushthoza, D. A., Dewi, N. P. J. L., & Tineh, S. (2023). Artificial intelligence and English classroom: The implications of AI toward EFL students' motivation. *Edumaspul*, *7*(2), 2444–2454. DOI: 10.33487/edumaspul.v7i2.6669

Namaziandost, E., Behbahani, H. K., & Naserpour, A. (2024). Peer support in language learning: Mitigating anxiety, enhancing achievement, cultivating growth mindsets, and increasing enjoyment. *Journal of Applied Learning & Teaching*, *7*(2), 1–18. DOI: 10.37074/jalt.2024.7.2.40

Osterman, K. F. (2023). Teacher practice and students' sense of belonging. In Lovat, T., Toomey, R., Clement, N., & Dally, K. (Eds.), *Second international research handbook on values education and student wellbeing* (2nd ed., pp. 971–993). Springer. DOI: 10.1007/978-3-031-24420-9_54

Pham, Q. H. P. (2017). Group dynamics: Building a sense of belonging in the EFL classroom. *English Teaching Forum, 55*(1), 14-21.

Rezai, A., Soyoof, A., & Reynolds, B. L. (2024). Disclosing the correlation between using ChatGPT and well-being in EFL learners: Considering the mediating role of emotion regulation. *European Journal of Education*, *59*(4), 1–12. DOI: 10.1111/ejed.12752

Shao, K., Pekrun, R., & Nicholson, L. J. (2019). Emotions in classroom language learning: What can we learn from achievement emotion research? *System*, *86*, 102121. Advance online publication. DOI: 10.1016/j.system.2019.102121

Shen, Y., & Guo, H. (2024). "I feel AI is neither too good nor too bad": Unveiling Chinese EFL teachers' perceived emotions in generative AI-mediated L2 classes. *Computers in Human Behavior, 161*, 1–7. DOI: 10.1016/j.chb.2024.108429

Solhi, M. (2024). Do L2 teacher support and peer support predict L2 speaking motivation in online classes? *The Asia-Pacific Education Researcher*, *33*(4), 829–842. DOI: 10.1007/s40299-023-00767-5

Son, J.-B., Ružić, N. K., & Philpott, A. (2023). Artificial intelligence technologies and applications for language learning and teaching. *Journal of China Computer-Assisted Language Learning*, •••, 1–19. DOI: 10.1515/jccall-2023-0015

Sumakul, D. T. Y. G., Hamied, F. A., & Sukyadi, D. (2022). Artificial intelligence in EFL classrooms: Friend or foe? *LEARN Journal: Language Education and Acquisition Research Network*, *15*(1), 232–256.

Sun, Y., & Shi, W. (2022). On the role of teacher-student rapport and teacher support as predictors of Chinese EFL students' affective learning. *Frontiers in Psychology*, *13*, 1–9. DOI: 10.3389/fpsyg.2022.856430 PMID: 35360642

Tian, J., Zhang, M., Zhou, H., & Wu, J. (2021). College satisfaction, sense of achievement, student happiness and sense of belonging of freshmen in Chinese private colleges: Mediation effect of emotion regulation. *International Journal of Environmental Research and Public Health, 18*(22), 1–14. DOI: 10.3390/ijerph182211736 PMID: 34831492

Wang, Y., & Xue, L. (2024). Using AI-driven chatbots to foster Chinese EFL students' academic engagement: An intervention study. *Computers in Human Behavior, 159*, 1–8. DOI: 10.1016/j.chb.2024.108353

Wei, L. (2023). Artificial intelligence in language instruction: Impact on English learning achievement, L2 motivation, and self-regulated learning. *Frontiers in Psychology, 14*, 1–14. DOI: 10.3389/fpsyg.2023.1261955 PMID: 38023040

Wentzel, K. R. (1998). Social relationships and motivation in middle school: The roles of parents, teachers and peers. *Journal of Educational Psychology, 90*(2), 202–209. DOI: 10.1037/0022-0663.90.2.202

Wright, T. (2012). Managing the classroom. In Burns, A., & Richards, J. C. (Eds.), *The Cambridge guide to pedagogy and practice in second language teaching* (pp. 60–67). Cambridge University Press. DOI: 10.1017/9781009024778.009

Wu, X.-Y. (2024). Artificial Intelligence in L2 learning: A meta-analysis of contextual, instructional, and social-emotional moderators. *System, 126*, 1–20. DOI: 10.1016/j.system.2024.103498

Xiao, T., Yi, S., & Akhter, S. (2024). AI-supported online language learning: Learners' self-esteem, cognitive-emotion regulation, academic enjoyment, and language success. *International Review of Research in Open and Distance Learning, 25*(3), 77–96. DOI: 10.19173/irrodl.v25i3.7666

Yang, L., & Zhao, S. (2024). AI-induced emotions in L2 education: Exploring EFL students' perceived emotions and regulation strategies. *Computers in Human Behavior, 159*, 1–8. DOI: 10.1016/j.chb.2024.108337

Yoon, S. Y. (2019). Student readiness for AI instruction: Perspectives on AI in university EFL classrooms. *Multimedia-Assisted Language Learning, 24*(4), 134–160. DOI: 10.15702/mall.2019.22.4.134

Yüksel, H. G., Solhi, M., Özcan, E., & Giritlioğlu, N. B. (2024). The associations between EFL learners' L2 class belongingness, emotion regulation strategies, and perceived L2 proficiency in an online learning context. *Language Learning Journal*, 1–17. Advance online publication. DOI: 10.1080/09571736.2024.2403463

Zengilowski, A., Lee, J., Gaines, R. E., Park, H., Choi, E., & Schallert, D. L. (2023). The collective classroom "we": The role of students' sense of belonging on their affective, cognitive, and discourse experiences of online and face-to-face discussions. *Linguistics and Education, 73*, 1–14. DOI: 10.1016/j.linged.2022.101142

Zhai, X., Zhao, R., Jiang, Y., & Wu, H. (2024). Unpacking the dynamics of AI-based language learning: Flow, grit, and resilience in Chinese EFL contexts. *Behavioral Sciences (Basel, Switzerland), 14*(9), 838. Advance online publication. DOI: 10.3390/bs14090838 PMID: 39336053

Zhang, B. (2023). The relationship between teacher-student rapport and EFL learners' engagement in online scaffolding setting. *Journal of Psycholinguistic Research, 52*(5), 1685–1705. DOI: 10.1007/s10936-023-09954-3 PMID: 37171685

Zhang, Y. (2023). EFL learners' boredom coping strategies: The role of teacher-student rapport and support. *BMC Psychology, 11*(1), 1–10. DOI: 10.1186/s40359-023-01446-2 PMID: 37978568

Zhi, R., & Wang, Y. (2024). On the relationship between EFL students' attitudes toward artificial intelligence, teachers' immediacy and teacher-student rapport, and their willingness to communicate. *System, 124*, 1–15. DOI: 10.1016/j.system.2024.103341

Zhou, C., & Hou, F. (2024). Can AI empower L2 education? Exploring its influence on the behavioral, cognitive and emotional engagement of EFL teachers and language learners. *European Journal of Education, 59*(4), 1–13. DOI: 10.1111/ejed.12750

## ADDITIONAL READING

Jiang, Q. (2025). Revisiting classroom climate: Exploring the relationship between EFL students' disengagement and demotivation. *Language Related Research, 16*(1), 29–57. DOI: 10.29252/LRR.16.1.2

Lettieri, M. (2025). Embracing empathy: How AI technologies enhance the pedagogy of kindness in education. In Lobalsamo, T., & Segreti, D. (Eds.), *Redefining education with pandemic pedagogies* (pp. 167–188). IGI Global., DOI: 10.4018/979-8-3693-3695-3.ch006

Xin, Z., & Derakhshan, A. (2025). From excitement to anxiety: Exploring English as a foreign language learners' emotional experiences in the artificial intelligence-powered classrooms. *European Journal of Education, 60*(1), 1–12. DOI: 10.1111/ejed.12845

Yuan, L., & Liu, X. (2025). The effect of artificial intelligence tools on EFL learners' engagement, enjoyment, and motivation. *Computers in Human Behavior, 162*, 1–10. DOI: 10.1016/j.chb.2024.108474

Zong, Y., & Yang, L. (2025). How AI-enhanced social-emotional learning framework transforms EFL students' engagement and emotional well-being. *European Journal of Education*, *60*(1), 1–12. DOI: 10.1111/ejed.12925

## KEY TERMS AND DEFINITIONS

**Artificial intelligence in education:** The adoption of artificial intelligence technologies such as chatbots, virtual assistants, interactive games, content creation tools and adaptive learning platforms that support teachers' performance and promote students' learning outcomes and positive attitudes toward learning.

**Classroom management:** Teachers' activities and strategies for handling students, monitoring their classroom behaviors, and facilitating the learning process to create a positive classroom atmosphere.

**Classroom rapport:** Relationships with teachers and peer students that facilitate classroom interaction and support learners' cognitive and affective development.

**Engagement:** The extent to which learners are involved in classroom interaction that entails learners' cognitive, affective and behavioral dimensions.

**Sense of belonging:** Learners' perceptions of being personally and academically accepted, valued, and supported by teachers and peers.

# Compilation of References


AbdAlgane, M., & Jabir Othman, K. A. (2023). Utilizing artificial intelligence technologies in Saudi EFL tertiary level classrooms. *Journal of Intercultural Communication, 23*(1).

Abd-Alrazaq, A., AlSaad, R., Alhuwail, D., Ahmed, A., Healy, P. M., Latifi, S., Aziz, S., Damseh, R., Alabed Alrazak, S., & Sheikh, J. (2023). Large language models in medical education: Opportunities, challenges, and future directions. *JMIR Medical Education, 9*(1), e48291. DOI: 10.2196/48291 PMID: 37261894

Abd-Elsalam, K. A., & Abdel-Momen, S. M. (2023). Artificial Intelligence's Development and Challenges in Scientific Writing. *Egyptian Journal of Agricultural Research, 101*(3), 714–717. DOI: 10.21608/ejar.2023.220363.1414

Abdi Ali, A., AlQarni, K., Migdadi, H. F., Aldosemani, T. I., & Alshraah, S. M. (2024). Addressing the Challenge of Hybrid Learning Environment in Foreign Language Education: Training Lecturers for Blended Teaching Approaches. [TPLS]. *Theory and Practice in Language Studies, 14*(5).

Ableson, F. W., Collins, C., & Sen, R. (2009). Unlocking Android. Manning Publications 2009. Available Online at https://www.manning.com/ableson/SampleChapter1.pdf

Adams, D., & Chuah, K.-M. (2022). Artificial Intelligence-Based Tools in Research Writing : Current Trends and Future Potentials. In *Artificial Intelligence in Higher Education* (pp. 169–184). CRC Press. https://doi.org/DOI: 10.1201/9781003184157-9

Adipat, S., Laksana, K., Busayanon, K., Asawasowan, A., & Adipat, B. (2021). Engaging students in the learning process with game-based learning: The fundamental concepts. *International Journal of Technology in Education, 4*(3), 542–552. DOI: 10.46328/ijte.169

Ahmed, A. A. A., Widodo, M., Komariah, A., Hassan, I., Sukmana, N., Ali, M. H., Abbas, A. K., & Rohi, A. (2022). Assessing the effects of gamification on developing EFL Learners' idiomatic knowledge: Do attitudinal factors contribute to the learning of the idioms with the game? *Education Research International, 2022*(1), 2482570. DOI: 10.1155/2022/2482570

Ahn, M. Y., & Davis, H. H. (2020). Four domains of students' sense of belonging to university. *Studies in Higher Education, 45*(3), 622–634. DOI: 10.1080/03075079.2018.1564902

Akbana, Y. E., & Yavuz, A. (2020). Global issues in efl teaching: Efl lecturers' voices at a state university. *Kahramanmaraş Sütçü İmam Üniversitesi Eğitim Dergisi, 2*(1), 83–102.

Akbari, R. (2007). Reflections on reflection: A critical appraisal of reflective practices in L2 teacher education. *System, 35*(2), 192–207. DOI: 10.1016/j.system.2006.12.008

Akinrinola, O., Okoye, C. C., Ofodile, O. C., & Ugochukwu, C. E. (2024). Navigating and reviewing ethical dilemmas in AI development: Strategies for transparency, fairness, and accountability. *GSC Advanced Research and Reviews, 18*(3), 50–58. DOI: 10.30574/gscarr.2024.18.3.0088

Al Khatri, A. M. (2019). *How Omani teachers perceive the process of integrating 21st century competencies and skills into the EFL curriculum: A step forward.* University of Exeter.

Ala, H. A. R. R. A. T. N. R. (2024). *Investigating the relationship between audiovisual-based media and EFL learners' intercultural knowledge* [Unpublished Master's thesis]. University of 8 May 1945 Guelma, Algeria.

Alalawi, K., Athauda, R., & Chiong, R. (2024). An extended learning analytics framework integrating machine learning and pedagogical approaches for student performance prediction and intervention. *International Journal of Artificial Intelligence in Education,* •••, 1–49. DOI: 10.1007/s40593-024-00429-7

Alam, A., & Mohanty, A. (2023). Educational technology: Exploring the convergence of technology and pedagogy through mobility, interactivity, AI, and learning tools. *Cogent Engineering, 10*(2), 2283282. DOI: 10.1080/23311916.2023.2283282

Alasmari, N. J., & Althaqafi, A. S. A. (2021). Teachers' practices of proactive and reactive classroom management strategies and the relationship to their self-efficacy. *Language Teaching Research, 28*(6), 2158–2189. Advance online publication. DOI: 10.1177/13621688211046351

Aldoseri, A., Al-Khalifa, K. N., & Hamouda, A. M. (2023). Re-thinking data strategy and integration for artificial intelligence: Concepts, opportunities, and challenges. *Applied Sciences (Basel, Switzerland), 13*(12), 7082. DOI: 10.3390/app13127082

Alfredo, R., Echeverria, V., Jin, Y., Yan, L., Swiecki, Z., Gašević, D., & Martinez-Maldonado, R. (2024). Human-centred learning analytics and AI in education: A systematic literature review. Computers and Education: Artificial Intelligence, 100215.

Alghamdy, R. Z. (2023). Pedagogical and ethical implications of artificial intelligence in EFL context: A review study. *English Language Teaching, 16*(10), 87–98. DOI: 10.5539/elt.v16n10p87

Alharbi, W. (2023). AI in the foreign language classroom: A pedagogical overview of automated writing assistance tools. *Education Research International, 2023*, 1–15. DOI: 10.1155/2023/4253331

Alharthi, A. (2021). Exploring the use of intonation in Arabic varieties, particularly in Oman. *International Journal of Linguistics, 12*(3), 67–81.

Alisoy, H., & Sadiqzade, Z. (2024). Mobile-assisted language learning (MALL): Revolutionizing language education. *Luminis Applied Science and Engineering, 1*(1), 60–72. DOI: 10.69760/lumin.202400002

Allen, K. A., Slaten, C. D., Arslan, G., Roffey, S., Craig, H., & Vella-Brodrick, D. A. (2021). School belonging: The importance of student and teacher relationships. In *The Palgrave handbook of positive education* (pp. 525–550). Springer International Publishing.

Allen, K.-A., Kern, M. L., Slaten, C., D'Argenio, E., Arslan, G., & Reardon, J. (2024). Student belonging in focus: Bridging research, theory, and practice with contextual relevance to enhance well-being and academic outcomes. In Arslan, G., & Yıldırım, M. (Eds.), *Handbook of positive school psychology: Evidence-based strategies for youth well-being* (pp. 55–71). Springer. DOI: 10.1007/978-3-031-54295-4_5

Allen, K., Kern, M. L., Vella-Brodrick, D., Hattie, J., & Waters, L. (2018). What schools need to know about fostering school belonging: A meta-analysis. *Educational Psychology Review, 30*(1), 1–34. DOI: 10.1007/s10648-016-9389-8

Ally, M., & Wark, N. (2020). Sustainable development and education in the fourth industrial revolution (4IR).

Al-Shallakh, I., & Ahmad, M. (2024). Embedding Artificial Intelligent Applications in Higher Educational Institutions to Improve Students' Pronunciation Performance. [TPLS]. *Theory and Practice in Language Studies, 14*(6).

Alshumaimeri, Y. A., & Alshememry, A. K. (2024). The Extent of AI Applications in EFL Learning and Teaching. *IEEE Transactions on Learning Technologies, 17*, 653–663. DOI: 10.1109/TLT.2023.3322128

AlTwijri, L., & Alghizzi, T. M. (2024). Investigating the integration of artificial intelligence in English as foreign language classes for enhancing learners' affective factors: A systematic review. *Heliyon, 10*(10), e31053. Advance online publication. DOI: 10.1016/j.heliyon.2024.e31053 PMID: 38778968

Alzubaidi, L., Bai, J., Al-Sabaawi, A., Santamaría, J., Albahri, A. S., Al-dabbagh, B. S. N., Fadhel, M. A., Manoufali, M., Zhang, J., Al-Timemy, A. H., Duan, Y., Abdullah, A., Farhan, L., Lu, Y., Gupta, A., Albu, F., Abbosh, A., & Gu, Y. (2023). A survey on deep learning tools dealing with data scarcity : Definitions, challenges, solutions, tips, and applications. *Journal of Big Data, 10*(1), 46. DOI: 10.1186/s40537-023-00727-2

Anchimbe, E. A. (2020). *Globalizing English and the English classroom: Perspectives from African contexts*. Routledge.

Anh, P. T. (2017). Intonation and stress in English: Issues and challenges for EFL learners. *Journal of English Language Teaching, 22*(3), 14–28.

An, X., Chai, C. S., Li, Y., Zhou, Y., Shen, X., Zheng, C., & Chen, M. (2023). Modeling English teachers' behavioral intention to use artificial intelligence in middle schools. *Education and Information Technologies, 28*(5), 5187–5208. DOI: 10.1007/s10639-022-11286-z

Arefian, M. H., Çomoğlu, I., & Dikilitaş, K. (2024). Understanding EFL teachers' experiences of ChatGPT-driven collaborative reflective practice through a community of practice lens. *Innovation in Language Learning and Teaching*, •••, 1–16. DOI: 10.1080/17501229.2024.2412769

Artificial Intelligence Index Report (2024). URL: https:// aiindex.stanford.edu/wp-content/uploads/2024/04/HAI_2024_AI-Index-Report.pdf

Asaad Hamza Sheerah, H. (2020). Using blended learning to support the teaching of English as a foreign language. Arab World English Journal (AWEJ) Special Issue on CALL, (6).

Attali, Y., & Burstein, J. (2006). Automated essay scoring with e-rater® v.2. *The Journal of Technology, Learning, and Assessment, 4*(3), 1–30.

August, D., & Shanahan, T. (Eds.). (2006). *Developing literacy in second-language learners: Report of the National Literacy Panel on language-minority children and youth*. Erlbaum.

Aydin, I., Diebel-Fischer, H., Freiberger, V., Möller-Klapperich, J., Buchmann, E., Färber, M., Lauber-Rönsberg, A., & Platow, B. (2024). Assessing privacy policies with AI: Ethical, legal, and technical challenges. *arXiv. https://doi.org//arXiv.2410.08381.*DOI: 10.48550

Aysu, S. (2024). The use of AI-Powered Tools in Language Learning. Dil Eğitimi ve Öğretiminde, 1.

Azzahra, S., Syarfina, T., & Sembiring, F. E. D. R. B. (2024). Comparative formants analysis of English vowels using PRAAT. *Journal of English Language and Pedagogy*, *7*(2), 260–266. DOI: 10.33503/journey.v7i2.838

Bachman, L. F. (1990). *Fundamental considerations in language testing*. Oxford University Press.

Badia van Pelt, M. Y. (2020). *Rise and fall of a hero: Teaching English through literature and cinema* [Unpublished Master's thesis]. University of the Balearic Islands, Majorca.

Bailey, D., & Cassidy, R. (2019). Online peer feedback tasks: Training for improved L2 writing proficiency, anxiety reduction, and language learning strategies. *Computer-Assisted Language Learning Electronic Journal*, *20*(2), 70–88.

Baker, R. S., Martin, T., & Rossi, L. M. (2016). Educational data mining and learning analytics. *The Wiley handbook of cognition and assessment: Frameworks, methodologies, and applications*, 379-396.

Baker, T., & Smith, L. (2019). Educ-AI-tion rebooted? Exploring the future of artificial intelligence in schools and colleges. Retrieved from Nesta Foundation website: https://media.nesta.org.uk/documents/Future_of_AI_and_education_v5_WEB.pdf

Baker, A. (2021). Assessing EFL pronunciation with PRAAT: Methods and applications. *Linguistic Studies Journal*, *18*(1), 49–66.

Baker, A., & Trofimovich, P. (2022). The role of PRAAT in evaluating EFL learners' pronunciation: A comprehensive guide. *Language Learning & Technology*, *26*(2), 35–50.

Baker, R. S., & Hawn, A. (2022). Algorithmic bias in education. *International Journal of Artificial Intelligence in Education*, •••, 1–41.

Bálint, K., Sukalla, F., & Rooney, B. (2022). Personal relevance and state empathy with a character facilitates self-disclosure in film viewers. *Frontiers in Communication*, *7*, 984341. DOI: 10.3389/fcomm.2022.984341

Baltazani, M., Armostis, S., & Payne, E. (2024). The intonation of polar questions in Cypriot Arabic: Prosodic contact in an endangered language. *Speech Prosody (Urbana, Ill.), 1–5*, 502–506. Advance online publication. DOI: 10.21437/Speech-Prosody.2024-102

Banik, B. G., & Gullapelly, A. (2025). AI-Powered Gamification and Interactive Learning Tools for Enhancing Student Engagement. In Driving Quality Education Through AI and Data Science (pp. 283-310). IGI Global Scientific Publishing.

Barber, W., Harrison, R., VanOostveen, R., & Childs, E. (2021). Building better online communities in the post pandemic world. In *ECEL 2021 20th European Conference on e-Learning*. Academic Conferences International limited.

Bardovi-Harlig, K. (1999). Exploring the interlanguage of interlanguage pragmatics: The case of requests. *Studies in Second Language Acquisition, 21*(3), 341–377. DOI: 10.1017/S0272263199003010

Barr, D., & Feigenberg, L. (2017). Artificial intelligence in the classroom. *Journal of Educational Technology Systems, 45*(1), 27–45.

Bashir, A. (2024). Acoustic analysis of the English diphthongs /ou/ and /ei/ among Hausa native speakers in Northwest and Northeast Nigeria. *International Journal of Innovation in Literature, Language & Arts Studies, 12(2), 34–46. Retrieved from*https://www.seahipublications.org/wp-content/uploads/2024/04/IJILLAS-J-4-2024.pdf

Bassiouney, R. (Ed.). (2009). *Arabic sociolinguistics: Topics in diglossia, gender, identity, and politics*. Georgetown University Press. DOI: 10.3366/edinburgh/9780748623730.001.0001

Bates, A. W. (2015). *Teaching in a digital age: Guidelines for designing teaching and learning*. Tony Bates Associates Ltd.

Bax, S. (2019). *The Past, Present, and Future of CALL: An Overview of Selected Literature*. Routledge.

Bearman, M., Ryan, J., & Ajjawi, R. (2023). Discourses of artificial intelligence in higher education: A critical literature review. *Higher Education, 86*(2), 369–385. DOI: 10.1007/s10734-022-00937-2

Beck, I., & McKeown, M. (2007). Increasing young low-income children's oral vocabulary repertoires through rich and focused instruction. *The Elementary School Journal, 107*(3), 251–271. DOI: 10.1086/511706

Beijaard, D., Meijer, P. C., & Verloop, N. (2004). Reconsidering research on teachers' professional identity. *Teaching and Teacher Education, 20*(2), 107–128. DOI: 10.1016/j.tate.2003.07.001

Bender, E. M., Gebru, T., McMillan-Major, A., & Shmitchell, S. (2021, March). On the dangers of stochastic parrots: Can language models be too big? . In *Proceedings of the 2021 ACM conference on fairness, accountability, and transparency* (pp. 610-623). DOI: 10.1145/3442188.3445922

Bengsch, G. (2024). Redefining traditional pedagogy: The integration of machine learning in the contemporary language education classroom. In AI in Language Teaching, Learning, and Assessment (pp. 195-221). IGI Global Scientific Publishing.

Berens, P., Cranmer, K., Lawrence, N. D., von Luxburg, U., & Montgomery, J. (2023). *AI for Science : An Emerging Agenda* (arXiv:2303.04217). arXiv. http://arxiv.org/abs/2303.04217

Bettega, S. (2019a). Tense, Modality and Aspect in Omani Arabic. Naples: Università degli Studi di Napoli 'L'Orientale'.

Bettega, S. (2019b). 'Genitive markers in Omani Arabic'. In RomanoArabica 19: 223–37.

Betti, M. J., & Ulaiwi, W. A. (2018). Stress in English and Arabic: A contrastive study. *English Language and Literature Studies, 8*(1), 83–91.

Bialystok, E. (2001). *Bilingualism in Development: Language, Literacy, and Cognition*. Cambridge University Press. DOI: 10.1017/CBO9780511605963

Bialystok, E. (2007). Acquisition of literacy in bilingual children: A framework for research. *Language Learning, 57*(s1), 45–77. DOI: 10.1111/j.1467-9922.2007.00412.x

Biemiller, A. (2006). Vocabulary development and instruction: A prerequisite for school learning. In Dickinson, D., & Neuman, S. B. (Eds.), *Handbook of early literacy research* (Vol. II, pp. 41–51). Guilford.

Bin-Hady, W. R. A., Ali, J. K. M., & Al-humari, M. A. (2024). The effect of ChatGPT on EFL students' social and emotional learning. *Journal of Research in Innovative Teaching & Learning, 17*(2), 243–255. DOI: 10.1108/JRIT-02-2024-0036

Blair, C. (2002). School readiness: Integrating cognition and emotion in a neurobiological conceptualization of children's functioning at school entry. *The American Psychologist, 57*(2), 111–127. DOI: 10.1037/0003-066X.57.2.111 PMID: 11899554

Blum-Kulka, S., House, J., & Kasper, G. (1989). *Cross-cultural pragmatics: Requests and apologies*. Ablex Publishing.

Bobkina, J., & Dominguez Romero, E. (2023). Towards a quality standardized technological education in Spain: A case study with EFL preservice teachers. *Journal of Research in Applied Linguistics, 14*(2), 55–66. DOI: 10.22055/rals.2023.43480.3035

Boersma, P., & Weenink, D. (2024). PRAAT: Doing phonetics by computer (Version 6.1). University of Amsterdam. https://www.praat.org

Boersma, P. (2023). *PRAAT: An introduction to speech analysis*. Cambridge University Press.

Boeru, M. (2024). Exploring the use of AI Tools in Teaching English for Specific Purposes (ESP). Scientific Bulletin'Mircea cel Batran'Naval Academy, 27(1).

Boud, D., Keogh, R., & Walker, D. (2013). *Reflection: Turning experience into learning*. Routledge. DOI: 10.4324/9781315059051

Bowers, E., Laster, B., Gurvitz, D., Ryan, T., Cobb, J., & Vazzano, J. (2017). Using video for teacher reflection: Reading clinics in action. *Reflective Theory and Practice in Teacher Education*, 141-160.

Brandenburg, R., & Jones, M. (2017). Toward transformative reflective practice in teacher education. *Reflective Theory and Practice in Teacher Education*, 259-273.

Braun, V., & Clarke, V. (2006). Using thematic analysis in psychology. *Qualitative Research in Psychology, 3*(2), 77–101. DOI: 10.1191/1478088706qp063oa

Brookfield, S. D. (2015). *The skillful teacher: On technique, trust, and responsiveness in the classroom*. John Wiley & Sons.

Brown, G., & Hellmuth, S. (2024). Computational modelling of segmental and prosodic levels of analysis for capturing variation across Arabic dialects. *Journal of Phonetics, 89*, 101–118.

Brown, P., & Levinson, S. C. (1987). *Politeness: Some universals in language usage*. Cambridge University Press. DOI: 10.1017/CBO9780511813085

Brynjolfsson, E., & McAfee, A. (2017). *Machine, platform, crowd: Harnessing our digital future*. W. W. Norton & Company.

Budiarta, I. K., & Krismayani, N. W. (2024). Post-pandemic shifts in English language teaching: Challenges and perceptions in online learning environments. *Voices of English Language Education Society, 8*(1), 241–252. DOI: 10.29408/veles.v8i1.25678

Burns, A., & Richards, J. C. (Eds.). (2009). *Cambridge guide to second language teacher education*. Cambridge University Press. DOI: 10.1017/9781139042710

Byram, M. (1997). *Teaching and assessing intercultural communicative competence*. Multilingual Matters.

Byram, M. (2021). *Teaching and assessing intercultural communicative competence: Revisited*. Multilingual Matters., DOI: 10.21832/9781800410251

Cabero-Almenara, J., Palacios-Rodríguez, A., Loaiza-Aguirre, M. I., & Rivas-Manzano, M. D. R. D. (2024). Acceptance of educational artificial intelligence by teachers and its relationship with some variables and pedagogical beliefs. *Education Sciences*, *14*(7), 740. DOI: 10.3390/educsci14070740

Cabrero-Daniel, B., & Cabrero, A. S. (2023). Perceived Trustworthiness of Natural Language Generators. *Proceedings of the First International Symposium on Trustworthy Autonomous Systems*, (pp. 1–9). https://doi.org/DOI: 10.1145/3597512.3599715

Çakır, İ. (2022). TV serials and movies to boost intercultural communicative competence in Turkish EFL context. *International Journal of Applied Linguistics*, *32*(3), 397–410. DOI: 10.1111/ijal.12425

Çakmak, F. (2022). Chatbot-human interaction and its effects on EFL students' L2 speaking performance and anxiety.

Calogerakou, C., & Vlachos, K. (2011). Films and blogs: An authentic approach to improve the writing skill-an intercultural project-based framework in the Senior High State School. *Research Papers in Language Teaching and Learning*, *2*(1), 98–110.

Carter, G. M. (1982). *The Arabic dialect of Oman*. Curzon Press.

Castillo, R., Lin, C., & Zhang, Y. (2023). The effects of neural machine translation tools on vocabulary acquisition and learner confidence in EFL contexts. *Computer Assisted Language Learning*, *36*(2), 145–160. DOI: 10.1080/09588221.2022.2100212

Cenoz, J., & Gorter, D. (2019). Focus on multilingualism in language teaching and learning: An introduction to the special issue. *Language Teaching*, *52*(1), 1–14. DOI: 10.1017/S0261444818000320

Cevallos, L. F. E., & Soto, S. T. (2020). EFL classroom management. *MEXTESOL Journal*, *44*(2), 1–11.

Chang, C. C., Hwang, G. J., & Tu, Y. F. (2023). Roles, applications, and trends of concept map-supported learning: A systematic review and bibliometric analysis of publications from 1992 to 2020 in selected educational technology journals. *Interactive Learning Environments*, *31*(9), 5995–6016. DOI: 10.1080/10494820.2022.2027457

Chang, T. S., Li, Y., Huang, H. W., & Whitfield, B. (2021). Exploring EFL students' writing performance and their acceptance of AI-based automated writing feedback. In *Proceedings of the 2021 2nd International Conference on Education Development and Studies*. DOI: 10.1145/3459043.3459065

Chang, W.-L., & Sun, J. C.-Y. (2024). Evaluating AI's impact on self-regulated language learning: A systematic review. *System*, *126*, 1–16. DOI: 10.1016/j.system.2024.103484

Chao, T. C. (2013). A diary study of university EFL learners' intercultural learning through foreign films. *Language, Culture and Curriculum*, *26*(3), 247–265. DOI: 10.1080/07908318.2013.833936

Chapelle, C. A. (2001). *Computer Applications in Second Language Acquisition: Foundations for Teaching, Testing, and Research*. Cambridge University Press. DOI: 10.1017/CBO9781139524681

Chapman, L. R. (2024). Students' experience of sense of belonging in a diversity class: A model and practice recommendations. *Teaching and Learning in Communication Sciences & Disorders*, *8*(2), 1–29. DOI: 10.61403/2689-6443.1313

Chen, C.-H., Koong, C.-S., & Liao, C. (2022). Influences of integrating dynamic assessment into a speech recognition learning design to support pupils' English speaking skills, learning anxiety and cognitive load. *Journal of Educational Technology & Society*, *25*(1), 1–14. https://eric.ed.gov/?id=EJ1335942

Chen, G. M. (2014). Intercultural communication competence: Summary of 30-year research and directions for future study. In Dai, X.-D., & Chen, G. M. (Eds.), *Intercultural communication competence: Conceptualization and its development in cultural contexts and interactions* (pp. 14–40). Cambridge Scholars Publishing.

Chen, G. M., & Starosta, J. W. (1996). Intercultural communication competence: A synthesis. *Annals of the International Communication Association*, *19*(1), 353–383. DOI: 10.1080/23808985.1996.11678935

Chen, G. M., & Starosta, W. J. (1998). *Foundations of intercultural communication*. Allyn & Bacon.

Chen, H., Sun, J., & Li, X. (2020). Meta-analysis of AI-assisted language learning: A review of recent developments. *Journal of Educational Technology & Society*, *23*(4), 100–113. https://www.jstor.org/stable/26915413

Chen, L., Chen, P., & Lin, Z. (2020). Artificial intelligence in education: A review. *IEEE Access : Practical Innovations, Open Solutions*, *8*, 75264–75278. DOI: 10.1109/ACCESS.2020.2988510

Chen, M. (2022). Computer-aided feedback on the pronunciation of Mandarin Chinese tones: Using Praat to promote multimedia foreign language learning. *Computer Assisted Language Learning*, *35*(3), 363–388. DOI: 10.1080/09588221.2022.2037652

Chen, X., Wang, Y., & Li, J. (2020). Automated essay scoring in rural and urban Chinese schools: Adoption and challenges. *Asia Pacific Education Review*, *21*(4), 567–580. DOI: 10.1007/s12564-020-09658-6

Chen, X., Zou, D., Xie, H., & Cheng, G. (2021). Twenty years of personalized language learning. *Journal of Educational Technology & Society*, *24*(1), 205–222.

Chen, X., Zou, D., Xie, H., Cheng, G., & Liu, C. (2022). Two decades of artificial intelligence in education. *Journal of Educational Technology & Society*, *25*, 28–47. https:// www.jstor.org/stable/48647028#metadata_info_tab_contents

Chen, Y., Liu, Y., & Zhang, Y. (2020). Exploring the potential of AI in language learning: A meta-analysis of empirical studies. *Educational Technology Research and Development*, *68*(4), 1795–1812.

Chen, Y., Liu, Y., & Zhang, Y. (2022). Exploring the effects of artificial intelligence-driven personalized learning on language learners' performance. *Educational Technology Research and Development*, *70*(1), 213–230.

Chen, Y., Smith, T. J., York, C. S., & Mayall, H. J. (2020). Google earth virtual reality and expository writing for young english learners from a funds of knowledge perspective. *Computer Assisted Language Learning*, *33*(1-2), 1–25. DOI: 10.1080/09588221.2018.1544151

Chiappini, R., & Mansur, E. (2020, July 9). *Mediating a text: A practical guide to task creation*. https://www.macmillanenglish.com/gr/blog-resources/article/advancing-learning-mediating-a-text-a-practical-guide-to-task-creation

Chien, S.-Y., Hwang, G.-J., & Jong, M. S.-Y. (2020). Effects of peer assessment within the context of spherical video-based virtual reality on efl students' englishspeaking performance and learning perceptions. *Computers & Education*, *146*, 103751. DOI: 10.1016/j.compedu.2019.103751

Chinta, S. V., Wang, Z., Yin, Z., Hoang, N., Gonzalez, M., Quy, T. L., & Zhang, W. (2024). FairAIED: Navigating fairness, bias, and ethics in educational AI applications. *arXiv preprint arXiv:2407.18745*.

Chiu, T. K. F., Chen, J. M., & Chung, S. (2023). Artificial intelligence in language education: A systematic review and research agenda. *British Journal of Educational Technology*, *54*(1), 5–28. DOI: 10.1111/bjet.13232

Chiu, T. K. F., & Ching, Y. H. (2018). The effectiveness of AI-driven feedback in language learning: A systematic review. *Computer Assisted Language Learning, 31*(5-6), 486–508.

Chiu, T. K. F., Moorhouse, B. L., Chai, C. S., & Ismailov, M. (2024). Teacher support and student motivation to learn with Artificial Intelligence (AI) based chatbot. *Interactive Learning Environments, 32*(7), 3240–3256. DOI: 10.1080/10494820.2023.2172044

Chow, J. C., & Li, K. (2024). Ethical considerations in human-centered AI: Advancing oncology chatbots through large language models. *JMIR Bioinformatics and Biotechnology, 5*, e64406. DOI: 10.2196/64406 PMID: 39321336

Christopher, O. (2013). Availability of Information Resources for Research Output : Perception of Academic Staff Members in Nigerian Federal Universities. *International Journal of Computer Science and Telecommunications, 4*(8), 1–6.

Chung, E., Subramaniam, G., & Dass, L. C. (2020). Online learning readiness among university students in Malaysia amidst COVID-19. *Asian Journal of University Education, 16*(2), 46–58. DOI: 10.24191/ajue.v16i2.10294

Churi, P. P., Joshi, S., Elhoseny, M., & Omrane, A. (2022). *Artificial Intelligence in Higher Education : A Practical Approach* (1re éd.). CRC Press. https://doi.org/ DOI: 10.1201/9781003184157

Clark, R. (2023). *Meaningful games: Exploring language with game theory*. MIT Press.

Coniam, D., & Falvey, P. (2018). Comparing human and automated scoring of summary writing. *Language Testing, 35*(3), 309–332.

Corp, I. B. M. (2023). *IBM SPSS Statistics for Windows* (Version 29.0) [Computer software]. IBM Corp.

Corrigan, S. (2024). Top 7 AI tools for language teachers and language learners. URL: https://epale.ec.europa.eu/en/blog/top-7-ai-tools-language-teachers-and-language-learners

Coşkun, F., & Gülleroğlu, H. D. (2021). Yapay zekânın tarih içindeki gelişimi ve eğitimde kullanılması. [JFES]. *Ankara University Journal of Faculty of Educational Sciences, 54*(3), 947–966.

Council of Europe. (2001). *Common European Framework of Reference for Languages: Learning, Teaching, Assessment.* Cambridge University Press.

Cowie, N., & Alizadeh, M. (2022). The affordances and challenges of virtual reality for language teaching. *Int. J. TESOL Stud., 4*, 50–65. DOI: 10.46451/ijts.2022.03.05

Crawford, J., Allen, K.-A., Pani, B., & Cowling, M. (2024). When artificial intelligence substitutes humans in higher education: The cost of loneliness, student success, and retention. *Studies in Higher Education, 49*(5), 883–897. DOI: 10.1080/03075079.2024.2326956

Creswell, J. W. (1986). *Measuring faculty research performance*. Jossey-Bass.

Crompton, H., & Burke, D. (2023). Artificial intelligence in higher education: The state of the field. *International Journal of Educational Technology in Higher Education*, *20*(1), 22.

Cukurova, M., Kralj, L., Hertz, B., & Saltidou, E. (2024, January). *Professional development for teachers in the age of AI.*https://discovery.ucl.ac.uk/id/eprint/10186881/

Dakakni, D., & Safa, N. (2023). Artificial intelligence in the L2 classroom: Implications and challenges on ethics and equity in higher education: A 21st century Pandora's box. *Computers and Education: Artificial Intelligence*, *5*, 1–10. DOI: 10.1016/j.caeai.2023.100179

Dandee, N.. (2022). Prosody in English language teaching: The importance of rhythm, intonation, and stress. *TESOL Quarterly*, *56*(1), 89–102.

Daraselia, M., & Jojua, T. (2025). The importance of using movies in EFL classrooms. *Jurnal Pendidikan Guru Sekolah Dasar*, *2*(2), 1–7. DOI: 10.47134/pgsd.v2i2.1177

Darling-Hammond, L., & Bransford, J. (Eds.). (2007). *Preparing teachers for a changing world: What teachers should learn and be able to do*. John Wiley & Sons.

De la Vall, R. R. F., & Araya, F. G. (2023). Exploring the benefits and challenges of AI-language learning tools. *International Journal of Social Sciences and Humanities Invention*, *10*(01), 7569–7576. DOI: 10.18535/ijsshi/v10i01.02

Delahunty, J., Verenikina, I., & Jones, P. (2014). Socio-emotional connections: Identity, belonging and learning in online interactions. A literature review. *Technology, Pedagogy and Education*, *23*(2), 243–265. DOI: 10.1080/1475939X.2013.813405

Delorme Benites, A., & Lehr, C. (2022). Neural machine translation and language teaching: possible implications for the cefr. Bull. Suisse de Linguist. Appliquée 2021, 47–66. DOI: 10.21256/zhaw-24716

Dengiz, Y. (2023). *Innovative effects of artificial intelligence on teacher education* (774595) [Master's thesis, Muğla Sıtkı Koçman University]. Council of Higher Education Thesis Center.

Dergaa, I., Chamari, K., Zmijewski, P., & Ben Saad, H. (2023). From human writing to artificial intelligence generated text : Examining the prospects and potential threats of ChatGPT in academic writing. *Biology of Sport*, *40*(2), 615–622. DOI: 10.5114/biolsport.2023.125623 PMID: 37077800

Derwing, T. M. (2021). Pronunciation instruction and its impact on second language learners. *Journal of Second Language Pronunciation*, *7*(4), 377–390.

Dimitriadou, E., & Lanitis, A. (2023). A critical evaluation, challenges, and future perspectives of using artificial intelligence and emerging technologies in smart classrooms. *Smart Learning Environments*, *10*(1), 1–26. DOI: 10.1186/s40561-023-00231-3

Ding, A. C. E., Shi, L., Yang, H., & Choi, I. (2024). Enhancing teacher AI literacy and integration through different types of cases in teacher professional development. *Computers and Education Open*, *6*, 100178. DOI: 10.1016/j.caeo.2024.100178

Dizon, G., & Gayed, J. M. (2021). Examining the impact of Grammarly on the quality of mobile l2 writing. *The JALT CALL Journal*, *17*(2), 74–92. DOI: 10.29140/jaltcall.v17n2.336

Dizon, G., & Tang, D. (2020). Intelligent personal assistants for autonomous second language learning: An investigation of Alexa. *The JALT CALL Journal*, *16*(2), 107–120. DOI: 10.29140/jaltcall.v16n2.273

Doherty, S., & Kenny, D. (2014). The design and evaluation of a statistical machine translation syllabus for translation students. *The Interpreter and Translator Trainer*, *8*(2), 295–315. DOI: 10.1080/1750399X.2014.937571

Dong, D., Wu, H., He, W., Yu, D., & Wang, H. (2015). "Multi-task learning for multiple language translation," in Proceedings of the 53rd Annual Meeting of the Association for Computational Linguistics and the 7th International Joint Conference on Natural Language Processing (Volume 1: Long Papers) (Beijing), 1723–1732.

Dong, S., Wang, P., & Abbas, K. (2021). A survey on deep learning and its applications. *Computer Science Review*, *40*, 100379. DOI: 10.1016/j.cosrev.2021.100379

Dong, Y., Chiang, C., Truong, H., & Qiu, Y. (2021). Enhancing language learning through AI-driven inclusive design. *Journal of Educational Technology & Society*, *24*(2), 191–204.

Dong, Y., Hou, J., Zhang, N., & Zhang, M. (2020). Research on how human intelligence, consciousness, and cognitive computing affect the development of artificial intelligence. *Complexity*, *2020*(1), 1680845. DOI: 10.1155/2020/1680845

Dörnyei, Z., & Ushioda, E. (2011). *Teaching and Researching Motivation*. Pearson Education Limited.

Duff, P. A., & Uchida, Y. (1997). The negotiation of teachers' sociocultural identities and practices in postsecondary EFL classrooms. *TESOL Quarterly*, *31*(3), 451–486. DOI: 10.2307/3587834

DuFour, R., & Eaker, R. (Eds.). (2009). *On common ground: The power of professional learning communities*. Solution Tree Press.

Dupps, W. J. (2023). Artificial intelligence and academic publishing. *Journal of Cataract and Refractive Surgery*, *49*(7), 655–656. DOI: 10.1097/j.jcrs.0000000000001223 PMID: 37390321

Dusek, O., Gurevych, I., Riezler, S., & Arnold, T. (2020). What is the essence of a claim? Cross-domain claim identification. *Natural Language Engineering*, *26*(2), 191–211.

Dusmukhamedova, S., Rasulova, F., Shukurov, Y., Zukhra, Q., Matchanova, M., & Narkabilova, G. (2024, May). A Novel Based Design of AI kind of Models for Gami-Fication in Enhanced Learning type of Environment. In 2024 4th International Conference on Advance Computing and Innovative Technologies in Engineering (ICACITE) (pp. 584-588). IEEE. DOI: 10.1109/ICACITE60783.2024.10617373

Du, Y., & Gao, H. (2022). Determinants affecting teachers' adoption of aibased applications in efl context: An analysis of analytic hierarchy process. *Education and Information Technologies*, *27*(7), 9357–9384. DOI: 10.1007/s10639-022-11001-y

Ebadijalal, M., & Yousofi, N. (2023). The impact of mobile-assisted peer feedback on EFL learners' speaking performance and anxiety: Does language make a difference? *Language Learning Journal*, *51*(1), 112–130. DOI: 10.1080/09571736.2021.1957990

Ebadi, S., & Ebadijalal, M. (2020). The effect of google expeditions virtual reality on efl learners' willingness to communicate and oral proficiency. *Computer Assisted Language Learning*, *33*, 1–25. DOI: 10.1080/09588221.2020.1854311

Edmett, A., Ichaporia, N., Crompton, H., & Crichton, R. (2024). *Artificial intelligence and English language teaching. Preparing for the future*. https://www.teachingenglish .org.uk/sites/teacheng/files/2024-08/AI_and_ELT_Jul_2024.pdf

Edmett, A., Ichaporia, N., Crompton, H., Crichton, R. (2023). Artificial intelligence and English language teaching: Preparing for the future. British Council. URL: DOI: 10.57884/78EA-3C69

Edwards, L., Eales, F., & Oakes, S. (2023). Speak out 3rd Edition, Student's book and eBook with online practice, Pearson Education Limited, 176 p.

Ekanayake, K., Khatibi, A., & Azam, F. (2020). The impact of teacher education and English language education in fostering global citizenship education: A review of literature. *International Journal of Advances in Scientific Research and Engineering*, *6*(7), 30–40. DOI: 10.31695/IJASRE.2020.33847

Eldot, S. G. (2023). *English as a second language teachers' lived experience of transitioning from remote learning to the traditional classroom setting: A phenomenological study* (4743). [Doctoral dissertation, Libery Univesity].

El-Garawany, M. S. M. (2021). Using Praat to develop English majors' EFL intonation production. Educational Journal of the Faculty of Education. *Sohag University*, *92*(92), 91–125. DOI: 10.21608/edusohag.2021.208708

Ellikkal, A., & Rajamohan, S. (2024). *AI-enabled personalized learning: empowering management students for improving engagement and academic performance.* Vilakshan-XIMB Journal of Management.

El, M. (2023). UNVEILING THE DYNAMIC POWER OF GAMIFICATION IN STUDENT LEARNING THROUGH NOVEL CONCEPTUAL AND THEORETICAL FRAMEWORKS. Journal of Studies in Language [JSLCS]. *Cultura e Scuola*, *6*(2), 1–19.

Elsayed, M., Al-Khalili, M., & Al-Maqbali, K. (2021). The transfer of intonation patterns from Omani Arabic to English. *International Journal of Linguistics*, *13*(2), 71–89.

Engel, F., Keary, A., Berwind, K., Bornschlegl, M. X., & Hemmje, M. (2017). "The role of reproducibility in affective computing," in *2017 IEEE International Conference on Bioinformatics and Biomedicine (BIBM)* (Kansas City, MO: IEEE), 2008–2014. DOI: 10.1109/BIBM.2017.8217969

Erin, J. (2025). *Opportunities and challenges for plurilingual and intercultural education in times of AI* [Webinar]. European Centre for Modern Languages of the Council of Europe. https://www.youtube.com/live/byO8nno1jmk

Eslit, E. R. (2023). Voices of resiliency: exploring the transformative journey of educators and students in the post-pandemic education era. *Preprints*. DOI: 10.20944/preprints202305.1514.v1

Etri, W. (2022). Intercultural sensitivity and its effects on ELT curricula–Teacher insights. *Higher Education Evaluation and Development*, *16*(1), 32–46. DOI: 10.1108/HEED-03-2021-0027

European Commission. (2012). *Multilingualism: An Asset for Europe and a Shared Commitment*. European Commission.

Fahlevi, R., & Bako, E. N. (2022). Characteristics and moral values from "Encanto" Disney as an enhancing strategy in character building. [English Language Teaching Prima Journal]. *ELT*, *4*(2), 147–160. DOI: 10.34012/elt.v%25vi%25i.3461

Fakhar, H., Lamrabet, M., Echantoufi, N., & Ajana, L. (2024). Towards a new artificial intelligence-based framework for teachers' online continuous professional development programs: Systematic Review. *International Journal of Advanced Computer Science and Applications*, *15*(4). Advance online publication. DOI: 10.14569/IJACSA.2024.0150450

Fakher Ajabshir, Z. (2023). A review of the affordances and challenges of artificial intelligence technologies in second language learning. *Technology Assisted Language Education*, *1*(4), 92–111.

Farrell, T. (2013). *Reflective practice in ESL teacher development groups: From practices to principles*. Springer. DOI: 10.1057/9781137317193

Farrell, T. S. (2022). *Reflective practice in language teaching*. Cambridge University Press. DOI: 10.1017/9781009028783

Félix-Brasdefer, J. C., & Koike, D. A. (2012). *Pragmatic variation in service encounters and behind the scenes: A cross-cultural study of interactions in Spanish and English*. Routledge.

Feng, J., & Zhang, L. (2024). An assessment of different Praat versions for acoustic measures. *Journal of Voice*, *38*(3), 432.e1–432.e9. DOI: 10.1016/j.jvoice.2023.07.004

Ferikoğlu, D. (2021). *An artificial intelligence awareness level scale for teachers: A reliability and validity study* (684964) [Master's thesis, Bahçeşehir University]. Council of Higher Education Thesis Center.

Ferrara, E. (2024). The butterfly effect in artificial intelligence systems: Implications for AI bias and fairness. *Machine Learning with Applications*, *15*, 100525. DOI: 10.1016/j.mlwa.2024.100525

Finley, A. M. (2018). Fostering success: Belongingness pedagogy for English language learners. *BC TEAL Journal*, *3*(1), 37–48.

Firmansyah, F. H., & Rosmansyah, Y. (2024). Exploring Collaboration in Multiplayer Gamification: A Systematic Literature Review. *IEEE Access : Practical Innovations, Open Solutions*.

Fleming, N. D., & Mills, C. (1992). Not another inventory, rather a catalyst for reflection. *To Improve the Academy*, *11*(1), 137–155. DOI: 10.1002/j.2334-4822.1992.tb00213.x

Fokides, E., & Peristeraki, E. (2024). Comparing ChatGPT's correction and feedback comments with that of educators in the context of primary students' short essays written in English and Greek. *Education and Information Technologies*, •••, 1–45. DOI: 10.1007/s10639-024-12912-8

Foster, A., Khazanchi, P., & Khazanchi, R. (2024). MagicSchool.ai: A Personal Assistant. In J. Cohen & G. Solano (Eds.), *Proceedings of Society for Information Technology & Teacher Education International Conference* (pp. 74-80). Association for the Advancement of Computing in Education (AACE).

Freeman, T. M., Anderman, L. H., & Jensen, J. M. (2007). Sense of belonging in college freshmen at the classroom and campus levels. *75*(3), 203-220. DOI: 10.3200/JEXE.75.3.203-220

Freiermuth, M. R., & Huang, H. C. (2021). Zooming across cultures: Can a telecollaborative video exchange between language learning partners further the development of intercultural competences? *Foreign Language Annals*, *54*(1), 185–206. DOI: 10.1111/flan.12504

Fryer, L. K., Bovee, H. N., & Hennessy, S. (2022). The role of chatbots in language learning. *International Journal of Educational Technology in Higher Education*, *19*(1), 1–13. PMID: 35013716

Furrer, C., & Skinner, E. (2003). Sense of relatedness as a factor in children's academic engagement and performance. *Journal of Educational Psychology*, *95*(1), 148–162. DOI: 10.1037/0022-0663.95.1.148

Fu, Y., Zhang, Z., & Yang, H. (2023). Design of Oral English Teaching Assistant System based on deep belief networks. *Soft Computing*, *27*(22), 17403–17418.

Gamlath, S. (2022). Peer learning and the undergraduate journey: A framework for student success. *Higher Education Research & Development*, *41*(3), 699–713. DOI: 10.1080/07294360.2021.1877625

Gao, J. (2021). Exploring the feedback quality of an automated writing evaluation system pigai. *International Journal of Emerging Technologies in Learning*, *16*(11), 322–330. DOI: 10.3991/ijet.v16i11.19657

García-Peñalvo, F. J., Corell, A., Abella-García, V., Grande, M., & Morales, E. (2020). Artificial intelligence in the classroom: A scoping review of AI-driven language learning tools. *Journal of Educational Technology & Society*, *23*(3), 161–175.

Gass, S. M., & Selinker, L. (2008). *Second language acquisition: An introductory course* (3rd ed.). Routledge. DOI: 10.4324/9780203932841

Gessinger, I., Seaborn, K., Steeds, M., Doyle, P., & Cowan, B. R. (2023, June 28). ChatGPT and me: Is ChatGPT perceived as a communication partner? https://doi.org/DOI: 10.17605/OSF.IO/R7P2A

Ghafouri, M. (2024). ChatGPT: The catalyst for teacher-student rapport and grit development in L2 class. *System*, *120*, 1–11. DOI: 10.1016/j.system.2023.103209

Gholami, K., Faraji, S., Meijer, P. C., & Tirri, K. (2021). Construction and deconstruction of student teachers' professional identity: A narrative study. *Teaching and Teacher Education*, *97*, 103142. DOI: 10.1016/j.tate.2020.103142

Ghosh, S. S. (2024). Assessing the Efficacy of Intelligent Tutoring Systems in Language Teacher Education: A Quantitative Study. *Computers in the Schools*, •••, 1–24. DOI: 10.1080/07380569.2024.2435308

Gillen-O'Neel, C. (2021). Sense of belonging and student engagement: A daily study of first- and continuing-generation college students. *Research in Higher Education*, *62*(1), 45–71. DOI: 10.1007/s11162-019-09570-y

Glasswell, K., & Ryan, J. (2017). Reflective practice in teacher professional standards: Reflection as mandatory practice. *Reflective Theory and Practice in Teacher Education*, 3-26.

Godde, D., Bosses, M., & Bailly, G. (2020). The role of prosody in the comprehension of spoken language. *Language and Speech*, *63*(2), 231–250.

Godwin-Jones, R. (2015). Contributing, creating, curating: Digital literacies for language learners. *Language Learning & Technology*, *19*, 8–20.

Goksel, N., & Bozkurt, A. (2019). Artificial intelligence in education: Current insights and future perspectives. In *Handbook of Research on Learning in the Age of Transhumanism* (pp. 224–236). IGI Global. DOI: 10.4018/978-1-5225-8431-5.ch014

Goodfellow, I., Bengio, Y., & Courville, A. (2016). *Deep learning*. The MIT Press.

Greipl, S., Moeller, K., & Ninaus, M. (2020). Potential and limits of game-based learning. *International Journal of Technology Enhanced Learning*, *12*(4), 363–389. DOI: 10.1504/IJTEL.2020.110047

Griffiths, D., & Goddard, T. (2015). An explanatory framework for understanding teachers' resistance to adopting educational technology. *Kybernetes*, *44*(8/9), 1240–1250. DOI: 10.1108/K-11-2014-0274

Groves, M., & Mundt, K. (2015). Friend or foe? google translate in language for academic purposes. *English for Specific Purposes*, *37*, 112–121. DOI: 10.1016/j.esp.2014.09.001

Guan, C., Mou, J., & Jiang, Z. (2020). Artificial intelligence innovation in education: A twenty-year data-driven historical analysis. *Int. J. Innovat. Stud.*, *4*(4), 134–147. DOI: 10.1016/j.ijis.2020.09.001

Guan, J. Q., Ying, S. F., Zhang, M. L., & Hwang, G. J. (2024). From experience to empathy: An empathetic VR-based learning approach to improving EFL learners' empathy and writing performance. *Computers & Education*, *220*, 105120. DOI: 10.1016/j.compedu.2024.105120

Gu, J., Wang, Z., Kuen, J., Ma, L., Shahroudy, A., Shuai, B., Liu, T., Wang, X., Wang, G., Cai, J., & Chen, T. (2018). Recent advances in convolutional neural networks. *Pattern Recognition*, *77*, 354–377. DOI: 10.1016/j.patcog.2017.10.013

Guo, K., Wang, J., & Chu, S. K. W. (2022). Using chatbots to scaffold efl students argumentative writing. *Assessing Writing*, *54*, 100666. DOI: 10.1016/j.asw.2022.100666

Guo, K., Zhong, Y., Qin, J., & Chu, S. K. W. (2025). Investigating EFL teachers' lesson planning for chatbot-assisted learning of argumentative writing: A TPACK perspective. *Interactive Learning Environments*, *33*(2), 1520–1541.

Guo, Y., & Wang, Y. (2025). Exploring the Effects of Artificial Intelligence Application on EFL Students' Academic Engagement and Emotional Experiences: A mixed-methods study. *European Journal of Education*, *60*(1), e12812. DOI: 10.1111/ejed.12812

Gupta, M., & Singh, A. (2023). Emerging trends in artificial intelligence education: Advancements, opportunities, and impact on educational technology. *Quanta Research*, *1*(1), 20–26.

Gupta, Y., Saini, A., & Saxena, A. K. (2013). A review on important aspects of information retrieval. *International. Journal of Computing and Information Science in Engineering*, *7*(12), 940–948.

Gutiérrez-Colón, M., Pérez-Moreno, J. A., Moreno-Ger, P., & Martínez-Ortiz, I. (2020). Addressing language diversity in AI-driven language learning platforms: Challenges and opportunities. *Computer Assisted Language Learning*, *33*(7), 813–833.

Hakulinen, L., Auvinen, T., & Bauters, M. (2019). Predicting language learning outcomes with neural networks: An exploratory study. *Journal of Computer Assisted Learning*, *35*(5), 623–632.

Hambarde, K. A., & Proenca, H. (2023). Information Retrieval : Recent Advances and Beyond. *IEEE Access : Practical Innovations, Open Solutions, 11*, 76581–76604. DOI: 10.1109/ACCESS.2023.3295776

Hanyi, X., Wensheng, G., Zhenlian, Q., Jiayang, W., & Philip, S. Y. (2023). Large language models for education: A survey. *arXiv preprint arXiv:2302.12345*. https://arxiv.org/abs/2302.12345

Hardaker, G., & Glenn, L. E. (2025). Artificial intelligence for personalized learning: A systematic literature review. *The International Journal of Information and Learning Technology, 42*(1), 1–14. DOI: 10.1108/IJILT-07-2024-0160

Haristiani, N. (2019). Artificial intelligence (ai) chatbot as language learning medium: An inquiry. *Journal of Physics: Conference Series, 1387*(1), 012020. DOI: 10.1088/1742-6596/1387/1/012020

Harrison, K., & Vass, R. (2022). Stress patterns in English: Acoustic analysis and its impact on prosody. *Journal of Phonetic Research, 35*(3), 212–224.

Harry, A. (2023). Role of AI in Education. [INJURITY]. *Interdiciplinary Journal and Hummanity, 2*(3), 260–268.

Hasan, M. A., Noor, N. F. M., Rahman, S. S. B. A., & Rahman, M. M. (2020). The transition from intelligent to affective tutoring system: A review and open issues. *IEEE Access : Practical Innovations, Open Solutions, 8*, 204612–204638. DOI: 10.1109/ACCESS.2020.3036990

Hastuti, F. D., Linda, L., Olyvia, O., & Tomy, T. (2022). The effects of family values in overcoming conflicts in the "Coco" film. *BLESS, 2*(2), 58–69.

Hayat, A. (2025). Language classroom management: Underprivileges of ChatGPT. *Journal of Management World, 2025*(1), 159–165. DOI: 10.53935/jomw.v2024i4.632

Hayes, A. F. (2022). *PROCESS macro for SPSS, SAS, and R* (Version 4.2) [Computer software]. http://www.processmacro.org

Hayes, A. F. (2022). *Introduction to mediation, moderation, and conditional process analysis: A regression-based approach* (3rd ed.). Guilford Press.

Heffernan, N., & Heffernan, C. (2014). The ASSISTments ecosystem: Building a platform that brings scientists and teachers together for minimally invasive research on human learning and teaching. *International Journal of Artificial Intelligence in Education, 24*(4), 470–497. DOI: 10.1007/s40593-014-0024-x

Heift, T., & Schulze, M. (2007). *Error Detection and Correction in CALL: A Comprehensive Guide*. John Benjamins Publishing.

Higgins, J., Xiao, Z., & Nunan, D. (2012). *The Cambridge Guide to Pedagogy and Practice in Second Language Teaching*. Cambridge University Press.

Hinojo-Lucena, F.-J., Aznar-Díaz, I., Cáceres-Reche, M.-P., & Romero-Rodríguez, J.-M. (2019). Artificial intelligence in higher education: A bibliometric study on its impact in the scientific literature. *Education Sciences*, *9*(1), 51. DOI: 10.3390/educsci9010051

Hochstein, A., & Green, J. (2018). Using AI to improve language learning. Memrise Blog. https://blog.memrise. com/using-ai-to-improve-language-learning/

Hodges, C. B., Moore, S., Lockee, B. B., Trust, T., & Bond, M. A. (2020). *The difference between emergency remote teaching and online learning*. Educause.

Holes, C. (2004). *Arabic dialectology: A guide to the study of the regional varieties of Arabic*. Routledge.

Holmes, W., & Tuomi, I. (2022). State of the Art and Practice in AI in Education. *European Journal of Education*, 57(4), 542–570. URL: DOI: 10.1111/ejed.12533

Holmes, W., Bialik, M., & Fadel, C. (2021). *Artificial Intelligence in Education: Promises and Implications for Teaching and Learning*. Center for Curriculum Redesign.

Holmes, W., Bialik, M., & Fadel, C. (2022). *Artificial intelligence in education: Promises and implications for teaching and learning* (2nd ed.). Center for Curriculum Redesign.

Holstein, K., Gómez, P., & Lee, M. J. (2020). AI in education: Ethical considerations for equitable access and participation. *British Journal of Educational Technology*, *51*(4), 1354–1369.

Holstein, K., McLaren, B. M., & Aleven, V. (2017). "Spacle: investigating learning across virtual and physical spaces using spatial replays," in *Proceedings of the Seventh International Learning Analytics and Knowledge Conference* (Vancouver, CA), 358–367. DOI: 10.1145/3027385.3027450

Hoofnagle, C. J., Van Der Sloot, B., & Borgesius, F. Z. (2019). The European Union general data protection regulation: What it is and what it means. *Information & Communications Technology Law*, *28*(1), 65–98. DOI: 10.1080/13600834.2019.1573501

Hopcan, S., Türkmen, G., & Polat, E. (2024). Exploring the artificial intelligence anxiety and machine learning attitudes of teacher candidates. *Education and Information Technologies*, *29*(6), 7281–7301. DOI: 10.1007/s10639-023-12086-9

Hord, S. M. (1997). *Professional learning communities: Communities of continuous inquiry and improvement*. SEDL.

Hosseini, M., Resnik, D. B., & Holmes, K. (2023). The ethics of disclosing the use of artificial intelligence tools in writing scholarly manuscripts. *Research Ethics*, *19*(4), 449–465. DOI: 10.1177/17470161231180449 PMID: 39749232

Howard, S. K. (2013). Risk-aversion: Understanding teachers' resistance to technology integration. *Technology, Pedagogy and Education*, *22*(3), 357–372. DOI: 10.1080/1475939X.2013.802995

Huang, Y., Al-Rfou, R., Pottier, L., & Adams, K. (2015). Natural language processing with small feed-forward networks. Association for Computational Linguistics. https://www.aclweb.org/anthology/D15-1266.pdf

Huang, L., Al-Rashidi, A. H., & Bayat, S. (2024). Teacher support in language learning: A picture of the effects on language progress, academic immunity, and academic enjoyment. *BMC Psychology*, *12*(1), 1–8. DOI: 10.1186/s40359-024-01602-2 PMID: 38439089

Huang, S. (2019). Using computer-assisted language learning (CALL) for teaching pronunciation. *Language Teaching Research*, *23*(5), 12–31.

Huang, X., Zou, D., Cheng, G., Chen, X., & Xie, H. (2023). Trends, research issues and applications of artificial intelligence in language education. *Journal of Educational Technology & Society*, *26*(1), 112–131.

Huang, Y. (2023). Examining the relationship between peer support and foreign language emotions in online learning: The mediating effect of self-efficacy. *Frontiers in Psychology*, *14*, 1–11. DOI: 10.3389/fpsyg.2023.1148472 PMID: 37842693

Huda, M. (2019). Empowering application strategy in the technology adoption: Insights from professional and ethical engagement. *Journal of Science and Technology Policy Management*, *10*(1), 172–192. DOI: 10.1108/JSTPM-09-2017-0044

Hughes, S. (2023). Why AI makes traditional education models obsolete – and what to do about it. *World Economic Forum*. URL: https://www.weforum.org/stories/2023/09/higher-education-model-for-ai/

Hussain, T., Shah, D., & Zhang, X. (2021). Chatbots in language education: A comprehensive review. *Journal of Language Learning and Technology*, *25*(1), 45–63.

Hu, Z., & McGrath, I. (2012). Integrating ICT into college English: An implementation study of a national reform. *Education and Information Technologies*, *17*(2), 147–165. DOI: 10.1007/s10639-011-9153-0

Hwang, Y., Lee, J. H., & Shin, D. (2023). What is prompt literacy? An exploratory study of language learners' development of new literacy skill using generative AI. *arXiv preprint arXiv:2311.05373.*

Hwang, G. J., Xie, H., Wah, B. W., & Gašević, D. (2020). Vision, challenges, roles and research issues of Artificial Intelligence in Education. *Computers and Education: Artificial Intelligence, 1*, 100001. DOI: 10.1016/j.caeai.2020.100001

Hwang, S. I., Lim, J. S., Lee, R. W., Matsui, Y., Iguchi, T., Hiraki, T., & Ahn, H. (2023). Is ChatGPT a "Fire of Prometheus" for Non-Native English-Speaking Researchers in Academic Writing? *Korean Journal of Radiology, 24*(10), 952. DOI: 10.3348/kjr.2023.0773 PMID: 37793668

Idris, N. (2014). Using non-native English films to promote multiculturalism in ELT classroom. *Journal of NELTA, 19*(1-2), 65–76. DOI: 10.3126/nelta.v19i1-2.12081

IEEE. (2023). *Ethically aligned design: A vision for prioritizing human well-being with autonomous and intelligent systems* (2nd ed.). IEEE Standards Association. https://standards.ieee.org/industry-connections/ec/autonomous-systems/

Inomjonov, A. (2024). IMPACT OF GLOBALIZATION IN ELT. University Research Base, 134-139.

Ishihara, N., & Tarone, E. (2009). Pragmatics and language learning. In Ellis, N. C., & Larsen-Freeman, D. (Eds.), *Language as a complex adaptive system* (pp. 307–324). Wiley-Blackwell.

Iswandari, Y. A., & Ardi, P. (2022). Intercultural Communicative Competence in EFL Setting: A Systematic Review. *Reflections: The SoL Journal, 29*(2), 361–380. DOI: 10.61508/refl.v29i2.260249

Jabbari, N., & Eslami, Z. R. (2019). Second language learning in the context of massively multiplayer online games: A scoping review. *ReCALL, 31*(1), 92–113. DOI: 10.1017/S0958344018000058

Jacobs, G. M. (2004). *Cooperative learning: Theory, principles, and techniques* [Paper presentation/Online Submission]. *The International Online Conference on Second and Foreign Language Teaching and Research, Online.*

Jahanbin, P. (2025). Modeling L1 influence on L2 pronunciation: An MFCC-based framework for explainable machine learning and pedagogical feedback. *arXiv*.https://arxiv.org/abs/2504.13765

Jameer, M. R., & Narra, P. L. (2024). Augmenting EFL/ESL education: The outcome of technology on contemporary language learning. *Educational Administration: Theory and Practice*, *30*(5), 2196–2202.

Jaques, Z. (2021). Intergenerational dialogue in Disney-Pixar animation. In Deszcz-Tryhubczak, J., & Jaques, Z. (Eds.), *Intergenerational solidarity in children's literature and film* (pp. 85–100). University Press of Mississippi.

Jegede, O. O. (2021). Mobile-Assisted Language Learning and Online Cooperative Language Learning: Merits and Demerits. A. A. Robbin, O. B. Jolaoso & O. B. Bakare (Eds.) Management of Education for Sustainable Development in a Changing World: A Festschrift in Honour of Professor Afolakemi Olasumbo Oredein, pp. 55-58. Ibadan: College Press

Jegede, O. O. (2024). Artificial Intelligence and English Language Learning: Exploring the Roles of AI-Driven Tools in Personalizing Learning and Providing Instant Feedback. Universal Library of Languages and Literatures, 1(2).

Jegede, O. O., & Adesina, O. (2022). Digitising English Language Teaching and Learning for e-Generation Students in Nigeria. B. A. Adeyemi, P. O. Yara & M. D. Oyetade (Eds.) (2022). Pastoral Psychology in Education for Sustainable Development: A Book of Readings in Honour of Professor Donald Abidemi Odeleye (pp. 204212). Ibadan: College Press.

Jeon, J. (2024). Exploring AI chatbot affordances in the EFL classroom: Young learners' experiences and perspectives. *Computer Assisted Language Learning*, *37*(1-2), 1–26. DOI: 10.1080/09588221.2021.2021241

Jiang, R. (2022). How does artificial intelligence empower EFL teaching and learning nowadays? A review on artificial intelligence in the EFL context. *Frontiers in Psychology*, *13*, 1049401. DOI: 10.3389/fpsyg.2022.1049401 PMID: 36467167

Jiang, X., Peters, R., Plonsky, L., & Pajak, B. (2024). *The Effectiveness of Duolingo English Courses in Developing Reading and Listening Proficiency. CALICO, 2024.* URL., DOI: 10.1558/cj.26704

Job, M. A. (2021). Automating and Optimizing Software Testing using Artificial Intelligence Techniques. *International Journal of Advanced Computer Science and Applications*, *12*(5). Advance online publication. DOI: 10.14569/IJACSA.2021.0120571

John, D., Hussin, N., Zaini, M. K., Ametefe, D. S., Aliu, A. A., & Caliskan, A. (2023). Gamification equilibrium: the fulcrum for balanced intrinsic motivation and extrinsic rewards in learning systems: immersive gamification in Muhamad Khairulnizam Zaini Learning system. *International Journal of Serious Games, 10*(3), 83–116. DOI: 10.17083/ijsg.v10i3.633

Johnson, K. E. (2009). *Second language teacher education: A sociocultural perspective*. Routledge. DOI: 10.4324/9780203878033

Johnson, K. E. (2016). Language teacher education. In *The Routledge handbook of English language teaching* (pp. 121–134). Routledge. DOI: 10.4324/9781315676203-12

Johnson, K. E., & Golombek, P. R. (2016). *Mindful L2 teacher education: A sociocultural perspective on cultivating teachers' professional development*. Routledge. DOI: 10.4324/9781315641447

Johnson, M., McCarty, T., & Wilson, D. (2019). Ethical implications of AI in education: The challenges of privacy, data security, and human interaction. *Journal of Educational Technology & Society, 22*(3), 78–88. DOI: 10.1007/s11528-019-00353-9

John, T., & Davies, F. (1983). Text as a vehicle for information: The classroom use of written texts in teaching reading in a foreign language. *Reading in a Foreign Language, 1*(1), 1–19.

Jones, A., Smith, B., & Johnson, C. (2018). The impact of AI-driven language learning tools on student motivation and engagement. *Computers & Education, 125*, 247–256.

Jones, K. S. (1999). Information retrieval and artificial intelligence. *Artificial Intelligence, 114*(1-2), 257–281. DOI: 10.1016/S0004-3702(99)00075-2

Kadlubar, A. (2024, February 26). *Making The Grade: How Central Texas public schools are using artificial intelligence chat bots in the classroom*. https://www.kwtx.com/2024/02/26/making-grade-how-central-texas-public-schools-are-using-artificial-intelligence-chat-bots-classroom/

Kalantzis, M., & Cope, B. (2025). Literacy in the time of Artificial Intelligence. *Reading Research Quarterly, 60*(1), e591. DOI: 10.1002/rrq.591

Kang, H., & Chen, H. (2024). Effects of teachers' rapport-building strategies on EFL learners' cognitive load and computer-assisted language learning motivation. *Education and Information Technologies*, •••, 1–42. DOI: 10.1007/s10639-024-12961-z

Kanu, I. A. (2020). The philosophy of language and code-switching: A Nigerian perspective. *Journal of African Languages and Linguistics, 41*(2), 123–140. DOI: 10.1515/jall-2020-0006

Karakaya, K., & Bozkurt, A. (2022). Mobile-assisted language learning (MALL) research trends and patterns through bibliometric analysis: Empowering language learners through ubiquitous educational technologies. *System, 110*, 102925. DOI: 10.1016/j.system.2022.102925

Karatay, Y., & Karatay, L. (2024). Automated writing evaluation use in second language classrooms: A research synthesis. *System, 123*, 103332. DOI: 10.1016/j.system.2024.103332

Karras, I. (2021). Raising intercultural awareness in teaching young learners in EFL classes. *Research Papers in Language Teaching and Learning, 11*(1), 173–184.

Karras, I. D. (2020). *The culture and communication interface*. Diavlos Publishing.

Kartal, G. (2023). From digital literacy to AI literacy in language teaching: Embracing the artificial intelligence age. In Kartal, G. (Ed.), *Transforming the language teaching experience in the age of AI* (pp. 125–140). IGI Global., DOI: 10.4018/978-1-6684-9893-4.ch008

Kartikasari, Y. D. N., Retnaningdyah, P., & Musthofa, A. (2019). Using film in fostering intercultural awareness for high school students in the Efl classroom. *Jurnal Education and Development, 7*(2), 58–58. DOI: 10.37081/ed.v7i2.871

Kayabaş, İ. (2010). Usabilty of artificial intelligent conversational agents as student support service in distance education (263179) [Master's thesis, Anadolu University]. Council of Higher Education Thesis Center.

Kayyali, M. (2021). Positive impact of high technology on higher education.

Kayyali, M. (2024). Future possibilities and challenges of AI in education. In *Transforming education with generative AI: Prompt engineering and synthetic content creation* (pp. 118–137). IGI Global. DOI: 10.4018/979-8-3693-1351-0.ch006

Kazu, I. Y., & Kuvvetli, M. (2023). The influence of pronunciation education via artificial intelligence technology on vocabulary acquisition in learning English. *International Journal of Psychology and Educational Studies, 10*(2), 480–493. DOI: 10.52380/ijpes.2023.10.2.1044

Keegan, S. (2019). Busuu language app: Full review and tips for using. The Mimic Method. https://www. mimicmethod.com/busuu-language-app-review/

Kern, R. (2021). Digital language learning: A research agenda. *Modern Language Journal, 105*(3), 612–628.

Kerridge, S. (2023). Embracing the potential of AI in education: Moving beyond fear and resistance. *Metaphor*, (3), 24-26. https://search.informit.org/doi/10.3316/informit.275737987896285

Kessler, G. (2021). AI and pragmatics: Bridging the gap between form and function in second language learning. *Pragmatics & Language Learning, 13*(1), 115–128. DOI: 10.2307/41599193

Kessler, G. (2021). The role of artificial intelligence in language learning. *Journal of Language and Linguistic Studies, 17*(2), 327–345. DOI: 10.52462/jlls.2021.008

Khalifa, M., & Albadawy, M. (2024). Using artificial intelligence in academic writing and research: An essential productivity tool. *Computer Methods and Programs in Biomedicine Update, 100145*, 100145. Advance online publication. DOI: 10.1016/j.cmpbup.2024.100145

Khiem, H. G., Huong, H. L., Triet, M. N., Khanh, H. V., Phuc, N. T., Khoa, T. D., . . . Quy, T. L. (2023, November). Generative AI in English education: Harnessing ChatGPT for digital learning. In International Symposium on Emerging Technologies for Education (pp. 147-157). Singapore: Springer Nature Singapore.

Khotbi, T., Belbouah, A., & Bouguerba, T. (2023). Navigating multicultural curriculum reform: EFL Teachers' use of movie-based cultural content. *British Journal of Teacher Education and Pedagogy, 2*(3), 01-08. https://doi.org/DOI: 10.32996/bjtep.2023.2.3.1

Kim, H., Quinn, K., & Petscher, Y. (2020). The role of prosody in the language learning process. *Applied Linguistics Review, 32*(1), 105–122.

Kim, J. (2024). Leading teachers' perspective on teacher-AI collaboration in education. *Education and Information Technologies, 29*(7), 8693–8724. DOI: 10.1007/s10639-023-12109-5

Kim, J., Park, S., & Lee, H. (2020). An experimental study on the effectiveness of AI-driven feedback in language learning. *Language Learning & Technology, 24*(1), 120–136.

Kim, N. Y. (2022). AI-Integrated Mobile-Assisted Language Learning: Is It an Effective Way of Preparing for the TOEIC Test in Classroom Environments? *English Teaching, 77*(3), 79–102.

Kirby, L. A. J., & Thomas, C. L. (2022). High-impact teaching practices foster a greater sense of belonging in the college classroom. *Journal of Further and Higher Education, 46*(3), 368–381. DOI: 10.1080/0309877X.2021.1950659

Kizilcec, R. F. (2024). To advance AI use in education, focus on understanding educators. *International Journal of Artificial Intelligence in Education, 34*(1), 12–19. DOI: 10.1007/s40593-023-00351-4 PMID: 37359103

Klimova, B., Pikhart, M., Benites, A. D., Lehr, C., & Sanchez-Stockhammer, C. (2023). Neural machine translation in foreign language teaching and learning: A systematic review. *Education and Information Technologies, 28*(1), 663–682. DOI: 10.1007/s10639-022-11194-2

Koç, F. Ş., & Savaş, P. (2024). The use of artificially intelligent chatbots in English language learning: A systematic meta-synthesis study of articles published between 2010 and 2024. *ReCALL.*

Kong, S. C. (2018). Integration of learner interests and multimedia materials in language learning: A crosscultural study of Hong Kong and Korean learners. *Computer Assisted Language Learning, 31*(3), 264–287.

Korell, T. (2020). How Babbel is using AI to personalize language learning. Medium. https://medium.com/ babbel-engineering/how-babbel-is-using-ai-topersonalize-language-learning-7981b0d7c48f

Kormos, J. (2022). The importance of intonation and stress in second language speech. *Language Learning Journal, 44*(3), 312–328.

Kovari, A. (2025). A systematic review of AI-powered collaborative learning in higher education: Trends and outcomes from the last decade. *Social Sciences & Humanities Open, 11*, 101335. DOI: 10.1016/j.ssaho.2025.101335

Kozlowski, R., Nascimento, L., & McMullen, L. (2021). Understanding sarcasm and irony: AI in second language acquisition. *Journal of Applied Linguistics and Language Research, 8*(2), 33–47. DOI: 10.5861/jallr.2021.1001

Krashen, S. D. (1982). *Principles and Practice in Second Language Acquisition.* Pergamon Press.

Krishnan, R., & Zaini, M. (2025). Large language models in EFL classrooms: Opportunities and overreliance. [Add DOI if available]. *Journal of AI and Education, 12*(1), 33–52.

Kristiawan, D., Bashar, K., & Pradana, D. A. (2024). Artificial intelligence in English language learning: A systematic review of ai tools, applications, and pedagogical outcomes. [TATEFL]. *The Art of Teaching English as a Foreign Language*, *5*(2), 207–218. DOI: 10.36663/tatefl.v5i2.912

Kuhn, M., & Schwanenflugel, P. (2019). Prosody and reading comprehension: The importance of rhythm and intonation. *Reading Research Quarterly*, *54*(1), 41–56.

Kuhn, T., & Atkinson, R. (2020). Pragmatics in AI-driven feedback: Current practices and limitations. *Computers & Education*, *149*, 103790. DOI: 10.1016/j.compedu.2020.103790

Kukulska-Hulme, A. (2021). Mobile language learning: What we know and what we need to know. *Language Learning & Technology*, *25*(2), 5–18.

Kukulska-Hulme, A., & Lee, H. (2020). Intelligent assistants in language learning: Analysis of features and limitations. *CALL for Widening Participation: Short Papers from EUROCALL*, *1*(1), 172–176. DOI: 10.14705/rpnet.2020.48.1184

Kukulska-Hulme, A., Lee, H., & Norris, L. (2020). Machine feedback in EFL writing: Teacher perceptions and learner challenges. *Language Learning & Technology*, *24*(3), 15–34. https://www.lltjournal.org/item/3102

Kukulska-Hulme, A., Lee, H., & Norris, L. (2021). *Mobile Learning Revolution: Implications for Language Pedagogy*. Cambridge University Press.

Kumaravadivelu, B. (1994). The postmethod condition: (E)merging strategies for second/foreign language teaching. *TESOL Quarterly*, *28*(1), 27. DOI: 10.2307/3587197

Kuo, Y. C., Lee, J. M., & Wu, Y. S. (2022). The impact of a chatbot on English conversation skills. *Journal of Computer Assisted Learning*, *38*(1), 1–14.

Kusmawan, U. (2023). Redefining teacher training: The promise of AI-supported teaching practices. *Journal of Advances in Education and Philosophy*, *7*(9), 332–335. DOI: 10.36348/jaep.2023.v07i09.001

Labadie, C., & Legner, C. (2023). Building data management capabilities to address data protection regulations: Learnings from EU-GDPR. *Journal of Information Technology*, *38*(1), 16–44. DOI: 10.1177/02683962221141456

Ladefoged, P. (2006). *A course in phonetics* (5th ed.). Wadsworth.

Lai, C., Chen, Q., Wang, Y., & Qi, X. (2024). Individual interest, self-regulation, and self-directed language learning with technology beyond the classroom. *British Journal of Educational Technology*, *55*(1), 379–397. DOI: 10.1111/bjet.13366

Lalengmawia, R., & Shukla, A. (2017). Theoretical Perspectives of Research Output based on Literature Review. *Library Waves, 3*(2), 108–118. Retrieved from https://www.librarywaves.com/index.php/lw/article/view/57

Lambert, J. (2024). Why writing by hand beats typing for thinking and learning. URL: npr.org

Lan, Y. J. (2020). Immersion, interaction, and experience-oriented learning: AI-enhanced virtual reality for EFL students. *ReCALL, 32*(1), 71–87. DOI: 10.1017/S0958344019000209

Larina, T.. (2021). The impact of L1 language on L2 prosody. *Journal of Second Language Acquisition, 23*(2), 54–69.

Lave, J., & Wenger, E. (1991). *Situated learning: Legitimate peripheral participation.* Cambridge University Press. DOI: 10.1017/CBO9780511815355

Layali, K., & Al-Shlowiy, A. (2020). Students perceptions of e-learning for esl/efl in saudi universities at time of coronavirus: A literature review. *Indonesian EFL J., 6*(2), 97–108. DOI: 10.25134/ieflj.v6i2.3378

Leech, G. N. (1983). *Principles of pragmatics.* Longman.

Lee, H., & Park, S. (2020). AI-powered language learning: Investigating the impact of an AI-based writing tool on second language learners' accuracy. *Language Learning & Technology, 24*(3), 90–107. DOI: 10.1016/j.jacad.2020.04.004

Lee, J., & Lee, S. (2021). Exploring the role of adaptive learning systems in AI-mediated language education. *Computer Assisted Language Learning, 34*(5), 524–538.

Lee, K. R., & Reinders, H. (2020). *Language learning with technology: Ideas for the classroom* (2nd ed.). Oxford University Press.

Lee, U., Jung, H., & Jeon, Y.. (2024). Few-shot is enough: exploring ChatGPT prompt engineering method for automatic question generation in English education. In *Education and Information Technologies* (Vol. 29, pp. 11483–11515). URL., DOI: 10.1007/s10639-023-12249-8

Lee, Y. H., Park, M. J., & Kwon, H. J. (2022). Chatbots and motivation in language learning. *Language Learning & Technology, 26*(3), 63–81.

Leitch, R., & Day, C. (2000). Action research and reflective practice: Towards a holistic view. *Educational Action Research, 8*(1), 179–193. DOI: 10.1080/09650790000200108

L'Enfant, J. (2024). AI as a reflective coach in graduate ESL practicum: activity theory insights into student-teacher development. *European Journal of Open, Distance & E-Learning, 26*(1).

Leong, D., Tse, S. K., & Chan, C. K. (2020). Enhancing accessibility of AI-driven language learning tools for learners with disabilities. *International Journal of Artificial Intelligence in Education*, *30*(4), 506–525.

Levy, M., & Stockwell, G. (2006). *CALL Dimensions: Options and Issues in Computer-Assisted Language Learning*. Lawrence Erlbaum Associates.

Li, C. (2024). A review of theories, pedagogies and vocabulary learning tasks of English vocabulary learning apps for Chinese EFL learners. *Journal of China Computer-Assisted Language Learning*, *4*(2), 346–375. DOI: 10.1515/jccall-2023-0026

Li, J., Zong, H., Wu, E., Wu, R., Peng, Z., Zhao, J., & Shen, B. (2024). Exploring the potential of artificial intelligence to enhance the writing of english academic papers by non-native english-speaking medical students-the educational application of ChatGPT. *BMC Medical Education*, *24*(1), 736.

Limonova, V., Santos, A., São Mamede, H., & Filipe, V. (2023). The research context of artificial intelligence and gamification to improve student engagement and attendance in higher education. RE@ D–Revista de Educação a Distância e eLearning.

Lin, C. C. (2021). Using virtual exchange to foster global competence and collaborative leadership in teacher education. Dual Language Research and Practice Journal, 4(1).

Lin, C.-C., Liu, G.-Z., & Wang, T.-I. (2017). Development and usability test of an e-learning tool for engineering graduates to develop academic writing in english: A case study. *Journal of Educational Technology & Society*, *20*, 148–161. https://www. jstor.org/stable/26229213#metadata_info_tab_contents

Lin, H.-C. K., Wang, C.-H., Chao, C.-J., & Chien, M.-K. (2012). Employing textual and facial emotion recognition to design an affective tutoring system. *The Turkish Online Journal of Educational Technology*, *11*, 418–426. https://files.eric. ed.gov/fulltext/EJ989317.pdf

Lin, S., & Huang, J. (2022). Can AI detect politeness? A study on pragmatic feedback in automated writing evaluation tools. *Computer Assisted Language Learning*. Advance online publication. DOI: 10.1080/09588221.2022.2048013

Little, J. W. (1990). The persistence of privacy: Autonomy and initiative in teachers' professional relations. *Teachers College Record*, *91*(4), 509–536. DOI: 10.1177/016146819009100403

Liu, C. C., Hwang, G. J., Yu, P., Tu, Y. F., & Wang, Y. (2025). Effects of an automated corrective feedback-based peer assessment approach on students' learning achievement, motivation, and self-regulated learning conceptions in foreign language pronunciation. *Educational Technology Research and Development*, •••, 1–22. DOI: 10.1007/s11423-025-10484-z

Liu, H., & Fan, J. (2025). AI-mediated communication in EFL classrooms: The role of technical and pedagogical stimuli and the mediating effects of AI literacy and enjoyment. *European Journal of Education*, *60*(1), 1–13. DOI: 10.1111/ejed.12813

Liu, L. (2024). Impact of AI gamification on EFL learning outcomes and nonlinear dynamic motivation: Comparing adaptive learning paths, conversational agents, and storytelling. *Education and Information Technologies*, •••, 1–40. DOI: 10.1007/s10639-024-13296-5

Liu, S. C., & Hung, P. Y. (2016). Teaching pronunciation with computer assisted pronunciation instruction in a technological university. *Universal Journal of Educational Research*, *4*(9), 1939–1943.

Liu, S., & Kunnan, A. J. (2016). Investigating the application of automated writing evaluation to chinese undergraduate english majors: A case study of" writetolearn. *CALICO Journal*, *33*(1), 71–91. DOI: 10.1558/cj.v33i1.26380

Liu, Z. L. (2025). Preparation knowledge: Basics of AI. In *Artificial Intelligence for Engineers: Basics and Implementations* (pp. 1–43). Springer Nature Switzerland. DOI: 10.1007/978-3-031-75953-6_1

Li, X., & Wang, Y. (2025). Acoustic voice quality index and acoustic breathiness index as two indicators of voice disorders. *Journal of Voice*, *39*(1), 102.e1–102.e8.

Li, X., Wu, H., & Zhang, Q. (2023). Equity considerations in the use of AI-driven language learning tools. *Journal of Educational Computing Research*, *61*(1), 34–48.

Loda, T., Erschens, R., Loenneker, H., Keifenheim, K. E., Nikendei, C., Junne, F., Zipfel, S., & Herrmann-Werner, A. (2019). Cognitive and social congruence in peer-assisted learning – A scoping review. *PLoS One*, *14*(9), 1–15. DOI: 10.1371/journal.pone.0222224 PMID: 31498826

Loewen, S. (2020). *Introduction to instructed second language acquisition*. Routledge. DOI: 10.4324/9781315616797

López, J. L., & Munoz, R. (2020). Gamification in chatbot-based language learning. *Language Learning & Technology*, *24*(2), 22–39.

Lotze, N. (2018). Goodbye to classroom teaching. Artificial intelligence in language learning. Translation: Chris Cave. Copyright: Goethe-Institut e. V., Redaktion Magazin Sprache. Available online at: https://www.goethe.de/en/spr/mag/dsk/ 21290629.html

Luckin, R. (2017). Towards artificial intelligence-based assessment systems. *Nature Human Behaviour, 1*(3), 0028.

Luckin, R., Holmes, W., Griffiths, M., & Forcier, L. B. (2016). Intelligence unleashed. *An Argument for AI in Education, 18.*

Luckin, R., Holmes, W., Griffiths, M., & Forcier, L. B. (2016). *Intelligence unleashed: An argument for AI in education.* Pearson. https://www.pearson.com/content/dam/one-dot-com/one-dot-com/global/Files/about-pearson/innovation/open-ideas/Intelligence-Unleashed-Publication.pdf

Luckin, R. (2018). *Machine Learning and Human Intelligence. The future of education for the 21st century.* UCL Institute of Education Press.

Luckin, R., Holmes, W., Griffiths, M., & Forcier, L. B. (2020). *Intelligence Unleashed: An Argument for AI in Education.* Pearson Education.

Luck, M., & Aylett, R. (2000). Applying artificial intelligence to virtual reality: Intelligent virtual environments. *Applied Artificial Intelligence, 14*(1), 3–32. DOI: 10.1080/088395100117142

Luckyardi, S., Karin, J., Rosmaladewi, R., Hufad, A., & Haristiani, N. (2024). Chatbots as digital language tutors: Revolutionizing education through AI. *Indonesian Journal of Science and Technology, 9*(3), 885–908. DOI: 10.17509/ijost.v9i3.79514

Luu, N. (2024). AI-powered gamification for boosting second language acquisition efficiency.

Magic School AI. https://app.magicschool.ai/tools

Malik, A. R., Pratiwi, Y., Andajani, K., Numertayasa, I. W., Suharti, S., Darwis, A., & Marzuki, . (2023). Exploring Artificial Intelligence in Academic Essay : Higher Education Student's Perspective. *International Journal of Educational Research Open, 5*, 100296. DOI: 10.1016/j.ijedro.2023.100296

Mandl, T. (2009). Artificial Intelligence for Information Retrieval. In Rabuñal Dopico, J. R., Dorado, J., & Pazos, A. (Eds.), *Encyclopedia of Artificial Intelligence* (pp. 151–156). IGI Global., DOI: 10.4018/978-1-59904-849-9.ch023

Ma, Q., Crosthwaite, P., Sun, D., & Zou, D. (2024). Exploring ChatGPT literacy in language education: A global perspective and comprehensive approach. *Computers and education. Artificial Intelligence, 7*, 100278. DOI: 10.1016/j.caeai.2024.100278

Marienko, M., Nosenko, Y., Sukhikh, A., Tataurov, V., & Shyshkina, M. (2020). Personalization of learning through adaptive technologies in the context of sustainable development of teachers education. *arXiv preprint arXiv:2006.05810*.

Marinucci, L., Mazzuca, C., & Gangemi, A. (2023). Exposing implicit biases and stereotypes in human and artificial intelligence: State of the art and challenges with a focus on gender. *AI & Society*, *38*(2), 747–761. DOI: 10.1007/s00146-022-01474-3

Martin, F., Zhuang, M., & Schaefer, D. (2024). Systematic review of research on artificial intelligence in K-12 education (2017–2022). *Computers and Education: Artificial Intelligence*, *6*, 100195. DOI: 10.1016/j.caeai.2023.100195

Martin, N. K., & Sass, D. A. (2010). Construct validation of the behavior and instructional management scale. *Teaching and Teacher Education*, *26*(5), 1124–1135. DOI: 10.1016/j.tate.2009.12.001

Marzuki, M., Widiati, U., Rusdin, D., Darwin, D., & Indrawati, I. (2023). The impact of AI writing tools on the content and organization of students' writing : EFL teachers' perspective. *Cogent Education*, *10*(2), 2236469. DOI: 10.1080/2331186X.2023.2236469

Matthew, U. O., Bakare, K. M., Ebong, G. N., Ndukwu, C. C., & Nwanakwaugwu, A. C. (2023). GenerativeArtificial Intelligence (AI) Educational Pedagogy Development:Conversational AI with User-Centric ChatGPT4. *Journal ofTrends in ComputerScience and Smart Technology*, *5*(4), 401–418. DOI: 10.36548/jtcsst.2023.4.003

Matthew, U. O., Kazaure, A. S., Kazaure, J. S., Hassan, I. M., Nwanakwaugwu, A. C., & Okafor, N. U. (2022). Educational Technology Adaptation & Implication for MediaTechnology Adoption in the Period of COVID-19. *Journal of Trends in ComputerScience and Smart Technology*, *4*(4), 226–245. DOI: 10.36548/jtcsst.2022.4.002

Matthew, U. O., & Kazaure, J. S. (2020). Multimedia e-learning education in nigeriaand developing countries of Africa for achieving SDG4. [IJICTHD]. *International Journal of Information Communication Technologies and Human Development*, *12*(1), 40–62. DOI: 10.4018/IJICTHD.2020010103

Mauroner, O. (2019). Gamification in management and other non-game contexts—Understanding game elements, motivation, reward systems, and user types. *Open Journal ofBusiness and Management*, *7*(4), 1815–1830. DOI: 10.4236/ojbm.2019.74125

Ma, Y. C., & Lin, H.-C.-K. (2017). "The development of an affective tutoring system for japanese language learners," in *International Symposium on Emerging Technologies for Education* (Cape Town: Springer), 363–371. DOI: 10.1007/978-3-319-71084-6_41

Ma, Y., & Chen, M. (2024). AI-empowered applications effects on EFL learners' engagement in the classroom and academic procrastination. *BMC Psychology*, *12*(1), 1–11. DOI: 10.1186/s40359-024-02248-w PMID: 39695837

McCrocklin, S. (2019). Learners' feedback regarding asr-based dictation practice for pronunciation learning. *CALICO Journal*, *36*(2), 119–137. DOI: 10.1558/cj.34738

Mehrabi, N., Morstatter, F., Saxena, N., Lerman, K., & Galstyan, A. (2021). A survey on bias and fairness in machine learning. *ACM Computing Surveys*, *54*(6), 1–35. DOI: 10.1145/3457607

Melchor-Couto, S. (2017). Foreign language anxiety levels in second life oral interaction. *ReCALL*, *29*(1), 99–119. DOI: 10.1017/S0958344016000185

Memon, F. N., & Memon, S. N. (2025). Digital divide and equity in education: Bridging gaps to ensure inclusive learning. In *Impact of Digitalization on Education and Social Sustainability* (pp. 107–130). IGI Global.

Meylani, R. (2024). Artificial intelligence in the education of teachers: A qualitative synthesis of the cutting-edge research literature. *Journal of Computer and Education Research*, *12*(24), 600–637. DOI: 10.18009/jcer.1477709

Mi, Y., Rong, M., & Chen, X. (2025). Exploring the affordances and challenges of GenAI feedback in L2 writing instruction: A comparative analysis with peer feedback. *ECNU Review of Education*, 1-26. DOI: 10.1177/20965311241310883

Miao, F., Holmes, W., Huang, R., & Zhang, H. (2021). *AI and education: A guidance for policymakers*. UNESCO Publishing.

Mikhaylov, S. J., Esteve, M., & Campion, A. (2018). Artificial intelligence for the public sector: Opportunities and challenges of cross-sector collaboration. *Philosophical Transactions. Series A, Mathematical, Physical, and Engineering Sciences*, *376*(2128), 20170357. DOI: 10.1098/rsta.2017.0357 PMID: 30082303

Mikolov, T., Kombrink, S., & Burget, L., Cernockˇ y, J., and Khudanpur, S.` (2011). "Extensions of recurrent neural network language model," in 2011 IEEE International Conference on Acoustics, Speech and Signal Processing (ICASSP) (Prague: IEEE), 5528–5531. DOI: 10.1109/ICASSP.2011.5947611

Mitchell, M. (2025). AI is spreading old stereotypes to new languages and cultures. Wired. https://www.wired.com/story/ai-bias-spreading-stereotypes-across-languages-and-cultures-margaret-mitchell

Mitchell, T. M. (1997). *Machine Learning*. McGraw-Hill.

Mohamed, A., Faisal, R., & Shaalan, K. (2024). Exploring the impact of ai-driven virtual assistants in AR and VR environments for special needs education: A quantitative analysis. In Proceedings of the *International Conference on Extended Reality*. Cham: Springer Nature Switzerland. DOI: 10.1007/978-3-031-71713-0_8

Mohamed, A. M. (2024). Exploring the potential of an AI-based Chatbot (ChatGPT) in enhancing English as a Foreign Language (EFL) teaching: Perceptions of EFL Faculty Members. *Education and Information Technologies*, *29*(3), 3195–3217.

Mohamed, A. M. (2024). Exploring the potential of an AI-based chatbot (ChatGPT) in enhancing English as a Foreign Language (EFL) teaching: Perceptions of EFL faculty members. *Education and Information Technologies*, *29*(3), 3195–3217. DOI: 10.1007/s10639-023-11917-z

Mohamed, H., & Lamia, M. (2018). Implementing flipped classroom that used an intelligent tutoring system into learning process. *Computers & Education*, *124*, 62–76. DOI: 10.1016/j.compedu.2018.05.011

Mohammadzadeh, A., & Sarkhosh, M. (2018). The effects of selfregulatory learning through computer-assisted intelligent tutoring system on the improvement of efl learners' speaking ability. *International Journal of Instruction*, *11*(2), 167–184. DOI: 10.12973/iji.2018.11212a

Mohebbi, A. (2025). Enabling learner independence and self-regulation in language education using AI tools: A systematic review. *Cogent Education*, *12*(1), 1–18. DOI: 10.1080/2331186X.2024.2433814

Morano, R. (2024). Diachronic variation in the Omani Arabic vernacular of the Al-ʿAwābī district: From Carl Reinhardt (1894) to the present day. Journal Name, Volume(Issue), page range. DOI or URL (if available).

Mora-Pablo, I., & Goodwin, D. (2023). Identity construction during emergency remote teaching reflections of novice teachers in a teacher education program. *MEXTESOL Journal*, *47*(3), n3. DOI: 10.61871/mj.v47n3-11

Morshedian, M., Ghanizadeh, A., & Mirzaee, S. (2023). Smart classroom management: How does it influence EFL learners' anxiety, engagement, and language achievement. *MEXTESOL Journal, 47*(2).

Moybeka, A. M. S., Syariatin, N., Tatipang, D. P., Mushthoza, D. A., Dewi, N. P. J. L., & Tineh, S. (2023). Artificial intelligence and English classroom: The implications of AI toward EFL students' motivation. *Edumaspul*, *7*(2), 2444–2454. DOI: 10.33487/edumaspul.v7i2.6669

Moybeka, A. M., Syariatin, N., Tatipang, D. P., Mushthoza, D. A., Dewi, N. P. J. L., & Tineh, S. (2023). Artificial Intelligence and English classroom: The implications of AI toward EFL students' motivation. Edumaspul. *Jurnal Pendidikan*, *7*(2), 2444–2454.

Muawanah, U., Marini, A., & Sarifah, I. (2024). The interconnection between digital literacy, artificial intelligence, and the use of E-learning applications in enhancing the sustainability of Regional Languages: Evidence from Indonesia. *Social Sciences & Humanities Open*, *10*, 101169. DOI: 10.1016/j.ssaho.2024.101169

Munday, P. (2016). *Introducing translation studies: Theories and applications* (4th ed.). Routledge. DOI: 10.4324/9781315691862

Munro, M. J. (2021). Focused on how intonation and stress placement are affected by L1 transfer. *Journal of Linguistic Studies*, *19*(4), 132–144.

Munro, M. J. (2022). The use of PRAAT in phonetic research: A case study on vowel quality and prosody. *Journal of Speech Sciences*, *39*(2), 221–235.

Mustafa, H. M., Mahmoud, S. S., Abouelnaga, H. M., Tayfour, M., Metwally, A. B. M., & Shehata, S. M. (2024). The effect of the training of using Magic School AI on self-efficacy in teaching and information overload among Arabic teachers. *Migration Letters : An International Journal of Migration Studies*, *21*(S9), 1361–1370.

Mykytka, I. (2023). The use of Quizlet to enhance L2 vocabulary acquisition. *Encuentro Journal*, *31*, 56–69.

Nafa, M. S. (2023). *A broad guide to teaching the skills of listening and speaking*. Cambridge Scholars Publishing.

Nagro, S. A. (2021). The role of artificial intelligence techniqies in improving the behavior and practices of faculty members when switching to e-learning in light of the COVID-19 crisis. *Int. J. Educ. Pract.*, *9*(4), 687–714. DOI: 10.18488/journal.61.2021.94.687.714

Namaziandost, E., Behbahani, H. K., & Naserpour, A. (2024). Peer support in language learning: Mitigating anxiety, enhancing achievement, cultivating growth mindsets, and increasing enjoyment. *Journal of Applied Learning & Teaching*, *7*(2), 1–18. DOI: 10.37074/jalt.2024.7.2.40

Nassaji, H. (2016). The role and importance of lower-level processes in second language reading. *Language Teaching*, *49*(1), 67–80.

Neff, J., Arciaga, K., & Burri, M. (2024). EFL students' and teachers' perceptions of the ethical uses of AI tools. *Technology in Language Teaching & Learning*, *6*(3), 1714. Advance online publication. DOI: 10.29140/tltl.v6n3.1714

Negrila, A. M. C. (2023). The new revolution in language learning: The power of artificial intelligence and education 4.0. Bulletin of" Carol I [EN]. *National Defence University, 12*(02), 16–27. DOI: 10.53477/2284-9378-23-17

Ngo, T. T. N., Chen, H. H. J., & Lai, K. K. W. (2024). The effectiveness of automatic speech recognition in ESL/EFL pronunciation: A meta-analysis. *ReCALL, 36*(1), 4–21. DOI: 10.1017/S0958344023000113

Nguyen, A., Hong, Y., Dang, B., & Huang, X. (2024). Human-AI collaboration patterns in AI-assisted academic writing. *Studies in Higher Education*, *49*(5), 847–864. DOI: 10.1080/03075079.2024.2323593

Nguyen, A., Ngo, H. N., Hong, Y., Dang, B., & Nguyen, B.-P. T. (2023). Ethical-principles for artificial intelligence in education. *Education and Information Technologies*, *28*(4), 4221–4241. DOI: 10.1007/s10639-022-11316-w PMID: 36254344

Nguyen, L. T., & Ikeda, M. (2021). Automated feedback and EFL learners' writing performance: A comparative study. *System*, *99*, 102514. DOI: 10.1016/j.system.2021.102514

Nguyen, P.. (2008). Exploring language transfer and prosody in second language learners. *Journal of Applied Linguistics*, *10*(1), 44–58.

Nguyen, T. T. H., & Ikeda, M. (2021). Artificial intelligence in EFL learning: Enhancing writing skills with automated feedback. *Language Learning & Technology*, *25*(3), 130–146. https://www.lltjournal.org/item/3242

Nikolic, S., Sandison, C., Haque, R., Daniel, S., Grundy, S., Belkina, M., Lyden, S., Hassan, G. M., & Neal, P. (2024). ChatGPT, Copilot, Gemini, SciSpace andWolfram versus higher education assessments: An updated multi-institutional studyof the academic integrity impacts of Generative Artificial Intelligence (GenAI) onassessment, teaching and learning in engineering. *Australasian Journal of Engineering Education*, *29*(2), 1–28. DOI: 10.1080/22054952.2024.2372154

Nikolopoulou, K. (2024). *ChatGPT for educational-academic activities: Preschool student teachers' experiences*. Intelligent Technologies in Education., DOI: 10.70770/r5aett21

Nobrega, F. A., & Rozenfeld, C. C. D. F. (2019). Virtual reality in the teaching of fle in a brazilian public school. *Languages (Basel, Switzerland)*, *4*(2), 36. DOI: 10.3390/languages4020036

Noël, R., Miranda, D., Cechinel, C., Riquelme, F., Primo, T. T., & Munoz, R. (2022). Visualizing collaboration in teamwork: A multimodal learning analytics platform for non-verbal communication. *Applied Sciences (Basel, Switzerland)*, *12*(15), 7499. DOI: 10.3390/app12157499

Nogues, J. (2024). Unlocking potential: harnessing AI for language teaching and learning. URL: https://www.fraubastowmfl.co.uk/post/unlocking-potential-harnessing-ai-for-language-teaching-and-learning

Norte, N. (2023). ELAN: An annotation tool for multimodal discourse analysis. *Proceedings of the 2nd International Conference on Digital Linguistics*.https://www.researchgate.net/publication/373458287_ELAN_An_annotation_tool_for_multimodal_discourse_analysis

Norton, B. (2013). *Identity and language learning: Extending the conversation*. Multilingual matters.

Nushi, M., & Eqbali, M. H. (2017). Duolingo: A mobile application to assist second language learning. *Teaching English with Technology*, *17*(1), 89–98.

Nwanakwaugwu, A. C., Andrew-Vitalis, N., Kwakpovwe, P., Emakporuena, D., & Eboesomi, E. (2025). Personalizing Medicine for Fake Drug Prevention With AI-Driven Digital Twins. In B. S. & S. Kadry (Eds.), *AI-Powered Digital Twins for Predictive Healthcare: Creating Virtual Replicas of Humans* (pp. 325-358). IGI Global Scientific Publishing. DOI: 10.4018/979-8-3373-0538-7.ch010

Nwanakwaugwu, A. C., Matthew, U. O., Okey, O. D., Kazaure, J. S., & Nwamouh, U. C. (2023). News Reporting in Drone Internet of Things Digital Journalism: Drones Technology for Intelligence Gathering in Journalism. [IJICST]. *International Journal of Interactive Communication Systems and Technologies*, *12*(1), 1–22. DOI: 10.4018/ijicst.320181

Nyholm, S. (2024). Artificial intelligence and human enhancement: Can AI technologies make us more (artificially) intelligent? *Cambridge Quarterly of Healthcare Ethics*, *33*(1), 76–88. DOI: 10.1017/S0963180123000464 PMID: 37646146

Obari, H. (2020). "The integration of ai and virtual learning in teaching efl under COVID-19," in *ICERI2020 Proceedings (IATED)*, 7866–7872. DOI: 10.21125/iceri.2020.1740

Ogundele, R. A. (2023). AI-POWERED THESPIAN: DEVELOPING AN INNOVATIVE CONVERSATIONAL ENGINE (Doctoral dissertation, Doctoral dissertation, MANCHESTER METROPOLITAN UNIVERSITY).

Olatunji, A. P., Ajibola, O. S., & Agunbiade, N. O. (2024). Leveraging AI-driven training programs for enhanced organizational security awareness. *International Journal of Science and Research Archive, 13*(1), 301–311. DOI: 10.30574/ijsra.2024.13.1.1649

Oluwatola, K., & Akingbade, L. (2022). *Information Retrieval Skills as Correlate of Scholarly Research Among Postgraduate Students in Selected Universities in Oyo and Lagos States.*

Onah, J. C., Mr, I. O. A., Okonkwo, E. A., & Onyebuchi, G. U. (2020). Information retrieval skills as it correlates to undergraduate use of library information resources at a Nigerian university. *Library Philosophy and Practice (e-journal)*, 4567.

Onu, P., Ikumapayi, O. M., Omole, E. O., Amoyedo, F. E., Ajewole, K. P., Jacob, A. S., . . . Mbohwa, C. (2024). Science, Technology, Engineering and Mathematics(STEM) Education and the Influence of Industry 4.0. Paper presented at the 2024International Conference on Science, Engineering and Business for Driving Sus-tainable Development Goals (SEB4SDG)

Osterman, K. F. (2023). Teacher practice and students' sense of belonging. In Lovat, T., Toomey, R., Clement, N., & Dally, K. (Eds.), *Second international research handbook on values education and student wellbeing* (2nd ed., pp. 971–993). Springer. DOI: 10.1007/978-3-031-24420-9_54

Owan, V. J., Abang, K. B., Idika, D. O., Etta, E. O., & Bassey, B. A. (2023). Exploring the potential of artificial intelligence tools in educational measurement and assessment. *Eurasia Journal of Mathematics, Science and Technology Education, 19*(8), em2307. Advance online publication. DOI: 10.29333/ejmste/13428

Oyekunle, D., Matthew, U., Waliu, A., & Fatai, L. (2024). Healthcare applicationsof Augmented Reality (AR) and Virtual Real-ity (VR) simulation in clinical cedu-cation. *Journal of Clinical Images and Medical Case Reports, 5*(6), 3141.

Özdemir, O., & Seçkin, H. (2024). Quantifying cognitive and affective impacts of Quizlet on learning outcomes: A systematic review and comprehensive meta-analysis. *Frontiers in Psychology, 15*, 1349835.

Panagiotidis, P. (2021). Augmented and mixed reality in language learning. *European Journal of Education, 4*(2), 27–43. DOI: 10.26417/501ibq23c

Papadimitriou, S. (2025). *Artificial Intelligence—Based Games as Novel Holistic Educational Environments to Teach 21st Century Skills.* Springer Nature. DOI: 10.1007/978-3-031-77464-5

Peachey, N. (2023). *ChatGPT in the language classroom.* Peachey Publications Ltd.

Pedro, F., Subosa, M., Rivas, A., & Valverde, P. (2019). Artificial intelligence in education: Challenges and opportunities for sustainable development. UNESCO. https://repositorio.minedu.gob.pe/bitstream/handle/20.500.12799/6533/Artificial%20intelligence%20in%20education%20challenges%20and%20opportunities%20for%20sustainable%20development.pdf?sequence=1&isAllowed=y

Peeters, D. (2019). Virtual reality: A game-changing method for the language sciences. *Psychonomic Bulletin & Review, 26*(3), 894–900. DOI: 10.3758/s13423-019-01571-3 PMID: 30734158

Perdana, I., Manullang, S. O., & Masri, F. A. (2021). Effectiveness of online Grammarly application in improving academic writing : Review of experts experience. *The International Journal of Social Sciences (Islamabad), 4*(1), 122–130. DOI: 10.31295/ijss.v4n1.1444

Pérez, J. F., & García, S. (2020). Adaptive learning with AI-powered chatbots. *Journal of Educational Technology & Society, 23*(4), 56–70.

Permatasari, D., & Aryani, F. (2023). Duolingo: An enchanting application to learn English for college students. *ELTR Journal, 7*(2), 101–109.

Phadatare, T. S., & Naik, P. (2023). AI Based Disease Prediction. *International Journal of Advanced Research in Science. Tongxin Jishu*, •••, 621–628. DOI: 10.48175/IJARSCT-12094

Pham, Q. H. P. (2017). Group dynamics: Building a sense of belonging in the EFL classroom. *English Teaching Forum, 55*(1), 14-21.

Pinto-Santos, A. R., Pérez Garcias, A., & Darder Mesquida, A. (2022). Development of teaching digital competence in initial teacher training: A Systematic Review. *World Journal on Educational Technology: Current Issues, 14*(1), 1–15.

Pokrivčáková, S. (2019). Preparing teachers for the application of AI-powered technologies in foreign language education. *Journal of language and cultural education, 7*(3), 135-153. https://doi:DOI: 10.2478/jolace-2019-0025

Popenici, S. A., & Kerr, S. (2017). Exploring the impact of artificial intelligence on teaching and learning in higher education. *Research and Practice in Technology Enhanced Learning, 12*(1), 22. DOI: 10.1186/s41039-017-0062-8 PMID: 30595727

Puglisi, B. (2018, May 29). Build character empathy in your first few pages. WRITERS HELPING WRITERS. https://writershelpingwriters.net/2018/05/creating-characterempathy/

Qian, L., Yang, Y., & Zhao, Y. (2021). Syntactic complexity revisited: Sensitivity of china's aes-generated scores to syntactic measures, effects of discourse-mode and topic. *Reading and Writing*, *34*(3), 681–704. DOI: 10.1007/s11145-020-10087-5

Radanliev, P., De Roure, D., Page, K., Van Kleek, M., Santos, O., Maddox, L. T., Burnap, P., Anthi, E., & Maple, C. (2020). Design of a dynamic and self-adapting system, supported with artificial intelligence, machine learning and real-time intelligence for predictive cyber risk analytics in extreme environments–cyber risk in the colonisation of Mars. *Safety in Extreme Environments*, *2*(3), 219–230. DOI: 10.1007/s42797-021-00025-1

Rahimi, M., Fathi, J., & Zou, D. (2024). Exploring the impact of automated written corrective feedback on the academic writing skills of EFL learners: An activity theory perspective. *Education and Information Technologies*, •••, 1–45.

Rahim, M. N. (2019). The use of blended learning approach in EFL education. *International Journal of Engineering and Advanced Technology*, *8*(5), 1165–1168. DOI: 10.35940/ijeat.E1163.0585C19

Rahim, N. A., Hanum, A. Z. A., Bhakti, M. A. C., & Wandy, W. (2023). Artificial Intelligence Tools in Higher Education Students Usage Analysis – Case Study : Sampoerna University. *Jurnal Teknologi*, *16*(2), 137–145. DOI: 10.34151/jurtek.v16i2.4544

Rajak, L., Chauhan, S., & Bara, S. (2024). Transforming English Pedagogy with Artificial Intelligence: Enroute to Enhanced Language Learning. In T. Khan., M. Singh., & S. Raza (Eds.), *Artificial Intelligence: A Multidisciplinary Approach towards Teaching and Learning* (pp. 216-241). Bentham Science Publishers.

Ramnani, S. (2024). Exploring ethical considerations of Artificial Intelligence in educational settings: An examination of bias, privacy, and accountability. [IJNRD]. *International Journal of Novel Research and Development*, *9*(2), 2456–4184.

Rapti, C., & Panagiotidis, P. (2024). Teachers' attitudes towards AI integration in foreign language learning: Supporting differentiated instruction and flipped classroom. *European Journal of Education*, *7*(2), 88–104. DOI: 10.26417/171oob60e

Ravichandran, K., Virgin, B. A., Patil, S., Fatma, G., Rengarajan, M., & Bala, B. K. (2024, July). Gamifying Language Learning: Applying Augmented Reality and Gamification Strategies for Enhanced English Language Acquisition. In *2024 Third International Conference on Smart Technologies and Systems for Next Generation Computing (ICSTSN)* (pp. 1-6). IEEE. DOI: 10.1109/ICSTSN61422.2024.10670787

Renacido, J. M. D., & Biray, E. T. (2025). Enhancing Peer Engagement and Student Motivation Through AI-Gamified Interactive Learning Tools. In Advancing Sustainable Development Goals With Educational Technology (pp. 277-342). IGI Global Scientific Publishing.

Rezai, A., Soyoof, A., & Reynolds, B. L. (2024). Disclosing the correlation between using ChatGPT and well-being in EFL learners: Considering the mediating role of emotion regulation. *European Journal of Education*, *59*(4), e12752. DOI: 10.1111/ejed.12752

Richards, J. C. (2005). *Professional development for language teachers: Strategies for teacher learning*. Ernst Klett Sprachen. DOI: 10.1017/CBO9780511667237

Roach, P. (2009). *English phonetics and phonology: A practical course* (4th ed.). Cambridge University Press.

Roach, P. (2018). Lexical stress placement in disyllabic and polysyllabic words in English. *Journal of Phonetics*, *23*(4), 132–144.

Rodgers, C. R., & Scott, K. H. (2008). The development of the personal self and professional identity in learning to teach. In Cochran-Smith, M., Feiman-Nemser, S., McIntyre, J., & Demers, K. E. (Eds.), *Handbook of research on teacher education* (pp. 732–755). Routledge.

Rodrigues, A. L. (2023). Innovative hybrid learning: a new paradigm in teacher education for transformative learning. In Lytras, M. D. (Ed.), *Active and transformative learning in STEAM disciplines: From curriculum design to social impact* (pp. 153–175). Emerald Publishing Limited. DOI: 10.1108/978-1-83753-618-420231008

Rodríguez, L. M. G., & Gerke, A. E. (2022). Using foreign films to foster pre-service teachers' intercultural awareness in an EFL context. In García-Sánchez, S., & Clouet, R. (Eds.), *Intercultural communication and ubiquitous learning in multimodal English language education* (pp. 45–67). IGI Global., DOI: 10.4018/978-1-7998-8852-9.ch003

Roe, J., Renandya, W. A., & Jacobs, G. M. (2023). A Review of AI-Powered Writing Tools and Their Implications for Academic Integrity in the Language Classroom. *Journal of English and Applied Linguistics*, *2*(1). Advance online publication. DOI: 10.59588/2961-3094.1035

Roell, C. (2010). Intercultural training with films. *English Teaching Forum, 48*(2), 2-15.

Rogers, C. (2023). Mediation in the ELT classroom. *Humanising language teaching*, 4. https://www.hltmag.co.uk/aug23/mediation-in-the-elt-classroom

Roh, Y., Heo, G., & Whang, S. E. (2019). A survey on data collection for machine learning: A big data-ai integration perspective. *IEEE Transactions on Knowledge and Data Engineering, 33*(4), 1328–1347. DOI: 10.1109/TKDE.2019.2946162

Rojas, J. P. (2024). *Enhancing English Language Teaching through AI: The case of Magic School AI.* Universidad Distrital Francisco José de Caldas.

Romero, M. (2021). The role of intonation in spoken language communication. *Language and Linguistics Compass, 15*(8), e12349.

Rosé, C. P., Martínez-Maldonado, R., Hoppe, H. U., Luckin, R., Mavrikis, M., Porayska-Pomsta, K., & Du Boulay, B. (Eds.). (2018). *Artificial Intelligence in Education.InProceedings, Part I* (Vol. 10947) *of the 19th International Conference, AIED,* Springer.

Roshan, S., Iqbal, S. Z., & Qing, Z. (2024). Teacher training and professional development for implementing ai-based educational tools. *Journal of Asian Development Studies, 13*(2), 1972–1987. DOI: 10.62345/jads.2024.13.2.154

Rovai, A., & Pfingsthorn, J. (2022). "Good foreign language teachers pay attention to heterogeneity": Conceptualizations of differentiation and effective teaching practice in inclusive EFL classrooms by German pre-service teachers. *Languages (Basel, Switzerland), 7*(3), 162. DOI: 10.3390/languages7030162

Rudnik, Y. (2024). The Use of Artificial Intelligence Chatbots in Teaching Foreign Languages as an Innovative Interactive Technology. Educological discourse, 45(2).

Russell, T., & Martin, A. K. (2017). Reflective practice: Epistemological perspectives on learning from experience in teacher education. *Reflective Theory and Practice in Teacher Education*, 27-47.

Russell, S., Norvig, P., Popineau, F., Miclet, L., & Cadet, C. (2021). *Intelligence artificielle: Une approche moderne (4 édition).* Pearson France.

Ruusunen, V. (2011). *Using movies in EFL teaching: The point of view of teachers* [Unpublished Master's thesis]. University of Jyväskylä, Finland.

Saeed, M. A. (2021). Learner autonomy: Learners' perceptions on strategies to achieve autonomy in an EFL classroom. International Journal of Linguistics. *Literature and Translation, 4*(3), 150–158.

Samantray, K., İZGİ, F. D., Ocampo, M. B., Dehghan, M., Mohammadpour, S., Siriphaprapagon, Y., ... & Babu, S. D. (2024). The Power of Words in AI-Driven World: Exploring the Interplay of Language, Culture, and Communication. SKET-SAMEDIA.

Sardabi, N., Biria, R., & Golestan, A. A. (2018). Reshaping teacher professional identity through critical pedagogy-informed teacher education. *International Journal of Instruction, 11*(3), 617–634. DOI: 10.12973/iji.2018.11342a

Sarker, I. H. (2022). AI-Based Modeling : Techniques, Applications and Research Issues Towards Automation, Intelligent and Smart Systems. *SN Computer Science, 3*(2), 158. DOI: 10.1007/s42979-022-01043-x PMID: 35194580

Sato, K. (2022). PRAAT and its applications in EFL pronunciation instruction. *Pronunciation Journal, 9*(3), 115–130.

Schmidt, T., & Strasser, T. (2022). Artificial intelligence in foreign language learning and teaching: A CALL for intelligent practice. Anglistik. *International Journal of English Studies, 33*(1), 165–184.

Scrivener, J. (2005). *Learning Teaching: The Essential Guide to English Language Teaching*. Macmillan Education.

Searle, J. R. (1969). *Speech acts: An essay in the philosophy of language*. Cambridge University Press. DOI: 10.1017/CBO9781139173438

Seiradakis, E. V. (2025). ChatGPT use: Drivers and barriers in English for Academic Purposes among migrant students with learning disabilities. In Stevkovska, M., Klemenchich, M., & Kavaklı Ulutaş, N. (Eds.), *Reimagining Intelligent Computer-Assisted Language Education* (pp. 309–330). IGI Global., DOI: 10.4018/979-8-3693-4310-4.ch011

Selwyn, N. (2019). *Should robots replace teachers? AI and the future of education.* Polity Press.

Seo, J. Y. (2024). Generative AI as a virtual conversation partner in language learning. *International Journal of Advanced Culture Technology, 12*(2), 7–15. DOI: 10.17703/IJACT.2024.12.2.7

Setyaningsih, E., Asrori, M., Zainnuri, H., & Hariyanti, Y. (2024). Exploring High School EFL teachers' experiences with Magic School AI in lesson planning: Benefits and insights. *Voices of English Language Education Society, 8*(3), 685–700. DOI: 10.29408/veles.v8i3.27700

Seyyedali, S., Barati, H., & Nouri, M. (2022). The cultural implications of AI tools in language teaching: A review of the literature. *Language Learning & Technology, 26*(1), 54–75. DOI: 10.1016/j.langed.2022.05.008

Shah, P. (2023). *AI and the Future of Education: Teaching in the age of artificial intelligence*. John Wiley & Sons.

Shah, P., Gadekar, N. A., & Taylor, S. S. (2024). Escape From Passive Learning: Harnessing Gamified Digital Educational Escape Rooms for Immersive Marketing Education. *Journal of Marketing Education*, •••, 02734753241306093. DOI: 10.1177/02734753241306093

Shalev, T., Gonzalez, G., & Tuan, M. (2020). Chatbots in language learning: A review of literature. *International Journal of Artificial Intelligence in Education*, *30*(3), 367–383.

Shao, K., Pekrun, R., & Nicholson, L. J. (2019). Emotions in classroom language learning: What can we learn from achievement emotion research? *System*, *86*, 102121. Advance online publication. DOI: 10.1016/j.system.2019.102121

Sharma, L., & Srivastava, V. (2017). Performance enhancement of information retrieval via artificial intelligence. [IJSRSET]. *International Journal of Scientific Research in Science, Engineering and Technology*, *3*(1), 187–192.

Sheldon, K. M., & Prentice, M. (2019). Self-determination theory as a foundation for personality researchers. *Journal of Personality*, *87*(1), 5–14. DOI: 10.1111/jopy.12360 PMID: 29144550

Shen, Y., & Guo, H. (2024). "I feel AI is neither too good nor too bad": Unveiling Chinese EFL teachers' perceived emotions in generative AI-mediated L2 classes. *Computers in Human Behavior*, *161*, 1–7. DOI: 10.1016/j.chb.2024.108429

Shue, Y., & Keating, P. (2024). Comparative analysis of acoustic measures using Praat and VoiceSauce. *The Journal of the Acoustical Society of America*, *156*(4), 2112–2123.

Shumeiko, N. (2024). Exploiting the potential of Artificial Intelligence in teaching English: some scientific aspects. ZBORNÍK konferencie XXXVII DidMatTech 2024. Proceedings of XXXVII DidMatTech 2024 Conference "New Methods and Technologies in Education, Research and Practice," J. Selye University - Komárno, Trnava University in Trnava, p.46-57. Article. ISBN 978-80-568-0698-2. http://didmattech.ujs.sk/proceeding/

Shumeiko, N. V., & Osadcha, K. P. (2024, October). Application of artificial intelligence in higher education institutions for developing soft skills of future specialists in the sphere of information technology. [). IOP Publishing.]. *Journal of Physics: Conference Series*, *2871*(1), 012027.

Siedentop, D., Hastie, P., & Van der Mars, H. (2019). *Complete guide to sport education*. Human Kinetics.

Situmorang, K., Nugroho, D. Y., & Pramusita, S. M. (2020). English teachers' preparedness in technology enhanced language learning during covid-19 pandemic–students' voice. *Jo-ELT (Journal of English Language Teaching). Fakultas Pendidikan Bahasa & Seni Prodi Pendidikan Bahasa Inggris IKIP*, *7*(2), 57–67.

Sobehrad, S., & Francis, R. (2024, March). Indistinguishable from Magic: AI for educators. In J. Cohen & G. Solano (Eds.), *Proceedings of Society for Information Technology & Teacher Education International Conference* (pp. 2278-2283). Association for the Advancement of Computing in Education (AACE).

Soe, T. H. (2021). *AI video editing tools. What editors want and how far is AI from delivering?* (arXiv:2109.07809). arXiv. http://arxiv.org/abs/2109.07809

Solhi, M. (2024). Do L2 teacher support and peer support predict L2 speaking motivation in online classes? *The Asia-Pacific Education Researcher*, *33*(4), 829–842. DOI: 10.1007/s40299-023-00767-5

Son, J.-B., Ružić, N. K., & Philpott, A. (2023). Artificial intelligence technologies and applications for language learning and teaching. *Journal of China Computer-Assisted Language Learning*, •••, 1–19. DOI: 10.1515/jccall-2023-0015

Sperber, D., & Wilson, D. (1986). *Relevance: Communication and cognition.* Blackwell.

Sperling, K., Stenberg, C. J., McGrath, C., Åkerfeldt, A., Heintz, F., & Stenliden, L. (2024). In search of artificial intelligence (AI) literacy in teacher education: A scoping review. *Computers and Education Open*, *100169*, 100169. Advance online publication. DOI: 10.1016/j.caeo.2024.100169

Statista, (2024). URL: https://www.statista.com/statistics/1239522/top-language -learning-apps-downloads/

Stiller, K. D., & Schworm, S. (2019, March). Game-based learning of the structure and functioning of body cells in a foreign language: Effects on motivation, cognitive load, and performance. [). Frontiers Media SA.]. *Frontiers in Education*, *4*, 18. DOI: 10.3389/feduc.2019.00018

Storch, N. (2002). Patterns of interaction in ESL pair work. *Language Learning*, *52*(1), 119–158. DOI: 10.1111/1467-9922.00179

Styler, W. (2025). Using Praat for linguistic research. *Retrieved from*https://wstyler .ucsd.edu/praat/

Sumakul, D. T. Y. G., Hamied, F. A., & Sukyadi, D. (2022). Artificial intelligence in EFL classrooms: Friend or foe? *LEARN Journal: Language Education and Acquisition Research Network*, *15*(1), 232–256.

Sun, Y., & Shi, W. (2022). On the role of teacher-student rapport and teacher support as predictors of Chinese EFL students' affective learning. *Frontiers in Psychology*, *13*, 1–9. DOI: 10.3389/fpsyg.2022.856430 PMID: 35360642

Su, Y., Luo, M., & Zhong, C. (2025). To Chat or Not: Pre-Service English Teachers' Perceptions of and Needs in Chatbot's Educational Application. *SAGE Open*, *15*(1), 21582440251321853. DOI: 10.1177/21582440251321853

Swaroop, S., Buçinca, Z., Gajos, K. Z., & Doshi-Velez, F. (2024). *Accuracy-Time Tradeoffs in AI-Assisted Decision Making under Time Pressure*. https://doi.org/DOI: 10.1145/3640543.3645206

Sykes, J. M. (2019). Digital games and language learning: Theory, development, and implementation. *Foreign Language Annals*, *52*(1), 76–90.

Tai, T. Y., & Chen, H. H. J. (2024). Improving elementary EFL speaking skills with generative AI chatbots: Exploring individual and paired interactions. *Computers & Education*, *220*, 105112. DOI: 10.1016/j.compedu.2024.105112

Tariq, U. (2024). Challenges in AI-Powered educational technologies: Teacher perspectives and resistance. *Journal of AI in Education: Innovations, Opportunities, Challenges, and Future Directions*, *1*(3), 1–10.

Thakur, A. (2020). The role of stress patterns in Omani Arabic. *Journal of Arabic Linguistics*, *32*(1), 74–89.

Thomas, J. (1983). Cross-cultural pragmatic failure. *Applied Linguistics*, *4*(2), 91–112. DOI: 10.1093/applin/4.2.91

Thornhill-Miller, B., Camarda, A., Mercier, M., Burkhardt, J. M., Morisseau, T., Bourgeois-Bougrine, S., Vinchon, F., El Hayek, S., Augereau-Landais, M., Mourey, F., Feybesse, C., Sundquist, D., & Lubart, T. (2023). Creativity, critical thinking, communication, and collaboration: Assessment, certification, and promotion of 21st century skills for the future of work and education. *Journal of Intelligence*, *11*(3), 54. DOI: 10.3390/jintelligence11030054 PMID: 36976147

Thuker, A. (2020). Examined the use of falling tunes for tag-question endings. *Journal of Linguistics*, *15*(3), 98–112.

Tian, J., Zhang, M., Zhou, H., & Wu, J. (2021). College satisfaction, sense of achievement, student happiness and sense of belonging of freshmen in Chinese private colleges: Mediation effect of emotion regulation. *International Journal of Environmental Research and Public Health, 18*(22), 1–14. DOI: 10.3390/ijerph182211736 PMID: 34831492

Toosi, A., Bottino, A. G., Saboury, B., Siegel, E., & Rahmim, A. (2021). A brief history of AI: How to prevent another winter (a critical review). *PET Clinics, 16*(4), 449–469. DOI: 10.1016/j.cpet.2021.07.001 PMID: 34537126

Trofimovich, P. (2020). The use of PRAAT in second language phonology research: Applications and techniques. *Studies in Second Language Acquisition, 42*(4), 735–754.

Trofimovich, P., & Baker, A. (2023). PRAAT and the evaluation of EFL learners' prosody. *Language Learning Journal, 41*(2), 312–328.

Tsui, A. B. (2007). Complexities of identity formation: A narrative inquiry of an EFL teacher. *TESOL Quarterly, 41*(4), 657–680. DOI: 10.1002/j.1545-7249.2007.tb00098.x

Tulsiani, R. (2024). Data privacy in AI-driven learning and ethical considerations. eLearning Industry. https://elearningindustry.com/ensuring-data-privacy-and-ethical-considerations-in-ai-driven-learning

UNESCO. (2023). *Technology in education: A tool on whose terms? Global Education Monitoring Report 2023*. https://www.unesco.org/gem-report/en/2023

UNESCO. (2024). *AI and education: Guidance for policy makers*. United Nations Educational, Scientific and Cultural Organization. https://unesdoc.unesco.org/ark:/48223/pf0000382000

Unkrich, L., & Molina, A. (Directors). (2017). *Coco* [Film]. Pixar Animation Studios.

Varghese, M., Morgan, B., Johnston, B., & Johnson, K. A. (2005). Theorizing language teacher identity: Three perspectives and beyond. *Journal of Language, Identity, and Education, 4*(1), 21–44. DOI: 10.1207/s15327701jlie0401_2

Vesselinov, R., & Grego, J. (2021). Improving second language acquisition through AI tools. *Computers in Human Behavior, 115*, 106535. DOI: 10.1016/j.chb.2020.106535

Vetrivel, S. C., Arun, V. P., Maheswari, R., & Saravanan, T. P. (2024). Technology Integration in Online Learning Platforms: Blended Learning Gamification. In Transdisciplinary Teaching and Technological Integration for Improved Learning: Case Studies and Practical Approaches (pp. 219-247). IGI Global.

Visser, W. (2010). Schön: Design as a reflective practice. *Collection*, (2), 21–25.

Vygotsky, L. S. (1978). *Mind in society: The development of higher psychological processes* (Vol. 86). Harvard University Press.

Wafula, L. (2025). The evolving roles of faculty in modern classrooms: A shift from lecturer to facilitator. In Areba, G. N., Gisore, B. N., & Njurai, E. W. (Eds.), *Creating dynamic space in higher education: Modern shifts in policy, competencies, and governance* (pp. 253–282). IGI Global Scientific Publishing.

Wang, J., & Kabashima, H. (2022). Artificial general ıntelligence in human ınterface—ıts ımpact on society and human being. In Lütge, C., Uhl, M., Kriebitz, A., & Max, R. (Eds.), *Business ethics and digitization*. Springer Nature., DOI: 10.1007/978-3-662-64094-4_3

Wang, Y., & Kabilan, M. K. (2024). Integrating technology into English learning in higher education: A bibliometric analysis. *Cogent Education, 11*(1), 2404201. DOI: 10.1080/2331186X.2024.2404201

Wang, Y., & Spector, J. M. (2023). AI-powered chatbots in language learning: A systematic review. *Computers & Education, 194*, 104739. DOI: 10.1016/j.compedu.2023.104739

Wang, Y., Wu, J., Chen, F., Wang, Z., Li, J., & Wang, L. (2024). Empirical assessment of AI-powered tools for vocabulary acquisition in EFL instruction. *IEEE Access : Practical Innovations, Open Solutions, 12*, 131892–131905. DOI: 10.1109/ACCESS.2024.3446657

Wang, Y., & Wu, M. (2025). Analysis of English Mofun Show based on the theory of second language acquisition. In *Addressing Global Challenges-Exploring Socio-Cultural Dynamics and Sustainable Solutions in a Changing World* (pp. 283–288). Routledge.

Wang, Y., & Xue, L. (2024). Using AI-driven chatbots to foster Chinese EFL students' academic engagement: An intervention study. *Computers in Human Behavior, 159*, 1–8. DOI: 10.1016/j.chb.2024.108353

Watson, J. C. E. (2004). *The phonology of Arabic*. Oxford University Press.

Watt, H. M., & Richardson, P. W. (2023). Supportive school Workplaces for beginning teachers' motivations and career satisfaction. In Urdan, T., & Gonida, E. N. (Eds.), *Remembering the life, work, and influence of Stuart A. Karabenick: A legacy of research on self-Regulation, help Seeking, teacher motivation, and more* (pp. 115–138). Emerald Publishing Limited. DOI: 10.1108/S0749-742320230000022009

Wei, L. (2023). Artificial intelligence in language instruction: Impact on English learning achievement, L2 motivation, and self-regulated learning. *Frontiers in Psychology*, *14*, 1–14. DOI: 10.3389/fpsyg.2023.1261955 PMID: 38023040

Wentzel, K. R. (1998). Social relationships and motivation in middle school: The roles of parents, teachers and peers. *Journal of Educational Psychology*, *90*(2), 202–209. DOI: 10.1037/0022-0663.90.2.202

Whalen, J. (2020). Should teachers be trained in emergency remote teaching? Lessons learned from the COVID-19 pandemic. *Journal of Technology and Teacher Education*, *28*(2), 189–199. DOI: 10.70725/307718pkpjuu

Widayanti, A., & Pramudya, I. (2022). Audacity software analysis in analyzing the frequency and character of the sound spectrum. *Journal of Physical Education (Maringá)*, *3*(1), 45–52. https://www.researchgate.net/publication/357770757_Audacity_Software_Analysis_In_Analyzing_The_Frequency_And_Character_Of_The_Sound_Spectrum

Williamson, B. (2024). The social life of AI in education. *International Journal of Artificial Intelligence in Education*, *34*(1), 97–104.

Williamson, B., & Eynon, R. (2020). Historical threads, missing links, and future directions in AI in education. *Learning, Media and Technology*, *45*(3), 223–235. DOI: 10.1080/17439884.2020.1798995

Williamson, B., Eynon, R., & Potter, J. (2020). Pandemic politics, pedagogical continuity and edtech: Disturbing trajectories in education. *Learning, Media and Technology*, *45*(2), 107–114. DOI: 10.1080/17439884.2020.1761641

Wilson, B. (2005). PRAAT software and its application in language learning. *Computer Assisted Language Learning*, *18*(2), 109–125.

Woodrum, C. (2024, May). ChatGPT and Language Translation: A Small Case Study Evaluating English–Mandarin Translation. In International Conference on Human-Computer Interaction (pp. 147-157). Cham: Springer Nature Switzerland.

Wright, T. (2012). Managing the classroom. In Burns, A., & Richards, J. C. (Eds.), *The Cambridge guide to pedagogy and practice in second language teaching* (pp. 60–67). Cambridge University Press. DOI: 10.1017/9781009024778.009

Wulantari, N. P., Rachman, A., Sari, M. N., Uktolseja, L. J., & Rofi'i, A. (2023). The Role Of Gamification In English Language Teaching: A Literature. *Journal of Education*, *6*(01), 2847–2856.

Wu, X.-Y. (2024). Artificial Intelligence in L2 learning: A meta-analysis of contextual, instructional, and social-emotional moderators. *System*, *126*, 1–20. DOI: 10.1016/j.system.2024.103498

Xiao, T., Yi, S., & Akhter, S. (2024). AI-supported online language learning: Learners' self-esteem, cognitive-emotion regulation, academic enjoyment, and language success. *International Review of Research in Open and Distance Learning*, *25*(3), 77–96. DOI: 10.19173/irrodl.v25i3.7666

Xia, Y., Shin, S. Y., & Kim, J. C. (2024). Cross-cultural intelligent language learning system (CILS): Leveraging AI to facilitate language learning strategies in cross-cultural communication. *Applied Sciences (Basel, Switzerland)*, *14*(13), 5651. DOI: 10.3390/app14135651

Xi, J., & Lantolf, J. P. (2021). Scaffolding and the zone of proximal development: A problematic relationship. *Journal for the Theory of Social Behaviour*, *51*(1), 25–48. DOI: 10.1111/jtsb.12260

Xu, T., Zhang, Y. F., Chu, Z., Wang, S., & Wen, Q. (2024). Ai-driven virtual teacher for enhanced educational efficiency: Leveraging large pretrain models for autonomous error analysis and correction. arXiv preprint arXiv:2409.09403.

Xu, H. (2024). *Language teachers' social cognition: Elements in critical issues in teacher education*. Cambridge University Press. DOI: 10.1017/9781009377720

Yalcin, N. (2013). Using movies in language classrooms as means of understanding cultural diversity. *Epiphany.Journal of Transdisciplinary Studies*, *6*(1), 259–271.

Yamashita, Y., Sakamoto, Y., & Nakagawa, H. (2023). Comparison of Praat and Computerized Speech Lab for formant analysis in maxillectomy patients. *Frontiers in Neuroscience*, *17*, 1098197. DOI: 10.3389/fnins.2023.1098197 PMID: 36816122

Yang, H., Gao, C., & Shen, H. Z. (2024). Learner interaction with, and response to, AI-programmed automated writing evaluation feedback in EFL writing: An exploratory study. *Education and Information Technologies*, *29*(4), 3837–3858. DOI: 10.1007/s10639-023-11991-3

Yang, L., & Zhao, S. (2024). AI-induced emotions in L2 education: Exploring EFL students' perceived emotions and regulation strategies. *Computers in Human Behavior*, *159*, 1–8. DOI: 10.1016/j.chb.2024.108337

Yan, L., Echeverria, V., Jin, Y., Fernandez-Nieto, G., Zhao, L., Li, X., Alfredo, R., Swiecki, Z., Gašević, D., & Martinez-Maldonado, R. (2024). Evidence-based multimodal learning analytics for feedback and reflection in collaborative learning. *British Journal of Educational Technology*, *55*(5), 1900–1925. DOI: 10.1111/bjet.13498

Yarovenko, H., Kuzior, A., Norek, T., & Lopatka, A. (2024). The future of artificial intelligence: Fear, hope or indifference? *Human Technology*, *20*(3), 611–639. DOI: 10.14254/1795-6889.2024.20-3.10

Yoon, H., & Nguyen, C. T. (2021). Evaluating the effectiveness of AI in correcting L2 pragmatics: A case study of automated writing feedback. *ReCALL*, *33*(2), 147–165. DOI: 10.1017/S0958344020000351

Yoon, S. Y. (2019). Student readiness for AI instruction: Perspectives on AI in university EFL classrooms. *Multimedia-Assisted Language Learning*, *24*(4), 134–160. DOI: 10.15702/mall.2019.22.4.134

Ypsilanti, A., & Karras, I. (2024). Introducing Pixar shorts in the Greek EFL classroom as a means to enhancing empathy among High School students. *Proceedings of the IAFOR International Conference on Arts & Humanities in Hawaii (IICAH2024)* (pp. 165-175). https://doi.org/DOI: 10.22492/issn.2432-4604.2024.15

Yuan, X., Zhao, F., & Xie, Y. (2021). Pragmatics and artificial intelligence in language education: Current practices and future directions. *Journal of Language Teaching & Research*, *12*(5), 1021–1034. DOI: 10.17507/jltr.1205.01

Yue, J. (2019). Use of foreign films in cultivating intercultural communicative competence in ELT—A case study. *Theory and Practice in Language Studies*, *9*(2), 198–203. DOI: 10.17507/tpls.0902.09

Yüksel, H. G., Solhi, M., Özcan, E., & Giritlioğlu, N. B. (2024). The associations between EFL learners' L2 class belongingness, emotion regulation strategies, and perceived L2 proficiency in an online learning context. *Language Learning Journal*, 1–17. Advance online publication. DOI: 10.1080/09571736.2024.2403463

Yürük, N. (2016). Films as a multimodal way to improve learners reading skills and enhance cultural awareness in English Language and Literature Departments [Unpublished doctoral dissertation]. Hacettepe University, Turkey.

Zainuddin, Z., Chu, S. K. W., & Perera, C. J. (2024). Gamification in Education. In *Gamification in A Flipped Classroom: Pedagogical Methods and Best Practices* (pp. 67–113). Springer Nature Singapore. DOI: 10.1007/978-981-97-2219-8_3

Zamiri, M., & Esmaeili, A. (2024). Methods and technologies for supporting knowledge sharing within learning communities: A systematic literature review. *Administrative Sciences*, *14*(1), 17. DOI: 10.3390/admsci14010017

Zawacki-Richter, O., Marín, V. I., Bond, M., & Gouverneur, F. (2019). Systematic review of research on artificial intelligence applications in higher education: Where are the educators? *International Journal of Educational Technology in Higher Education, 16*(1), 39. Advance online publication. DOI: 10.1186/s41239-019-0171-0

Zawacki-Richter, O., Marín, V. I., Bond, M., & Gouverneur, F. (2020). Systematic Review of Research on Artificial Intelligence Applications in Higher Education. *International Journal of Educational Technology in Higher Education, 17*(1), 1–27.

Zeng, W., & Huang, Y. (2025). On the effectiveness of visual speech software Praat in English pronunciation teaching research. In M. Atiquzzaman, N. Yen, & Z. Xu (Eds.), *Proceedings of the 5th International Conference on Big Data Analytics for Cyber-Physical System in Smart City—Volume 2 (pp. 1–9). Springer. https://doi .org/*DOI: 10.1007/978-981-96-0211-7_1

Zeng, C., & Fisher, L. (2024). Opening the "black box": How out-of-class use of Duolingo impacts Chinese junior high school students' intrinsic motivation for English. *ECNU Review of Education, 7*(2), 283–307.

Zengilowski, A., Lee, J., Gaines, R. E., Park, H., Choi, E., & Schallert, D. L. (2023). The collective classroom "we": The role of students' sense of belonging on their affective, cognitive, and discourse experiences of online and face-to-face discussions. *Linguistics and Education, 73*, 1–14. DOI: 10.1016/j.linged.2022.101142

Zhai, X., Zhao, R., Jiang, Y., & Wu, H. (2024). Unpacking the dynamics of AI-based language learning: Flow, grit, and resilience in Chinese EFL contexts. *Behavioral Sciences (Basel, Switzerland), 14*(9), 838. Advance online publication. DOI: 10.3390/bs14090838 PMID: 39336053

Zhang, B. (2023). The relationship between teacher-student rapport and EFL learners' engagement in online scaffolding setting. *Journal of Psycholinguistic Research, 52*(5), 1685–1705. DOI: 10.1007/s10936-023-09954-3 PMID: 37171685

Zhang, C. B., Li, T. G., Li, Y. N., Chang, Y., & Zhang, Z. P. (2024). Fostering well-being: Exploring the influence of user-AI assistant relationship types on subjective well-being. *International Journal of Information Management, 79*, 102822. DOI: 10.1016/j.ijinfomgt.2024.102822

Zhang, H., & Liu, J. (2024). Analysis of voice in Parkinson's disease utilizing the Acoustic Voice Quality Index. *Journal of Clinical Neuroscience, 82*, 56–61. DOI: 10.1016/j.jocn.2024.02.019

Zhang, L., & Li, X. (2024). Guidance to the Praat, a software for speech and acoustic analysis. *Journal of Speech Science and Technology, 14*(1), 22–30. DOI: 10.1016/j.jsst.2024.03.001

Zhang, R., & Zou, D. (2022). Types, purposes, and effectiveness of state-of-the-art technologies for second and foreign language learning. *Computer Assisted Language Learning, 35*(4), 696–742. DOI: 10.1080/09588221.2020.1744666

Zhang, S., Huang, J., & Zhang, X. (2021). AI-based language learning applications for pragmatic competence. *Language Learning & Technology, 25*(2), 54–69. DOI: 10.1016/j.jacad.2021.05.004

Zhang, X. (2021). Using visual feedback in language teaching: Insights from PRAAT. *Language Education Research, 8*(2), 45–58.

Zhang, Y. (2023). EFL learners' boredom coping strategies: The role of teacher-student rapport and support. *BMC Psychology, 11*(1), 1–10. DOI: 10.1186/s40359-023-01446-2 PMID: 37978568

Zhao, Z. (2021). Decipher the Effect of Gamification in Harnessing Boredom and Improving Performance.

Zhi, R., & Wang, Y. (2024). On the relationship between EFL students' attitudes toward artificial intelligence, teachers' immediacy and teacher-student rapport, and their willingness to communicate. *System, 124*, 1–15. DOI: 10.1016/j.system.2024.103341

Zhou, C., & Hou, F. (2024). Can AI empower L2 education? Exploring its influence on the behavioral, cognitive and emotional engagement of EFL teachers and language learners. *European Journal of Education, 59*(4), 1–13. DOI: 10.1111/ejed.12750

Zovko, V., & Gudlin, M. (2019). Artificial intelligence as a disruptive technology in education. In *Conference Proceedings of The Future of Education(*2019*)*.

Zulfugarova, M. (2018). Intonation in language: A prosodic perspective. *Journal of Linguistics and Language Studies, 15*(2), 25–38.

# About the Contributors

**Youssef Baba Khouya** is a Moroccan educator and researcher specializing in English language teaching and applied linguistics, currently a professor at the University of Hassan I, Morocco. He holds a Doctorate in English Didactics from Inje University, South Korea, funded by the Korean Government Scholarship, with a focus on the link between personality factors and English language anxiety across cultural contexts. Prof. Baba Khouya has published extensively on topics like language anxiety, demotivation, and EFL pedagogy, presenting at international conferences and serving on academic committees. Proficient in Arabic, English, French, and Korean, he brings a multilingual, multicultural perspective to his teaching and research, with experience in medical and specialized English instruction in both Morocco and South Korea.

**Abderrahmane Ismaili-Alaoui** serves as an Assistant Professor of Linguistics at Hassan II University in Casablanca, Morocco. He held a PhD in Linguistics from Sidi Mohamed Ben Abdellah University, Fes, Morocco. Dr. Ismaili-Alaoui's academic contributions are notable and diverse, ranging from published books to influential peer-reviewed articles in respected journals and international conferences.

***

**Meletius Igbokwe** is a cybersecurity-focused Modern Workplace Engineer with a strong passion for protecting organizational data and identities in today's cloud-driven world. With expertise spanning cloud security, infrastructure, and automation, he is dedicated to helping organizations adopt modern technologies while maintaining a strong security posture. A professional member of BCS, The Chartered Institute for IT, and a holder of a Master's degree in Cloud and Network Security from the University of Bolton, Meletius is deeply invested in advancing cybersecurity through research, innovation, and real-world application. His interests include the intersection of AI and cybersecurity, digital forensics, identity security, and securing enterprise environments using industry best practices.

**Ioannis Karras** is Professor in Applied Linguistics & Intercultural Communication at Ionian University, Greece. He has lectured at universities around the world, has delivered talks at international conferences and has conducted seminars/workshops with international audiences. He has authored a book, a number of edited book chapters and articles in journals and conference proceedings.

**Peter Kwakpovwe** is an innovative Data Scientist with a Master's degree in Data Science from the University of Salford, UK, where he graduated with distinction. He is driven by a passion for unlocking the potential of data and artificial intelligence to create groundbreaking solutions that address complex business challenges. His expertise spans predictive analytics, machine learning, and the development of AI-driven systems such as digital twins, all aimed at optimizing processes and improving efficiency across various sectors. Peter's career is defined by his ability to transform data into actionable insights that enhance decision-making, improve user experiences, and drive operational efficiencies across industries like retail, financial services, and healthcare. He is also deeply committed to the peer review process and scientific publication, viewing these activities as essential for research integrity, knowledge sharing, and the advancement of the field. In addition to his professional accomplishments, Peter has founded Draco Intelligence Ltd, a cutting-edge company that is redefining business intelligence. Draco Intelligence leverages AI-powered platforms to enable businesses to capture and analyze real-time data, improve product offerings, optimize customer engagement, and make better-informed decisions. With tailored solutions across industries such as manufacturing, construction, finance, real estate, and healthcare, Draco Intelligence is revolutionizing how businesses use data to drive growth and innovation. Peter's work is positioned at the intersection of AI, machine learning, and business strategy, and he is constantly exploring new ways to harness technology for positive change. Through his pioneering efforts, Peter continues to push the boundaries of what data and AI can achieve, solving real-world problems and creating lasting value.

**Manuel Macías Borrego** is a university professor in the area of English Philology at the URJC (Universidad Rey Juan Carlos), in the Department of Foreign Philology and Translation and Interpretation. He is considered a specialist in Applied Linguistics, particularly in Pragmatics and Error Analysis in the acquisition of English as a second language. He holds a PhD in English Philology from the Complutense University of Madrid, with the highest honors (Cum Laude), and has a Master's degree in Digital and Contemporary Humanities. His training includes studies in Corpus Linguistics and the teaching of English as a Foreign Language and as a Second Language.

**Papi Naidu Mavidi** is currently working as Asst. Professor of English in the Department of English at Aditya Institute of Technology and Management, Tekkali, Andhra Pradesh. He completed MA in English Language and Literature from Andhra University M.Phil&Ph.D from Acharya Nagarjuna University. He also got qualified APSET. His interested research areas are Indian Writing in English, English Language Teaching and Black Literature. He has passion for creative reading and writing. He has been training thousands of students in terms of academic English as well as communicative English for many years. He has published 20 research papers and 3 book chapters in international journals. He is also one of the authors for the text books prepared for B.Tech students entitled "Preparing for the Future" and "Studying for the Success"(2013).His area of research interest is English language teaching and Indian writing in English.

**Obinna Emmanuel Obi-Akwari** is a Lawyer and Software Developer, currently working as a Front-End Developer. With expertise in Javascript, Typescript, React, and Node.js, he is passionate about building scalable, user-friendly applications. A future founder, driven to develop innovative software solutions. He is also an avid researcher in software development and AI. He has experience in API integrations, full-stack development, and software testing principles to enhance quality and performance.

**Ene Ojaide** is an accomplished data scientist and AI researcher with a strong background in machine learning, predictive analytics, and data driven problem-solving. Holding an MSc in Data Science from Nottingham Trent University, UK, Ene has expertise spanning data science, cybersecurity, Finance, ecommerce and healthcare AI, with notable work in network intrusion detection, churn prediction, and multimodal deep learning for breast cancer prediction. A dedicated contributor to the field, Ene is a scholar who actively bridges the gap between theoretical research and real-world applications, strongly focusing on leveraging machine learning and AI for societal impact, interpretability, ethical AI, and data-driven decision-making. Beyond research, Ene plays a key role in fostering knowledge exchange and upholding high academic standards. She contributes to industry discussions, mentors aspiring data scientists, and promotes diversity in tech. As the founder of ThinkData, she is committed to bridging the gap between underrepresented communities and opportunities in technology. She is also a member of the Institute of Analytics, Women in Data UK, and Rewriting the Code, advocating for inclusive AI and equitable access to technology. Her expertise and commitment to advancing the field make her a valuable contributor to academic and industry discourse, ensuring that the latest advancements in AI and data science are rigorously evaluated and widely accessible.

**Cuong Huy Pham** is currently Dean of Faculty of English, Ho Chi Minh City University of Economics and Finance, Vietnam. He obtained his PhD in Applied Linguistics from Massey University, New Zealand. He has profound teaching and research experience in both EAP and ESP contexts in New Zealand and Vietnam. His research interests include affective factors in language learning and teaching, language learning spaces, and curriculum development. Email: cuongph@uef.edu.vn

**Natalia Shumeiko** is a Researcher and Assistant Professor at the Department of English Language at the Bratislava University of Economics and Business. She teaches Business English, and her research interests focus on using information and communication technologies (ICT) to have a good command of the English language, blended and online learning formats, and foreign language teaching in multicultural environments.

**Angeliki Ypsilanti** is an EFL teacher in Secondary Education. She holds two B.A. degrees, one in English Language and Literature from the University of Athens and the other in Hispanic Language and Civilization Studies from the Hellenic Open University as well as an M.Ed. in TEFL/TEIL from the Hellenic Open University. She is currently a PhD candidate in the Department of Foreign Languages, Translation and Interpreting at Ionian University. Her research focuses on cultural discourse analysis of Disney movie scripts, with a particular interest in intergenerational conflicts. She has presented her work at international conferences and published in leading academic journals and conference proceedings.

# Index

## A



## C

## D



## E



## F



## G

## Q



## R



## S



## T



## W

www.ingramcontent.com/pod-product-compliance
Lightning Source LLC
LaVergne TN
LVHW080612300926
849162LV00005B/1126